Essentials of Strategic Management

Essentials of Strategic Management

The Quest for Competitive Advantage

John E. Gamble
University of South Alabama

Arthur A. Thompson, Jr.
The University of Alabama

McGraw-Hill Irwin

Boston   Burr Ridge, IL   Dubuque, IA   New York   San Francisco   St. Louis
Bangkok   Bogotá   Caracas   Kuala Lumpur   Lisbon   London   Madrid   Mexico City
Milan   Montreal   New Delhi   Santiago   Seoul   Singapore   Sydney   Taipei   Toronto

McGraw-Hill
Irwin

ESSENTIALS OF STRATEGIC MANAGEMENT: THE QUEST FOR COMPETITIVE ADVANTAGE

Published by McGraw-Hill/Irwin, a business unit of The McGraw-Hill Companies, Inc., 1221 Avenue of the Americas, New York, NY, 10020.

Some ancillaries, including electronic and print components, may not be available to customers outside the United States.

This book is printed on acid-free paper.

4 5 6 7 8 9 0 WCK/WCK 0 9

ISBN 978-0-07-353030-7
MHID 0-07-353030-1

Senior sponsoring editor: *Michael Ablassmeir*
Developmental editor: *Laura Griffin*
Senior marketing manager: *Anke Braun Weekes*
Marketing coordinator: *Michael Gedatus*
Senior project manager: *Harvey Yep*
Lead production supervisor: *Carol A. Bielski*
Senior designer: *Cara Hawthorne*
Senior media project manager: *Susan Lombardi*
Cover design: *Pam Verros*
Cover image: *©iStockphoto*
Typeface: *10.5/12 Palatino*
Compositor: *Laserwords Private Limited*
Printer: *Quebecor World Versailles Inc.*

Library of Congress Cataloging-in-Publication Data

Gamble, John (John E.)
    Essentials of strategic management : the quest for competitive advantage/John E. Gamble, Arthur A. Thompson, Jr.—1st ed.
        p. cm.
    Includes bibliographical references and index.
    ISBN-13: 978-0-07-353030-7 (alk. paper)
    ISBN-10: 0-07-353030-1 (alk. paper)
    1. Strategic planning. 2. Business planning. 3. Competition. 4. Strategic planning—Case studies. I. Thompson, Arthur A., 1940- II. Title.
HD30.28.G353 2009
658.4'012-422—dc22

                                                                2008003390

www.mhhe.com

Dedication

To our families and especially our wives:
Debra and Hasseline

About the Authors

John E. Gamble is currently Associate Dean and Professor of Management in the Mitchell College of Business at the University of South Alabama. His teaching specialty at USA is strategic management and he also conducts a course in strategic management in Germany, which is sponsored by the University of Applied Sciences in Worms.

Dr. Gamble's research interests center on strategic issues in entrepreneurial, health care, and manufacturing settings. His work has been published in various scholarly journals and he is the author or co-author of more than 30 case studies published in an assortment of strategic management and strategic marketing texts. He has done consulting on industry and market analysis for clients in a diverse mix of industries.

Professor Gamble received his Ph.D. in management from The University of Alabama in 1995. Dr. Gamble also has a Bachelor of Science degree and a Master of Arts degree from The University of Alabama.

Arthur A. Thompson, Jr., earned his B.S. and Ph.D. degrees in economics from The University of Tennessee, spent three years on the economics faculty at Virginia Tech, and served on the faculty of The University of Alabama's College of Commerce and Business Administration for 25 years. In 1974 and again in 1982, Dr. Thompson spent semester-long sabbaticals as a visiting scholar at the Harvard Business School.

His areas of specialization are business strategy, competition and market analysis, and the economics of business enterprises. In addition to publishing over 30 articles in some 25 different professional and trade publications, he has authored or co-authored five textbooks and six computer-based simulation exercises that are used in colleges and universities worldwide.

Dr. Thompson spends much of his off-campus time giving presentations, putting on management development programs, working with companies, and helping operate a business simulation enterprise in which he is a major partner.

Dr. Thompson and his wife of 48 years have two daughters, two grandchildren, and a Yorkshire terrier.

Preface

*E*ssentials of Strategic Management responds head-on to the growing requests by business faculty for a concise, conceptually strong strategic management text with mainstream coverage. This first edition text was written with four objectives in mind: (1) To provide students with an up-to-date and thorough understanding of essential strategic management concepts and analytic tools; (2) To simplify the task of demonstrating student learning through course-embedded assessment; (3) To provide an attractive set of contemporary cases that involve headline strategic issues and that give students ample opportunities to apply what they read in the chapters; and (4) To complement use of a business strategy simulation.

The nine-chapter presentation provides coverage of essential topics expected by the vast majority of faculty teaching undergraduate and MBA strategic management courses. But the coverage is not skimpy or definition driven. We've provided solid explanations and real-world illustrations of strategies keyed to industry positioning, corporate-level strategy, and various strategic management analytical tools. In addition, we believe our coverage of resource-based strategies and Kaplan and Norton's Balanced Scorecard and Strategy Maps is unmatched by other "essential" texts in the field.

Through our experiences as college of business faculty members and administrators, we also fully understand the assessment demands on faculty teaching strategic management courses. In many institutions, capstone courses have emerged as the logical home for assessing student achievement of program learning objectives. *Essentials of Strategic Management* includes a number of interesting Assurance of Learning Exercises at the end of each chapter that you can use as a basis for class discussion or to demonstrate student learning through written assignments and/or team presentations. Instructors can easily pair the Assurance of Learning Exercises with instructor-developed scoring rubrics to assess course or program learning outcomes.

Complementing the text presentation is a truly appealing lineup of 14 diverse, timely, and thoughtfully crafted cases. All of the cases are tightly linked to the content of the nine chapters, thus pushing students to apply the concepts and analytical tools they have read about. Twelve of the 14 cases were written by the coauthors to illustrate specific tools of analysis or distinct strategic management theories. The two cases included in the text not written by the coauthors were chosen because of their exceptional linkage to strategic management concepts presented in the text. We are confident you will be impressed with how well each of the 14 cases in the collection will work in the classroom and the amount of student interest they will spark.

This book by no means "requires" parallel use of a simulation but it fits the needs of simulation users perfectly. The relatively short length of each chapter gives students more time for simulation activities that illustrate the application of chapter concepts. In addition, each chapter contains an Assurance of Learning Exercise designed to drive home the linkage between the strategic management concepts presented in the chapter and the decision-making challenges of running a simulation company.

We've done our very best to ensure that the *Essentials of Strategic Management* package will work especially well for you in the classroom, help you economize on the time needed to be well-prepared for each class, and cause students to conclude that your course is one of the very best they have ever taken—from the standpoint of both enjoyment and learning.

Organization, Content, and Features of the Nine Text Chapters

The following rundown summarizes the topical focus of each *Essentials of Strategic Management* chapter:

- Chapter 1 focuses on the central questions of *"Where are we now?" "Where do we want to go?" and "How are we going to get there?"* In putting these questions into the context of business strategy, we introduce students to the primary approaches to building competitive advantage and the key elements of business-level strategy. Following Henry Mintzberg's pioneering research, we also stress why a company's strategy is partly planned and partly reactive and why this strategy tends to evolve over time. The chapter also discusses the relationship between a company's business model and its business strategy. This brief chapter is the perfect accompaniment to your opening day lecture on what the course is all about and why it matters.

- Chapter 2 lays out a five-stage strategic management process and examines the role of leadership in fostering corporate intrapreneurship, setting the long-term direction of the company, crafting its strategy, and leading the execution process. Students are introduced to such core concepts as strategic visions, mission statements, strategic versus financial objectives, and strategic intent. The chapter's treatment of objective setting is framed by the key tenets of *Kaplan and Norton's Balanced Scorecard. The chapter goes on to explain how Kaplan and Norton's Strategy Maps can be effective tools to illustrate connections between the company's strategies, operating activities, and financial and strategic results.* The chapter winds up with a section on conditions for good corporate governance.

- Chapter 3 deals with a company's quest for competitive advantage through *strategies keyed to industry positioning and/or the deployment of bundled or standalone competitively important resources.* Topics covered in this chapter include the *four classic generic competitive strategies*—overall low-cost leadership, broad differentiation, focused differentiation, and focused low cost. The chapter's topical coverage also includes the necessary conditions for a *competence- and resource-based competitive advantage and how strategic alliances and collaborative partnerships may be used to supplement the company's portfolio of resources.*

- Chapter 4 sets forth the now-familiar analytical tools and concepts of industry and competitive analysis and demonstrates the importance of tailoring strategy to fit the circumstances of a company's industry and competitive environment. *The standout feature of this chapter is a presentation of Michael Porter's "five forces model of competition" that we think is the clearest, most straightforward discussion of any text in the field.* Our discussion of evaluating the competitive positions of strategic groups and the *identification of Blue Ocean opportunities* is also unique among strategic management texts, in our opinion.

- Chapter 5 establishes the equal importance of doing solid company situation analysis as a basis for matching strategy to organizational resources, competencies, and competitive capabilities. SWOT analysis is cast as a simple, easy-to-use way to assess a company's resources and overall situation. Our coverage of value chain analysis, benchmarking, and competitive strength assessments provides a comprehensive view of the factors affecting a company's internal situation. We have cast the discussion of vertical integration and outsourcing as strategic approaches to building a competitively superior value chain. *We propose that superior value chain configurations can open opportunities for a "best cost" positioning strategy that incorporates differentiating features at a low cost.* We have also included a table showing how key financial and operating ratios are calculated and how to interpret them; students will find this table handy in doing the number-crunching needed to evaluate whether a company's strategy is delivering good financial performance.

- Chapter 6 focuses on the tasks involved with implementing and executing the chosen strategy. *Implementation topics are anchored by Kaplan and Norton's Balanced Scorecard and Strategy Map perspectives that include human capital, information capital, and organizational capital.* The following implementation topics are included in the chapter's discussion of strategy implementation: (1) Adopting an organizational structure that supports strategies intended to create customer value; (2) ensuring that policies and procedures facilitate rather than impede effective execution; (3) creating a company culture that supports successful strategy execution; (4) pushing for continuous improvement in how value chain activities are performed; (5) allocating ample resources to strategy critical activities; (6) tying rewards and incentives directly to the achievement of performance objectives; (7) staffing the organization to provide the needed skills and expertise; and (8) installing information and operating systems that enable company personnel to perform essential activities.

- Chapter 7 reflects the very latest in the literature on (1) a company's *duty to operate according to ethical standards;* (2) a company's *obligation to demonstrate socially responsible behavior and corporate citizenship;* and (3) why more companies are *limiting strategic initiatives to those that meet the needs of consumers without harming future generations.* The opening section of the chapter outlines drivers of unethical strategies and business behavior and discusses the *business case supporting a strong commitment to business ethics.* This discussion includes approaches to ensuring consistent ethical standards for companies with international operations. Following this section, we discuss *corporate social responsibility and corporate citizenship theories* and the growing efforts of corporations in many industries to limit strategies and operating practices to those that are *environmentally sustainable.*

- Chapter 8 explores the full range of strategy options for competing in foreign markets: export strategies; licensing; franchising; localized multi-country strategies; global strategies; and collaborative strategies involving heavy reliance on strategic alliances and joint ventures. There's also coverage of strategy considerations in international markets and common approaches to using international operations to improve overall competitiveness. Key topics in this discussion include locational advantages, cross-border coordination, profit sanctuaries, and cross-market subsidization.

- Chapter 9 examines strategies for building shareholder value in multibusiness enterprises. Corporate strategy topics covered in the chapter include methods of entering new businesses, related diversification, unrelated diversification, combined related and unrelated diversification approaches, and strategic options for improving the overall performance of an already diversified company. The chapter's analytical spotlight is trained on the techniques and procedures for assessing a diversified company's business portfolio—the relative attractiveness of the various businesses the company has diversified into, the company's competitive strength in each of its business lines, and the *strategic fits* and *resource fits* among a diversified company's different businesses. The chapter concludes with a brief survey of a company's four main post-diversification strategy alternatives: (1) sticking closely with the existing business lineup, (2) broadening the diversification base, (3) divesting some businesses and retrenching to a narrower diversification base, and (4) restructuring the makeup of the company's business lineup.

We have done our best to ensure that the nine chapters convey the best thinking of academics and practitioners in the field of strategic management and hit the bull's-eye in topical coverage for senior- and MBA-level strategy courses. We are confident you'll find the nine-chapter presentation is among the best strategic management texts in terms of coverage, readability, quality illustrations, and carefully crafted case studies. The ultimate test of the text, of course, is the positive pedagogical impact it has in the classroom. If this text sets a more effective stage for your lectures and does a better job of helping you persuade students that the discipline of strategy merits their rapt attention, then it will have fulfilled its purpose.

The Case Collection

Essentials of Strategic Management features a case collection flush with interesting companies and valuable lessons for students in the art and science of crafting and executing strategy. Twelve of the 14 cases were researched and written by the text coauthors; we made a conscientious effort to keep the length of cases relatively short (all but two are less than 20 pages), while offering plenty for students to chew on. Each case allows you to utilize a full complement of analytical tools and illustrate a range of strategic management concepts.

Almost all of the 14 cases involve companies or products that students will have heard of, know about from personal experience, or can easily identify with. All but two of the cases illustrate competence- and resource-based strategies as well as strategies keyed to industry positioning. There are four cases that provide students with insight into the special demands of competing in industry environments where technological developments are an everyday event, product life cycles are short, and competitive maneuvering among rivals comes fast and furious. Scattered throughout the lineup are nine cases concerning globally competitive industries and/or cross-cultural situations. We've also included two cases dealing with the strategic problems of relatively small entrepreneurial businesses and one case that zeroes in on business ethics and corporate social responsibility issues. All of the cases are accompanied by Case-Tutor case preparation exercises or a list of assignment questions linked to text concepts.

We believe you will find the collection of 14 cases quite appealing, eminently teachable, and very suitable for drilling students in the use of the concepts and analytical treatments in Chapters 1 through 9. With this case lineup, you should have no difficulty whatsoever assigning cases that will capture the interest of students from start to finish.

The Two Companion Strategy Simulations

The Business Strategy Game and *GLO-BUS: Developing Winning Competitive Strategies*—two Web-based strategy simulations that feature automated decision processing and performance grading—are being marketed by the publisher as companion supplements for use with this and other texts in the field. *The Business Strategy Game* is the world's leading strategy simulation, having been played by over 450,000 students at more than 500 universities worldwide. *GLO-BUS,* a somewhat streamlined online strategy simulation that was introduced in 2004, has been played by over 40,000 students at more than 150 universities across the world. Both simulations allow students to apply strategy making and analysis concepts presented in the text and may be used as part of a comprehensive effort to assess undergraduate or graduate program learning objectives.

The Compelling Case for Incorporating a Strategy Simulation

There are four powerful, convincing reasons for using a simulation in strategy courses for seniors and MBA students:

- Assigning students to run a company that competes head-to-head against companies run by other class members *gives students the immediate opportunity to experiment with various strategy options and to gain proficiency in applying the core concepts and analytical tools that they have been reading about.*

- *A competition-based strategy simulation adds an enormous amount of student interest and excitement.* Being an active manager in running a company in which they have a stake makes the students' task of learning about crafting and executing winning strategies more enjoyable. Their company becomes "real" and takes on a life of its own as the simulation unfolds—and it doesn't take long for students to establish a healthy rivalry with other class members who are running rival companies.

- Strategy simulations like *The Business Strategy Game* or *GLO-BUS* that have exceptionally close ties between the industry and company circumstances in the simulation and the topics covered in the text chapters *provide instructors with a host of first-rate examples of how the material in the text applies both to the simulation experience and to real-world management.*

- Because a simulation involves making decisions related to production operations, worker compensation and training, sales and marketing, distribution, customer service, and finance and requires analysis of company financial statements and market data, *the simulation helps students synthesize the knowledge gained in a variety of different business courses. The cross-functional, integrative nature of a strategy simulation helps make courses in strategy much more of a true capstone experience.*

In sum, *a three-pronged text-case-simulation course model has significantly more teaching/learning power than the traditional text-case model.* And, happily, there's another positive side benefit to using a simulation—*it lightens the grading burden for instructors.* Most adopters trim the total number of assigned cases to allow for classroom time to explain the mechanics of the simulation and to challenge students about the strength of their competitive advantage and what changes might be considered to their strategies or operations. This results in less time spent grading because both *The Business Strategy Game* and *GLO-BUS* have built-in grading features that require no instructor effort (beyond setting the grading weights).

Administration and Operating Features of the Two Companion Simulations

The Internet delivery and user-friendly designs of both *BSG* and *GLO-BUS* make them incredibly easy to administer, even for first-time users. And the menus and controls are so similar that you can readily switch between the two simulations or use one in your undergraduate class and the other in a graduate class. If you have not yet used either of the two simulations, you may find the following of particular interest:

- Time requirements for instructors are minimal. Setting up the simulation for your course is done online and takes about 10–15 minutes. Once set-up is completed, no other administrative actions are required beyond that of moving participants to a different team (should the need arise) and monitoring the progress of the simulation (to whatever extent desired).

- There's no software for students or administrators to download and no disks to fool with. All work must be done online and the speed for participants using dial-up modems is quite satisfactory. The servers dedicated to hosting the two simulations have appropriate back-up capability and are maintained by a prominent Web-hosting service that guarantees 99.99% reliability on a 24/7/365 basis—as long as students or instructors are connected to the Internet, the servers are virtually guaranteed to be operational.

- Participant's Guides are delivered at the Web site—students can read it on their monitors or print out a copy, as they prefer.

- There are extensive built-in "Help" screens explaining (a) each decision entry, (b) the information on each page of the Industry Reports, and (c) the numbers presented in the Company Reports. *The Help screens allow company co-managers to figure things out for themselves, thereby curbing the need for students to always run to the instructor with questions about "how things work."*

- The results of each decision are processed automatically and are typically available to all participants *15 minutes* after the decision deadline specified by the instructor/game administrator.

- Participants and instructors are notified via e-mail when the results are ready.

- Decision schedules are instructor-determined. Decisions can be made once per week, twice per week, or even twice daily, depending on how instructors want to conduct the exercise. One popular decision schedule involves 1 or 2 practice decisions and 6–10 weekly decisions across the remainder of the term. A second popular schedule is 1 or 2 practice decisions during weeks 3 and 4 of the course, followed by 2 decisions per week during last 4 to 6 weeks of the course. A third popular schedule is to use the simulation as a "final written assignment" for the course, where student teams are required to prepare a report discussing their strategy, operations, and performance during the simulation. The simulation is also well suited to executive courses where 5–8 decisions are made over a 3- to 5-day period.

- Instructors have the flexibility to prescribe 0, 1, or 2 practice decisions and from 4 to 10 regular decisions.

- Company teams can be composed of 1 to 5 players each and the number of companies competing head-to-head in a single industry can range from 4 to 12. If your class size is too large for a single industry, then it is a simple matter to create two or more industries for a single class section.

- Following each decision round, participants are provided with a complete set of reports—a six-page Industry Report, a one-page Competitive Intelligence report for each geographic region that includes strategic group maps and bulleted lists of competitive strengths and weaknesses, and a set of Company Reports (income statement, balance sheet, cash flow statement, and assorted production, marketing, and cost statistics).

- Two "open-book" multiple choice tests of 20 questions (optional, but strongly recommended) are included as part of each of the two simulations. The quizzes are taken online and automatically graded, with scores reported instantaneously to participants and automatically recorded in the instructor's electronic grade book. Students are provided with three sample questions for each test.

- Both simulations contain a three-year strategic plan option that you can assign. Scores on the plan are automatically recorded in the instructor's online grade book.

- At the end of the simulation, you can have students complete online peer evaluations (again, the scores are automatically recorded in your online grade book).

- Both simulations have a Company Presentation feature that enables students to easily prepare PowerPoint slides for use in describing their strategy and summarizing their company's performance in a presentation either to the class, the instructor, or an "outside" board of directors.

- *A Learning Assurance Report provides you with hard data concerning how well your students performed vis-à-vis students playing the simulation worldwide over the past 12 months.* The report is based on eight measures of student proficiency, business know-how, and decision-making skill and can also be used in evaluating the extent to which your school's academic curriculum produces the desired degree of student learning insofar as accreditation standards are concerned.

For more details on either simulation, please consult the Instructor's Manual or visit the simulation Web sites (www.bsg-online.com and www.glo-bus .com). Once you register (there's no obligation), you'll be able to access the Instructor's Guide and a set of PowerPoint Presentation slides that you can skim to preview the two simulations in some depth. The simulation authors will be glad to provide you with a personal tour of either or both Web sites (while you are on your PC) and walk you through the many features that are built into the simulations. You can arrange such a demonstration by contacting the simulation authors at (205) 722-9140. We think you'll be quite impressed with the capabilities that have been programmed into *The Business Strategy Game* and *GLO-BUS,* the simplicity with which both simulations can be administered, and their exceptionally tight connection to the text chapters, core concepts, and standard analytical tools.

Adopters of the text who also want to incorporate use of one of the two simulation supplements can either have students register at the simulation Web site via a credit card or instruct the campus bookstore to order the "book-simulation package"—the publisher has a special ISBN number for new texts that contain a special card shrink-wrapped with each text; printed on the enclosed card is a prepaid access code that students can use to register for either simulation and gain full access to the student portion of the simulation Web site.

Student Support Materials

Key Points Summaries

At the end of each chapter is a synopsis of the core concepts, analytical tools, and other key points discussed in the chapter. These chapter-end synopses help students focus on basic strategy principles, digest the messages of each chapter, and prepare for tests.

Online Learning Center (OLC)

The following helpful aids are available to students via the publisher's OLC at www.mhhe.com/gamble:

- **Case-Tutor Software** One of the most important and useful student aids available as premium content at the Web site is a set of downloadable files called **Case-Tutor** that consists of (1) files containing assignment questions for all 14 cases in the text and (2) files containing analytically structured exercises for eight of the cases—these eight "case preparation exercises" coach students in doing the strategic thinking needed to arrive at solid answers to the assignment questions for that case. Conscientious completion of the case preparation exercises helps students gain quicker command of the concepts and analytical techniques and points them toward doing good strategic analysis. The eight cases with an accompanying case preparation exercise are indicated by the Case-Tutor logo in the case listing section of the Table of Contents (the Case-Tutor logo also appears on the first page of cases for which there is an exercise).

  All the directions that students need to use the Case-Tutor files appear on the opening screens, and the menus are self-evident and intuitive. The Case-Tutor courseware can be used only on Windows-based PCs loaded with Microsoft Excel (either the Office 2000, Office XP, Office 2003, or Office 2007 versions).

- **Self-Graded Chapter Quizzes** The OLC contains 20-question quizzes for each chapter to allow students to measure their grasp of the material presented in each of the nine chapters.

- **Guide to Case Analysis** Explains what a case is, why cases are a standard part of courses in strategy, how to prepare for a class discussion of a case, how to prepare a written case analysis, what is expected in an oral presentation, and how to use financial ratio analysis to assess a company's financial condition. We suggest having students read this Guide prior to the first class discussion of a case.

- PowerPoint slides for each chapter.
- A selection of case-related videos.

Instructor Support Materials

Online Learning Center (OLC)

In addition to the student resources, the instructor section of www.mhhe .com/gamble also includes the Instructor's Manual and other instructional resources. Your McGraw-Hill representative can arrange delivery of instructor support materials in a format-ready Standard Cartridge for Blackboard, WebCT, and other Web-based educational platforms.

Instructor's Manual and Case Teaching Notes

The accompanying IM was prepared exclusively by the text coauthors. We've included a section on suggestions for organizing and structuring your course, sample syllabi and course outlines used by the coauthors, a copy of the test bank, and comprehensive teaching notes for each of the cases. All of the teaching notes were written by the text coauthors and reflect their analysis and insight into how to best teach each case.

Test Bank

There is a test bank prepared by the coauthors that contains over 500 multiple choice questions and short-answer/essay questions. It has been tagged with learning objectives, level of difficulty, Bloom's Taxonomy, and AACSB criteria. The AACSB tags allow instructors to sort questions by the various standards and create reports that provide evidence the curriculum satisfies accreditation standards.

PowerPoint Slides

To facilitate delivery and preparation of your lectures and to serve as chapter outlines, you'll have access to the PowerPoint presentations that the authors have developed for their own classes. The collection includes approximately 250 professional-looking slides displaying core concepts, analytical procedures, key points, and all the figures in the text chapters.

Accompanying Case Videos

Six of the cases (Costco, The Battle in Radio Broadcasting, Competition in the Bottled Water Industry in 2006, Blue Nile, Panera Bread, and Competition in Video Game Consoles) have accompanying videotape segments that can be

shown in conjunction with the case discussions. Suggestions for using each video are contained in the teaching notes for that case.

Instructor's Resource CD-ROM

All instructor supplements are available to text adopters in this one-stop multimedia resource, including the Instructor's Manual, EZ Test software, PowerPoint presentations, and case videos.

Acknowledgments

We heartily acknowledge the contributions of the outside case researchers whose case-writing efforts appear herein and the companies whose cooperation made the cases possible. We cannot overstate the importance of timely, carefully researched cases in contributing to a substantive study of strategic management issues and practices. From a research standpoint, strategy related cases are invaluable in exposing the generic kinds of strategic issues that companies face, in forming hypotheses about strategic behavior, and in drawing experience-based generalizations about the practice of strategic management. From an instructional standpoint, strategy cases give students essential practice in diagnosing and evaluating the strategic situations of companies and organizations, in applying the concepts and tools of strategic analysis, in weighing strategic options and crafting strategies, and in tackling the challenges of successful strategy execution. Without a continuing stream of fresh, well-researched, and well-conceived cases, the discipline of strategic management would lose its close ties to the very institutions whose strategic actions and behavior it is aimed at explaining. There's no question, therefore, that first-class case research constitutes a valuable scholarly contribution to the theory and practice of strategic management.

In addition, a great number of colleagues and students at various universities, business acquaintances, and people at McGraw-Hill provided inspiration, encouragement, and counsel during the course of this project. Like all text authors in the strategy field, we are intellectually indebted to the many academics whose research and writing have blazed new trails and advanced the discipline of strategic management.

As always, we value your recommendations and thoughts about the book. Your comments regarding coverage and content will be taken to heart, and we always are grateful for the time you take to call our attention to printing errors, deficiencies, and other shortcomings. Please e-mail us at **jgamble@usouthal.edu** or **athompso@cba.ua.edu;** fax us at (251) 460-6529; or write us at 104 Mitchell College of Business, The University of South Alabama, Mobile, Alabama 36688.

John E. Gamble

Arthur A. Thompson, Jr.

Brief Table of Contents

Table of Contents

Chapter 3: Competitive Strategy and Advantage in the Marketplace *34*

PART THREE: Executing the Strategy

Chapter 6:   Superior Strategy Execution—Another Path to Competitive Advantage   *116*

Chapter 7: Ethical Business Strategies, Corporate Social Responsibility, and Environmental Sustainability *143*

PART FOUR: Beyond Competitive Strategy

Chapter 8: Strategies for Competing in International Markets *162*

Chapter 9: Strategies for Multibusiness Corporations *184*

PART FIVE: Cases In Strategic Management

Indexes

Chapter 1

Strategy and the Quest for Competitive Advantage

Chapter Learning Objectives

LO1. Understand the need for having a sound strategy for achieving organizational objectives.

LO2. Develop an awareness of how companies can develop and sustain competitive advantage.

LO3. Understand why a company's strategy tends to evolve over time.

LO4. Understand what is meant by the term "business model" and why a company's business model is important in generating revenues sufficient to cover operating expenses.

The Importance of Managing Strategically

Three questions must be answered by managers of all types of organizations—small family-owned businesses, rapidly growing entrepreneurial firms, not-for-profit organizations, and the world's leading multinational corporations. These three critical questions are:

- *Where are we now?*
- *Where do we want to go?*
- *How are we going to get there?*

"Where are we now?" is answered by examining the company's current financial performance and market standing, its resource strengths and capabilities, its competitive weaknesses, and changing industry conditions that might affect the company. The answer to the question, *"Where do we want to go?"* lies within management's vision of the company's future direction. Only management is in the position to determine what changes are needed in its business makeup. It is management's responsibility as well to answer the question *"How are we going to get there?"*. In settling upon *"Where do we want to go?"*, management must craft and execute a strategy that moves the company in the intended direction and achieves the targeted levels of strategic and financial performance.

A company's **strategy** consists of the competitive moves and approaches management has developed to attract and please customers, conduct operations, grow the business, and achieve performance objectives.

Developing clear answers to the question *"How are we going to get there?"* is the essence of managing strategically. Rather than relying on the status quo as a roadmap and dealing with new opportunities or threats as they emerge, managing strategically involves developing a business game plan. Management's game plan must answer several *"how"* questions: *how* to outcompete rivals, *how* to respond to changing market conditions, *how* to manage each functional piece of the business, *how* to develop important competencies and capabilities, *how* to take advantage of growth opportunities, and *how* to achieve strategic and financial objectives.

In this opening chapter, we define the concepts of strategy and competitive advantage. The chapter will explain what makes up a company's strategy, explain why strategies are partly proactive and partly reactive, and discuss the relationship between a company's strategy and its business model. The chapter will also introduce you to the kinds of competitive strategies that can give a company an advantage over rivals in attracting customers and earning above-average profits. The chapter concludes by discussing three tests of a winning strategy. While there is no one surefire winning strategy that will always work for every organization in every situation, all top-notch strategies are well-matched to a company's external and internal situation, help build a competitive advantage over rivals, and produce good financial performance. By the end of this chapter, you will have a pretty clear idea of why managing strategically is always the beginning point in the quest for competitive advantage.

Answering the Question, "How Are We Going to Get There?"

The specific elements that comprise management's answer to the question *"How are we going to get there?"* define a company's business strategy. The company's business strategy lays out how management intends to compete in the industry, manage the functional areas of the business, and develop new capabilities and assemble resources to strengthen the company's prospects for long-term success. There's virtually no area of a company's operations that isn't involved in its business strategy and helps answer the question, *"How are we going to get there?"* Management must have deliberate plans for addressing such issues as:

LO1

Understand the need for having a sound strategy for achieving organizational objectives.

- Changing market conditions.
- Features and attributes to be included in the company's products or services.
- Pricing of the company's products or services.
- Distribution channels selected for the company's products.
- Reactions to offensive moves by rival sellers.
- Allocation of the company's financial resources.
- Acquisition of new physical assets and resources.
- Development of internal competencies, capabilities, and resource strengths.
- Development of alliances and joint ventures to supplement the company's competencies and capabilities.

Of course, business strategy includes planning for topics not included in the list above. The important thing to recognize is that every activity involved in delivering a business's product or service should be guided by strategic thinking. There's really no single activity, process, department, or functional area that should be left to chance. Figure 1.1 presents a diagram showing actions and approaches that make up a company's business strategy. Concepts & Connections 1.1 describes the various elements of the business strategy used at Whole Foods Market that have allowed it to become North America's largest organic and natural foods retailer. The capsule should make it clear how the business strategy includes actions related to such operating issues as produce displays and store site selection.

Competitive Strategy and Advantage over Rivals

The most important aspect of a company's business strategy is its approach to competing in the marketplace. It is imperative that a company's strategy strengthen its long-term competitive position and allow it to gain a competitive edge over rivals. In Concepts & Connections 1.1, it's evident that Whole Foods Market has attempted to gain a competitive advantage over rivals by

FIGURE 1.1   **Elements of a Company's Business Strategy**

A company achieves **sustainable competitive advantage** when an attractively large number of buyers develop a long-lasting preference for its products or services over the offerings of competitors.

creating a unique shopping experience for consumers. The company's merchandise selection, store locations, store layouts, and outstanding customer service are deliberate actions and policies meant to differentiate Whole Foods Market from competing natural and organic foods stores. A creative, distinctive strategy such as that used by Whole Foods Market is a company's most reliable ticket for developing a sustainable competitive advantage. A **sustainable competitive advantage** allows a company to attract sufficiently large numbers of buyers who have a lasting preference for its products or services over those offered by rivals. This enduring demand for a company's products or services is the key to a company's ability to earn ongoing above-average profits.

L02

Develop an awareness of how companies can develop and sustain competitive advantage.

Four proven strategic approaches to setting a company apart from rivals and winning a sustainable competitive advantage are:

1. *Developing a cost-based advantage.* Wal-Mart and Southwest Airlines have utilized low-cost provider strategies to earn strong market positions in their respective industries. Achieving lower costs than rivals can produce a durable competitive edge because lower costs allow a company to underprice rivals or earn larger profit margins than rivals. Kmart's poor performance in the discount retailing industry came about largely because of its unsuccessful attempts to emulate Wal-Mart's frugal operating practices, super-efficient distribution systems, and its finely honed supply chain approaches.

WHOLE FOODS MARKET'S BUSINESS STRATEGY IN NATURAL AND ORGANIC FOODS RETAILING

Founded in 1980 as a local supermarket for natural and health foods in Austin, Texas, Whole Foods Market had by 2007 evolved into the world's largest retail chain of natural and organic foods supermarkets. The company had 194 stores in the United States, Canada, and Great Britain and 2006 sales of $5.6 billion; revenues had grown at a compound annual rate of 20 percent since 2002. John Mackey, the company's co-founder and CEO, believed Whole Foods's rapid growth and market success had much to do with its having "remained a uniquely mission-driven company—highly selective about what we sell, dedicated to our core values and stringent quality standards, and committed to sustainable agriculture." The company's stated mission was to promote vitality and well-being for all individuals by offering the highest quality, least processed, most flavorful and naturally preserved foods available.

During its 26-year history, Whole Foods Market had been a leader in the natural and organic foods movement across the United States, helping the industry gain acceptance among growing numbers of consumers. Its stores were highly appealing places to shop. Whole Foods put considerable emphasis on attractive stores, a colorful décor, and appealing product displays. The company got very high marks from merchandising experts and customers for its presentation—from the bright colors and hand-stacked fruits to the quality of the foods and customer service to the wide aisles and cleanliness. Most stores featured hand-stacked produce, in-store chefs and open kitchens, scratch bakeries, prepared foods stations, European-style charcuterie departments, sampling displays, and everchanging selections and merchandise displays. Whole Foods's merchandising skills were said to be a prime factor in its success in luring shoppers back time and again. Whole Foods's long-term objectives were to have 400 stores and sales of $10 billion by 2010.

Key elements of the business strategy included:

- Most stores were in high-traffic shopping locations, some were freestanding and some were in strip centers.

- Whole Foods stressed a wide selection of natural and organic foods that appealed to both natural foods and gourmet shoppers—the company's product line included roughly 26,000 food and nonfood items, including fresh produce, a selection of daily baked goods, prepared foods, and an olive bar.

- Whole Foods stocked conventional household products so its stores could function as a one-stop grocery shopping destination where people could get everything on their shopping list.

- Competent, knowledgeable, and friendly service was a hallmark of shopping at a Whole Foods Market. The aim was to turn highly satisfied customers into advocates for Whole Foods, talking to close friends and acquaintances about their positive experiences shopping at Whole Foods.

2. *Creating a differentiation-based advantage.* Companies such as Harley-Davidson, Chanel, Rolex, and BMW have achieved competitive advantage by building their brands on such differentiating features as higher quality, a distinctive image, attractive styling, or superior engineering. Amazon.com has used its wide selection of merchandise to successfully differentiate itself from rival booksellers and other Internet retailers. Companies pursuing differentiation strategies must continually seek new innovations, undertake continuing efforts to add to the prestige of a brand, or strive for higher levels of value-adding services to defend against rivals' attempts to imitate the features of a successful differentiator's product offering.

3. *Focusing on a narrow market niche within an industry.* Many companies have developed a competitive advantage by serving the special needs

and tastes of only a small segment of an industry's buyers rather than attempting to appeal to all buyers in an industry. Prominent companies that enjoy competitive success in a specialized market niche include Google in search-based Internet advertising, eBay in online auctions, Jiffy Lube International in quick oil changes, McAfee in virus protection software, and The Weather Channel in cable TV.

4. *Developing unmatched resource strengths and competitive capabilities.* FedEx has developed a resource-based competitive advantage through its superior distribution capabilities that allow it to promise next-day delivery of small packages within the United States. Over the years, Toyota has developed a sophisticated production system that allows it to produce reliable, largely defect-free vehicles at low cost. Ritz Carlton and Four Seasons have uniquely strong capabilities in providing their hotel guests with highly personalized services. Very often, winning a durable competitive edge over rivals hinges more on building competitively valuable resource strengths and capabilities than it does on having a distinctive product. Clever rivals can nearly always copy the features of a popular product, but it's much more difficult for rivals to match experience, know-how, or specialized resources that a company has developed and perfected over a long period of time.

Why a Company's Strategy Evolves over Time

LO3

Understand why a company's strategy tends to evolve over time.

The appeal of a strategy that yields a sustainable competitive advantage is that it offers the potential for an enduring edge over rivals. However, managers of every company must be willing and ready to modify its strategy in response to the unexpected moves of competitors, shifting buyer needs and preferences, emerging market opportunities, new ideas for improving the strategy, and mounting evidence that the strategy is not working well. Managers should avoid dramatic departures from a proven competitive strategy if at all possible, but it should be expected that the strategy will be fine-tuned and tweaked on a regular basis. Therefore, *a company's strategy is not a one-time event, but is always a work in progress.*

Even though it's expected that a company's strategy will evolve incrementally, on occasion, major strategy shifts are called for, such as when a strategy is clearly failing and the company faces a financial crisis. In some industries, conditions change at a fairly slow pace, making it feasible for a strategy to remain in place for many years. But in industries where industry and competitive conditions change frequently and in sometimes dramatic ways, the life-cycle of a given strategy is short. Industry environments characterized by *high-velocity change* require companies to repeatedly adapt their strategies.[1] For example, companies in industries with rapid-fire advances in technology like medical equipment, electronics, and wireless devices often find it essential to adjust key elements of their strategies several times a year.

---

[1] For an excellent treatment of the strategic challenges posed by high velocity changes, see Shona L. Brown and Kathleen M. Eisenhardt, *Competing on the Edge: Strategy as Structured Chaos.* Boston, MA: Harvard Business School Press, 1998, Chapter 1.

FIGURE 1.2   **A Company's Strategy Is a Blend of Planned Initiatives and Unplanned Reactive Adjustments**

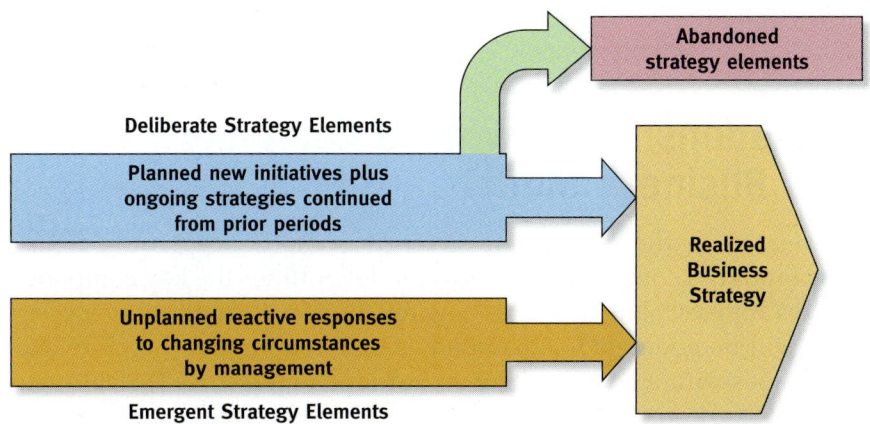

Regardless of whether a company's strategy changes gradually or swiftly, the important point is that a company's present strategy is always fluid. The evolving nature of a company's strategy means that the typical company strategy is a blend of (1) proactive moves to improve the company's financial performance and secure a competitive edge and (2) as-needed reactions to unanticipated developments and fresh market conditions—see Figure 1.2.[2] The biggest portion of a company's current strategy flows from ongoing actions that have proven themselves in the marketplace and newly launched initiatives aimed at building a larger lead over rivals and further boosting financial performance. This part of management's action plan for running the company is its proactive, **deliberate strategy.**

At times, components of a company's deliberate strategy will fail in the marketplace and become **abandoned strategy elements.** Although strategy flows from an analysis of the industry and the company's internal capabilities, planned strategies don't always play out as expected. In these cases, it makes much more sense to abandon a losing plan than to blindly adhere to strategy elements destined to fail. Although most elements of the company's deliberate strategy should be expected to survive, some portion of the realized strategy will be in response to unplanned reactions to unanticipated developments. It should be assumed that there will be occasions when market and competitive conditions take unexpected turns that call for some kind of strategic reaction. Novel strategic moves on the part of rival firms, unexpected shifts in customer preferences, fast-changing technological developments,

---

[2] See Henry Mintzberg and Joseph Lampel, "Reflecting on the Strategy Process, *Sloan Management Review* 40, no. 3 (Spring 1999), pp. 21–30; Henry Mintzberg and J. A. Waters, "Of Strategies, Deliberate and Emergent," *Strategic Management Journal* 6 (1985), pp. 257–272; Costas Markides, "Strategy as Balance: From 'Either-Or' to 'And,'" *Business Strategy Review* 12, no. 3 (September 2001), pp. 1–10; Henry Mintzberg, Bruce Ahlstrand, and Joseph Lampel, *Strategy Safari: A Guided Tour through the Wilds of Strategic Management* (New York: Free Press, 1998), Chapters 2, 5, and 7; and C. K. Prahalad and Gary Hamel, "The Core Competence of the Corporation," *Harvard Business Review* 70, no. 3 (May–June 1990), pp. 79–93.

and new market opportunities call for reactive adjustments that form the company's **emergent strategy.** As shown in Figure 1.2, a company's **realized strategy** tends to be a *combination* of deliberate planned elements and unplanned, emergent elements.

The Relationship Between a Company's Strategy and Its Business Model

LO4

Understand what is meant by the term "business model" and why a company's business model is important in generating revenues sufficient to cover operating expenses.

Closely related to the concept of strategy is the concept of a company's **business model.** A company's business model outlines the key components of its business approach and indicates how revenues sufficient to cover operating expenses will be generated. A company's business model therefore explains how its business strategy will deliver value to customers in a profitable manner.[3] The concept of a company's business model is, consequently, more narrowly focused than the concept of a company's business strategy. A company's strategy *relates broadly to its action plan for running the business,* while a company's business model zeros in on *the principle business components that will allow the business to generate revenues sufficient to cover costs.* It should be expected that a company's strategy should be based upon a business model capable of *producing attractive profits.* Absent the ability to deliver good profits, the strategy and business model are flawed and are incapable of producing a flourishing business.

A company's **business model** indicates how its strategy will generate revenues sufficient to cover operating expenses. Absent the ability to deliver good profitability, the strategy is not viable and the survival of the business is in doubt.

Magazines and newspapers employ a business model based on generating sufficient subscriptions and advertising to cover the costs of delivering their products to readers. Cable TV companies, mobile phone providers, satellite radio companies, and broadband providers also employ subscription-based business models. The business model of radio broadcasters provides free programming to audiences and then generates revenues from fees charged to advertisers. Gillette's business model in razor blades involves selling razors at attractively low prices and then making high profits on repeat purchases of razor blades. Printer manufacturers like Hewlett-Packard, Lexmark, and Epson pursue much the same business model as Gillette—selling printers at a low (virtually breakeven) price and making large profit margins on the repeat purchases of ink and toner cartridges. Concepts & Connections 1.2 discusses the contrasting business models of Microsoft and Red Hat Linux.

The Three Tests of a Winning Strategy

Three questions can be used to distinguish a winning strategy from a so-so or flawed strategy:

1. ***Does the strategy fit the company's situation?*** To qualify as a winner, a strategy has to be well matched to the company's external and internal

[3] Joan Magretta, "Why Business Models Matter," *Harvard Business Review* 80, no. 5 (May 2002), p. 87.

Concepts & Connections 1.2

MICROSOFT AND RED HAT LINUX: TWO CONTRASTING BUSINESS MODELS

The strategies of rival companies are often predicated on strikingly different business models. Consider, for example, the business models for Microsoft and Red Hat Linux in operating system software for PCs.

Microsoft's business model for making money from its operating system products is based on the following revenue-cost-profit economics:

- Employ highly skilled programmers to develop proprietary code; keep the source code hidden to keep the inner workings of the software proprietary.

- Sell the resulting operating system and software package to personal computer (PC) makers and to PC users at relatively attractive prices (around $75 to PC makers and about $100 at retail to PC users); strive to maintain a 90 percent or more market share of the 150 million PCs sold annually worldwide.

- Most of Microsoft's costs arise on the front end in developing the software and are thus "fixed"; the variable costs of producing and packaging the CDs provided to users are only a couple of dollars per copy—once the breakeven volume is reached, Microsoft's revenues from additional sales are almost pure profit.

- Provide a modest level of technical support to users at no cost.

- Keep rejuvenating revenues by periodically introducing next-generation software versions with features that will induce PC users to upgrade the operating system on previously purchased PCs to the new version.

Red Hat Linux, a company formed to market its own version of the open-source Linux operating system, employs a business model based on sharply different revenue-cost-profit economics:

- Rely on the collaborative efforts of volunteer programmers from all over the world who contribute bits and pieces of code to improve and polish the Linux system. The global community of thousands of programmers who work on Linux in their spare time do what they do because they love it, because they are fervent believers that all software should be free (as in free speech), and, in some cases, because they are anti-Microsoft and want to have a part in undoing what they see as a Microsoft monopoly.

- Collect and test enhancements and new applications submitted by the open-source community of volunteer programmers. Linux's originator, Linus Torvalds, and a team of 300-plus Red Hat engineers and software developers evaluate which incoming submissions merit inclusion in new releases of Red Hat Linux—the evaluation and integration of new submissions are Red Hat's only up-front product development costs.

- Market the upgraded and tested family of Red Hat Linux products to large enterprises and charge them a subscription fee that includes 24/7 support within one hour in seven languages. Provide subscribers with updated versions of Red Hat Linux every 12–18 months to maintain the subscriber base.

- Capitalize on the specialized expertise required to use Linux in multiserver, multiprocessor applications by providing fee-based training, consulting, software customization, and client-directed engineering to Red Hat Linux users.

Microsoft's business model—sell proprietary code software and give service away free—is a proven money-maker that generates billions in profits annually. On the other hand, the jury is still out on Red Hat's business model of selling subscriptions to open-source software to large corporations and deriving substantial revenues from the sales of technical support, training, consulting, software customization, and engineering to generate revenues sufficient to cover costs and yield a profit. Red Hat's fiscal 2007 revenues of $400 million and net income of $60 million are quite meager in comparison.

Source: Company documents and information posted on their Web sites.

situations. The strategy must fit competitive conditions in the industry and other aspects of the enterprise's external environment. At the same time, it should be tailored to the company's resource strengths, competencies, and competitive capabilities. It's unwise to build a strategy upon the company's weaknesses or pursue a strategic approach that requires resources that are deficient in the company. Unless a strategy exhibits tight fit with both the external and internal aspects of a company's overall situation, it is unlikely to produce respectable first-rate business results.

2. ***Has the strategy yielded a sustainable competitive advantage?*** Strategies that fail to achieve a durable competitive advantage over rivals are unlikely to produce superior performance for more than a brief period of time. Winning strategies enable a company to achieve a competitive advantage over key rivals that is long lasting.

3. ***Has the strategy produced good financial performance?*** It would be difficult to categorize a strategy as a "winning strategy" unless it produces excellent company performance. Two kinds of performance improvements tell the most about the caliber of a company's strategy: (1) gains in profitability and financial performance and (2) advances in the company's competitive strength and market standing.

Managing strategically involves considering the three tests of a winning strategy when evaluating proposed or existing strategies. New initiatives that don't seem to match the company's internal and external situation should be scrapped before they come to fruition, while existing strategies must be scrutinized on a regular basis to ensure they have good fit, offer a competitive advantage, and have contributed to above-average performance. Strategies that come up short on one or more of the above tests are plainly less appealing than strategies passing all three tests with flying colors.

Key Points

1. A company's strategy is management's game plan to stake out a market position, conduct its operations, attract and please customers, compete successfully, and achieve organizational objectives.

2. The central thrust of a company's strategy is undertaking moves to build and strengthen the company's long-term competitive position and financial performance. Ideally, this results in a competitive advantage over rivals that then becomes the company's ticket to above-average profitability.

3. A company's strategy typically evolves over time, arising from a blend of (1) proactive and deliberate actions on the part of company managers and (2) as-needed emergent reactions to unanticipated developments and fresh market conditions.

4. Closely related to the concept of strategy is the concept of a company's business model. A business model is management's storyline for how the company's strategy will generate a revenue stream sufficient to cover its cost structure and produce attractive earnings and return on investment.

5. A winning strategy fits the circumstances of a company's external situation and its internal resource strengths and competitive capabilities, builds competitive advantage, and boosts company performance.

LO1 1. Please view and analyze Avon's archived investor presentations and the Management's Discussion and Analysis of Financial Condition section of its latest 10-K at www.avoncompany.com/investor. Using the information in the company's presentations and financial filings, please explain how the company's business strategy is moving Avon in an intended direction and accomplishing targeted levels of performance. What are management's actions to gain sales and market share, enter new geographic or product markets, and strengthen its market standing? Also, what actions and approaches does the company use in managing R&D, production, sales and marketing, finance, and other key activities? Please use Figure 1.1 as a reference for your report.

LO4 2. Go to www.redhat.com and check whether the company's recent financial reports indicate that its business model is working. Is the company sufficiently profitable to validate its business model and strategy? Is its revenue stream from selling training and consulting and engineering services growing or declining as a percentage of total revenues? Does your review of the company's recent financial performance suggest that its business model and strategy are changing? Read the company's latest statement about its business model and about why it is pursuing the subscription approach (as compared to Microsoft's approach of selling copies of its operating software directly to PC manufacturers and individuals).

LO1
LO2 This chapter discusses three questions that must be answered by managers of organizations of all sizes. Please read the Participant's Guide or Player's Manual for the business simulation that you will participate in this academic term. You and your simulation team should develop specific answers to the following three questions prior to completing your first decision. While the answers to the first of the three questions can be determined by reading your simulation manual, the second and third questions require strategic thinking.

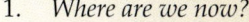

1. *Where are we now?*
2. *Where do we want to go?*
3. *How are we going to get there?*

Chapter 2

Leadership and the Strategic Management Process

Chapter Learning Objectives

LO1. Grasp why it is critical for company managers to have a clear strategic vision of where a company needs to head and why.

LO2. Understand the importance of setting both financial and strategic objectives and using a Balanced Scorecard to track performance.

LO3. Recognize the importance of tightly coordinating strategic initiatives at the corporate, business, functional, and operating levels.

LO4. Learn what a company needs to do to execute its chosen strategy in a proficient, results-producing fashion.

LO5. Become aware of the leadership skills that are required for good strategy execution.

LO6. Understand why the strategic management process is an ongoing process.

LO7. Learn about the role and responsibilities of a company's board of directors in overseeing the strategic management process.

Corporate Leaders as Chief Entrepreneurs and Strategy Makers

You are undoubtedly familiar with the names of famous entrepreneurs who have launched new ventures that have become successful corporations with sales and operations around the world. In many of these companies, the founder CEO single-handedly shaped the direction and strategy of the company and was largely responsible for many of the key decisions that led to the company's success. You are familiar, as well, with the names of non-founder CEOs known for their strategy-making capabilities and abilities to spot new business opportunities. Whether becoming CEO as the founder or as a professional manager, many chief executives such as Larry Ellison at Oracle, Meg Whitman at eBay, Andrea Jung at Avon, Jeffrey Immelt at General Electric, Steve Jobs at Apple, and Howard Schultz at Starbucks have wielded a heavy hand in shaping their company's future direction and strategy. In most companies, however, strategy is the product of more than just the CEO's handiwork. Typically, other senior executives—business unit heads, the chief financial officer, and vice presidents for production, marketing, human resources, and other functional departments—have influential strategy-making roles.

But even here it is a mistake to view strategy-making as a *top* management function limited to owner-entrepreneurs, CEOs, and other senior executives. In most of today's companies *every company manager typically has a strategy-making role for the area he or she heads.* It is not the least bit typical that strategy-making is the domain of top management and that midlevel and frontline personnel merely carry out the strategic directives of senior managers. In companies with wide-ranging operations, it is far more accurate to view strategy-making as a **collaborative team effort** involving managers (and sometimes key employees) down through the whole organizational hierarchy.[1]

> In most companies, crafting and executing strategy is a **collaborative team effort** that includes managers in various positions and a various organizational levels. Crafting and executing strategy is rarely something only high-level executives do.

Involving individuals throughout the organization in strategy-making also unleashes the talents and energies of promising "corporate intrapreneurs." Executive-level management in many companies encourages employees to try out untested business ideas and gives them room to pursue new strategic initiatives. W. L. Gore and Associates, a privately owned company famous for its Gore-Tex waterproofing film, is an avid and highly successful practitioner of the corporate intrapreneur approach to strategy-making. Gore expects all employees to initiate improvements and to display innovativeness. Each employee's intrapreneurial contributions are prime considerations in determining raises, stock option bonuses, and promotions. W. L. Gore's commitment to intrapreneurship has produced a stream of product innovations and new strategic initiatives that has kept the company vibrant and growing for nearly two decades.

---

[1] The strategy-making, strategy-implementing roles of middle managers are thoroughly discussed and documented in Steven W. Floyd and Bill Wooldridge, *The Strategic Middle Manager* (San Francisco: Jossey-Bass Publishers, 1996), Chapters 2 and 3.

Along with identifying innovations, another valuable strength of collaborative strategy-making is that, in most cases, the team of people charged with crafting the strategy will also be charged with executing it. Giving people an influential stake in crafting the strategy they must later help execute not only builds motivation and commitment, but also heightens their accountability for putting the strategy into place and making it work.

The Strategic Management Process

The managerial process of crafting and executing a company's strategy consists of five integrated stages:

1. *Developing a strategic vision* of the company's future direction and focus.
2. *Setting objectives* to measure progress toward achieving the strategic vision.
3. *Crafting a strategy* to achieve the objectives.
4. *Implementing and executing the chosen strategy* efficiently and effectively.
5. *Evaluating performance and initiating corrective adjustments* that are needed in the company's long-term direction, objectives, strategy, or approach to strategy execution.

Figure 2.1 displays this five-stage process. The model illustrates the need for management to evaluate performance on an ongoing basis once the strategy has entered the implementation phase. Any indication that the company is failing to achieve its objectives calls for corrective adjustments in one of the first four

FIGURE 2.1   **The Strategic Management Process**

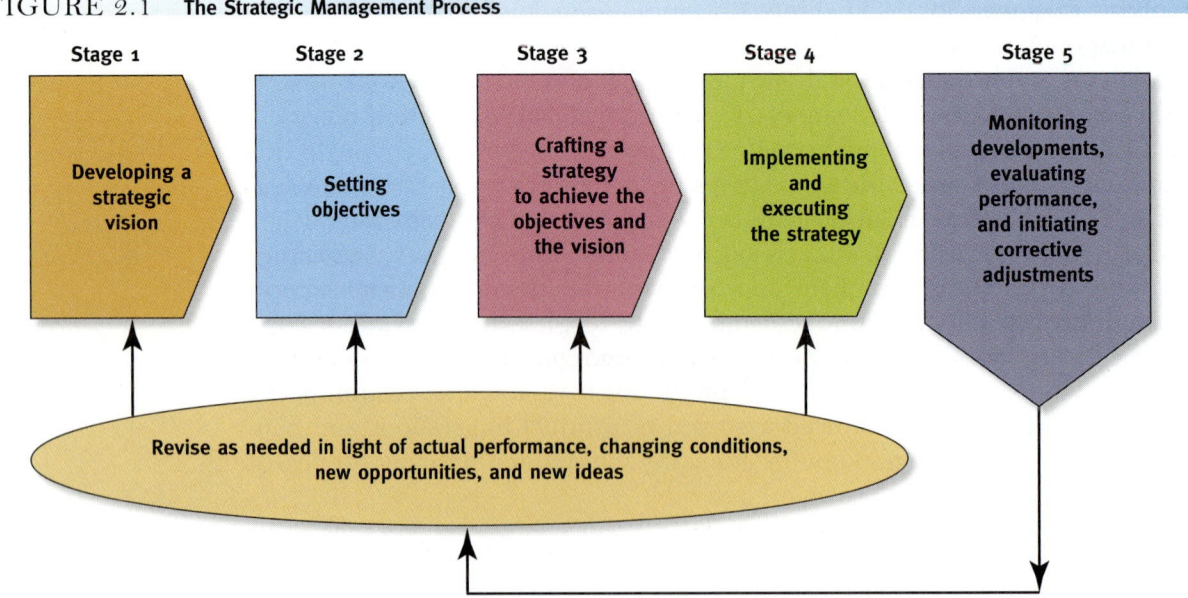

stages of the process. It's quite possible that the company's implementation efforts have fallen short and that new tactics must be devised to fully exploit the potential of the company's strategy. If management determines that the company's execution efforts are sufficient, it should challenge the assumptions underlying the company's business strategy and alter the strategy to better fit competitive conditions and the company's internal capabilities. If the company's strategic approach to competition is rated as sound, then perhaps management set overly ambitious targets for the company's performance.

The evaluation stage of the strategic management process shown in Figure 2.1 also allows for a change in the company's vision, but this should only be necessary when it becomes evident to management that the industry has changed in a significant way that renders its vision obsolete. Such occasions can be referred to as **strategic inflection points.** When a company reaches a strategic inflection point, management has some tough decisions to make about the company's direction, because abandoning an established course carries considerable risk. However, responding to unfolding changes in the marketplace in timely fashion lessens a company's chances of becoming trapped in a stagnant or declining business or letting attractive new growth opportunities slip away.

The first three stages of the strategic management process make up a strategic plan. A **strategic plan** maps out where a company is headed, establishes strategic and financial targets, and outlines the competitive moves and approaches to be used in achieving the desired business results.[2]

Stage 1 of the Strategic Management Process: Developing a Strategic Vision

Top management's views about the company's direction and future product-customer-market-technology focus constitute a **strategic vision** for the company. A clearly articulated strategic vision communicates management's aspirations to stakeholders about "where we are going" and helps steer the energies of company

> A **strategic vision** describes "where we are going"—the course and direction management has charted and the company's future product-customer-market-technology focus.

personnel in a common direction. For instance, Henry Ford's vision of a car in every garage had power because it captured the imagination of others, aided internal efforts to mobilize the Ford Motor Company's resources, and served as a reference point for gauging the merits of the company's strategic actions.

Well-conceived visions are *specific* to a particular organization; they avoid generic, feel-good statements like "We will become a global leader and the

LO1

Grasp why it is critical for company managers to have a clear strategic vision of where a company needs to head and why.

[2] For an excellent discussion of why a strategic plan needs to be more than a list of bullet points and should in fact tell an engaging, insightful, stage-setting story that lays out the industry and competitive situation as well as the vision, objectives, and strategy, see Gordon Shaw, Robert Brown, and Philip Bromiley, "Strategic Stories: How 3M Is Rewriting Business Planning," *Harvard Business Review* 76, no. 3 (May–June 1998), pp. 41–50.

Table 2.1

Characteristics of Effectively Worded Vision Statements

Graphic—Paints a picture of the kind of company that management is trying to create and the market position(s) the company is striving to stake out.

Directional—Is forward looking; describes the strategic course that management has charted and the kinds of product-market-customer-technology changes that will help the company prepare for the future.

Focused—Is specific enough to provide managers with guidance in making decisions and allocating resources.

Flexible—Is not so focused that it makes it difficult for management to adjust to changing circumstances in markets, customer preferences, or technology.

Feasible—Is within the realm of what the company can reasonably expect to achieve.

Desirable—Indicates why the directional path makes good business sense.

Easy to communicate—Is explainable in 5–10 minutes and, ideally, can be reduced to a simple, memorable "slogan" (like Henry Ford's famous vision of "a car in every garage").

Source: Based partly on John P. Kotter, *Leading Change* (Boston: Harvard Business School Press, 1996), p. 72.

first choice of customers in every market we choose to serve"—which could apply to any of hundreds of organizations.[3] And they are not the product of a committee charged with coming up with an innocuous but well-meaning one sentence vision that wins consensus approval from various stakeholders. Nicely worded vision statements with no specifics about the company's product-market-customer-technology focus fall well short of what it takes for a vision to measure up.

For a strategic vision to function as a valuable managerial tool, it must provide understanding of what management wants its business to look like and provide managers with a reference point in making strategic decisions. It must say something definitive about how the company's leaders intend to position the company beyond where it is today. Table 2.1 lists some characteristics of effective vision statements.

A surprising number of the vision statements found on company Web sites and in annual reports are vague and unrevealing, saying very little about the company's future product-market-customer-technology focus. Some could apply to most any company in any industry. Many read like a public relations statement—lofty words that someone came up with

[3] For a more in-depth discussion of the challenges of developing a well-conceived vision, as well as some good examples, see Hugh Davidson, *The Committed Enterprise: How to Make Vision and Values Work* (Oxford: Butterworth Heinemann, 2002), Chapter 2; W. Chan Kim and Renée Mauborgne, "Charting Your Company's Future," *Harvard Business Review* 80, no. 6 (June 2002), pp. 77–83; James C. Collins and Jerry I. Porras, "Building Your Company's Vision," *Harvard Business Review* 74, no. 5 (September–October 1996), pp. 65–77; Jim Collins and Jerry Porras, *Built to Last: Successful Habits of Visionary Companies* (New York: HarperCollins, 1994), Chapter 11; and Michel Robert, *Strategy Pure and Simple II* (New York: McGraw-Hill, 1998), Chapters 2, 3, and 6.

Table 2.2

Common Shortcomings in Company Vision Statements

Vague or incomplete—Short on specifics about where the company is headed or what the company is doing to prepare for the future.

Not forward looking—Doesn't indicate whether or how management intends to alter the company's current product-market-customer-technology focus.

Too broad—So all-inclusive that the company could head in most any direction, pursue most any opportunity, or enter most any business.

Bland or uninspiring—Lacks the power to motivate company personnel or inspire shareholder confidence about the company's direction.

Not distinctive—Provides no unique company identity; could apply to companies in any of several industries (including rivals operating in the same market arena).

Too reliant on superlatives—Doesn't say anything specific about the company's strategic course beyond the pursuit of such distinctions as being a recognized leader, a global or worldwide leader, or the first choice of customers.

Sources: Based on information in Hugh Davidson, *The Committed Enterprise* (Oxford: Butterworth Heinemann, 2002, Chapter 2), and Michel Robert, *Strategy Pure and Simple II* (New York: McGraw-Hill, 1998, Chapters 2, 3, and 6).

because it is fashionable for companies to have an official vision statement.[4] Table 2.2 provides a list of the most common shortcomings in company vision statements. Like any tool, vision statements can be used properly or improperly, either clearly conveying a company's strategic course or not. Concepts & Connections 2.1 presents vision statements of several well-known companies.

How a Strategic Vision Differs from a Mission Statement

The defining characteristic of a well-conceived strategic vision is what it says about the company's *future strategic course—"where we are headed and what our future product-customer-market-technology focus will be."* The mission statements of most companies say much more about the enterprise's *present* business scope and purpose—"who we are, what we do, and why we are here." Very few mission statements are forward looking in content or emphasis. Consider, for example, the mission statement of Trader Joe's (a specialty grocery chain):

> The distinction between a strategic vision and a mission statement is fairly clear-cut: A strategic vision portrays a company's **future business scope** ("where we are going") whereas a company's mission typically describes its **present business and purpose** ("who we are, what we do, and why we are here").

> The mission of Trader Joe's is to give our customers the best food and beverage values that they can find anywhere and to provide them with the information required for informed buying decisions. We provide these with a dedication to the highest quality of customer satisfaction delivered with a sense of warmth, friendliness, fun, individual pride, and company spirit.

[4] Hugh Davidson, *The Committed Enterprise* (Oxford: Butterworth Heinemann, 2002), pp. 20 and 54.

Concepts & Connections 2.1

EXAMPLES OF STRATEGIC VISIONS

UBS

We are determined to be the best global financial services company. We focus on wealth and asset management, and on investment banking and securities businesses. We continually earn recognition and trust from clients, shareholders, and staff through our ability to anticipate, learn and shape our future. We share a common ambition to succeed by delivering quality in what we do. Our purpose is to help our clients make financial decisions with confidence. We use our resources to develop effective solutions and services for our clients. We foster a distinctive, meritocratic culture of ambition, performance and learning as this attracts, retains and develops the best talent for our company. By growing both our client and our talent franchises, we add sustainable value for our shareholders.

Red Hat Linux

To extend our position as the most trusted Linux and open source provider to the enterprise. We intend to grow the market for Linux through a complete range of enterprise Red Hat Linux software, a powerful Internet management platform, and associated support and services.

Hilton Hotels Corporation

Our vision is to be the first choice of the world's travelers. Hilton intends to build on the rich heritage and strength of our brands by:

- Consistently delighting our customers.
- Investing in our team members.
- Delivering innovative products and services.
- Continuously improving performance.
- Increasing shareholder value.
- Creating a culture of pride.
- Strengthening the loyalty of our constituents.

eBay

Provide a global trading platform where practically anyone can trade practically anything.

Chevron

To be *the* global energy company most admired for its people, partnership and performance. Our vision means we:

- Provide energy products vital to sustainable economic progress and human development throughout the world.
- Are people and an organization with superior capabilities and commitment.
- Are the partner of choice.
- Deliver world-class performance.
- Earn the admiration of all our stakeholders—investors, customers, host governments, local communities and our employees—not only for the goals we achieve but how we achieve them.

Note that Trader Joe's mission statement does a good job of conveying "who we are, what we do, and why we are here," but it provides no sense of "where we are headed." (Some companies use the term *business purpose* instead of *mission statement* in describing themselves; in actual practice, there seems to be no meaningful difference between the terms mission statement and business purpose—which one is used is a matter of preference.)

To reflect common management practice, we will use the term *mission statement* to refer to an enterprise's description of its *present* business and its purpose for existence. Ideally, a company mission statement is sufficiently descriptive to:

- *Identify the company's products or services.*
- *Specify the buyer needs it seeks to satisfy.*

- *Specify the customer groups or markets it is endeavoring to serve.*
- *Specify its approach to pleasing customers.*

Occasionally, companies state their mission is to simply earn a profit. This is misguided. Profit is more correctly an *objective* and a *result* of what a company does.

An example of a well-stated mission statement with ample specifics about what the organization does is that of the Occupational Safety and Health Administration (OSHA): "to assure the safety and health of America's workers by setting and enforcing standards; providing training, outreach, and education; establishing partnerships; and encouraging continual improvement in workplace safety and health." Google's mission statement, while short, still captures the essence of what the company is about: "to organize the world's information and make it universally accessible and useful." An example of a not-so-revealing mission statement is that of Microsoft. "To help people and businesses throughout the world realize their full potential" says nothing about its products or business makeup and could apply to many companies in many different industries. A mission statement that provides scant indication of "who we are and what we do" has no apparent value.

The Importance of Communicating the Strategic Vision

A strategic vision has little value to the organization unless it's effectively communicated down the line to lower-level managers and employees. It would be difficult for a vision statement to provide direction to decision makers and energize employees toward achieving long-term strategic intent unless they know of the vision and observe management's commitment to that vision. Communicating the vision to organization members nearly always means putting "where we are going and why" in writing, distributing the statement organizationwide, and having executives personally explain the vision and its rationale to as many people as feasible. Ideally, executives should present their vision for the company in a manner that reaches out and grabs people's attention. An engaging and convincing strategic vision has enormous motivational value—for the same reason that a stone mason is inspired by building a great cathedral for the ages. Therefore, an executive's ability to paint a convincing and inspiring picture of a company's journey to a future destination is an important element of effective strategic leadership.[5]

The Benefits of an Effective Strategic Vision

In sum, a well-conceived, effectively communicated strategic vision pays off in several respects: (1) it crystallizes senior executives' own views about the firm's long-term direction; (2) it reduces the risk of rudderless decision making by management at all levels; (3) it is a tool for winning the support of employees to help make the vision a reality; (4) it provides a beacon for lower-level managers in forming departmental missions; and (5) it helps an organization prepare for the future.

[5] Ibid, pp. 36, 54.

Stage 2 of the Strategic Management Process: Setting Objectives

LO2

Understand the importance of setting both financial and strategic objectives and using a Balanced Scorecard to track performance.

The managerial purpose of setting **objectives** is to convert the strategic vision into specific performance targets. Well-stated objectives are *quantifiable,* or *measurable,* and contain a *deadline for achievement.* Concrete, measurable objectives are managerially valuable because they serve as yardsticks for tracking a company's performance and progress toward its vision. Vague targets like "maximize profits," "reduce costs," "become more efficient," or "increase sales," which specify neither how much nor when offer little value as a management tool to improve company performance. Ideally, managers should develop *challenging,* yet *achievable* objectives that *stretch an organization to perform at its full potential.* As Mitchell Leibovitz, former CEO of the auto parts and service retailer Pep Boys, once said, "If you want to have ho-hum results, have ho-hum objectives."

What Kinds of Objectives to Set—The Need for a Balanced Scorecard

Two very distinct types of performance yardsticks are required: those relating to financial performance and those relating to strategic performance. **Financial objectives** communicate management's targets for financial performance. Common financial objectives relate to revenue growth, profitability, and return on investment. **Strategic objectives** are related to a company's marketing standing and competitive vitality. The importance of attaining financial objectives is intuitive. Without adequate profitability and financial strength, a company's long-term health and ultimate survival is jeopardized. Furthermore, sub-par earnings and a weak balance sheet alarm shareholders and creditors and put the jobs of senior executives at risk. However, good financial performance, by itself, is not enough.

A company's financial objectives are really *lagging indicators* that reflect the results of past decisions and organizational activities.[6] The results of past decisions and organizational activities are not reliable indicators of a company's future prospects. Companies that have been poor financial performers are sometimes able to turn things around and good financial performers on occasion fall upon hard times. Hence, the best and most reliable predictors of a company's success in the marketplace and future financial performance are strategic objectives. Strategic outcomes are *leading indicators* of a company's future financial performance and business prospects. The accomplishment of strategic objectives signals the company is well-positioned to sustain or improve its performance. For instance, if a company is achieving ambitious strategic objectives, then there's reason to expect that its *future* financial performance will be better than its current or past performance. If a company begins to lose competitive strength and fails to

---

[6] Robert S. Kaplan and David P. Norton, *The Strategy-Focused Organization* (Boston: Harvard Business School Press, 2001), p. 3.

achieve important strategic objectives, then its ability to maintain its present profitability is highly suspect.

Consequently, utilizing a performance measurement system that strikes a *balance* between financial objectives and strategic objectives is optimal.[7] The balanced scorecard approach used by companies such as BMW, Walt Disney, Verizon, and Ann Taylor Stores involves financial performance targets and strategic performance targets in three areas: (1) external **customer-related** issues such as customer satisfaction, brand loyalty, and on-time delivery, (2) internal **business processes** that are necessary to allow the company to attract and retain customers, and (3) internal **learning and growth** activities related to human resources, information technology, and organizational qualities such as teamwork.[8] Representative examples of financial and strategic objectives that companies often include in a balanced scorecard approach to measuring their performance are displayed in the following table:

FINANCIAL OBJECTIVES	STRATEGIC OBJECTIVES		
	Customer	**Internal Business Process**	**Learning and Growth**
• An x percent increase in annual revenues • Annual increases in earnings per share of x percent • An x percent return on capital employed (ROCE) or shareholder investment (ROE) • Dividend increases of x percent • Bond and credit ratings of x • Internal cash flows of x to fund new capital investment	• Winning an x percent market share • Achieving customer satisfaction rates of x percent • Achieving a customer retention rate of x percent • Acquire x number of new customers • Lower service failure rate to x percent • Shorten order fulfillment time to x hours • Reduce out-of-stock items to x percent	• Reduce product defects to x percent • Introduction of x number of new products in the next three years • Reduce product development times to x months • Increase percentage of sales coming from new products to x percent • Improve post-sale service process by reducing the cycle time from customer request to problem resolution to x hours	• Improve employee satisfaction rate to x • Reduce turnover to x percent per year • Increase employee training to x hours per year • Improve information systems capabilities to give frontline managers defect information in x minutes • Improve teamwork by increasing the number of projects involving more than one business unit to x

SHORT-TERM AND LONG-TERM OBJECTIVES   A company's set of financial and strategic objectives should include both near-term and long-term performance targets. Short-term objectives focus attention on delivering performance improvements in the current period, while long-term targets force

[7] *Ibid.*, p. 7. Also, see Robert S. Kaplan and David P. Norton, *The Balanced Scorecard: Translating Strategy into Action* (Boston: Harvard Business School Press, 1996), p. 10.; Kevin B. Hendricks, Larry Menor, and Christine Wiedman, "The Balanced Scorecard: To Adopt or Not to Adopt," *Ivey Business Journal* 69, no. 2 (November–December 2004), pp. 1–7; and Sandy Richardson, "The Key Elements of Balanced Scorecard Success," *Ivey Business Journal* 69, no. 2 (November–December 2004), pp. 7–9.

[8] Kaplan and Norton, *The Balanced Scorecard: Translating Strategy into Action*, pp. 25–29.

the organization to consider how actions currently under way will affect the company at a later date. Specifically, long-term objectives stand as a barrier to a nearsighted management philosophy and an undue focus on short-term results. When trade-offs have to be made between achieving long-run and short-run objectives, long-run objectives should take precedence (unless the achievement of one or more short-run performance targets has unique importance).

THE NEED FOR OBJECTIVES AT ALL ORGANIZATIONAL LEVELS

Objective setting should not stop with the establishment of companywide performance targets. Company objectives need to be broken down into performance targets for each of the organization's separate businesses, product lines, functional departments, and individual work units. Employees within various functional areas and operating levels will be guided much better by narrow objectives relating directly to their departmental activities than broad organizational level goals. Objective setting is thus a top-down process that must extend to the lowest organizational levels. And it means that each organizational unit must take care to set performance targets that support—rather than conflict with or negate—the achievement of companywide strategic and financial objectives.

Stage 3 of the Strategic Management Process: Crafting Corporate and Business Strategies

LO3

Recognize the importance of tightly coordinating strategic initiatives at the corporate, business, functional, and operating levels.

Management's strategic approach to achieving organizational objectives, competing successfully, and building competitively important capabilities creates *a collection of strategic initiatives and actions* that encompass all levels of the organization. Ideally, the pieces of a company's strategy should be cohesive and mutually reinforcing, fitting together like a jigsaw puzzle. To achieve such unity, top executives must clearly articulate key strategic themes to guide lower-level strategy makers. For example, functional area managers of a company pursuing a cost-based advantage must adopt unit-level strategies that minimize cost. Figure 2.2 illustrates the strategy levels of a single business company with a relatively simple business structure. A diversified, multibusiness company would also have an overarching corporate-level strategy beyond what is shown in Figure 2.2 to ensure consistency in strategy among all businesses in its portfolio.

A key element of the strategy-making hierarchy shown in Figure 2.2 is the two-way influence between management at various levels of the organization in crafting the business strategy. Managers at the top of the organization might have conceptualized a ground breaking strategy possible of yielding significant marketplace advantages, but such plans may not match the current competitive capabilities of the organization. In many ways, managers closest to operations are in the best position to determine if an organization is capable of executing a planned strategy. You should conclude from examining the figure that strategy-making efforts require collaboration among managers throughout the organization and must be coordinated across functional areas to have a good chance of bringing success to the organization.

FIGURE 2.2   **Strategy-Making Hierarchy for a Single Business Company**

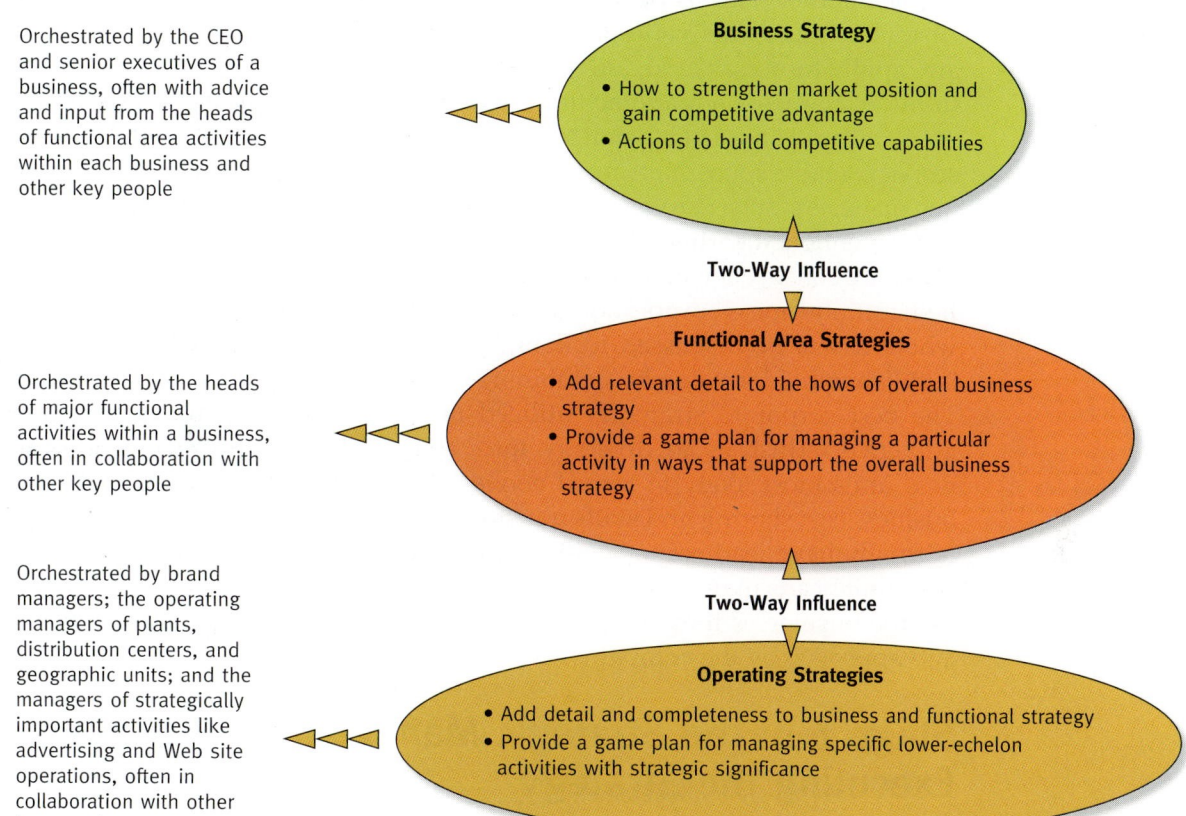

Orchestrated by the CEO and senior executives of a business, often with advice and input from the heads of functional area activities within each business and other key people

Business Strategy

- How to strengthen market position and gain competitive advantage
- Actions to build competitive capabilities

Two-Way Influence

Orchestrated by the heads of major functional activities within a business, often in collaboration with other key people

Functional Area Strategies

- Add relevant detail to the hows of overall business strategy
- Provide a game plan for managing a particular activity in ways that support the overall business strategy

Two-Way Influence

Orchestrated by brand managers; the operating managers of plants, distribution centers, and geographic units; and the managers of strategically important activities like advertising and Web site operations, often in collaboration with other key people

Operating Strategies

- Add detail and completeness to business and functional strategy
- Provide a game plan for managing specific lower-echelon activities with strategic significance

As shown in Figure 2.2, a company's **business strategy** is the responsibility of the CEO and other senior executives and is primarily concerned with strengthening the company's market position and building competitive advantage. **Functional-area strategies** concern the actions related to particular functions or processes within a business. A company's product development strategy, for example, represents the managerial game plan for creating new products that are in tune with what buyers are looking for. Functional strategies add detail to the company's business-level strategy and specify what resources and organizational capabilities are needed to put the company's overall business strategy into action. Lead responsibility for functional strategies within a business is normally delegated to the heads of the respective functions, with the general manager of the business having final approval over functional strategies. For the overall business strategy to have maximum impact, a business's marketing strategy, production strategy, finance strategy, customer service strategy, product development strategy, and human resources strategy should be compatible and mutually reinforcing rather than each serving its own narrower purpose.

Operating strategies concern the relatively narrow strategic initiatives and approaches for managing key operating units (plants, distribution centers, geographic units) and specific operating activities such as materials purchasing or Internet sales. A distribution center manager of a company promising customers speedy deliveries must have a strategy to ensure that finished goods are rapidly turned around and shipped out to customers once they are received from the company's manufacturing facilities. Operating strategies are limited in scope, but add further detail to functional strategies and the overall business strategy. Lead responsibility for operating strategies is usually delegated to front-line managers, subject to review and approval by higher ranking managers.

As mentioned earlier in this section, the purpose of a **corporate strategy** is to ensure consistency in strategic approach among the businesses of a diversified, multibusiness corporation. Corporate strategy is the subject of Chapter 9, where it will be discussed in detail. In short, winning corporate strategies build shareholder value by combining businesses to yield a $1 + 1 = 3$ effect. The best corporate strategies utilized in multibusiness companies identify attractive industries to diversify into, allocate financial resources to business units most likely to record above-average earnings, and capture cross-business cost sharing and skills transfer synergies. Senior corporate executives normally have lead responsibility for devising corporate strategy. Key business-unit heads may also be influential, especially in strategic decisions affecting the businesses they head. Major strategic decisions are usually reviewed and approved by the company's board of directors.

Stage 4 of the Strategic Management Process: Executing the Strategy

LO4

Learn what a company needs to do to execute its chosen strategy in a proficient, results-producing fashion.

Managing the implementation and execution of strategy is easily the most demanding and time-consuming part of the strategic management process. In most situations, managing the strategy execution process includes the following principal aspects:

- Staffing the organization to provide needed skills and expertise.
- Allocating ample resources to activities critical to good strategy execution.
- Ensuring that policies and procedures facilitate rather than impede effective execution.
- Installing information and operating systems that enable company personnel to perform essential activities.
- Pushing for continuous improvement in how value chain activities are performed.
- Tying rewards and incentives directly to the achievement of performance objectives.
- Creating a company culture and work climate conducive to successful strategy execution.
- Exerting the internal leadership needed to propel implementation forward.

Many large companies with complex strategies utilize **strategy maps** to explain to lower-level managers and other employees how effective strategy implementation drives revenue growth and profitability. Strategy maps bridge the gap between strategy formulation and implementation by visually describing the connections between operating level activities and broad organizational strategies. Strategy maps are tied to balanced scorecard objectives and organize the company's key activities by the *four perspectives of the Balanced Scorecard—financial, customer, internal process, and learning and growth.* Figure 2.3 shows how *product or service attributes* such as price and quality, *customer relationships,* and *brand image* drive revenue growth and shareholder value. The figure also identifies internal processes related to *operations, customer management, innovation,* and *regulatory and social* issues that affect the company's ability to deliver valuable products and services to customers. Ultimately, the company's ability to effectively execute its strategy rests with its performance of learning and growth activities that build the skills, talent, and know-how of *human capital,* provide necessary *information systems,* and develop *organizational capital* such as a strategy-supportive culture, leadership depth, and teamwork.[9]

[9] Robert S. Kaplan and David P. Norton, *Strategy Maps: Converting Intangible Assets into Tangible Outcomes* (Boston: Harvard Business School Press, 2004), pp. 29–32. Also, see Robert S. Kaplan and David P. Norton, "Mastering the Management System," *Harvard Business Review* 86, no. 1 (January 2008), pp. 68–70; and Cam Scholey, "Strategy Maps: A Step-by-Step Guide to Measuring, Managing and Communicating the Plan," *Journal of Business Strategy* 26, no. 3 (2005), pp. 12–19.

FIGURE 2.3 **Strategy Map Illustrating Relationships Between Business Strategy, Strategy Implementation, and Achievement of Balanced Scorecard Performance Targets**

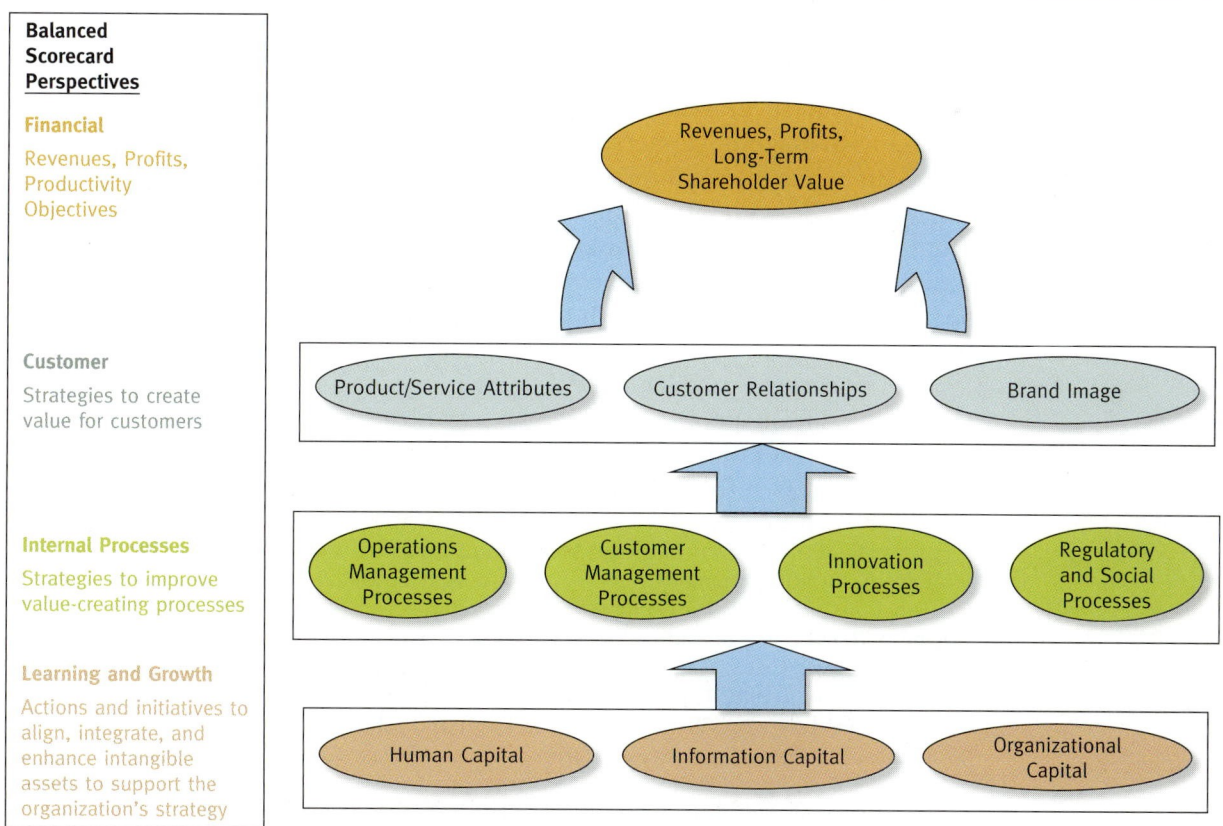

Leading the Strategy Execution Process

LO5

Become aware of the leadership skills that are required for good strategy execution.

Strategy maps are effective communication tools to help employees understand how activities in their departments or units contribute to the company's game plan for competing in the industry, but managers throughout the organization must exert leadership to drive the implementation of functional- and operating-level strategies forward. In general, leading the campaign for good strategy execution and operating excellence calls for three actions on the part of the manager-in-charge.[10]

1. Stay on top of what is happening and identify obstacles to good strategy execution.

2. Push organizational units to achieve good results and operating excellence.

3. Display ethical integrity and spearhead social responsibility initiatives.

STAYING ON TOP OF HOW WELL THINGS ARE GOING   One of the best ways for executives to stay on top of the strategy execution process is by making regular visits to the field and talking with many different people at many different levels—a technique often labeled *managing by walking around* **(MBWA).** Wal-Mart executives have had a long-standing practice of spending two to three days every week visiting Wal-Mart's stores and talking with store managers and employees. Sam Walton, Wal-Mart's founder, insisted, "The key is to get out into the store and listen to what the associates have to say." Jack Welch, the highly effective CEO of General Electric (GE) from 1980 to 2001, not only spent several days each month personally visiting GE operations and talking with major customers, but also arranged his schedule so that he could spend time exchanging information and ideas with GE managers from all over the world who were attending classes at the company's leadership development center near GE's headquarters. Jeff Bezos, Amazon.com's CEO, is noted for his frequent facilities visits and his insistence that other Amazon managers spend time in the trenches with their people to prevent overly abstract thinking and getting disconnected from the reality of what's happening.[11]

Most managers practice MBWA, attaching great importance on gathering information from people at different organizational levels about how well various aspects of the strategy execution process are going. They believe facilities visits and face-to-face contacts give them a good feel for what progress is

---

[10] For excellent discussions of the problems and pitfalls in leading the transition to a new strategy and to fundamentally new ways of doing business, see Larry Bossidy and Ram Charan, *Confronting Reality: Doing What Matters to Get Things Right* (New York: Crown Business, 2004); Larry Bossidy and Ram Charan, *Execution: The Discipline of Getting Things Done* (New York: Crown Business, 2002), especially Chapters 3 and 5; John P. Kotter, "Leading Change: Why Transformation Efforts Fail," *Harvard Business Review* 73, no. 2 (March–April 1995), pp. 59–67; Thomas M. Hout and John C. Carter, "Getting It Done: New Roles for Senior Executives," *Harvard Business Review* 73, no. 6 (November–December 1995), pp. 133–45; and Sumantra Ghoshal and Christopher A. Bartlett, "Changing the Role of Top Management: Beyond Structure to Processes," *Harvard Business Review* 73, no. 1 (January–February 1995), pp. 86–96.

[11] Fred Vogelstein, "Winning the Amazon Way," *Fortune*, May 26, 2003, p. 64.

being made, what problems are being encountered, and whether additional resources or different approaches may be needed. Just as important, MBWA provides opportunities to give encouragement, lift spirits, shift attention from old to new priorities, and create excitement—all of which help mobilize organizational efforts behind strategy execution.

PUSHING ORGANIZATION UNITS TO ACHIEVE GOOD RESULTS AND OPERATING EXCELLENCE Managers have to be out front in mobilizing the effort for good strategy execution and operating excellence. Part of the leadership requirement here entails fostering a results-oriented work climate, where performance standards are high and a spirit of achievement is pervasive. Organizational leaders who succeed in creating a results-oriented work climate typically are intensely people-oriented, and they are skilled users of people-management practices that win the emotional commitment of company personnel and inspire them to do their best.[12] They understand that treating employees well generally leads to increased teamwork, higher morale, greater loyalty, and increased employee commitment to making a contribution. All of these foster an esprit de corps that energizes organizational members to contribute to the drive for operating excellence and proficient strategy execution.

Successfully leading the effort to instill a spirit of high achievement into the culture generally entails such leadership actions and managerial practices as:

- *Treating employees with dignity and respect.*
- *Encouraging employees to use initiative and creativity in performing their work.*
- *Setting stretch objectives* and clearly communicating an expectation that company personnel are to give their best in achieving performance targets.
- *Focusing attention on continuous improvement.*
- *Using the full range of motivational techniques and compensation incentives to reward high performance.*
- *Celebrating individual, group, and company successes.* Top management should miss no opportunity to express respect for individual employees and show their appreciation of extraordinary individual and group effort.[13]

While leadership efforts to instill a results-oriented, high performance culture usually accentuate the positive, there are negative reinforcers too. Low-performing workers and people who reject the results-oriented cultural emphasis have to be weeded out or at least moved to out-of-the-way positions. Average performers have to be candidly counseled that they have limited career potential unless they show more progress in the form of additional effort, better skills, and improved ability to deliver good results. In addition, managers whose units consistently perform poorly have to be replaced.

[12] For a more in-depth discussion of the leader's role in creating a results-oriented culture that nurtures success, see Benjamin Schneider, Sarah K. Gunnarson, and Kathryn Niles-Jolly, "Creating the Climate and Culture of Success," *Organizational Dynamics,* Summer 1994, pp. 17–29.

[13] Jeffrey Pfeffer, "Producing Sustainable Competitive Advantage through the Effective Management of People," *Academy of Management Executive* 9, no. 1 (February 1995), pp. 55–69.

DISPLAYING ETHICAL INTEGRITY AND LEADING SOCIAL RESPONSIBILITY INITIATIVES   For an organization to avoid the pitfalls of scandal and disgrace related to unethical business practices, management must be openly and unswervingly committed to ethical conduct and socially redeeming business principles. Leading the effort to operate the company's business in an ethically principled fashion has three pieces.

- First and foremost, the CEO and other senior executives must set an excellent example in their own ethical behavior, demonstrating character and personal integrity in their actions and decisions. The behavior of senior executives is always watched carefully, sending a clear message to company personnel regarding what the "real" standards of personal conduct are.

- Second, top management must declare unequivocal support of the company's ethical code and take an uncompromising stand on expecting all company personnel to adhere to the company's ethical principles.

- Third, top management must be prepared to act as the final arbiter on hard calls; this means removing people from key positions or terminating them when they are guilty of a violation. It also means reprimanding those who have been lax in enforcing ethical compliance. Failure to act swiftly and decisively in punishing ethical misconduct is interpreted as a lack of real commitment.

LEADING SOCIAL RESPONSIBILITY INITIATIVES   The exercise of social responsibility, just as with observance of ethical principles, requires top executive leadership. What separates companies that make a sincere effort to be good corporate citizens from companies that are content to do only what is legally required are company leaders who believe strongly that just making a profit is not good enough. Such leaders are committed to a higher standard of performance that includes social and environmental metrics as well as financial and strategic metrics. The strength of the commitment from the top—typically a company's CEO and board of directors—ultimately determines whether a company will implement and execute a full-fledged strategy of social responsibility that protects the environment, actively participates in community affairs, supports charitable causes, and has a positive impact on workforce diversity and the overall well-being of employees.

LO6

Understand why the strategic management process is an ongoing process.

Evaluating Performance and Initiating Corrective Adjustments: Stage 5 of the Strategy-Making, Strategy-Executing Process

The fifth stage of the strategy management process—monitoring new external developments, evaluating the company's progress, and making corrective adjustments—is the trigger point for deciding whether to continue or change the company's vision, objectives, strategy, and/or strategy execution methods. So long as the company's direction and strategy seem well matched to industry and competitive conditions and performance targets are being met, company executives may well decide to stay the course. Simply fine-tuning the strategic plan and continuing with efforts to improve strategy execution are sufficient.

But whenever a company encounters disruptive changes in its environment, questions need to be raised about the appropriateness of its direction and strategy. If a company experiences a downturn in its market position or persistent shortfalls in performance, then company managers are obligated to ferret out the causes—do they relate to poor strategy, poor strategy execution, or both?—and take timely corrective action. A company's direction, objectives, and strategy have to be revisited any time external or internal conditions warrant.

The leadership challenge of making corrective adjustments is twofold: deciding when adjustments are needed and deciding what adjustments to make.[14] Both decisions are a normal and necessary part of managing the strategy execution process. The *process* of making corrective adjustments varies according to the situation. In a crisis, it is typical for leaders to have key subordinates gather information, identify and evaluate options, and perhaps prepare a preliminary set of recommended actions for consideration. The organizational leader then usually meets with key subordinates to evaluate strategic options and try to build a quick consensus among members of the executive inner circle. If no consensus emerges and action is required immediately, the burden falls on the manager in charge to choose the response and urge its support. When the situation is less urgent, most managers seem to prefer a process of incrementally solidifying commitment to a particular course of action.[15] The process that managers go through in deciding on corrective adjustments is essentially the same for both proactive and reactive changes.[16] The time frame for deciding what corrective changes to initiate can take a few hours, a few days, a few weeks, or even a few months if the situation is particularly complicated.

Corporate Governance: The Role of the Board of Directors in the Strategic Management Process

Although senior managers have *lead responsibility* for crafting and executing a company's strategy, it is the duty of the board of directors to exercise strong oversight and see that the five tasks of strategic management are done in a manner that benefits shareholders (in the case of investor-owned enterprises) or stakeholders (in the case of not-for-profit organizations). In watching over management's strategy-making, strategy-executing actions, a company's board of directors has four important obligations to fulfill:

LO7

Learn about the role and responsibilities of a company's board of directors in overseeing the strategic management process.

1. *Be inquiring critics and oversee the company's direction, strategy, and business approaches.* Board members must ask probing questions and draw on their business acumen to make independent judgments about whether strategy proposals have been adequately analyzed and whether proposed strategic actions appear to have greater promise than alternatives.

[14] For an excellent discussion of the leader's role in developing a dynamic strategy-making process involving continuous creation and recreation, see Cynthia A. Montgomery, "Putting Leadership Back into Strategy," *Harvard Business Review* 86, no. 1 (January 2008), pp. 54–60.

[15] James Brian Quinn, *Strategies for Change: Logical Incrementalism* (Homewood, IL: Richard D. Irwin, 1980), pp. 20–22.

[16] Ibid., p. 146.

2. *Evaluate the caliber of senior executives' strategy-making and strategy-executing skills.* The board is always responsible for determining whether the current CEO is doing a good job of strategic leadership.

3. *Institute a compensation plan for top executives that rewards them for actions and results that serve stakeholder interests, and most especially those of shareholders.* A basic principle of corporate governance is that the owners of a corporation delegate managerial control to top management in return for compensation. In their role as an *agent* of shareholders, top executives have a duty to make decisions and operate the company in accord with shareholder interests. Boards of directors must develop salary and incentive compensation plans that make it in the self-interest of executives to operate the business in a manner that benefits the owners. It is also incumbent on the board of directors to prevent management from gaining executive perks and privileges that simply line the financial pockets of executives. Numerous media reports have recounted instances in which boards of directors have gone along with opportunistic executive efforts to secure excessive, if not downright obscene, compensation of one kind or another (multimillion-dollar interest-free loans, personal use of corporate aircraft, lucrative severance and retirement packages, outsized stock incentive awards, and so on).

4. *Oversee the company's financial accounting and financial reporting practices.* While top management, particularly the company's CEO and CFO (chief financial officer), is primarily responsible for seeing that the company's financial statements accurately report the results of the company's operations, board members have a fiduciary duty to protect shareholders by exercising oversight of the company's financial practices. In addition, corporate boards must ensure that generally acceptable accounting principles are properly used in preparing the company's financial statements and determine whether proper financial controls are in place to prevent fraud and misuse of funds.

Every corporation should have a strong, independent board of directors that (1) is well-informed about the company's performance, (2) guides and judges the CEO and other top executives, (3) has the courage to curb management actions they believe are inappropriate or unduly risky, (4) certifies to shareholders that the CEO is doing what the board expects, (5) provides insight and advice to management, and (6) is intensely involved in debating the pros and cons of key decisions and actions.[17] Boards of directors that lack the backbone to challenge a strong-willed or "imperial" CEO or that rubberstamp most anything the CEO recommends without probing inquiry and debate abandon their duty to represent and protect shareholder interests.

---

[17] For a discussion of what it takes for the corporate governance system to function properly, see David A. Nadler, "Building Better Boards," *Harvard Business Review* 82, no. 5 (May 2004), pp. 102–105; Cynthia A. Montgomery and Rhonda Kaufman, "The Board's Missing Link," *Harvard Business Review* 81, no. 3 (March 2003), pp. 86–93; and John Carver, "What Continues to Be Wrong with Corporate Governance and How to Fix It," *Ivey Business Journal* 68, no. 1 (September/October 2003), pp. 1–5. See also Gordon Donaldson, "A New Tool for Boards: The Strategic Audit," *Harvard Business Review* 73, no. 4 (July–August 1995), pp. 99–107.

Key Points

The strategic management process consists of five interrelated and integrated stages:

1. *Developing a strategic vision* of where the company needs to head and what its future product-customer-market-technology focus should be. This managerial step provides long-term direction, infuses the organization with a sense of purposeful action, and communicates to stakeholders management's aspirations for the company.

2. *Setting objectives* and using the targeted results as yardsticks for measuring the company's performance. Objectives need to spell out *how much* of *what kind* of performance *by when*. A *balanced scorecard* approach for measuring company performance entails setting both *financial objectives and strategic objectives.*

3. *Crafting a strategy to achieve the objectives* and move the company along the strategic course that management has charted. Crafting strategy is concerned principally with forming responses to changes underway in the external environment, devising competitive moves and market approaches aimed at producing sustainable competitive advantage, building competitively valuable competencies and capabilities, and uniting the strategic actions initiated in various parts of the company. Strategy-making is a *collaborative team effort* involving managers and company personnel at many organizational levels. The total strategy that emerges is really a collection of strategic actions and business approaches initiated partly by senior company executives, partly by the heads of major business divisions, partly by functional-area managers, and partly by operating managers on the frontlines. A single business enterprise has three levels of strategy—business strategy for the company as a whole, functional-area strategies for each main area within the business, and operating strategies undertaken by lower-echelon managers. In diversified, multibusiness companies, the strategy-making task involves four distinct types or levels of strategy: corporate strategy for the company as a whole, business strategy (one for each business the company has diversified into), functional-area strategies within each business, and operating strategies. Typically, the strategy-making task is more top-down than bottom-up, with higher-level strategies serving as the guide for developing lower-level strategies.

4. *Implementing and executing the chosen strategy efficiently and effectively.* Managing the implementation and execution of strategy is an operations-oriented, make-things-happen activity aimed at shaping the performance of core business activities in a strategy supportive manner. Management's handling of the strategy implementation process can be considered successful if things go smoothly enough that the company meets or beats its strategic and financial performance targets and shows good progress in achieving management's strategic vision.

5. *Evaluating performance and initiating corrective adjustments* in vision, long-term direction, objectives, strategy, or execution in light of actual experience, changing conditions, new ideas, and new opportunities. This stage of the strategy management process is the trigger point for deciding whether to continue or change the company's vision, objectives, strategy, and/or strategy execution methods.

The sum of a company's strategic vision, objectives, and strategy constitute a *strategic plan.*

Many large companies with complex strategies utilize *strategy maps* to bridge the gap between strategy formulation and implementation by visually describing the connections between operating level activities and broad organizational strategies. Strategy maps are tied to balanced scorecard objectives and organize the company's key activities by the four perspectives of the Balanced Scorecard—financial, customer, internal process, and learning and growth.

Managers must demonstrate strong leadership to push strategy implementation and execution forward. In general, leading the drive for good strategy execution and operating excellence calls for three actions on the part of the manager in charge:

1. Stay on top of what is happening and identify obstacles to good strategy execution.

2. Push organizational units to achieve good results and operating excellence.

3. Display ethical integrity and spearhead social responsibility initiatives.

Boards of directors have a duty to shareholders to play a vigilant role in overseeing management's handling of a company's strategy-making, strategy-executing process. A company's board is obligated to (1) critically appraise and ultimately approve strategic action plans, (2) evaluate the strategic leadership skills of the CEO, (3) institute a compensation plan for top executives that rewards them for actions and results that serve stakeholder interests, most especially those of shareholders, and (4) ensure that the company issues accurate financial reports and has adequate financial controls.

Assurance of Learning Exercises

1. Examples of strategic visions of several prominent companies are listed below. Which ones are mostly meaningless or nice-sounding and which ones are managerially useful in communicating "where we are headed and the kind of company we are trying to become." Please improve upon the vision statements that you believe are ineffective in communicating the future direction of the company.

LO1

Wells Fargo
We want to satisfy all of our customers' financial needs, help them succeed financially, be the premier provider of financial services in every one of our markets, and be known as one of America's great companies.

The Dental Products Division of 3M Corporation
Become THE supplier of choice to the global dental professional markets, providing world-class quality and innovative products.

   [Note: All employees of the division wear badges bearing these words, and whenever a new product or business procedure is being considered, management asks, "Is this representative of THE leading dental company?"]

Caterpillar
Be the global leader in customer value.

H. J. Heinz Company
Be the world's premier food company, offering nutritious, superior tasting foods to people everywhere. Being the premier food company does not mean being the biggest but it does mean being the best in terms of consumer value, customer service, employee talent, and consistent and predictable growth.

Best Buy
Make life fun and easy!

Source: Company Web sites and annual reports.

L05 2. Go to www.dell.com/speeches and read Michael Dell's recent speeches. Do Michael Dell's speeches provide evidence that he is an effective leader at Dell Computer? Is there evidence he is concerned with (1) staying on top of what is happening and identifying obstacles to good strategy execution, (2) pushing the organization to achieve good results and operating excellence, and (3) displaying ethical integrity and spearheading social responsibility initiatives?

L07 3. Go to www.dell.com/leadership and read the section dedicated to corporate governance at Dell Computer. Is there evidence of effective governance at Dell in regard to (1) a critical appraisal of strategic action plans, (2) evaluation of the strategic leadership skills of the CEO, (3) executive compensation, and (4) accurate financial reports and controls?

L03
L04 Using information in your Player's Manual or Participant's Guide, please prepare a strategy map outlining how your simulation company will generate revenue growth and profits that meet investor expectations. Please use Figure 2.3 as a guide to outline strategies to create value for customers, strategies to improve value-creating processes, and activities to align, integrate, and enhance intangible assets to support the company's business strategy. The game manual should contain all of the information needed to describe the strategies your company will undertake regarding customer and internal process perspectives. Learning and growth perspectives may include topics discussed in your simulation manual or qualities and characteristics possessed by your team members.

Exercise for Business Simulation Users

Chapter 3

Competitive Strategy and Advantage in the Marketplace

Chapter Learning Objectives

LO1. Gain an understanding of competitive strategies frequently used to provide distinctive industry positioning and competitive advantage in the marketplace.

LO2. Recognize industry conditions that favor a market target that is either broad or narrow and that indicate whether the company should pursue a competitive advantage linked to low costs or product differentiation.

LO3. Understand the role of resource-based strategies in supplementing generic strategies and achieving competitive advantage.

LO4. Learn how strategic alliances and partnerships can be used to add to a firm's collection of resources and competencies.

In Chapter 1 we introduced the concept of competitive strategy and its importance in attaining a sustainable competitive advantage in the marketplace. The chapter exposed you to proven approaches to winning a sustainable competitive advantage, including strategies keyed to lower costs, differentiating features, a focus on a narrow market niche, and developing unmatched resource strengths and competitive capabilities. Regardless of approach, a company's **competitive strategy** *deals exclusively with the specifics of management's game plan for securing a competitive advantage vis-à-vis rivals.*

There are many routes to competitive advantage, but they all involve giving buyers what they perceive as superior value compared to the offerings of rival sellers. Superior value can mean offering a good product at a lower price, a superior product that is worth paying more for, or an attractive combination of price, features, quality, service, and other appealing attributes. This chapter examines approaches to providing customers with superior value, including strategies that yield distinctive industry positioning and strategies keyed to exploiting unsurpassed resources and competencies.

Competitive Strategies and Industry Positioning

There are countless variations in the competitive strategies that companies employ, mainly because each company's strategic approach entails custom-designed actions to fit its own circumstances and industry environment. The custom-tailored nature of each company's strategy is also the result of management's efforts to uniquely position the company in its industry. Companies are much more likely to achieve competitive advantage and earn above-average profits if they are able to find a unique way of delivering superior value to customers. For example, during the 1990s, Starbucks' convenient locations, flavorful coffee drinks, superior customer service, and appealing store ambiance made it stand out among other restaurants selling coffee and gave it a competitive advantage in the ready-to-drink coffee industry. There have since been an untold number of coffeeshops that have attempted to imitate Starbucks' competitive strategy, but none have been able to achieve a comparable level of success. By choosing a unique approach to providing value to customers and striving for operational excellence, Starbucks has achieved an enduring brand loyalty that makes it difficult for others to triumph by merely copying its strategic approach. "Me too" strategies can rarely be expected to deliver competitive advantage and stellar performance unless the imitator possesses resources or competencies that allow it to provide greater value to customers than that offered by firms with similar strategic approaches.

Competitive strategies that provide distinctive industry positioning and competitive advantage in the marketplace involve choosing between (1) a market target that is either broad or narrow, and (2) whether the company should pursue a competitive advantage linked to low costs or product differentiation. Figure 3.1 presents four proven competitive strategies keyed to

LO1

Gain an understanding of competitive strategies frequently used to provide distinctive industry positioning and competitive advantage in the marketplace.

FIGURE 3.1   **The Four Generic Competitive Strategies**

Type of Competitive Advantage Pursued

	Value Creation Keyed to Lower Cost	Value Creation Keyed to Differentiating Features
Presence in a Broad Range of Market Segments	**Overall Low-Cost Provider Strategy**	**Broad Differentiation Strategy**
Presence in a Limited Number of Market Segments	**Focused Low-Cost Strategy**	**Focused Differentiation Strategy**

*(Left axis label: **Market Coverage**)*

Source: This is an author-expanded version of a 3-strategy classification discussed in Michael E. Porter, *Competitive Strategy* (New York: Free Press, 1980), pp. 35–40.

industry positioning.[1] The general approach to competing and operating the business is notably different for each of the four competitive strategies. The four generic strategies are:

1. *A low-cost provider strategy*—striving to achieve lower overall costs than rivals and appealing to a broad spectrum of customers, usually by under-pricing rivals.

2. *A broad differentiation strategy*—seeking to differentiate the company's product or service from rivals' in ways that will appeal to a broad spectrum of buyers.

3. *A focused low-cost strategy*—concentrating on a narrow buyer segment (or market niche) and outcompeting rivals by having lower costs than rivals and thus being able to serve niche members at a lower price.

4. *A focused differentiation strategy*—concentrating on a narrow buyer segment (or market niche) and outcompeting rivals by offering niche members customized attributes that meet their tastes and requirements better than rivals' products.

Each of these four generic competitive approaches stakes out a different market position. The following sections explore the ins and outs of the four generic competitive strategies and how they differ.

[1] This classification scheme is an adaptation of a narrower three-strategy classification presented in Michael E. Porter, *Competitive Strategy: Techniques for Analyzing Industries and Competitors* (New York: Free Press, 1980), Chapter 2, especially pp. 35–40 and 44–46. For a discussion of the different ways that companies can position themselves in the marketplace, see Michael E. Porter, "What Is Strategy?" *Harvard Business Review* 74, no. 6 (November–December 1996), pp. 65–67.

Low-Cost Provider Strategies

Striving to be the industry's overall low-cost provider is a powerful competitive approach in markets with many price-sensitive buyers. A company achieves low-cost leadership when it becomes the industry's lowest-cost provider rather than just being one of perhaps several competitors with low costs. Successful low-cost providers boast meaningfully lower costs than rivals—but not necessarily the absolutely lowest possible cost. In striving for a cost advantage over rivals, managers must take care to include features and services that buyers consider essential—*a product offering that is too frills-free can be viewed by consumers as offering little value even if it is priced lower than competing products.*

A company has two options for translating a low-cost advantage over rivals into attractive profit performance. Option 1 is to use the lower-cost edge to underprice competitors and attract price-sensitive buyers in great enough numbers to increase total profits. Option 2 is to maintain the present price, be content with the present market share, and use the lower-cost edge to earn a higher profit margin on each unit sold, thereby raising the firm's total profits and overall return on investment. For maximum effectiveness, companies employing a low-cost provider strategy need to achieve their cost advantage in ways difficult for rivals to copy or match. If rivals find it relatively easy or inexpensive to imitate the leader's low-cost methods, then the leader's advantage will be too short-lived to yield a valuable edge in the marketplace.

Achieving Low-Cost Leadership

To succeed with a low-cost provider strategy, company managers have to scrutinize each cost-creating activity and determine what factors cause costs to be high or low. Then they have to use this knowledge to keep the unit costs of each activity low. They have to be proactive in eliminating nonessential work steps and low-value activities. Normally, low-cost producers work diligently to create cost-conscious corporate cultures that feature broad employee participation in continuous cost improvement efforts and limited perks and frills for executives. They strive to operate with exceptionally small corporate staffs to keep administrative costs to a minimum. Many successful low-cost leaders also use benchmarking to keep close tabs on how their costs compare with rivals and firms performing comparable activities in other industries.

> Success in achieving a low-cost edge over rivals comes from outmanaging rivals in performing essential activities and eliminating or curbing "nonessential" activities.

But while low-cost providers are champions of frugality, they usually don't scrimp on investing in resources that promise to drive costs out of the business. Wal-Mart, one of the foremost practitioners of low-cost leadership, has invested in state-of-the-art technology throughout its operations—its distribution facilities are an automated showcase, it uses online systems to order goods from suppliers and manage inventories, it equips its stores with cutting-edge sales-tracking and checkout systems, and it sends daily point-of-sale data to 4,000 vendors. Wal-Mart's information and communications systems and capabilities are more sophisticated than those of virtually any other retail chain in the world.

Market Conditions Favoring a Low-Cost Provider Strategy

LO2

Recognize industry conditions that favor a market target that is either broad or narrow and that indicate whether the company should pursue a competitive advantage linked to low costs or product differentiation.

A competitive strategy predicated on low-cost leadership is particularly powerful when:

1. *Price competition among rival sellers is especially vigorous*—Low-cost providers are in the best position to compete offensively on the basis of price and to survive price wars.

2. *The products of rival sellers are essentially identical and are readily available from several sellers*—Commodity-like products and/or ample supplies set the stage for lively price competition; in such markets, it is the less efficient, higher-cost companies that are most vulnerable.

3. *There are few ways to achieve product differentiation that have value to buyers*—When the product or service differences between brands do not matter much to buyers, buyers nearly always shop the market for the best price.

4. *Buyers incur low costs in switching their purchases from one seller to another*—Low switching costs give buyers the flexibility to shift purchases to lower-priced sellers having equally good products. A low-cost leader is well positioned to use low price to induce its customers not to switch to rival brands.

5. *The majority of industry sales are made to a few, large volume buyers*—Low-cost providers are in the best position among sellers in bargaining with high-volume buyers because they are able to beat rivals' pricing to land a high volume sale while maintaining an acceptable profit margin.

6. *Industry newcomers use introductory low prices to attract buyers and build a customer base*—The low-cost leader can use price cuts of its own to make it harder for a new rival to win customers.

As a rule, the more price-sensitive buyers are, the more appealing a low-cost strategy becomes. A low-cost company's ability to set the industry's price floor and still earn a profit erects protective barriers around its market position.

The Hazards of a Low-Cost Provider Strategy

Perhaps the biggest pitfall of a low-cost provider strategy is getting carried away with *overly aggressive price cutting* and ending up with lower, rather than higher, profitability. A low-cost/low-price advantage results in superior profitability only if (1) prices are cut by less than the size of the cost advantage or (2) the added volume is large enough to bring in a bigger total profit despite lower margins per unit sold. Thus, a company with a 5 percent cost advantage cannot cut prices 20 percent, end up with a volume gain of only 10 percent, and still expect to earn higher profits!

A second big pitfall is *relying on an approach to reduce costs that can be easily copied by rivals.* The value of a cost advantage depends on its sustainability. Sustainability, in turn, hinges on whether the company achieves its cost advantage in ways difficult for rivals to replicate or match. A third pitfall is becoming *too fixated on cost reduction.* Low costs cannot be pursued so zealously that a firm's offering ends up being too features-poor to gain the interests of buyers. Furthermore, a company driving hard to push its costs down has to guard against misreading or ignoring increased buyer preferences for added features or declining buyer price sensitivity. Even if these mistakes are avoided, a low-cost competitive approach still carries risk. Cost-saving technological breakthroughs or process improvements can nullify a low-cost leader's hard-won position.

Broad Differentiation Strategies

Differentiation strategies are attractive whenever buyers' needs and preferences are too diverse to be fully satisfied by a standardized product or service. A company attempting to succeed through differentiation must study buyers' needs and behavior carefully to learn what buyers think has value and what they are willing to pay for. Then the company must include these desirable features to clearly set itself apart from rivals lacking such product or service attributes.

Successful differentiation allows a firm to:

- Command a premium price, and/or
- Increase unit sales (because additional buyers are won over by the differentiating features), and/or
- Gain buyer loyalty to its brand (because some buyers are strongly attracted to the differentiating features and bond with the company and its products).

Differentiation enhances profitability whenever the extra price the product commands outweighs the added costs of achieving the differentiation. Company differentiation strategies fail when buyers don't value the brand's uniqueness and/or when a company's approach to differentiation is easily copied or matched by its rivals.

Approaches to Differentiation

Companies can pursue differentiation from many angles: a unique taste (Dr Pepper, Listerine); multiple features (Microsoft Vista, Microsoft Office); wide selection and one-stop shopping (Home Depot, Amazon.com); superior service (FedEx); spare parts availability (Caterpillar guarantees 48-hour spare parts delivery to any customer anywhere in the world or else the part is furnished free); engineering design and performance (Mercedes, BMW); prestige and distinctiveness (Rolex); product reliability (Whirlpool and GE in large home appliances); quality manufacturing (Michelin in tires, Toyota and Honda in automobiles); technological leadership (3M Corporation in bonding and coating products); a full range of services (Charles Schwab in stock brokerage); a complete line of products (Campbell's soups); and top-of-the-line image and reputation (Ralph Lauren and Starbucks).

Easy-to-copy differentiating features cannot produce sustainable competitive advantage; differentiation based on hard-to-copy competencies and capabilities tends to be more sustainable.

The most appealing approaches to differentiation are those that are hard or expensive for rivals to duplicate. Indeed, resourceful competitors can, in time, clone almost any product or feature or attribute. If Coca-Cola introduces a vanilla-flavored soft drink, so can Pepsi; if Nokia introduces mobile phones with cameras and Internet capability, so can Motorola and Samsung. As a rule, differentiation yields a longer-lasting and more profitable competitive edge when it is based on product innovation, technical superiority, product quality and reliability, comprehensive customer service, and unique competitive capabilities. Such differentiating attributes tend to be tough for rivals to copy or offset profitably and buyers widely perceive them as having value.

Creating Value for Customers through Differentiation

While it is easy enough to grasp that a successful differentiation strategy must offer value in ways unmatched by rivals, a big issue in crafting a differentiation strategy is deciding what is valuable to customers. Typically, value can be delivered to customers in three basic ways.

1. *Include product attributes and user features that lower the buyer's costs.* Commercial buyers value products that can reduce their cost of doing business. For example, making a company's product more economical for a buyer to use can be done by reducing the buyer's raw materials waste (providing cut-to-size components), reducing a buyer's inventory requirements (providing just-in-time deliveries), increasing product reliability to lower a buyer's repair and maintenance costs, and providing free technical support. Similarly, consumers find value in differentiating features that will reduce their expenses. The recent increase in gasoline prices in the United States has spurred the sales of hybrid-powered automobiles that have higher sales prices than similar gasoline models, but offer better fuel economy.

2. *Incorporate features that improve product performance.*[2] Commercial buyers and consumers alike value higher levels of performance in many types of products. Product reliability, output, durability, convenience, or ease of use are aspects of product performance that differentiate products offered to buyers. Mobile phone manufacturers are currently in a race to improve the performance of their products through the introduction of next-generation phones with a more appealing, trend-setting set of user features and options.

3. *Incorporate features that enhance buyer satisfaction in noneconomic or intangible ways.* Goodyear's Aquatred tire design appeals to safety conscious motorists wary of slick roads. Bentley, Ralph Lauren, Louis Vuitton, Tiffany, Cartier, and Rolex have differentiation-based competitive advantages linked to buyer desires for status, image, prestige, upscale fashion, superior craftsmanship, and the finer things in life. L. L. Bean makes its mail-order customers feel secure in their purchases by providing an unconditional guarantee with no time limit.

Where to Look for Opportunities to Differentiate

Differentiation is not something hatched in marketing and advertising departments, nor is it limited to quality and service. Differentiation opportunities

[2] Ibid., pp. 135–38.

can exist in activities that affect the value of a product or service; possibilities include the following:

- *Supply chain activities* that ultimately spill over to affect the performance or quality of the company's end product. Starbucks gets high ratings on its coffees partly because it has very strict specifications on the coffee beans purchased from suppliers.

- *Product R&D activities* that aim at improved product designs and performance, more frequent first-to-market victories, added user safety, or enhanced environmental protection.

- *Production R&D and technology related activities* that permit the manufacture of customized products at an efficient cost; make production methods safer for the environment; or improve product quality, reliability, and appearance. Dell Computer's build-to-order production process continues to be a strong differentiating feature for the company that appeals to many corporate and individual PC buyers.

- *Manufacturing activities* that reduce product defects, extend product life, allow better warranty coverages, or enhance product appearance. The quality edge enjoyed by Japanese automakers stems partly from their distinctive competence in performing assembly line activities.

- *Distribution and shipping activities* that allow for fewer warehouse and on-the-shelf stockouts, quicker delivery to customers, more accurate order filling, and/or lower shipping costs.

- *Marketing, sales, and customer service activities* that result in superior technical assistance to buyers, faster maintenance and repair services, better credit terms, or greater customer convenience.

Perceived Value and the Importance of Signaling Value

The price premium commanded by a differentiation strategy reflects *the value actually delivered* to the buyer and *the value perceived* by the buyer. The value of certain differentiating features is rather easy for buyers to detect, but in some instances buyers may have trouble assessing what their experience with the product will be.[3] Successful differentiators go to great lengths to make buyers knowledgeable about a product's value and incorporate signals of value such as attractive packaging, extensive ad campaigns (i.e., how well-known the product is), the quality of brochures and sales presentations, the seller's list of customers, the length of time the firm has been in business, and the professionalism, appearance, and personality of the seller's employees. Such signals of value may be as important as actual value (1) when the nature of differentiation is subjective or hard to quantify, (2) when buyers are making a first-time purchase, (3) when repurchase is infrequent, and (4) when buyers are unsophisticated.

---

[3] The relevance of perceived value and signaling is discussed in more detail in Porter, *Competitive Advantage: Creating and Sustaining Superior Performance*, (New York: Simon & Schuster, 1996), pp. 138–142.

Market Conditions Favoring a Differentiation Strategy

LO2

Recognize industry conditions that favor a market target that is either broad or narrow and that indicate whether the company should pursue a competitive advantage linked to low costs or product differentiation.

Differentiation strategies tend to work best in market circumstances where:

1. *Buyer needs and uses of the product are diverse*—Diverse buyer preferences allow industry rivals to set themselves apart with product attributes that appeal to particular buyers. For instance, the diversity of consumer preferences for menu selection, ambience, pricing, and customer service gives restaurants exceptionally wide latitude in creating differentiated concepts. Other industries offering opportunities for differentiation based upon diverse buyer needs and uses include magazine publishing, automobile manufacturing, footwear, and computers.

2. *There are many ways to differentiate the product or service that have value to buyers*—Industries that allow competitors to add features to product attributes are well suited to differentiation strategies. For example, hotel chains can differentiate on such features as location, size of room, range of guest services, in-hotel dining, and the quality and luxuriousness of bedding and furnishings. Similarly, cosmetics producers are able to differentiate based upon prestige and image, formulations that fight the signs of aging, UV light protection, exclusivity of retail locations, the inclusion of antioxidants and natural ingredients, or prohibitions against animal testing.

3. *Few rival firms are following a similar differentiation approach*—The best differentiation approaches involve trying to appeal to buyers on the basis of attributes that rivals are not emphasizing. A differentiator encounters less head-to-head rivalry when it goes its own separate way to create uniqueness and does not try to outdifferentiate rivals on the very same attributes. When many rivals are all claiming "ours tastes better than theirs" or "ours gets your clothes cleaner than theirs," competitors tend to end up chasing the same buyers with very similar product offerings.

4. *Technological change is fast-paced and competition revolves around rapidly evolving product features*—Rapid product innovation and frequent introductions of next-version products heighten buyer interest and provide space for companies to pursue distinct differentiating paths. In video game hardware and video games, golf equipment, PCs, mobile phones, and MP3 players, competitors are locked into an ongoing battle to set themselves apart by introducing the best next-generation products— companies that fail to come up with new and improved products and distinctive performance features quickly lose out in the marketplace.

The Hazards of a Differentiation Strategy

Differentiation strategies can fail for any of several reasons. *A differentiation strategy keyed to product or service attributes that are easily and quickly copied is always suspect.* Rapid imitation means that no rival achieves meaningful differentiation, because whatever new feature one firm introduces that strikes the fancy of buyers is almost immediately added by rivals. This is why a firm must search out sources of uniqueness that are time-consuming or burdensome for rivals to match if it hopes to use differentiation to win a sustainable competitive edge over rivals.

Differentiation strategies can also fail when buyers see little value in the unique attributes of a company's product. Thus even if a company sets the attributes of its brand apart from its rivals' brands, its strategy can fail because of trying to differentiate on the basis of something that does not deliver adequate value to buyers. For example, consumers may have a "so what" attitude about the Adidas 1 running shoe that utilizes a 20 MHz microprocessor to make adjustments to pavement and ground surfaces. Adidas may find buyers will decide the computer-controlled running shoes are not worth the $250 retail price and sales will be disappointingly low.

Overspending on efforts to differentiate is a strategy flaw that can end up eroding profitability. Company efforts to achieve differentiation nearly always raise costs. The trick to profitable differentiation is either to keep the costs of achieving differentiation below the price premium the differentiating attributes can command in the marketplace or to offset thinner profit margins by selling enough additional units to increase total profits. If a company goes overboard in pursuing costly differentiation, it could be saddled with unacceptably thin profit margins or even losses. The need to contain differentiation costs is why many companies add little touches of differentiation that add to buyer satisfaction but are inexpensive to institute.

Other common pitfalls and mistakes in crafting a differentiation strategy include:[4]

- *Overdifferentiating so that product quality or service levels exceed buyers' needs.* Even if buyers "like" the differentiating extras, they may not find them sufficiently valuable to pay extra for them.
- *Trying to charge too high a price premium.* Even if buyers view certain extras or deluxe features as "nice to have," they may still conclude that the added cost is excessive relative to the value they deliver.
- *Being timid and not striving to open up meaningful gaps in quality or service or performance features vis-à-vis the products of rivals*—tiny differences between rivals' product offerings may not be visible or important to buyers.

A low-cost provider strategy can always defeat a differentiation strategy when buyers are satisfied with a basic product and don't think "extra" attributes are worth a higher price.

Focused (or Market Niche) Strategies

LO2

Recognize industry conditions that favor a market target that is either broad or narrow and that indicate whether the company should pursue a competitive advantage linked to low costs or product differentiation.

What sets focused strategies apart from low-cost leadership or broad differentiation strategies is a concentration on a narrow piece of the total market. The targeted segment, or niche, can be defined by geographic uniqueness or by special product attributes that appeal only to niche members. The advantages of focusing a company's entire competitive effort on a single market niche are considerable, especially for smaller and medium-sized companies that may lack the breadth and depth of resources to tackle going after a national customer base with a "something for everyone" lineup of models, styles, and product selection. Community Coffee, the largest family-owned specialty coffee

[4] Porter, *Competitive Advantage*, pp. 160–162.

retailer in the United States, has a geographic focus on the state of Louisiana and communities across the Gulf of Mexico. Community holds only a 1.1 percent share of the national coffee market, but has recorded sales in excess of $100 million and has won a 50 percent share of the coffee business in the 11-state region where it is distributed. Examples of firms that concentrate on a well-defined market niche keyed to a particular product or buyer segment include Animal Planet and the History Channel (in cable TV); Google (in Internet search engines); Porsche (in sports cars); and Bandag (a specialist in truck tire recapping that promotes its recaps aggressively at over 1,000 truck stops).

A Focused Low-Cost Strategy

A focused strategy based on low cost aims at securing a competitive advantage by serving buyers in the target market niche at a lower cost and a lower price than rival competitors. This strategy has considerable attraction when a firm can lower costs significantly by limiting its customer base to a well-defined buyer segment. The avenues to achieving a cost advantage over rivals also serving the target market niche are the same as for low-cost leadership—outmanage rivals in keeping the costs to a bare minimum and searching for innovative ways to bypass or reduce nonessential activities. The only real difference between a low-cost provider strategy and a focused low-cost strategy is the size of the buyer group to which a company is appealing.

Focused low-cost strategies are fairly common. Producers of private-label goods are able to achieve low costs in product development, marketing, distribution, and advertising by concentrating on making generic items similar to name-brand merchandise and selling directly to retail chains wanting a low-priced store brand. The Perrigo Company has become a leading manufacturer of over-the-counter health care products with 2006 sales of more than $1.4 billion by focusing on producing private-label brands for retailers such as Wal-Mart, CVS, Walgreen, Rite-Aid, and Safeway. Even though Perrigo doesn't make branded products, a focused low-cost strategy is appropriate for the makers of branded products as well. Concepts & Connections 3.1 describes how Motel 6 has kept its costs low in catering to budget-conscious travelers.

A Focused Differentiation Strategy

Focused differentiation strategies are keyed to offering carefully designed products or services to appeal to the unique preferences and needs of a narrow, well-defined group of buyers (as opposed to a broad differentiation strategy aimed at many buyer groups and market segments). Companies like Four Seasons Hotels and Resorts, Chanel, Gucci, and Ferrari employ successful differentiation-based focused strategies targeted at affluent buyers wanting products and services with world-class attributes. Glaceau Vitamin Water and Under Armour have found success by offering performance-oriented products for athletes and fitness buffs. Orvis has become a leading seller of high-quality sporting goods equipment by focusing on sportsmen dedicated to fly fishing and bird hunting. Indeed, most markets contain a buyer segment willing to pay a price premium for the very finest items available, thus opening the

Concepts & Connections 3.1

MOTEL 6's FOCUSED LOW-COST STRATEGY

Motel 6 caters to price-conscious travelers who want a clean, no-frills place to spend the night. To be a low-cost provider of overnight lodging, Motel 6 (1) selects relatively inexpensive sites on which to construct its units (usually near interstate exits and high traffic locations but far enough away to avoid paying prime site prices); (2) builds only basic facilities (no restaurant or bar and only rarely a swimming pool); (3) relies on standard architectural designs that incorporate inexpensive materials and low-cost construction techniques; and (4) provides simple room furnishings and decorations. These approaches lower both investment and operating costs. Without restaurants, bars,

and all kinds of guest services, a Motel 6 unit can operate with just front-desk personnel, room cleanup crews, and skeleton building-and-grounds maintenance.

To promote the Motel 6 concept with travelers who have simple overnight requirements, the chain uses unique, recognizable radio ads done by nationally syndicated radio personality Tom Bodett; the ads describe Motel 6's clean rooms, no-frills facilities, friendly atmosphere, and dependably low rates (usually under $40 a night).

Motel 6's basis for competitive advantage is lower costs than competitors in providing basic, economical overnight accommodations to price-constrained travelers.

strategic window for some competitors to pursue differentiation-based focused strategies aimed at the very top of the market pyramid.

Conditions Making a Focused Low-Cost or Focused Differentiation Strategy Viable

A focused strategy aimed at securing a competitive edge based either on low cost or differentiation becomes increasingly attractive as more of the following conditions are met:

- The target market niche is big enough to be profitable and offers good growth potential.
- Industry leaders have chosen not to compete in the niche—in which case focusers can avoid battling head-to-head against the industry's biggest and strongest competitors.
- It is costly or difficult for multisegment competitors to meet the specialized needs of niche buyers and at the same time satisfy the expectations of mainstream customers.
- The industry has many different niches and segments, thereby allowing a focuser to pick a niche suited to its resource strengths and capabilities.
- Few, if any, other rivals are attempting to specialize in the same target segment.

The Hazards of a Focused Low-Cost or Focused Differentiation Strategy

Focusing carries several risks. The *first major risk* is the chance that competitors will find effective ways to match the focused firm's capabilities in serving the target niche. In the lodging business, large chains like Marriott and Hilton have launched multibrand strategies that allow them to compete effectively in several lodging segments simultaneously. Marriott has flagship hotels with a full complement of services and amenities that allow it to attract travelers and vacationers going to major resorts; it has J.W. Marriott and Ritz-Carlton hotels that provide deluxe comfort and service to business and leisure travelers; it has Courtyard by Marriott and SpringHill Suites brands for business travelers looking for moderately priced lodging; it has Marriott Residence Inns and TownePlace Suites designed as a "home away from home" for travelers staying five or more nights; and it has 520 Fairfield Inn locations that cater to travelers looking for quality lodging at an "affordable" price. Similarly, Hilton has a lineup of brands (Conrad Hotels, Doubletree Hotels, Embassy Suites Hotels, Hampton Inns, Hilton Hotels, Hilton Garden Inns, and Homewood Suites) that enable it to compete in multiple segments and compete head-to-head against lodging chains that operate only in a single segment. Multibrand strategies are attractive to large companies like Marriott and Hilton precisely because they enable a company to enter a market niche and siphon business away from companies that employ a focus strategy.

A *second risk* of employing a focus strategy is the potential for the preferences and needs of niche members to shift over time toward the product attributes desired by the majority of buyers. An erosion of the differences across buyer segments lowers entry barriers into a focuser's market niche and provides an open invitation for rivals in adjacent segments to begin competing for the focuser's customers. A *third risk* is that the segment may become so attractive it is soon inundated with competitors, intensifying rivalry and splintering segment profits.

The Peril of Adopting a "Stuck in the Middle" Strategy

Each of the four generic competitive strategies positions the company differently in its market and competitive environment. Each establishes a central theme for how the company will endeavor to outcompete rivals. Each creates some boundaries or guidelines for maneuvering as market circumstances unfold and as ideas for improving the strategy are debated. Thus, settling on which generic strategy to employ is perhaps the most important strategic commitment a company makes—it tends to drive the rest of a company's strategic actions.

One of the big dangers in crafting a competitive strategy is that managers, torn between the pros and cons of the various generic strategies, will opt for *"stuck in the middle"* strategies that represent compromises between lower costs and greater differentiation and between broad and narrow market appeal. Compromise or middle-ground strategies rarely produce sustainable competitive advantage or a distinctive competitive position. Usually, companies with compromise strategies end up with a middle-of-the-pack industry ranking—they have average costs, some but not a lot of product differentiation relative to rivals, an average image and reputation, and little prospect of industry leadership.

Resource- and Competence-Based Strategic Approaches to Competitive Advantage

LO3

Understand the role of resource-based strategies in supplementing generic strategies and achieving competitive advantage.

Companies are able to supplement strategies keyed to unique industry positioning with strategies that rely on valuable and rare resources possessed by the firm. **Resource-based strategies** attempt to exploit company resources in a manner that offers value to customers in ways rivals are unable to match. For example, a company pursuing a broad low-cost strategy might build its strategy around unique resources that allow it to produce or distribute products at a lower cost than rivals. Dell Computer has amassed a variety of valuable resource strengths that have yielded a considerable cost advantage in the PC industry. Dell Computer's supplier relationships and build-to-order manufacturing capabilities allowed it to operate with no more than two hours of PC components inventory in 2006. Also at that time, its direct selling business model and Internet sales capabilities allowed it to average just 3 to 4 days worth of finished goods inventory, while its rivals typically held as much as 30 days of finished goods inventory. The inability of Dell's rivals to match its supplier-, manufacturing-, and sales-related resource strengths made it difficult for them to match Dell's pricing and earn comparable profit margins.

A **resource-based strategy** utilizes a company's resources and competitive capabilities to achieve a cost-based advantage or differentiation. The most successful resource-based strategies offer value to customers in ways that are unmatched by rivals.

Resource strengths and competitive capabilities can also facilitate differentiation in the marketplace. Because Fox News and CNN have the capability to devote more air time to breaking news stories and get reporters on the scene very quickly compared to the major networks, many viewers turn to the cable networks when a major news event occurs. Microsoft has stronger capabilities to design, create, distribute, and advertise an array of software products for PC applications than any of its rivals. Avon and Mary Kay Cosmetics have differentiated themselves from other cosmetics and personal care companies by assembling a salesforce numbering in the hundreds of thousands that gives them direct sales capability—their sales associates can demonstrate products to interested buyers, take their orders on the spot, and deliver the items to buyers' homes.[5]

A Company's Resources, Capabilities, and Competencies as the Basis for Competitive Advantage

One of the most important aspects of identifying resource strengths and competitive capabilities that can become the basis for competitive advantage has to do with a company's competence level in performing key pieces of its business—such as supply chain management, R&D, production, distribution, sales and marketing, and customer service. A company's proficiency

---

[5] For a more detailed discussion, see George Stalk, Jr., Philip Evans, and Lawrence E. Schulman, "Competing on Capabilities: The New Rules of Corporate Strategy," *Harvard Business Review* 70, no. 2 (March–April 1992), pp. 57–69.

in conducting different facets of its operations can range from merely a competence in performing an activity to a core competence to a distinctive competence:

1. A **competence** is an internal activity an organization is good at doing. Some competencies relate to fairly specific skills and expertise (like just-in-time inventory control or picking locations for new stores) and may be performed in a single department or organizational unit. Other competencies, however, are inherently multidisciplinary and cross-functional. A competence in continuous product innovation, for example, comes from teaming the efforts of people and groups with expertise in market research, new product R&D, design and engineering, cost-effective manufacturing, and market testing.

> A **competence** is an activity that a company performs well.

2. A **core competence** is a proficiently performed internal activity that is *central* to a company's strategy and competitiveness. A core competence is a highly valuable resource strength because of the contribution it makes to the company's success in the marketplace. A company may have more than one core competence in its resource portfolio, but rare is the company that can legitimately claim more than two or three core competencies. Most often, *a core competence is knowledge-based, residing in people and in a company's intellectual capital and not in its assets on the balance sheet.* Moreover, a core competence is more likely to be grounded in cross-department combinations of knowledge and expertise rather than being the product of a single department or work group. 3M Corporation has a core competence in product innovation—its record of introducing new products goes back several decades and new product introduction is central to 3M's strategy for growing its business.

> A **core competence** is a competitively important activity that a company performs better than other internal activities.

3. A **distinctive competence** is a competitively valuable activity that a company *performs better than its rivals.* Because a distinctive competence represents a uniquely strong capability relative to rival companies, it qualifies as a *competitively superior resource strength* with competitive advantage potential. This is particularly true when the distinctive competence enables a company to deliver standout value to customers (in the form of lower prices or better product performance or superior service). Toyota has worked diligently over several decades to establish a distinctive competence in low-cost, high-quality manufacturing of motor vehicles; its "lean production" system is far superior to that of any other automaker's and the company is pushing the boundaries of its production advantage with a new Global Body assembly line. Toyota's new assembly line costs 50 percent less to install and can be changed to accommodate a new model for 70 percent less than its previous production system.[6]

> A **distinctive competence** is a competitively important activity that a company performs better than its rivals—therefore offering the potential for competitive advantage.

[6] George Stalk, Jr. and Rob Lachenauer, "Hard Ball: Five Killer Strategies for Trouncing the Competition," *Harvard Business Review* 82, no. 4 (April 2004), p. 65.

The conceptual differences between a competence, a core competence, and a distinctive competence draw attention to the fact that a company's resource strengths and competitive capabilities are not all equal.[7] Some competencies and competitive capabilities merely enable market survival because most rivals have them. Core competencies are *competitively* more important resource strengths than competencies because they add power to the company's strategy and have a bigger positive impact on its market position and profitability. Distinctive competencies are even more competitively important. A distinctive competence is a competitively potent resource strength for three reasons: (1) it gives a company competitively valuable capability that is unmatched by rivals, (2) it has potential for being the cornerstone of the company's strategy, and (3) it can produce a competitive edge in the marketplace.

Determining the Competitive Power of a Resource Strength

What is most telling about a company's resource strengths is how powerful they are in the marketplace. The competitive power of a resource strength is measured by how many of the following four tests it can pass:[8]

1. *Is the resource really competitively valuable?* All companies possess a collection of resources and competencies—some have the potential to contribute to a competitive advantage while others may not. Apple's operating system for its MacIntosh PCs is by most accounts a world beater (compared to Windows XP) but Apple has failed miserably in converting its resource strength in operating system design into competitive success in the global PC market—it's an industry laggard with a two percent worldwide market share.

2. *Is the resource strength rare—is it something rivals lack?* Companies have to guard against pridefully believing that their core competences are distinctive competences or that their brand name is more powerful than those of their rivals. Who can really say whether Coca-Cola's consumer marketing prowess is better than Pepsi-Cola's or whether the Mercedes-Benz brand name is more powerful than that of BMW or Lexus? Although many retailers claim to be quite proficient in product selection and in-store merchandising, a number run into trouble in the marketplace because

[7] For a more extensive discussion of how to identify and evaluate the competitive power of a company's capabilities, see David W. Birchall and George Tovstiga, "The Strategic Potential of a Firm's Knowledge Portfolio," *Journal of General Management* 25, no. 1 (Autumn 1999), pp. 1–16 and David Teece, "Capturing Value from Knowledge Assets: The New Economy, Markets for Know-How, and Intangible Assets," *California Management Review* 40, no. 3 (Spring 1998), pp. 55–79.

[8] See Jay B. Barney, "Firm Resources and Sustained Competitive Advantage," *Journal of Management* 17, no. 1 (1991), pp. 105–109; and Jay B. Barney and Delwyn N. Clark, *Resource-Based Theory: Creating and Sustaining Competitive Advantage* (New York: Oxford University Press, 2007). Also see M. A. Peteraf, "The Cornerstones of Competitive Advantage: A Resource-Based View," *Strategic Management Journal* 14 (1993), pp. 179–191; and David J. Collis and Cynthia A. Montgomery, "Competing on Resources: Strategy in the 1990s," *Harvard Business Review* 73, no. 4 (July–August 1995), pp. 120–23.

they encounter rivals whose competencies in product selection and in-store merchandising are equal to or better than theirs.

3. *Is the resource strength hard to copy?* The more difficult and more expensive it is to imitate a company's resource strength, the greater its potential competitive value. Resources tend to be difficult to copy when they are unique (a fantastic real estate location, patent protection), when they must be built over time (a brand name, a strategy supportive organizational culture), and when they carry big capital requirements (a cost-effective plant to manufacture cutting-edge microprocessors). Wal-Mart's competitors have failed miserably in their attempts over the past two decades to match its state-of-the-art distribution capabilities.

4. *Can the resource strength be trumped by substitute resource strengths and competitive capabilities?* Resources that are competitively valuable, rare, and costly to imitate lose their ability to offer competitive advantage if rivals possess equivalent substitute resources. For example, manufacturers relying on automation to gain a cost-based advantage in production activities may find their technology based advantage nullified by rivals' use of low-wage offshore manufacturing. Resources can contribute to a competitive advantage only when resource substitutes don't exist.

Understanding the nature of competitively important resources allows managers to identify resources or capabilities that should be further developed to play an important role in the company's future strategies. In addition, management may determine that it doesn't possess a resource that independently passes all four tests listed here with high marks, but does have a bundle of resources that can be leveraged to develop a core competence. Although Callaway Golf Company's engineering and market research capabilities are matched relatively well by rivals Cobra Golf and Ping Golf, its cross-functional development skills allow it to consistently outperform both rivals in the marketplace. Callaway Golf's technological capabilities, understanding of consumer preferences, and collaborative organizational culture have allowed it to remain the largest seller of golf equipment for more than a decade. The company's bundling of resources used in its product development process qualifies as a distinctive competence and is the basis of the company's competitive advantage.

> Companies may lack stand-alone resource strengths capable of contributing to competitive advantage, but may develop a distinctive competence through **bundled resource strengths.**

Resource-based strategies can also be directed at undermining a rival's competitively valuable resources by identifying **substitute resources** to accomplish the same objective. Amazon.com lacks the broad network of retail stores operated by rival Barnes & Noble, but it is able to make its products readily available to anyone with Internet access. Amazon.com's free shipping on orders over $25 and searchable index of books and other merchandise is much more appealing than visiting a big-box bookstore for many busy consumers.

> **Substitute resources** may be developed to allow companies to offset resource weaknesses or deficiencies in performing competitively critical activities.

Supplementing Resources and Competencies through Strategic Alliances and Collaborative Partnerships

Companies in all types of industries have elected to form strategic alliances and partnerships to add to their collections of resources and competencies. This is an about-face from times past, when the vast majority of companies were confident they could independently develop whatever resources were needed to be successful in their industries. But globalization of the world economy, revolutionary advances in technology, and rapid growth in emerging markets in Asia, Latin America, and Eastern Europe have made strategic partnerships commonplace in most industries.[9] Even the largest and most financially sound companies have concluded that simultaneously running the races for global market leadership and for a stake in the industries of the future requires more diverse skills, resources, technological expertise, and competitive capabilities than they can assemble alone. Such companies, along with others that are missing the resources and competitive capabilities needed to pursue promising opportunities, have determined that the fastest way to fill the gap is often to form alliances with enterprises having the desired strengths. Consequently, these companies form **strategic alliances** or collaborative partnerships in which two or more companies jointly work to achieve mutually beneficial strategic outcomes. Thus, *a strategic alliance is a formal agreement between two or more separate companies in which there is strategically relevant collaboration of some sort, joint contribution of resources, shared risk, shared control, and mutual dependence.* Often, alliances involve joint marketing, joint sales or distribution, joint production, design collaboration, joint research, or projects to jointly develop new technologies or products. The relationship between the partners may be contractual or merely collaborative; the arrangement commonly stops short of formal ownership ties between the partners (although there are a few strategic alliances where one or more allies have minority ownership in certain of the other alliance members). Five factors make an alliance "strategic," as opposed to just a convenient business arrangement:[10]

1. It is critical to the company's achievement of an important objective.

2. It helps build, sustain, or enhance a core competence or competitive advantage.

3. It helps block a competitive threat.

4. It helps open up important new market opportunities.

5. It mitigates a significant risk to a company's business.

Companies in many different industries all across the world have made strategic alliances a core part of their overall strategy; U.S. companies alone announced nearly 68,000 alliances from 1996 through 2003.[11] In the personal

> ### LO4
>
> Learn how strategic alliances and partnerships can be used to add to a firm's collection of resources and competencies.

---

[9] Yves L. Doz and Gary Hamel, *Alliance Advantage: The Art of Creating Value through Partnering* (Boston: Harvard Business School Press, 1998), pp. xiii, xiv.

[10] Jason Wakeam, "The Five Factors of a Strategic Alliance," *Ivey Business Journal* 68, no. 3 (May–June 2003), pp. 1–4.

[11] Jeffrey H. Dyer, Prashant Kale, and Harbir Singh, "When to Ally and When to Acquire," *Harvard Business Review* 82, no. 7/8 (July–August 2004), p. 109.

computer (PC) industry, alliances are pervasive because PC components and software are supplied by so many different companies—one set of companies provides the microprocessors, another group makes the circuit boards, another the monitors, another the disk drives, another the memory chips, and so on. Moreover, their facilities are scattered across the United States, Japan, Taiwan, Singapore, Malaysia, and parts of Europe. Strategic alliances among companies in the various parts of the PC industry facilitate the close cross-company collaboration required on next-generation product development, logistics, production, and the timing of new product releases.

During the 1998–2004 period, Samsung Electronics, a South Korean corporation with $54 billion in sales, entered into over 50 major strategic alliances involving such companies as Sony, Yahoo, Hewlett-Packard, Nokia, Motorola, Intel, Microsoft, Dell, Mitsubishi, Disney, IBM, Maytag, and Rockwell Automation; the alliances involved joint investments, technology transfer arrangements, joint R&D projects, and agreements to supply parts and components—all of which facilitated Samsung's strategic efforts to transform itself into a global enterprise and establish itself as a leader in the worldwide electronics industry.

Studies indicate that large corporations are commonly involved in 30 to 50 alliances and that a number have hundreds of alliances. One recent study estimated that about 35 percent of corporate revenues in 2003 came from activities involving strategic alliances, up from 15 percent in 1995.[12] Another study reported that the typical large corporation relied on alliances for 15 to 20 percent of its revenues, assets, or income.[13] Companies that have formed a host of alliances have a need to manage their alliances like a portfolio—terminating those that no longer serve a useful purpose or that have produced meager results, forming promising new alliances, and restructuring certain existing alliances to correct performance problems and/or redirect the collaborative effort.[14]

How Strategic Alliances Build Resource Strengths and Core Competencies

The most common reasons why companies enter into strategic alliances are to expedite the development of promising new technologies or products, to overcome deficits in their own technical and manufacturing expertise, to bring together the personnel and expertise needed to create new skill sets, to improve supply chain efficiency, to gain economies of scale in production, and to acquire or improve market access through joint marketing agreements.[15] In bringing together firms with different skills and knowledge bases, alliances

---

[12] Salvatore Parise and Lisa Sasson, "Leveraging Knowledge Management across Strategic Alliances," *Ivey Business Journal* 66, no. 4 (March–April 2002), p. 42.

[13] David Ernst and James Bamford, "Your Alliances Are Too Stable," *Harvard Business Review* 83, no. 6 (June 2005), p. 133.

[14] An excellent discussion of the portfolio approach to managing multiple alliances and how to restructure a faltering alliance is presented in Ernst and Bamford, "Your Alliances Are Too Stable," pp. 133–141.

[15] Michael E. Porter, *The Competitive Advantage of Nations* (New York: Free Press, 1990), p. 66. For a discussion of how to realize the advantages of strategic partnerships, see Nancy J. Kaplan and Jonathan Hurd, "Realizing the Promise of Partnerships," *Journal of Business Strategy* 23, no. 3 (May–June 2002), pp. 38–42; Parise and Sasson, "Leveraging Knowledge Management across Strategic Alliances," pp. 41–47; and Ernst and Bamford, "Your Alliances Are Too Stable," pp. 133–141.

open up learning opportunities that help partner firms better leverage their own resource strengths.[16]

Allies can learn much from one another in performing joint research, sharing technological know-how, and collaborating on complementary new technologies and products.[17] Manufacturers frequently pursue alliances with parts and components suppliers to gain the efficiencies of better supply chain management

> The competitive attraction of alliances is in allowing companies to bundle competencies and resources that are more valuable in a joint effort than when kept separate.

and to speed new products to market. By joining forces in components production and/or final assembly, companies may be able to realize cost savings not achievable with their own small volumes—German automakers Volkswagen AG, Audi AG, and Porsche AG formed a strategic alliance to spur mutual development of a gasoline-electric hybrid engine and transmission system that they could each then incorporate into their motor vehicle models; BMW, General Motors, and Daimler AG formed a similar partnership. Both alliances were aimed at closing the gap on Toyota, generally said to be the world leader in fuel-efficient hybrid engines. Johnson & Johnson and Merck entered into an alliance to market Pepcid AC; Merck developed the stomach distress remedy and Johnson & Johnson functioned as marketer—the alliance made Pepcid products the best-selling remedies for acid indigestion and heartburn.

FAILED STRATEGIC ALLIANCES AND COOPERATIVE PARTNERSHIPS

Most alliances that aim at technology sharing or providing market access turn out to be temporary, fulfilling their purpose after a few years because the benefits of mutual learning have occurred. Although long-term alliances sometimes prove mutually beneficial, most partners don't hesitate to terminate the alliance and go it alone when the payoffs run out. Alliances are more likely to be long-lasting when (1) they involve collaboration with suppliers or distribution allies, or (2) both parties conclude that continued collaboration is in their mutual interest, perhaps because new opportunities for learning are emerging.

Whether intended for long-term or temporary purposes, a surprising number of alliances fail to benefit either partner. In 2004, McKinsey & Co. estimated that the overall success rate of alliances was around 50 percent, based on whether the alliance achieved the stated objectives.[18] Many alliances are dissolved after a few years. The high "divorce rate" among strategic allies has several causes, the most common of which are:[19]

- Diverging objectives and priorities.
- An inability to work well together.
- Changing conditions that make the purpose of the alliance obsolete.
- The emergence of more attractive technological paths.
- Marketplace rivalry between one or more allies.

[16] A. Inkpen, "Learning, Knowledge Acquisition, and Strategic Alliances," *European Management Journal* 16, no. 2 (April 1998), pp. 223–229.

[17] For a discussion of how to raise the chances that a strategic alliance will produce strategically important outcomes, see M. Koza and A. Lewin, "Managing Partnerships and Strategic Alliances: Raising the Odds of Success," *European Management Journal* 18, no. 2 (April 2000), pp. 146–151.

[18] This same 50 percent success rate for alliances was also cited in Ernst and Bamford, "Your Alliances Are Too Stable," p. 133; both co-authors of this *HBR* article were McKinsey personnel.

[19] Doz and Hamel, *Alliance Advantage,* pp. 16–18.

Experience indicates that *alliances stand a reasonable chance of helping a company reduce competitive disadvantage but very rarely have they proved a strategic option for gaining a durable competitive edge over rivals.*

THE STRATEGIC DANGERS OF RELYING ON ALLIANCES FOR KEY RESOURCE STRENGTHS The Achilles heel of alliances and cooperative strategies is becoming dependent on other companies for *essential* expertise and capabilities. To be a market leader (and perhaps even a serious market contender), a company must ultimately develop its own capabilities in areas where internal strategic control is pivotal to protecting its competitiveness and building competitive advantage. Moreover, some alliances hold only limited potential because the partner guards its most valuable skills and expertise; in such instances, acquiring or merging with a company possessing the desired know-how and resources is a better solution.

Key Points

1. Early in the process of crafting a strategy, company managers have to decide which of the four basic competitive strategies to employ—overall low-cost, broad differentiation, focused low-cost, or focused differentiation.

2. In employing a low-cost provider strategy, a company must do a better job than rivals of cost-effectively managing internal activities and/or it must find innovative ways to eliminate or bypass cost-producing activities. Low-cost provider strategies work particularly well when price competition is strong and the products of rival sellers are very weakly differentiated. Other conditions favoring a low-cost provider strategy are when supplies are readily available from eager sellers, when there are not many ways to differentiate that have value to buyers, when the majority of industry sales are made to a few, large buyers, when buyer switching costs are low, and when industry newcomers are likely to use a low introductory price to build market share.

3. Broad differentiation strategies seek to produce a competitive edge by incorporating attributes and features that set a company's product/service offering apart from rivals in ways that buyers consider valuable and worth paying for. Successful differentiation allows a firm to (1) command a premium price for its product, (2) increase unit sales (because additional buyers are won over by the differentiating features), and/or (3) gain buyer loyalty to its brand (because some buyers are strongly attracted to the differentiating features and bond with the company and its products). Differentiation strategies work best in markets with diverse buyer preferences where there are big windows of opportunity to strongly differentiate a company's product offering from those of rival brands, in situations where few other rivals are pursuing a similar differentiation approach, and in circumstances where technological change is fast-paced and competition centers on rapidly evolving product features. A differentiation strategy is doomed when competitors are able to quickly copy most or all of the appealing product attributes a company comes up with, when a company's differentiation efforts meet

with a ho-hum or so what market reception, or when a company erodes profitability by overspending on efforts to differentiate its product offering.

4. A focus strategy delivers competitive advantage either by achieving lower costs than rivals in serving buyers comprising the target market niche or by offering niche buyers an appealingly differentiated product or service that meets their needs better than rival brands. A focused strategy becomes increasingly attractive when the target market niche is big enough to be profitable and offers good growth potential, when it is costly or difficult for multisegment competitors to put capabilities in place to meet the specialized needs of the target market niche and at the same time satisfy the expectations of their mainstream customers, when there are one or more niches that present a good match with a focuser's resource strengths and capabilities, and when few other rivals are attempting to specialize in the same target segment.

5. Deciding which generic strategy to employ is perhaps the most important strategic commitment a company makes—it tends to drive the rest of the strategic actions a company decides to undertake and it sets the whole tone for the pursuit of a competitive advantage over rivals.

6. Companies are able to supplement the four generic strategies with strategies that rely on valuable and rare resources possessed by the firm. Resource-based strategies attempt to exploit company resources in a manner that offers value to customers in ways rivals are unable to match. A company's resource strengths and competitive capabilities can contribute to an organizational competence, core competence, or distinctive competence. A distinctive competence is a competitively potent resource strength for three reasons: (1) it gives a company competitively valuable capability that is unmatched by rivals, (2) it can underpin and add real punch to a company's strategy, and (3) it is a basis for sustainable competitive advantage. Companies lacking important standalone resource strengths capable of contributing to competitive advantage may find advantage through bundled resource strengths or substitute resources.

7. Companies lacking key resource strengths or competences may also form alliances with enterprises having the desired strengths. Consequently, these companies form strategic alliances or collaborative partnerships in which two or more companies jointly work to achieve mutually beneficial strategic outcomes. Strategic alliances are formal agreements between two or more separate companies in which there is strategically relevant collaboration of some sort, joint contribution of resources, shared risk, shared control, and mutual dependence. Alliances are more likely to be long-lasting when (1) they involve collaboration with suppliers or distribution allies, or (2) both parties conclude that continued collaboration is in their mutual interest, perhaps because new opportunities for learning are emerging.

LO1 1. Progressive Insurance has fashioned a strategy in auto insurance focused on people with a record of traffic violations who drive high-performance cars, drivers with accident histories, motorcyclists, teenagers, and other so-called high-risk categories of drivers that most auto insurance companies steer away from. Progressive discovered that some of these high-risk drivers are affluent and pressed for time, making them less sensitive to paying premium rates for their car insurance. Management learned that it could charge such drivers high enough premiums to cover the added risks. Progressive also is known for its expedited application process and friendly application policies toward higher-risk drivers.

Assurance
of Learning
Exercises

Progressive also pioneered the low-cost direct sales model of allowing customers to purchase insurance online and over the phone.

Progressive also studied the market segments for insurance carefully enough to discover that some motorcycle owners were not especially risky (middle-aged suburbanites who sometimes commuted to work or used their motorcycles mainly for recreational trips with their friends). Progressive's strategy allowed it to become a leader in the market for luxury car insurance for customers who appreciated Progressive's streamlined approach to doing business. The company also maintains roving claims adjusters who arrive at accident scenes to assess claims and issue checks for repairs on the spot. Progressive introduced 24-hour claims reporting, which has become an industry standard.

How would you characterize Progressive Insurance's competitive strategy? Does it appear that Progressive is pursuing a cost-based advantage or differentiation? Has it focused on a niche within the insurance industry or is it pursuing a broad range of customer groups? Please support your assessment with facts from the information provided above.

Sources: www.progressiveinsurance.com; Ian C. McMillan, Alexander van Putten, and Rita Gunther McGrath, "Global Gamesmanship," *Harvard Business Review* 81, no. 5 (May 2003), p. 68; and *Fortune*, May 16, 2005, p. 34.

2. Go to www.bmwgroup.com and then click on the link for www.bmwgroup.com. The site you find provides an overview of the company's key functional areas, including research & development and production activities. Explore each of the links on the Research & Development page to better understand the company's approach to People & Networks, Innovation & Technology, and Mobility & Traffic. Also review the statements under Production focusing on Vehicle Production and Sustainable Production. How do these activities contribute to BMW's differentiation strategy and the unique position in the industry that BMW has achieved? **LO1**

3. Review the discussion of GE's innovation capabilities at www.ge.com/research. Explain how the company has bundled its technology resources to contribute to competitive advantage in its businesses. Is there evidence the company's deployment of resources has given it a distinctive competence in the area of innovation? Explain why or why not. **LO3**

Exercise for Business Simulation Users

The exercise for simulation users presented in Chapter 2 asked that you prepare a strategy map for your simulation company. Please refer to the strategy map that you prepared in that exercise and describe key resources that your strategy will rely upon to create customer value. Specifically, what human capital and organizational capital resources must your simulation company possess to support internal processes? Also, which of the four generic strategies best characterize the product attributes and brand image choices presented in your strategy map? **LO1 LO3**

Chapter 4

Industry and Competitive Analysis

Chapter Learning Objectives

LO1. Recognize the importance of crafting strategies that have a good fit with a company's external environment.

LO2. Gain an understanding of the analytical tools utilized to assess a company's industry and competitive environment.

LO3. Learn what kinds of conditions cause an industry to be more or less attractive from the standpoint of earning good profits and presenting good long-term business opportunity.

As indicated in the opening section of Chapter 1, one of the three central questions that managers must address in evaluating their company's business prospects is *"Where are we now?"* Management must address this question from two perspectives: (1) the industry and competitive environment in which the company operates and (2) the company's own market position and competitiveness—its resource strengths and capabilities, its resource deficiencies and competitive liabilities, the success of its alliances and partnerships, the strength of its leadership, the health of its culture, and its cost position. Developing answers to the questions *"Where do we want to go?"* and *"How are we going to get there?"* without first gaining an understanding of the company's external environment and internal situation hamstrings attempts to build competitive advantage and boost company performance. Indeed, the first test of a winning strategy inquires *"Does the strategy fit the company's situation?"*

This chapter presents the concepts and analytical tools for assessing a single-business company's external environment that should be considered in making strategic choices. Analysis of the external environment centers on the defining economic and business characteristics of the industry, the industry's competitive forces, the drivers of change in the industry, industry key success factors, and the actions of rivals. In Chapter 5 we explore the methods of evaluating a company's internal circumstances and competitiveness.

Company Performance and the "Macroenvironment"

The performance of all companies is affected by such external factors as the economy at large, population demographics, societal values and lifestyles, governmental legislation and regulation, and technological factors. Strictly speaking, a company's "macroenvironment" includes *all relevant factors and influences* outside the company's boundaries; by *relevant,* we mean these factors are important enough that they should shape management's decisions regarding the company's long-term direction, objectives, strategy, and business model. Figure 4.1 presents a depiction of macroenvironmental factors with a high potential to affect a company's business situation. The impact of outer-ring factors on a company's choice of strategy can range from big to small. But even if the factors in the outer ring of the macroenvironment change slowly or likely have a low impact on the company's business situation, they still merit a watchful eye. Motor vehicle companies must adapt their strategies to current customer concerns about carbon emissions and high gasoline prices. The demographics of an aging population and longer life expectancies will have a dramatic impact on the health care and prescription drug industries in the next few decades. As company managers scan the external environment, they must be alert for potentially important outer-ring developments, assess their impact and influence, and adapt the company's direction and strategy as needed.

However, the factors and forces in a company's macroenvironment that have the *biggest* strategy-shaping impact typically pertain to the company's immediate industry and competitive environment—competitive pressures,

FIGURE 4.1 **The Components of a Company's Macroenvironment**

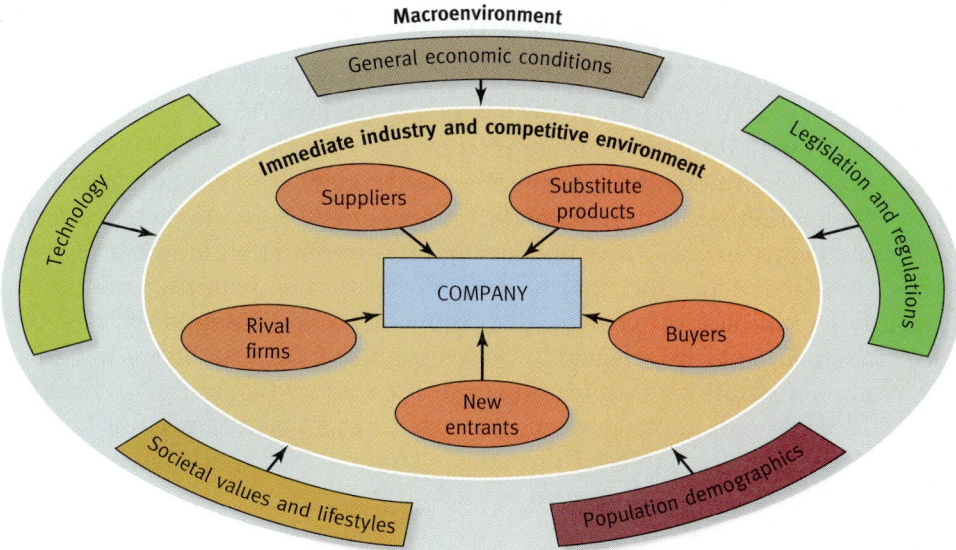

the actions of rivals firms, buyer behavior, supplier-related considerations, and so on. Consequently, it is on a company's industry and competitive environment that we concentrate our attention in this chapter.

Assessing the Company's Industry and Competitive Environment

Thinking strategically about a company's industry and competitive environment entails using some well-validated concepts and analytical tools to get clear answers to seven questions:

1. What are the industry's dominant economic characteristics?

2. What kinds of competitive forces are industry members facing, and how strong is each force?

3. What forces are driving industry change, and what impact will these changes have on competitive intensity and industry profitability?

4. What market positions do industry rivals occupy—who is strongly positioned and who is not?

5. What strategic moves are rivals likely to make next?

6. What are the key factors of competitive success?

7. Does the industry outlook offer good prospects for profitability?

Analysis-based answers to these questions are prerequisites for a strategy offering good fit with the external situation. The remainder of this chapter is devoted to describing the methods of obtaining solid answers to the seven questions above.

LO2

Gain an understanding of the analytical tools utilized to assess a company's industry and competitive environment.

Industry Analysis Question 1: What Are the Industry's Dominant Economic Characteristics?

Analyzing a company's industry and competitive environment begins with identifying the industry's dominant economic characteristics. An industry's dominant economic features are defined by such factors as market size and growth rate, the number and size of buyers and sellers, the geographic boundaries of the market (which can extend from local to worldwide), whether sellers' products are virtually identical or highly differentiated, number of rival sellers, the pace of product innovation, market demand-supply conditions, the pace of technological change, the extent of vertical integration, and the extent to which costs are affected by scale economies (i.e., situations in which large-volume operations result in lower unit costs) and learning/experience curve effects (i.e., situations in which costs decline as a company gains knowledge and experience). Table 4.1 provides a summary of analytical questions that define the industry's dominant economic features.

Getting a handle on an industry's distinguishing economic features not only provides a broad overview of the attractiveness of the industry, but also promotes understanding of the kinds of strategic moves that industry members are likely to employ. For example, industries characterized by rapid product innovations require substantial investments in R&D and the development of strong product innovation capabilities—continuous product innovation is primarily a survival strategy in such industries as video games, computers, and pharmaceuticals. Industries with strong *learning/experience curve* effects are unlikely to experience entry of new competitors because any newcomer would be at a competitive disadvantage for an extended period of time. The microprocessor industry is an excellent example of how learning/experience curves put new entrants at a substantial cost disadvantage. Manufacturing unit costs for microprocessors tends to decline about 20 percent each time *cumulative* production volume doubles. With a 20 percent experience curve effect, if the first 1 million chips cost $100 each, once production volume reaches 2 million the unit cost would fall to $80 (80 percent of $100), and by a production volume of 4 million the unit cost would be $64 (80 percent of $80).[1] The bigger the learning or experience curve effect, the bigger the cost advantage of the company with the largest *cumulative* production volume.

Industry Analysis Question 2: How Strong Are the Industry's Competitive Forces?

After gaining an understanding of the industry's general economic characteristics, industry and competitive analysis should focus on the competitive dynamics of the industry. The nature and subtleties of competitive forces are

[1] There are a large number of studies on the size of the cost reductions associated with experience; the median cost reduction associated with a doubling of cumulative production volume is approximately 15%, but there is a wide variation from industry to industry. For a good discussion of the economies of experience and learning, see Pankaj Ghemawat, "Building Strategy on the Experience Curve," *Harvard Business Review 64*, no. 2 (March–April 1985), pp. 143–149.

Table 4.1

Analytical Questions that Point to an Industry's Key Economic Characteristics

ECONOMIC CHARACTERISTIC	QUESTIONS TO ANSWER
Market size and growth rate	• How big is the industry and how fast is it growing? • What does the industry's position in the life-cycle (early development, rapid growth and takeoff, early maturity and slowing growth, saturation and stagnation, decline) reveal about the industry's growth prospects?
Number of rivals	• Is the industry fragmented into many small companies or concentrated and dominated by a few large companies? • Is the industry going through a period of consolidation to a smaller number of competitors?
Scope of competitive rivalry	• Is the geographic area over which most companies compete local, regional, national, multinational, or global?
Number of buyers	• Is market demand fragmented among many buyers?
Degree of product differentiation	• Are the products of rivals becoming more differentiated or less differentiated?
Product innovation	• Is the industry characterized by rapid product innovation and short product life-cycles? • How important is R&D and product innovation? • Are there opportunities to overtake key rivals by being first-to-market with next-generation products?
Demand-supply conditions	• Is a surplus of capacity pushing prices and profit margins down? • Is the industry overcrowded with too many competitors?
Pace of technological change	• What role does advancing technology play in this industry? • Do most industry members have or need strong technological capabilities? Why?
Vertical integration	• Do most competitors operate in only one stage of the industry (parts and components production, manufacturing and assembly, distribution, retailing) or do some competitors operate in multiple stages? • Is there any cost or competitive advantage or disadvantage associated with being fully or partially integrated?
Economies of scale	• Is the industry characterized by economies of scale in purchasing, manufacturing, advertising, shipping, or other activities? • Do companies with large-scale operations have an important cost advantage over small-scale firms?
Learning and experience curve effects	• Are certain industry activities characterized by strong learning and experience curve effects? • Do any companies have significant cost advantages because of their learning/experience in performing particular activities?

never the same from one industry to another and must be wholly understood to accurately form answers to the question, *"Where are we now?"* Far and away the most powerful and widely used tool for assessing the strength of the industry's competitive forces is the *five-forces model of competition*.[2] This model, as

[2] The five-forces model of competition is the creation of Professor Michael Porter of the Harvard Business School. For his original presentation of the model, see Michael E. Porter, "How Competitive Forces Shape Strategy," *Harvard Business Review* 57, no. 2 (March–April 1979), pp. 137–45. A more thorough discussion can be found in Michael E. Porter, *Competitive Strategy: Techniques for Analyzing Industries and Competitors* (New York: Free Press, 1980), Chapter 1. Porter's five-forces model of competition is reaffirmed and extended in "The Five Competitive Forces that Shape Strategy," *Harvard Business Review* 86, no.1 (Sannary 2008), pp. 78–93.

FIGURE 4.2   The Five-Forces Model of Competition

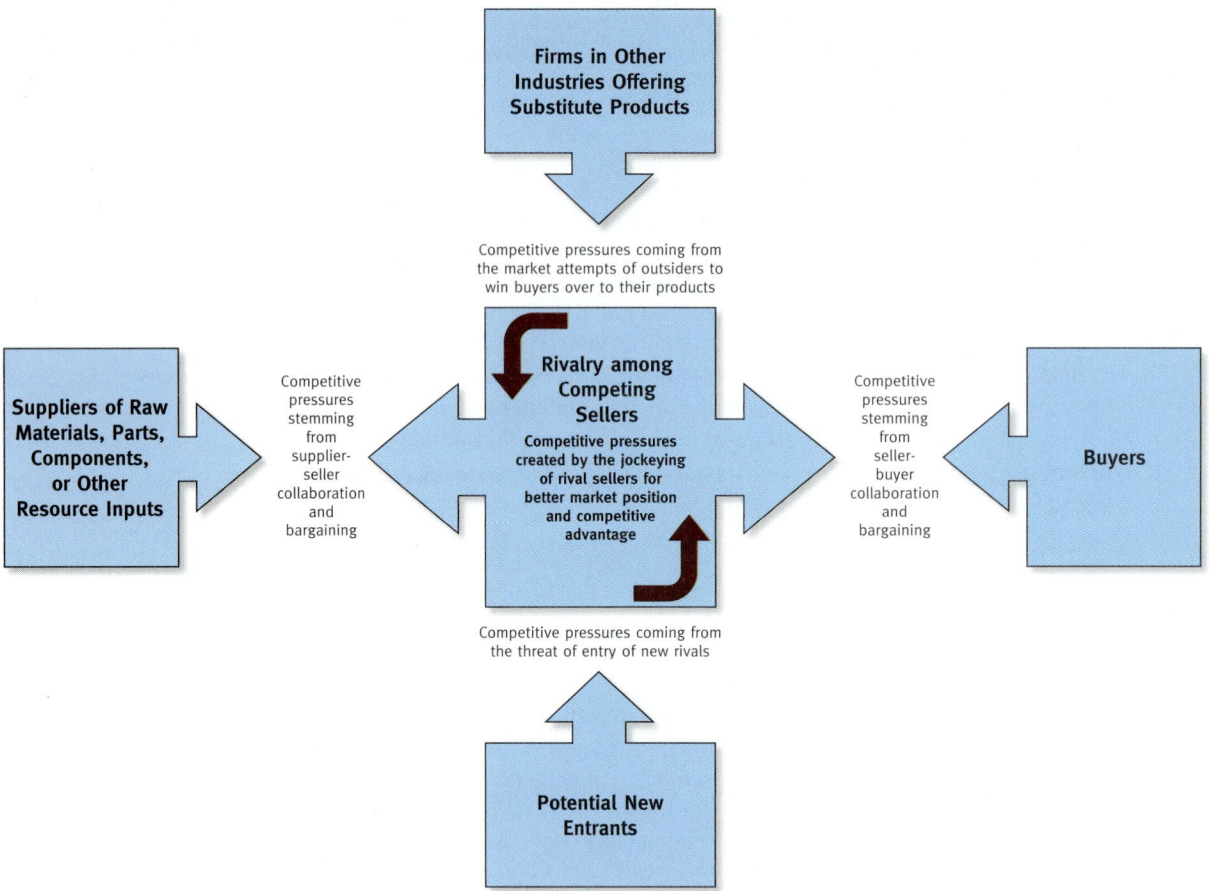

Source: Based on Michael E. Porter, "How Competitive Forces Shape Strategy," *Harvard Business Review* 57, no. 2 (March–April 1979), pp. 137–45 and Michael E. Porter, "The Five Competitive Forces that Shape Strategy," *Harvard Business Review* 86, no.1 (January 2008), pp. 80–86.

depicted in Figure 4.2, holds that competitive forces affecting industry attractiveness go beyond rivalry among competing sellers and include pressures stemming from four coexisting sources. The five competitive forces affecting industry attractiveness are listed below.

1. Competitive pressures stemming from *buyer* bargaining power and seller-buyer collaboration.

2. Competitive pressures coming from companies in other industries to win buyers over to *substitute products.*

3. Competitive pressures stemming from *supplier* bargaining power and supplier-seller collaboration.

4. Competitive pressures associated with the threat of *new entrants* into the market.

5. Competitive pressures associated with *rivalry among competing sellers* to attract customers. This is usually the strongest of the five competitive forces.

The Competitive Force of Buyer Bargaining Power and Seller-Buyer Collaboration

Whether seller-buyer relationships represent a minor or significant competitive force depends on (1) whether some or many buyers have sufficient bargaining leverage to obtain price concessions and other favorable terms, and (2) the extent and importance of seller-buyer strategic partnerships in the industry.

FACTORS AFFECTING BUYER BARGAINING POWER The leverage that buyers have in negotiating favorable terms of the sale can range from weak to strong. Individual consumers, for example, rarely have much bargaining power in negotiating price concessions or other favorable terms with sellers. The primary exceptions involve situations in which price haggling is customary, such as the purchase of new and used motor vehicles, homes, and other big-ticket items like jewelry and pleasure boats. For most consumer goods and services, individual buyers have no bargaining leverage—their option is to pay the seller's posted price, delay their purchase until prices and terms improve, or take their business elsewhere.

In contrast, large retail chains like Wal-Mart, Best Buy, Staples, and Home Depot typically have considerable negotiating leverage in purchasing products from manufacturers because retailers usually stock just two or three competing brands of a product and rarely carry all competing brands. In addition, the strong bargaining power of major supermarket chains like Kroger, Safeway, and Albertsons allows them to demand promotional allowances and lump-sum payments (called slotting fees) from food products manufacturers in return for stocking certain brands or putting them in the best shelf locations. Motor vehicle manufacturers have strong bargaining power in negotiating to buy original equipment tires from Goodyear, Michelin, Bridgestone/Firestone, Continental, and Pirelli not only because they buy in large quantities, but also because tire makers have judged original equipment tires to be important contributors to brand awareness and brand loyalty.

Even if buyers do not purchase in large quantities or offer a seller important market exposure or prestige, they gain a degree of bargaining leverage in the following circumstances:[3]

- *If buyers' costs of switching to competing brands or substitutes are relatively low*—Buyers who can readily switch between several sellers have more negotiating leverage than buyers who have high switching costs. When the products of rival sellers are virtually identical, it is relatively easy for buyers to switch from seller to seller at little or no cost. For example, the screws, rivets, steel, and capacitors used in the production of large home appliances like washers and dryers are all commodity-like and available from many sellers. The potential for buyers to easily switch from one seller to another encourages sellers to make concessions to win or retain a buyer's business.

[3] Porter, *Competitive Strategy*, pp. 24–27, and Porter, "The Five Competitive Forces that Shape Strategy," pp. 83–84.

- *If the number of buyers is small or if a customer is particularly important to a seller*—The smaller the number of buyers, the less easy it is for sellers to find alternative buyers when a customer is lost to a competitor. The prospect of losing a customer who is not easily replaced often makes a seller more willing to grant concessions of one kind or another. Because of the relatively small number of digital camera brands, the sellers of lenses and other components used in the manufacture of digital cameras are in a weak bargaining position in their negotiations with buyers of their components.

- *If buyer demand is weak*—Weak or declining demand creates a "buyers' market"; conversely, strong or rapidly growing demand creates a "sellers' market" and shifts bargaining power to sellers.

- *If buyers are well-informed about sellers' products, prices, and costs*—The more information buyers have, the better bargaining position they are in. The mushrooming availability of product information on the Internet is giving added bargaining power to individuals. It has become commonplace for automobile shoppers to arrive at dealerships armed with invoice prices, dealer holdback information, a summary of incentives, and manufacturers' financing terms.

- *If buyers pose a credible threat of integrating backward into the business of sellers*—Companies like Anheuser-Busch, Coors, and Heinz have integrated backward into metal can manufacturing to gain bargaining power in obtaining the balance of their can requirements from otherwise powerful metal can manufacturers.

Figure 4.3 provides a summary of factors causing buyer bargaining power to be strong or weak.

FIGURE 4.3   **Factors Affecting the Strength of Buyer Bargaining Power**

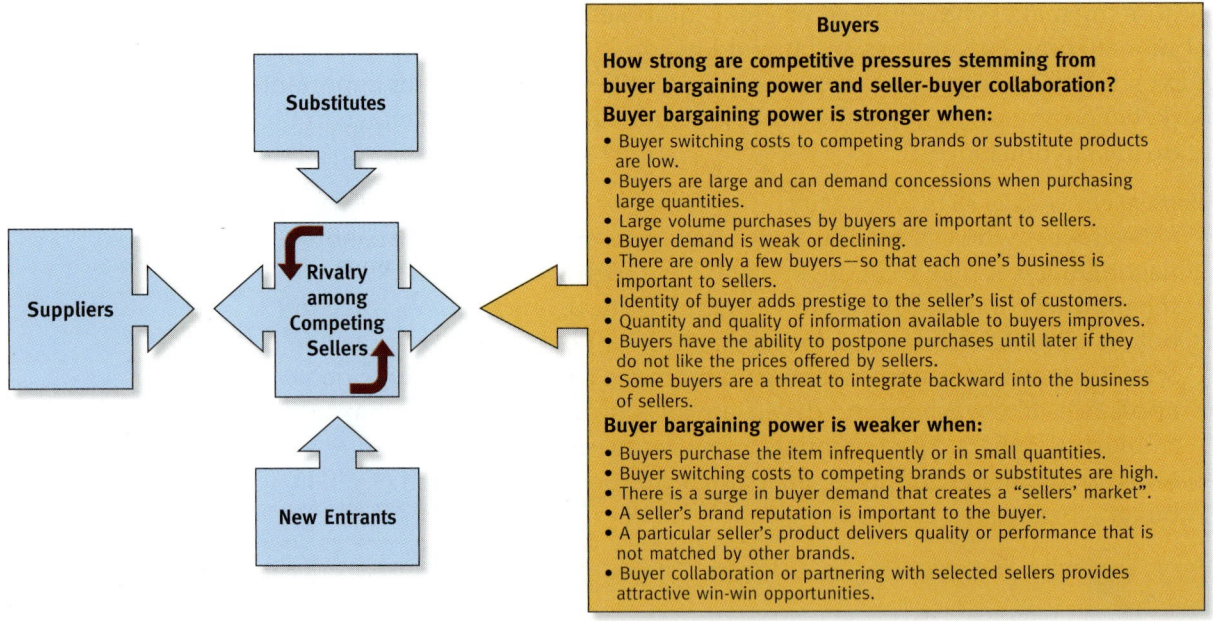

A final point to keep in mind is that *not all buyers of an industry's product have equal degrees of bargaining power with sellers,* and some may be less sensitive than others to price, quality, or service differences. For example, apparel manufacturers confront significant bargaining power when selling to big retailers like Macy's, T. J. Maxx, or Target, but they can command much better prices selling to small owner-managed apparel boutiques.

SELLER-BUYER PARTNERSHIPS AND THE COMPETITIVE POWER OF BUYERS Partnerships between sellers and buyers are an increasingly important element of the competitive picture in *business-to-business relationships* (as opposed to business-to-consumer relationships). Many sellers that provide items to business customers have found it in their mutual interest to collaborate closely with buyers on such matters as just-in-time deliveries, order processing, electronic invoice payments, and data sharing. Wal-Mart, for example, has entered into partnerships with the manufacturers of products sold in its stores to ensure that merchandise is in stock and to lower its inventory costs. Wal-Mart allows its vendors like Procter & Gamble, Sara Lee, or Unilever to monitor store bar code scanner data to determine when and what sized shipments to Wal-Mart's distribution centers are needed. In some instances, sellers ship inventory directly to each Wal-Mart store as merchandise is sold and shelves become depleted. Wal-Mart's planned transition from bar coded merchandise to radio frequency identification (RFID) will assist sellers further in boosting the sale of their products in Wal-Mart stores. Wal-Mart's RFID system uses receivers located in each store or distribution center to determine an exact inventory count and the actual location of the inventory by reading the wireless radio transmissions of each RFID tag. Procter & Gamble and other sellers are able to connect to Wal-Mart's computer networks to watch inventory flow in real-time and make just-in-time shipments to prevent inventory stockouts.

The Competitive Force of Substitute Products

Companies in one industry are vulnerable to competitive pressure from the actions of companies in another industry whenever buyers view the products of the two industries as good substitutes. For instance, the producers of sugar experience competitive pressures from the sales and marketing efforts of the makers of artificial sweeteners. McNeil Nutritionals has achieved considerable success with its Splenda brand of calorie-free sweetener because many consumers consider Splenda an acceptable substitute for sugar. The brand's tagline of "made from sugar, so it tastes like sugar" has resonated with consumers who dislike the bitter aftertaste of most artificial sweeteners, but prefer to avoid the calories associated with the use of sugar. Splenda is not only commonly used to sweeten coffee or tea, but is also used by consumers to bake sugar-free cookies, pies, and muffins and make sugar-free glazes and sweet sauces. Splenda's success as a sugar substitute has been so noteworthy that The Sugar Association, a sugar industry trade group in the United States., has filed suit against McNeil in hopes of preventing Splenda from using its "made from sugar" catchphrase.

Just how strong the competitive pressures are from the sellers of substitute products depends on three factors:

1. *Whether substitutes are readily available and attractively priced.* The presence of readily available and attractively priced substitutes creates competitive pressure by placing a ceiling on the prices industry members can charge.[4] The producers of metal cans are becoming increasingly engaged in a battle with the makers of retort pouches for the business of companies producing packaged fruits, vegetables, meats, and pet foods. Retort pouches, which are multilayer packages made from polypropylene, aluminum foil, and polyester, are more attractively priced than metal cans because they are less expensive to produce and ship.

2. *Whether buyers view the substitutes as comparable or better in terms of quality, performance, and other relevant attributes.* Customers are prone to compare performance and other attributes as well as price. For example, consumers have found digital cameras to be a superior substitute to film cameras because of the superior ease of use, the ability to download images to a home computer, and the ability to delete bad shots without paying for film developing.

3. *Whether the costs that buyers incur in switching to the substitutes are high or low.* High switching costs deter switching to substitutes while low switching costs make it easier for the sellers of attractive substitutes to lure buyers to their products.[5] Typical switching costs include the inconvenience of switching to a substitute, the costs of additional equipment, the psychological costs of severing old supplier relationships, and employee retraining costs.

Figure 4.4 summarizes the conditions that determine whether the competitive pressures from substitute products are strong, moderate, or weak. As a rule, the lower the price of substitutes, the higher their quality and performance, and the lower the user's switching costs, the more intense the competitive pressures posed by substitute products.

The Competitive Force of Supplier Bargaining Power and Supplier-Seller Collaboration

Whether supplier-seller relationships represent a weak or strong competitive force depends on (1) the extent to which suppliers are able to shape the terms and conditions of sales of the items they supply to an industry and (2) the nature and extent of supplier-seller collaboration in the industry.

FACTORS INFLUENCING SUPPLIER BARGAINING POWER   Certain conditions exist that make it possible for industry suppliers to exert competitive pressure on one or more rival sellers. For instance, Microsoft and Intel, both of whom supply PC makers with essential components, are known for using their dominant market status not only to charge PC makers premium prices but also to leverage PC makers in other ways. Microsoft pressures PC makers to load only Microsoft products on the PCs they ship and to position the icons

---

[4] Porter, "How Competitive Forces Shape Strategy," p. 142; Porter, *Competitive Strategy*, pp. 23–24; and Porter, "The Five Competitive Forces that Shape Strategy," pp. 82–83.

[5] Porter, *Competitive Strategy*, p. 10; and Porter, "The Five Competitive Forces that Shape Strategy," p. 85.

FIGURE 4.4   **Factors Affecting Competition from Substitute Products**

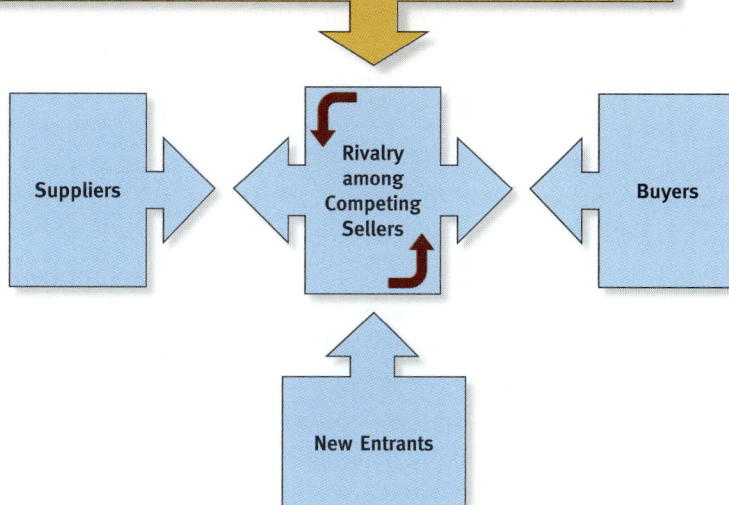

Firms in Other Industries Offering Substitute Products

How strong are competitive pressures coming from substitute products from outside the industry?

Competitive pressures from substitutes are stronger when:
- Good substitutes are readily available or new ones are emerging.
- Substitutes are attractively priced.
- Substitutes have comparable or better performance features.
- End users have low costs in switching to substitutes.
- End users grow more comfortable with using substitutes.

Competitive pressures from substitutes are weaker when:
- Good substitutes are not readily available or don't exist.
- Substitutes are higher priced relative to the performance they deliver.
- End users have high costs in switching to substitutes.

Signs that Competition from Substitutes Is Strong
- Sales of substitutes are growing faster than sales of the industry being analyzed (an indication that the sellers of substitutes are drawing customers away from the industry in question).
- Producers of substitutes are moving to add new capacity.
- Profits of the producers of substitutes are on the rise.

Suppliers

Rivalry among Competing Sellers

Buyers

New Entrants

for Microsoft software prominently on the screens of new computers that come with factory-loaded software. Intel tends to give PC makers who use the biggest percentages of Intel chips in their PC models top priority in filling orders for newly introduced Intel chips. Being on Intel's list of preferred customers helps a PC maker get an allocation of the first production runs of Intel's latest and greatest chips and thus get new PC models to market ahead of rivals. The ability of Microsoft and Intel to pressure PC makers for preferential treatment of one kind or another in turn affects competition among rival PC makers.

The factors that determine whether any of the industry suppliers are in a position to exert substantial bargaining power or leverage are fairly clear-cut:[6]

- *If the item being supplied is a commodity that is readily available from many suppliers.* Suppliers have little or no bargaining power or leverage whenever industry members have the ability to source from any of several alternative and eager suppliers.

[6] Porter, *Competitive Strategy,* pp. 27–28; and Porter, "The Five Competitive Forces that Shape Strategy," pp. 82–83.

- *The number of suppliers of a particular item.* Suppliers are in good positions to negotiate for price increases when only a small number of suppliers exist.

- *The ability of industry members to switch their purchases from one supplier to another or to switch to attractive substitutes.* High switching costs signal strong bargaining power on the part of suppliers, whereas low switching costs and ready availability of good substitute inputs signal weak bargaining power.

- *Whether certain needed inputs are in short supply.* Suppliers of items in short supply have some degree of pricing power.

- *If certain suppliers provide a differentiated input that enhances the performance or quality of the industry's product.* The greater the ability of a particular input to enhance a product's performance or quality, the more bargaining leverage its suppliers are likely to possess.

- *Whether certain suppliers provide equipment or services that deliver cost savings to industry members in conducting their operations.* Suppliers who provide cost-saving equipment or services are likely to possess bargaining leverage.

- *The fraction of the costs of the industry's product accounted for by the cost of a particular input.* The bigger the cost of a specific part or component, the more opportunity for competition in the marketplace to be affected by the actions of suppliers to raise or lower their prices.

- *If industry members are major customers of suppliers.* As a rule, suppliers have less bargaining leverage when their sales to members of this one industry constitute a big percentage of their total sales. In such cases, the well-being of suppliers is closely tied to the well-being of their major customers.

- *Whether it makes good economic sense for industry members to vertically integrate backward.* The make-or-buy decision generally boils down to whether suppliers are able to supply a particular component at a lower cost than industry members could achieve if they were to integrate backward.

Figure 4.5 summarizes the conditions that tend to make supplier bargaining power strong or weak.

HOW SELLER-SUPPLIER PARTNERSHIPS AFFECT COMPETITIVE PRESSURES Just as sellers benefit from strategic partnerships with buyers, collaboration with suppliers may also prove rewarding for sellers. Seller-buyer partnerships have the ability to help a seller cement its relationships with buyers, reduce order fulfillment costs, and boost sales volume. In many industries, strategic partnerships with suppliers allow sellers to (1) reduce inventory and logistics costs (e.g., through just-in-time deliveries), (2) speed the availability of next-generation components, (3) enhance the quality of the parts and components being supplied, and (4) squeeze out important cost savings for both themselves and their suppliers. Dell Computer has entered into strategic partnerships with its key suppliers to ensure its just-in-time deliveries of PC components arrive when needed. In some instances, Dell receives just-in-time delivery of computer parts every few hours. Many of Dell's key suppliers have built plants and distribution centers within a few miles of Dell

FIGURE 4.5   **Factors Affecting the Strength of Supplier Bargaining Power**

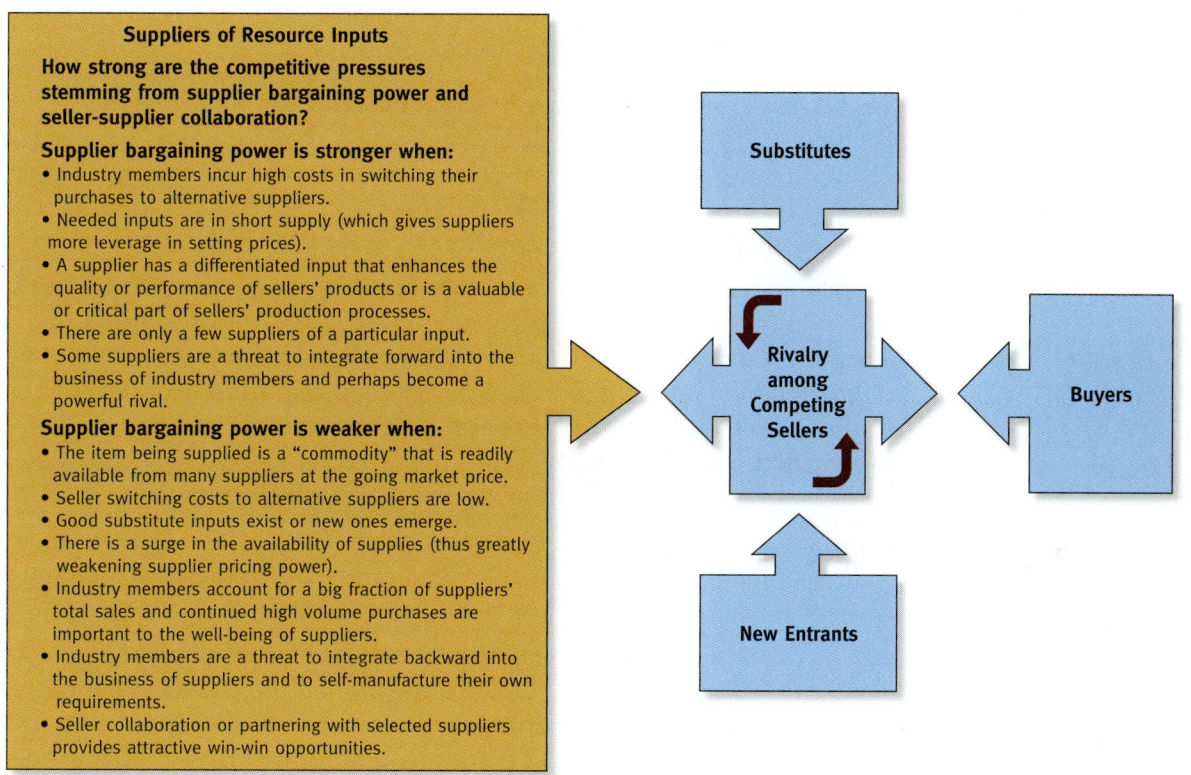

assembly plants to meet these demanding delivery requirements. In addition, close relationships with suppliers allow Dell Computer to reduce the likelihood of recalled computers or production slowdowns. Many Dell suppliers assign engineers to Dell assembly plants to quickly resolve production-related problems as they occur. The more opportunities that exist for win-win efforts between a company and its suppliers, the less their relationship is characterized by who has the upper hand in bargaining with the other.

The Competitive Force of Potential New Entrants

Several factors determine whether the threat of new companies entering the marketplace presents a significant competitive pressure. One factor relates to the size of the pool of likely entry candidates and the resources at their command. As a rule, the bigger the pool of entry candidates, the stronger the threat of potential entry. This is especially true when some of the likely entry candidates have ample resources to support entry into a new line of business. Frequently, the strongest competitive pressures associated with potential entry come not from outsiders but from current industry participants looking for growth opportunities. *Existing industry members are often strong candidates to enter market segments or geographic areas where they currently do not have a market presence.*

A second factor concerns whether the likely entry candidates face high or low entry barriers. High barriers reduce the competitive threat of potential entry, while low barriers make entry more likely, especially if the industry is growing and offers attractive profit opportunities. The most widely encountered barriers that entry candidates must hurdle include:[7]

- *The presence of sizable economies of scale in production or other areas of operation*—When incumbent companies enjoy cost advantages associated with large-scale operations, outsiders must either enter on a large scale (a costly and perhaps risky move) or accept a cost disadvantage and consequently lower profitability.

- *Cost and resource disadvantages not related to scale of operation*—Aside from enjoying economies of scale, there are other reasons why existing firms may have low unit costs that are hard to replicate by newcomers. Industry incumbents can have cost advantages that stem from experience/learning curve effects, the possession of proprietary technology, partnerships with the best and cheapest suppliers, and low fixed costs (because they have older facilities that have been mostly depreciated).

- *Strong brand preferences and high degrees of customer loyalty*—The stronger the attachment of buyers to established brands, the harder it is for a newcomer to break into the marketplace.

- *High capital requirements*—The larger the total dollar investment needed to enter the market successfully, the more limited the pool of potential entrants. The most obvious capital requirements for new entrants relate to manufacturing facilities and equipment, introductory advertising and sales promotion campaigns, working capital to finance inventories and customer credit, and sufficient cash to cover start-up costs.

- *The difficulties of building a network of distributors-retailers and securing adequate space on retailers' shelves*—A potential entrant can face numerous distribution channel challenges. Wholesale distributors may be reluctant to take on a product that lacks buyer recognition. Retailers have to be recruited and convinced to give a new brand ample display space and an adequate trial period. Potential entrants sometimes have to "buy" their way into wholesale or retail channels by cutting their prices to provide dealers and distributors with higher markups and profit margins or by giving them big advertising and promotional allowances.

- *Restrictive regulatory policies*—Government agencies can limit or even bar entry by requiring licenses and permits. Regulated industries like cable TV, telecommunications, electric and gas utilities, and radio and television broadcasting entail government-controlled entry.

- *Tariffs and international trade restrictions*—National governments commonly use tariffs and trade restrictions (antidumping rules, local content

---

[7] The role of entry barriers in shaping the strength of competition in a particular market has long been a standard topic in the literature of microeconomics. For a discussion of how entry barriers affect competitive pressures associated with potential entry, see J. S. Bain, *Barriers to New Competition* (Cambridge: Harvard University Press, 1956); F. M. Scherer, *Industrial Market Structure and Economic Performance* (Chicago: Rand McNally & Co., 1971), pp. 216–220, 226–233; Porter, *Competitive Strategy*, pp. 7–17; and Porter, "The Five Competitive Forces that Shape Strategy," pp. 80–82.

requirements, local ownership requirements, quotas, etc.) to raise entry barriers for foreign firms and protect domestic producers from outside competition.

- *The ability and willingness of industry incumbents to launch vigorous initiatives to block a newcomer's successful entry*—Even if a potential entrant has or can acquire the needed competencies and resources to attempt entry, it must still worry about the reaction of existing firms.[8] Sometimes, there's little that incumbents can do to throw obstacles in an entrant's path. But there are times when incumbents use price cuts, increase advertising, introduce product improvements, and launch legal attacks to prevent the entrant from building a clientele. Cable TV companies have vigorously fought the entry of satellite TV into the industry by seeking government intervention to delay satellite providers in offering local stations, offering satellite customers discounts to switch back to cable, and charging satellite customers high monthly rates for cable Internet access.

In evaluating the overall effect of barriers to entry in preventing newcomers from entering the industry, company managers must also look at how attractive the growth and profit prospects are for new entrants. *Rapidly growing market demand and high potential profits act as magnets, motivating potential entrants to commit the resources needed to hurdle entry barriers.*[9] When profits are sufficiently attractive, entry barriers are unlikely to be an effective entry deterrent. Hence, *the best test of whether potential entry is a strong or weak competitive force in the marketplace is to ask if the industry's growth and profit prospects are strongly attractive to potential entry candidates.*

Figure 4.6 summarizes conditions making the threat of entry strong or weak.

The Competitive Force of Rivalry Among Competing Sellers

The strongest of the five competitive forces is nearly always the rivalry among competing sellers of a product or service. In effect, *a market is a competitive battlefield* where there's no end to the campaign for buyer patronage. Rival sellers are prone to employ whatever weapons they have in their business arsenal to improve their market positions, strengthen their market position with buyers, and earn good profits. The strategy-making challenge is to craft a competitive strategy that, at the very least, allows a company to hold its own against rivals and that, ideally, *produces a competitive edge over rivals.* But competitive contests are ongoing and dynamic. When one firm makes a strategic move that produces good results, its rivals typically respond with offensive or defensive countermoves of their own. This pattern of action and reaction produces a continually evolving competitive landscape where the market battle ebbs and flows, sometimes takes unpredictable twists and turns, and produces winners and losers.

---

[8] Porter, "How Competitive Forces Shape Strategy, p. 140; Porter, *Competitive Strategy*, pp. 14–15; and Porter, "The Five Competitive Forces that Shape Strategy," p. 82.

[9] For a good discussion of this point, see George S. Yip, "Gateways to Entry," *Harvard Business Review* 60, no. 5 (September–October 1982), pp. 85–93.

FIGURE 4.6   **Factors Affecting the Threat of Entry**

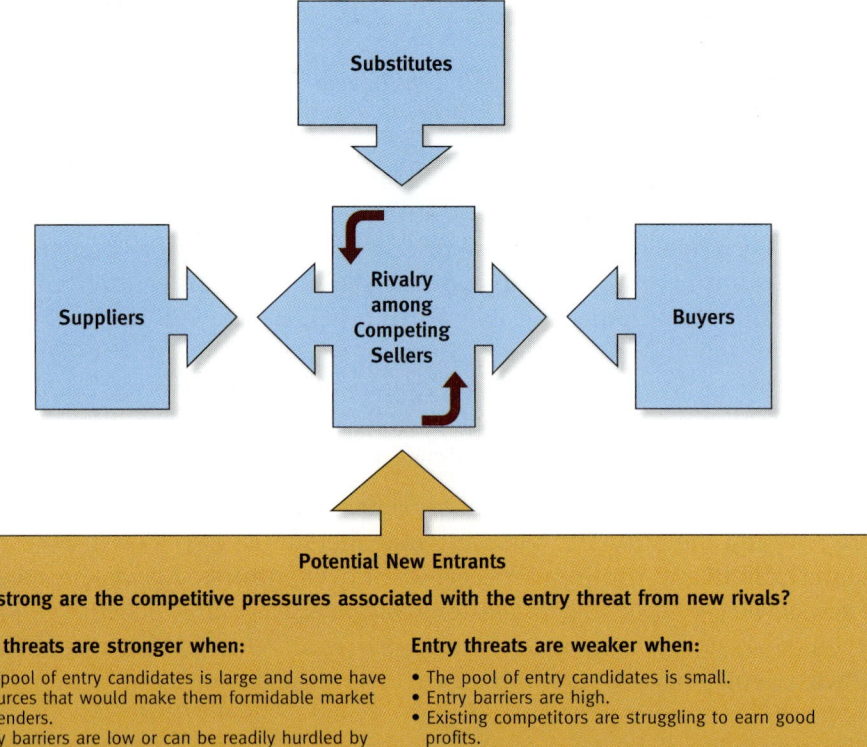

Potential New Entrants

How strong are the competitive pressures associated with the entry threat from new rivals?

Entry threats are stronger when:

- The pool of entry candidates is large and some have resources that would make them formidable market contenders.
- Entry barriers are low or can be readily hurdled by the likely entry candidates.
- Existing industry members are looking to expand their market reach by entering product segments or geographic areas where they currently do not have a presence.
- Newcomers can expect to earn attractive profits.
- Buyer demand is growing rapidly.
- Industry members are unable (or unwilling) to strongly contest the entry of newcomers.

Entry threats are weaker when:

- The pool of entry candidates is small.
- Entry barriers are high.
- Existing competitors are struggling to earn good profits.
- The industry's outlook is risky or uncertain.
- Buyer demand is growing slowly or is stagnant.
- Industry members will strongly contest the efforts of new entrants to gain a market foothold.

Figure 4.7 shows a sampling of competitive weapons that firms can deploy in battling rivals and indicates the factors that influence the intensity of their rivalry. Some of the factors that influence the tempo of rivalry among industry competitors include:[10]

- *Rivalry intensifies when competing sellers regularly launch fresh actions to boost their market standing and business performance.* Normally, competitive jockeying among rival sellers is fairly intense. Indicators of strong competitive rivalry include lively price competition, the rapid introduction of next-generation products, and moves to differentiate products by offering better performance features, higher quality, improved customer service, or a wider product selection. Other common tactics used to temporarily boost sales include special sales promotions, heavy advertising, rebates, or low-interest-rate financing.

- *Rivalry is stronger in industries where competitors are equal in size and capability.* Competitive rivalry in the quick service restaurant industry is particularly

---

[10] Many of these indicators of whether rivalry produces intense competitive pressures are based on Porter, *Competitive Strategy*, pp. 17–21 and Porter, "The Five Competitive Forces that Shape Strategy," pp. 85–86.

FIGURE 4.7   **Factors Affecting the Strength of Competitive Rivalry**

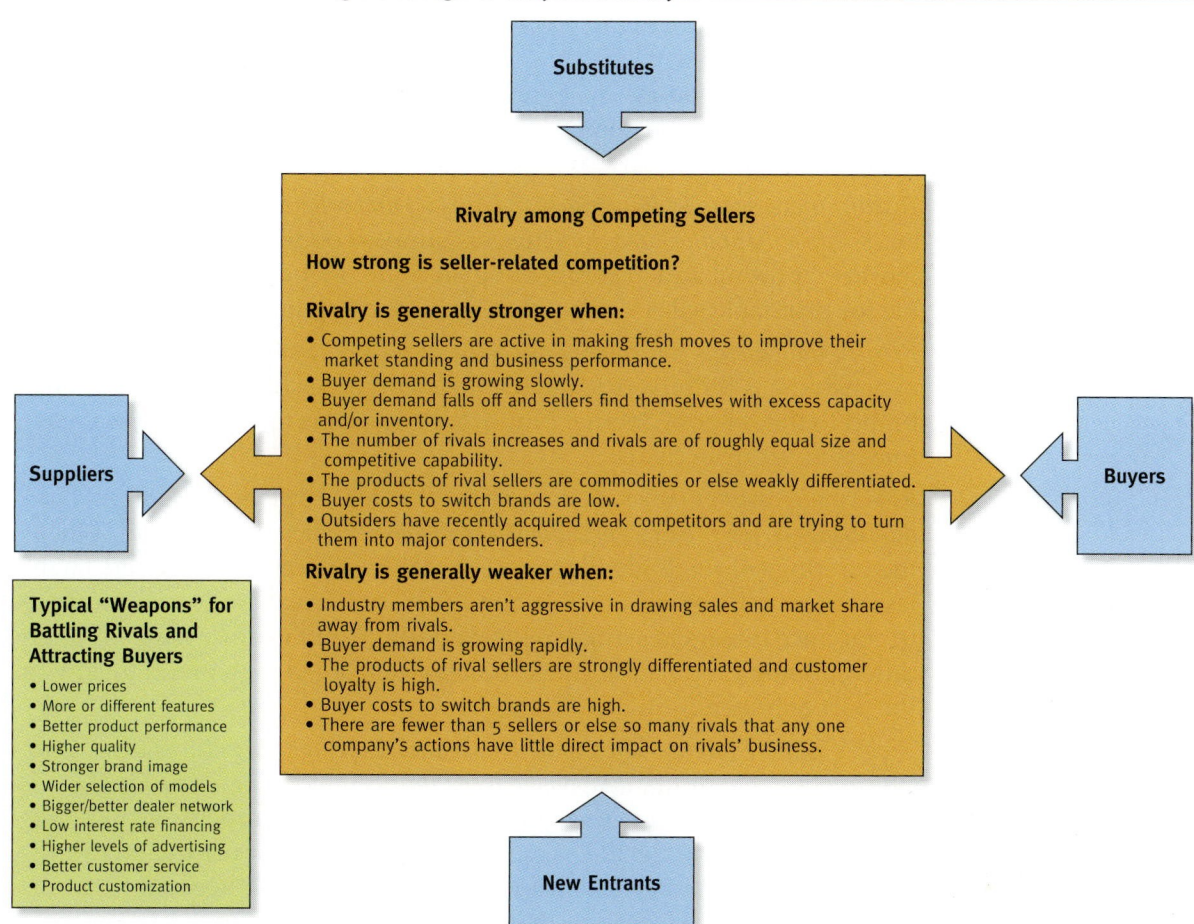

strong, where there are numerous relatively equal-sized hamburger, deli sandwich, chicken, and taco chains. For the most part, McDonald's, Burger King, Taco Bell, KFC, Arby's, and other national fast food chains have comparable capabilities and are required to compete aggressively to hold their own in the industry.

- *Rivalry is usually stronger in slow-growing markets and weaker in fast-growing markets.* Rapidly expanding buyer demand produces enough new business for all industry members to grow. But in markets where growth is sluggish or where buyer demand drops off unexpectedly, it is not uncommon for competitive rivalry to intensify significantly as rivals battle for market share and volume gains.

- *Rivalry is usually weaker in industries comprised of vast numbers of small rivals; likewise, it is often weak when there are fewer than five competitors.* Head-to-head rivalry tends to be weak once an industry becomes populated with so many rivals that the strategic moves of any one competitor have little discernible impact on the success of rivals. Rivalry also *tends* to be weak if an industry consists of just two to four sellers. In a market with few rivals, each competitor soon learns that aggressive moves to grow its sales and market share can have an immediate adverse impact on rivals' businesses, almost certainly provoking vigorous retaliation. However, some caution must be exercised in concluding that rivalry is weak just because there are only a few competitors. The fierceness of the current battle between Linux and Microsoft and the decades-long war between Coca-Cola and Pepsi are prime examples.

- *Rivalry increases when buyer demand falls off and sellers find themselves with excess capacity and/or inventory.* Excess supply conditions create a "buyers' market," putting added competitive pressure on industry rivals to scramble for profitable sales levels (often by price discounting).

- *Rivalry increases as it becomes less costly for buyers to switch brands.* The less expensive it is for buyers to switch their purchases from the seller of one brand to the seller of another brand, the easier it is for sellers to steal customers away from rivals.

- *Rivalry increases as the products of rival sellers become more standardized and diminishes as the products of industry rivals become more differentiated.* When the offerings of rivals are identical or weakly differentiated, buyers have less reason to be brand loyal—a condition which makes it easier for rivals to convince buyers to switch to their offering. On the other hand, strongly differentiated product offerings among rivals breed high brand loyalty on the part of buyers.

- *Rivalry is more intense when industry conditions tempt competitors to use price cuts or other competitive weapons to boost unit volume.* When a product is perishable, seasonal, or costly to hold in inventory, competitive pressures build quickly any time one or more firms decide to cut prices and dump supplies on the market. Likewise, whenever fixed costs account for a large fraction of total cost, so that unit costs tend to be lowest at or near full capacity, firms come under significant pressure to cut prices or otherwise try to boost sales whenever they are operating below full capacity.

- *Rivalry increases when one or more competitors become dissatisfied with their market position.* Firms that are losing ground or in financial trouble often pursue aggressive (or perhaps desperate) turnaround strategies that can involve price discounts, greater advertising, or merger with other rivals. Such strategies can turn competitive pressures up a notch.

- *Rivalry increases when strong companies outside the industry acquire weak firms in the industry and launch aggressive, well-funded moves to build market share.* A concerted effort to turn a weak rival into a market leader nearly always entails launching well-financed strategic initiatives to dramatically improve the competitor's product offering, excite buyer interest, and win a much bigger market share—actions that, if successful, put added pressure on rivals to counter with fresh strategic moves of their own.

Rivalry can be characterized as *cutthroat* or *brutal* when competitors engage in protracted price wars or habitually employ other aggressive tactics that are mutually destructive to profitability. Rivalry can be considered *fierce* to *strong* when the battle for market share is so vigorous that the profit margins of most industry members are squeezed to bare-bones levels. Rivalry can be characterized as *moderate* or *normal* when the maneuvering among industry members, while lively and healthy, still allows most industry members to earn acceptable profits. Rivalry is *weak* when most companies in the industry are relatively well satisfied with their sales growth and market share and rarely undertake offensives to steal customers away from one another.

The Collective Strengths of the Five Competitive Forces and Industry Profitability

Scrutinizing each of the five competitive forces one by one provides a powerful diagnosis of what competition is like in a given market. Once the strategist has gained an understanding of the competitive pressures associated with each of the five forces, the next step is to evaluate the collective strength of the five forces and determine if companies in this industry should reasonably expect to earn decent profits.

As a rule, the stronger the collective impact of the five competitive forces, the lower the combined profitability of industry participants. The most extreme case of a "competitively unattractive" industry is when all five forces are producing strong competitive pressures: rivalry among sellers is vigorous, low entry barriers allow new rivals to gain a market foothold, competition from substitutes is intense, and both suppliers and customers are able to exercise considerable bargaining leverage. Fierce to strong competitive pressures coming from all five directions nearly always drive industry profitability to unacceptably low levels, frequently producing losses for many industry members and forcing some out of business. But an industry can be competitively unattractive without all five competitive forces being strong. Intense competitive pressures from just two or three of the five forces may suffice to destroy the conditions for good profitability. The manufacture of disk drives, for example, is brutally competitive; IBM recently announced the sale of its disk drive business to Hitachi, taking a loss of over $2 billion on its exit from the business.

In contrast, when the collective impact of the five competitive forces is moderate to weak, an industry is competitively attractive in the sense that industry members can reasonably expect to earn good profits and a nice return on investment. The ideal competitive environment for earning superior profits is one in which both suppliers and customers are in weak bargaining positions, there are no good substitutes, high barriers block further entry, and rivalry among present sellers generates only moderate competitive pressures. Weak competition is the best of all possible worlds for companies with mediocre strategies and second-rate implementation because even they can expect a decent profit.

Industry Analysis Question 3: What Are the Industry's Driving Forces of Change and What Impact Will They Have?

The intensity of competitive forces and the level of industry attractiveness are almost always fluid and subject to change. It is essential for strategy makers to understand the current competitive dynamics of the industry, but it is equally important for strategy makers to consider how the industry is changing and the effect of industry changes that are underway. Any strategies devised by management will play out in a dynamic industry environment, so it's imperative that such plans consider what the industry environment might look like during the near term.

The Concept of Industry Driving Forces

Driving forces are the major underlying causes of change in industry and competitive conditions.

Industry and competitive conditions change because forces are enticing or pressuring certain industry participants (competitors, customers, suppliers) to alter their actions in important ways.[11] The most powerful of the change agents are called **driving forces** because they have the biggest influences in reshaping the industry landscape and altering competitive conditions. Some driving forces originate in the outer ring of the company's macroenvironment (see Figure 4.1) but most originate in the company's more immediate industry and competitive environment.

Driving forces analysis has three steps: (1) identifying what the driving forces are, (2) assessing whether the drivers of change are, individually or collectively, acting to make the industry more or less attractive, and (3) determining what strategy changes are needed to prepare for the impact of the driving forces.

Identifying an Industry's Driving Forces

Many developments can affect an industry powerfully enough to qualify as driving forces. Some drivers of change are unique and specific to a particular industry situation, but most drivers of industry and competitive change fall into one of the following categories:[12]

- *Changes in an industry's long-term growth rate*—Shifts in industry growth are a driving force for industry change, affecting the balance between industry supply and buyer demand, entry and exit, and the character and strength of competition. An upsurge in buyer demand triggers a race among established firms and newcomers to capture the new sales opportunities. A slowdown in the growth of demand nearly always brings an increase in rivalry and increased efforts by some firms to maintain their high rates of growth by taking sales and market share away from rivals.

- *Increasing globalization*—Globalization of competition really starts to take hold when one or more ambitious companies launch a race for worldwide market leadership. The forces of globalization are sometimes such a strong driver that companies find it highly advantageous, if not necessary, to spread their operating reach into more and more country markets. Globalization is very much a driver of industry change in such industries as credit cards, mobile phones, digital cameras, golf and ski equipment, motor vehicles, steel, petroleum, personal computers, and videogames.

[11] Porter, *Competitive Strategy*, p. 162.

[12] Most of the driving forces described here are based on the discussion in Porter, *Competitive Strategy*, pp. 164–83.

- *Emerging new Internet capabilities and applications*—Since the late 1990s, the Internet has woven its way into everyday business operations and the social fabric of life all across the world. Mushrooming Internet use, growing acceptance of Internet shopping, the emergence of high-speed Internet service and Voice Over Internet Protocol (VoIP) technology, and an evergrowing series of Internet applications and capabilities have been major drivers of change in industry after industry. Companies are increasingly using online technology to (1) collaborate closely with suppliers and streamline their supply chains and (2) revamp internal operations and squeeze out cost savings. But Internet-related impacts vary from industry to industry. The challenges here are to assess precisely how emerging Internet developments are altering a particular industry's landscape and to factor these impacts into the strategy-making equation.

- *Changes in who buys the product and how they use it*—Shifts in buyer demographics and the ways products are used can alter competition by affecting how customers perceive value, how customers make purchasing decisions, and where customers purchase the product. The burgeoning popularity of downloading music from the Internet has significantly changed the recording industry. Consumers largely don't purchase every track offered on an album, often consider format compatibility with iPods, MP3 players, or mobile phones, and may acquire the track either legally through an online store or illegally through a file sharing network. According to Nielsen SoundScan, album sales have declined from 785.1 million units in 2000 to 588.2 units in 2006. The changing nature of consumer music purchases led to digital single sales by Web sites such as iTunes Store, MSN Music, and Yahoo! Music to reach 582 million downloads in 2006. Consumers also purchased ringtones totaling more than $600 million in 2006.

- *Product innovation*—An ongoing stream of product innovations tends to alter the pattern of competition in an industry by attracting more first-time buyers, rejuvenating industry growth, and/or creating wider or narrower product differentiation among rival sellers. Product innovation has been a key driving force in such industries as computers, digital cameras, televisions, video games, and prescription drugs.

- *Technological change and manufacturing process innovation*—Advances in technology can dramatically alter an industry's landscape, making it possible to produce new and better products at lower cost and opening up whole new industry frontiers. In the steel industry, ongoing advances in electric arc mini-mill technology (which involves recycling scrap steel to make new products) have allowed steelmakers with state-of-the-art mini-mills to gradually expand into the production of more and more steel products and steadily take sales and market share from higher-cost integrated producers (which make steel from scratch using iron ore, coke, and traditional blast furnace technology). Nucor, the leader of the mini-mill technology revolution in the United States, began operations in 1970 and has ridden the wave of technological advances in mini-mill technology to become the biggest U.S. steel producer with 2006 revenues of nearly $15 billion.

- *Marketing innovation*—When firms are successful in introducing *new ways* to market their products, they can spark a burst of buyer interest, widen industry demand, increase product differentiation, and lower unit costs—any or all of which can alter the competitive positions of rival firms and force strategy revisions.

- *Entry or exit of major firms*—The entry of one or more foreign companies into a geographic market once dominated by domestic firms nearly always shakes up competitive conditions. Likewise, when an established domestic firm from another industry attempts entry either by acquisition or by launching its own start-up venture, it usually pushes competition in new directions.

- *Diffusion of technical know-how across more companies and more countries*—As knowledge about how to perform a particular activity or execute a particular manufacturing technology spreads, the competitive advantage held by firms originally possessing this know-how erodes. Knowledge diffusion can occur through scientific journals, trade publications, onsite plant tours, word of mouth among suppliers and customers, employee migration, and Internet sources. In recent years, *rapid technology transfer across national boundaries has been a prime factor in causing industries to become more globally competitive.*

- *Changes in cost and efficiency*—Widening or shrinking differences in the costs among key competitors tend to dramatically alter the state of competition. Shrinking cost differences in producing multifeatured mobile phones is turning the mobile phone market into a commodity business and causing more buyers to base their purchase decisions on price.

- *Growing buyer preferences for differentiated products instead of a commodity product (or for a more standardized product instead of strongly differentiated products)*—When a shift from standardized to differentiated products occurs, rivals must adopt strategies to outdifferentiate one another. However, buyers sometimes decide that a standardized, budget-priced product suits their requirements as well as a premium-priced product with lots of snappy features and personalized services. Online brokers, for example, have used the lure of cheap commissions to attract many investors willing to place their own buy-sell orders via the Internet.

- *Regulatory influences and government policy changes*—Government regulatory actions can often force significant changes in industry practices and strategic approaches. Deregulation has proved to be a potent pro-competitive force in the airline, banking, natural gas, telecommunications, and electric utility industries.

- *Changing societal concerns, attitudes, and lifestyles*—Emerging social issues and changing attitudes and lifestyles can be powerful instigators of industry change. Consumer concerns about salt, sugar, chemical additives, saturated fat, cholesterol, carbohydrates, and nutritional value have forced food producers to revamp food-processing techniques, redirect R&D efforts into the use of healthier ingredients, and compete in developing nutritious, good-tasting products.

While many forces of change may be at work in a given industry, *no more than three or four* are likely to be true driving forces powerful enough to qualify as the *major determinants* of why and how the industry is changing. Thus company strategists must resist the temptation to label every change they see as a driving force. Table 4.2 lists the most common driving forces.

Assessing the Impact of the Industry Driving Forces

The second step in driving forces analysis is to determine whether the prevailing driving forces are acting to make the industry environment more or less attractive. Getting a handle on the collective impact of the driving forces usually requires looking at the likely effects of each force separately, because the driving forces may not all be pushing change in the same direction. For example, two driving forces may be acting to spur demand for the industry's product while one driving force may be working to curtail demand. Whether the net effect on industry demand is up or down hinges on which driving forces are the more powerful.

> An important part of driving forces analysis is to determine whether the individual or collective impact of the driving forces will be to increase or decrease market demand, make competition more or less intense, and lead to higher or lower industry profitability.

Determining Strategy Changes Needed to Prepare for the Impact of Driving Forces

The third step of driving forces analysis—where the real payoff for strategy-making comes—is for managers to draw some conclusions about what strategy adjustments will be needed to deal with the impact of the driving forces. Without understanding the forces driving industry change and the impacts these forces will have on the industry environment over the next one to three years, managers are ill-prepared to craft a strategy tightly matched to emerging

Table 4.2

Common Driving Forces

1. Changes in the long-term industry growth rate.
2. Increasing globalization.
3. Emerging new Internet capabilities and applications.
4. Changes in who buys the product and how they use it.
5. Product innovation.
6. Technological change and manufacturing process innovation.
7. Marketing innovation.
8. Entry or exit of major firms.
9. Diffusion of technical know-how across more companies and more countries.
10. Changes in cost and efficiency.
11. Growing buyer preferences for differentiated products instead of a standardized commodity product (or for a more standardized product instead of strongly differentiated products).
12. Regulatory influences and government policy changes.
13. Changing societal concerns, attitudes, and lifestyles.

conditions. Similarly, if managers are uncertain about the implications of one or more driving forces, or if their views are off-base, it will be difficult for them to craft a strategy that is responsive to the consequences of driving forces. So driving forces analysis is not something to take lightly; it has practical value and is basic to the task of thinking strategically about where the industry is headed and how to prepare for the changes ahead.

Industry Analysis Question 4: How Are Industry Rivals Positioned?

The nature of competitive strategy inherently positions companies competing in an industry into strategic groups with diverse price/quality ranges, different distribution channels, varying product features, and different geographic coverages. The best technique for revealing the market positions of industry competitors is **strategic group mapping.**[13] This analytical tool is useful for comparing the market positions of industry competitors or for grouping industry combatants into like positions.

Using Strategic Group Maps to Assess the Positioning of Key Competitors

A **strategic group** consists of those industry members with similar competitive approaches and positions in the market.[14] Companies in the same strategic group can resemble one another in any of several ways—they may have comparable product-line breadth, sell in the same price/quality range, emphasize the same distribution channels, use essentially the same product attributes to appeal to similar types of buyers, depend on identical technological approaches, or offer buyers similar services and technical assistance.[15] An industry with a commodity-like product may contain only one strategic group whereby all sellers pursue essentially identical strategies and have comparable market positions. But even with commodity products, there is likely some attempt at differentiation taking place in the form of varying delivery times, financing terms, or levels of customer service. Most industries offer a host of competitive approaches that allow companies to find unique industry positioning and avoid fierce competition in a crowded strategic group. Evaluating strategy options entails examining what strategic groups exist, which companies exist within each group, and determining if a competitive "white space" exists where industry competitors are able to pursue a "blue ocean" strategy.

The procedure for constructing a *strategic group map* is straightforward:

- Identify the competitive characteristics that delineate strategic approaches used in the industry. Typical variables used in creating strategic group maps are the price/quality range (high, medium, low), geographic

---

[13] Porter, *Competitive Strategy*, Chapter 7.

[14] Ibid., pp. 129–30.

[15] For an excellent discussion of how to identify the factors that define strategic groups, see Mary Ellen Gordon and George R. Milne, "Selecting the Dimensions that Define Strategic Groups: A Novel Market-Driven Approach," *Journal of Managerial Issues* 11, no. 2 (Summer 1999), pp. 213–33.

Concepts & Connections 4.1

COMPARATIVE MARKET POSITIONS OF SELECTED RETAIL CHAINS: A STRATEGIC GROUP MAP APPLICATION

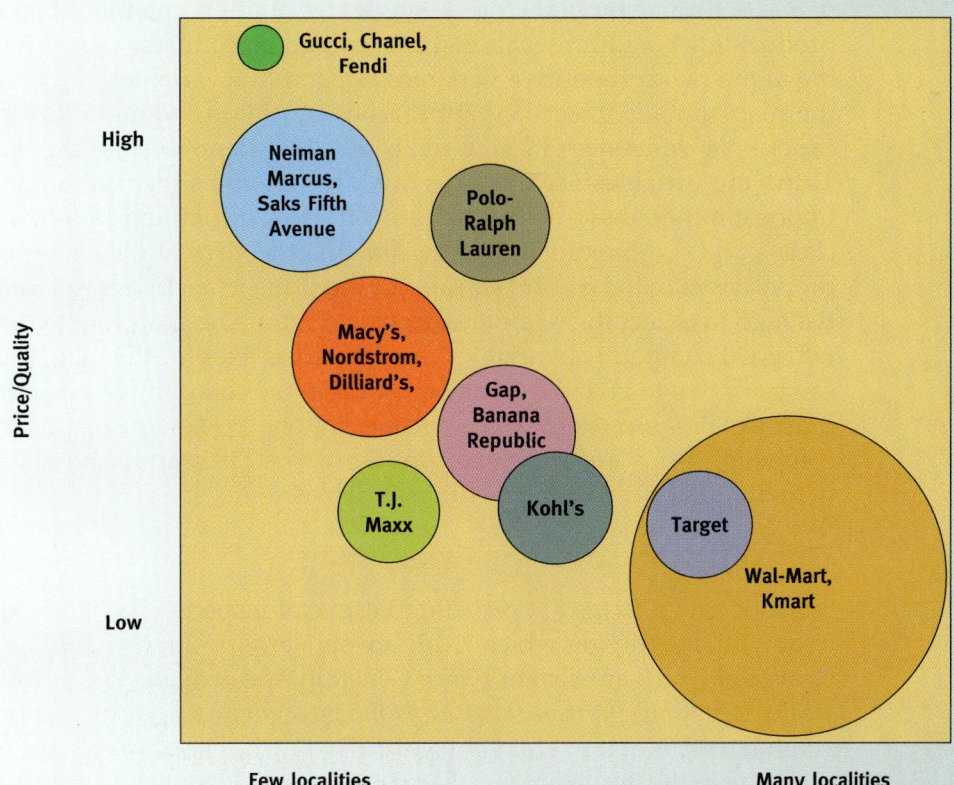

Note: Circles are drawn roughly proportional to the sizes of the chains, based on revenues.

coverage (local, regional, national, global), degree of vertical integration (none, partial, full), product-line breadth (wide, narrow), choice of distribution channels (retail, wholesale, Internet, multiple channels), and degree of service offered (no-frills, limited, full).

- Plot firms on a two-variable map based upon their strategic approaches.
- Assign firms occupying the same map location to a common strategic group.
- Draw circles around each strategic group, making the circles proportional to the size of the group's share of total industry sales revenues.

This produces a two-dimensional diagram like the one for the retailing industry in Concepts & Connections 4.1.

Several guidelines need to be observed in creating strategic group maps.[16] First, the two variables selected as axes for the map should *not* be highly correlated; if they are, the circles on the map will fall along a diagonal and strategy makers will learn nothing more about the relative positions of competitors than they would by considering just one of the variables. For instance, if companies with broad product lines use multiple distribution channels while companies with narrow lines use a single distribution channel, then looking at product line breadth reveals just as much about industry positioning as looking at the two competitive variables. Second, the variables chosen as axes for the map should reflect key approaches to offering value to customers and expose big differences in how rivals position themselves in the marketplace. Third, the variables used as axes don't have to be either quantitative or continuous; rather, they can be discrete variables or defined in terms of distinct classes and combinations. Fourth, drawing the sizes of the circles on the map proportional to the combined sales of the firms in each strategic group allows the map to reflect the relative sizes of each strategic group. Fifth, if more than two good competitive variables can be used as axes for the map, several maps can be drawn to give different exposures to the competitive positioning in the industry. Because there is not necessarily one best map for portraying how competing firms are positioned in the market, it is advisable to experiment with different pairs of competitive variables.

The Value of Strategic Group Maps

Strategic group maps are revealing in several respects. The *most important* has to do with identifying which rivals are similarly positioned and are thus close rivals and which are distant rivals. Generally speaking, *the closer strategic groups are to each other on the map, the stronger the cross-group competitive rivalry tends to be.* Although firms in the same strategic group are the closest rivals, the next closest rivals are in the immediately adjacent groups.[17] Often, firms in strategic groups that are far apart on the map hardly compete at all. For instance, Wal-Mart's clientele, merchandise selection, and pricing points are much too different to justify calling them close competitors of Neiman Marcus or Saks Fifth Avenue in retailing. For the same reason, Timex is not a meaningful competitive rival of Rolex, and Kia is not a close competitor of Porsche or Hummer.

The second thing to be gleaned from strategic group mapping is that *not all positions on the map are equally attractive.* Two reasons account for why some positions can be more attractive than others:

1. *Industry driving forces may favor some strategic groups and hurt others.*[18]
    Driving forces in an industry may be acting to grow the demand for the

---

[16] Porter, *Competitive Strategy*, pp. 152–54.

[17] Strategic groups act as good reference points for predicting the evolution of an industry's competitive structure. See Avi Fiegenbaum and Howard Thomas, "Strategic Groups as Reference Groups: Theory, Modeling and Empirical Examination of Industry and Competitive Strategy," *Strategic Management Journal* 16 (1995), pp. 461–76. For a study of how strategic group analysis helps identify the variables that lead to sustainable competitive advantage, see S. Ade Olusoga, Michael P. Mokwa, and Charles H. Noble, "Strategic Groups, Mobility Barriers, and Competitive Advantage," *Journal of Business Research* 33 (1995), pp. 153–64.

[18] Ibid., pp. 130,132–38, and 154–55.

products of firms in some strategic groups and shrink the demand for the products of firms in other strategic groups—as is the case in the news industry where Internet news services and cable news networks are gaining ground at the expense of newspapers and network television. The industry driving forces of emerging Internet capabilities and applications, changes in who buys the product and how they use it, and changing societal concerns, attitudes, and lifestyles are making it increasingly difficult for traditional media to increase audiences and attract new advertisers.

2. *Competitive pressures may cause the profit potential of different strategic groups to vary.* The profit prospects of firms in different strategic groups can vary from good to poor because of differing degrees of competitive rivalry within strategic groups, differing degrees of exposure to competition from substitute products outside the industry, and differing degrees of supplier or customer bargaining power from group to group. For instance, the competitive battle among Wal-Mart, Target, and Sears/Kmart (Kmart merged with Sears to form Sears Holdings Corporation in 2005) is more intense (with consequently smaller profit margins) than the rivalry among the flagship stores of couture brands such as Versace, Chanel, and Givenchy.

A third benefit of preparing strategic group maps is that strategy makers may identify competitive "white spaces" where customer needs have gone unmet. The identification of a white space or "blue ocean" gives expansion-oriented companies opportunities to pursue new industry segments that may offer high growth and profits. While a competitive white space may present additional growth opportunities for industry leaders, the discovery of a blue ocean may be critical to the survival of companies faltering in the "red ocean" of a crowded strategic group. A **blue ocean strategy** seeks to gain a competitive advantage *by discovering or inventing a new industry or distinctive market segment that allows a company to create and capture altogether new demand.*[19]

This strategy views the business universe as consisting of two distinct types of market space. One is where industry boundaries are well-defined, the competitive rules have been decided, and companies try to outperform rivals by capturing a bigger share of existing demand. The second type of market space is where the

> **Blue ocean strategies** offer growth in revenues and profits by discovering or inventing new industry segments that create altogether new demand.

industry or industry segment does not really exist yet, is untainted by competition, and offers wide open opportunity for profitable and rapid growth. A terrific example of such wide open or blue ocean market space is the online auction industry that eBay created and now dominates.

Another company that has employed a blue ocean strategy is Cirque du Soleil, which has achieved remarkable success in the circus business—an industry that had been in long-term decline for 20 years. Cirque du Soleil has created a blue ocean by "reinventing the circus" with new venues for its performances (Las Vegas night clubs and theater type settings), and by appealing to a new group of customers. Most patrons of a Cirque du Soleil performance

---

[19] W. Chan Kim and Renée Mauborgne, "Blue Ocean Strategy," *Harvard Business Review* 82, no. 10 (October 2004), pp. 76–84.

are vacationing adults and businesspeople attending corporate meetings who pay several times more than the price of a conventional circus ticket to have an "entertainment experience." Cirque performances feature sophisticated clowns and star-quality acrobatic acts in a comfortable tent-like atmosphere. The company has avoided the use of animals because of costs and concerns over the treatment of circus animals. Cirque's market research led management to conclude that the lasting allure of the traditional circus came down to just three factors: the clowns, classic acrobatic acts, and a tent-like stage. As of 2007, Cirque du Soleil was presenting 15 different shows, each with its own theme and story line, was performing before audiences of about 10 million people annually, and had performed 250 engagements in 100 cities since its formation in 1984.

Industry Analysis Question 5: What Strategic Moves Are Rivals Likely to Make Next?

As in sports, scouting the business opposition is an essential part of game plan development. **Competitive intelligence** about rivals' strategies, their latest actions and announcements, their resource strengths and weaknesses, and the thinking and leadership styles of their executives is valuable for predicting the strategic moves competitors are likely to make next. Having good information to predict the likely moves of key competitors allows a company to prepare defensive countermoves and to exploit any openings that arise from competitors' missteps.

Predicting the Moves of Industry Rivals

Considerations in trying to predict what strategic moves rivals are likely to make next include the following:

- What executives are saying about where the industry is headed, the firm's situation, and their past actions and leadership styles.
- Identifying trends in the timing of new product launches or marketing promotions.
- Determining which rivals badly need to increase unit sales and market share.
- Considering which rivals have a strong incentive, along with the resources, to make major strategic changes.
- Knowing which rivals are likely to enter new geographic markets.
- Deciding which rivals are strong candidates to expand their product offerings and enter new product segments.

To succeed in predicting a competitor's next moves, company strategists need to have a good feel for each rival's situation, how its managers think, and what the rival's best strategic options are. Doing the necessary detective work can be tedious and time-consuming, but scouting competitors well enough to anticipate their next moves allows managers to prepare effective countermoves and to take rivals' probable actions into account in crafting their own offensive strategies.

BUSINESS ETHICS AND COMPETITIVE INTELLIGENCE   Those who gather competitive intelligence on rivals, however, can sometimes cross the fine line between honest inquiry and unethical or even illegal behavior. For example, calling rivals to get information about prices, the dates of new product introductions, or wage and salary levels is legal, but misrepresenting one's company affiliation during such calls is unethical. Pumping rivals' representatives at trade shows is ethical only if one wears a name tag with accurate company affiliation indicated. Avon Products at one point secured information about its biggest rival, Mary Kay Cosmetics (MKC), by having its personnel search through the garbage bins outside MKC's headquarters.[20] When MKC officials learned of the action and sued, Avon claimed it did nothing illegal, since a 1988 Supreme Court case had ruled that trash left on public property (in this case, a sidewalk) was anyone's for the taking. Avon even produced a videotape of its removal of the trash at the MKC site. Avon won the lawsuit— but Avon's action, while legal, scarcely qualifies as ethical.

Industry Analysis Question 6: What Are the Industry Key Success Factors?

An industry's **key success factors (KSFs)** are those competitive factors that most affect industry members' ability to prosper in the marketplace. Key success factors may include specific product attributes, resources, competencies, competitive capabilities, or intangible assets. KSFs by their very nature are so important to future competitive success that *all firms* in the industry must pay close attention to them or risk an eventual exit from the industry.

> **Key success factors** are the product attributes, competencies, competitive capabilities, or intangible assets with the greatest impact on future success in the marketplace.

In the ready-to-wear apparel industry, the KSFs are appealing designs and color combinations, low-cost manufacturing, a strong network of retailers or company-owned stores, distribution capabilities that allow stores to keep the best-selling items in stock, and advertisements that effectively convey the brand's image. These attributes and capabilities apply to all brands of apparel ranging from private-label brands sold by discounters to premium-priced ready-to-wear brands sold by upscale department stores. Table 4.3 lists the most common types of industry key success factors.

An industry's key success factors can usually be deduced through identifying the industry's dominant characteristics, assessing the five competitive forces, considering the impacts of the driving forces, comparing the market positions of industry members, and forecasting the likely next moves of key rivals. In addition, the answers to the following three questions help identify an industry's key success factors:

1. On what basis do buyers of the industry's product choose between the competing brands of sellers? That is, what product attributes are crucial?

2. Given the nature of the competitive forces prevailing in the marketplace, what resources and competitive capabilities does a company need to have to be competitively successful?

---

[20] Larry Kahaner, *Competitive Intelligence*, (New York: Simon and Schuster, 1996) pp. 84–85.

Table 4.3

Common Types of Industry Key Success Factors

Technology-related KSFs	• Expertise in a particular technology or in scientific research (important in pharmaceuticals, Internet applications, mobile communications, and most "high-tech" industries) • Proven ability to improve production processes (important in industries where advancing technology opens the way for higher manufacturing efficiency and lower production costs)
Manufacturing-related KSFs	• Ability to achieve scale economies and/or capture experience curve effects (important to achieving low production costs) • Quality control know-how (important in industries where customers insist on product reliability) • High utilization of fixed assets (important in capital-intensive/high-fixed-cost industries) • Access to attractive supplies of skilled labor • High labor productivity (important for items with high labor content) • Low-cost product design and engineering (reduces manufacturing costs) • Ability to manufacture or assemble products that are customized to buyer specifications
Distribution-related KSFs	• A strong network of wholesale distributors/dealers • Strong direct sales capabilities via the Internet and/or having company-owned retail outlets • Ability to secure favorable display space on retailer shelves
Marketing-related KSFs	• Breadth of product line and product selection • A well-known and well-respected brand name • Fast, accurate technical assistance • Courteous, personalized customer service • Accurate filling of buyer orders (few back orders or mistakes) • Customer guarantees and warranties (important in mail-order and online retailing, big-ticket purchases, and new product introductions) • Clever advertising
Skills- and capability-related KSFs	• A talented workforce (superior talent is important in professional services like accounting and investment banking) • National or global distribution capabilities • Product innovation capabilities (important in industries where rivals are racing to be first-to-market with new product attributes or performance features) • Design expertise (important in fashion and apparel industries) • Short delivery time capability • Supply chain management capabilities • Strong e-commerce capabilities—a user-friendly Web site and/or skills in using Internet technology applications to streamline internal operations
Other types of KSFs	• Overall low costs (not just in manufacturing) to be able to meet low price expectations of customers • Convenient locations (important in many retailing businesses) • Ability to provide fast, convenient, after-the-sale repairs and service • A strong balance sheet and access to financial capital (important in newly emerging industries with high degrees of business risk and in capital-intensive industries) • Patent protection

3. What shortcomings are almost certain to put a company at a significant competitive disadvantage?

Only rarely are there more than five or six key factors for future competitive success. Managers should therefore resist the temptation to label a factor that has only minor importance a KSF. To compile a list of every factor that matters even a little bit defeats the purpose of concentrating management attention on the factors truly critical to long-term competitive success.

Industry Analysis Question 7: Does the Industry Offer Good Prospects for Attractive Profits?

The final step in evaluating the industry and competitive environment is boiling down the results of the analyses performed in Questions 1–6 to determine if the industry offers a company strong prospects for attractive profits.

The important factors on which to base such a conclusion include:

- The industry's growth potential.

- Whether powerful competitive forces are squeezing industry profitability to subpar levels and whether competition appears destined to grow stronger or weaker.

- Whether industry profitability will be favorably or unfavorably affected by the prevailing driving forces.

- The company's competitive position in the industry vis-à-vis rivals. (Well-entrenched leaders or strongly positioned contenders have a much better chance of earning attractive margins than those fighting a steep uphill battle.)

- How competently the company performs industry key success factors.

LO3

Learn what kinds of conditions cause an industry to be more or less attractive from the standpoint of earning good profits and presenting good long-term business opportunity.

It is a mistake to think of a particular industry as being equally attractive or unattractive to all industry participants and all potential entrants. Conclusions have to be drawn from the perspective of a particular company. Industries attractive to insiders may be unattractive to outsiders. Industry environments unattractive to weak competitors may be attractive to strong competitors. A favorably positioned company may survey a business environment and see a host of opportunities that weak competitors cannot capture.

> The degree to which an industry is attractive or unattractive is not the same for all industry participants and potential new entrants. The attractiveness of an industry depends on the degree of fit between a company's competitive capabilities and industry key success factors.

When a company decides an industry is fundamentally attractive, a strong case can be made that it should invest aggressively to capture the opportunities it sees. When a strong competitor concludes an industry is relatively unattractive, it may elect to simply protect its present position, investing cautiously if at all, and begin looking for opportunities in other industries. A competitively weak company in an unattractive industry may see its best option as finding a buyer, perhaps a rival, to acquire its business.

Key Points

Thinking strategically about a company's external situation involves probing for answers to the following seven questions:

1. *What are the industry's dominant economic features?* Industries differ significantly on such factors as market size and growth rate, the number and relative sizes of both buyers and sellers, the geographic scope of competitive rivalry, the degree of product differentiation, the speed of product innovation, demand-supply conditions, the extent of vertical integration, and the extent of scale economies and learning curve effects.

2. *What kinds of competitive forces are industry members facing, and how strong is each force?* The strength of competition is a composite of five forces: (1) competitive pressures stemming from buyer bargaining power and seller-buyer collaboration, (2) competitive pressures associated with the sellers of substitutes, (3) competitive pressures stemming from supplier bargaining power and supplier-seller collaboration, (4) competitive pressures associated with the threat of new entrants into the market, and (5) competitive pressures stemming from the competitive jockeying among industry rivals.

3. *What forces are driving changes in the industry, and what impact will these changes have on competitive intensity and industry profitability?* Industry and competitive conditions change because forces are in motion that create incentives or pressures for change. The first phase is to identify the forces that are driving industry change. The second phase of driving forces analysis is to determine whether the driving forces, taken together, are acting to make the industry environment more or less attractive.

4. *What market positions do industry rivals occupy—who is strongly positioned and who is not?* Strategic group mapping is a valuable tool for understanding the similarities and differences inherent in the market positions of rival companies. Rivals in the same or nearby strategic groups are close competitors, whereas companies in distant strategic groups usually pose little or no immediate threat. Some strategic groups are more favorable than others. The profit potential of different strategic groups may not be the same because industry driving forces and competitive forces likely have varying effects on the industry's distinct strategic groups. Strategic groups also help strategy makers discover opportunities for "blue ocean" strategies.

5. *What strategic moves are rivals likely to make next?* Scouting competitors well enough to anticipate their actions can help a company prepare effective countermoves (perhaps even beating a rival to the punch) and allows managers to take rivals' probable actions into account in designing their own company's best course of action.

6. *What are the key factors for competitive success?* An industry's key success factors (KSFs) are the particular product attributes, competitive capabilities, and intangible assets that spell the difference between being a strong competitor and a weak competitor—and sometimes between profit and loss. KSFs by their very nature are so important to competitive success that *all firms* in the industry must pay close attention to them or risk being driven out of the industry.

7. *Does the outlook for the industry present the company with sufficiently attractive prospects for profitability?* Conclusions regarding industry attractiveness are a major driver of company strategy. When a company decides an industry is

fundamentally attractive and presents good opportunities, a strong case can be made that it should invest aggressively to capture the opportunities it sees. When a strong competitor concludes an industry is relatively unattractive and lacking in opportunity, it may elect to simply protect its present position, investing cautiously if at all and looking for opportunities in other industries. A competitively weak company in an unattractive industry may see its best option as finding a buyer, perhaps a rival, to acquire its business. On occasion, an industry that is unattractive overall is still very attractive to a favorably situated company with the skills and resources to take business away from weaker rivals.

Assurance of Learning Exercises

LO2 1. Prepare a brief analysis of the ready-to-drink coffee industry (e.g., Starbucks) using the information provided on industry trade association Web sites. Based upon information provided on the Web sites of these associations, draw a five-forces diagram for the ready-to-drink coffee industry and briefly discuss the nature and strength of each of the five competitive forces. What driving forces of change are taking shape in the industry?

LO2 2. Consider the strategic group map in Concepts & Connections 4.1. Who are Polo-Ralph Lauren's closest competitors? Between which two strategic groups is competition the strongest? Why do you think no retailers are positioned in the upper right corner of the map? Which company/strategic group faces the weakest competition from the members of other strategic groups?

LO2 3. Using the information provided in Table 4.2 and your knowledge as a casual dining patron, what are the key success factors for restaurants such as Outback Steakhouse or Carrabba's Italian Grill? Your list should contain no more than six industry key success factors. In deciding on your list, it's important to distinguish between factors critical to success in the industry and factors that enhance a company's overall well-being.

Exercise for Business Simulation Users

LO1 Use the strategic group mapping capability of your simulation to develop strategic groups for the competitors in your simulation. Which companies are your key rivals? Which are near rivals that may migrate toward your strategic group? Are there strategic white spaces in your industry that present the opportunity for a blue ocean strategy?

LO2 In addition, use the competitor tracking capability of your simulation to identify trends in your key rivals' strategic and tactical decisions. What do you predict their next moves to be? Discuss strategy changes that are warranted based upon your understanding of the market positions of the competitors in your industry and their likely planned strategic moves.

Chapter 5

Analyzing a Company's Competitive Strength and Cost Structure

Chapter Learning Objectives

LO1. Recognize the importance of crafting strategies that are well-matched to a company's resource strengths and competitive capabilities.

LO2. Understand why a company's overall cost position is determined both by internally-performed activities and those performed externally by its suppliers and distribution allies.

LO3. Learn to use the analytical tools for determining a company's competitive strength relative to its rivals in the industry.

LO4. Learn why a sound analysis of a company's external and internal situation is the most reliable methodology for identifying front-burner strategic issues and problems that require prompt managerial attention.

In Chapter 4 we described how to use the tools of industry and competitive analysis to assess a company's external environment and lay the groundwork for matching a company's strategy to its external situation. In this chapter we discuss the techniques of evaluating a company's resource capabilities, relative cost position, and competitive strength versus its rivals. The analytical spotlight will be trained on five questions:

1. How well is the company's strategy working?
2. What are the company's resource strengths and weaknesses and its external opportunities and threats?
3. Are the company's prices and costs competitive?
4. Is the company competitively stronger or weaker than key rivals?
5. What strategic issues and problems merit front-burner managerial attention?

The answers to these five questions complete management's understanding of *"Where are we now?"* and positions the company for a good strategy situation fit required of the *"Three Tests of a Winning Strategy"* (see Chapter 1, pages 8–10).

Situation Analysis Question 1: How Well Is the Company's Strategy Working?

The two best indicators of how well a company's strategy is working are (1) whether the company is achieving its stated financial and strategic objectives and (2) whether the company is an above-average industry performer. Persistent shortfalls in meeting company performance targets and weak performance relative to rivals are reliable warning signs that the company suffers from poor strategy-making, less-than-competent strategy execution, or both. Other indicators of how well a company's strategy is working include:

- Trends in the company's sales and earnings growth.
- Trends in the company's stock price.
- The company's overall financial strength.
- The company's customer retention rate.
- The rate at which new customers are acquired.
- Changes in the company's image and reputation with customers.
- Evidence of improvement in internal processes such as defect rate, order fulfillment, delivery times, days of inventory, and employee productivity.

The stronger a company's current overall performance, the less likely the need for radical changes in strategy. The weaker a company's financial performance and market standing, the more its current strategy must be questioned.

Table 5.1 provides a compilation of the financial ratios most commonly used to evaluate a company's financial performance and balance sheet strength.

Table 5.1

Key Ratios to Assess a Company's Financial Performance

RATIO	HOW CALCULATED	WHAT IT SHOWS
Profitability Ratios		
1. Gross profit margin	$$\frac{\text{Sales} - \text{Cost of goods sold}}{\text{Sales}}$$	Shows the percent of revenues available to cover operating expenses and yield a profit. Higher is better and the trend should be upward.
2. Operating profit margin (or return on sales)	$$\frac{\text{Sales} - \text{Operating expenses}}{\text{Sales}}$$ or $$\frac{\text{Operating income}}{\text{Sales}}$$	Shows the profitability of current operations without regard to interest charges and income taxes. Higher is better and the trend should be upward.
3. Net profit margin (or net return on sales)	$$\frac{\text{Profits after taxes}}{\text{Sales}}$$	Shows after-tax profits per dollar of sales. Higher is better and the trend should be upward.
4. Return on total assets	$$\frac{\text{Profits after taxes} + \text{Interest}}{\text{Total assets}}$$	A measure of the return on total investment in the enterprise. Interest is added to after-tax profits to form the numerator since total assets are financed by creditors as well as by stockholders. Higher is better and the trend should be upward.
5. Return on stockholders' equity	$$\frac{\text{Profits after taxes}}{\text{Total stockholders' equity}}$$	Shows the return stockholders are earning on their investment in the enterprise. A return in the 12–15% range is "average" and the trend should be upward.
6. Earnings per share	$$\frac{\text{Profits after taxes}}{\text{Number of shares of common stock outstanding}}$$	Shows the earnings for each share of common stock outstanding. The trend should be upward, and the bigger the annual percentage gains, the better.
Liquidity Ratios		
1. Current ratio	$$\frac{\text{Current assets}}{\text{Current liabilities}}$$	Shows a firm's ability to pay current liabilities using assets that can be converted to cash in the near term. Ratio should definitely be higher than 1.0; ratios of 2 or higher are better still.
2. Quick ratio (or acid-test ratio)	$$\frac{\text{Current assets} - \text{Inventory}}{\text{Current liabilities}}$$	Shows a firm's ability to pay current liabilities without relying on the sale of its inventories.
3. Working capital	$\text{Current assets} - \text{Current liabilities}$	Bigger amounts are better because the company has more internal funds available to (1) pay its current liabilities on a timely basis and (2) finance inventory expansion, additional accounts receivable, and a larger base of operations without resorting to borrowing or raising more equity capital.
Leverage Ratios		
1. Debt-to-assets ratio	$$\frac{\text{Total debt}}{\text{Total assets}}$$	Measures the extent to which borrowed funds have been used to finance the firm's operations. Low fractions or ratios are better—high fractions indicate overuse of debt and greater risk of bankruptcy.

Table 5.1   (*concluded*)

2. Debt-to-equity ratio	$\dfrac{\text{Total debt}}{\text{Total stockholders' equity}}$	Should usually be less than 1.0. High ratios (especially above 1.0) signal excessive debt, lower creditworthiness, and weaker balance sheet strength.
3. Long-term debt-to-equity ratio	$\dfrac{\text{Long-term debt}}{\text{Total stockholders' equity}}$	Shows the balance between debt and equity in the firm's *long-term* capital structure. Low ratios indicate greater capacity to borrow additional funds if needed.
4. Times-interest-earned (or coverage) ratio	$\dfrac{\text{Operating income}}{\text{Interest expenses}}$	Measures the ability to pay annual interest charges. Lenders usually insist on a minimum ratio of 2.0, but ratios above 3.0 signal better creditworthiness.

Activity Ratios

1. Days of inventory	$\dfrac{\text{Inventory}}{\text{Cost of goods sold} \div 365}$	Measures inventory management efficiency. Fewer days of inventory are usually better.
2. Inventory turnover	$\dfrac{\text{Cost of goods sold}}{\text{Inventory}}$	Measures the number of inventory turns per year. Higher is better.
3. Average collection period	$\dfrac{\text{Accounts receivable}}{\text{Total sales} \div 365}$ or $\dfrac{\text{Accounts receivable}}{\text{Average daily sales}}$	Indicates the average length of time the firm must wait after making a sale to receive cash payment. A shorter collection time is better.

Other Important Measures of Financial Performance

1. Dividend yield on common stock	$\dfrac{\text{Annual dividends per share}}{\text{Current market price per share}}$	A measure of the return to owners received in the form of dividends.
2. Price/Earnings ratio	$\dfrac{\text{Current market price per share}}{\text{Earnings per share}}$	P/E ratios above 20 indicate strong investor confidence in a firm's outlook and earnings growth; firms whose future earnings are at risk or likely to grow slowly typically have ratios below 12.
3. Dividend payout ratio	$\dfrac{\text{Annual dividends per share}}{\text{Earnings per share}}$	Indicates the percentage of after-tax profits paid out as dividends.
4. Internal cash flow	After-tax profits + Depreciation	A quick and rough estimate of the cash a company's business is generating after payment of operating expenses, interest, and taxes. Such amounts can be used for dividend payments or funding capital expenditures.

Situation Analysis Question 2: What Are the Company's Internal Strengths and Weaknesses and Its External Opportunities and Threats?

Appraising a company's resource <u>s</u>trengths and <u>w</u>eaknesses and its external <u>o</u>pportunities and <u>t</u>hreats, commonly known as **SWOT analysis,** provides a good overview of whether its overall situation is fundamentally healthy or unhealthy. Just as important, a first-rate SWOT analysis provides the basis for

LO1

Recognize the importance of crafting strategies that are well-matched to a company's resource strengths and competitive capabilities.

crafting a strategy that capitalizes on the company's strengths, aims squarely at capturing the company's best opportunities, and defends against the threats to its well-being.

Identifying Company Resource Strengths, Competitive Capabilities, and Competencies

SWOT analysis is a simple but powerful tool for sizing up a company's resource strengths and competitive deficiencies, its market opportunities, and the external threats to its future well-being.

As discussed in Chapter 3, resources that are competitively valuable, rare, hard to copy, and have no good substitutes can function as the cornerstone of a company's competitive strategy.[1] Common types of resource strengths, competitive capabilities, and competencies that management should consider when developing a SWOT analysis include:

- *A skill, specialized expertise, or competitively important capability*—Examples include skills in low-cost operations, proven capabilities in creating and introducing innovative products, cutting-edge supply chain management capabilities, expertise in getting new products to market quickly, and expertise in providing consistently good customer service.

- *Valuable physical assets*—Such as state-of-the-art plants and equipment, attractive real estate locations, or ownership of valuable natural resource deposits.

- *Valuable human assets and intellectual capital*—an experienced and capable workforce, talented employees in key areas, collective learning embedded in the organization, or proven managerial know-how.[2]

- *Valuable organizational assets*—proven quality control systems, proprietary technology, key patents, and a strong network of distributors or retail dealers.

- *Valuable intangible assets*—a powerful or well-known brand name or strong buyer loyalty.

- *Competitively valuable alliances or cooperative ventures*—alliances or joint ventures that provide access to valuable technologies, specialized know-how, or geographic markets.

Identifying Company Resource Weaknesses and Competitive Deficiencies

A *resource weakness* or *competitive liability* is something a company lacks or does poorly or a condition that puts it at a disadvantage in the marketplace. As a rule, strategies that place heavy demands on areas where the company

---

[1] See Jay B. Barney and Delwyn N. Clark, Resource-Based Theory: Creating and Sustaining Competitive Advantage, (New York: Oxford University Press, 2007), pp. 57–69.

[2] Many business organizations are coming to view cutting-edge knowledge and the intellectual resources of company personnel as a valuable competitive asset and have concluded that explicitly managing these assets is an essential part of their strategy. See Michael H. Zack, "Developing a Knowledge Strategy," *California Management Review* 41, no. 3 (Spring 1999), pp. 125–45; and Shaker A. Zahra, Anders P. Nielsen, and William C. Bogner, "Corporate Entrepreneurship, Knowledge, and Competence Development," *Entrepreneurship Theory and Practice*, Spring 1999, pp. 169–89.

is weakest or has unproven ability are suspect and should be avoided. A company's resource weaknesses can relate to:

- Inferior or unproven skills, expertise, or intellectual capital in competitively important areas of the business;
- Deficiencies in competitively important physical, organizational, or intangible assets; or
- Missing or competitively inferior capabilities in key areas.

Nearly all companies have competitive liabilities of one kind or another. Whether a company's resource weaknesses make it competitively vulnerable depends on how much they matter in the marketplace and whether they are offset by the company's resource strengths. Sizing up a company's complement of resource capabilities and deficiencies is akin to constructing a *strategic balance sheet*, where resource strengths represent *competitive assets* and resource weaknesses represent *competitive liabilities.*

Identifying a Company's Market Opportunities

Managers can't properly tailor strategy to the company's situation without first identifying its market opportunities and appraising the growth and profit potential each one holds. Depending on the prevailing circumstances, a company's opportunities can be plentiful or scarce and can range from wildly attractive to unsuitable.

In evaluating the attractiveness of a company's market opportunities, managers have to guard against viewing every *industry* opportunity as a suitable opportunity. Not every company is equipped with the resources to successfully pursue each opportunity that exists in its industry. Some companies are more capable of going after particular opportunities than others. *The market opportunities most relevant to a company are those that match up well with the company's financial and organizational resource capabilities, offer the best growth and profitability, and present the most potential for competitive advantage.*

Identifying Threats to a Company's Future Profitability

Often, certain factors in a company's external environment pose *threats* to its profitability and competitive well-being. Threats can stem from the emergence of cheaper or better technologies, rivals' introduction of new or improved products, the entry of lower-cost foreign competitors into a company's market stronghold, new regulations that are more burdensome to a company than to its competitors, vulnerability to a rise in interest rates, the potential of a hostile takeover, unfavorable demographic shifts, or adverse changes in foreign exchange rates.

External threats may pose no more than a moderate degree of adversity or they may be so imposing as to make a company's situation and outlook quite tenuous. On rare occasions, market shocks can throw a company into an immediate crisis and battle to survive. Many of the world's major airlines have been plunged into unprecedented financial crisis by a perfect storm of 9/11, rising prices for jet fuel, mounting competition from low-fare carriers, shifting traveler preferences for low fares as opposed to lots of in-flight amenities, and "out-of-control" labor costs. It is management's job to identify the threats to the company's future prospects and to evaluate what strategic actions can be taken to neutralize or lessen their impact.

The Value of a SWOT Analysis

A SWOT analysis involves more than making four lists. The most important parts of SWOT analysis are:

1. Drawing conclusions from the SWOT listings about the company's overall situation.
2. Matching the company's strategy to its resource strengths and market opportunities, correcting problematic weaknesses, and defending against worrisome external threats.

Table 5.2 lists examples of factors that should be considered in compiling a SWOT analysis.

Situation Analysis Question 3: How Competitive Is the Company's Cost Position and Pricing?

LO2

Understand why a company's overall cost position is determined both by internally-performed activities and those performed externally by its suppliers and distribution allies.

Company managers are often stunned when a competitor cuts its price to "unbelievably low" levels or when a new market entrant comes on strong with a very low price. The competitor may not, however, be buying its way into the market with super-low prices that are below its costs—it may simply have substantially lower costs. One of the most telling signs of whether a company's business position is strong or precarious is whether its prices and costs are competitive with industry rivals.

Price–cost comparisons are especially critical in industries where price competition is typically the ruling market force. But even in industries where products are differentiated, rival companies have to keep their costs *in line* with rivals in their strategic group or those offering a similar mix of differentiating features. Two analytical tools are particularly useful in determining whether a company's prices and costs are competitive: value chain analysis and benchmarking.

Company Value Chains

Every company's business consists of a collection of activities undertaken in the course of designing, producing, marketing, delivering, and supporting its product or service. All of the various activities that a company performs

A company's **value chain** identifies the primary activities that create customer value and related support activities.

internally combine to form a **value chain**—so-called because the underlying intent of a company's activities is to do things that ultimately *create value for buyers.* A company's value chain also includes an allowance for profit because it is customarily part of the price (or total cost) borne by buyers.

Table 5.2

Factors to Consider When Identifying a Company's Strengths, Weaknesses, Opportunities, and Threats

Potential Resource Strengths and Competitive Capabilities

- Core competencies in _____.
- A strong financial condition; ample financial resources to grow the business.
- Strong brand name image/company reputation.
- Economy of scale and/or learning and experience curve advantages over rivals.
- Proprietary technology/superior technological skills/important patents.
- Cost advantages over rivals.
- Product innovation capabilities.
- Proven capabilities in improving production processes.
- Good supply chain management capabilities.
- Good customer service capabilities.
- Better product quality relative to rivals.
- Wide geographic coverage and/or strong global distribution capability.
- Alliances/joint ventures with other firms that provide access to valuable technology, competencies, and/or attractive geographic markets.

Potential Market Opportunities

- Serving additional customer groups or market segments.
- Expanding into new geographic markets.
- Expanding the company's product line to meet a broader range of customer needs.
- Utilizing existing company skills or technological know-how to enter new product lines or new businesses.
- Falling trade barriers in attractive foreign markets.
- Acquiring rival firms or companies with attractive technological expertise or capabilities.

Potential Resource Weaknesses and Competitive Deficiencies

- No clear strategic direction.
- No well-developed or proven core competencies.
- A weak balance sheet; burdened with too much debt.
- Higher overall unit costs relative to key competitors.
- A product/service with features and attributes that are inferior to those of rivals.
- Too narrow a product line relative to rivals.
- Weak brand image or reputation.
- Weaker dealer network than key rivals.
- Behind on product quality, R&D, and/or technological know-how.
- Lack of management depth.
- Short on financial resources to grow the business and pursue promising initiatives.

Potential External Threats to a Company's Future Prospects

- Increasing intensity of competition among industry rivals—may squeeze profit margins.
- Slowdowns in market growth.
- Likely entry of potent new competitors.
- Growing bargaining power of customers or suppliers.
- A shift in buyer needs and tastes away from the industry's product.
- Adverse demographic changes that threaten to curtail demand for the industry's product.
- Vulnerability to unfavorable industry driving forces.
- Restrictive trade policies on the part of foreign governments.
- Costly new regulatory requirements.

As shown in Figure 5.1, a company's value chain consists of two broad categories of activities: the *primary activities* that are foremost in creating value for customers and the requisite *support activities* that facilitate and enhance the performance of the primary activities.[3] For example, the primary activities for a department store retailer include merchandise selection and buying, store layout and product display, advertising, and customer service; its support activities include site selection, hiring and training, store maintenance, plus the usual assortment of administrative activities. A hotel chain's primary activities and costs are in site selection and construction, reservations, operation of its hotel properties (check-in and check-out, maintenance and housekeeping, dining and room service, and conventions and meetings), and management of its lineup of hotel locations; principal support activities include accounting, hiring and training hotel staff, advertising, building a brand and reputation, and general administration. Whether an activity is classified as primary or supporting varies with each company's business model and strategy, so it is important to view the listing of the primary and support activities in Figure 5.1 as illustrative rather than definitive.

Using Activity-Based Costing to Determine the Cost of Performing Value Chain Activities

Once the major value chain activities are identified, the next step in evaluating a company's cost-competitiveness involves using the company's cost accounting system to determine the costs of performing specific value chain activities, using what accountants call activity-based costing.[4] *Traditional cost accounting* classifies expenses into broad categories—wages and salaries, employee benefits, supplies, maintenance, utilities, travel, depreciation, R&D, interest, general administration, and so on. But activity-based cost accounting involves establishing expense categories for specific value chain activities and assigning costs to the activity responsible for creating the cost. An illustrative example is shown in Table 5.3. Perhaps 25 percent of the companies that have explored the feasibility of activity-based costing have adopted this accounting approach.

The degree to which a company's costs should be disaggregated into specific activities depends on how valuable it is to develop cross-company cost comparisons. Generally speaking, cost estimates are needed for, at least, each broad category of primary and support activities, but finer classifications may be needed if a company discovers that it has a problematic cost disadvantage. Once a company has developed good cost estimates for each of the major activities in its value chain (and perhaps cost estimates for sub-activities within its value chain), then it is ready to see how its costs for these activities compare with the costs of rival firms.

---

[3] The value chain concept was developed and articulated by professor Michael Porter at the Harvard Business School and is described at greater length in Michael E. Porter, *Competitive Advantage* (New York: Free Press, 1985), Chapters 2 and 3.

[4] For discussions of the accounting challenges in calculating the costs of value chain activities, see John K. Shank and Vijay Govindarajan, *Strategic Cost Management* (New York: Free Press, 1993), especially Chapters 2–6, 10, and 11; Robin Cooper and Robert S. Kaplan, "Measure Costs Right: Make the Right Decisions," *Harvard Business Review* 66, no. 5 (September–October 1988), pp. 96–103; and Joseph A. Ness and Thomas G. Cucuzza, "Tapping the Full Potential of ABC," *Harvard Business Review* 73, no. 4 (July–August 1995), pp. 130–38.

FIGURE 5.1 **Illustration of a Company Value Chain**

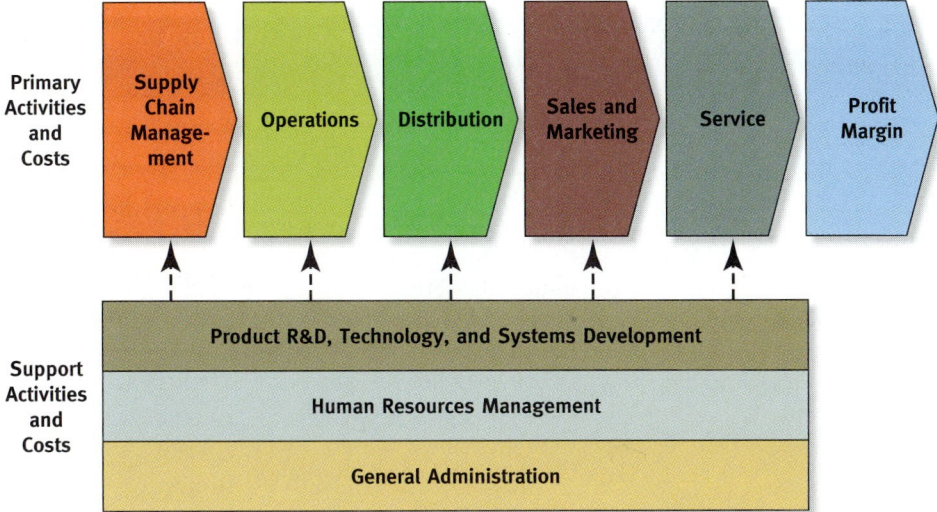

PRIMARY ACTIVITIES

- **Supply Chain Management**—Activities, costs, and assets associated with purchasing fuel, energy, raw materials, parts and components, merchandise, and consumable items from vendors; receiving, storing, and disseminating inputs from suppliers; inspection; and inventory management.

- **Operations**—Activities, costs, and assets associated with converting inputs into final product form (production, assembly, packaging, equipment maintenance, facilities, operations, quality assurance, environmental protection).

- **Distribution**—Activities, costs, and assets dealing with physically distributing the product to buyers (finished goods warehousing, order processing, order picking and packing, shipping, delivery vehicle operations, establishing and maintaining a network of dealers and distributors).

- **Sales and Marketing**—Activities, costs, and assets related to sales force efforts, advertising and promotion, market research and planning, and dealer/distributor support.

- **Service**—Activities, costs, and assets associated with providing assistance to buyers, such as installation, spare parts delivery, maintenance and repair, technical assistance, buyer inquiries, and complaints.

SUPPORT ACTIVITIES

- **Product R&D, Technology, and Systems Development**—Activities, costs, and assets relating to product R&D, process R&D, process design improvement, equipment design, computer software development, telecommunications systems, computer-assisted design and engineering, database capabilities, and development of computerized support systems.

- **Human Resources Management**—Activities, costs, and assets associated with the recruitment, hiring, training, development, and compensation of all types of personnel; labor relations activities; and development of knowledge-based skills and core competencies.

- **General Administration**—Activities, costs, and assets relating to general management, accounting and finance, legal and regulatory affairs, safety and security, management information systems, forming strategic alliances and collaborating with strategic partners, and other "overhead" functions.

Source: Based on the discussion in Michael E. Porter, *Competitive Advantage* (New York: Free Press, 1985), pp. 37–43.

Benchmarking Activity Costs

Benchmarking entails comparing how different companies perform various value chain activities—how materials are purchased, how inventories are managed, how products are assembled, how customer orders are filled and shipped, and how maintenance is performed—and then making cross-company

Table 5.3

Cost Reporting Using Traditional Cost Accounting and Activity-Based Costing: A Supply Chain Activity Example

Traditional Cost Accounting Categories for Supply Chain Activities		Cost of Performing Specific Supply Chain Activities Using Activity Based Cost Accounting	
Wages and salaries	$450,000	Evaluate supplier capabilities	$ 150,000
Employee benefits	95,000	Process purchase orders	92,000
Supplies	21,500	Collaborate with suppliers on just-in-time deliveries	180,000
Travel	12,250	Share data with suppliers	69,000
Depreciation	19,000	Check quality of items purchased	94,000
Other fixed charges (office space, utilities)	112,000	Check incoming deliveries against purchase orders	50,000
Miscellaneous operating expenses	40,250	Resolve disputes	15,000
		Conduct internal administration	100,000
	$750,000		$750,000

Source: Developed from information in Terence P. Par, "A New Tool for Managing Costs," *Fortune* (June 14, 1993), pp. 124–29.

comparisons of the costs of these activities.[5] The objectives of benchmarking are to identify the best practices in performing an activity and to emulate those best practices when they are possessed by others.

Xerox became one of the first companies to use benchmarking in 1979 when Japanese manufacturers began selling midsize copiers in the United States for $9,600 each—less than Xerox's production costs.[6] Xerox management sent a team of line managers and its head of manufacturing to Japan to study competitors' business processes and costs. With the aid of Xerox's joint venture partner in Japan (Fuji-Xerox), who knew the competitors well, the team found that Xerox's costs were excessive due to gross inefficiencies in the company's manufacturing processes and business practices. The findings triggered a major internal effort at Xerox to become cost-competitive and prompted Xerox to begin benchmarking 67 of its key work processes. Xerox quickly decided not to restrict its benchmarking efforts to its office equipment rivals but to extend them to any company regarded as "world class" in performing *any activity* relevant to Xerox's business. Other companies quickly picked up on Xerox's approach. Toyota managers got their idea for just-in-time inventory deliveries by studying how U.S. supermarkets replenished their shelves. Southwest Airlines reduced the turnaround time of its aircraft at each scheduled stop by studying pit crews on the auto racing circuit. Over 80 percent of Fortune

[5] For more details, see Gregory H. Watson, *Strategic Benchmarking: How to Rate Your Company's Performance Against the World's Best* (New York: John Wiley, 1993); Robert C. Camp, *Benchmarking: The Search for Industry Best Practices That Lead to Superior Performance* (Milwaukee: ASQC Quality Press, 1989); Christopher E. Bogan and Michael J. English, *Benchmarking for Best Practices: Winning through Innovative Adaptation* (New York: McGraw-Hill, 1994); and Dawn Iacobucci and Christie Nordhielm, "Creative Benchmarking," *Harvard Business Review* 78, no. 6 (November–December 2000), pp. 24–25.

[6] Jeremy Main, "How to Steal the Best Ideas Around," *Fortune* (October 19, 1992), pp. 102–3.

500 companies reportedly use benchmarking for comparing themselves against rivals on cost and other competitively important measures.

The tough part of benchmarking is not whether to do it, but rather how to gain access to information about other companies' practices and costs. Sometimes benchmarking can be accomplished by collecting information from published reports, trade groups, and industry research firms and by talking to knowledgeable industry analysts, customers, and suppliers. Sometimes field trips to the facilities of competing or noncompeting companies can be arranged to observe how things are done, compare practices and processes, and perhaps exchange data on productivity and other cost components. However, such companies, even if they agree to host facilities tours and answer questions, are unlikely to share competitively sensitive cost information. Furthermore, comparing two companies' costs may not involve comparing apples to apples if the two companies employ different cost accounting principles to calculate the costs of particular activities.

However, a fairly reliable source of benchmarking information has emerged. The explosive interest of companies in benchmarking costs and identifying best practices has prompted consulting organizations (e.g., Accenture, A. T. Kearney, Benchnet—The Benchmarking Exchange, Towers Perrin, and Best Practices, LLC) and several councils and associations (e.g., the American Productivity & Quality Center, the Qualserve Benchmarking Clearinghouse, and the Strategic Planning Institute's Council on Benchmarking) to gather benchmarking data, distribute information about best practices, and provide comparative cost data without identifying the names of particular companies. Having an independent group gather the information and report it in a manner that disguises the names of individual companies avoids the disclosure of competitively sensitive data and lessens the potential for unethical behavior on the part of company personnel in gathering their own data about competitors.

Industry Value Chain Systems

A company's value chain is embedded in a larger system of activities that includes the value chains of its suppliers and the value chains of whatever distribution channel allies it utilizes in getting its product or service to end users.[7] The value chains of forward channel partners are relevant because (1) the costs and margins of a company's distributors and retail dealers are part of the price the consumer ultimately pays, and (2) the activities that distribution allies perform affect customer satisfaction. For these reasons, companies normally work closely with their suppliers and forward channel allies to perform value chain activities in mutually beneficial ways. For instance, motor vehicle manufacturers work closely with their forward channel allies (local automobile dealers) to ensure that owners are satisfied with dealers' repair and maintenance services.[8] Also, many automotive parts suppliers have built plants near the auto

[7] Porter, *Competitive Advantage*, p. 34.

[8] M. Hegert and D. Morris, "Accounting Data for Value Chain Analysis," *Strategic Management Journal* 10 (1989), p. 180; Robin Cooper and Robert S. Kaplan, "Measure Costs Right: Make the Right Decisions," *Harvard Business Review* 66, no. 5 (September–October 1988), pp. 96–103; and John K. Shank and Vijay Govindarajan, *Strategic Cost Management* (New York: Free Press, 1993), especially Chapters 2–6, 10.

assembly plants they supply to facilitate just-in-time deliveries, reduce warehousing and shipping costs, and promote close collaboration on parts design and production scheduling. The lesson here is that a company's value chain activities are often closely linked to the value chains of their suppliers and the forward allies.

As a consequence, *accurately assessing a company's competitiveness requires that company managers understand an industry's entire value chain system for delivering a product or service to customers, not just the company's own value chain.* A typical industry value chain that incorporates the activities, costs, and margins of suppliers and forward channel allies (if any) is shown in Figure 5.2. However, industry value chains vary significantly by industry. For example, the primary value chain activities in the pulp and paper industry (timber farming, logging, pulp mills, and papermaking) differ from the primary value chain activities in the home appliance industry (parts and components manufacture, assembly, wholesale distribution, and retail sales). Concepts & Connections 5.1 shows representative costs for various activities performed by the producers and marketers of music CDs.

Vertical Integration: Operating Across More Industry Value Chain Segments

Vertical integration extends a firm's competitive and operating scope within the same industry. It involves expanding the firm's range of value chain activities backward into sources of supply and/or forward toward end users. Thus, if a manufacturer invests in facilities to produce certain component parts that it formerly purchased from outside suppliers, it remains in essentially the same industry as before. The only change is that it has operations in two stages of the industry value chain. Similarly, if a paint manufacturer, Sherwin-Williams for example, elects to integrate forward by opening 100 retail stores to market its paint products directly to consumers, it remains in the paint business even though its competitive scope extends from manufacturing to retailing.

Vertical integration strategies can aim at *full integration* (participating in all stages of the industry value chain) or *partial integration* (building positions in

FIGURE 5.2   **Representative Value Chain for an Entire Industry**

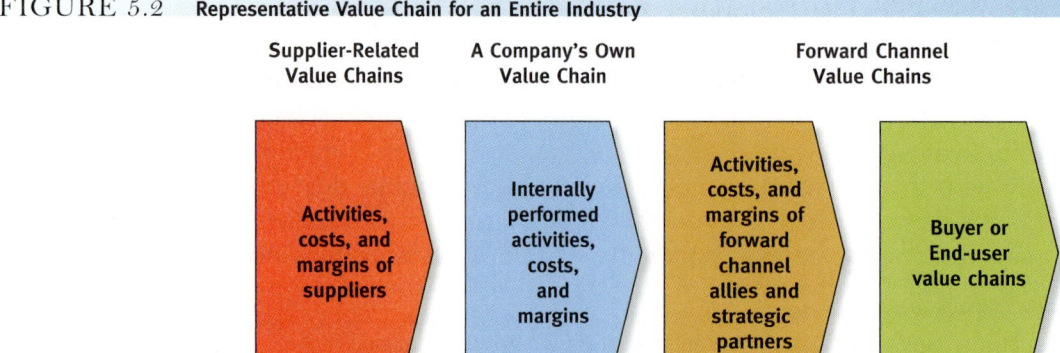

Source: Based in part on the single-industry value chain displayed in Michael E. Porter, *Competitive Advantage* (New York: Free Press, 1985), p. 35.

Concepts & Connections 5.1

ESTIMATED COSTS FOR VALUE CHAIN ACTIVITIES IN THE RECORDING INDUSTRY

The table below presents the representative costs and markups associated with producing and distributing a music CD retailing for $15 in music stores (as opposed to Internet sources).

Value Chain Activities and Costs in Producing and Distributing a CD		
1. Record company direct production costs:		$ 2.40
Artists and repertoire	$0.75	
Pressing of CD and packaging	1.65	
2. Royalties		.99
3. Record company marketing expenses		1.50
4. Record company overhead		1.50
5. Total record company costs		6.39
6. Record company's operating profit		1.86
7. Record company's selling price to distributor/wholesaler		8.25
8. Average wholesale distributor markup to cover distribution activities and profit margins		1.50
9. Average wholesale price charged to retailer		9.75
10. Average retail markup over wholesale cost		5.25
11. Average price to consumer at retail		$15.00

Source: Developed from information in "Fight the Power," a case study prepared by Adrian Aleyne, Babson College, 1999.

selected stages of the industry's total value chain). A firm can pursue vertical integration by starting its own operations in other stages in the industry's activity chain or by acquiring a company already performing the activities.

The Advantages of a Vertical Integration Strategy

The two best reasons for investing company resources in vertical integration are to strengthen the firm's competitive position and/or boost its profitability.[9] Vertical integration has no real payoff unless it produces sufficient cost savings to justify the extra investment, adds materially to a company's technological and competitive strengths, and/or helps differentiate the company's product offering.

INTEGRATING BACKWARD TO ACHIEVE GREATER COMPETITIVE-NESS It is harder than one might think to generate cost savings or boost profitability by integrating backward into activities such as parts and components manufacture. For backward integration to be a viable and profitable strategy, a company must be able to (1) achieve the same scale economies as outside

[9] See Kathryn R. Harrigan, "Matching Vertical Integration Strategies to Competitive Conditions," *Strategic Management Journal* 7, no. 6 (November–December 1986), pp. 535–56; for a more extensive discussion of the advantages and disadvantages of vertical integration, see John Stuckey and David White, "When and When Not to Vertically Integrate," *Sloan Management Review* (Spring 1993), pp. 71–83.

suppliers and (2) match or beat suppliers' production efficiency with no drop-off in quality. Neither outcome is easily achieved. To begin with, a company's in-house requirements are often too small to reach the optimum size for low-cost operation—for instance, if it takes a minimum production volume of 1 million units to achieve scale economies and a company's in-house requirements are just 250,000 units, then it falls way short of being able to match the costs of outside suppliers (who may readily find buyers for 1 million or more units).

But that said, there are still occasions when a company can improve its cost position and competitiveness by performing a broader range of value chain activities in-house rather than having these activities performed by outside suppliers. The best potential for being able to reduce costs via a backward integration strategy exists in situations where suppliers have very large profit margins, where the item being supplied is a major cost component, and where the requisite technological skills are easily mastered or acquired. Backward vertical integration can produce a differentiation-based competitive advantage when performing activities internally contributes to a better-quality product/service offering, improves the caliber of customer service, or in other ways enhances the performance of a final product. Other potential advantages of backward integration include sparing a company the uncertainty of being dependent on suppliers for crucial components or support services and lessening a company's vulnerability to powerful suppliers inclined to raise prices at every opportunity.

INTEGRATING FORWARD TO ENHANCE COMPETITIVENESS

Vertical integration into forward stages of the industry value chain allows manufacturers to gain better access to end users, improve market visibility, and to include the end user's purchasing experience as a differentiating feature. In many industries, independent sales agents, wholesalers, and retailers handle competing brands of the same product and have no allegiance to any one company's brand—they tend to push whatever offers the biggest profits. An independent insurance agency, for example, represents a number of different insurance companies and tries to find the best match between a customer's insurance requirements and the policies of alternative insurance companies. Under this arrangement, it is possible an agent will develop a preference for one company's policies or underwriting practices and neglect other represented insurance companies. An insurance company may conclude, therefore, that it is better off integrating forward and setting up its own local sales offices. The insurance company also has the ability to make consumers' interactions with local agents and office personnel a differentiating feature.

The Disadvantages of a Vertical Integration Strategy

Vertical integration has some substantial drawbacks, however.[10] Specific drawbacks to vertical integration include:

- Vertical integration *boosts a firm's capital investment* in the industry.
- Integrating into more industry value chain segments *increases business risk* if industry growth and profitability sour.

[10] The resilience of vertical integration strategies despite the disadvantages is discussed in Thomas Osegowitsch and Anoop Madhok, "Vertical Integration Is Dead, or Is It?" *Business Horizons* 46, no. 2 (March–April 2003), pp. 25–35.

- Vertically integrated companies are often *slow to embrace technological advances* or more efficient production methods when they are saddled with older technology or facilities.

- Integrating backward potentially results in less flexibility in accommodating shifting buyer preferences when a new product design doesn't include parts and components that the company makes in-house.

> In today's world of close relationships with suppliers and efficient supply chain management, very few businesses can make a case for integrating backward into the business of suppliers.

- Vertical integration poses all kinds of *capacity matching problems.* In motor vehicle manufacturing, for example, the most efficient scale of operation for making axles is different from the most economic volume for radiators, and different yet again for both engines and transmissions. Consequently, integrating across several production stages in ways that achieve the lowest feasible costs can be a monumental challenge.

- Integration forward or backward often requires the *development of new skills and business capabilities.* Parts and components manufacturing, assembly operations, wholesale distribution and retailing, and direct sales via the Internet are different businesses with different key success factors.

THE CASE FOR OUTSOURCING   Absent the ability to strengthen the firm's competitive position and/or boost its profitability, integrating forward or backward into additional industry value chain stages is not likely to be an attractive strategy option. Outsourcing forgoes attempts to perform certain value chain activities internally and instead farms them out to outside specialists and strategic allies. Outsourcing makes strategic sense whenever:

- *An activity can be performed better or more cheaply by outside specialists.*

- *The activity is not crucial to the firm's ability to achieve sustainable competitive advantage and won't hollow out its core competencies, capabilities, or technical know-how.* Outsourcing of support activities such as maintenance services, data processing and data storage, fringe benefit management, and Web site operations has become commonplace.

- *It improves a company's ability to innovate.* Collaborative partnerships with world-class suppliers who have cutting-edge intellectual capital and are early adopters of the latest technology give a company access to ever better parts and components.

- *It allows a company to concentrate on its core business, leverage its key resources, and do even better what it already does best.* A company is better able to build and develop its own competitively valuable competencies and capabilities when it concentrates its full resources and energies on performing those activities. Cisco Systems, for example, devotes its energy to designing new generations of switches, routers, and other Internet-related equipment, opting to outsource the more mundane activities of producing and assembling its routers and switching equipment to contract manufacturers. Cisco's contract suppliers work so closely with Cisco that they can ship Cisco products to Cisco customers without a Cisco employee ever touching the gear. This system of alliances saves $500 million to $800 million annually.[11]

The biggest danger of outsourcing is that a company will farm out the wrong types of activities and thereby hollow out its own capabilities.[12] In such cases, a company loses touch with the very activities and expertise that over the long run determine its success. But most companies are alert to this danger and take actions to protect against being held hostage by outside suppliers. Cisco Systems guards against loss of control and protects its manufacturing expertise by designing the production methods that its contract manufacturers must use. Cisco keeps the source code for its designs proprietary, thereby controlling the initiation of all improvements and safeguarding its innovations from imitation. Further, Cisco uses the Internet to monitor the factory operations of contract manufacturers around the clock, and can therefore know immediately when problems arise and whether to get involved.

Building a Competitively Superior Value Chain

There are three main areas in a company's overall value chain where important differences in the costs of competing firms can occur: a company's own activity segments, suppliers' part of the industry value chain, and the forward channel portion of the industry chain.

CORRECTING INTERNAL COST DISADVANTAGES When a company's cost disadvantage stems from performing internal value chain activities at a higher cost than key rivals, then managers can pursue any of several strategic approaches to restore cost parity:[13]

1. *Implement the use of best practices* throughout the company, particularly for high-cost activities.

2. *Try to eliminate some cost-producing activities altogether* by revamping the value chain. Many retailers have found that donating returned items to charitable organizations and taking the appropriate tax deduction results in a smaller loss than incurring the costs of the value chain activities involved in reverse logistics.

3. *Relocate high-cost activities* (such as manufacturing) to geographic areas like China, Latin America, or Eastern Europe where they can be performed more cheaply.

4. *See if certain internally performed activities can be outsourced* from vendors or performed by contractors more cheaply than they can be done in-house.

5. *Invest in productivity enhancing, cost-saving technological improvements* (robotics, flexible manufacturing techniques, state-of-the-art electronic networking).

[11] "The Internet Age," *BusinessWeek*, October 4, 1999, p. 104.

[12] For a good discussion of the problems that can arise from outsourcing, see Jérôme Barthélemy, "The Seven Deadly Sins of Outsourcing," *Academy of Management Executive* 17, no. 2 (May 2003), pp. 87–100.

[13] Some of these options are discussed in more detail in Porter, *Competitive Advantage*, Chapter 3.

6. *Find ways to detour around the activities or items where costs are high*—computer chip makers regularly design around the patents held by others to avoid paying royalties; automakers have substituted lower-cost plastic and rubber for metal at many exterior body locations.

7. Redesign the product and/or some of its components to facilitate speedier and more economical manufacture or assembly.

8. Try to make up the internal cost disadvantage by reducing costs in the supplier or forward channel portions of the industry value chain—usually a last resort.

CORRECTING SUPPLIER-RELATED COST DISADVANTAGES   Supplier-related cost disadvantages can be attacked by pressuring suppliers for lower prices, switching to lower-priced substitute inputs, and collaborating closely with suppliers to identify mutual cost-saving opportunities.[14] For example, just-in-time deliveries from suppliers can lower a company's inventory and internal logistics costs, eliminate capital expenditures for additional warehouse space, and improve cash flow and financial ratios by reducing accounts payable. In a few instances, companies may find that it is cheaper to integrate backward into the business of high-cost suppliers and make the item in-house instead of buying it from outsiders.

CORRECTING COST DISADVANTAGES ASSOCIATED WITH FORWARD CHANNEL ALLIES   There are three main ways to combat a cost disadvantage in the forward portion of the industry value chain: (1) pressure dealer-distributors and other forward channel allies to reduce their costs and markups, (2) work closely with forward channel allies to identify win-win opportunities to reduce costs—for example, a chocolate manufacturer learned that by shipping its bulk chocolate in liquid form in tank cars instead of 10-pound molded bars, it could not only save its candy bar manufacturing customers the costs associated with unpacking and melting but also eliminate its own costs of molding bars and packing them, and (3) change to a more economical distribution strategy or perhaps integrate forward into company-owned retail outlets. Dell Computer has eliminated all activities, costs, and margins of forward channel allies by adopting a direct sales business model that allows buyers to purchase customized PCs directly from the manufacturer. The direct sales model allows Dell to easily match competitors' prices, while earning larger profit margins.

Translating Proficient Performance of Value Chain Activities into a Best-Cost Advantage

A company that does a *first rate job* of managing its value chain activities *relative to competitors* is in position to craft a powerful strategy keyed to exceeding buyers' expectations on both price and product or service attributes.

[14] An example of how Whirlpool Corporation transformed its supply chain from a competitive liability to a competitive asset is discussed in Reuben E. Stone, "Leading a Supply Chain Turnaround," *Harvard Business Review* 82, no. 10 (October 2004), pp. 114–121.

A **best-cost provider strategy** yields distinctive industry positioning by offering more value-adding features than the industry's low-cost providers and lower prices than those pursuing differentiation.

> A **best-cost provider strategy** is a hybrid of a low-cost and differentiation strategy that exploits value chain efficiencies to exceed buyers' expectations for differentiating features and low prices.

The ability to execute a best-cost provider strategy is contingent on (1) a superior value chain configuration and (2) unmatched efficiency in managing value chain activities. What makes a best-cost provider strategy so appealing is being able to incorporate differentiating attributes at a lower cost than rivals and then underpricing rivals whose products have similar differentiating attributes.

Toyota Motor Company, which is the world's low-cost producer of automobiles and the world's largest seller of automobiles, has utilized a best-cost provider strategy to compete in the luxury segment of the automobile industry. When Toyota launched its Lexus brand in 1989, it drew upon the company's core competencies in supply chain management and low-cost production processes. Toyota added to its traditional strengths with new skills in design and engineering in a quest to match Audi, BMW, and Jaguar in terms of quality and performance, but at a much lower cost per car. Toyota used its best-cost advantage to price Lexus models substantially lower than comparably equipped models built by its key rivals in the luxury car segment. Lexus's pricing advantage over Mercedes and BMW was sometimes quite significant. For example, in 2008 the Lexus RX 350, a mid-sized SUV, carried a sticker price in the $37,000–$48,000 range (depending on how it was equipped), whereas variously equipped Mercedes ML 350 SUVs had price tags in the $42,000–$85,000 range and a BMW X5 SUV could range anywhere from $46,000 to $75,000, depending on the optional equipment chosen. Lexus's best-cost strategy allowed it to become the number-one-selling luxury car brand worldwide in 2000—a distinction it has held through 2007.

THE DANGER OF AN UNSOUND BEST-COST PROVIDER STRATEGY

A company's biggest vulnerability in employing a best-cost provider strategy is not having the requisite efficiencies in managing value chain activities to support the addition of differentiating features without significantly increasing costs. A company with a modest degree of differentiation and no real cost advantage will most likely find itself squeezed between the firms using low-cost strategies and those using differentiation strategies. Low-cost providers may be able to siphon customers away with the appeal of a lower price (despite having marginally less appealing product attributes). High-end differentiators may be able to steal customers away with the appeal of appreciably better product attributes (even though their products carry a higher price tag). Thus, a successful best-cost provider must offer buyers *significantly* better product attributes in order to justify a price above what low-cost leaders are charging. Likewise, it has to achieve significantly lower costs in providing upscale features so that it can outcompete high-end differentiators on the basis of a *significantly* lower price.

Situation Analysis Question 4: What Is the Company's Competitive Strength Relative to Key Rivals?

An additional component of evaluating a company's situation is developing a comprehensive assessment of the company's overall competitive strength. Making this determination requires answers to two questions:

1. How does the company rank relative to competitors on each of the important factors that determine market success?

2. All things considered, does the company have a net competitive advantage or disadvantage versus major competitors?

LO3

Learn to use the analytical tools for determining a company's competitive strength relative to its rivals in the industry.

Step 1 in doing a competitive strength assessment is to make a list of the industry's key success factors and other telling measures of competitive strength or weakness (6 to 10 measures usually suffice). Step 2 is to rate the firm and its rivals on each factor on a scale from 1 to 10, where 1 is very weak and 10 is very strong. Step 3 is to sum the strength ratings on each factor to get an overall measure of competitive strength for each company being rated. Step 4 is to use the overall strength ratings to draw conclusions about the size and extent of the company's net competitive advantage or disadvantage and to take specific note of areas of strength and weakness.

Table 5.4 provides two examples of competitive strength assessment, using the hypothetical ABC Company against four rivals. The first example employs an *unweighted rating system.* With unweighted ratings, each key success factor/competitive strength measure is assumed to be equally important. Whichever company has the highest strength rating on a given measure has an implied competitive edge on that factor. Summing a company's ratings on all the measures produces an overall strength rating. The bigger the difference between a company's overall rating and the scores of *lower-rated* rivals, the greater its implied *net competitive advantage.* Thus, ABC's total score of 61 (see the top half of Table 5.4) signals a much greater net competitive advantage over Rival 4 (with a score of 32) than over Rival 1 (with a score of 58) but indicates a moderate net competitive disadvantage against Rival 2 (with an overall score of 71).

However, a better method is a *weighted rating system* (shown in the bottom half of Table 5.4) because the different measures of competitive strength are unlikely to be equally important. In an industry where the products/services of rivals are virtually identical, for instance, having low unit costs relative to rivals is nearly always the most important determinant of competitive strength. In an industry with strong product differentiation, the most significant measures of competitive strength may be brand awareness, amount of advertising, product attractiveness, and distribution capability. In a weighted rating system each measure of competitive strength is assigned a weight based on its perceived importance in shaping competitive success. No matter whether the differences between the importance weights are big or little, *the sum of the weights must add up to 1.0.*

Weighted strength ratings are calculated by rating each competitor on each strength measure (using the 1 to 10 rating scale) and multiplying the assigned

Table 5.4

Illustrations of Unweighted and Weighted Competitive Strength Assessments

A. Sample of an Unweighted Competitive Strength Assessment

Key Success Factor/Strength Measure	Strength Rating (Scale: 1 = Very Weak; 10 = Very Strong)				
	ABC CO.	RIVAL 1	RIVAL 2	RIVAL 3	RIVAL 4
Quality/product performance	8	5	10	1	6
Reputation/image	8	7	10	1	6
Manufacturing capability	2	10	4	5	1
Technological skills	10	1	7	3	8
Dealer network/distribution capability	9	4	10	5	1
New product innovation capability	9	4	10	5	1
Financial resources	5	10	7	3	1
Relative cost position	5	10	3	1	4
Customer service capabilities	5	7	10	1	4
Unweighted overall strength rating	**61**	**58**	**71**	**25**	**32**

B. Sample of a Weighted Competitive Strength Assessment
[Rating Scale: 1 = Very Weak; 10 = Very Strong]

Key Success Factor/Strength Measure	Importance Weight	ABC CO.		RIVAL 1		RIVAL 2		RIVAL 3		RIVAL 4	
		Strength Rating	Score	Strength Rating	Score	Strength Rating	Score	Strength Rating	Score	Strength Rating	Score
Quality/product performance	0.10	8	0.80	5	0.50	10	1.00	1	0.10	6	0.60
Reputation/image	0.10	8	0.80	7	0.70	10	1.00	1	0.10	6	0.60
Manufacturing capability	0.10	2	0.20	10	1.00	4	0.40	5	0.50	1	0.10
Technological skills	0.05	10	0.50	1	0.05	7	0.35	3	0.15	8	0.40
Dealer network/distribution capability	0.05	9	0.45	4	0.20	10	0.50	5	0.25	1	0.05
New product innovation capability	0.05	9	0.45	4	0.20	10	0.50	5	0.25	1	0.05
Financial resources	0.10	5	0.50	10	1.00	7	0.70	3	0.30	1	0.10
Relative cost position	0.30	5	1.50	10	3.00	3	0.95	1	0.30	4	1.20
Customer service capabilities	0.15	5	0.75	7	1.05	10	1.50	1	0.15	4	0.60
Sum of importance weights	**1.00**										
Weighted overall strength rating		61	**5.95**	58	**7.70**	71	**6.85**	25	**2.10**	32	**3.70**

rating by the assigned weight. Again, the company with the highest rating on a given measure has an implied competitive edge on that measure. The weight attached to the measure indicates how important the edge is. Summing a company's weighted strength ratings for all the measures yields an overall strength rating. Comparisons of the weighted overall strength scores indicate which competitors are in the strongest and weakest competitive positions.

Note in Table 5.4 that the unweighted and weighted rating schemes may produce different orderings of the companies. In the weighted system, ABC Company drops from second to third in strength, and Rival 1 jumps from third into first because of its high strength ratings on the two most important factors. Weighting the importance of the strength measures can thus make a significant difference in the outcome of the assessment.

> A weighted competitive strength analysis is conceptually stronger than an unweighted analysis because of the inherent weakness in assuming that all the strength measures are equally important.

INTERPRETING THE COMPETITIVE STRENGTH ASSESSMENTS

Competitive strength assessments provide useful conclusions about a company's competitive situation. The ratings show how a company compares against rivals, factor by factor or capability by capability, thus revealing where it is strongest and weakest. Moreover, the overall competitive strength scores indicate how all the different factors add up—whether the company is at a net competitive advantage or disadvantage against each rival.

In addition, the strength ratings provide guidelines for designing wise offensive and defensive strategies. For example, consider the ratings and weighted scores in the bottom half of Table 5.4. If ABC Co. wants to go on the offensive to win additional sales and market share, such an offensive probably needs to be aimed directly at winning customers away from Rivals 3 and 4 (which have lower overall strength scores) rather than Rivals 1 and 2 (which have higher overall strength scores). ABC's advantages over Rival 4 tends to be in areas that are moderately important to competitive success in the industry, but ABC outclasses Rival 3 on the two most heavily weighted strength factors—relative cost position and customer service capabilities. Therefore, Rival 3 should be viewed as the primary target of ABC's offensive strategies, with Rival 4 being a secondary target.

The point here is that a competitively astute company should utilize the strength scores in deciding what strategic moves to make. When a company has important competitive strengths in areas where one or more rivals are weak, it makes sense to consider offensive moves to exploit rivals' competitive weaknesses. When a company has important competitive weaknesses in areas where one or more rivals are strong, it makes sense to consider defensive moves to curtail its vulnerability.

Situation Analysis Question 5: What Strategic Issues and Problems Must Be Addressed by Management?

The final and most important analytical step is to zero in on exactly what strategic issues company managers need to address. This step involves drawing on the results of both industry and competitive analysis and the evaluations of the company's internal situation. The task here is to get a clear fix on exactly what industry and competitive challenges confront the company, which of the company's internal weaknesses need fixing, and what specific problems merit front-burner attention by company managers. *Pinpointing the precise things that management needs to worry about sets the agenda for deciding what actions to take next to improve the company's performance and business outlook.*

If the items on management's "worry list" are relatively minor, which suggests the company's strategy is mostly on track and reasonably well matched to the company's overall situation, company managers seldom need to go much beyond fine-tuning the present strategy. If, however, the issues and problems confronting the company are serious and indicate the present strategy is not well suited for the road ahead, the task of crafting a better strategy has got to go to the top of management's action agenda.

Compiling a "worry list" of problems and issues creates an agenda for managerial strategy-making.

Key Points

There are five key questions to consider in analyzing a company's own particular competitive circumstances and its competitive position vis-à-vis key rivals:

1. *How well is the present strategy working?* This involves evaluating the strategy from a qualitative standpoint (completeness, internal consistency, rationale, and suitability to the situation) and also from a quantitative standpoint (the strategic and financial results the strategy is producing). The stronger a company's current overall performance, the less likely the need for radical strategy changes. The weaker a company's performance and/or the faster the changes in its external situation (which can be gleaned from industry and competitive analysis), the more its current strategy must be questioned.

2. *What are the company's resource strengths and weaknesses, and its external opportunities and threats?* A SWOT analysis provides an overview of a firm's situation and is an essential component of crafting a strategy tightly matched to the company's situation. A company's resource strengths, competencies, and competitive capabilities are strategically relevant because they are the most logical and appealing building blocks for strategy; resource weaknesses are important because they may represent vulnerabilities that need correction. External opportunities and threats come into play because a good strategy necessarily aims at capturing a company's most attractive opportunities and at defending against threats to its well-being.

3. *Are the company's prices and costs competitive?* One telling sign of whether a company's situation is strong or precarious is whether its prices and costs are competitive with those of industry rivals. Value chain analysis and benchmarking are essential tools in determining whether the company is performing particular functions and activities cost-effectively, learning whether its costs are in line with competitors, and deciding which internal activities and business processes need to be scrutinized for improvement. Value chain analysis teaches that how competently a company manages its value chain activities relative to rivals is a

key to building a competitive advantage based on either better competencies and competitive capabilities or lower costs than rivals. A company that does a first rate job of managing its value chain activities relative to competitors is in position to craft a *best-cost provider* strategy keyed to exceeding buyers' expectations on both price and product or service attributes.

4. *Is the company competitively stronger or weaker than key rivals?* The key appraisals here involve how the company matches up against key rivals on industry key success factors and other chief determinants of competitive success and whether and why the company has a competitive advantage or disadvantage. Quantitative competitive strength assessments, using the method presented in Table 5.4, indicate where a company is competitively strong and weak and provide insight into the company's ability to defend or enhance its market position. As a rule a company's competitive strategy should be built around its competitive strengths and should aim at shoring up areas where it is competitively vulnerable. When a company has important competitive strengths in areas where one or more rivals are weak, it makes sense to consider offensive moves to exploit rivals' competitive weaknesses. When a company has important competitive weaknesses in areas where one or more rivals are strong, it makes sense to consider defensive moves to curtail its vulnerability.

5. *What strategic issues and problems merit front-burner managerial attention?* This analytical step zeros in on the strategic issues and problems that stand in the way of the company's success. It involves using the results of both industry and competitive analysis and company situation analysis to identify a "worry list" of issues to be resolved in order for the company to be financially and competitively successful in the years ahead. Actually deciding upon a strategy and what specific actions to take is what comes after the list of strategic issues and problems that merit front-burner management attention has been developed.

Good company situation analysis, like good industry and competitive analysis, is a valuable precondition for good strategy-making.

LO2 1. Review the information in Concepts & Connections 5.1 concerning the costs of the different value chain activities associated with recording and distributing music CDs through traditional brick-and-mortar retail outlets. Then answer the following questions:

    a. Does the growing popularity of downloading music from the Internet give rise to a new music industry value chain that differs considerably from the traditional value chain? Explain why or why not.

    b. What costs would be cut out of the traditional value chain or bypassed in the event recording studios sell downloadable files of artists' recordings direct to online buyers?

    c. What happens to the traditional value chain if more and more consumers use peer-to-peer file-sharing software to download music from the Internet rather than purchase CDs or downloadable files?

LO1 2. Using the information in Table 5.1 and the financial statement information for Avon Products below, calculate the following ratios for Avon for both 2005 and 2006:

    a. Gross profit margin

    b. Operating profit margin

Assurance
of Learning
Exercises

c. Net profit margin.

d. Times interest earned coverage

e. Return on shareholders' equity

f. Return on assets

g. Debt-to-equity ratio

h. Days of inventory

i. Inventory turnover ratio

j. Average collection period

Based on these ratios, did Avon's financial performance improve, weaken, or remain about the same from 2005 to 2006?

AVON PRODUCTS, INC.
CONSOLIDATED STATEMENTS OF INCOME
(In millions, except per share data)
Years ended December 31

	2006	2005
Net sales	$ 8,677.3	$8,065.2
Other revenue	86.6	84.4
Total revenue	8,763.9	8,149.6
Costs, expenses and other:		
Cost of sales	3,434.6	3,133.7
Selling, general and administrative expenses	4,567.9	3,866.9
Operating profit	761.4	1,149.0
Interest expense	(99.6)	(54.1)
Interest income	55.3	37.3
Other expense, net	(13.6)	(8.0)
Total other expenses	(57.9)	(24.8)
Income before taxes and minority interest	703.5	1,124.2
Income taxes	(223.4)	(269.7)
Income before minority interest	480.1	854.5
Minority interest	(2.5)	(6.9)
Net income	$ 477.6	$ 847.6
Earnings per share:		
Basic	$ 1.07	$ 1.82
Diluted	$ 1.06	$ 1.81
Weighted-average shares outstanding:		
Basic	447.40	466.28
Diluted	449.16	469.47

AVON PRODUCTS, INC.
CONSOLIDATED BALANCE SHEETS
(In millions, except per share data)
December 31

	2006	2005
Assets		
Current assets		
Cash, including cash equivalents of $825.1 and $721.6	$ 1,198.9	$1,058.7
Accounts receivable (less allowances of $119.1 and $110.1)	700.4	634.1
Inventories	900.3	801.7

(concluded)

Prepaid expenses and other	534.8	424.5
Total current assets	3,334.4	2,919.0
Property, plant and equipment, at cost		
Land	65.3	61.9
Buildings and improvements	910.0	901.3
Equipment	1,137.0	1,033.7
	2,112.3	1,996.9
Less accumulated depreciation	(1,012.1)	(946.1)
	1,100.2	1,050.8
Other assets	803.6	791.6
Total assets	$ 5,238.2	$ 4,761.4
Liabilities and Shareholders' Equity		
Current liabilities		
Debt maturing within one year	$ 615.6	$ 882.5
Accounts payable	655.8	538.2
Accrued compensation	266.9	236.1
Other accrued liabilities	601.6	446.3
Sales and taxes other than income	201.0	172.4
Income taxes	209.2	224.2
Total current liabilities	2,550.1	2,499.7
Long-term debt	1,170.7	766.5
Employee benefit plans	504.9	484.2
Deferred income taxes	30.1	34.3
Other liabilities (including minority interest of $37.0 and $39.9)	192.0	182.5
Total liabilities	$ 4,447.8	$ 3,967.2
Commitments and contingencies (Notes 12 and 14)		
Shareholders' equity		
Common stock, par value $.25 — authorized 1,500 shares; issued 732.7 and 731.4 shares	183.5	182.9
Additional paid-in capital	1,549.8	1,448.7
Retained earnings	3,396.8	3,233.1
Accumulated other comprehensive loss	(656.3)	(740.9)
Treasury stock, at cost – 291.4 and 279.9 shares	(3,683.4)	(3,329.6)
Total shareholders' equity	790.4	794.2
Total liabilities and shareholders' equity	$ 5,238.2	$ 4,761.4

Source: Avon Products, Inc. 2006, 10-K.

LO1
LO3

Prepare a SWOT analysis for your simulation company. Which of your company's resource strengths are most valuable to your competitive approach? Do you have resource weaknesses that make you vulnerable to attack by key rivals?

Also, what do your cost reports and benchmarking reports tell you about your company's cost competitiveness relative to key rivals?

Exercise for
Simulation
Users

Chapter 6

Superior Strategy Execution—Another Path to Competitive Advantage

Chapter Learning Objectives

LO1. Gain an understanding of why and how internal leadership, strategy-supportive policies and organizational structure, corporate culture and a commitment to continuous improvement and incentive compensation contribute to superior strategy execution.

LO2. Understand why and how information and operating systems contribute to superior strategy execution.

LO3. Learn about the key managerial tools and techniques that a company can use to promote operating excellence and superior strategy execution.

Chapters 4 and 5 described the tasks involved in analyzing a company's external and internal environments to ensure the good strategy-situation fit required of the *"Three Tests of a Winning Strategy"* (see Chapter 1, pages 8–10). A solid fit between a company's situation and its strategy puts the company in a strong position to develop a sustainable competitive advantage, but the difference between winning and losing in the marketplace also lies with management's ability to execute its strategy. An impressive strategic approach coupled with shoddy implementation can hardly be assumed to yield an advantage over rivals. In addition, almost every industry contains rivals bunched into common strategic groups where each vies for customer allegiance through either a mix of differentiating features or low prices. When rivals engage in head-to-head battles using similar strategic approaches, the rival most capable of proficiently executing its strategy usually triumphs.

Superior strategy execution calls for creating the specific kinds of *human capital, information capital,* and *organizational capital* needed to proficiently execute the key elements of the company's business strategy. The relationships between these three *learning and growth* perspectives of the balanced scorecard and the performance of value-creating internal processes were discussed in Chapter 2 and illustrated in the strategy map presented in Figure 2.3. Just how efficiently and effectively a company is able to implement and execute its strategy boils down to management's ability to create and deploy the following three types of resources in a manner that drives and supports efficient, effective strategy execution.[1]

1. *Human Capital—intangible assets such as skills, knowledge, and values required by the strategy.* Actions and initiatives to align, integrate, and enhance human capital include:

   - Staffing the organization with people having the right skills and expertise.

2. *Information Capital—intangible assets such as systems, databases, and networks that support the strategy.* Actions and initiatives to align, integrate, and enhance information capital include:

   - Installing information and operating systems that enable company personnel to perform essential activities.

3. *Organizational Capital—strategy supportive intangible assets such as leadership, alignment of goals, and teamwork.* Actions and initiatives to align, integrate, and enhance organizational capital include:

   - Exerting the internal leadership needed to propel implementation forward.

   - Adopting an organizational structure that supports strategies intended to create customer value.

[1] The process of aligning an organization's intangible capital assets with value-creating internal processes is discussed at length in chapter 7 of *Strategy Maps: Converting Intangible Assets into Tangible Outcomes,* by Robert S. Kaplan and David P. Norton, Harvard Business School Publishing Corporation (2004), pp. 199–224.

- Ensuring that policies and procedures facilitate rather than impede effective execution.
- Creating a company culture and work climate that support successful strategy execution.
- Pushing for continuous improvement in how value chain activities are performed.
- Allocating ample resources to strategy-critical activities.
- Tying rewards and incentives directly to the achievement of performance objectives.

Organizational Capital and Superior Strategy Execution

L01

Gain an understanding of why and how internal leadership, strategy-supportive policies and organizational structure, corporate culture and a commitment to continuous improvement and incentive compensation contribute to superior strategy execution.

The organizational capital components of executing the chosen strategy relate to the quality and depth of an organization's leadership, its organizational structure, its culture, policies that align the behavior of organizational personnel with the chosen strategy, commitment to continuous improvement and best practices, and rewards and incentives.

Internal Leadership

The task of exerting effective internal leadership was discussed in Chapter 2, where it was stressed that managers in charge must carry out three ongoing actions:

1. Stay on top of what is happening and identify obstacles to good strategy execution.
2. Push organizational units to achieve good results and operating excellence.
3. Display ethical integrity and spearhead social responsibility initiatives.

The absence of any one of these three qualities of management severely limits the prospects of good strategy execution and operating excellence.

Matching Organizational Structure to the Strategy

The aspects of strategy implementation listed above rely on an organizational structure that lays out lines of authority and reporting relationships in a manner that supports the company's key strategic initiatives. The best approach to settling on an organizational structure is to first consider the key value chain activities that deliver value to the customer. In any business, some activities in the value chain are always more critical than others. For instance, hotel/motel enterprises have to be good at fast check-in/check-out, housekeeping, food service, and creating a pleasant ambience. In discount stock brokerage, the strategy-critical activities include fast access to information, accurate order execution, efficient transactions processing, and good customer service. It is important for management to build its organization structure around proficient performance of these activities, making them the centerpieces or main building blocks on the organization chart.

The rationale for making strategy-critical activities the main building blocks in structuring a business is compelling: If activities crucial to strategic success are to have the resources, decision-making influence, and organizational impact they need, they have to be centerpieces in the organizational scheme. In addition, a new or changed strategy is likely to entail new or different key activities, competencies, or capabilities and therefore to require a new or different organizational structure.[2] Attempting to carry out a new strategy with an old organizational structure is usually unwise.

TYPES OF ORGANIZATIONAL STRUCTURES   It is common for companies engaged in a single line of business to utilize a **departmental organizational structure** that organizes strategy-critical activities into distinct *functional, product, geographic, process,* or *customer* groups. For instance, a discount retailer may organize around such functional units as purchasing, warehousing and distribution, store operations, advertising, merchandising and promotion, customer service, and corporate administrative services. A company with operations scattered across a large geographic area or many countries may organize activities and reporting relationships by geography. Many diversified companies utilize a **divisional organizational structure.** A divisional structure is appropriate for a diversified sporting goods company that designs, produces, and markets golf equipment, ski equipment, apparel, and footwear. The divisional structure organizes all of the value chain activities involved with making each type of sporting goods equipment available to consumers into a common division and makes each division an independent profit center. **Matrix organizational structures** allow companies to specify dual reporting relationships for various value-creating building blocks. For example, in the diversified sporting goods company just mentioned, a matrix structure could require the marketing department for the golf equipment division to report to both the corporate marketing department and the chief manager of the golf equipment division.

ORGANIZATIONAL STRUCTURE AND AUTHORITY IN DECISION MAKING   Responsibility for results of decisions made throughout the organization ultimately lies with managers at the top of the organizational structure, but in practice, lower level managers might possess a great deal of authority in decision making. Companies vary in the degree of authority delegated to managers of each organization unit and how much decision-making latitude

---

[2] The importance of matching organization design and structure to the particular needs of strategy was first brought to the forefront in a landmark study of 70 large corporations conducted by Professor Alfred Chandler of Harvard University. Chandler's research revealed that changes in an organization's strategy bring about new administrative problems that, in turn, require a new or refashioned structure for the new strategy to be successfully implemented. He found that structure tends to follow the growth strategy of the firm—but often not until inefficiency and internal operating problems provoke a structural adjustment. The experiences of these firms followed a consistent sequential pattern: new strategy creation, emergence of new administrative problems, a decline in profitability and performance, a shift to a more appropriate organizational structure, and then recovery to more profitable levels and improved strategy execution. See Alfred Chandler, *Strategy and Structure* (Cambridge, MA: MIT Press, 1962).

given to individual employees in performing their jobs. The two extremes are to *centralize decision making* at the top (the CEO and a few close lieutenants) or to *decentralize decision making* by giving managers and employees considerable decision-making latitude in their areas of responsibility. The two approaches are based on sharply different underlying principles and beliefs, with each having its pros and cons. *In a highly decentralized organization, decision-making authority is pushed down to the lowest organizational level capable of making timely, informed, competent decisions.* The objective is to put adequate decision-making authority in the hands of the people closest to and most familiar with the situation and train them to weigh all the factors and exercise good judgment. Decentralized decision making means that the managers of each organizational unit are delegated lead responsibility for deciding how best to execute strategy.

The case for empowering down-the-line managers and employees to make decisions related to daily operations and executing the strategy is based on the belief that a company that draws on the combined intellectual capital of all its employees can outperform a command-and-control company.[3] Decentralized decision making means, for example, employees with customer contact may be empowered to do what it takes to please customers. At Starbucks, for example, employees are encouraged to exercise initiative in promoting customer satisfaction—there's the story of a store employee who, when the computerized cash register system went offline, enthusiastically offered free coffee to waiting customers.[4]

Pushing decision-making authority deep down into the organization structure and empowering employees presents its own organizing challenge: *how to exercise adequate control over the actions of empowered employees so that the business is not put at risk at the same time that the benefits of empowerment are realized.*[5] Maintaining adequate organizational control over empowered employees is generally accomplished by placing limits on the authority that empowered personnel can exercise, holding people accountable for their decisions, instituting compensation incentives that reward people for doing their jobs in a manner that contributes to good company performance, and creating a corporate culture where there's strong peer pressure on individuals to act responsibly.

---

[3] The importance of empowering workers in executing strategy and the value of creating a great working environment are discussed in Stanley E. Fawcett, Gary K. Rhoads, and Phillip Burnah, "People as the Bridge to Competitiveness: Benchmarking the 'ABCs' of an Empowered Workforce," *Benchmarking: An International Journal* 11, no. 4 (2004), pp. 346–360.

[4] Iain Somerville and John Edward Mroz, "New Competencies for a New World," in *The Organization of the Future,* ed. Frances Hesselbein, Marshall Goldsmith, and Richard Beckard (San Francisco: Jossey-Bass, 1997), p. 70.

[5] Exercising adequate control over empowered employees is a serious issue. For example, a prominent Wall Street securities firm lost $350 million when a trader allegedly booked fictitious profits; Sears took a $60 million write-off after admitting that employees in its automobile service departments recommended unnecessary repairs to customers. Several makers of memory chips paid fines of over $500 million when over a dozen of their employees conspired to fix prices and operate a global cartel—some of the guilty employees were sentenced to jail. For a discussion of the problems and possible solutions, see Robert Simons, "Control in an Age of Empowerment," *Harvard Business Review* 73 (March–April 1995), pp. 80–88.

In a highly centralized organization structure, top executives retain authority for most strategic and operating decisions and keep a tight rein on business-unit heads, department heads, and the managers of key operating units; comparatively little discretionary authority is granted to frontline supervisors and rank-and-file employees. The command-and-control paradigm of centralized structures is based on the underlying assumption that frontline personnel have neither the time nor the inclination to direct and properly control the work they are performing, and that they lack the knowledge and judgment to make wise decisions about how best to do it.

The big advantage of an authoritarian structure is that it is easy to know who is accountable when things do not go well. But there are some serious disadvantages. Hierarchical command-and-control structures make an organization sluggish in responding to changing conditions because of the time it takes for the review/approval process to run up all the layers of the management bureaucracy. Also, centralized decision making is often impractical—the larger the company and the more scattered its operations, the more that decision-making authority has to be delegated to managers closer to the scene of the action.

Allocating Resources to Strategy-Critical Activities

Early in the process of implementing and executing a new or different strategy, top management must determine what funding is needed to execute new strategic initiatives, to bolster value-creating processes, and to strengthen the company's competencies and capabilities. This includes careful screening of requests for more people and new facilities and equipment, approving those that hold promise for making a contribution to strategy execution, and turning down those that don't. Should internal cash flows prove insufficient to fund the planned strategic initiatives, then management must raise additional funds through borrowing or selling additional shares of stock to willing investors.

A company's ability to marshal the resources needed to support new strategic initiatives has a major impact on the strategy execution process. Too little funding slows progress and impedes the efforts of organizational units to execute their pieces of the strategic plan proficiently. Too much funding wastes organizational resources and reduces financial performance. Both outcomes argue for managers to be deeply involved in reviewing budget proposals and directing the proper amounts of resources to strategy critical organization units.

A change in strategy nearly always calls for budget reallocations and resource shifting. Previously important units having a lesser role in the new strategy may need downsizing. Units that now have a bigger strategic role may need more people, new equipment, additional facilities, and above-average increases in their operating budgets. Strategy implementers need to be active and forceful in shifting resources, not only to amply fund activities with a critical role in the new strategy, but also to avoid inefficiency and achieve profit projections. They have to exercise their power to put enough resources behind new strategic initiatives to make things happen, and they have to make the tough decisions to kill projects and activities that are no longer justified.

Instituting Strategy-Supportive Policies and Procedures

A company's policies and procedures can either assist or become a barrier to good strategy execution. Anytime a company makes changes to its business strategy, managers are well advised to carefully review existing policies and procedures and revise or discard those that are out of sync. Well-conceived policies and operating procedures act to facilitate strategy execution in three ways:

1. *Instituting policies and procedures provides top-down guidance regarding how certain things now need to be done.* Asking people to alter established habits and procedures, of course, always upsets the internal order of things. It is normal for pockets of resistance to develop and for people to exhibit some degree of stress and anxiety about how the changes will affect them, especially when the changes may eliminate jobs. Policies are a particularly useful way to counteract tendencies for some people to resist change—most people refrain from violating company policy or going against recommended practices and procedures without first gaining clearance or having strong justification.

2. *Policies and procedures help enforce needed consistency in how particular strategy critical activities are performed.* Standardization and strict conformity are sometimes desirable components of good strategy execution. Eliminating significant differences in the operating practices of different plants, sales regions, or customer service centers helps a company deliver consistent product quality and service to customers.

3. *Well-conceived policies and procedures promote a work climate that facilitates good strategy execution.* Managers can use the policy changing process as a powerful lever for changing the corporate culture in ways that produce a stronger fit with the new strategy.

McDonald's policy manual spells out detailed procedures that personnel in each McDonald's unit are expected to observe to ensure consistent quality across its 31,000 units. For example, "Cooks must turn, never flip, hamburgers. If they haven't been purchased, Big Macs must be discarded in 10 minutes after being cooked and French fries in 7 minutes." To get store personnel to dedicate themselves to outstanding customer service, Nordstrom has a policy of promoting only those people whose personnel records contain evidence of "heroic acts" to please customers—especially customers who may have made "unreasonable requests" that require special efforts.

One of the big policy making issues concerns what activities need to be rigidly prescribed and what activities allow room for independent action on the part of empowered personnel. Few companies need thick policy manuals to prescribe exactly how daily operations are to be conducted. Too much policy can be confusing and erect obstacles to good strategy implementation. There is wisdom in a middle approach: *Prescribe enough policies to place boundaries on employees' actions, then empower them to act within these boundaries in whatever way they think makes sense.* Allowing company personnel to act anywhere between the "white lines" is especially appropriate when individual creativity and initiative are more essential to good strategy execution than standardization and strict conformity.

Corporate Cultures and Superior Strategy Execution

Every company has its own unique culture. The character of a company's culture or work climate is a product of the work practices and behaviors that define "how we do things around here," its approach to people management, and the "chemistry" that permeates its work environment. The meshing together of stated core values, beliefs, business principles, style of operating, ingrained behaviors and attitudes, and work climate define a company's **corporate culture.** A company's culture is important because it influences the organization's actions and approaches to conducting business—in a very real sense, the culture is the company's organizational DNA.[6]

> **Corporate culture** is a company's internal work climate and is shaped by its core values, beliefs, business principles, traditions, work practices, and style of operating.

The psyche of corporate cultures varies widely. For instance, the bedrock of Wal-Mart's culture is dedication to customer satisfaction, zealous pursuit of low costs and frugal operating practices, a strong work ethic, ritualistic Saturday-morning headquarters meetings to exchange ideas and review problems, and company executives' commitment to visiting stores, listening to customers, and soliciting suggestions from employees. General Electric's culture is founded on a hard-driving, results-oriented atmosphere (where all of the company's business divisions are held to a standard of being number one or two in their industries as well as achieving good business results); extensive cross-business sharing of ideas, best practices, and learning; the reliance on "workout sessions" to identify, debate, and resolve burning issues; a commitment to Six Sigma quality; and globalization of the company.

Unhealthy Corporate Cultures

The distinctive characteristic of an unhealthy corporate culture is the presence of counterproductive cultural traits that adversely impact the work climate and company performance.[7] The following four traits are particularly unhealthy:

1. A highly politicized internal environment in which many issues get resolved and decisions are made on the basis of which individuals or groups have the most political clout.

2. Hostility to change and a general wariness of people who champion new ways of doing things.

3. An insular "not-invented-here" mindset that makes company personnel averse to looking outside the company for best practices, new managerial approaches, and innovative ideas.

4. A disregard for high ethical standards and an overzealous pursuit of wealth and status on the part of key executives.

[6] Joanne Reid and Victoria Hubbell, "Creating a Performance Culture," *Ivey Business Journal* 69, no. 4 (March/April 2005), p. 1.

[7] John P. Kotter and James L. Heskett, *Corporate Culture and Performance* (New York: Free Press, 1992), chapter 6.

POLITICIZED CULTURES What makes a politicized internal environment so unhealthy is that political infighting consumes a great deal of organizational energy and often results in the company's strategic agenda taking a backseat to political maneuvering. In companies where internal politics pervades the work climate, empire-building managers pursue their own agendas and the positions they take on issues are usually aimed at protecting or expanding their turf. When an important proposal moves to the front burner, advocates try to ram it through and opponents try to alter it in significant ways or else kill it altogether. The support or opposition of politically influential executives and/or coalitions among departments with vested interests in a particular outcome typically weighs heavily in deciding what actions the company takes. All this maneuvering takes away from efforts to execute strategy with real proficiency and frustrates company personnel who are less political and more inclined to do what is in the company's best interests.

CHANGE-RESISTANT CULTURES Change-resistant cultures encourage a number of undesirable or unhealthy behaviors—avoiding risks, hesitation in pursuing emerging opportunities, and widespread aversion to continuous improvement in performing value chain activities. Change-resistant companies have little appetite for being first-movers or fast-followers, believing that being in the forefront of change is too risky and that acting too quickly increases vulnerability to costly mistakes. They are more inclined to adopt a wait-and-see posture, learn from the missteps of early movers, and then move forward cautiously with initiatives that are deemed safe. Hostility to change is most often found in companies with multilayered management bureaucracies that have enjoyed considerable market success in years past and that are wedded to the "We have done it this way for years" syndrome.

General Motors, IBM, Sears, and Eastman Kodak are classic examples of companies whose change-resistant bureaucracies have damaged their market standings and financial performance; clinging to what made them successful, they were reluctant to alter operating practices and modify their business approaches when signals of market change first sounded. As strategies of gradual change won out over bold innovation, all four lost market share to rivals that quickly moved to institute changes more in tune with evolving market conditions and buyer preferences. These companies have now made changes needed for market success, but are still struggling to recoup lost ground.

INSULAR, INWARDLY FOCUSED CULTURES Sometimes a company reigns as an industry leader or enjoys great market success for so long that its personnel start to believe they have all the answers or can develop them on their own. There is a strong tendency to neglect what customers are saying and how their needs and expectations are changing. Such confidence breeds arrogance—company personnel discount the merits of what outsiders are doing and what can be learned by studying best-in-class performers. Benchmarking and a search for the best practices of outsiders are seen as offering little payoff. Any market share gains on the part of up-and-coming rivals are regarded as temporary setbacks, soon to be reversed by the company's own forthcoming initiatives. The big risk of a must-be-invented-here mindset insular cultural thinking is that the company can underestimate the competencies and accomplishments of rival companies and overestimate its own progress—with a resulting loss of competitive advantage over time.

UNETHICAL AND GREED-DRIVEN CULTURES Companies that have little regard for ethical standards or that are run by executives driven by greed and ego-gratification are scandals waiting to happen. Enron's collapse in 2001 was largely the product of an ethically dysfunctional corporate culture—while Enron's culture embraced the positives of product innovation, aggressive risk-taking, and a driving ambition to lead global change in the energy business, its executives exuded the negatives of arrogance, ego, greed, and an "ends-justify-the-means" mentality in pursuing stretch revenue and profitability targets.[8] A number of Enron's senior managers were all too willing to wink at unethical behavior, to cross over the line to unethical (and sometimes criminal) behavior themselves, and to deliberately stretch generally accepted accounting principles to make Enron's financial performance look far better than it really was. In the end, Enron came unglued because a few top executives chose unethical and illegal paths to pursue corporate revenue and profitability targets. Unethical cultures and executive greed have produced scandals at WorldCom, Quest, HealthSouth, Adelphia, Tyco, McWane, Parmalat, Rite Aid, Hollinger International, Refco, and Marsh & McLennan, with executives indicted and/or convicted of criminal behavior.

High-Performance Cultures

Some companies have so-called "high-performance" cultures where the standout cultural traits are a "can-do" spirit, pride in doing things right, no-excuses accountability, and a pervasive results-oriented work climate where people go the extra mile to meet or beat stretch objectives. In high-performance cultures, there's a strong sense of involvement on the part of company personnel and emphasis on individual initiative and creativity. Performance expectations are clearly stated for the company as a whole, for each organizational unit, and for each individual. Issues and problems are promptly addressed—there's a razor-sharp focus on what needs to be done. A high-performance culture where there's constructive pressure to achieve good results is a valuable contributor to good strategy execution and operating excellence. Results-oriented cultures are permeated with a spirit of achievement and have a good track record in meeting or beating performance targets.[9]

The challenge in creating a high-performance culture is to inspire high loyalty and dedication on the part of employees, such that they are energized to put forth their very best efforts to do things right. Managers have to take pains to reinforce constructive behavior, reward top performers, and purge habits and behaviors that stand in the way of good results. They must work at knowing the strengths and weaknesses of their subordinates, so as to better match

[8] See Kurt Eichenwald, *Conspiracy of Fools: A True Story* (New York: Broadway Books, 2005).

[9] For a good discussion of how a strategy-supportive, high-performance culture can contribute to competitive advantage, see Jay B. Barney and Delwyn N. Clark, *Resource-Based Theory: Creating and Sustaining Competitive Advantage*, (New York: Oxford University Press, 2007), chapter 4.

talent with task. In sum, there has to be an overall disciplined, performance-focused approach to managing the organization.[10]

Adaptive Cultures

The hallmark of adaptive corporate cultures is willingness on the part of organizational members to accept change and take on the challenge of introducing and executing new strategies.[11] In direct contrast to change-resistant cultures, **adaptive cultures** are very supportive of managers and employees at all ranks who propose or help initiate useful change. Internal entrepreneurship on the part of individuals and groups is encouraged and rewarded. Senior executives seek out, support, and promote individuals who exercise initiative, spot opportunities for improvement, and display the skills to implement them. As in high-performance cultures, the company exhibits a proactive approach to identifying issues, evaluating the implications and options, and quickly moving ahead with workable solutions.

Adaptive cultures are exceptionally well-suited to companies competing in fast-changing market environments.

But why is change so willingly embraced in an adaptive culture? The answer lies in its two distinctive and dominant traits: (1) Any changes in operating practices and behaviors must *not* compromise core values and long-standing business principles, and (2) the changes that are instituted must satisfy the legitimate interests of stakeholders—customers, employees, share-owners, suppliers, and the communities where the company operates.[12] In other words, what sustains an adaptive culture is that organization members perceive the changes that management is trying to institute as legitimate and in keeping with the organization's core values.[13]

Technology companies, software companies, and dot-coms are good illustrations of organizations with adaptive cultures. Such companies thrive on change—driving it, leading it, and capitalizing on it (but sometimes also succumbing to change when they make the wrong move or are swamped by better technologies or the superior business models of rivals). Companies like Google, Intel, Cisco Systems, eBay, Nokia, Amazon.com, and Dell cultivate the capability to act and react rapidly. They are avid practitioners of entrepreneurship and innovation, with a demonstrated willingness to take bold risks to create altogether new products, new businesses, and new industries. To create and nurture a culture that can adapt rapidly to changing or shifting business conditions,

---

[10] Reid and Hubbell, "Creating a Performance Culture," pp. 2 and 5.

[11] This section draws heavily on the discussion of Kotter and Heskett, *Corporate Culture and Performance*, Chapter 4.

[12] There's no inherent reason why new strategic initiatives should conflict with core values and business principles. While conflict is always possible, most strategy makers lean toward choosing strategic initiatives that are compatible with the company's character and culture and that don't go against ingrained values and beliefs. After all, the company's culture is usually something that strategy makers have had a hand in building and perpetuating, so they are not often anxious to undermine core values and business principles without serious soul-searching and compelling business reasons.

[13] For a more in-depth discussion of using values as boundaries rather than traditional managerial controls, see Rosabeth Moss Kanter, "Transforming Giants," *Harvard Business Review* 86, no. 1 (January 2008), pp. 43–52.

they make a point of staffing their organizations with people who are proactive, who rise to the challenge of change, and who have an aptitude for adapting.

In fast-changing business environments, a corporate culture that is receptive to altering organizational practices and behaviors is a virtual necessity. However, adaptive cultures work to the advantage of all companies, not just those in rapid-change environments. Every company operates in a market and business climate that is changing to one degree or another. *As a company's strategy evolves, an adaptive culture is a definite ally in the strategy implementing, strategy executing process as compared to cultures that have to be coaxed and cajoled to change.*

Changing a Problem Culture

Changing a company culture that impedes proficient strategy execution is among the toughest management tasks. It is natural for company personnel to cling to familiar practices and to be wary, if not hostile, to new approaches of how things are to be done. Consequently, it takes concerted management action over a period of time to root out certain unwanted behaviors and replace an out-of-sync culture with more effective ways of doing things. *The single most visible factor that distinguishes successful culture-change efforts from failed attempts is competent leadership at the top.* Great power is needed to force major cultural change and overcome the unremitting resistance of entrenched cultures—and great power is possessed only by the most senior executives, especially the CEO. However, while top management must be out front leading the culture change effort, instilling new cultural behaviors is a job for the whole management team. Middle managers and frontline supervisors play a key role in implementing the new work practices and operating approaches, helping win rank-and-file acceptance of and support for the changes, and instilling the desired behavioral norms.

As shown in Figure 6.1, the first step in fixing a problem culture is for top management to identify those facets of the present culture that pose obstacles to executing new strategic initiatives. Second, managers have to clearly define the desired new behaviors and features of the culture they want to create. Third, managers have to convince company personnel why the present culture poses problems and why and how new behaviors and operating approaches will improve company performance. Finally, all the talk about remodeling the present culture has to be followed swiftly by visible, forceful actions on the part of management to promote the desired new behaviors and work practices.

DEVELOPING SUPPORT FOR CULTURE CHANGE The place for management to begin a major remodeling of the corporate culture is by selling company personnel on the need for new-style behaviors and work practices. This means making a compelling case for why the company's new strategic direction and culture-remodeling efforts are in the organization's best interests and why company personnel should wholeheartedly join the effort to do things somewhat differently. Skeptics and opinion leaders must be convinced that all is not well with the status quo. This can be done by:

- Citing reasons why the current strategy has to be modified and why new strategic initiatives are being undertaken. The case for altering the old strategy usually needs to be predicated on its shortcomings—why sales are growing slowly, why rivals are doing so much better, why too many customers are opting to go with the products of rivals, why costs are too high, why the company's price has to be lowered, and so on. There may be merit in holding events where managers and other key personnel are forced to listen to dissatisfied customers or the complaints of strategic allies.

- Citing why and how certain behavioral norms and work practices in the current culture pose obstacles to good execution of new strategic initiatives.

- Explaining why new behaviors and work practices have important roles in the new culture and will produce better results.

Top executives and department heads have to play the lead role in explaining the behaviors, practices, and operating approaches to be introduced and why they are beneficial. For the culture-change effort to be successful, frontline supervisors and employee opinion leaders must be won over to the cause, which means convincing them of the merits of *enforcing* new cultural norms at the lowest levels in the organization. Until a big majority of employees accept the need for a new culture and agree that different work practices and behaviors are called for, there's more work to be done in selling company personnel on the whys and wherefores of culture change.

Management's efforts to make a persuasive case for changing what is deemed to be a problem culture must be *quickly followed* by forceful, high-profile actions across several fronts. The actions to implant the new culture must be both substantive and symbolic.

SUBSTANTIVE CULTURE-CHANGING ACTIONS No culture change effort can get very far by just talking about the need for different actions, behaviors, and work practices. Company executives have to give

FIGURE 6.1   **Steps in Changing a Problem Culture**

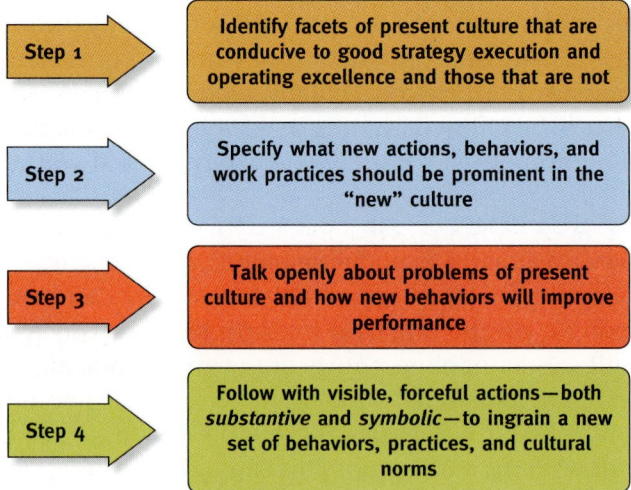

Step 1 — Identify facets of present culture that are conducive to good strategy execution and operating excellence and those that are not

Step 2 — Specify what new actions, behaviors, and work practices should be prominent in the "new" culture

Step 3 — Talk openly about problems of present culture and how new behaviors will improve performance

Step 4 — Follow with visible, forceful actions—both *substantive* and *symbolic*—to ingrain a new set of behaviors, practices, and cultural norms

the culture-change effort some teeth by initiating *a series of actions* that company personnel will see as unmistakable support for the change program. The strongest signs that management is truly committed to instilling a new culture include:

1. Replacing key executives who stonewall needed organizational and cultural changes.

2. Promoting individuals who have stepped forward to advocate the shift to a different culture and who can serve as role models for the desired cultural behavior.

3. Appointing outsiders with the desired cultural attributes to high-profile positions—bringing in new-breed managers sends an unambiguous message that a new era is dawning and acts to reinforce company personnel who have already accepted the culture-change effort.

4. Screening all candidates for new positions carefully, hiring only those who appear to fit in with the new culture.

5. Mandating that all company personnel attend culture-training programs to better understand the culture-related actions and behaviors that are expected.

6. Designing compensation incentives that boost the pay of teams and individuals who display the desired cultural behaviors, while hitting change-resisters in the pocketbook.

7. Revising policies and procedures in ways that will help drive cultural change.

Executives must take care to launch enough companywide culture-change actions at the outset to leave no room for doubt that management is dead serious about changing the present culture and that a cultural transformation is inevitable. To convince doubters and skeptics that they cannot just wait things out in hopes the culture-change initiative will die, the opening series of actions initiated by top management must be followed by unrelenting efforts to firmly establish the new work practices and style of operating as "standard."

SYMBOLIC CULTURE-CHANGING ACTIONS   There's also an important place for symbolic managerial actions to alter a problem culture and tighten the strategy–culture fit. The most important symbolic actions are those that top executives take to *lead by example*. For instance, if the organization's strategy involves a drive to become the industry's low-cost producer, senior managers must display frugality in their own actions and decisions: inexpensive decorations in the executive suite, conservative expense accounts and entertainment allowances, a lean staff in the corporate office, scrutiny of budget requests, few executive perks, and so on. At Wal-Mart, all the executive offices are simply decorated; executives are habitually frugal in their own actions, and they are zealous in their own efforts to control costs and promote greater efficiency. At Nucor, one of the world's low-cost producers of steel products, executives fly coach class and use taxis at airports rather than limousines. Top executives must be alert to the fact that company personnel will be watching their actions and decisions to see if they are walking the talk.[14]

Another category of symbolic actions includes holding ceremonial events to single out and honor people whose actions and performance exemplify what is called for in the new culture. A point is made of holding events to celebrate each culture-change success. Executives sensitive to their role in promoting the strategy–culture fit make a habit of appearing at ceremonial functions to praise individuals and groups that get with the program. They show up at employee training programs to stress strategic priorities, values, ethical principles, and cultural norms. Every group gathering is seen as an opportunity to repeat and ingrain values, praise good deeds, and cite instances of how the new work practices and operating approaches have led to improved results.

The use of symbols in culture-building is widespread. Many universities give outstanding teacher awards each year to symbolize their commitment to good teaching and their esteem for instructors who display exceptional classroom talents. Numerous businesses have employee-of-the-month awards. The military has a long-standing custom of awarding ribbons and medals for exemplary actions. Mary Kay Cosmetics awards an array of prizes—from ribbons to automobiles—to its beauty consultants for reaching various sales plateaus.

Striving for Continuous Improvement in Internal Processes

Company managers can significantly advance the cause of superior strategy execution by pushing organization units and company personnel to strive for continuous improvement in how value chain activities are performed. One of the most widely used and effective tools for improving the performance of internal processes entails benchmarking the company's performance of value chain activities against "best-in-industry" and "best-in-world" performers.[15] It can also be useful to look at "best-in-company" performers of an activity if a company has a number of different organizational units performing much the same function at different locations. Identifying, analyzing, and understanding how top companies or individuals perform particular *best practices* provides useful yardsticks for judging the effectiveness and efficiency of internal operations and setting performance standards for organization units to meet or beat.

In striving for operating excellence, many companies have also come to rely on three other potent management tools: business process reengineering, total

---

[14] Judy D. Olian and Sara L. Rynes, "Making Total Quality Work: Aligning Organizational Processes, Performance Measures, and Stakeholders," *Human Resource Management* 30, no. 3 (Fall 1991), p. 324.

[15] For a discussion of the value of benchmarking in implementing strategy, see Christopher E. Bogan and Michael J. English, *Benchmarking for Best Practices: Winning through Innovative Adaptation* (New York: McGraw-Hill, 1994), Chapters 2 and 6; Mustafa Ungan, "Factors Affecting the Adoption of Manufacturing Best Practices," *Benchmarking: An International Journal* 11, no. 5 (2004), pp. 504–520; Paul Hyland and Ron Beckett, "Learning to Compete: The Value of Internal Benchmarking," *Benchmarking: An International Journal* 9, no. 3 (2002), pp. 293–304; and Yoshinobu Ohinata, "Benchmarking: The Japanese Experience," *Long-Range Planning* 27, no. 4 (August 1994), pp. 48–53.

quality management (TQM) programs, and Six Sigma quality control techniques. *Business process reengineering* involves pulling the pieces of strategy-critical activities out of different departments and unifying their performance in a single department or cross-functional work group.[16] When done properly, business process reengineering can produce dramatic operating benefits. In the order-processing section of General Electric's circuit breaker division, elapsed time from order receipt to delivery was cut from three weeks to three days by consolidating six production units into one, reducing a variety of former inventory and handling steps, automating the design system to replace a human custom-design process, and cutting the organizational layers between managers and workers from three to one. Productivity rose 20 percent in one year, and unit manufacturing costs dropped 30 percent.[17]

Total quality management (TQM) is a philosophy of managing a set of business practices that emphasizes continuous improvement in all phases of operations, 100 percent accuracy in performing tasks, involvement and empowerment of employees at all levels, team-based work design, benchmarking, and total customer satisfaction.[18] While TQM concentrates on the production of quality goods and fully satisfying customer expectations, it achieves its biggest successes when it is extended to employee efforts in *all departments*—human resources, billing, R&D, engineering, accounting and records, and information systems. It involves reforming the corporate culture and shifting to a total quality/continuous improvement business philosophy that permeates every facet of the organization.[19] TQM doctrine preaches that there's no such thing as "good enough" and that everyone has a responsibility to participate in continuous improvement. TQM is thus a race without a finish. Success comes from making little steps forward each day, a process that the Japanese call *kaizen.*

Six Sigma quality control consists of a disciplined, statistics-based system aimed at producing not more than 3.4 defects per million iterations for any business process—from manufacturing to customer transactions.[20] The Six

---

[16] Michael Hammer and James Champy, *Reengineering the Corporation,* (New York: Harper Business, 1993) pp. 26–27.

[17] Gene Hall, Jim Rosenthal, and Judy Wade, "How to Make Reengineering Really Work," *Harvard Business Review* 71, no. 6 (November–December 1993), pp. 119–131.

[18] For some of the seminal discussions regarding what TQM is and how it works, see M. Walton, *The Deming Management Method* (New York: Pedigree, 1986); J. Juran, *Juran on Quality by Design* (New York: Free Press, 1992); Philip Crosby, *Quality Is Free: The Act of Making Quality Certain* (New York: McGraw-Hill, 1979); and S. George, *The Baldrige Quality System* (New York: Wiley, 1992). For a critique of TQM, see Mark J. Zbaracki, "The Rhetoric and Reality of Total Quality Management," *Administrative Science Quarterly* 43, no. 3 (September 1998), pp. 602–636.

[19] For a discussion of the shift in work environment and culture that TQM entails, see Robert T. Amsden, Thomas W. Ferratt, and Davida M. Amsden, "TQM: Core Paradigm Changes," *Business Horizons* 39, no. 6 (November–December 1996), pp. 6–14.

[20] For easy to understand overviews of what Six Sigma is all about, see Peter S. Pande and Larry Holpp, *What Is Six Sigma?* (New York: McGraw-Hill, 2002); Jiju Antony, "Some Pros and Cons of Six Sigma: An Academic Perspective," *The TQM Magazine* 16, no. 4 (2004), pp. 303–306; Peter S. Pande, Robert P. Neuman, and Roland R. Cavanagh, *The Six Sigma Way: How GE, Motorola and Other Top Companies Are Honing Their Performance* (New York: McGraw-Hill, 2000); and Joseph Gordon and M. Joseph Gordon, Jr., *Six Sigma Quality for Business and Manufacture* (New York: Elsevier, 2002). For how Six Sigma can be used in smaller companies, see Godecke Wessel and Peter Burcher, "Six Sigma for Small and Medium-sized Enterprises," *The TQM Magazine* 16, no. 4 (2004), pp. 264–272.

Sigma process of define, measure, analyze, improve, and control (DMAIC) is an improvement system for existing processes falling below specification. The Six Sigma DMADV (define, measure, analyze, design, and verify) methodology is used to develop *new* processes or products at Six Sigma quality levels.[21] The statistical thinking underlying Six Sigma is based on the following three principles: All work is a process, all processes have variability, and all processes create data that explain variability.[22] To illustrate how these three principles work, consider the case of a Milwaukee hospital that used Six Sigma to map the prescription filling process. Prescriptions written in the hospital originated with a doctor's write-up, were filled by the hospital pharmacy, and then administered by nurses. DMAIC analysis revealed that most mistakes came from misreading the doctor's handwriting.[23] The hospital implemented a program requiring doctors to type the prescription into a computer, which slashed the number of errors dramatically.

THE DIFFERENCE BETWEEN BUSINESS PROCESS REENGINEERING AND CONTINUOUS IMPROVEMENT PROGRAMS LIKE SIX SIGMA AND TQM

Business process reengineering and continuous improvement efforts like TQM and Six Sigma both aim at improved efficiency, better product quality, and greater customer satisfaction. The essential difference between business process reengineering and continuous improvement programs is that reengineering aims at *quantum gains* on the order of 30 to 50 percent or more whereas total quality programs stress *incremental progress*—striving for inch-by-inch gains again and again in a neverending stream. The two approaches to improved performance of value chain activities and operating excellence are not mutually exclusive; it makes sense to use them in tandem. Reengineering can be used first to produce a good basic design that yields quick, dramatic improvements in performing a business process. Total quality programs can then be used as a follow-up to deliver continuing improvements.

A NOTE ON INITIATIVES TO IMPROVE OPERATIONS

Usually the biggest beneficiaries of benchmarking and best practice initiatives, reengineering, TQM, and Six Sigma are companies that view such programs not as ends in themselves but as tools for implementing and executing company strategy more effectively. The skimpiest payoffs occur when company managers seize them as novel ideas that could improve things. In most such instances, they result in strategy blind efforts to simply manage better. There's an important lesson here. Best practices, TQM, Six Sigma, and reengineering all need to be seen and used as part of a bigger picture effort to execute strategy proficiently. Only strategy can point to which value chain activities matter and what performance targets make the

> The purpose of using benchmarking, best practices, business process reengineering, TQM, Six Sigma, or other operational improvement programs is to improve the performance of strategy-critical activities and promote superior strategy execution.

[21] Based on information posted at www.sixsigma.com, November 4, 2002.

[22] Kennedy Smith "Six Sigma for the Service Sector," *Quality Digest Magazine*, May 2003, posted at www.qualitydigest.com, accessed September 28, 2003.

[23] Del Jones, "Taking the Six Sigma Approach," *USA Today*, October 31, 2002, p. 5B.

most sense. Absent a strategic framework, managers lack the context in which to fix things that really matter to business-unit performance and competitive success.

Using Rewards and Incentives to Promote Better Strategy Execution

To create a strategy supportive system of rewards and incentives, a company must emphasize rewarding people for accomplishing results related to creating value for customers, not for just dutifully performing assigned tasks. Focusing jobholders' attention and energy on what to *achieve* as opposed to what to *do* makes the work environment results-oriented. It is flawed management to tie incentives and rewards to satisfactory performance of duties and activities instead of desired business outcomes and company achievements.[24] In any job, performing assigned tasks is not equivalent to achieving intended outcomes. Diligently showing up for work and attending to job assignment does not, by itself, guarantee results. As any student knows, the fact that an instructor teaches and students go to class doesn't necessarily mean that the students are learning.

MOTIVATION AND REWARD SYSTEMS   It is important for both organization units and individuals to be properly aligned with strategic priorities and enthusiastically committed to executing strategy. *To get employees' sustained, energetic commitment, management has to be resourceful in designing and using motivational incentives—both monetary and nonmonetary.* The more a manager understands what motivates subordinates and is able to use appropriate motivational incentives, the greater will be employees' commitment to good day-in, day-out strategy execution and achievement of performance targets.[25]

> A properly designed reward structure is management's most powerful tool for gaining employee commitment to superior strategy execution and excellent operating results.

GUIDELINES FOR DESIGNING MONETARY INCENTIVE SYSTEMS   Guidelines for creating incentive compensation systems that link employee behavior to organizational objectives include:

1. *Make the performance payoff a major, not minor, piece of the total compensation package.* Payoffs must be at least 10 to 12 percent of base salary to have much impact. Moreover, the payoff for high-performing individuals and teams must be meaningfully greater than the payoff for average performers, and the payoff for average performers meaningfully bigger than for below-average performers.

---

[24] See Steven Kerr, "On the Folly of Rewarding A While Hoping for B," *Academy of Management Executive* 9, no. 1 (February 1995), pp. 7–14; Steven Kerr, "Risky Business: The New Pay Game," *Fortune*, July 22, 1996, pp. 93–96; and Doran Twer, "Linking Pay to Business Objectives," *Journal of Business Strategy* 15, no. 4 (July–August 1994), pp. 15–18.

[25] The importance of motivating and empowering workers to create a working environment that is highly conducive to good strategy execution is discussed in Stanley E. Fawcett, Gary K. Rhoads, and Phillip Burnah, "People as the Bridge to Competitiveness: Benchmarking the 'ABCs' of an Empowered Workforce," *Benchmarking: An International Journal* 11, no. 4 (2004), pp. 346–360.

2. *Have incentives that extend to all managers and all workers, not just top management.* Lower-level managers and employees are just as likely as senior executives to be motivated by the possibility of lucrative rewards.

3. *Administer the reward system with scrupulous objectivity and fairness.* If performance standards are set unrealistically high or if individual/group performance evaluations are not accurate and well documented, dissatisfaction with the system will overcome any positive benefits.

4. *Tie incentives to performance outcomes directly linked to good strategy execution and financial performance.* Incentives should never be paid just because people are thought to be "doing a good job" or because they "work hard."

5. *Make sure that the performance targets each individual or team is expected to achieve involve outcomes that the individual or team can personally affect.* The role of incentives is to enhance individual commitment and channel behavior in beneficial directions.

6. *Keep the time between achieving the target performance outcome and the payment of the reward as short as possible.* Companies like Nucor and Continental Airlines have discovered that weekly or monthly payments for good performance work much better than annual payments. Nucor pays weekly bonuses based on prior-week production levels; Continental awards employees a monthly bonus for each month that on-time flight performance meets or beats a specified percentage companywide. Annual bonus payouts work best for higher-level managers and for situations where target outcome relates to overall company profitability or stock price performance.

7. *Absolutely avoid skirting the system to find ways to reward effort rather than results.* An argument can be made that exceptions should be made in giving rewards to people who've tried hard, gone the extra mile, yet still come up short because of circumstances beyond their control. The problem with making exceptions for unknowable, uncontrollable, or unforeseeable circumstances is that once good excuses start to creep into justifying rewards for subpar results, the door is open for all kinds of reasons why actual performance failed to match targeted performance.

Once the incentives are designed, they have to be communicated and explained. Everybody needs to understand how their incentive compensation is calculated and how individual/group performance targets contribute to organizational performance targets.

NONMONETARY REWARDS Financial incentives generally head the list of motivating tools for trying to gain wholehearted employee commitment to good strategy execution and operating excellence. Monetary rewards generally include some combination of base pay increases, performance bonuses, profit sharing plans, stock awards, and company contributions to employee 401(k) or retirement plans. But most successful companies also make extensive use of such nonmonetary incentives as frequent words of praise, special recognition at company gatherings or in the company newsletter, job security, stimulating assignments, opportunities to transfer to attractive locations, and the prospect of timely promotions. Some of the most important nonmonetary approaches used to enhance motivation are listed below:[26]

- *Provide attractive perks and fringe benefits*—The various options include full coverage of health insurance premiums; full tuition reimbursement for work on college degrees; paid vacation time; on-site child care; on-site fitness centers; subsidized cafeterias and free lunches; casual dress every day; paid sabbaticals; maternity leaves; paid leaves to care for ill family members; telecommuting; compressed workweeks (four 10-hour days instead of five 8-hour days); and college scholarships for children.

- *Adopt promotion from within policies*—This practice helps bind workers to their employers and employers to their workers; plus, it is an incentive for good performance.

- *Act on suggestions from employees*—Many companies find that their best ideas for nuts-and-bolts operating improvements come from their employees' suggestions. Moreover, research indicates that the moves of many companies to push decision making down the line and empower employees increases employee motivation and satisfaction, as well as boosting productivity.

- *Create a work atmosphere in which there is genuine sincerity, caring, and mutual respect among workers and between management and employees*—A "family" work environment where people are on a first-name basis and there is strong camaraderie promotes teamwork and cross-unit collaboration.

- *Share information with employees about financial performance, strategy, operational measures, market conditions, and competitors' actions*—Broad disclosure and prompt communication send the message that managers trust their workers.

- *Have attractive office spaces and facilities*—A workplace environment with appealing features and amenities usually has decidedly positive effects on employee morale and productivity.

The Importance of Information Capital in Strategy Execution

Company strategies and value-creating internal processes can't be executed well without a number of internal operating systems. FedEx has internal communication systems that allow it to coordinate its 70,000-plus vehicles in handling an average of 5.5 million packages a day. Its leading-edge flight operations systems allow a single controller to direct as many as 200 of FedEx's 650 aircraft simultaneously, overriding their flight plans should weather or other special emergencies arise. In addition, FedEx has created a series of e-business tools for customers that allow them to ship and track packages online, review

LO2

Understand why and how information and operating systems contribute to superior strategy execution.

---

[26] Jeffrey Pfeffer and John F. Veiga, "Putting People First for Organizational Success," *Academy of Management Executive* 13, no. 2 (May 1999), pp. 37–45. Linda K. Stroh and Paula M. Caliguiri, "Increasing Global Competitiveness through Effective People Management," *Journal of World Business* 33, no. 1 (Spring 1998), pp. 1–16; and articles in *Fortune* on the 100 best companies to work for (various issues).

shipping history, generate custom reports, simplify customer billing, reduce internal warehousing and inventory management costs, and purchase goods and services from suppliers. All of FedEx's systems support the company's strategy of providing businesses and individuals with a broad array of package delivery services (from premium next-day to economical five-day deliveries) and boosting its competitiveness against United Parcel Service, Airborne Express, and the U.S. Postal Service.

Most telephone companies, electric utilities, and TV broadcasting systems have online monitoring systems to spot transmission problems within seconds and increase the reliability of their services. At eBay, there are systems for real-time monitoring of new listings, bidding activity, Web site traffic, and page views. Kaiser Permanente spent $3 billion to digitize the medical records of its 8.2 million members so that it could manage patient care more efficiently.[27] IBM has created a database of 36,000 employee profiles that enable it to better assign the most qualified IBM consultant to the projects it is doing for clients. Many companies have cataloged best-practice information on their intranets to promote faster transfer and implementation organizationwide.[28]

Information systems need to cover five broad areas: (1) customer data, (2) operations data, (3) employee data, (4) supplier/partner/collaborative ally data, and (5) financial performance data. All key strategic performance indicators have to be tracked and reported as often as practical. Long the norm, monthly profit-and-loss statements and monthly statistical summaries are fast being replaced with daily statistical updates and even up-to-the-minute performance monitoring. Many retail companies have automated online systems that generate daily sales reports for each store and maintain up-to-the-minute inventory and sales records on each item. Manufacturing plants typically generate daily production reports and track labor productivity on every shift. Many retailers and manufacturers have online data systems connecting them with their suppliers that monitor the status of inventories, track shipments and deliveries, and measure defect rates. Regardless of the industry, real-time information systems permit company managers to stay on top of implementation initiatives and daily operations, and to intervene if things seem to be drifting off course.

Human Capital and Superior Strategy Execution

LO3

Learn about the key managerial tools and techniques that a company can use to promote operating excellence and superior strategy execution.

Organizational capital and information capital are critical to good strategy execution, but no company can hope to perform the activities required for successful strategy execution without attracting and retaining talented managers and employees. Indeed, the essence of a company's culture, continuous improvement initiatives, intellectual capital, and core competencies resides within its human capital.

[27] Steve Hamm, "Motivating the Troops," *BusinessWeek*, November 21, 2005, pp. 87–88.

[28] Such systems speed organizational learning by providing fast, efficient communication, creating an organizational memory for collecting and retaining best-practice information, and permitting people all across the organization to exchange information and updated solutions. See Paul S. Goodman and Erie D. Darr, "Exchanging Best Practices Information through Computer-Aided Systems," *Academy of Management Executive* 10, no. 2 (May 1996) pp. 7–17.

BUILDING MANAGERIAL TALENT Assembling a capable management team is a cornerstone of the organization-building task.[29] While company circumstances sometimes call for different mixes of backgrounds, experiences, management styles, and know-how, *the most important consideration is to fill key managerial slots with people who are good at figuring out what needs to be done and skilled in "making it happen" and delivering good results.*[30] The task of implementing and executing challenging strategic initiatives must be assigned to executives who have the skills and talents to turn their decisions into results that meet or beat the established performance targets. Without a smart, capable, results-oriented management team, the implementation-execution process ends up being hampered by missed deadlines, misdirected or wasteful efforts, and/or managerial ineptness.[31] Weak executives are serious impediments to getting optimal results because they are unable to differentiate between ideas that have merit and those that are misguided.[32] In contrast, managers with strong strategy implementing capabilities have a talent for asking tough, incisive questions. They know enough about the details of the business to be able to challenge and ensure the soundness of the approaches of the people around them, and they can discern whether the resources people are asking for make sense strategically. They are good at getting things done through others, typically by making sure they have the right people under them and that these people are put in the right jobs.[33] They consistently follow through on issues and do not let important details slip through the cracks.

Sometimes a company's existing management team is suitable; at other times it may need to be strengthened or expanded by promoting qualified people from within or by bringing in outsiders. The overriding aim in building a management team should be to assemble a *critical mass* of talented managers who can function as agents of change and further the cause of first-rate strategy execution.[34] When a first-rate manager enjoys the help and support of other first-rate managers, it's possible to create a managerial whole that is greater than the sum of individual efforts—talented managers who work well together as a team can produce organizational results that are dramatically better than what one or two star managers acting individually can achieve.[35]

---

[29] For an insightful discussion of how important it is to staff an organization with the right people, see Christopher A. Bartlett and Sumantra Ghoshal, "Building Competitive Advantage through People," *MIT Sloan Management Review* 43, no. 2 (Winter 2002), pp. 34–41.

[30] The importance of assembling an executive team with exceptional ability to see what needs to be done and an instinctive talent for figuring out how to get it done is discussed in Justin Menkes, "Hiring for Smarts," *Harvard Business Review* 83, no. 11 (November 2005), pp. 100–109; and Justin Menkes, *Executive Intelligence* (New York: HarperCollins, 2005), especially Chapters 1–4.

[31] See Larry Bossidy and Ram Charan, *Execution: The Discipline of Getting Things Done*, (New York: Crown Business, 2002) Chapter 1.

[32] Menkes, *Executive Intelligence*, pp. 68, 76.

[33] Bossidy and Charan, *Execution: The Discipline of Getting Things Done*, Chapter 5.

[34] Menkes, *Executive Intelligence*, pp. 65–71.

[35] Jim Collins, *Good to Great* (New York: HarperBusiness, 2001), p. 44.

RECRUITING AND RETAINING A CAPABLE WORKFORCE

Assembling a capable management team is not enough. Staffing the organization with the right kinds of people must go much deeper than managerial jobs in order for value chain activities to be performed competently. *The quality of an organization's people is always an essential ingredient of successful strategy execution—knowledgeable, engaged employees are a company's best source of creative ideas for the nuts-and-bolts operating improvements that lead to operating excellence.* Companies like Microsoft and Southwest Airlines make a concerted effort to recruit the best and brightest people they can find and then retain them with excellent compensation packages, opportunities for rapid advancement and professional growth, and challenging and interesting assignments. Having a pool of "A players" with strong skill sets and lots of brainpower is essential to their business. Microsoft makes a point of hiring the very brightest and most talented programmers it can find and motivating them with both good monetary incentives and the challenge of working on cutting-edge software design projects. The leading global accounting firms screen candidates not only on the basis of their accounting expertise but also on whether they possess the people skills needed to relate well with clients and colleagues. Southwest Airlines goes to considerable lengths to hire people who can have fun and be fun on the job; it uses special interviewing and screening methods to gauge whether applicants for customer-contact jobs have outgoing personality traits that match its strategy of creating a high-spirited, fun-loving, in-flight atmosphere for passengers. Southwest Airlines is so selective that only about 3 percent of the people who apply are offered jobs.

The tactics listed below are common among companies dedicated to staffing jobs with the best people they can find:

1. Putting forth considerable effort in screening and evaluating job applicants—selecting only those with suitable skill sets, energy, initiative, judgment, aptitudes for learning, and adaptability to the company's culture.

2. Investing in training programs that continue throughout employees' careers.

3. Providing promising employees with challenging, interesting, and skill-stretching assignments.

4. Rotating people through jobs that span functional and geographic boundaries.

5. Making the work environment stimulating and engaging such that employees will consider the company a great place to work.

6. Striving to retain talented, high-performing employees via promotions, salary increases, performance bonuses, stock options and equity ownership, fringe benefit packages, and other perks.

7. Coaching average performers to improve their skills and capabilities, while weeding out underperformers and benchwarmers.

It is very difficult for a company to competently execute its strategy and achieve operating excellence without a large band of capable employees.

Key Points

1. Implementing strategy is an operation-driven activity revolving around creating and deploying a company's *human capital, information capital,* and *organizational capital* in a manner calculated to produce first-rate execution of every key element of its overall business strategy. These three types of resources directly influence the company's ability to perform value chain activities and achieve good strategic and financial results. Shortfalls in performance signal weak strategy, weak execution, or both.

2. Actions and initiatives to align, integrate, and enhance human capital involved in strategy implementation include staffing the organization to provide the needed skills and expertise.

3. Actions and initiatives to align, integrate, and enhance information capital involved in strategy implementation include installing information and operating systems that enable company personnel to perform essential activities.

4. Actions and initiatives to align, integrate, and enhance organizational capital involved in strategy implementation include:

    - Exerting the internal leadership needed to propel implementation forward.
    - Adopting an organizational structure that supports strategies intended to create customer value.
    - Allocating ample resources to strategy-critical activities.
    - Ensuring that policies and procedures facilitate rather than impede effective execution.
    - Creating a company culture and work climate that support successful strategy execution.
    - Pushing for continuous improvement in how value chain activities are performed.
    - Tying rewards and incentives directly to the achievement of performance objectives.

5. Leading the drive for good strategy execution and operating excellence calls for three actions on the part of the manager in charge:

    - Staying on top of what is happening and learning what obstacles lie in the path of good execution.
    - Putting constructive pressure on the organization to achieve good results and operating excellence.
    - Displaying ethical integrity and leading social responsibility initiatives.

6. Structuring the organization and organizing the work effort in a strategy supportive fashion involves making internally performed strategy-critical activities the main building blocks in the organization structure and deciding how much authority to centralize at the top and how much to delegate to down-the-line managers and employees.

7. Managers implementing and executing a new or different strategy must identify the resource requirements of each new strategic initiative and then consider whether current resource allocations sufficiently support the various subunit budgetary needs.

8. Anytime a company alters its strategy, managers should review existing policies and operating procedures, proactively revise or discard those that are out of sync, and formulate new ones to facilitate execution of new strategic initiatives. Prescribing new or freshly revised policies and operating procedures aids strategy execution by:

- Providing top-down guidance to operating managers, supervisory personnel, and employees regarding how certain things need to be done and what the boundaries are on independent actions and decisions.

- Enforcing consistency in how particular strategy-critical activities are performed in geographically scattered operating units.

- Creating a work climate and corporate culture that promotes good strategy execution.

9. The character of a company's culture is a product of the core values and business principles that define "how we do things around here" and the "chemistry" and the "personality" that permeates its work environment. A company's culture is important because it influences the organization's actions and approaches to conducting business—in a very real sense, the culture is the company's "operating system" or organizational DNA.[36]

10. There are four types of unhealthy cultures: (1) those that are highly political and characterized by empire building, (2) those that are change resistant, (3) those that are insular and inwardly focused, and (4) those that are ethically unprincipled and driven by greed. High-performance cultures and adaptive cultures both have positive features that are conducive to good strategy execution.

11. Changing a company's culture, especially a strong one with traits that don't fit a new strategy's requirements, is a tough and often time-consuming challenge. Changing a culture requires competent leadership at the top. It requires symbolic and substantive actions that unmistakably indicate serious commitment on the part of top management.

12. Competent strategy execution entails visible, unyielding managerial commitment to best practices and continuous improvement. Benchmarking, the discovery and adoption of best practices, reengineering core business processes, and continuous improvement initiatives like total quality management (TQM) and Six Sigma all aim at improved efficiency, lower costs, better product quality, and greater customer satisfaction.

13. Strategy supportive motivational practices and reward systems are powerful management tools for gaining employee commitment. The key to creating a reward system that promotes good strategy execution is to make strategically relevant measures of performance *the dominating basis* for designing incentives, evaluating individual and group efforts, and handing out rewards.

14. For an incentive compensation system to work well (1) the monetary payoff should be a major percentage of the compensation package, (2) the use of incentives should extend to all managers and workers, (3) the system should be administered with care and fairness, (4) the incentives should be linked to performance targets spelled out in the strategic plan, (5) each individual's performance targets should involve outcomes the person can personally affect, (6) rewards should promptly follow the determination of good performance, (7) monetary rewards should be

[36] Joanne Reid and Victoria Hubbell, "Creating a Performance Culture," *Ivey Business Journal* 69, no. 4 (March/April 2005), p. 1.

supplemented with liberal use of nonmonetary rewards, and (8) skirting the system to reward nonperformers or subpar results should be scrupulously avoided.

15. Company strategies can't be implemented or executed well without a number of information support systems to carry on business operations. Well-conceived state-of-the-art support systems not only facilitate better strategy execution but also strengthen organizational capabilities enough to provide a competitive edge over rivals. Real-time information and control systems further aid the cause of good strategy execution.

16. Building an organization capable of good strategy execution requires staffing the organization with a can-do management team with the right mix of experiences, skills, and abilities to get things done. The overriding aim in building a management team should be to assemble a *critical mass* of talented managers who can function as agents of change and further the cause of first-rate strategy execution.[37]

17. Staffing the organization with the right kinds of people must go much deeper than managerial jobs in order for value chain activities to be performed competently. The quality of an organization's people is always an essential ingredient of successful strategy execution. Companies dedicated to staffing jobs with the best people they can find frequently rely on the following tactics to recruit and retain "A player" employees:

- Putting forth considerable effort in screening and evaluating job applicants—selecting only those with suitable skill sets, energy, initiative, judgment, aptitudes for learning, and adaptability to the company's culture.

- Investing in training programs that continue throughout employees' careers.

- Providing promising employees with challenging, interesting, and skill-stretching assignments.

- Rotating people through jobs that span functional and geographic boundaries.

- Making the work environment stimulating and engaging such that employees will consider the company a great place to work.

- Striving to retain talented, high-performing employees via promotions, salary increases, performance bonuses, stock options and equity ownership, fringe benefit packages, and other perks.

- Coaching average performers to improve their skills and capabilities, while weeding out underperformers and benchwarmers.

[37] Menkes, *Executive Intelligence*, pp. 65–71.

LO2 1. Go to www.dell.com/casestudies and read how Dell's clients have utilized information capital to facilitate good strategy execution. Choose one of the case studies provided in PDF format and describe how the information systems solution improved the effectiveness of the client's value-creating business processes.

LO3 2. Go to www.google.com/jobs and review Google's approach to recruiting employees. How might Google's comments appeal to job candidates likely to enhance the company's human capital?

LO1 3. Go to www.google.com. Click on the "About Google" link and then on the "Corporate Info" link. Read what Google has to say about its culture under the "Culture" link. Also, read the "Ten things Google has found to be true" in the "Our Philosophy" section. How do the "Ten Things" and Google's culture help align organizational capital with the company's strategy?

Discuss the actions and initiatives your simulation management team has taken to align, integrate, and enhance intangible assets to support the implementation of your company's strategy. Specifically, how have you chosen to allocate resources to strategy critical activities? Also, how have you tied rewards and incentives to the achievement of operating objectives?

LO1

Chapter 7

Ethical Business Strategies, Corporate Social Responsibility, and Environmental Sustainability

Chapter Learning Objectives

LO1. Understand why the standards of ethical behavior in business are no different from the ethical standards and norms of the larger society and culture in which a company operates.

LO2. Recognize conditions that give rise to unethical business strategies and behavior.

LO3. Gain an understanding of why the failure of companies to operate in an ethical manner can be so costly.

LO4. Become familiar with how companies that operate in countries with different cultures and ethical norms deal with the need for company personnel to observe uniform ethical standards worldwide.

LO5. Gain an understanding of the concepts of corporate social responsibility, corporate citizenship, and corporate sustainability.

Clearly, a company has a responsibility to make a profit and grow the business, but just as clearly, a company and its personnel also have a duty to obey the law and play by the rules of fair competition. But does a company have a duty to go beyond legal requirements and operate according to the ethical norms of the societies in which it operates? And does it have a duty or obligation to contribute to the betterment of society independent of the needs and preferences of the customers it serves? Should a company display a social conscience and devote a portion of its resources to bettering society? Should its strategic initiatives be screened for possible negative effects on future generations of the world's population?

The focus of this chapter is to examine what link, if any, there should be between a company's efforts to craft and execute a winning strategy and its duties to (1) conduct its activities in an ethical manner, (2) demonstrate socially responsible behavior by being a committed corporate citizen, and (3) limit its strategic initiatives to those that meet the needs of consumers without harming future generations.

Business Ethics and the Tasks of Crafting and Executing Strategy

LO1

Understand why the standards of ethical behavior in business are no different from the ethical standards and norms of the larger society and culture in which a company operates.

Business ethics is the application of ethical principles and standards to business behavior.[1] Ethical principles in business are not materially different from ethical principles in general because business actions have to be judged in the context of society's standards of right and wrong. There is not a special set of rules that business people decide to apply to their own conduct. If dishonesty is considered unethical and immoral, then dishonest behavior in business— whether it relates to customers, suppliers, employees or shareholders—qualifies as equally unethical and immoral. If being ethical entails adhering to generally accepted norms about conduct that is right and wrong, then managers must consider such norms when crafting and executing strategy.

While most company managers are careful to ensure that a company's strategy is within the bounds of what is legal, evidence indicates they are not always so careful to ensure that their strategies are within the bounds of what is considered ethical. In recent years, there has been an ongoing series of revelations where managers at such companies as Enron, Tyco International, HealthSouth, Adelphia, Parmalat (an Italy-based food products company), Mexican oil giant Pemex, several leading brokerage houses and investment banking firms, and a host of mutual fund companies have deliberately ignored society's ethical norms. The consequences of crafting strategies that cannot pass the test of moral scrutiny are manifested in sharp drops in stock price that cost shareholders billions of dollars, devastating public relations hits, sizeable fines, and criminal indictments and convictions of company executives. Concepts & Connections 7.1 details the ethically flawed strategy at the world's leading insurance broker and the resulting consequences to those concerned.

Business ethics involves the application of ethical standards and principles to business activities, behavior, and decisions.

[1] James E. Post, Anne T. Lawrence, and James Weber, *Business and Society: Corporate Strategy, Public Policy, Ethics*, 10th edition (Burr Ridge, IL: McGraw-Hill Irwin, 2002), p. 103.

Concepts & Connections 7.1

MARSH & MCLENNAN'S ETHICALLY FLAWED STRATEGY

In October 2004, *Wall Street Journal* headlines trumpeted that a cartel among insurance brokers had been busted. Among the ringleaders was worldwide industry leader Marsh & McLennan Cos., Inc., with 2003 revenues of $11.5 billion and a U.S. market share of close to 20 percent. The gist of the cartel was to cheat corporate clients by rigging the bids brokers solicited for insurance policies and thereby collecting big fees (called "contingent commissions") from major insurance companies for steering business their way. Two family members of Marsh & McLennan CEO Jeffery Greenberg were CEOs of major insurance companies to which Marsh sometimes steered business. Greenberg's father was CEO of insurance giant AIG, which had total revenues of $81 billion and insurance premium revenues of $28 billion in 2003. Greenberg's younger brother was CEO of ACE, Ltd., the 24th biggest property casualty insurer in the United States, with 2003 revenues of $10.7 billion and insurance premium revenues of more than $5 billion worldwide.

The cartel scheme arose from the practice of large corporations hiring the services of such brokers as Marsh & McLennan, Aon Corp., A.J. Gallaher & Co., Wells Fargo, or BB&T Insurance Services to manage their risks and take out appropriate property and casualty insurance on their behalf. The broker's job was to solicit bids from several insurers and obtain the best policies at the lowest prices for the client.

Marsh's insurance brokerage strategy was to solicit artificially high bids from some insurance companies so it could guarantee that the bid of a preferred insurer on a given deal would win the bid. The scheme involved Marsh brokers calling underwriters at various insurers, often including AIG and ACE, and asking for "B" quotes—bids that were deliberately high. Insurers that were asked for B quotes knew that Marsh wanted another insurer to win the business, but were willing to participate because Marsh could on other policy solicitations end up steering the business to them via Marsh's B quote strategy. Sometimes Marsh even asked underwriters that were providing B quotes to attend a meeting with Marsh's client and make a presentation regarding their policy to help bolster the credibility of their inflated bid.

Marsh's B quote solicitation strategy allowed it to steer business to those insurers paying the largest contingent commissions—these contingent commissions were in addition to the fees the broker earned from the corporate client for conducting the bidding process. Marsh's contingent commissions generated revenues of close to $1.5 billion over the 2001–2003 period, including $845 million in 2003 (without these commission revenues, Marsh's $1.5 billion in net profits would have been close to 40 percent lower in 2003). In addition, a substantial fraction of the policies that Marsh steered were to two Bermuda-based insurance companies that it helped start up and in which it also had ownership interests. These two insurance companies received 30–40 percent of their total business from policies that were steered to them by Marsh.

Within days of headlines about the cartel bust, Marsh's stock price had fallen by 48 percent (costing shareholders about $11.5 billion in market value), and the company was looking down the barrel of a criminal indictment. To stave off the criminal indictment (something no company had ever survived), board members forced Jeffrey Greenberg to resign as CEO. Another top executive was suspended. Criminal charges against several Marsh executives for their roles in the bid-rigging scheme were filed several weeks thereafter.

In an attempt to lead industry reform, Greenberg's successor quickly announced a new business model for Marsh that included not accepting any contingent commissions from insurers. Marsh's new strategy and business model involved charging fees only to its corporate clients for soliciting bids, placing their insurance, and otherwise managing clients' risks and crises. This eliminated the conflict of interest Marsh had in earning fees from both sides of the transactions it made on behalf of its corporate clients. Marsh also committed to provide upfront disclosure to clients of the fees it would earn on their business (in the past such fees had been murky and incomplete). Even so, the company was faced with a number of lawsuits—including a suit filed by the New York State Attorney General that the company settled for $850 million in 2005. More than a dozen cases remained unsettled in 2007.

Sources: Monica Langley and Theo Francis, "Insurers Reel from Bust of a 'Cartel'," *Wall Street Journal,* October 18, 2004, pp. A1 and A14; Monica Langley and Ian McDonald, "Marsh Averts Criminal Case with New CEO," *Wall Street Journal,* October 26, 2004, pp. A1 and A10; Christopher Oster and Theo Francis, "Marsh and Aon Have Holdings in Two Insurers," *Wall Street Journal,* November 1, 2004, p. C1; and Marcia Vickers, "The Secret World of Marsh Mac," *BusinessWeek,* November 1, 2004, pp. 78–89.

Drivers of Unethical Strategies and Business Behavior

LO2

Recognize conditions that give rise to unethical business strategies and behavior.

Apart from "the business of business is business, not ethics" kind of thinking apparent in recent high-profile business scandals, three other main drivers of unethical business behavior also stand out:[2]

- Faulty oversight by top management and the board of directors that implicitly allows the overzealous pursuit of personal gain, wealth, and other self-interests.
- Heavy pressures on company managers to meet or beat performance targets.
- A company culture that puts profitability and good business performance ahead of ethical behavior.

OVERZEALOUS PURSUIT OF PERSONAL GAIN, WEALTH, AND SELF-INTERESTS   People who are obsessed with wealth accumulation, greed, power, status, and other self-interests often push ethical principles aside in their quest for personal gain. Driven by their ambitions, they exhibit few qualms in skirting the rules or doing whatever is necessary to achieve their goals. A general disregard for business ethics can prompt all kinds of unethical strategic maneuvers and behaviors at companies. Andrew Fastow, Enron's chief financial officer (CFO), set himself up as the manager of one of Enron's off-the-books partnerships and as the part-owner of another, allegedly earning extra compensation of $30 million for his owner-manager roles in the two partnerships; Enron's board of directors facilitated Fastow's greed-driven agenda by agreeing to suspend the company's conflict-of-interest rules designed to protect the company from this very kind of executive self-dealing.

According to a civil complaint filed by the Securities and Exchange Commission, the chief executive officer (CEO) of Tyco International, a well-known $35.6 billion manufacturing and services company, conspired with the company's CFO to steal more than $170 million, including a company-paid $2 million birthday party for the CEO's wife held on Sardinia, an island off the coast of Italy; a $7 million Park Avenue apartment for his wife; and secret low-interest and interest-free loans to fund private businesses and investments and purchase lavish artwork, yachts, estate jewelry, and vacation homes in New Hampshire, Connecticut, Nantucket, and Park City, Utah. Also, the CEO allegedly lived rent-free in a $31 million Fifth Avenue apartment that Tyco purchased in his name, directed millions of dollars of charitable contributions in his own name using Tyco funds, diverted company funds to finance his personal businesses and investments, and sold millions of dollars of Tyco stock back to Tyco itself through Tyco subsidiaries located in offshore bank-secrecy jurisdictions. Tyco's CEO and CFO were further charged with conspiring to reap more than $430 million from sales of stock, using questionable accounting to hide their actions, and engaging in deceptive accounting practices to distort the company's financial condition from 1995 to 2002.

---

[2] For survey data on what managers say about why they sometimes behave unethically, see John F. Veiga, Timothy D. Golden, and Kathleen Dechant, "Why Managers Bend Company Rules," *Academy of Management Executive* 18, no. 2 (May 2004), pp. 84–89.

HEAVY PRESSURES ON COMPANY MANAGERS TO MEET OR BEAT EARNINGS TARGETS   Performance expectations of Wall Street analysts and investors may create enormous pressure on management to do whatever it takes to sustain the company's reputation for delivering good financial performance. Executives at high-performing companies know that investors will see the slightest sign of a slowdown in earnings growth as a red flag, which could begin a mass sell-off of the company's stock. In addition, slowing growth or declining profits could lead to a downgrade of the company's credit rating if it has used lots of debt to finance its growth. The pressure to watch the scoreboard and "never miss a quarter"—so as not to upset the expectations of Wall Street analysts, stock market investors, and creditors—prompts near-sighted managers to cut discretionary costs that create greater customer value, squeeze extra sales out of early deliveries, and engage in other short-term maneuvers to make the numbers. As the pressure builds to "meet or beat the numbers," company personnel start stretching the rules further and further, until the limits of ethical conduct are overlooked.[3]

Several top executives at WorldCom (now MCI, a company built with scores of acquisitions in exchange for WorldCom stock) allegedly concocted a fraudulent $11 billion accounting scheme to hide costs and inflate revenues and profit over several years; the scheme was said to have helped the company keep its stock price propped up high enough to make additional acquisitions, support its nearly $30 billion debt load, and allow executives to cash in on their lucrative stock options. At Bristol-Myers Squibb, the world's fifth largest drug maker, management apparently engaged in a series of numbers-game maneuvers to meet earnings targets, including such actions as:

- Offering special end-of-quarter discounts to induce distributors and local pharmacies to stock up on certain prescription drugs—a practice known as "channel stuffing."
- Issuing last-minute price increase alerts to spur purchases and beef up operating profits.
- Setting up excessive reserves for restructuring charges and then reversing some of the charges as needed to bolster operating profits.
- Making repeated asset sales small enough that the gains could be reported as additions to operating profit rather than being flagged as one-time gains.

Such numbers games were said to be a common "earnings management" practice at Bristol-Myers and, according to one former executive, "sent a huge message across the organization that you make your numbers at all costs."[4]

The fundamental problem with a "make the numbers and move on" syndrome is that a company doesn't really create additional value for customers or improve its competitiveness in the marketplace, which are the most reliable drivers of higher profits and added shareholder value. Cutting ethical

---

[3] For more details see Ronald R. Sims and Johannes Brinkmann, "Enron Ethics (Or: Culture Matters More than Codes)," *Journal of Business Ethics* 45, no. 3 (July 2003), pp. 244–246.

[4] As reported in Gardiner Harris, "At Bristol-Myers, Ex-Executives Tell of Numbers Games," *Wall Street Journal*, December 12, 2002, pp. A1 and A13.

corners or stooping to downright illegal actions in the name of profits first carries exceptionally high risk for shareholders—a steep stock price decline and a tarnished brand image that leaves a company worth much less than before.

COMPANY CULTURES THAT PUT THE BOTTOM LINE AHEAD OF ETHICAL BEHAVIOR   When a company's culture spawns an ethically corrupt or amoral work climate, people have a company approved license to ignore "what's right" and engage in most any behavior they think they can get away with.[5] At such companies, ethically immoral or amoral people are given free reign and otherwise honorable people may succumb to the many opportunities around them to engage in unethical practices. A perfect example of a company culture gone awry on ethics is Enron.[6] Enron's annual "rank and yank" performance evaluation process where the 15 to 20 percent lowest-ranking employees were let go or encouraged to seek other employment made it abundantly clear that bottom-line results were what mattered most. Survival at Enron relied, to some extent, on devising clever ways to boost revenues and earnings—even if it sometimes meant operating outside established policies and without the knowledge of superiors.

The underpinnings of Enron's culture that encouraged unethical behavior was also linked to its reward system. Employees who produced the best bottom-line results received impressively large incentives and bonuses (amounting to as much as $1 million for traders and even more for senior executives). On Car Day at Enron, an array of luxury sports cars arrived for presentation to the most successful employees. Understandably, employees wanted to be seen as part of Enron's star team and partake in the benefits granted to Enron's best and smartest employees. The high monetary rewards, the ambitious and hard-driving people that the company hired and promoted, and the competitive, results-oriented culture combined to give Enron a reputation not only for trampling competitors at every opportunity but also for internal ruthlessness. The company's super-aggressiveness and win-at-all-costs mindset nurtured a culture that gradually and then more rapidly fostered the erosion of ethical standards, eventually making a mockery of the company's stated values of integrity and respect. When it became evident in the fall of 2001 that Enron was a house of cards propped up by deceitful accounting and a myriad of unsavory practices, the company imploded in a matter of weeks—the biggest bankruptcy of all time cost investors $64 billion in losses.

LO3

Gain an understanding of why the failure of companies to operate in an ethical manner can be so costly.

The Business Case for Ethical Strategies and Ethical Operating Practices

There are solid business reasons to adopt ethical strategies even if most company managers are not of strong moral character and personally committed to high ethical standards. Pursuing unethical strategies not only damages a company's reputation but it can also have costly consequences that are

[5] Veiga, Golden, and Dechant, "Why Managers Bend Company Rules," p. 85.

[6] The following account is based largely on the discussion and analysis in Sims and Brinkmann, "Enron Ethics," pp. 245–252. Perhaps the definitive book-length account of the corrupt Enron culture is Kurt Eichenwald, *Conspiracy of Fools: A True Story* (New York: Broadway Books, 2005).

FIGURE 7.1   **The Costs of Business Ethics Failures**

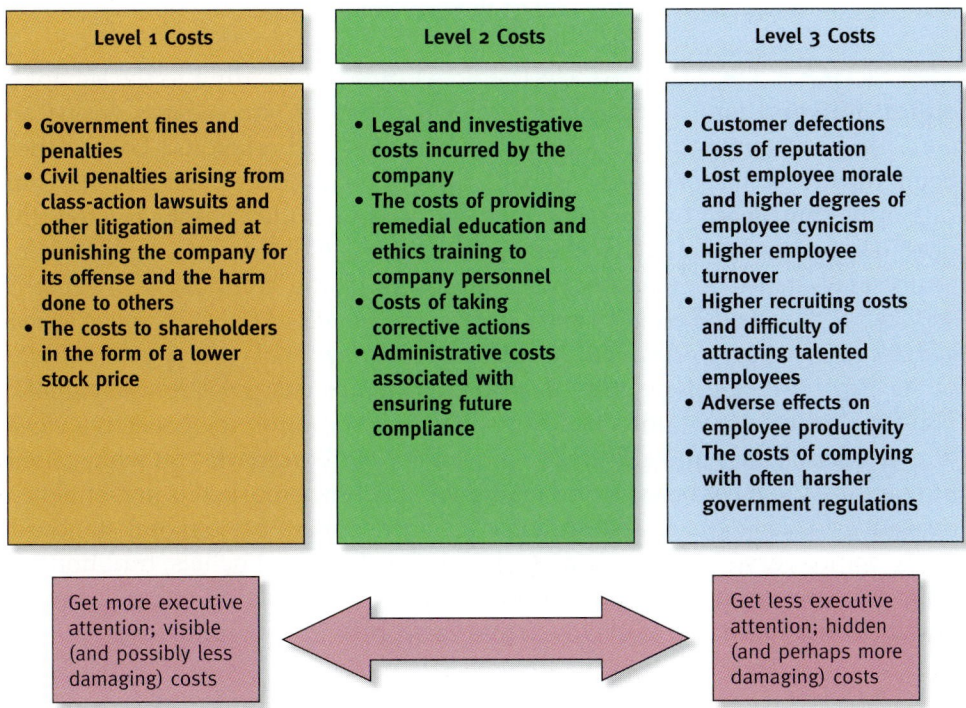

Level 1 Costs	Level 2 Costs	Level 3 Costs
• Government fines and penalties • Civil penalties arising from class-action lawsuits and other litigation aimed at punishing the company for its offense and the harm done to others • The costs to shareholders in the form of a lower stock price	• Legal and investigative costs incurred by the company • The costs of providing remedial education and ethics training to company personnel • Costs of taking corrective actions • Administrative costs associated with ensuring future compliance	• Customer defections • Loss of reputation • Lost employee morale and higher degrees of employee cynicism • Higher employee turnover • Higher recruiting costs and difficulty of attracting talented employees • Adverse effects on employee productivity • The costs of complying with often harsher government regulations

Get more executive attention; visible (and possibly less damaging) costs ⟷ Get less executive attention; hidden (and perhaps more damaging) costs

Source: Adapted from Terry Thomas, John R. Schermerhorn, and John W. Dienhart, "Strategic Leadership of Ethical Behavior," *Academy of Management Executive* 18, no. 2 (May 2004), p. 58.

wide-ranging. Some of the costs are readily visible; others are hidden and difficult to track down—as shown in Figure 7.1. The costs of fines and penalties and any declines in the stock price are easy enough to calculate. The administrative "cleanup" (or Level 2) costs are usually buried in the general costs of doing business and can be difficult to ascribe to any one ethical misdeed. Level 3 costs can be quite difficult to quantify but can sometimes be the most devastating—the aftermath of the Enron debacle left Arthur Andersen's reputation in shreds and led to the once-revered accounting firm's almost immediate demise. It remains to be seen whether Marsh & McLennan can overcome the problems described in Concepts & Connections 7.1 or whether Merck, once one of the world's most respected pharmaceutical firms, can survive the revelation that senior management deliberately concealed that its Vioxx painkiller, which the company pulled off the market in September 2004, was tied to much greater risk of heart attack and strokes.[7]

Ensuring a Strong Commitment to Business Ethics in Companies with International Operations

Notions of right and wrong, fair and unfair, moral and immoral, ethical and unethical are present in all societies, organizations, and individuals. But there are three schools of thought about the extent to which the ethical standards

[7] Anna Wilde Mathews and Barbara Martinez, "E-Mails Suggest Merck Knew Vioxx's Dangers at Early Stage," *The Wall Street Journal*, November 1, 2004, pp. A1 and A10.

travel across cultures and whether multinational companies can apply the same set of ethical standards in all of the locations where they operate.

THE SCHOOL OF ETHICAL UNIVERSALISM According to the school of **ethical universalism,** some concepts of what is right and what is wrong are *universal* and transcend most all cultures, societies, and religions.[8] For instance, being truthful strikes a chord of what's right in the peoples of all nations. Ethical norms considered universal by many ethicists include honesty, trustworthiness, respecting the rights of others, practicing the Golden Rule, and avoiding unnecessary harm to workers or to the users of the company's product or service.[9] *To the extent there is common moral agreement about right and wrong actions and behaviors across multiple cultures and countries, there exists a set of universal ethical standards to which all societies, companies, and individuals can be held accountable.* The strength of ethical universalism is that it draws upon the collective views of multiple societies and cultures to put some clear boundaries on what constitutes ethical business behavior no matter what country market its personnel are operating in. This means that in those instances where basic moral standards really do not vary significantly according to local cultural beliefs, traditions, or religious convictions, a multinational company can develop a code of ethics that it applies more or less evenly across its worldwide operations.[10]

THE SCHOOL OF ETHICAL RELATIVISM Beyond widely accepted ethical norms, many ethical standards likely vary from one country to another because of divergent religious beliefs, social customs, and prevailing political and economic doctrines (whether a country leans more toward a capitalistic market economy or one heavily dominated by socialistic or communistic principles). The school of **ethical relativism** holds that when there are cross-country or cross-cultural differences in what is deemed an ethical or unethical business situation, it is appropriate for local moral standards to take precedence over what the ethical standards may be in a company's home market. The thesis is that whatever a culture thinks is right or wrong really is right or wrong for that culture.[11]

A company that adopts the principle of ethical relativism and holds company personnel to local ethical standards necessarily assumes that what prevails as local morality is an adequate guide to ethical behavior. This can be ethically dangerous—it leads to the conclusion that if a country's culture is accepting of bribery or environmental degradation or exposing workers to dangerous conditions, then managers in that country are free to engage in such activities. Adopting such a position places a company in a perilous position

[8] For research on what are the universal moral values (six are identified—trustworthiness, respect, responsibility, fairness, caring, and citizenship), see Mark S. Schwartz, "Universal Moral Values for Corporate Codes of Ethics," *Journal of Business Ethics* 59, no. 1 (June 2005), pp. 27–44.

[9] See, for instance, Mark. S. Schwartz, "A Code of Ethics for Corporate Codes of Ethics," *Journal of Business Ethics* 41, nos. 1–2 (November–December 2002), pp. 27–43.

[10] For more discussion of this point, see Schwartz, "A Code of Ethics for Corporate Codes of Ethics," pp. 29–30.

[11] T. L. Beauchamp and N. E. Bowie, *Ethical Theory and Business* (Upper Saddle River, N.J.: Prentice-Hall, 2001), p. 8.

if it is required to defend these activities to its stakeholders in countries with higher ethical expectations. Moreover, from a global markets perspective, ethical relativism results in a maze of conflicting ethical standards for multinational companies. Imagine, for example, that a multinational company in the name of ethical relativism takes the position that it is okay for company personnel to pay bribes and kickbacks in countries where such payments are customary but forbids company personnel from making such payments in those countries where bribes and kickbacks are considered unethical or illegal. Having thus adopted conflicting ethical standards for operating in different countries, company managers have little moral basis for enforcing ethical standards companywide—rather, the clear message to employees would be that the company has no ethical standards or principles of its own, preferring to let its practices be governed by the countries in which it operates. Table 7.1 presents results of the 2006 Global Corruption Report, which illustrates the impracticality of tailoring a multinational company's ethical standards to local expectations.

INTEGRATIVE SOCIAL CONTRACTS THEORY   Social contract theory provides yet a middle position between the opposing views of universalism and relativism.[12] According to **integrative social contracts theory,** the ethical standards a company should try to uphold are governed both by (1) a limited number of universal ethical principles that are widely recognized as putting legitimate ethical boundaries on actions and behavior in *all* situations and (2) the circumstances of local cultures, traditions, and shared values that further prescribe what constitutes ethically permissible behavior and what does not. This "social contract" by which managers in all situations have a duty to serve provides that *"first-order" universal ethical norms always take precedence over "second-order" local ethical norms in circumstances where local ethical norms are more permissive.* Integrated social contracts theory offers managers in multinational companies clear guidance in resolving cross-country ethical differences: those parts of the company's code of ethics that involve universal ethical norms must be enforced worldwide, but within these boundaries there is room for ethical diversity and opportunity for host country cultures to exert *some* influence in setting their own moral and ethical standards.

A good example of the application of integrated social contracts theory involves the payment of bribes and kickbacks. Yes, bribes and kickbacks seem to be common in some countries, but does this justify paying them? Just because bribery flourishes in a country does not mean that it is an authentic or legitimate ethical norm. Virtually all of the world's major religions (Buddhism, Christianity, Confucianism, Hinduism, Islam, Judaism, Sikhism, and Taoism)

[12] Two of the definitive treatments of integrated social contracts theory as applied to ethics are Thomas Donaldson and Thomas W. Dunfee, "Towards a Unified Conception of Business Ethics: Integrative Social Contracts Theory," *Academy of Management Review* 19, no.2 (April 1994), pp. 252–284; and Thomas Donaldson and Thomas W. Dunfee, *Ties that Bind: A Social Contracts Approach to Business Ethics* (Boston: Harvard Business School Press, 1999) especially Chapters 3, 4, and 6. See, also, Andrew Spicer, Thomas W. Dunfee, and Wendy J. Bailey, "Does National Context Matter in Ethical Decision Making? An Empirical Test of Integrative Social Contracts Theory," *Academy of Management Journal* 47, no. 4 (August 2004), p. 610.

Table 7.1

Corruption Perceptions Index, Selected Countries, 2006

COUNTRY RANK	COUNTRY	2006 CPI SCORE*	HIGH-LOW RANGE	COUNTRY RANK	COUNTRY	2006 CPI SCORE*	HIGH-LOW RANGE
1	Finland	9.6	9.2–9.8	34	Taiwan	5.9	5.2–6.6
1 (tie)	Iceland	9.6	9.2–9.8	42	South Korea	5.1	4.0–6.0
1 (tie)	New Zealand	9.6	9.2–9.7	45	Italy	4.9	4.0–6.1
4	Denmark	9.5	9.2–9.7	51	South Africa	4.6	3.2–6.2
5	Singapore	9.4	8.9–9.7	54	Greece	4.4	3.6–5.8
6	Sweden	9.2	8.8–9.4	60	Turkey	3.8	2.3–4.9
7	Switzerland	9.1	8.6–9.4	70	Brazil	3.3	2.7–3.9
8	Norway	8.8	7.7–9.3	70 (tie)	China	3.3	2.2–4.2
9	Australia	8.7	7.7–9.4	70 (tie)	India	3.3	2.7–4.3
9 (tie)	Netherlands	8.7	7.7–9.3	70 (tie)	Mexico	3.3	2.7–3.5
11	Austria	8.6	7.7–9.2	93	Argentina	2.9	2.4–3.5
11 (tie)	Luxembourg	8.6	7.7–9.7	105	Iran	2.7	2.3–3.2
11 (tie)	United Kingdom	8.6	7.7–9.2	111	Vietnam	2.6	1.9–3.5
14	Canada	8.5	7.6–9.3	121	Russia	2.5	1.9–2.7
15	Hong Kong	8.3	6.7–9.3	130	Zimbabwe	2.4	1.6–3.2
16	Germany	8.0	7.5–9.1	138	Venezuela	2.3	2.1–2.5
17	Japan	7.6	5.4–8.9	142	Nigeria	2.2	1.8–2.7
18	France	7.4	5.5–8.5	151	Belarus	2.1	1.8–2.3
18 (tie)	Ireland	7.4	5.5–8.4	151 (tie)	Uzbekistan	2.1	1.6–2.3
20	Belgium	7.3	5.5–8.9	156	Bangladesh	2.0	1.4–2.3
20 (tie)	United States	7.3	5.1–8.6	156 (tie)	Chad	2.0	1.5–2.7
20 (tie)	Chile	7.3	5.5–7.7	156 (tie)	Sudan	2.0	1.8–2.3
23	Spain	6.8	5.5–7.7	160 (tie)	Iraq	1.9	1.6–2.3
24	Barbados	6.7	5.8–7.7	160 (tie)	Myanmar	1.9	1.7–2.3
24 (tie)	Estonia	6.7	5.4–8.9	163	Haiti	1.8	1.7–1.9

*The CPI scores range between 10 (highly clean) and 0 (highly corrupt); the data were collected between 2005 and 2006 and represent a composite of 12 data sources from 9 institutions, as indicated in the number of surveys used. The CPI score represents the perceptions of the degree of corruption as seen by business people, academics, and risk analysts. CPI scores were reported for 163 countries.

Source: Reprinted from *2006 Global Corruption Report.* Copyright © 2006 Transparency International: The global coalition against corruption. Used with permission. For further information, visit http://www.transparency.org.

and all moral schools of thought condemn bribery and corruption.[13] Bribery is commonplace in India but interviews with Indian CEOs whose companies constantly engaged in payoffs indicated disgust for the practice and they expressed no illusions about its impropriety.[14] Therefore, a multinational company might reasonably conclude that the right ethical standard is one of refusing to condone bribery and kickbacks on the part of company personnel no matter what the local custom is and no matter what the sales consequences are. But even with the guidance provided by integrated social contracts theory, there are many

[13] P. M. Nichols, "Outlawing Transnational Bribery through the World Trade Organization," *Law and Policy in International Business* 28, no. 2 (1997), pp. 321–322.

[14] Thomas Donaldson and Thomas W. Dunfee, "When Ethics Travel: The Promise and Peril of Global Business Ethics," *California Management Review,* 41, no. 4 (Summer 1999), pp. 55–56.

instances where cross-country differences in ethical norms create "gray areas" where it is tough to draw a line in the sand between right and wrong decisions, actions, and business practices.

Social Responsibility and Corporate Citizenship

The idea that businesses have an obligation to foster social betterment, a much-debated topic in the past 40 years, took root in the 19th century when progressive companies in the aftermath of the industrial revolution began to provide workers with housing and other amenities. The notion that corporate executives should balance the interests of all stakeholders—shareholders, employees, customers, suppliers, the communities in which they operated, and society at large—began to blossom in the 1960s. The essence of the theory of **corporate social responsibility** is that a company should strive for balance between (1) its *economic responsibility* to reward shareholders with profits, (2) its *legal responsibility* to comply with the laws of countries where it operates, (3) the *ethical responsibility* to abide by society's norms of what is moral and just, and (4) a *philanthropic responsibility* to contribute to the noneconomic needs of society.[15]

L05

Gain an understanding of the concepts of corporate social responsibility, corporate citizenship, and corporate sustainability.

There is unanimous agreement among chief managers of the world's most notable companies that economic, legal, and ethical responsibilities are a *duty* of management and are not subject to debate. In addition, even though such activities are discretionary, most chief managers agree that corporations have a duty to engage in philanthropic activities. Acting in a socially responsible manner thus involves undertaking actions that earn trust and respect from all stakeholders—operating in an honorable and ethical manner, striving to make the company a great place to work, demonstrating genuine respect for the environment, and trying to make a difference in bettering society. Common corporate social responsibility programs involve:

Corporate social responsibility calls for companies to strive for balance between (1) the *economic responsibility* to reward shareholders with profits, (2) the *legal responsibility* to comply with the laws of countries where it operates, (3) the *ethical responsibility* to abide by society's norms of what is moral and just, and (4) the discretionary *philanthropic responsibility* to contribute to the noneconomic needs of society.

- *Actions to protect the environment and, in particular, to minimize or eliminate any adverse impact on the environment stemming from the company's own business activities*—Social responsibility as it applies to environmental protection means doing more than what is legally required. From a social responsibility perspective, companies have an obligation to be stewards of the environment.

- *Actions to create a work environment that enhances the quality of life for employees*—Numerous companies exert extra efforts to enhance the quality of life for their employees, both at work and at home. This can include onsite day care, flexible work schedules for single parents, workplace exercise facilities, special leaves to care for sick family members, work-at-home opportunities, gender pay equity, and the like.

[15] Archie B. Carroll, "A Three-Dimensional Conceptual Model of Corporate Performance," *Academy of Management Review* 4, no. 4 (1979), pp. 497–505.

- *Actions to build a workforce that is diverse with respect to gender, race, national origin, and perhaps other aspects that different people bring to the workplace—* Most large companies in the United States have established workforce diversity programs, and some go the extra mile to ensure that their workplaces are attractive to ethnic minorities and inclusive of all groups and perspectives. The pursuit of workforce diversity can be good business. At Coca-Cola, where strategic success depends on getting people all over the world to become loyal consumers of the company's beverages, efforts to build a public persona of inclusiveness for people of all races, religions, nationalities, interests, and talents has considerable strategic value.

Corporate citizenship requires a corporate commitment to go beyond meeting society's expectations for ethical strategies and business behavior to demonstrating good citizenship by addressing unmet non-economic needs of society.

Some companies use the terms corporate social responsibility and **corporate citizenship** interchangeably, but there is a body of thought that only companies pursuing discretionary activities in the pursuit of bettering society can be described as good corporate citizens. Adherents of corporate citizenship theories suggest that corporations, as citizens of the communities in which they operate, have an obligation to contribute to society where government chose not to focus its efforts or has fallen short.[16] For instance, McDonald's sponsors the Ronald McDonald House Charities program, which provides a home away from home for the families of critically ill children receiving treatment at nearby hospitals. The first Ronald McDonald House was founded in 1974 in Philadelphia through the efforts of Philadelphia Eagles football player Fred Hill and his wife, Fran, during their child's treatment for leukemia. During their visits to the hospital, the Hills became acutely aware of the need for housing for families of children being treated for cancer and other serious illnesses. McDonald's commitment to the project came about informally through the involvement of a McDonald's regional manager in a fundraising campaign to help the Hills purchase an old house near the hospital. News of the efforts to open a Ronald McDonald House in Philadelphia spread quickly among franchisees and McDonald's franchisees in Chicago and Houston soon launched efforts to build Ronald McDonald Houses near hospitals in their cities. McDonald's eventually helped establish the Ronald McDonald House Charities to support the development of Ronald McDonald houses across the United States and in other countries. By 2007, McDonald's and other sponsors had donated more than $430 million to 245 Ronald McDonald Houses in 28 countries.

Corporate citizenship is also a commitment of British Telecom, which gives 1 percent of its profits directly to communities, largely for education—teacher training, in-school workshops, and digital technology. Leading prescription drugmaker GlaxoSmithKline and other pharmaceutical companies practice corporate citizenship by either donating or heavily discounting medicines for distribution in the least-developed nations. Companies frequently reinforce their philanthropic efforts by encouraging employees to support charitable

---

[16] Dirk Matten and Andrew Crane, "Corporate Citizenship: Toward an Extended Theoretical Conceptualization," *Academy of Management Review* 30, no. 1 (2005), pp. 166–179.

causes and participate in community affairs, often through programs that match employee contributions.

Corporate Sustainability and the Environment

There is a rapidly growing set of multinational companies that are expanding their understanding of societal responsibilities to include the impact of their strategies and operations on future generations. **Corporate sustainability** theories expect that companies will meet the needs of current era customers, suppliers, shareholders, employees, and other stakeholders, while protecting, and perhaps enhancing, the resources needed by future generations. Sustainability initiatives undertaken by companies are directed at improving the company's "Triple-P" performance—people, planet, and profit.[17] Unilever, a diversified producer of processed foods, personal care, and home cleaning products, is among the most committed corporations pursuing sustainable business practices. The company tracks 11 sustainable agricultural indicators in its processed foods business and has launched a variety of programs to improve the environmental performance of its suppliers. Examples of such programs include special low-rate financing for tomato suppliers choosing to switch to water-conserving irrigation systems and training programs in India that have allowed contract cucumber growers to reduce pesticide use by 90%, while improving yields by 78%.

Unilever has also reengineered many internal processes to improve the company's overall performance on sustainability measures. For example, the company's factories have reduced water usage by 50% and manufacturing waste by 14% through the implementation of sustainability initiatives. Unilever has also redesigned packaging for many of its products to conserve natural resources and reduce the volume of consumer waste. The company's Suave shampoo bottles in the U.S. were reshaped to save almost 150 tons of plastic resin per year, which is the equivalent of 15 million fewer empty bottles making it to landfills annually. Also, the width of Unilever's Lipton soup cartons was reduced to save 154 tons of cardboard per year. Because 40% of Unilever's sales are made to consumers in developing countries, the company also is committed to addressing societal needs of consumers in those countries. Examples of the company's social performance include free laundries in poor neighborhoods in developing countries, start-up assistance for women-owned micro businesses in India, and free drinking water provided to villages in Ghana.

Profitability is an equally important goal of corporate sustainability. Procter & Gamble's Swiffer cleaning system is an example of a sustainable product that has become a market success, not because of its earth-friendly design, but because it outperforms less ecologically friendly alternatives. In fact, most consumers probably aren't aware that the Swiffer mop is a sustainable product. Consumers purchase Swiffer mops because they prefer Swiffer's disposable

> **LO5**
>
> Gain an understanding of the concepts of corporate social responsibility, corporate citizenship, and corporate sustainability.

> **Corporate sustainability** involves strategic efforts to meet the needs of today's customers, suppliers, shareholders, employees, and other stakeholders, while protecting, and perhaps, enhancing, the resources needed by future generations.

[17] Gerald I. J., M. Zetsloot, and Marcel N. A. van Marrewijk, "From Quality to Sustainability," *Journal of Business Ethics* 55 (2004), PP. 79–82.

cleaning sheets to filling and refilling a mop bucket and wringing out a wet mop until the floor is clean. The fact that the Swiffer reduces demands on municipal water sources, save electricity that would be needed to heat mop water, and doesn't add to the amount of detergent making its way into waterways and waste treatment facilities are likely viewed by consumers as residual benefits to the product's efficiency and ease of use.

Most well-known companies discuss their sustainability strategies and results in press releases and special sustainability reports for consumers and investors to review. Just as investment firms have created mutual funds made up of companies passing some threshold of social responsibility, a number of sustainability funds have been created in recent years for environmentally and socially aware investors to purchase. The Dow Jones Sustainability World Index is made up of the top 10% of the 2,500 companies listed in the Dow Jones World Index in terms of economic performance, environmental performance, and social performance. Table 7.2 lists the worldwide supersector leaders within the Dow Jones Sustainability World Index for 2006/2007. However, achieving a prominent ranking in sustainability indexes is no guarantee that a company will outperform industry rivals when it comes to social responsibility. For example, BP's $8 billion investment into alternative energy sources and its strong involvement in community and environmental groups had allowed it to consistently rank near the top among sustainability indexes,

Table 7.2

Worldwide Sustainability Leaders Listed in the Dow Jones Sustainability World Index, 2006/2007

NAME	MARKET SECTOR	COUNTRY
Bayerische Motoren Werke AG (BMW)	Automobiles & Parts	Germany
Westpac Banking Corp.	Banks	Australia
Norsk Hydro	Basic Resources	Norway
DSM NV	Chemicals	Netherlands
Holcim	Construction & Materials	Switzerland
Sodexho Alliance SA	Travel & Leisure	France
Statoil	Oil & Gas	Norway
Investa Property Group	Financial Services	Australia
Unilever	Food & Beverage	Netherlands
Novartis	Health Care	Switzerland
3M Company	Industrial Goods & Services	USA
Allianz	Insurance	Germany
ITV Plc	Media	UK
Procter & Gamble Co.	Personal & Household Goods	USA
Kesko	Retail	Finland
Intel Corp.	Technology	USA
BT Group Plc	Telecommunications	UK
Veolia Environment	Utilities	France

Sources: Dow Jones Indexes, STOXX Limited, and SAM Group. Accessed at http://www.sustainability-indexes.com/07_htmle/indexes/djsiworld_supersectorleaders.html on September 14, 2007.

but between 2005 and 2007, the company was fined for safety violations at an Ohio refinery, was investigated by the U.S. Department of Justice for suspected manipulation of oil prices, had a major oil pipeline leak in Alaska, and was hit with a refinery explosion in Texas that claimed the lives of 15 employees.[18]

The Business Case for Socially Responsible Behavior

Whatever the moral arguments for socially responsible business behavior, it has long been recognized that it is in the enlightened self-interest of companies to be good citizens and devote some of their energies and resources to the betterment of employees, the communities in which they operate, and society in general. In short, there are several reasons why the exercise of corporate social responsibility and corporate citizenship is good business:

- *It generates internal benefits (particularly concerning employee recruiting, workforce retention, and training costs)*—Companies with good reputations for contributing time and money to the betterment of society are better able to attract and retain employees compared to companies with tarnished reputations. Some employees just feel better about working for a company committed to improving society.[19] This can contribute to lower turnover and better worker productivity. Other direct and indirect economic benefits include lower costs for staff recruitment and training. For example, Starbucks is said to enjoy much lower rates of employee turnover because of its full benefits package for both full-time and part-time employees, management efforts to make Starbucks a great place to work, and the company's socially responsible practices.

- *It reduces the risk of reputation-damaging incidents and can lead to increased buyer patronage*—Firms may well be penalized by employees, consumers, and shareholders for actions that are not considered socially responsible. Consumer, environmental, and human rights activist groups are quick to criticize businesses whose behavior they consider to be out of line, and they are adept at getting their message into the media and onto the Internet. Pressure groups can generate widespread adverse publicity, promote boycotts, and influence like-minded or sympathetic buyers to avoid an offender's products. Research has shown that product boycott announcements are associated with a decline in a company's stock price.[20] In contrast, to the extent that a company's socially responsible behavior wins

[18] BP's environmental record is discussed in "Beyond the Green Corporation," *BusinessWeek*, January 29, 2007, p. 50.

[19] N. Craig Smith, "Corporate Social Responsibility: Whether and How," *California Management Review* 45, no. 4 (Summer 2003), p. 63; see also, World Economic Forum, "Findings of a Survey on Global Corporate Leadership," accessed at www.weforum.org/corporatecitizenship, October 11, 2003.

[20] Wallace N. Davidson, Abuzar El-Jelly, and Dan L. Worrell, "Influencing Managers to Change Unpopular Corporate Behavior through Boycotts and Divestitures: A Stock Market Test," *Business and Society* 34, no. 2 (1995), pp. 171–196.

applause from consumers and fortifies its reputation, the company may win additional patronage. Some observers and executives are convinced that a strong, visible, social responsibility strategy gives a company an edge in differentiating itself from rivals and in appealing to those consumers who prefer to do business with companies that are solid corporate citizens. Whole Foods Market, Stonyfield Farm, and the Body Shop have definitely expanded their customer bases because of their visible and well-publicized activities as socially conscious companies. Yet there is only limited evidence that consumers go out of their way to patronize socially responsible companies if it means paying a higher price or purchasing an inferior product.[21]

- *It is in the best interest of shareholders*—Well-conceived social responsibility strategies help avoid or preempt legal and regulatory actions that could prove costly and otherwise burdensome. Taking the straight and narrow path has allowed the stock prices of companies rating high on social and environmental performance criteria to perform 35 to 45 percent better than the average of the 2,500 companies comprising the Dow Jones Global Index.[22] Nearly 100 studies have examined the relationship between corporate citizenship and corporate financial performance over the past 30 years; the majority point to a positive relationship. Of the 80 studies that examined whether a company's social performance is a good predictor of its financial performance, 42 concluded yes, 4 concluded no, and the remainder reported mixed or inconclusive findings.[23]

In sum, companies that take social responsibility seriously can improve their business reputations and operational efficiency while also reducing their risk exposure and encouraging loyalty and innovation. Overall, companies that take special pains to protect the environment (beyond what is required by law), are active in community affairs, and are generous supporters of charitable causes and projects that benefit society are more likely to be seen as good investments and as good companies to work for or do business with. Shareholders are likely to view the business case for social responsibility as a strong one, even though they certainly have a right to be concerned whether the time and money their company spends to carry out its social responsibility strategy outweighs the benefits and reduces the bottom line by an unjustified amount.

[21] Smith, "Corporate Social Responsibility," p. 62.

[22] See James C. Collins and Jerry I. Porras, *Built to Last: Successful Habits of Visionary Companies*, Third Edition (London: HarperBusiness, 2002); Sarah Roberts, Justin Keeble, and David Brown, "The Business Case for Corporate Citizenship," a study for the World Economic Forum, www.weforum.org/corporatecitizenship, October 14, 2003, p. 4; and Smith, "Corporate Social Responsibility," p. 63.

[23] Smith, "Corporate Social Responsibility," p. 65; Lee E. Preston and Douglas P. O'Bannon, "The Corporate Social-Financial Performance Relationship," *Business and Society* 36, no. 4 (December 1997), pp. 419–429; Ronald M. Roman, Sefa Hayibor, and Bradley R. Agle, "The Relationship between Social and Financial Performance: Repainting a Portrait," *Business and Society*, 38, no. 1 (March 1999), pp. 109–125; and Joshua D. Margolis and James P. Walsh, *People and Profits* (Mahwah, N.J.: Lawrence Erlbaum, 2001).

Key Points

Ethics involves concepts of right and wrong, fair and unfair, moral and immoral. Beliefs about what is ethical serve as a moral compass in guiding the actions and behaviors of individuals and organizations. Ethical principles in business are not materially different from ethical principles in general.

1. The three main drivers of unethical business behavior also stand out:

   - Overzealous or obsessive pursuit of personal gain, wealth, and other selfish interests.
   - Heavy pressures on company managers to meet or beat earnings targets.
   - A company culture that puts profitability and good business performance ahead of ethical behavior.

2. Business ethics failures can result in Level 1 costs (fines, penalties, civil penalties arising from lawsuits, stock price declines), the administrative "clean-up" (or Level 2) costs, and Level 3 costs (customer defections, loss of reputation, higher turnover, harsher government regulations).

3. There are three schools of thought about ethical standards for companies with international operations:

   - According to the *school of ethical universalism,* the same standards of what's ethical and unethical resonate with peoples of most societies regardless of local traditions and cultural norms; hence, common ethical standards can be used to judge the conduct of personnel at companies operating in a variety of international markets and cultural circumstances. According to the *school of ethical relativism,* different societal cultures and customs have divergent values and standards of right and wrong—thus what is ethical or unethical must be judged in the light of local customs and social mores and can vary from one culture or nation to another.
   - According to *integrated social contracts theory,* universal ethical principles or norms based on the collective views of multiple cultures and societies combine to form a "social contract" that all individuals in all situations have a duty to observe. Within the boundaries of this social contract, local cultures can specify other impermissible actions; however, universal ethical norms always take precedence over local ethical norms.

4. The concept of corporate social responsibility calls for companies to find balance between (1) their *economic responsibilities* to reward shareholders with profits, (2) *legal responsibilities* to comply with the laws of countries where they operate, (3) *ethical responsibilities* to abide by society's norms of what is moral and just, and (4) *philanthropic responsibilities* to contribute to the noneconomic needs of society.

5. Some companies use the terms corporate social responsibility and corporate citizenship interchangeably, but typically, corporate citizenship places expectations on companies to go beyond consistently demonstrating ethical strategies and business behavior by addressing unmet noneconomic needs of society.

6. Corporate sustainability involves strategic efforts to meet the needs of current customers, suppliers, shareholders, employees, and other stakeholders, while protecting, and perhaps enhancing, the resources needed by future generations.

7. The business case for corporate social responsibility is supported by the following benefits.

- *It generates internal benefits (particularly concerning employee recruiting, workforce retention, and training costs)*—Companies with good reputations for contributing time and money to the betterment of society are better able to attract and retain employees compared to companies with tarnished reputations. Other direct and indirect economic benefits include lower costs for staff recruitment and training.

- *It reduces the risk of reputation-damaging incidents and can lead to increased buyer patronage*—Firms may well be penalized by employees, consumers, and shareholders for actions that are not considered socially responsible. Consumer, environmental, and human rights activist groups are quick to criticize businesses whose behavior they consider to be out of line, and they are adept at getting their message into the media and onto the Internet. Pressure groups can generate widespread adverse publicity, promote boycotts, and influence like-minded or sympathetic buyers to avoid an offender's products.

- *It is in the best interest of shareholders*—Well-conceived social responsibility strategies help avoid or preempt legal and regulatory actions that could prove costly and otherwise burdensome. Taking the straight and narrow path has allowed the stock prices of companies rating high on social and environmental performance criteria to perform 35 to 45 percent better than the average of the 2,500 companies comprising the Dow Jones Global Index.[24]

[24] See James C. Collins and Jerry I. Porras, *Built to Last: Successful Habits of Visionary Companies*, Third Edition (London: HarperBusiness, 2002); Roberts, Keeble, and Brown, "The Business Case for Corporate Citizenship," p. 4; and Smith, "Corporate Social Responsibility," p. 63.

Assurance of Learning Exercises

1. Based on the description of Marsh & McLennan's strategy presented in Concepts & Connections 7.1, would it be fair to characterize the payment of contingent commissions by property casualty insurers as nothing more than thinly disguised kickbacks? Why or why not? If you were the manager of a company that hired Marsh & McLennan to provide risk management services, would you see that Marsh had a conflict of interest in steering your company's insurance policies to insurers in which it had an ownership interest? Using Internet research tools, determine the status of lawsuits against Marsh & McLennan that were unresolved in 2007. What is your assessment of the extent to which the conduct of company personnel damaged shareholders? **LO3**

2. Review Microsoft's statements about its corporate citizenship programs at www.microsoft.com/about/corporatecitizenship. How does the company's commitment to global citizenship provide positive benefits for its stakeholders? How does Microsoft plan to improve social and economic empowerment in developing countries through its Unlimited Potential program? Why is this important to Microsoft shareholders? **LO5**

3. Go to www.nestle.com and read the company's latest sustainability report. What are Nestlé's key sustainable environmental policies? How is the company addressing sustainable social development? How do these initiatives relate to the company's principles, values, and culture and its approach to competing in the food industry? **LO5**

LO1 Suppose you have been approached by members from a competing team in your business simulation to join in on a scheme to bring down the leading company in your industry. The plan has been hatched by two of the industry's runner-up firms, who are seeking a third company to aid them in their efforts to drive the number-one company to the bottom of the industry rankings. The plan calls for you to attack the leader in its key markets with deeply discounted prices designed to steal market share. The two co-conspirators would follow up your attack with loss-generating prices in the subsequent years. Those approaching you have suggested that the series of three straight predatory pricing attacks will result in market share losses for the industry leader from which it will be unable to recover. How will you respond to their offer to enter into the attack? What legal and ethical issues must you consider in making a decision?

Exercise for Business Simulation Users

Chapter 8

Strategies for Competing in International Markets

Chapter Learning Objectives

LO1. Gain an understanding of the primary reasons companies choose to compete in international markets.

LO2. Identify fundamental cross-country differences that shape strategy choices in international markets.

LO3. Gain familiarity with the strategic options for entering and competing in foreign markets.

LO4. Understand how multinational companies go about building competitive advantage in foreign markets.

Any company that aspires to industry leadership in the 21st century must think in terms of global, not domestic, market leadership. The world economy is globalizing at an accelerating pace as countries previously closed to foreign companies open up their markets, as countries with previously planned economies embrace market or mixed economies, as information technology shrinks the importance of geographic distance, and as ambitious, growth-minded companies race to build stronger competitive positions in the markets of more and more countries.

This chapter focuses on strategy options for expanding beyond domestic boundaries and competing in the markets of either a few or a great many countries. Some approaches to competing internationally allow for minimal investments abroad, while others involve establishing international operations. Regardless of a company's chosen line of attack for competing in international markets, managers must consider the following questions:

1. Will the company's home market offer sufficient opportunities for growth in revenues and profits or is it necessary to expand into international markets to achieve growth?

2. Does international expansion offer location-based advantages related to production costs, product distribution, or customer service operations?

3. How might the company efficiently transfer its resource strengths and competitive capabilities from one country to another in an effort to secure competitive advantage?

4. Will business risk be reduced or increased by electing to compete in additional country markets?

5. Is it better to employ essentially the same basic competitive strategy in all countries or modify the strategy country by country?

6. Will the company have sufficient capabilities to build competitive advantage in international markets or should it draw on the skills of local allies to help navigate competitive waters in foreign markets?

In the process of exploring these issues, we will introduce a number of core concepts—multicountry competition, global competition, profit sanctuaries, and cross-market subsidization. This chapter also includes sections on the appeal of international market expansion; cross-country differences in cultural, demographic, and market conditions; the growing role of alliances with foreign partners; the benefits of cross-border coordination; and the importance of locating operations in the most advantageous countries.

Why Expand into International Markets?

A company may opt to expand outside its domestic market for any of four major reasons:

1. *To gain access to new customers*—Expanding into foreign markets offers potential for increased revenues, profits, and long-term growth and becomes an especially attractive option when a company's home markets are mature. Firms like Cisco Systems, Dell, Sony, Nokia, Avon, and Toyota

LO1

Gain an understanding of the primary reasons companies choose to compete in international markets.

are moving rapidly to extend their market reach into all corners of the world.

2. *To achieve lower costs and enhance the firm's competitiveness*—Many companies are driven to sell in more than one country because domestic sales volume alone is not large enough to fully capture manufacturing economies of scale or learning-curve effects. The relatively small size of country markets in Europe explains why companies like Michelin, BMW, and Nestlé long ago began selling their products all across Europe and then moved into markets in North America and Latin America.

3. *To capitalize on its core competencies*—A company may be able to leverage its competencies and capabilities into a position of competitive advantage in foreign markets as well as domestic markets. Wal-Mart is capitalizing on its considerable expertise in discount retailing to expand into China, Latin America, and parts of Europe. Wal-Mart executives are particularly excited about the company's growth opportunities in China.

4. *To spread its business risk across a wider market base*—A company spreads business risk by operating in a number of different foreign countries rather than depending entirely on operations in its domestic market. Thus, if the economies of North American countries turn down for a period of time, a company with operations across much of the world may be sustained by buoyant sales in Latin America, Asia, or Europe.

In a few cases, companies in industries based on natural resources (e.g., oil and gas, minerals, rubber, and lumber) often find it necessary to operate in the international arena because attractive raw material supplies are located in foreign countries.

Strategy Considerations in International Markets

Assessing Cross-Country Differences in Cultural, Demographic, and Market Conditions

LO2

Identify fundamental cross-country differences that shape strategy choices in international markets.

Regardless of a company's motivation for expanding outside its domestic markets, the strategies it uses to compete in foreign markets must be situation-driven. Cultural, demographic, and market conditions vary significantly among the countries of the world.[1] *Cultures and lifestyles* are the most obvious areas in which countries differ; *market demographics* and *income levels* are close behind. For many product categories, consumers in Spain do not have the same tastes, preferences, and buying habits as consumers in Norway; buyers differ yet again in Greece, Chile, New Zealand, and Taiwan. Less than 20 percent of the populations of Brazil, India, and China have annual purchasing power equivalent to $25,000. Middle-class consumers represent a much smaller portion of the population in these and other emerging countries than in North America, Japan, and much of Western Europe—China's middle class

[1] For an insightful discussion of how much significance these kinds of demographic and market differences have, see C. K. Prahalad and Kenneth Lieberthal, "The End of Corporate Imperialism," *Harvard Business Review* 76, no. 4 (July–August 1998), pp. 68–79.

numbers about 125 million out of a population of 1.3 billion.[2] Sometimes, product designs suitable in one country are inappropriate in another—for example, in the United States electrical devices run on 110-volt electrical systems, but in some European countries the standard is a 220–240 volt electric system, necessitating the use of different electrical designs and components. In parts of Asia refrigerators are a status symbol and may be placed in the living room, leading to preferences for stylish designs and colors—in India bright blue and red are popular colors. In other Asian countries household space is constrained and many refrigerators are only four feet high so that the top can be used for storage. In Italy, most people use automatic washing machines but there is a strongly entrenched tradition and cultural preference for hanging the clothes out to dry on a clothesline and ironing them rather than using clothes dryers.

Similarly, *market growth* varies from country to country. In emerging markets like India, China, Brazil, and Malaysia, market growth potential is far higher than in the more mature economies of Britain, Denmark, Canada, and Japan. In automobiles, for example, the potential for market growth is explosive in China, where 2006 sales of new vehicles amounted to just less than 6 million in a country with 1.3 billion people. Market growth can be limited by the lack of infrastructure or established distribution and retail networks in emerging markets. In India, there are well-developed national channels for distribution of goods to the nation's three million retailers, whereas in China distribution is primarily local. Also, the competitive rivalry in some country marketplaces is only moderate, while others are characterized by strong or fierce competition.

One of the biggest concerns of companies competing in foreign markets is whether to customize their offerings in each different country market to match the tastes and preferences of local buyers or whether to offer a mostly standardized product worldwide. While making products closely matched to local tastes makes them more appealing to local buyers, customizing a company's products country by country may have the effect of raising production and distribution costs due to the greater variety of designs and components, shorter production runs, and the complications of added inventory handling and distribution logistics. *The tension between the market pressures to localize a company's product offerings country-by-country and the competitive pressures to lower costs is one of the big strategic issues that participants in foreign markets have to resolve.*

Aside from the basic cultural and market differences among countries, a company also has to pay special attention to location advantages that stem from country-to-country variations in manufacturing and distribution costs, the risks of adverse shifts in exchange rates, and the economic and political demands of host governments.

Location-Based Cost Drivers

Differences in wage rates, worker productivity, inflation rates, energy costs, tax rates, government regulations, and the like create sizable country-to-country variations in manufacturing costs. Plants in some countries have major

[2] Joseph Caron, "The Business of Doing Business with China: An Ambassador Reflects," *Ivey Business Journal* 69, no. 5 (May–June 2005), p. 2.

manufacturing cost advantages because of lower input costs (especially labor), relaxed government regulations, the proximity of suppliers, or unique natural resources. In such cases, the low-cost countries become principal production sites, with most of the output exported to markets in other parts of the world. Companies that build production facilities in low-cost countries (or that source their products from contract manufacturers in these countries) have a competitive advantage over rivals with plants in countries where costs are higher. The competitive role of low manufacturing costs is most evident in low-wage countries like China, India, Pakistan, Mexico, Brazil, and several countries in Africa that have become production havens for manufactured goods with high labor content (especially textiles and apparel). Hourly compensation costs in China averaged about $0.70 an hour in 2004–2005 versus about $6.00 in Hungary, $7.00 in Portugal, $2.50 in Mexico, $4.00 in Brazil, $24.00 in Canada, $23.50 in the U.S., $39.00 in Norway, and $33.00 in Germany.[3] China is fast becoming the manufacturing capital of the world—virtually all of the world's major manufacturing companies now have facilities in China. Likewise, concerns about short delivery times and low shipping costs make some countries better locations than others for establishing distribution centers.

The quality of a country's business environment also offers locational advantages—the governments of some countries are anxious to attract foreign investments and go all-out to create a business climate that outsiders will view as favorable. A good example is Ireland, which has one of the world's most pro-business environments. Ireland offers companies very low corporate tax rates, has a government that is responsive to the needs of industry, and aggressively recruits high-tech manufacturing facilities and multinational companies. Ireland's policies were a major factor in Intel's decision to locate a $2.5 billion chip manufacturing plant in Ireland that employs over 4,000 people. Another locational advantage is the clustering of suppliers of components and capital equipment, infrastructure suppliers (universities, vocational training providers, research enterprises), and makers of complementary products in close proximity to a company's major operations—such geographic clustering not only facilitates close collaboration but in many cases also produces significant cost savings.

The Effects of Shifting Exchange Rates

The volatility of exchange rates greatly complicates the issue of geographic cost advantages. Currency exchange rates often move up or down 20 to 40 percent annually. Changes of this magnitude can either totally wipe out a country's low-cost advantage or transform a former high-cost location into a competitive-cost location. For instance, in the mid-1980s, when the dollar was strong relative to the Japanese yen (meaning that $1 would purchase, say, 125 yen as opposed to only 100 yen), Japanese heavy-equipment maker Komatsu was able to undercut U.S.-based Caterpillar's prices by as much as 25 percent,

[3] "International Comparisons of Hourly Compensation Costs for Production Workers in Manufacturing, 2005," *U.S. Department of Labor Bureau of Labor Statistics Newsletter*, November 30, 2006.

causing Caterpillar to lose sales and market share. But starting in 1985, when shifting exchange rates caused the dollar to grow steadily weaker against the yen, Komatsu had to raise its prices to U.S. buyers six times over two years as its yen-based costs soared when converted into dollars. With its competitiveness against Komatsu restored because of the weaker dollar and Komatsu's higher prices, Caterpillar regained sales and market share. *The lesson of fluctuating exchange rates is that companies that export goods to foreign countries always gain in competitiveness when the currency of the country in which the goods are manufactured is weak. Exporters are disadvantaged when the currency of the country where goods are being manufactured grows stronger.*

Host Government Policies

National governments enact all kinds of measures affecting business conditions and the operations of foreign companies in their markets. Examples of host government policies affecting foreign-based companies include:

- Local content requirements on goods made inside their borders by foreign-based companies.
- Policies that protect local companies from foreign competition.
- Restrictions on exports because of national security concerns.
- Price regulation of imported and locally produced goods.
- Deliberately burdensome procedures and requirements for imported goods to pass customs inspection.
- Tariffs or quotas on the import of certain goods.
- Complex technical standards imposed on foreign-based companies.
- Subsidies and low-interest loans for domestic companies competing against foreign rivals.

Until 2002, when it joined the World Trade Organization, China imposed a 100 percent tariff on motor vehicle imports. The European Union imposes quotas on textile and apparel imports from China as a measure to protect European producers in southern Europe. India has imposed excise taxes on categories of imported goods ranging from wheat to automobiles. In 2005, India placed tariffs of 24 to 40 percent on imported automobiles—a policy that has significantly dampened the demand for new vehicles in India. In 2007, the United States House and Senate voted to ban all imports from Myanmar to protest human rights violations carried out by the military junta ruling that country.

Other governments, anxious to obtain new plants and jobs, offer foreign companies a helping hand in the form of subsidies, privileged market access, and technical assistance. All of these possibilities explain why the managers of companies opting to compete in foreign markets have to take a close look at a country's politics and policies toward business in general, and foreign companies in particular, when deciding which country markets to participate in and which ones to avoid.

Strategy Options for Entering and Competing in Foreign Markets

There are several general strategic options for a company that decides to expand outside its domestic market and compete internationally or globally:

1. *Maintain a national (one-country) production base and export goods to foreign markets,* using either company owned or foreign-controlled forward distribution channels.

2. *License foreign firms to use the company's technology or to produce and distribute the company's products.*

3. *Employ a franchising strategy.*

4. *Follow a multicountry strategy,* varying the company's strategic approach (perhaps a little, perhaps a lot) from country to country in accordance with local conditions and differing buyer tastes and preferences.

5. *Follow a global strategy,* using essentially the same competitive strategy approach in all country markets where the company has a presence.

6. *Use strategic alliances or joint ventures with foreign companies as the primary vehicle for entering foreign markets* and perhaps also use them as an ongoing strategic arrangement aimed at maintaining or strengthening the company's competitiveness.

The following sections discuss the six general options in more detail.

Export Strategies

Using domestic plants as a production base for exporting goods to foreign markets is an excellent initial strategy for pursuing international sales. It is a conservative way to test the international waters. The amount of capital needed to begin exporting is often quite minimal and existing production capacity may well be sufficient to make goods for export. With an export strategy, a manufacturer can limit its involvement in foreign markets by contracting with foreign wholesalers experienced in importing to handle the entire distribution and marketing function in their countries or regions of the world. If it is more advantageous to maintain control over these functions, however, a manufacturer can establish its own distribution and sales organizations in some or all of the target foreign markets. Either way, a home-based production and export strategy helps the firm minimize its direct investments in foreign countries. Such strategies are commonly favored by Chinese, Korean, and Italian companies—products are designed and manufactured at home and then distributed through local channels in the importing countries; the primary functions performed abroad relate chiefly to establishing a network of distributors and perhaps conducting sales promotion and brand awareness activities.

Whether an export strategy can be pursued successfully over the long run hinges on the relative cost-competitiveness of the home-country production base. In some industries, firms gain additional scale economies and learning-curve benefits from centralizing production in one location that exports to various international markets. However, an export strategy is vulnerable when (1) manufacturing costs in the home country are substantially higher than in foreign countries where rivals have plants, (2) the costs of shipping the product to distant foreign markets are relatively high, or (3) adverse shifts occur in currency exchange rates. Unless an exporter can both keep its production and shipping costs competitive with rivals and successfully hedge against unfavorable changes in currency exchange rates, its success will be limited.

Licensing Strategies

Licensing makes sense when a firm with valuable technical know-how or a unique patented product has neither the internal organizational capability nor the resources to enter foreign markets. Licensing also has the advantage of avoiding the risks of committing resources to country markets that are unfamiliar, politically volatile, economically unstable, or otherwise risky. By licensing the technology or the production rights to foreign-based firms, the firm does not have to bear the costs and risks of entering foreign markets on its own, yet it is able to generate income from royalties. The big disadvantage of licensing is the risk of providing valuable technological know-how to foreign companies and thereby losing some degree of control over its use. Also, monitoring licensees and safeguarding the company's proprietary know-how can prove quite difficult in some circumstances. But if the royalty potential is considerable and the companies to whom the licenses are being granted are both trustworthy and reputable, then licensing can be a very attractive option. Many software and pharmaceutical companies use licensing strategies.

Franchising Strategies

While licensing works well for manufacturers and owners of proprietary technology, franchising is often better suited to the global expansion efforts of service and retailing enterprises. McDonald's, Yum! Brands (the parent of A&W, Pizza Hut, KFC, Long John Silver's, and Taco Bell), the UPS Store, 7-Eleven, and Hilton Hotels have all used franchising to build a presence in international markets. Franchising has much the same advantages as licensing. The franchisee bears most of the costs and risks of establishing foreign locations, so a franchisor has to expend only the resources to recruit, train, support, and monitor franchisees. The big problem a franchisor faces is maintaining quality control. In many cases, foreign franchisees do not always exhibit strong commitment to consistency and standardization—especially when the local culture does not stress the same kinds of quality concerns. Another problem that can arise is whether to allow foreign franchisees to make modifications to the franchisor's product offering to better satisfy the tastes and expectations of local buyers. Should McDonald's allow its franchised units in Japan to modify Big Macs slightly to suit Japanese tastes? Should the franchised KFC units in China be permitted to substitute spices that appeal to Chinese consumers? Or should the same menu offerings be rigorously and unvaryingly required of all franchisees worldwide?

Establishing International Operations: Choosing Between Localized Multicountry Strategies or a Global Strategy

While exporting, licensing, and franchising rely upon the competencies and capabilities of allies in international markets to deliver goods or services to buyers, companies pursuing international expansion may elect to take responsibility for the performance of all essential value chain activities in foreign markets. Once a company chooses to establish operations in international markets, deciding upon the degree to vary its competitive approach to fit specific market conditions and buyer preferences in each host country is perhaps the foremost strategic issue that it must address. Figure 8.1 shows a company's options for resolving this issue.

THINK LOCAL, ACT LOCAL APPROACHES TO STRATEGY-MAKING A think local, act local approach to strategy-making is essential when there are significant country-to-country differences in customer preferences and buying habits, when there are significant cross-country differences in distribution channels and marketing methods, when host governments

FIGURE 8.1 **A Company's Strategic Options for Dealing with Cross-Country Variations in Buyer Preferences and Market Conditions**

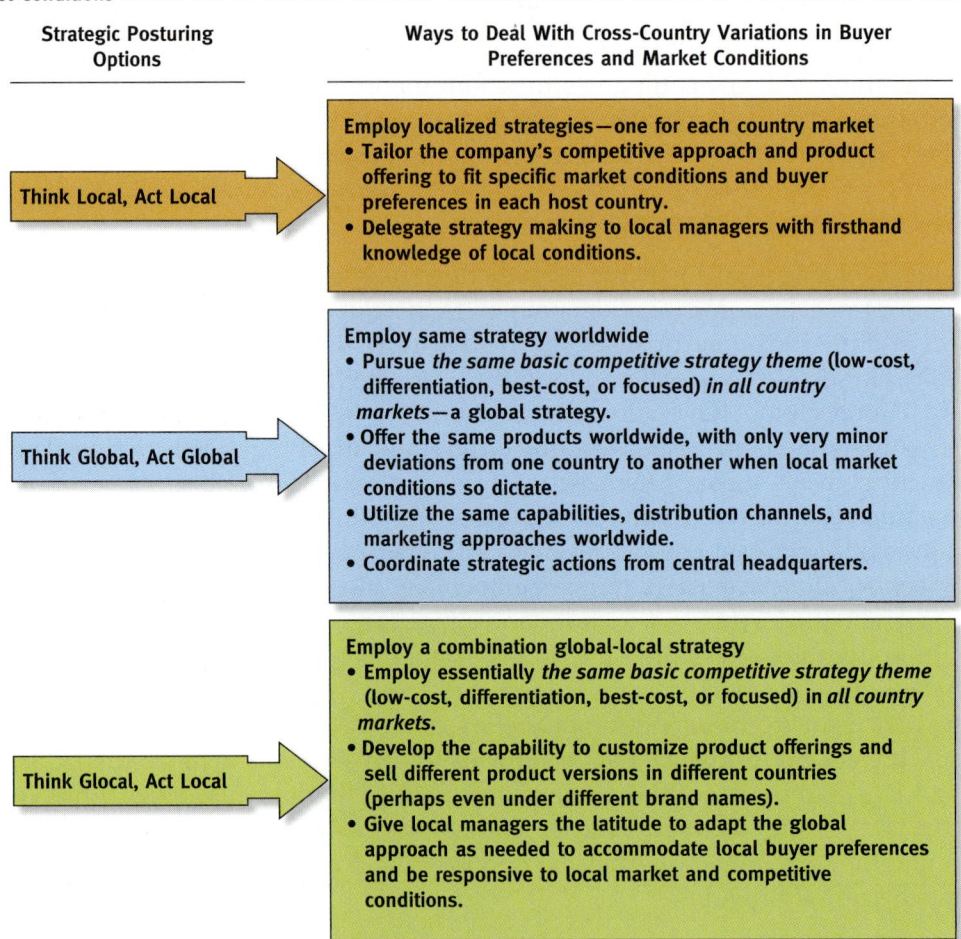

Strategic Posturing Options

Ways to Deal With Cross-Country Variations in Buyer Preferences and Market Conditions

Think Local, Act Local

Employ localized strategies—one for each country market
- Tailor the company's competitive approach and product offering to fit specific market conditions and buyer preferences in each host country.
- Delegate strategy making to local managers with firsthand knowledge of local conditions.

Think Global, Act Global

Employ same strategy worldwide
- Pursue *the same basic competitive strategy theme* (low-cost, differentiation, best-cost, or focused) *in all country markets*—a global strategy.
- Offer the same products worldwide, with only very minor deviations from one country to another when local market conditions so dictate.
- Utilize the same capabilities, distribution channels, and marketing approaches worldwide.
- Coordinate strategic actions from central headquarters.

Think Glocal, Act Local

Employ a combination global-local strategy
- Employ essentially *the same basic competitive strategy theme* (low-cost, differentiation, best-cost, or focused) in *all country markets*.
- Develop the capability to customize product offerings and sell different product versions in different countries (perhaps even under different brand names).
- Give local managers the latitude to adapt the global approach as needed to accommodate local buyer preferences and be responsive to local market and competitive conditions.

enact regulations requiring that products sold locally meet strict manufacturing specifications or performance standards, and when the trade restrictions of host governments are so diverse and complicated that they preclude a uniform, coordinated worldwide market approach. With localized strategies, a company often has different product versions for different countries and sometimes sells them under different brand names. In the food products industry, it is common for companies to vary the ingredients in their products and sell the localized versions under local brand names in order to cater to country-specific tastes and eating preferences. The strength of employing a set of **localized** or **multicountry strategies** is that the company's actions and business approaches are deliberately crafted to appeal to the tastes and expectations of buyers in each country and to stake out the most attractive market positions vis-à-vis local competitors.[4]

> **Localized or multicountry strategies** are necessary when there are significant cross-country differences in customer preferences, buyer purchasing habits, distribution channels, or marketing methods. **Think local, act local** strategy-making approaches are also essential when host government regulations or trade policies preclude a uniform, coordinated worldwide market approach.

However, **think local, act local** strategies have two big drawbacks: (1) They hinder transfer of a company's competencies and resources across country boundaries because the strategies in different host countries can be grounded in varying competencies and capabilities; and (2) they do not promote building a single, unified competitive advantage—especially one based on low cost. Companies employing highly localized or multicountry strategies face big hurdles in achieving low-cost leadership *unless* they find ways to customize their products and *still* be in a position to capture scale economies and learning-curve effects. Toyota's unique mass customization production capability has been key to its ability to effectively adapt product offerings to local buyer tastes, while maintaining low-cost leadership.

THINK GLOBAL, ACT GLOBAL APPROACHES TO STRATEGY-MAKING While multicountry or localized strategies are best suited for industries where a fairly high degree of local responsiveness is important, global strategies are best suited for globally standardized industries. A **global strategy** is one in which the company's approach is predominantly the same in all countries—it sells the same products under the same brand names everywhere, utilizes much the same distribution channels in all countries, and competes on the basis of the same capabilities and marketing approaches worldwide. Although the company's strategy or product offering may be adapted in very minor ways to accommodate specific situations in a few host countries, the compa-

> **Global strategies** are best suited to industries that are globally standardized in terms of customer preferences, buyer purchasing habits, distribution channels, or marketing methods.

ny's fundamental competitive approach (low-cost, differentiation, or focused) remains very much intact worldwide and local managers stick close to the global strategy. A **think global, act global** strategic theme prompts company managers to integrate and coordinate the company's strategic moves worldwide and to expand into most if not all nations where there is significant buyer

---

[4] For more details on the merits of and opportunities for cross-border transfer of successful strategy experiments, see C. A. Bartlett and S. Ghoshal, *Managing Across Borders: The Transnational Solution*, 2nd ed. (Boston: Harvard Business School Press, 1998), pp. 79–80 and Chapter 9.

demand. It puts considerable strategic emphasis on building a *global* brand name and aggressively pursuing opportunities to transfer ideas, new products, and capabilities from one country to another.

Whenever country-to-country differences are small enough to be accommodated within the framework of a global strategy, a global strategy is preferable to localized strategies because a company can more readily unify its operations and focus on establishing a brand image and reputation that is uniform from country to country. Moreover, with a global strategy a company is better able to focus its full resources on securing a sustainable low-cost or differentiation-based competitive advantage over both domestic rivals and global rivals.

THINK GLOBAL, ACT LOCAL APPROACHES TO STRATEGY-MAKING

Often, a company can accommodate cross-country variations in buyer tastes, local customs, and market conditions with a **think global, act local** approach to developing strategy. This middle ground approach entails utilizing the same basic competitive theme (low-cost, differentiation, or focused) in each country but allows local managers the latitude to (1) incorporate whatever country-specific variations in product attributes are needed to best satisfy local buyers and (2) make whatever adjustments in production, distribution, and marketing are needed to respond to local market conditions and compete successfully against local rivals.

Think global, act local strategy-making approaches involve employing essentially the same strategic theme (low-cost, differentiation, focused, best-cost) in all country markets, while allowing some country-to-country customization to fit local market conditions.

Slightly different product versions sold under the same brand name may suffice to satisfy local tastes, and it may be feasible to accommodate these versions rather economically in the course of designing and manufacturing the company's product offerings. The build-to-order component of Dell computer's strategy, for example, makes it simple for Dell to respond to how buyers in different parts of the world want their PCs equipped. However, Dell has not wavered in its strategy to sell direct to customers rather than through local retailers even though the majority of buyers in countries such as China are concerned about ordering online and prefer to personally inspect PCs at stores before making a purchase.

As a rule, most companies that operate multinationally endeavor to employ as global a strategy as customer needs and market conditions permit. Whirlpool has been globalizing its low-cost leadership strategy in home appliances for over 15 years, striving to standardize parts and components and move toward worldwide designs for as many of its appliance products as possible. But it has found it necessary to continue producing significantly different versions of refrigerators, washing machines, and cooking appliances for consumers in different regions of the world because sizes and designs have not converged sufficiently to permit worldwide product standardization. General Motors began an initiative in 2004 to insist that its worldwide units share basic parts and work together to design vehicles that can be sold, with modest variations, anywhere around the world; by reducing the types of radios used in its cars and trucks from 270 to 50, it expected to save 40 percent in radio costs.

Concepts and Connections 8.1 describes how two companies localize their strategies for competing in country markets across the world.

Concepts & Connections 8.1

MULTICOUNTRY STRATEGIES AT ELECTRONIC ARTS AND COCA-COLA

Electronic Arts' Multicountry Strategy in Video Games

Electronic Arts (EA), the world's largest independent developer and marketer of video games, designs games that are suited to the differing tastes of game players in different countries and also designs games in multiple languages. EA has two major design studios—one in Vancouver, British Columbia, and one in Los Angeles—and smaller design studios in San Francisco, Orlando, London, and Tokyo. This dispersion of design studios helps EA to design games that are specific to different cultures—for example, the London studio took the lead in designing the popular FIFA Soccer game to suit European tastes and to replicate the stadiums, signage, and team rosters; the U.S. studio took the lead in designing games involving NFL football, NBA basketball, and NASCAR racing. No other game software company had EA's ability to localize games or to launch games on multiple platforms in mul-

tiple countries in multiple languages. EA's *Harry Potter and the Chamber of Secrets* was released simultaneously in 75 countries, 31 languages, and on seven platforms.

Coca-Cola's Multicountry Strategy in Beverages

Coca-Cola strives to meet the demands of local tastes and cultures, offering 400 brands in over 200 countries. Its network of bottlers and distributors is distinctly local, and the company's products and brands are formulated to cater to local tastes. The ways in which Coca-Cola's local operating units bring products to market, the packaging that is used, and the advertising messages that are employed are all intended to match the local culture and fit in with local business practices. Many of the ingredients and supplies for Coca-Cola's products are sourced locally.

Sources: www.ea.com and www.thecoca-colacompany.com, accessed October 2007.

Using International Strategic Alliances and Joint Ventures to Build Competitive Strength in Foreign Markets

Strategic alliances, joint ventures, and other cooperative agreements with foreign companies are a favorite and potentially fruitful means for entering a foreign market or strengthening a firm's competitiveness in world markets.[5] Historically, export-minded firms in industrialized nations sought alliances with firms in less-developed countries to import and market their products locally—such arrangements were often necessary to win approval for entry from the host country's government. Both Japanese and American companies are actively forming alliances with European companies to strengthen their ability to compete in the 27-nation European Union (and the three countries that are candidates to become EU members) and to capitalize on the opening up of Eastern European markets. Many U.S. and European companies are allying with Asian companies in their efforts to enter markets in China, India, Malaysia, Thailand, and other Asian countries. Many foreign companies, of course, are particularly interested in strategic partnerships that will strengthen their ability to gain a foothold in the U.S. market.

[5] For two especially insightful studies of company experiences with cross-border alliances, see Joel Bleeke and David Ernst, "The Way to Win in Cross-Border Alliances," *Harvard Business Review* 69, no. 6 (November–December 1991), pp. 127–135; and Gary Hamel, Yves L. Doz, and C. K. Prahalad, "Collaborate with Your Competitors—and Win," *Harvard Business Review* 67, no. 1 (January–February 1989), pp. 133–139.

However, cooperative arrangements between domestic and foreign companies have strategic appeal for reasons besides gaining better access to attractive country markets.[6] A second big appeal of cross-border alliances is to capture economies of scale in production and/or marketing. By joining forces in producing components, assembling models, and marketing their products, companies can realize cost savings not achievable with their own small volumes. A third motivation for entering into a cross-border alliance is to fill gaps in technical expertise and/or knowledge of local markets (buying habits and product preferences of consumers, local customs, and so on). Allies learn much from one another in performing joint research, sharing technological know-how, studying one another's manufacturing methods, and understanding how to tailor sales and marketing approaches to fit local cultures and traditions. Indeed, one of the win-win benefits of an alliance is to learn from the skills, technological know-how, and capabilities of alliance partners and implant the knowledge and know-how of these partners in personnel throughout the company.

A fourth motivation for cross-border alliances is to share distribution facilities and dealer networks, and to mutually strengthen each partner's access to buyers. A fifth benefit is that cross-border allies can direct their competitive energies more toward mutual rivals and less toward one another; teaming up may help them close the gap on leading companies. A sixth driver of cross-border alliances comes into play when companies wanting to enter a new foreign market conclude that alliances with local companies are an effective way to establish working relationships with key officials in the host-country government.[7] And, finally, alliances can be a particularly useful way for companies across the world to gain agreement on important technical standards—they have been used to arrive at standards for DVD players, assorted PC devices, Internet-related technologies, high-definition televisions, and mobile phones.

What makes cross-border alliances an attractive strategic means of gaining the aforementioned types of benefits (as compared to acquiring or merging with foreign-based companies) is that entering into alliances and strategic partnerships allows a company to preserve its independence and avoid using perhaps scarce financial resources to fund acquisitions. Furthermore, an alliance offers the flexibility to readily disengage once its purpose has been served or if the benefits prove elusive, whereas an acquisition is a more permanent sort of arrangement.[8] Concepts & Connections 8.2 provides examples of cross-border strategic alliances.

THE RISKS OF STRATEGIC ALLIANCES WITH FOREIGN PARTNERS   Alliances and joint ventures with foreign partners have their pitfalls, however. Cross-border allies typically have to overcome language and

[6] See Yves L. Doz and Gary Hamel, *Alliance Advantage* (Boston, MA: Harvard Business School Press, 1998), especially Chapters 2–4; Bleeke and Ernst, "The Way to Win in Cross-Border Alliances," pp. 127–133; Hamel, Doz, and Prahalad, "Collaborate with Your Competitors—and Win," pp. 134–135; and Porter, *The Competitive Advantage of Nations*, (New York: Free Press, 1990), p. 66.

[7] H. Kurt Christensen, "Corporate Strategy: Managing a set of Businesses," in *The Portable MBA in Strategy*, ed. Liam Fahey and Robert M. Randall (New York: Wiley, 2001), p. 43.

[8] For an excellent presentation on the pros and cons of alliances versus acquisitions, see Jeffrey H. Dyer, Prashant Kale, and Harbir Singh, "When to Ally and When to Acquire," *Harvard Business Review* 82, no. 7/8 (July–August 2004), pp. 109–115.

EXAMPLES OF CROSS-BORDER STRATEGIC ALLIANCES

1. Intel, the world's largest chipmaker, has formed strategic alliances with leading software application providers based in Europe and Asia. Intel's partners in the effort to enhance Intel's next-generation products include SAP, Oracle, SAS, BEA, IBM, Hewlett-Packard, Dell, Microsoft, Cisco Systems, and Alcatel. One of the alliances between Intel and Cisco involves a collaborative effort in Hong Kong to build next-generation infrastructure for Radio Frequency Identification (RFID) solutions used to link manufacturers and logistics companies in the Hong Kong region with retailers worldwide. Intel and France-based Alcatel (which is a leading provider of fixed and mobile broadband access products) formed an alliance in 2004 to advance the definition, standardization, development, integration, and marketing of WiMAX broadband services solutions. WiMAX was seen as a cost-effective wireless or mobile broadband solution for markets where it was not feasible to provide customers with hardwired DSL broadband access.

2. Verio, a subsidiary of Japan-based NTT Communications and one of the leading global providers of Web hosting services and IP data transport, has developed an alliance-oriented business model that combines the company's core competencies with the skills and products of best-of-breed technology partners. Verio's foreign-based strategic partners include Accenture, Cisco Systems, Microsoft, Sun Microsystems, Oracle, Arsenal Digital Solutions (a provider of data storage services), Internet Security Systems (a provider of firewall and intrusion detection systems), and Mercantec (which develops storefront and shopping cart software). Verio management believes that its portfolio of international strategic alliances allows it to use innovative, best-of-class technologies in providing its customers with fast, efficient, accurate data transport and a complete set of Web hosting services. An independent panel of 12 judges recently selected Verio as the winner of the Best Technology Foresight Award for its efforts in pioneering new technologies.

3. Toyota and First Automotive Works, China's biggest automaker, entered into an alliance in 2002 to make luxury sedans, sport-utility vehicles, and minivehicles for the Chinese market. The intent was to make as many as 400,000 vehicles annually by 2010, an amount equal to the 2002 sales of market-leader Volkswagen. At the time of the announced alliance, Toyota was lagging behind Honda, General Motors, and Volkswagen in setting up production facilities in China. Capturing a bigger share of the Chinese market was seen as crucial to Toyota's success in achieving its strategic objective of having a 15 percent share of the world's automotive market by 2010.

4. Airbus Industrie was formed by an alliance of aerospace companies from Britain, Spain, Germany, and France that included British Aerospace, Daimler-Benz Aerospace, and Aerospatiale. The objective of the alliance was to create a European aircraft company capable of competing with U.S.-based Boeing Corp. The alliance has proved highly successful, infusing Airbus with the know-how and resources to compete head-to-head with Boeing for world leadership in large commercial aircraft (over 100 passengers).

5. General Motors, Daimler AG, and BMW have entered into an alliance to develop a hybrid gasoline-electric engine for future GM, Mercedes, and BMW models. Toyota, the acknowledged world leader in hybrid engines, is endeavoring to establish its design as the industry standard by signing up other automakers to use it. But the technology favored by the General Motors, Daimler AG, BMW alliance is said to be less costly to produce and easier to configure for large trucks and SUVs than Toyota's (although it is also less fuel efficient). Europe's largest automaker, Volkswagen, has allied with Porsche to pursue the development of hybrid engines. So far, Ford Motor and Honda have elected to go it alone in developing hybrid engine technology.

Sources: Company Web sites and press releases; Yves L. Doz and Gary Hamel, *Alliance Advantage: The Art of Creating Value through Partnering* (Boston, MA: Harvard Business School Press, 1998); and Norihiko Shirouzu and Jathon Sapsford, "As hybrid cars gain traction, industry battles over designs," *The Wall Street Journal*, October 19, 2005, pp. A1, A9B.

cultural barriers and figure out how to deal with diverse (or perhaps conflicting) operating practices. The communication, trust-building, and coordination costs are high in terms of management time.[9] It is not unusual for there to be little personal affinity among some of the key people on whom success or failure of the alliance depends. And even if allies are able to develop productive personal relationships, they can still have trouble reaching mutually agreeable ways to deal with key issues or resolve differences. There is a natural tendency for allies to struggle to collaborate effectively in competitively sensitive areas, thus spawning suspicions on both sides about forthright exchanges of information and expertise. Occasionally, the egos of corporate executives can clash—an alliance between Northwest Airlines and KLM Royal Dutch Airlines resulted in a bitter feud among both companies' top officials (who, according to some reports, refused to speak to each other).[10]

It is not unusual for partners to discover they have conflicting objectives and strategies, deep differences of opinion about how to proceed, or important differences in corporate values and ethical standards. Tensions build up, working relationships cool, and the hoped-for benefits never materialize. The recipe for successful alliances requires many meetings of many people working in good faith over a period of time to iron out what is to be shared, what is to remain proprietary, and how the cooperative arrangements will work.[11]

Even if the alliance becomes a win-win proposition for both parties, there is the danger of becoming overly dependent on foreign partners for essential expertise and competitive capabilities. If a company is aiming for global market leadership and needs to develop capabilities of its own, then at some juncture cross-border merger or acquisition may have to be substituted for cross-border alliances and joint ventures. One of the lessons about cross-border alliances is that they are more effective in helping a company establish a beachhead of new opportunity in world markets than they are in enabling a company to achieve and sustain global market leadership.

WHEN A CROSS-BORDER ALLIANCE MAY BE UNNECESSARY
Experienced multinational companies that market in 50 to 100 or more countries across the world find less need for entering into cross-border alliances than do companies in the early stages of globalizing their operations.[12] Multinational companies make it a point to develop senior managers who understand how "the system" works in different countries, plus they can enhance local know-how by simply hiring experienced local managers. The role of expatriate managers is to transfer technology, business practices, and the corporate culture into the company's operations in the new country market and to serve as conduits for the flow of information between the corporate office and local operations. The role of local managers is to contribute a necessary understanding of the

---

[9] For additional discussion of company experiences with alliances and partnerships, see Doz and Hamel, *Alliance Advantage*, Chapters 2–7, and Rosabeth Moss Kanter, "Collaborative Advantage: The Art of the Alliance," *Harvard Business Review* 72, no. 4 (July–August 1994), pp. 96–108.

[10] Details are reported in Shawn Tully, "The Alliance from Hell," *Fortune*, June 24, 1996, pp. 64–72.

[11] Jeremy Main, "Making Global Alliances Work," *Fortune*, December 19, 1990, p. 125.

[12] Prahalad and Lieberthal, "The End of Corporate Imperialism," p. 77.

local market conditions, local buying habits, and local ways of doing business and, often, to head up local operations. Such an approach avoids the hazards and hassles of allying with local businesses.

Using International Operations to Improve Overall Competitiveness

There are three important ways in which a firm can gain competitive advantage by expanding outside its domestic market.[13] One, it can use location to lower costs or help achieve greater product differentiation. Two, it can use cross-border coordination in ways that a domestic-only competitor cannot. And three, it can use profit sanctuaries and cross-market subsidization to wage a strategic offensive.

Using Location to Build Competitive Advantage

To use location to build competitive advantage, a company must consider two issues: (1) whether to concentrate each internal process in a few countries or to disperse performance of each process to many nations, and (2) in which countries to locate particular activities.[14]

LO4

Understand how multinational companies go about building competitive advantage in foreign markets.

WHEN TO CONCENTRATE INTERNAL PROCESSES IN A FEW LOCATIONS   Companies tend to concentrate their activities in a limited number of locations in the following circumstances:

- *When the costs of manufacturing or other activities are significantly lower in some geographic locations than in others*—For example, much of the world's athletic footwear is manufactured in Asia (China and Korea) because of low labor costs; much of the production of circuit boards for PCs is located in Taiwan because of both low costs and the high-caliber technical skills of the Taiwanese labor force.

- *When there are significant scale economies*—The presence of significant economies of scale in components production or final assembly means that a company can gain major cost savings from operating a few superefficient plants as opposed to a host of small plants scattered across the world. Makers of digital cameras, LCD TVs, and DVD players located in Japan, South Korea, and Taiwan have used their scale economies to establish a low-cost advantage.

- *When there is a steep learning curve associated with performing an activity*—In some industries learning-curve effects in parts manufacture or assembly are so great that a company establishes one or two large plants from which it serves the world market. The key to riding down the learning curve is to concentrate production in a few locations to increase the accumulated volume at a plant (and thus the experience of the plant's workforce) as rapidly as possible.

---

[13] Porter, *The Competitive Advantage of Nations*, pp. 53–55.

[14] Ibid., pp. 55–58.

- *When certain locations have superior resources, allow better coordination of related activities, or offer other valuable advantages*—A research unit or a sophisticated production facility may be situated in a particular nation because of its pool of technically trained personnel. Samsung became a leader in memory chip technology by establishing a major R&D facility in Silicon Valley and transferring the know-how it gained back to headquarters and its plants in South Korea.

WHEN TO DISPERSE INTERNAL PROCESSES ACROSS MANY LOCATIONS   There are several instances when dispersing a process is more advantageous than concentrating it in a single location. Buyer-related activities—such as distribution to dealers, sales and advertising, and after-sale service—usually must take place close to buyers. This makes it necessary to physically locate the capability to perform such activities in every country market where a global firm has major customers. For example, the four biggest public accounting firms have numerous international offices to service the foreign operations of their multinational corporate clients. A global competitor that effectively disperses its buyer-related activities can gain a service-based competitive edge in world markets over rivals whose buyer-related activities are more concentrated—this is one reason the Big Four public accounting firms (PricewaterhouseCoopers, KPMG, Deloitte & Touche, and Ernst & Young) have been so successful relative to regional and national firms. Dispersing activities to many locations is also competitively advantageous when high transportation costs, diseconomies of large size, and trade barriers make it too expensive to operate from a central location. In addition, it is strategically advantageous to disperse activities to hedge against the risks of fluctuating exchange rates and adverse political developments.

Using Cross-Border Coordination to Build Competitive Advantage

Multinational and global competitors are able to coordinate activities across different countries to build competitive advantage.[15] If a firm learns how to assemble its product more efficiently at, say, its Brazilian plant, the accumulated expertise and knowledge can be shared with assembly plants in other world locations. Also, knowledge gained in marketing a company's product in Great Britain, for instance, can readily be exchanged with company personnel in New Zealand or Australia. Other examples of cross-border coordination include shifting production from a plant in one country to a plant in another to take advantage of exchange rate fluctuations and to respond to changing wage rates, energy costs, or changes in tariffs and quotas.

Efficiencies can also be achieved by shifting workloads from where they are unusually heavy to locations where personnel are underutilized. Whirlpool's efforts to link its product R&D and manufacturing operations in North America,

[15] C. K. Prahalad and Yves L. Doz, *The Multinational Mission* (New York: Free Press, 1987), pp. 58–60.

Latin America, Europe, and Asia allowed it to accelerate the discovery of innovative appliance features, coordinate the introduction of these features in the appliance products marketed in different countries, and create a cost-efficient worldwide supply chain. Whirlpool's conscious efforts to integrate and coordinate its various operations around the world have helped it become a low-cost producer and also speed product innovations to market, thereby giving Whirlpool an edge over rivals worldwide.

Using Profit Sanctuaries and Cross-Market Subsidization to Wage a Strategic Offensive

Profit sanctuaries are country markets (or geographic regions) in which a company derives substantial profits because of its strong or protected market position. Nike, which markets its products in 160 countries, has two big profit sanctuaries: the United States (where it earned 38.7 percent of its pretax profits in 2007), and Europe, the Middle East, and Africa (where it earned 31.1 percent of 2007 pretax profits). Carrefour, the world's second largest retailer with over 12,500 stores in Europe, Asia, and the Americas, also has two principal profit sanctuaries: its biggest is in France (which in 2006 accounted for 47.8 percent of revenues and 52.3 percent of operating earnings) and its second biggest is in Europe outside of France (which in 2006 accounted for 38.3 percent of revenues and 37.1 percent of earnings before interest and taxes). Japan is the chief profit sanctuary for most Japanese companies because trade barriers erected by the Japanese government effectively block foreign companies from competing for a large share of Japanese sales. Protected from the threat of foreign competition in their home market, Japanese companies can safely charge somewhat higher prices to their Japanese customers and thus earn attractively large profits on sales made in Japan. In most cases, a company's biggest and most strategically crucial profit sanctuary is its home market, but international and global companies may also enjoy profit sanctuary status in other nations where they have a strong competitive position, big sales volume, and attractive profit margins. Companies that compete globally are likely to have more profit sanctuaries than companies that compete in just a few country markets; a domestic-only competitor, of course, can have only one profit sanctuary.

Profit sanctuaries are valuable competitive assets, providing the financial strength to support strategic offensives in selected country markets and fuel a company's race for global market leadership. The added financial capability afforded by multiple profit sanctuaries gives a global or multicountry competitor the financial strength to wage a market offensive against a domestic competitor. The global company has the flexibility of lowballing its prices or launching high-cost marketing campaigns in the domestic company's home market and grabbing market share at the domestic company's expense. Razor-thin margins or even losses in these markets can be subsidized with the healthy profits earned in its profit sanctuaries—a practice called **cross-market subsidization.** If the domestic company retaliates with matching price cuts or increased marketing expenses, its profits can be squeezed substantially and its competitive strength sapped, even if it is the domestic market leader.

The availability of profit sanctuaries and cross-market subsidization provides global competitors with two offensive strategies not readily at hand for domestic-only competitors.

- *Employ cross-market subsidization to support sales growth in country markets where the company is weak.* Competing in multiple country markets gives a company the luxury of drawing upon the resources, profits, and cash flows derived from its profit sanctuaries to fund efforts to boost sales and market share in selected country markets. In addition, a multinational with a diversified product line can shift resources from a product category that is competitively strong and resource-deep (say soft drinks) to add firepower to an offensive in those countries with bright growth prospects in another product category (say bottled water or energy drinks).

- *Employ cross-market subsidization to attack a foreign rival's profit sanctuaries.* Launching an offensive in a country market where a rival earns its biggest profits can put the rival on the defensive, forcing it to perhaps spend more on marketing/advertising, trim its prices, boost product innovation efforts, or otherwise undertake actions that raise its costs and erode its profits. If a company's offensive succeeds in eroding a rival's profits in its chief profit sanctuary, the rival's financial resources may be sufficiently weakened to enable the attacker to gain the upper hand and build market momentum in other markets. While attacking a rival's profit sanctuary violates the principle of attacking competitor weaknesses instead of competitor strengths, it can nonetheless prove valuable when there's special merit in pursuing actions that cut into a foreign rival's profit margins and force it to defend a market that is important to its competitive well-being.

When taken to the extreme, cut-rate pricing attacks made possible by cross-market subsidization draws charges of unfair dumping. A company is said to be dumping when it sells its goods in foreign markets at prices that are (1) well below the prices at which it normally sells in its home market or (2) well below its full costs per unit. Companies that engage in dumping usually keep their selling prices high enough to cover variable costs per unit, thereby limiting their losses on each unit to some percentage of fixed costs per unit.

Dumping can be a tempting offensive strategy in either of two instances. The first may be justified as a legitimate competitive practice, while the latter is usually viewed to be predatory in nature. A charge of unfair dumping is more easily defended when a company with unused production capacity discovers that it is cheaper to keep producing (as long as the selling prices cover average variable costs per unit) than it is to incur the costs associated with idle plant capacity. By keeping its plants operating at or near capacity, not only may a dumping company be able to cover variable costs and earn a contribution to fixed costs, but it also may be able to use its below-market prices to draw price-sensitive customers away from foreign rivals. It is wise for companies pursuing such an approach to court these new customers and retain their business when prices later begin a gradual rise back to normal market levels.

A company may use dumping to drive down the price so far in the targeted country that domestic firms are quickly put in dire financial straits or in danger of being driven out of business. However, using below-market pricing in this way runs a high risk of host government retaliation on behalf of the adversely affected domestic companies. Indeed, as the trade among nations has mushroomed over the past 10 years, most governments have joined the World Trade Organization (WTO), which promotes fair trade practices among nations and actively polices dumping. Most WTO member governments have enacted antidumping laws and readily take action against dumping wherever there is material injury to domestic competitors. Companies based in France and China were recently found guilty of dumping laminate flooring at unreasonably low prices in Canada to the detriment of Canadian producers.[16] Most all governments can be expected to retaliate against dumping by imposing special tariffs on goods being imported from the countries of the guilty companies. Companies deemed guilty of dumping frequently come under pressure from their government to cease and desist, especially if the tariffs adversely affect innocent companies based in the same country or if the advent of special tariffs raises the specter of a trade war.

[16] Canadian International Trade Tribunal, findings issued June 16, 2005, and posted at www.citt-tcce.gc.ca (accessed September 28, 2005).

Key Points

1. Competing in international markets allows multinational companies to (1) gain access to new customers, (2) achieve lower costs and enhance the firm's competitiveness by more easily capturing scale economies or learning-curve effects, (3) leverage core competencies refined domestically in additional country markets, and (4) spread business risk across a wider market base.

2. Companies electing to expand into international markets must consider cross-country differences in cultural, demographic, and market conditions, location-based cost drivers, adverse exchange rates, and host government policies when evaluating strategy options.

3. In posturing to compete in foreign markets, a company has three basic options: (1) a think local, act local approach to crafting a strategy, (2) a think global, act global approach to crafting a strategy, and (3) a combination think global, act local approach. A "think local, act local" or multicountry strategy is appropriate for industries or companies that must vary their product offerings and competitive approaches from country to country in order to accommodate differing buyer preferences and market conditions. A "think global, act global" approach (or global strategy) works best in markets that support employing the same basic competitive approach (low-cost, differentiation, focused) in all country markets and marketing essentially the same products under the same brand names in all countries where the company operates. A "think global, act local" approach can be used when it is feasible for a company to employ essentially the same basic competitive strategy in all markets, but still customize its product offering and some aspect of its operations to fit local market circumstances.

4. Other strategy options for competing in world markets include maintaining a national (one-country) production base and exporting goods to foreign markets, licensing foreign firms to use the company's technology or produce and distribute the company's products, employing a franchising strategy, and using strategic alliances or other collaborative partnerships to enter a foreign market or strengthen a firm's competitiveness in world markets.

5. Strategic alliances with foreign partners have appeal from several angles: gaining wider access to attractive country markets, allowing capture of economies of scale in production and/or marketing, filling gaps in technical expertise and/or knowledge of local markets, saving on costs by sharing distribution facilities and dealer networks, helping gain agreement on important technical standards, and helping combat the impact of alliances that rivals have formed. Cross-border strategic alliances are fast reshaping competition in world markets, pitting one group of allied global companies against other groups of allied global companies.

6. There are three general ways in which a firm can gain competitive advantage (or offset domestic disadvantages) in global markets. One way involves locating various value chain activities among nations in a manner that lowers costs or achieves greater product differentiation. A second way draws on a multinational or global competitor's ability to deepen or broaden its resource strengths and capabilities and to coordinate its dispersed activities in ways that a domestic-only competitor cannot. A third involves utilizing profit sanctuaries in protected markets to wage strategic offenses in various international markets. Profit sanctuaries are country markets in which a company derives substantial profits because of its strong or protected market position. They are valuable competitive assets. A company with multiple profit sanctuaries has the financial strength to support competitive offensives in one market with resources and profits diverted from its operations in other markets—a practice called *cross-market subsidization.* The ability of companies with multiple profit sanctuaries to employ cross-subsidization gives them a powerful offensive weapon and a competitive advantage over companies with a single sanctuary.

Assurance of Learning Exercises

1. Harley-Davidson has chosen to compete in various country markets in Europe and Asia using an export strategy. Read the sections of its latest annual report at www.harley-davidson.com related to its international operations. Why does it seem the company has avoided developing production facilities outside of the United States?   **LO3**

2. Log on to www.ford.co.uk and review the information provided under the Vehicles and Company pull-down menus. Based on this information and what you know about Ford's operations in North America, does it appear that Ford is pursuing a global strategy or a localized multicountry strategy? Support your answer.   **LO3**

3. The Hero Group is among the ten largest corporations in India with 19 business segments and annual revenues of $3.19 billion in fiscal 2005–2006. Many of the corporation's business units have utilized strategic alliances with foreign partners to compete in new product and geographic markets. Review the company's statements concerning its alliances and international business operations at www.herogroup.com/alliance.htm and prepare a two-page report that outlines the group's successful use of international strategic alliances.   **LO3**

LO3
LO4
In your simulation, you likely compete in major country markets in North America, Latin America, Europe/Africa, and Asia/Pacific. What factors did your group consider in choosing between a multicountry strategy and a global strategy? Explain.

Exercise for
Business
Simulation
Users

Chapter 9

Strategies for Multibusiness Corporations

Chapter Learning Objectives

LO1. Understand how diversifying into multiple businesses can enhance shareholder value.

LO2. Gain an understanding of how related diversification strategies can produce cross-business strategic fits capable of delivering competitive advantage.

LO3. Recognize conditions that cause a strategy of unrelated diversification to result in added shareholder value.

LO4. Understand the process for evaluating a company's diversification strategy.

LO5. Recognize a diversified company's strategy options for improving its overall performance.

In a one-business company, managers have to come up with a plan for competing successfully in a single industry environment. But in a diversified company, the strategy-making challenge involves assessing multiple industry environments and developing a set of business strategies—one for each industry arena in which the diversified company operates. As was discussed in Chapter 2, a multibusiness company must devise a *corporate strategy* for improving the performance of the company's overall business lineup and ensuring strategic consistency among individual businesses. In this chapter, we move beyond strategy-making considerations for single-business enterprises to strategy-making in a diversified enterprise.

As in a single-business company, strategy-making in multibusiness corporations involves two-way influence between corporate level executives and managers at other organizational levels. In most diversified companies, corporate-level executives delegate considerable strategy-making authority to the heads of each business, usually giving them the latitude to craft a business strategy suited to their particular industry and competitive circumstances and holding them accountable for producing good results. But the task of crafting a diversified company's overall or corporate strategy falls squarely in the lap of top-level executives and involves four distinct facets:

1. *Picking new industries to enter and deciding on the means of entry*—The decision to pursue business diversification requires that management decide what new industries offer the best growth prospects and whether to enter by starting a new business from the ground up, acquiring a company already in the target industry, or forming a joint venture or strategic alliance with another company.

2. *Pursuing opportunities to leverage cross-business value chain relationships into competitive advantage*—Companies that diversify into businesses with strategic fit across the value chains of its business units have a much better chance of gaining a $1 + 1 = 3$ effect than multibusiness companies lacking strategic fit.

3. *Steering corporate resources into the most attractive business units*—A diversified company's business units are usually not equally attractive from the standpoint of investing additional funds. It is incumbent on corporate management to channel resources into areas where earnings potentials are higher.

4. *Initiating actions to boost the combined performance of the corporation's collection of businesses*—Corporate strategists must craft moves to improve the overall performance of the corporation's business lineup and sustain increases in shareholder value. Strategic options for diversified corporations include (a) sticking closely with the existing business lineup and pursuing opportunities presented by these businesses, (b) broadening the scope of diversification by entering additional industries, (c) retrenching to a narrower scope of diversification by divesting poorly performing businesses, and (d) broadly restructuring the business lineup with multiple divestitures and/or acquisitions.

In the first portion of this chapter we describe the various means a company can use to diversify and explore the pros and cons of related versus unrelated diversification strategies. The second part of the chapter looks at how to evaluate the attractiveness of a diversified company's business lineup, decide whether it has a good diversification strategy, and identify ways to improve its future performance.

When Business Diversification Becomes a Consideration

LO1

Understand how diversifying into multiple businesses can enhance shareholder value.

So long as a single-business company can achieve profitable growth opportunities in its present industry, there is no urgency to pursue diversification. The big risk of a single-business company, of course, is having all of the firm's eggs in one industry basket. If demand for the industry's product is eroded or if the industry becomes competitively unattractive and unprofitable, then a company's prospects can quickly dim. Consider, for example, what digital cameras are doing to erode the revenues of companies dependent on film and film processing and what mobile phone companies and marketers of VoIP are doing to the revenues of long-distance providers such as AT&T, British Telecommunications, and NTT in Japan.

Thus, *diversifying into new industries always merits strong consideration whenever a single-business company encounters diminishing market opportunities and stagnating sales in its principal business.* But there are four other instances in which a company becomes a prime candidate for diversifying:[1]

1. When it spots opportunities for expanding into industries whose technologies and products complement its present business.

2. When it can leverage existing competencies and capabilities by expanding into industries where these same resource strengths are valuable competitive assets.

3. When diversifying into closely related businesses opens new avenues for reducing costs.

4. When it has a powerful and well-known brand name that can be transferred to the products of other businesses.

The decision to diversify presents wide-ranging possibilities. A company can diversify into closely related businesses or into totally unrelated businesses. It can diversify its present revenue and earning base to a small or major extent (such that new businesses produce 30 or more percent of revenues and profits). It can move into one or two large new businesses or a greater number of small ones. It can achieve diversification by acquiring an existing company, starting up a new business subsidiary from scratch, or forming a joint venture with one or more companies to enter new businesses.

---

[1] For a further discussion of when diversification makes good strategic sense, see Constantinos C. Markides, "To Diversify or Not to Diversify," *Harvard Business Review* 75, no. 6 (November–December 1997), pp. 93–99.

Building Shareholder Value: The Ultimate Justification for Business Diversification

Diversification must do more for a company than simply spread its business risk across various industries. In principle, diversification cannot be considered a success unless it results in *added shareholder value*—value that shareholders cannot capture on their own by spreading their investments across the stocks of companies in different industries.

Business diversification stands little chance of building shareholder value without passing the following three tests:[2]

1. *The industry attractiveness test*—The industry to be entered through diversification must offer an opportunity for profits and return on investment that is equal to or better than that of the company's present business(es).

2. *The cost-of-entry test*—The cost to enter the target industry must not be so high as to erode the potential for good profitability. A catch-22 can prevail here, however. The more attractive an industry's prospects are for growth and good long-term profitability, the more expensive it can be to enter. It's easy for acquisitions of companies in highly attractive industries to fail the cost-of-entry test.

3. *The better-off test*—Diversifying into a new business must offer potential for the company's existing businesses and the new business to perform better together under a single corporate umbrella than they would perform operating as independent, standalone businesses. For example, let's say that company A diversifies by purchasing company B in another industry. If A and B's consolidated profits in the years to come prove no greater than what each could have earned on its own, then A's diversification won't provide its shareholders with added value. Company A's shareholders could have achieved the same $1 + 1 = 2$ result by merely purchasing stock in company B. Shareholder value is not created by diversification unless it produces a $1 + 1 = 3$ effect.

Diversification moves that satisfy all three tests have the greatest potential to grow shareholder value over the long term. Diversification moves that can pass only one or two tests are suspect.

Approaches to Diversifying the Business Lineup

The means of entering new industries and lines of business can take any of three forms: acquisition, internal start-up, or joint ventures with other companies.

Diversification by Acquisition of an Existing Business

Acquisition is the most popular means of diversifying into another industry. Not only is it quicker than trying to launch a brand new operation, but it also

---

[2] Michael E. Porter, "From Competitive Advantage to Corporate Strategy," *Harvard Business Review* 45, no. 3 (May–June 1987), pp. 46–49.

offers an effective way to hurdle such entry barriers as acquiring technological know-how, establishing supplier relationships, achieving scale economies, building brand awareness, and securing adequate distribution. Buying an ongoing operation allows the acquirer to move directly to the task of building a strong market position in the target industry, rather than getting bogged down in the fine points of launching a start-up.

The big dilemma an acquisition-minded firm faces is whether to pay a premium price for a successful company or to buy a struggling company at a bargain price.[3] If the buying firm has little knowledge of the industry but has ample capital, it is often better off purchasing a capable, strongly positioned firm—unless the price of such an acquisition is prohibitive and flunks the cost-of-entry test. However, when the acquirer sees promising ways to transform a weak firm into a strong one, a struggling company can be the better long-term investment.

Entering a New Line of Business through Internal Start-Up

Achieving diversification through *internal start-up* involves building a new business subsidiary from scratch. Generally, forming a start-up subsidiary to enter a new business has appeal only when (1) the parent company already has in-house most or all of the skills and resources needed to compete effectively; (2) there is ample time to launch the business; (3) internal entry has lower costs than entry via acquisition; (4) the targeted industry is populated with many relatively small firms such that the new start-up does not have to compete against large, powerful rivals; (5) adding new production capacity will not adversely impact the supply–demand balance in the industry; and (6) incumbent firms are likely to be slow or ineffective in responding to a new entrant's efforts to crack the market.[4]

Using Joint Ventures to Achieve Diversification

A joint venture to enter a new business can be useful in at least two types of situations.[5] First, a joint venture is a good vehicle for pursuing an opportunity that is too complex, uneconomical, or risky for one company to pursue alone. Second, joint ventures make sense when the opportunities in a new industry require a broader range of competencies and know-how than an expansion-minded company can marshal. Many of the opportunities in biotechnology call for the coordinated development of complementary innovations and tackling an intricate web of technical, political, and regulatory factors simultaneously. In such cases, pooling the resources and competencies of two or more companies is a wiser and less risky way to proceed.

---

[3] Michael E. Porter, *Competitive Strategy: Techniques for Analyzing Industries and Competitors* (New York: Free Press, 1980), pp. 354–55.

[4] Ibid., pp. 344–45.

[5] Yves L. Doz and Gary Hamel, *Alliance Advantage: The Art of Creating Value through Partnering* (Boston: Harvard Business School Press, 1998), Chapters 1 and 2.

However, as discussed in Chapters 3 and 8, partnering with another company—either in the form of a joint venture or collaborative alliance—has significant drawbacks due to the potential for conflicting objectives, disagreements over how to best operate the venture, culture clashes, and so on. Joint ventures are generally the least durable of the entry options, usually lasting only until the partners decide to go their own ways.

Defining the Corporate Strategy: Diversification into Related or Unrelated Businesses?

Once a company decides to diversify, its first big corporate strategy decision is whether to diversify into **related businesses, unrelated businesses,** or some mix of both (see Figure 9.1). *Businesses are said to be related when their value chains possess competitively valuable cross-business relationships.* These value chain matchups present opportunities for the businesses to perform better under the same corporate umbrella than they could by operating as standalone entities. *Businesses are said to be unrelated when the activities comprising their respective value chains are so dissimilar that no competitively valuable cross-business relationships are present.*

The next two sections explore the ins and outs of related and unrelated diversification.

FIGURE 9.1 **Strategic Themes of Multibusiness Corporations**

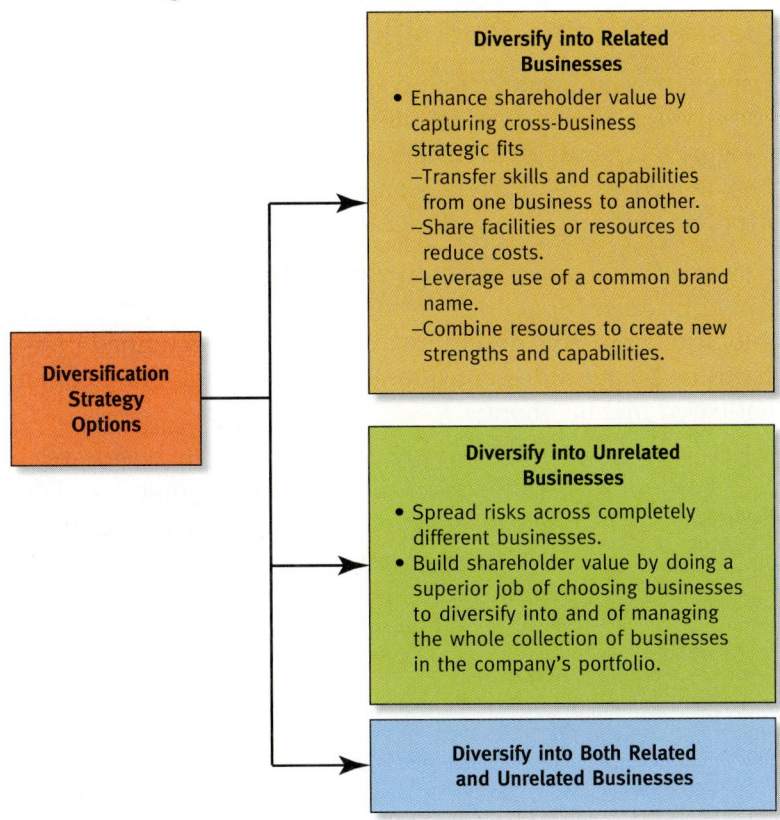

FIGURE 9.2 **Related Diversification Is Built Upon Competitively Valuable Strategic Fits in Value Chain Activities**

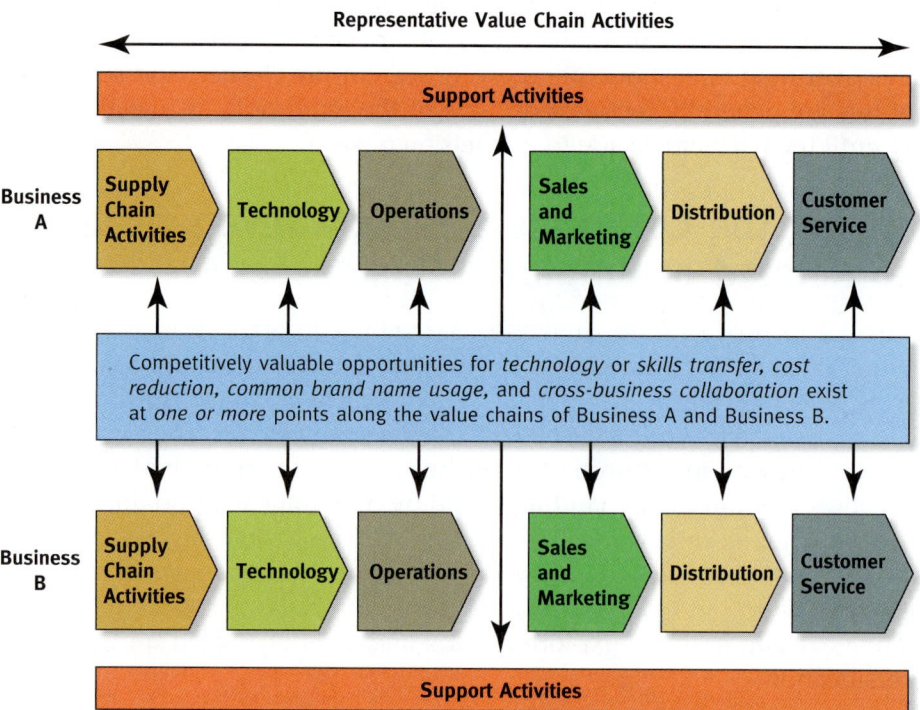

The Appeal of Related Diversification

A related diversification strategy involves building the company around businesses whose value chains possess competitively valuable strategic fits, as shown in Figure 9.2. **Strategic fit** exists whenever one or more activities comprising the value chains of different businesses are sufficiently similar to present opportunities for:[6]

- *Skills transfer* involving competitively valuable expertise, technological know-how, or other capabilities from one business to another. Google's technological know-how and innovation capabilities refined in its Internet search business have aided considerably in the development of an Internet-based mobile phone.

- *Cost sharing* between separate businesses where value chain activities can be combined. For example, diversified consumer products companies such as Unilever can use the same warehouses for shipping and distributing its oral care products, detergents, skin care products, and packaged foods.

[6] Michael E. Porter, *Competitive Advantage* (New York: Free Press, 1985), pp. 318–19 and pp. 337–53; and Porter, "From Competitive Advantage to Corporate Strategy," pp. 53–57. For an empirical study confirming that strategic fits are capable of enhancing performance (provided the resulting resource strengths are competitively valuable and difficult to duplicate by rivals), see Constantinos C. Markides and Peter J. Williamson, "Corporate Diversification and Organization Structure: A Resource-Based View," *Academy of Management Journal* 39, no. 2 (April 1996), pp. 340–67.

- *Brand sharing* between business units that have common customers or drawing upon common core competencies. For example, Honda's name in automobiles and motorcycles gave it instant credibility and recognition when entering the marine engine business and the powered lawn and garden equipment business.

Cross-business strategic fits can exist anywhere along the value chain—in R&D and technology activities, in supply chain activities, in manufacturing, in sales and marketing, or in distribution activities. Likewise, different businesses can often use the same administrative and customer service infrastructure. For instance, a cable operator that diversifies as a broadband provider can use the same customer data network, the same customer call centers and local offices, the same billing and customer accounting systems, and the same customer service infrastructure to support all of its products and services.[7]

STRATEGIC FIT AND ECONOMIES OF SCOPE   Strategic fit in the value chain activities of a diversified corporation's different businesses opens up opportunities for economies of scope—a concept distinct from *economies of scale*. Economies of *scale* are cost savings that accrue directly from a larger-sized operation; for example, unit costs may be lower in a large plant than in a small plant. Economies of *scope*, however, stem directly from cost-saving strategic fits along the value chains of related businesses. Such economies are open only to a multibusiness enterprise and are the result of a related diversification strategy that allows sibling businesses to share technology, perform R&D together, use common manufacturing or distribution facilities, share a common salesforce or distributor/dealer network, and/or share the same administrative infrastructure. *The greater the cross-business economies associated with cost-saving strategic fits, the greater the potential for a related diversification strategy to yield a competitive advantage based on lower costs than rivals.*

THE ABILITY OF RELATED DIVERSIFICATION TO DELIVER COMPETITIVE ADVANTAGE AND GAINS IN SHAREHOLDER VALUE   Economies of scope and the other strategic-fit benefits provide a dependable basis for earning higher profits and returns than what a diversified company's businesses could earn as standalone enterprises. Converting the competitive advantage potential into greater profitability is what fuels $1 + 1 = 3$ gains in shareholder value—the necessary outcome for satisfying the *better-off test*. There are three things to bear in mind here: (1) capturing cross-business strategic fits via related diversification builds shareholder value in ways that shareholders cannot replicate by simply owning a diversified portfolio of stocks; (2) the capture of cross-business strategic-fit benefits is possible only through related diversification; and (3) the benefits of

---

[7] For a discussion of the strategic significance of cross-business coordination of value chain activities and insight into how the process works, see Jeanne M. Liedtka, "Collaboration across Lines of Business for Competitive Advantage," *Academy of Management Executive* 10, no. 2 (May 1996), pp. 20–34.

cross-business strategic fits are not automatically realized—*the benefits materialize only after management has successfully pursued internal actions to capture them.*[8]

Diversifying into Unrelated Businesses

An unrelated diversification strategy discounts the importance of the *better-off test* and, instead, is focused on entering *attractive* industries where the *cost of entry* allows for acceptable returns on investment. *The basic premise of unrelated diversification is that any company or business that can be acquired on good financial terms and that has satisfactory growth and earnings potential represents a good business opportunity.* A corporate strategy based upon unrelated diversification makes no deliberate effort to capture strategic-fit opportunities between the value chains of the firm's various businesses.

Thus, with an unrelated diversification strategy, company managers spend much time and effort screening acquisition candidates and evaluating the pros and cons of keeping or divesting existing businesses, using such criteria as:

- Whether the business can meet corporate targets for profitability and return on investment.
- Whether the business is in an industry with attractive growth potential.
- Whether the business is big enough to contribute *significantly* to the parent firm's bottom line.
- Whether the business has burdensome capital requirements.
- Whether there is industry vulnerability to recession, inflation, high interest rates, tough government regulations concerning product safety or the environment, and other potentially negative factors.

Companies that pursue unrelated diversification nearly always enter new businesses by acquiring an established company rather than by forming a start-up. The premise of acquisition-minded corporations is that growth by acquisition can deliver enhanced shareholder value through upward-trending corporate revenues and earnings and a stock price that *on average* rises enough year after year to amply reward and please shareholders. Three types of acquisition candidates are usually of particular interest: (1) businesses that have bright growth prospects but are short on investment capital, (2) undervalued companies that can be acquired at a bargain price, and (3) struggling companies whose operations can be turned around with the aid of the parent company's financial resources and managerial know-how.

[8] For a discussion of what is involved in actually capturing strategic-fit benefits, see Kathleen M. Eisenhardt and D. Charles Galunic, "Coevolving: At Last, a Way to Make Synergies Work," *Harvard Business Review* 78, no. 1 (January–February 2000), pp. 91–101. Adeptness at capturing cross-business strategic fit positively impacts performance; see Constantinos C. Markides and Peter J. Williamson, "Related Diversification, Core Competencies and Corporate Performance," *Strategic Management Journal* 15 (Summer 1994), pp. 149–65.

Unrelated Diversification, Revenue and Earnings Growth, and Risk Reduction

A strategy of unrelated diversification is suggested to offer growth and reduced risk because of the following factors:

1. Business risk is scattered over a set of truly *diverse* industries. In comparison to related diversification, unrelated diversification more closely approximates *pure* diversification of financial and business risk because the company's investments are spread over businesses whose technologies and value chain activities bear no close relationship and whose markets are largely disconnected.[9]

2. The company's financial resources can be employed to maximum advantage by investing in *whatever industries* offer the best profit prospects (as opposed to considering only opportunities in industries with related value chain activities).

3. To the extent that corporate managers are exceptionally astute at spotting bargain-priced companies with big upside profit potential, shareholder wealth can be enhanced by buying distressed businesses at a low price, turning their operations around fairly quickly, and then enjoying a high return on investment on the newly acquired businesses.

4. Company profitability may prove somewhat less volatile over the course of economic upswings and downswings because market conditions in all industries don't move upward or downward simultaneously. In a broadly diversified company, there's a chance that market downtrends in some of the company's businesses will be partially offset by cyclical upswings in its other businesses. (In actual practice, however, there's no convincing evidence that the consolidated profits of firms with unrelated diversification strategies are more stable in periods of recession and economic stress than the profits of firms with related diversification strategies.)

Unrelated diversification certainly merits consideration when a firm is trapped in or overly dependent on an endangered or unattractive industry. Diversification into industries with closely related value chains might compound the effect of looming industry downturns on shareholder value.

BUILDING SHAREHOLDER VALUE THROUGH UNRELATED DIVERSIFICATION   Given the absence of cross-business strategic fits with which to capture added competitive advantage, the task of building shareholder value via unrelated diversification ultimately hinges on the business

---

[9] While the argument that unrelated diversification is a superior way to diversify financial risk has logical appeal, research shows that related diversification is less risky from a financial perspective than is unrelated diversification; see Michael Lubatkin and Sayan Chatterjee, "Extending Modern Portfolio Theory into the Domain of Corporate Diversification: Does It Apply?" *Academy of Management Journal* 37, no. 1 (February 1994), pp. 109–36.

acumen of corporate executives. To succeed with a corporate strategy keyed to unrelated diversification, corporate executives must:

- Do a superior job of identifying and acquiring new businesses that can produce consistently good earnings and returns on investment (thereby satisfying the attractiveness test).
- Do an excellent job of negotiating favorable acquisition prices (thereby satisfying the cost-of-entry test).
- Be shrewd in identifying when to shift resources out of businesses with dim profit prospects and into businesses with above-average prospects for growth and profitability.
- Be good at discerning when a business needs to be sold (because it is on the verge of confronting adverse industry and competitive conditions and probable declines in long-term profitability) and also finding buyers who will pay a price higher than the company's net investment in the business.

A case can be made that shareholder value has truly been enhanced if corporate executives are able to craft and execute a strategy of unrelated diversification that produces enough of the above outcomes to result in a greater than $1 + 1 = 2$ outcome.

The Pitfalls of Unrelated Diversification

Unrelated diversification strategies have two important negatives that undercut the pluses: very demanding managerial requirements and limited competitive advantage potential.

DEMANDING MANAGERIAL REQUIREMENTS Successfully managing a set of fundamentally different businesses operating in fundamentally different industry and competitive environments is an exceptionally difficult proposition for corporate-level managers. The greater the number of businesses a company is in and the more diverse they are, the more difficult it is for corporate managers to:

1. Stay abreast of what's happening in each industry and each subsidiary.
2. Pick business-unit heads having the requisite combination of managerial skills and know-how to drive gains in performance.
3. Be able to tell the difference between those strategic proposals of business-unit managers that are prudent and those that are risky or unlikely to succeed.
4. Know what to do if a business unit stumbles and its results suddenly head downhill.[10]

In a broadly diversified company like General Electric, corporate executives are challenged to stay abreast of industry developments and the strategic progress of each subsidiary, often depending on financial reports and briefings by business-level managers for many of the details. As a rule, the more

---

[10] For a review of the experiences of companies that have pursued unrelated diversification successfully, see Patricia L. Anslinger and Thomas E. Copeland, "Growth through Acquisitions: A Fresh Look," *Harvard Business Review* 74, no. 1 (January–February 1996), pp. 126–35.

unrelated businesses that a company has diversified into, the more corporate executives are forced to "manage by the numbers"—that is, keeping a close track on the financial and operating results of each subsidiary and assuming that the heads of the various subsidiaries have most everything under control so long as the latest key financial and operating measures look good.

> **Unrelated diversification** requires that corporate executives rely on the skills and expertise of business-level managers to build competitive advantage and boost the performance of individual businesses.

Managing by the numbers works okay if the heads of the various business units are quite capable and consistently meet their numbers. But the problem comes when things start to go awry and corporate management has to get deeply involved in turning around a business it does not know much about. As the former chairman of a Fortune 500 company advised, "Never acquire a business you don't know how to run."

Competently overseeing a set of widely diverse businesses can turn out to be much harder than it sounds. In practice, comparatively few companies have proved that they have top management capabilities that are up to the task. There are far more companies whose corporate executives have failed at delivering consistently good financial results with an unrelated diversification strategy than there are companies with corporate executives who have been successful.[11] The odds are that the result of unrelated diversification will be $1 + 1 = 2$ or less.

LIMITED COMPETITIVE ADVANTAGE POTENTIAL   The second big negative associated with unrelated diversification is that such a strategy *offers no potential for competitive advantage beyond what each individual business can generate on its own.* Unlike a related diversification strategy, there are no cross-business strategic fits to draw on for reducing costs, transferring skills and technology, or leveraging use of a powerful brand name and thereby adding to the competitive advantage possessed by individual businesses. *Without the competitive advantage potential of strategic fits, consolidated performance of an unrelated group of businesses is no better than the sum of what the individual business units could achieve independently.*

Corporate Strategies Combining Related and Unrelated Diversification

There's nothing to preclude a company from diversifying into both related and unrelated businesses. Indeed, the business makeup of diversified companies varies considerably. Some diversified companies are really *dominant-business enterprises*—one major "core" business accounts for 50 to 80 percent of total revenues and a collection of small related or unrelated businesses accounts for the remainder. Some diversified companies are *narrowly diversified* around a few (two to five) related or unrelated businesses. Others are *broadly diversified* around a wide-ranging collection of related businesses, unrelated businesses,

---

[11] For research evidence of broad diversification failure and the trend of companies to focus their diversification efforts more narrowly, see Lawrence G. Franko, "The Death of Diversification? The Focusing of the World's Industrial Firms, 1980–2000," *Business Horizons* 47, no. 4 (July–August 2004), pp. 41–50.

or a mixture of both. And a number of multibusiness enterprises have diversified into *several unrelated groups of related businesses.* There's ample room for companies to customize their diversification strategies to incorporate elements of both related and unrelated diversification.

Evaluating the Corporate Strategy of a Diversified Company

L04

Understand the process for evaluating a company's diversification strategy.

Strategic analysis of diversified companies builds on the methodology used for single-business companies but utilizes tools that streamline the overall process. The procedure for evaluating the pluses and minuses of a diversified company's strategy and deciding what actions to take to improve the company's performance involves six steps:

1. Assessing the attractiveness of the industries the company has diversified into.
2. Assessing the competitive strength of the company's business units.
3. Evaluating the extent of cross-business strategic fits along the value chains of the company's various business units.
4. Checking whether the firm's resources fit the requirements of its present business lineup.
5. Ranking the performance prospects of the businesses from best to worst and determining a priority for allocating resources.
6. Crafting new strategic moves to improve overall corporate performance.

The core concepts and analytical techniques underlying each of these steps are discussed further in this section of the chapter.

Step 1: Evaluating Industry Attractiveness

A principal consideration in evaluating the caliber of a diversified company's strategy is the attractiveness of the industries in which it has business operations. The more attractive the industries (both individually and as a group) a diversified company is in, the better its prospects for good long-term performance. A simple and reliable analytical tool for gauging industry attractiveness involves calculating quantitative industry attractiveness scores based upon the following measures.

- *Market size and projected growth rate*—Big industries are more attractive than small industries, and fast-growing industries tend to be more attractive than slow-growing industries, other things being equal.
- *The intensity of competition*—Industries where competitive pressures are relatively weak are more attractive than industries with strong competitive pressures.
- *Emerging opportunities and threats*—Industries with promising opportunities and minimal threats on the near horizon are more attractive than industries with modest opportunities and imposing threats.

- *The presence of cross-industry strategic fits*—The more the industry's value chain and resource requirements match up well with the value chain activities of other industries in which the company has operations, the more attractive the industry is to a firm pursuing related diversification. However, cross-industry strategic fits may be of no consequence to a company committed to a strategy of unrelated diversification.

- *Resource requirements*—Industries having resource requirements within the company's reach are more attractive than industries where capital and other resource requirements could strain corporate financial resources and organizational capabilities.

- *Seasonal and cyclical factors*—Industries where buyer demand is relatively steady year-round and not unduly vulnerable to economic ups and downs tend to be more attractive than industries with wide seasonal or cyclical swings in buyer demand.

- *Social, political, regulatory, and environmental factors*—Industries with significant problems in such areas as consumer health, safety, or environmental pollution or that are subject to intense regulation are less attractive than industries where such problems are not burning issues.

- *Industry profitability*—Industries with healthy profit margins are generally more attractive than industries where profits have historically been low or unstable.

- *Industry uncertainty and business risk*—Industries with less uncertainty on the horizon and lower overall business risk are more attractive than industries whose prospects for one reason or another are quite uncertain.

Each attractiveness measure should be assigned a weight reflecting its relative importance in determining an industry's attractiveness—it is weak methodology to assume that the various attractiveness measures are equally important. The intensity of competition in an industry should nearly always carry a high weight (say, 0.20 to 0.30). Strategic-fit considerations should be assigned a high weight in the case of companies with related diversification strategies; but, for companies with an unrelated diversification strategy, strategic fits with other industries may be given a low weight or even dropped from the list of attractiveness measures altogether. Seasonal and cyclical factors generally are assigned a low weight (or maybe even eliminated from the analysis) unless a company has diversified into industries strongly characterized by seasonal demand and/or heavy vulnerability to cyclical upswings and downswings. The importance weights must add up to 1.0.

Next, each industry is rated on each of the chosen industry attractiveness measures, using a rating scale of 1 to 10 (where 10 signifies *high* attractiveness and 1 signifies *low* attractiveness). Weighted attractiveness scores are then calculated by multiplying the industry's rating on each measure by the corresponding weight. For example, a rating of 8 times a weight of 0.25 gives a weighted attractiveness score of 2.00. The sum of the weighted scores for all the attractiveness measures provides an overall industry attractiveness score. This procedure is illustrated in Table 9.1.

Table 9.1

Calculating Weighted Industry Attractiveness Scores

[Rating scale: 1 = Very unattractive to company; 10 = Very attractive to company]

INDUSTRY ATTRACTIVENESS MEASURE	IMPORTANCE WEIGHT	INDUSTRY A RATING/SCORE	INDUSTRY B RATING/SCORE	INDUSTRY C RATING/SCORE	INDUSTRY D RATING/SCORE
Market size and projected growth rate	0.10	8/0.80	5/0.50	7/0.70	3/0.30
Intensity of competition	0.25	8/2.00	7/1.75	3/0.75	2/0.50
Emerging opportunities and threats	0.10	2/0.20	9/0.90	4/0.40	5/0.50
Cross-industry strategic fits	0.20	8/1.60	4/0.80	8/1.60	2/0.40
Resource requirements	0.10	9/0.90	7/0.70	10/1.00	5/0.50
Seasonal and cyclical influences	0.05	9/0.45	8/0.40	10/0.50	5/0.25
Societal, political, regulatory, and environmental factors	0.05	10/1.00	7/0.70	7/0.70	3/0.30
Industry profitability	0.10	5/0.50	10/1.00	3/0.30	3/0.30
Industry uncertainty and business risk	0.05	5/0.25	7/0.35	10/0.50	1/0.05
Sum of the assigned weights	1.00				
Overall weighted industry attractiveness scores		**7.70**	**7.10**	**5.45**	**3.10**

CALCULATING INDUSTRY ATTRACTIVENESS SCORES   There are two necessary conditions for producing valid industry attractiveness scores using this method. One is deciding on appropriate weights for the industry attractiveness measures. This is not always an easy task because different analysts have different views about which weights are most appropriate. Also, different weightings may be appropriate for different companies—based on their strategies, performance targets, and financial circumstances. For instance, placing a low weight on industry resource requirements may be justifiable for a cash-rich company, whereas a high weight may be more appropriate for a financially strapped company.

The second requirement for creating accurate attractiveness scores is to have sufficient knowledge to rate the industry on each attractiveness measure. It's usually rather easy to locate statistical data needed to compare industries on market size, growth rate, seasonal and cyclical influences, and industry profitability. Cross-industry fits and resource requirements are also fairly easy to judge. But the attractiveness measure that is toughest to rate is that of intensity of competition. It is not always easy to conclude whether competition in one industry is stronger or weaker than in another industry. In the event that the available information is too skimpy to confidently assign a rating value to an industry on a particular attractiveness measure, then it is usually best to use a score of 5, which avoids biasing the overall attractiveness score either up or down.

Despite the hurdles, calculating industry attractiveness scores is a systematic and reasonably reliable method for ranking a diversified company's industries from most to least attractive.

Step 2: Evaluating Business-Unit Competitive Strength

The second step in evaluating a diversified company is to determine how strongly positioned each of its business units are in their respective industries. Doing an appraisal of each business unit's strength and competitive position in its industry not only reveals its chances for industry success but also provides a basis for ranking the units from competitively strongest to weakest. Quantitative measures of each business unit's competitive strength can be calculated using a procedure similar to that for measuring industry attractiveness. The following factors may be used in quantifying the competitive strengths of a diversified company's business subsidiaries:

- *Relative market share*—A business unit's *relative market share* is defined as the ratio of its market share to the market share held by the largest rival firm in the industry, with market share measured in unit volume, not dollars. For instance, if business A has a market-leading share of 40 percent and its largest rival has 30 percent, A's relative market share is 1.33. If business B has a 15 percent market share and B's largest rival has 30 percent, B's relative market share is 0.5.

- *Costs relative to competitors' costs*—There's reason to expect that business units with higher relative market shares have lower unit costs than competitors with lower relative market shares because of the possibility of scale economies and experience or learning-curve effects. Another indicator of low cost can be a business unit's supply chain management capabilities.

- *Products or services that satisfy buyer expectations*—A company's competitiveness depends in part on being able to offer buyers appealing features, performance, reliability, and service attributes.

- *Ability to benefit from strategic fits with sibling businesses*—Strategic fits with other businesses within the company enhance a business unit's competitive strength and may provide a competitive edge.

- *Number and caliber of strategic alliances and collaborative partnerships*—Well-functioning alliances and partnerships may be a source of potential competitive advantage and thus add to a business's competitive strength.

- *Brand image and reputation*—A strong brand name is a valuable competitive asset in most industries.

- *Competitively valuable capabilities*—All industries contain a variety of important competitive capabilities related to product innovation, production capabilities, distribution capabilities, or marketing prowess.

- *Profitability relative to competitors*—Above-average returns on investment and large profit margins relative to rivals are usually accurate indicators of competitive advantage.

After settling on a set of competitive strength measures that are well matched to the circumstances of the various business units, weights indicating each measure's importance need to be assigned. As in the assignment of weights to industry attractiveness measures, the importance weights must add up to 1.0. Each business unit is then rated on each of the chosen strength measures,

Table 9.2

Calculating Weighted Competitive Strength Scores for A Diversified Company's Business Units

[Rating scale: 1 = Very weak; 10 = Very strong]

COMPETITIVE STRENGTH MEASURE	IMPORTANCE/ WEIGHT	BUSINESS A IN INDUSTRY A RATING/SCORE	BUSINESS B IN INDUSTRY B RATING/SCORE	BUSINESS C IN INDUSTRY C RATING/SCORE	BUSINESS D IN INDUSTRY D RATING/SCORE
Relative market share	0.15	10/1.50	1/0.15	6/0.90	2/0.30
Costs relative to competitors' costs	0.20	7/1.40	2/0.40	5/1.00	3/0.60
Ability to match or beat rivals on key product attributes	0.05	9/0.45	4/0.20	8/0.40	4/0.20
Ability to benefit from strategic fits with sibling businesses	0.20	8/1.60	4/0.80	8/0.80	2/0.60
Bargaining leverage with suppliers/ buyers; caliber of alliances	0.05	9/0.90	3/0.30	6/0.30	2/0.10
Brand image and reputation	0.10	9/0.90	2/0.20	7/0.70	5/0.50
Competitively valuable capabilities	0.15	7/1.05	2/0.20	5/0.75	3/0.45
Profitability relative to competitors	0.10	5/0.50	1/0.10	4/0.40	4/0.40
Sum of the assigned weights	1.00				
Overall weighted competitive strength scores		**8.30**	**2.35**	**5.25**	**3.15**

using a rating scale of 1 to 10 (where 10 signifies competitive *strength* and a 1 rating signifies competitive *weakness*). In the event that the available information is too skimpy to confidently assign a rating value to a business unit on a particular strength measure, then it is usually best to use a score of 5. Weighted strength ratings are calculated by multiplying the business unit's rating on each strength measure by the assigned weight. For example, a strength score of 6 times a weight of 0.15 gives a weighted strength rating of 0.90. The sum of weighted ratings across all the strength measures provides a quantitative measure of a business unit's overall market strength and competitive standing. Table 9.2 provides sample calculations of competitive strength ratings for 4 businesses.

USING A NINE-CELL MATRIX TO EVALUATE THE STRENGTH OF A DIVERSIFIED COMPANY'S BUSINESS LINEUP   The industry attractiveness and business strength scores can be used to portray the strategic positions of each business in a diversified company. Industry attractiveness is plotted on the vertical axis, and competitive strength on the horizontal axis. A nine-cell grid emerges from dividing the vertical axis into three regions (high, medium, and low attractiveness) and the horizontal axis into three regions (strong, average, and weak competitive strength). As shown in Figure 9.3, high attractiveness is associated with scores of 6.7 or greater on a rating scale of 1 to 10, medium attractiveness to scores of 3.3 to 6.7, and low attractiveness to scores below 3.3. Likewise, high competitive strength is defined as a score greater than 6.7, average strength as scores of 3.3 to 6.7, and low strength as

FIGURE 9.3   **A Nine-Cell Industry Attractiveness–Competitive Strength Matrix**

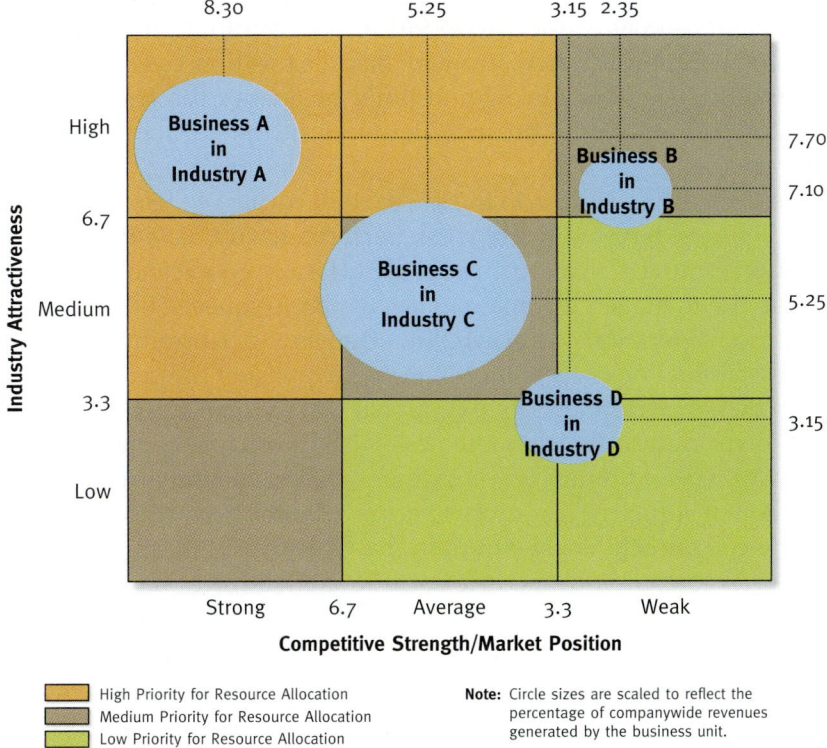

scores below 3.3. *Each business unit is plotted on the nine-cell matrix according to its overall attractiveness and strength scores, and then shown as a "bubble."* The size of each bubble is scaled to what percentage of revenues the business generates relative to total corporate revenues. The bubbles in Figure 9.3 were located on the grid using the four industry attractiveness scores from Table 9.1 and the strength scores for the four business units in Table 9.2.

The locations of the business units on the attractiveness–strength matrix provide valuable guidance in deploying corporate resources. In general, *a diversified company's best prospects for good overall performance involve concentrating corporate resources on business units having the greatest competitive strength and industry attractiveness.* Businesses plotted in the three cells in the upper left portion of the attractiveness–strength matrix have both favorable industry attractiveness and competitive strength and should receive a high investment priority. Business units plotted in these three cells (such as business A in Figure 9.3) are referred to as "grow and build" businesses because of their capability to drive future increases in shareholder value.

Next in priority come businesses positioned in the three diagonal cells stretching from the lower left to the upper right (businesses B and C in Figure 9.3). Such businesses usually merit medium or intermediate priority in the parent's resource allocation ranking. However, some businesses in the medium-priority diagonal cells may have brighter or dimmer prospects than others. For example, a small business in the upper right cell of the matrix (like business B), despite being in a highly attractive industry, may occupy too weak a competitive position in its industry to justify the investment and resources needed to turn it into a strong market contender. If, however, a business in the upper right cell has attractive opportunities for rapid growth and a good potential for winning a much stronger market position over time, management may designate it as a grow-and-build business—the strategic objective here would be to move the business leftward in the attractiveness–strength matrix over time.

Businesses in the three cells in the lower right corner of the matrix (like business D in Figure 9.3) typically are weak performers and have the lowest claim on corporate resources. Such businesses are typically good candidates for being divested or else managed in a manner calculated to squeeze out the maximum cash flows from operations. The cash flows from low-performing/low-potential businesses can then be diverted to financing expansion of business units with greater market opportunities. In exceptional cases where a business located in the three lower right cells is nonetheless fairly profitable or has the potential for good earnings and return on investment, the business merits retention and the allocation of sufficient resources to achieve better performance.

The nine-cell attractiveness–strength matrix provides clear, strong logic for why a diversified company needs to consider both industry attractiveness and business strength in allocating resources and investment capital to its different businesses. A good case can be made for concentrating resources in those businesses that enjoy higher degrees of attractiveness and competitive strength, being very selective in making investments in businesses with intermediate positions on the grid, and withdrawing resources from businesses that are lower in attractiveness and strength unless they offer exceptional profit or cash flow potential.

Step 3: Determining the Competitive Value of Strategic Fits in Multibusiness Companies

The greater the value of cross-business strategic fits in enhancing a company's performance in the marketplace or the bottom line, the more powerful is its strategy of unrelated diversification.

The potential for competitively important strategic fits is central to making conclusions about the effectiveness of a company's related diversification strategy. This step can be bypassed for diversified companies whose businesses are all unrelated (because, by design, no strategic fits are present). Checking the competitive advantage potential of cross-business strategic fits involves evaluating how much benefit a diversified company can gain from value chain matchups that present:

1. Opportunities to combine the performance of certain activities, thereby reducing costs and capturing economies of scope.

2. Opportunities to transfer skills, technology, or intellectual capital from one business to another.

3. Opportunities to share use of a well-respected brand name across multiple product and/or service categories.

But more than just strategic fit identification is needed. The real test is what competitive value can be generated from these fits. To what extent can cost savings be realized? How much competitive value will come from cross-business transfer of skills, technology, or intellectual capital? Will transferring a potent brand name to the products of sibling businesses grow sales significantly? Absent significant strategic fits and dedicated company efforts to capture the benefits, one has to be skeptical about the potential for a diversified company's businesses to perform better together than apart.

Step 4: Evaluating the Sufficiency of Corporate Resources in Diversified Companies

The businesses in a diversified company's lineup need to exhibit good resource fit. Resource fit exists when (1) businesses, individually, add to a company's collective resource strengths and (2) a company has sufficient resources to support its entire group of businesses without spreading itself too thin. One important dimension of resource fit concerns whether a diversified company can generate the internal cash flows sufficient to fund the capital requirements of its businesses, pay its dividends, meet its debt obligations, and otherwise remain financially healthy.

FINANCIAL RESOURCE FITS: CASH COWS VERSUS CASH HOGS Different businesses have different cash flow and investment characteristics. For example, business units in rapidly growing industries are often **cash hogs**—so labeled because the cash flows they are able to generate from internal operations aren't big enough to fund their expansion. To keep pace with rising buyer demand, rapid-growth businesses frequently need sizable annual capital infusions—for new facilities and equipment, for technology improvements, and for additional working capital to support inventory expansion. Because a cash hog's financial resources must be provided by the corporate parent, corporate managers have to decide whether it makes good financial and strategic sense to keep pouring new money into a cash hog business.

> A **cash hog** generates operating cash flows that are too small to fully fund its operations and growth; a cash hog must receive cash infusions from outside sources to cover its working capital and investment requirements.

In contrast, business units with leading market positions in mature industries may, however, be **cash cows**—businesses that generate substantial cash surpluses over what is needed to adequately fund their operations. Market leaders in slow-growth industries often generate sizable positive cash flows *over and above what is needed for growth and reinvestment* because the slow-growth nature of their industry often entails relatively modest annual investment requirements. Cash cows, though not always attractive from a growth standpoint, are valuable businesses from a financial resource perspective. The surplus cash flows they generate can be used to pay corporate dividends, finance acquisitions, and provide funds for investing in the company's promising cash hogs. It makes good financial and strategic sense for diversified companies to keep cash cows in healthy condition, fortifying and defending their market position to preserve their cash-generating

> A **cash cow** generates operating cash flows over and above its internal requirements, thereby providing financial resources that may be used to invest in cash hogs, finance new acquisitions, fund share buyback programs, or pay dividends.

capability over the long term and thereby have an ongoing source of financial resources to deploy elsewhere.

A diversified company has good financial resource fit when the excess cash generated by its cash cow businesses is sufficient to fund the investment requirements of promising cash hog businesses. Ideally, investing in promising cash hog businesses over time results in growing the hogs into self-supporting *star businesses* that have strong or market-leading competitive positions in attractive, high-growth markets and high levels of profitability. Star businesses are often the cash cows of the future—when the markets of star businesses begin to mature and their growth slows, their competitive strength should produce self-generated cash flows more than sufficient to cover their investment needs. The "success sequence" is thus cash hog to young star (but perhaps still a cash hog) to self-supporting star to cash cow.

If, however, a cash hog has questionable promise (either because of low industry attractiveness or a weak competitive position), then it becomes a logical candidate for divestiture. Aggressively investing in a cash hog with an uncertain future seldom makes sense because it requires the corporate parent to keep pumping more capital into the business with only a dim hope of turning the cash hog into a future star. Such businesses are a financial drain and fail the resource fit test because they strain the corporate parent's ability to adequately fund its other businesses. Divesting a less attractive cash hog business is usually the best alternative unless (1) it has highly valuable strategic fits with other business units or (2) the capital infusions needed from the corporate parent are modest relative to the funds available, and (3) there's a decent chance of growing the business into a solid bottom-line contributor.

Aside from cash flow considerations, there are two other factors to consider in assessing the financial resource fit for businesses in a diversified firm's portfolio:

- *Do individual businesses adequately contribute to achieving companywide performance targets?* A business exhibits poor financial fit if it soaks up a disproportionate share of the company's financial resources, while making subpar or insignificant contributions to the bottom line. Too many underperforming businesses reduce the company's overall performance and ultimately limit growth in shareholder value.

- *Does the corporation have adequate financial strength to fund its different businesses and maintain a healthy credit rating?* A diversified company's strategy fails the resource fit test when the resource needs of its portfolio unduly stretch the company's financial health and threaten to impair its credit rating. Time Warner, Royal Ahold, and AT&T, for example, have found themselves so financially overextended that they had to sell off some of their business units to raise the money to pay down burdensome debt obligations and continue to fund essential capital expenditures for the remaining businesses.

EXAMINING A DIVERSIFIED COMPANY'S NONFINANCIAL RESOURCE FITS   Diversified companies must also ensure that the nonfinancial resource needs of its portfolio of businesses are met by its corporate capabilities. Just as a diversified company must avoid allowing an excessive number of cash hungry businesses to jeopardize its financial stability, it should also avoid adding to the business lineup in ways that overly stretch such nonfinancial resources as managerial talent, technology and information systems, and marketing support.

> **Resource fit** extends beyond financial resources to include a good fit between the company's resource strengths and competencies and the key success factors of each industry it has diversified into.

- *Does the company have or can it develop the specific resource strengths and competitive capabilities needed to be successful in each of its businesses?*[12] Sometimes the resource strengths a company has accumulated in its core business prove to be a poor match with the competitive capabilities needed to succeed in businesses into which it has diversified. For instance, BTR, a multibusiness company in Great Britain, discovered that the company's resources and managerial skills were quite well suited for parenting industrial manufacturing businesses but not for parenting its distribution businesses (National Tyre Services and Texas-based Summers Group); as a consequence, BTR decided to divest its distribution businesses and focus exclusively on diversifying around small industrial manufacturing.[13] Thus, a mismatch between the company's resource strengths and the key success factors in a particular business can be serious enough to warrant divesting an existing business or not acquiring a new business. In contrast, when a company's resources and capabilities are a good match with the key success factors of industries it is not presently in, it makes sense to take a hard look at acquiring companies in these industries.

- *Are recently acquired businesses acting to strengthen a company's resource base and competitive capabilities or are they causing its competitive and managerial resources to be stretched too thinly?* A diversified company has to guard against overtaxing its resource strengths, a condition that can arise when (1) it goes on an acquisition spree and management is called upon to assimilate and oversee many new businesses very quickly or (2) when it lacks sufficient resource depth to do a creditable job of transferring skills and competencies from one of its businesses to another.

Step 5: Ranking Business Units and Setting a Priority for Resource Allocation

Once a diversified company's strategy has been evaluated from the perspective of industry attractiveness, competitive strength, strategic fit, and resource fit, the next step is to rank the performance prospects of the businesses from best to worst. Once this ranking has been established, management is in a good position to decide which businesses merit top priority for resource support and new capital investments by the corporate parent. The most important considerations in settling on resource allocation decisions is examining

---

[12] For an excellent discussion of what to look for in assessing these fits, see Andrew Campbell, Michael Gould, and Marcus Alexander, "Corporate Strategy: The Quest for Parenting Advantage," *Harvard Business Review* 73, no. 2 (March–April 1995), pp. 120–32.

[13] Ibid., p. 128.

business units' past performance in terms of sales growth, profit growth, contribution to company earnings, cash flow characteristics, and return on capital invested in the business. While past performance is not necessarily a good predictor of future performance, it does signal whether a business already has good to excellent performance or has problems to overcome.

Furthermore, the industry attractiveness/business strength evaluations provide a solid basis for judging a business's future prospects. Normally, strong business units in attractive industries have significantly better prospects of turning in stellar results than weak businesses in unattractive industries. And, normally, the revenue and earnings outlook for businesses in fast-growing industries is better than for businesses in slow-growing industries. One important exception is when a strong business in a slow-growing industry continues to draw sales and market share away from its rivals and thus achieves faster growth than the industry as a whole. As a rule, the prior analyses, taken together, signal which business units are likely to be strong performers on the road ahead and which are likely to be laggards. The task here is to decide which business units should have top priority for corporate resource support and new capital investment and which should carry the lowest priority. *Business units with the brightest profit and growth prospects and solid strategic and resource fits generally should head the list for corporate resource support.*

Step 6: Crafting New Strategic Moves to Improve the Overall Corporate Performance

LO5

Recognize a diversified company's strategy options for improving its overall performance.

The conclusions flowing from the five preceding analytical steps set the agenda for crafting strategic moves to improve a diversified company's overall performance. The strategic options boil down to four broad categories of actions:

1. Sticking closely with the existing business lineup and pursuing the opportunities these businesses present.
2. Broadening the company's business scope by making new acquisitions in new industries.
3. Divesting certain businesses and retrenching to a narrower base of business operations.
4. Restructuring the company's business lineup and putting a whole new face on the company's business makeup.

The option of sticking with the current business lineup makes sense when the company's present businesses offer attractive growth opportunities and can be counted on to generate good earnings and cash flows. As long as the company's set of existing businesses puts it in a good position for the future and these businesses have good strategic and/or resource fits, then rocking the boat with major changes in the company's business mix is usually unnecessary. Corporate executives can concentrate their attention on getting the best performance from each of the businesses, steering corporate resources into those areas of greatest potential and profitability. However, in the event that corporate executives are not entirely satisfied with the opportunities they see in the company's present set of businesses, they can opt for any of the three strategic alternatives listed in the following sections.

Broadening the Diversification Base

Diversified companies sometimes find it desirable to add to the diversification base for any one of the same reasons a single business company might pursue initial diversification. Sluggish growth in revenues or profits, vulnerability to seasonality or recessionary influences, potential for transferring resources and capabilities to other related businesses, or unfavorable driving forces facing core businesses are all reasons management of a diversified company might choose to broaden diversification. An additional, and often very important, motivating factor for adding new businesses is to complement and strengthen the market position and competitive capabilities of one or more of its present businesses. Procter & Gamble's recent acquisition of Gillette strengthened and extended P&G's reach into personal care and household products. At the time of the acquisition P&G boasted a portfolio of 16 billion-dollar brands including Crest, Bounty, Charmin, Tide, Clairol, Ivory, and Folgers. Gillette's business portfolio included Gillette razors and razor blades, Oral-B toothbrushes, Duracell batteries, Braun shavers and small appliances (coffeemakers, mixers, hair dryers, and electric toothbrushes), and toiletries (Right Guard, Foamy, Soft & Dry, White Rain, and Dry Idea). The $57 billion acquisition of Gillette delivered five additional billion-dollar brands to Procter & Gamble's business mix and made it the worldwide leader in the market for razors and blades, alkaline batteries, manual and electric toothbrushes, and foil electric shavers. Some companies depend on new acquisitions to drive a major portion of their growth in revenues and earnings, and thus are always on the acquisition trail. Cisco Systems built itself into a worldwide leader in networking systems for the Internet by making nearly 100 technology-based acquisitions during 1993–2007 to extend its market reach from routing and switching into IP telephony, home networking, wireless LAN, storage networking, network security, broadband, and optical and broadband systems.

Retrenching to a Narrower Diversification Base

A number of diversified firms have had difficulty managing a diverse group of businesses and have elected to get out of some of them. Retrenching to a narrower diversification base is usually undertaken when top management concludes that its diversification strategy has ranged too far afield and that the company can improve long-term performance by concentrating on building stronger positions in a smaller number of core businesses and industries. Hewlett-Packard spun off its testing and measurement businesses into a standalone company called Agilent Technologies so that it could better concentrate on its PC, workstation, server, printer and peripherals, and electronics businesses. PepsiCo divested its cash-hog group of restaurant businesses, consisting of Kentucky Fried Chicken, Pizza Hut, Taco Bell, and California Pizza Kitchens, to provide more resources for strengthening its beverage business

> Focusing corporate resources on a few core and mostly related businesses avoids the mistake of diversifying so broadly that resources and management attention are stretched too thin.

(soft drinks, Aquafina, Gatorade, Tropicana, and several others) and growing its highly profitable Frito-Lay snack foods business.

But there are other important reasons for divesting one or more of a company's present businesses. Sometimes divesting a business has to be considered because market conditions in a once-attractive industry have badly deteriorated. A business can become a prime candidate for divestiture because it lacks adequate strategic or resource fit, because it is a cash hog with questionable long-term potential, or because it is weakly positioned in its industry with little prospect of earning a decent return on investment. Sometimes a company acquires businesses that, down the road, just do not work out as expected even though management has tried all it can think of to make them profitable. Other business units, despite adequate financial performance, may not mesh as well with the rest of the firm as was originally thought.

There's evidence indicating that pruning businesses and narrowing a firm's diversification base improves corporate performance.[14] Corporate parents often end up selling off businesses too late and at too low a price, sacrificing shareholder value.[15] A useful guide to determine whether or when to divest a business subsidiary is to ask, "If we were not in this business today, would we want to get into it now?"[16] When the answer is no or probably not, divestiture should be considered. Another signal that a business should become a divestiture candidate is whether it is worth more to another company than to the present parent; in such cases, shareholders would be well served if the company were to sell the business and collect a premium price from the buyer for whom the business is a valuable fit.[17]

OPTIONS FOR DIVESTING A BUSINESS: SELL OR SPIN OFF?   Selling a business outright to another company is far and away the most frequently used option for divesting a business. However, finding a buyer can prove difficult or easy, depending on the business. As a rule, a company selling a troubled business should not ask, "How can we pawn this business off on someone, and what is the most we can get for it?"[18] Instead, it is wiser to ask, "For what sort of company would this business be a good fit, and under what conditions would it be viewed as a good deal?" But sometimes a business selected for divestiture has ample resource strengths to compete successfully on its own. In such cases, a corporate parent may elect to spin the unwanted business off as a financially and managerially independent company, either by selling shares to the investing public via an initial public offering or by

[14] See, for, example, Constantinos C. Markides, "Diversification, Restructuring, and Economic Performance," *Strategic Management Journal* 16 (February 1995), pp. 101–18.

[15] For a discussion of why divestiture needs to be a standard part of any company's diversification strategy, see Lee Dranikoff, Tim Koller, and Antoon Schneider, "Divestiture: Strategy's Missing Link," *Harvard Business Review* 80, no. 5 (May 2002), pp. 74–83.

[16] Peter F. Drucker, *Management: Tasks, Responsibilities, Practices*, (New York: Harper & Row, 1974), p. 94.

[17] See David J. Collis and Cynthia A. Montgomery, "Creating Corporate Advantage," *Harvard Business Review* 76, no. 3 (May–June 1998), pp. 72–80.

[18] Drucker, *Management: Tasks, Responsibilities, Practices*, p. 719.

distributing shares in the new company to existing shareholders of the corporate parent.

In 2005, Cendant announced it would split its diversified businesses into four separate publicly traded companies—one for vehicle rental services (which consisted of Avis and Budget car rental companies), one for real estate and mortgage services (which included Century 21, Coldwell Banker, ERA, Sotheby's International Realty, and NRT—a residential real estate brokerage company), one for hospitality and lodging (consisting of such hotels and motel chains as Wyndam, Ramada, Days Inn, Howard Johnson, Travelodge, AmeriHost Inn, and Knights Inn, plus an assortment of timeshare resort properties), and one for travel (consisting of various travel agencies, online ticket and vacation travel sites like Orbitz and Cheap Tickets, and vacation rental operations handling some 55,000 villas and condos). Cendant said the reason for the split-up was that shareholders would realize more value from operating the businesses independently—a clear sign that Cendant's diversification strategy had failed to deliver added shareholder value and that the parts were worth more than the whole.

When a corporate parent decides to spin off one of its businesses as a separate company, there's the issue of whether or not to retain partial ownership. Retaining partial ownership makes sense when the business to be divested has a hot product or technological capabilities that give it good profit prospects. When 3Com elected to divest its PalmPilot business, which investors then saw as having very promising profit potential, it elected to retain a substantial ownership interest in the new corporation. Of course, if the business is unable to support itself as an independent company and a buyer willing to pay an acceptable price cannot be found, then a company must decide whether to keep the business until a buyer appears or simply close it down and liquidate the remaining assets. Liquidation is obviously a last resort.

Broadly Restructuring the Business Lineup

Restructuring strategies involve divesting some businesses and acquiring others so as to put a whole new face on the company's business lineup. Performing radical surgery on a company's group of businesses is an appealing corporate strategy when its financial performance is squeezed or eroded by:

> **Restructuring** involves radically altering the business lineup by divesting businesses that lack strategic fit or are poor performers and acquiring new businesses that offer better promise for enhancing shareholder value.

- Too many businesses in slow-growth, declining, low-margin, or otherwise unattractive industries.
- Too many competitively weak businesses.
- An excessive debt burden with interest costs that eat deeply into profitability.
- Ill-chosen acquisitions that haven't lived up to expectations.

Candidates for divestiture in a corporate restructuring effort typically include not only weak or up-and-down performers or those in unattractive industries but also business units that lack strategic fit with the businesses to be retained, businesses that are cash hogs or that lack other types of resource fit, and businesses incompatible with the company's revised diversification strategy (even though they may be profitable or in an attractive industry). As businesses are divested, corporate restructuring generally involves aligning the remaining business units into groups with the best strategic fits and then redeploying the cash flows from the divested business to either pay down debt or make new acquisitions.[19] In a study of the performance of the 200 largest U.S. corporations from 1990 to 2000, McKinsey & Company found that those companies that actively managed their business portfolios through acquisitions and divestitures created substantially more shareholder value than those that kept a fixed lineup of businesses.[20]

Corporate restructuring has become a popular strategy at many diversified companies, especially those that have diversified broadly into many different industries and lines of business. For instance, PerkinElmer used a series of divestitures and new acquisitions to transform itself from a supplier of low-margin services sold to government agencies into an innovative high-tech company with operations in over 125 countries and businesses in four industry groups—life sciences (drug research and clinical screening), optoelectronics, medical instruments, and fluid control and containment services (for customers in aerospace, power generation, and semiconductors). In 2005 PerkinElmer took a second restructuring step by divesting its entire fluid control and containment business group so that it could concentrate on its higher growth health sciences and optoelectronics businesses; the company's CEO said, "while fluid services is an excellent business, it does not fit with our long-term strategy."[21]

During Jack Welch's first four years as CEO of General Electric (GE), the company divested 117 business units, accounting for about 20 percent of GE's assets. Then, during the 1990–2001 period, GE continued to reshuffle its business lineup, acquiring over 600 new companies, including 108 in 1998 and 64 during a 90-day period in 1999. In 2004, GE's new CEO, Jeffrey Immelt, further restructured GE's business lineup with three initiatives: (1) spending $10 billion to acquire British-based Amersham and extend GE's Medical Systems business into diagnostic pharmaceuticals and biosciences, (2) acquiring the entertainment assets of French media conglomerate Vivendi Universal Entertainment (Universal Studios, 5 Universal theme parks, USA Network, Sci-Fi Channel, the Trio cable channel, and Spanish-language broadcaster Telemundo) and integrating its operations into GE's NBC division, and (3) withdrawing from the insurance business by divesting several companies in its insurance division and spinning off its remaining life and mortgage insurance businesses through an IPO for a new company called Genworth Financial.

---

[19] Evidence that restructuring strategies tend to result in higher levels of performance is contained in Markides, "Diversification, Restructuring and Economic Performance," pp. 101–18.

[20] Dranikoff, Koller, and Schneider, "Divestiture: Strategy's Missing Link," p. 76.

[21] Company press release, October 6, 2005.

Key Points

1. The purpose of diversification is to build shareholder value. Diversification builds shareholder value when a diversified group of businesses can perform better under the auspices of a single corporate parent than they would as independent, standalone businesses—the goal is to achieve not just a $1 + 1 = 2$ result but rather to realize important $1 + 1 = 3$ performance benefits. Whether getting into a new business has potential to enhance shareholder value hinges on whether a company's entry into that business can pass the attractiveness test, the cost-of-entry test, and the better-off test.

2. Entry into new businesses can take any of three forms: acquisition, internal start-up, or joint venture/strategic partnership. Each has its pros and cons, but acquisition is the most frequently used; internal start-up takes the longest to produce home-run results, and joint venture/strategic partnership, though used second most frequently, is the least durable.

3. There are two fundamental approaches to diversification—into related businesses and into unrelated businesses. The rationale for *related* diversification is *strategic:* Diversify into businesses with strategic fits along their respective value chains, capitalize on strategic-fit relationships to gain competitive advantage, and then use competitive advantage to achieve the desired $1 + 1 = 3$ impact on shareholder value.

4. The basic premise of *unrelated* diversification is that any business that has good profit prospects and can be acquired on good financial terms is a good business to diversify into. Unrelated diversification strategies surrender the competitive advantage potential of strategic fit in return for such advantages as (1) spreading business risk over a variety of industries and (2) providing opportunities for financial gain (if candidate acquisitions have undervalued assets, are bargain-priced, or need the backing of a financially strong parent to capitalize on attractive opportunities). However, the greater the number of businesses a company has diversified into and the more diverse these businesses are, the harder it is for corporate executives to select capable managers to run each business, know when the major strategic proposals of business units are sound, or decide on a wise course of recovery when a business unit stumbles.

5. Analyzing how good a company's diversification strategy is a six-step process:

   - **Step 1:** *Evaluate the long-term attractiveness of the industries into which the firm has diversified.* Determining industry attractiveness involves developing a list of industry attractiveness measures, each of which might have a different importance weight.

   - **Step 2:** *Evaluate the relative competitive strength of each of the company's business units.* The purpose of rating each business's competitive strength is to gain clear understanding of which businesses are strong contenders in their industries, which are weak contenders, and the underlying reasons for their strength or weakness. The conclusions about industry attractiveness can be joined with the conclusions about competitive strength by drawing an industry attractiveness–competitive strength matrix that helps identify the prospects of each business and what priority each business should be given in allocating corporate resources and investment capital.

- **Step 3:** *Check for cross-business strategic fits.* A business is more attractive strategically when it has value chain relationships with sibling business units that offer the potential to (1) realize economies of scope or cost-saving efficiencies; (2) transfer technology, skills, know-how, or other resource capabilities from one business to another; and/or (3) leverage use of a well-known and trusted brand name. Cross-business strategic fits represent a significant avenue for producing competitive advantage beyond what any one business can achieve on its own.

- **Step 4:** *Check whether the firm's resource strengths fit the resource requirements of its present business lineup.* Resource fit exists when (1) businesses add to a company's resource strengths, either financially or strategically; and (2) a company has the resources to adequately support the resource requirements of its businesses as a group without spreading itself too thin. One important test of financial resource fit involves determining whether a company has ample cash cows and not too many cash hogs.

- **Step 5:** *Rank the performance prospects of the businesses from best to worst and determine what the corporate parent's priority should be in allocating resources to its various businesses.* The most important considerations in judging business-unit performance are sales growth, profit growth, contribution to company earnings, cash flow characteristics, and the return on capital invested in the business. Normally, strong business units in attractive industries should head the list for corporate resource support.

- **Step 6:** *Crafting new strategic moves to improve overall corporate performance.* This step entails using the results of the preceding analysis as the basis for selecting one of four different strategic paths for improving a diversified company's performance: (a) stick closely with the existing business lineup and pursue opportunities presented by these businesses, (b) broaden the scope of diversification by entering additional industries, (c) retrench to a narrower scope of diversification by divesting poorly performing businesses, and (d) broadly restructure the business lineup with multiple divestitures and/or acquisitions.

Assurance of Learning Exercises

1. See if you can identify the value chain relationships which make the businesses of the following companies related in competitively relevant ways. In particular, you should consider whether there are cross-business opportunities for (1) skills/technology transfer (2) combining related value chain activities to achieve lower costs, and/or (3) leveraging use of a well-respected brand name.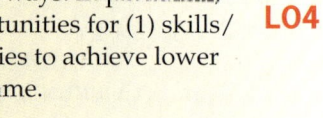

LO2

LO4

Outback Steakhouse
- Outback Steakhouse
- Carrabba's Italian Grill
- Roy's Restaurant (Hawaiian fusion cuisine)
- Bonefish Grill (Market-fresh fine seafood)
- Fleming's Prime Steakhouse & Wine Bar
- Lee Roy Selmon's (Southern comfort food)
- Cheeseburger in Paradise
- Blue Coral Seafood & Spirits (Fine seafood)

L'Oréal

- Maybelline, Lancôme, Helena Rubenstein, Kiehl's, Garner, and Shu Uemura cosmetics
- L'Oréal and Soft Sheen/Carson hair care products
- Redken, Matrix, L'Oréal Professional, and Kerastase Paris professional hair care and skin care products
- Ralph Lauren and Giorgio Armani fragrances
- Biotherm skincare products
- La Roche–Posay and Vichy Laboratories dermocosmetics

Johnson & Johnson

- Baby products (powder, shampoo, oil, lotion)
- Band-Aids and other first-aid products
- Women's health and personal care products (Stayfree, Carefree, Sure & Natural)
- Neutrogena and Aveeno skin care products
- Nonprescription drugs (Tylenol, Motrin, Pepcid AC, Mylanta, Monistat)
- Prescription drugs
- Prosthetic and other medical devices
- Surgical and hospital products
- Accuvue contact lenses

Source: Company Web sites, annual reports, and 10-K reports.

LO2
LO3
LO4

2. The Walt Disney Company is in the following businesses:
   - Theme parks
   - Disney Cruise Line
   - Resort properties
   - Movie, video, and theatrical productions (for both children and adults)
   - Television broadcasting (ABC, Disney Channel, Toon Disney, Classic Sports Network, ESPN and ESPN2, E!, Lifetime, and A&E networks)
   - Radio broadcasting (Disney Radio)
   - Musical recordings and sales of animation art
   - Anaheim Mighty Ducks NHL franchise
   - Anaheim Angels major league baseball franchise (25 percent ownership)
   - Books and magazine publishing
   - Interactive software and Internet sites
   - The Disney Store retail shops

   Based on the above listing, would you say that Walt Disney's business lineup reflects a strategy of related, unrelated, or a combination of related and unrelated diversification? Be prepared to justify and explain your answer in terms of the extent to which the value chains of Disney's different businesses seem to have competitively valuable cross-business relationships.

3. Explore the Web sites of the following companies and determine whether the company is pursuing a strategy of related diversification, unrelated diversification, or a mixture of both:

- Deere
- Altria Group
- Time Warner
- Motorola

LO2

LO3

LO4

Exercise for Simulation Users

Suppose that your instructor has given you two options: (1) continue in your current simulation and receive a grade based upon your final rank and score in the industry, or (2) participate in two or more simulations and average the scores from each simulation to determine a final grade. Which option would you prefer? Explain your answer based upon the chapter's discussion of the reasons companies may or may not pursue diversification.

LO1

+CASE TUTOR Costco Wholesale Corporation: Mission, Business Model, and Strategy

Arthur A. Thompson Jr.
The University of Alabama

Jim Sinegal, cofounder and CEO of Costco Wholesale, was the driving force behind Costco's 23-year march to become the fourth largest retailer in the United States and the seventh largest in the world. He was far from the stereotypical CEO. A grandfatherly 70-year-old, Sinegal dressed casually and unpretentiously, often going to the office or touring Costco stores wearing an open-collared cotton shirt that came from a Costco bargain rack and sporting a standard employee name tag that said, simply, "Jim." His informal dress, mustache, gray hair, and unimposing appearance made it easy for Costco shoppers to mistake him for a store clerk. He answered his own phone, once telling ABC News reporters, "If a customer's calling and they have a gripe, don't you think they kind of enjoy the fact that I picked up the phone and talked to them?"[1]

Sinegal spent much of his time touring Costco stores, using the company plane to fly from location to location and sometimes visiting 8 to 10 stores daily (the record for a single day was 12). Treated like a celebrity when he appeared at a store (the news "Jim's in the store" spread quickly), Sinegal made a point of greeting store employees. He observed, "The employees know that I want to say hello to them, because I like them. We have said from the very beginning:

'We're going to be a company that's on a first-name basis with everyone.'"[2] Employees genuinely seemed to like Sinegal. He talked quietly, in a commonsensical manner that suggested what he was saying was no big deal.[3] He came across as kind yet stern, but he was prone to display irritation when he disagreed sharply with what people were saying to him.

In touring a Costco store with the local store manager, Sinegal was very much the person-in-charge. He functioned as producer, director, and knowledgeable critic. He cut to the chase quickly, exhibiting intense attention to detail and pricing, wandering through store aisles firing a barrage of questions at store managers about sales volumes and stock levels of particular items, critiquing merchandising displays or the position of certain products in the stores, commenting on any aspect of store operations that caught his eye, and asking managers to do further research and get back to him with more information whenever he found their answers to his questions less than satisfying. It was readily apparent that Sinegal had tremendous merchandising savvy, that he demanded much of store managers and employees, and that his views about discount retailing set the tone for how the company operated. Knowledgeable observers regarded Jim Sinegal's merchandising expertise as being on a par with that of the legendary Sam Walton.

In 2006, Costco's sales totaled almost $59 billion at 496 stores in 37 states, Puerto Rico, Canada, the United Kingdom, Taiwan, Japan, Korea, and Mexico. About 26 million households and 5.2 million businesses had membership cards entitling them to shop at Costco, generating nearly $1.2 billion in membership fees for the company. Annual sales per store averaged about $128 million, nearly double the $67 million figure for Sam's Club, Costco's chief competitor in the membership warehouse retail segment.

Company Background

The membership warehouse concept was pioneered by discount merchandising sage Sol Price, who opened the first Price Club in a converted airplane hangar on Morena Boulevard in San Diego in 1976. Price Club lost $750,000 in its first year of operation, but by 1979 it had two stores, 900 employees, 200,000 members, and a $1 million profit. Years earlier, Sol Price had experimented with discount retailing at a San Diego store called Fed-Mart. Jim Sinegal got his start in retailing there at the age of 18, loading mattresses for $1.25 an hour while attending San Diego Community College. When Sol Price sold Fed-Mart, Sinegal left with Price to help him start the San Diego Price Club store; within a few years, Sol Price's Price Club emerged as the unchallenged leader in member warehouse retailing, with stores operating primarily on the West Coast.

Although he originally conceived Price Club as a place where small local businesses could obtain needed merchandise at economical prices, Sol Price soon concluded that his fledgling operation could achieve far greater sales volumes and gain buying clout with suppliers by also granting membership to individuals—a conclusion that launched the deep-discount warehouse club industry on a steep growth curve.

When Sinegal was 26, Sol Price made him the manager of the original San Diego store, which had become unprofitable. Price saw that Sinegal had a special knack for discount retailing and for spotting what a store was doing wrong (usually either not being in the right merchandise categories or not selling items at the right price points)—the very things that Sol Price was good at and that were at the root of the Price Club's growing success in the marketplace. Sinegal soon got the San Diego store back into the black. Over the next several years, Sinegal continued to build his prowess and talents for discount merchandising. He mirrored Sol Price's attention to detail and absorbed all the nuances and subtleties of his mentor's style of operating—constantly improving store operations, keeping operating costs and overhead low, stocking items that moved quickly, and charging ultra-low prices that kept customers coming back to shop. Realizing that he had mastered the tricks of running a successful membership warehouse business from Sol Price, Sinegal decided to leave Price Club and form his own warehouse club operation.

Costco was founded by Jim Sinegal and Seattle entrepreneur Jeff Brotman (now chairman of the board of directors). The first Costco store began operations in Seattle in 1983, the same year that Wal-Mart launched its warehouse membership format, Sam's Club. By the end of 1984, there were nine Costco stores in five states serving over 200,000 members. In December 1985, Costco became a public company, selling shares to the public and raising additional capital for expansion. Costco became the first ever U.S. company to reach $1 billion in sales in less than six years. In October 1993, Costco merged with Price Club. Jim Sinegal became CEO of the merged company, presiding over 206 PriceCostco locations, which in total generated $16 billion in annual sales. Jeff Brotman, who had functioned as Costco's chairman since the company's founding, became vice chairman of PriceCostco in 1993 and was elevated to chairman in December 1994. Brotman kept abreast of company operations but stayed in the background and concentrated on managing the company's $9 billion investment in real estate operations—in 2006, Costco owned the land and buildings for almost 80 percent of its stores.

In January 1997, after the spin-off of most of its nonwarehouse assets to Price Enterprises Inc., PriceCostco changed its name to Costco Companies Inc. When the company reincorporated from Delaware to Washington in August 1999, the name was changed to Costco Wholesale Corporation. The company's headquarters was in Issaquah, Washington, not far from Seattle.

Exhibit 1 contains a financial and operating summary for Costco for fiscal years 2000–2006.

Costco's Mission, Business Model, and Strategy

Costco's mission in the membership warehouse business read: "To continually provide our members with quality goods and services at the lowest possible prices." The company's business model was to generate high sales volumes and rapid inventory turnover by offering members low prices on a limited selection of nationally branded and selected private-label products in a wide range of merchandise categories. Management believed that rapid inventory turnover—when combined with the operating efficiencies achieved by volume purchasing, efficient distribution, and reduced handling of merchandise in no-frills, self-service warehouse facilities—enabled Costco to operate profitably at significantly lower gross margins than traditional wholesalers, mass merchandisers, supermarkets, and supercenters.

Examples of Costco's incredible annual sales volumes included 96,000 carats of diamonds (2006), 1.5 million televisions, $300 million worth of digital cameras, 28 million rotisserie chickens (over 500,000 weekly), 40 percent of the Tuscan olive oil bought in the United States, $16 million worth of pumpkin pies during the fall holiday season, $3 billion worth of gasoline, 21 million prescriptions, and 52 million $1.50 hot dog/soda pop combinations. Costco was also the world's largest seller of fine wines ($385 million out of total 2006 fine wine sales of $805 million).[4] At one of Costco's largest volume stores, which had annual sales of $285 million and 232,000 members, annual sales volume ran 283,000 rotisserie chickens, 375,000 gallons of milk, and 8.4 million rolls of toilet paper—this store had an average customer bill per trip of $150.[5]

Furthermore, Costco's high sales volume and rapid inventory turnover generally allowed it to sell and receive cash for inventory before it had to pay many of its merchandise vendors, even when vendor payments were made in time to take advantage of early payment discounts. Thus, Costco was able to finance a big percentage of its merchandise inventory through the payment terms provided by vendors rather than by having to maintain sizable working capital (defined as current assets minus current liabilities) to facilitate timely payment of suppliers.

Costco's Strategy

The cornerstones of Costco's strategy were low prices, limited selection, and a treasure-hunt shopping environment.

PRICING Costco was known for selling top-quality national and regional brands at prices consistently below traditional wholesale or retail outlets. The company stocked only those items that could be priced at bargain levels and thus provide members with significant cost savings; this was true even if an item was often requested by customers. A key element of Costco's pricing strategy was to cap its markup on brand-name merchandise at 14 percent (compared to 20 to 50 percent markups at other discounters and many supermarkets). Markups on Costco's 400 private-label (Kirkland Signature) items could be no higher than 15 percent, but the sometimes fractionally higher markups still resulted in Kirkland Signature items being priced about 20 percent below

Exhibit 1

Financial and Operating Summary, Costco Wholesale Corporation, Fiscal Years 2000–2006 ($ in millions, except for per share data)

	FISCAL YEARS ENDING ON SUNDAY CLOSEST TO AUGUST 31				
	2006	**2005**	**2004**	**2002**	**2000**
Income Statement Data					
Net sales	$58,963	$51,862	$47,146	$37,993	$31,621
Membership fees	1,188	1,073	961	769	544
Total revenue	60,151	52,935	48,107	38,762	32,164
Operating expenses					
Merchandise costs	52,745	46,347	42,092	33,983	28,322
Selling, general, and administrative	5,732	5,044	4,598	3,576	2,755
Preopening expenses	43	53	30	51	42
Provision for impaired assets and store closing costs	5	16	1	21	7
Operating income	1,626	1,474	1,386	1,132	1,037
Other income (expense)					
Interest expense	(13)	(34)	(37)	(29)	(39)
Interest income and other	138	109	52	36	54
Income before income taxes	1,751	1,549	1,401	1,138	1,052
Provision for income taxes	648	486	518	438	421
Net income	$ 1,103	$ 1,063	$ 882	$ 700	$ 631
Diluted net income per share	$ 2.30	$ 2.18	$ 1.85	$ 1.48	$ 1.35
Dividends per share	$ 0.49	$ 0.43	$ 0.20	$ 0.00	$ 0.00
Millions of shares used in per share calculations	480.3	492.0	482.5	479.3	475.7
Balance Sheet Data					
Cash and cash equivalents	$ 1,511	$ 2,063	$ 2,823	$ 806	$ 525
Merchandise inventories	4,569	4,015	3,644	3,127	2,490
Current assets	8,232	8,238	7,269	4,631	3,470
Current liabilities	7,819	6,761	6,170	4,450	3,404
Working capital	413	1,477	1,099	181	66
Net property and equipment	8,564	7,790	7,219	6,523	4,834
Total assets	17,495	16,514	15,093	11,620	8,634
Short-term borrowings	41	54	22	104	10
Long-term debt	215	711	994	1,211	790
Stockholders' equity	9,143	8,881	7,625	5,694	4,240
Cash Flow Data					
Net cash provided by operating activities	$ 1,827	$ 1,776	$ 2,096	$ 1,018	$ 1,070
Warehouses in Operation					
Beginning of year	433	417	397	345	292
Opened	28	21	20	35	25
Closed	(3)	(5)	—	(6)	(4)
End of year	458	433	417	374	313
Primary members at year-end					
Businesses (000s)	5,214	5,050	4,810	4,476	4,358
Gold Star members (000s)	17,338	16,233	15,018	14,597	12,737

Sources: Company 10-K reports 2006, 2005, 2002, and 2000.

comparable name-brand items. Kirkland Signature products—which included juice, cookies, coffee, tires, housewares, luggage, appliances, clothing, and detergent—were designed to be of equal or better quality than national brands.

Costco's philosophy was to keep customers coming in to shop by wowing them with low prices. Jim Sinegal explained the company's approach to pricing as follows:

> We always look to see how much of a gulf we can create between ourselves and the competition. So that the competitors eventually say, "These guys are crazy. We'll compete somewhere else." Some years ago, we were selling a hot brand of jeans for $29.99. They were $50 in a department store. We got a great deal on them and could have sold them for a higher price but we went down to $29.99. Why? We knew it would create a riot.[6]

At another time he said:

> We're very good merchants, and we offer value. The traditional retailer will say: "I'm selling this for $10. I wonder whether we can get $10.50 or $11." We say: "We're selling this for $9. How do we get it down to $8?" We understand that our members don't come and shop with us because of the window displays or the Santa Claus or the piano player. They come and shop with us because we offer great values.[7]

Indeed, Costco's markups and prices were so low that Wall Street analysts had criticized Costco management for going all out to please customers at the expense of increasing profits for shareholders. One retailing analyst said, "They could probably get more money for a lot of the items they sell."[8] Sinegal was unimpressed with Wall Street calls for Costco to abandon its ultra-low pricing strategy, commenting: "Those people are in the business of making money between now and next Tuesday. We're trying to build an organization that's going to be here 50 years from now."[9] He went on to explain why Costco's approach to pricing would remain unaltered during his tenure:

> When I started, Sears, Roebuck was the Costco of the country, but they allowed someone else to come in under them. We don't want to be one of the casualties. We don't want to turn around and say, "We got so fancy we've raised our prices, and all of a sudden a new competitor comes in and beats our prices."[10]

PRODUCT SELECTION Whereas typical supermarkets stocked about 40,000 items and a Wal-Mart Supercenter or a SuperTarget might have as many as 150,000 items for shoppers to choose from, Costco's merchandising strategy was to provide members with a selection of only about 4,000 items.

Costco's product range did cover a broad spectrum—rotisserie chicken, prime steaks, caviar, flat-screen televisions, digital cameras, fresh flowers, fine wines, caskets, baby strollers, toys and games, musical instruments, ceiling fans, vacuum cleaners, books, DVDs, chandeliers, stainless-steel cookware, seat-cover kits for autos, prescription drugs, gasoline, and one-hour photo finishing—but the company deliberately limited the selection in each product category to fast-selling models, sizes, and colors. Many consumable products like detergents, canned goods, office supplies, and soft drinks were sold only in big-container, case, carton, or multiple-pack quantities. For example, Costco stocked only a 325-count bottle of Advil—a size many shoppers might find too large for their needs. Sinegal explained the reason for the deliberately limited selection as follows:

> If you had ten customers come in to buy Advil, how many are not going to buy any because you just have one size? Maybe one or two. We refer to that as the intelligent loss of sales. We are prepared to give up that one customer. But if we had four or five sizes of Advil, as most grocery stores do, it would make our business more difficult to manage. Our business can only succeed if we are efficient. You can't go on selling at these margins if you are not.[11]

Costco's selections of appliances, equipment, and tools often included commercial and professional models because so many of its members were small businesses. The approximate percentage of net sales accounted for by each major category of items stocked by Costco is shown in the following table:

	2006	2005	2004	2003
Food (fresh produce, meats and fish, bakery and deli products, and dry and institutionally packaged foods)	30%	30%	31%	30%
Sundries (candy, snack foods, tobacco, alcoholic and nonalcoholic beverages, and cleaning and institutional supplies)	24	25	25	26
Hard lines (major appliances, electronics, health and beauty aids, hardware, office supplies, garden and patio, sporting goods, furniture, cameras and automotive supplies)	20	20	20	20
Soft lines (apparel, domestics, jewelry, housewares, media, home furnishings, and small appliances)	12	12	13	14
Ancillary and other (gasoline, pharmacy, food court, optical, one-hour photo, hearing aids, and travel)	14	13	11	10

To encourage members to shop at Costco more frequently, the company operated ancillary businesses within or next to most Costco warehouses; the number of ancillary businesses at Costco warehouses is shown in the following table:

	2006	2005	2004
Total number of warehouses	458	433	417
Warehouses having stores with			
Food court and hot dog stands	452	427	412
One-hour photo centers	450	423	408
Optical dispensing centers	442	414	397
Pharmacies	401	374	359
Gas stations	250	225	211
Hearing aid centers	196	168	143
Print shops and copy centers	9	10	10

TREASURE-HUNT MERCHANDISING

While Costco's product line consisted of approximately 4,000 items, about one-fourth of its product offerings were constantly changing. Costco's merchandise buyers remained on the lookout to make one-time purchases of items that would appeal to the company's clientele and that would sell out quickly. A sizable number of these items were high-end or name-brand products that carried big price tags—like $2,000–$3,500 big-screen HDTVs or $800 leather sofas. The idea was to entice shoppers to spend more than they might otherwise by offering irresistible deals on luxury items. According to Jim

Sinegal, "Of that 4,000, about 3,000 can be found on the floor all the time. The other 1,000 are the treasure-hunt stuff that's always changing. It's the type of item a customer knows they better buy because it will not be there next time, like Waterford crystal. We try to get that sense of urgency in our customers."[12]

In many cases, Costco did not obtain its luxury offerings directly from high-end manufacturers like Calvin Klein or Waterford (who were unlikely to want their merchandise marketed at deep discounts at places like Costco); rather, Costco buyers searched for opportunities to source such items legally on the gray market from other wholesalers or distressed retailers looking to get rid of excess or slow-selling inventory. Examples of treasure-hunt specials included $800 espresso machines, diamond rings and other jewelry items with price tags of anywhere from $5,000 to $250,000, Italian-made Hathaway shirts priced at $29.99, Movado watches, exotic cheeses, Coach bags, cashmere sports coats, $1,500 digital pianos, and Dom Perignon champagne.

MARKETING AND ADVERTISING Costco's low prices and its reputation for treasure-hunt shopping made it unnecessary for the company to engage in extensive advertising or sales campaigns. Marketing and promotional activities were generally limited to direct mail programs promoting selected merchandise to existing members, occasional direct mail marketing to prospective new members, and special campaigns for new warehouse openings. For new warehouse openings, marketing teams personally contacted businesses in the area that were potential wholesale members; these contacts were supplemented with direct mailings during the period immediately prior to opening. Potential Gold Star (individual) members were contacted by direct mail or by promotions at local employee associations and businesses with large numbers of employees. After a membership base was established in an area, most new memberships came from word of mouth (existing members telling friends and acquaintances about their shopping experiences at Costco), follow-up messages distributed through regular payroll or other organizational communications to employee groups, and ongoing direct solicitations to prospective business and Gold Star members. Management believed that its emphasis on direct mail advertising kept its marketing expenses low relative to those at typical retailers, discounters, and supermarkets.

GROWTH STRATEGY In recent years, Costco had opened an average 20–25 locations annually; most were in the United States, but expansion was under way internationally as well. The company opened 68 new warehouses in the United States in fiscal years 2002–2006; 16 new warehouses opened in the first four months of fiscal 2007 (between September 1 and December 31, 2006), and management planned to open another 20–24 by the end of fiscal 2007. Five new warehouses were opened outside the United States in fiscal 2005, five more were opened in fiscal 2006, and four were opened in the first four months of fiscal 2007. Going into 2007, Costco had a total of 102 wholly owned warehouses in operation outside the United States, including 70 in Canada, 18 in the United Kingdom, 5 in Korea, 5 in Japan, and 4 in Taiwan. Costco was a 50–50 partner in a venture to operate 30 Costco warehouses in Mexico. Exhibit 2 shows a breakdown of Costco's geographic operations for fiscal years 2003–2006. (The data for the 30 warehouses in Mexico are not included in the exhibit because the 50–50 venture in Mexico was accounted for using the equity method.)

Costco had recently opened two freestanding high-end furniture warehouse businesses called Costco Home. Sales in 2005 at these two locations increased by 132 percent over 2004 levels, and profits were up significantly. So far, however, rather than opening additional Costco Home stores, management had opted to experiment with adding about 45,000 square feet to the size of selected new Costco stores and using the extra space to stock a much bigger selection of furniture—furniture was one of the top three best-selling categories at Costco's Web site.

A third growth initiative was to expand the company's offerings of Kirkland Signature items. Management believed there were opportunities to expand its private-label offerings from the present level of 400 items to as many as 600 items over the next five years.

WEB SITE SALES Costco operated two Web sites—www.costco.com in the United States and www.costco.ca in Canada—both to provide another shopping alternative for members and to provide members with a way to purchase products and services that might not be available at the warehouse where they customarily shopped, especially such services as digital photo processing, prescription fulfillment, and travel and other membership services. At Costco's online photo center, customers could upload images and pick up the prints at their local warehouse in little over an hour; one-hour photo sales were up 10 percent in fiscal 2005, a year in which the industry overall had negative sales growth. Costco's e-commerce sales totaled $534 million in fiscal 2005 and $376 million in fiscal 2004. (Data for fiscal 2006 e-commerce sales were not available.)

Warehouse Operations

In Costco's 2005 annual report, Jim Sinegal summed up the company's approach to operations as follows:

> Costco is able to offer lower prices and better values by eliminating virtually all the frills and costs historically associated with conventional wholesalers and retailers, including salespeople, fancy buildings, delivery, billing, and accounts receivable.

Exhibit 2

Geographic Operating Data, Costco Wholesale Corporation, Fiscal Years 2003–2006 ($ in millions)

	UNITED STATES OPERATIONS	CANADIAN OPERATIONS	OTHER INTERNATIONAL OPERATIONS	TOTAL
Year Ended September 3, 2006				
Total revenue (including membership fees)	$48,465	$8,122	$3,564	$60,151
Operating income	1,246	293	87	1,626
Depreciation and amortization	413	61	41	515
Capital expenditures	934	188	90	1,213
Property and equipment	6,676	1,032	855	8,564
Total assets	14,009	1,914	1,572	17,495
Net assets	7,190	1,043	910	9,143
Number of warehouses	358	68	32	458
Year Ended August 28, 2005				
Total revenue (including membership fees)	$43,064	$6,732	$3,155	$52,952
Operating income	1,168	242	65	1,474
Depreciation and amortization	389	51	42	482
Capital expenditures	734	140	122	995
Property and equipment	6,171	834	786	7,790
Total assets	13,203	2,034	1,428	16,665
Net assets	6,769	1,285	827	8,881
Number of warehouses	338	65	30	433
Year Ended August 29, 2004				
Total revenue (including membership fees)	$39,430	$6,043	$2,637	$48,110
Operating income	1,121	215	50	1,386
Depreciation and amortization	364	40	36	441
Capital expenditures	560	90	55	706
Property and equipment	5,853	676	691	7,220
Total assets	12,108	1,718	1,267	15,093
Net assets	5,871	1,012	742	7,625
Number of warehouses	327	63	27	417
Year Ended August 31, 2003				
Total revenue (including membership fees)	$35,119	$5,237	$2,189	$42,546
Operating income	928	199	30	1,157
Depreciation and amortization	324	34	34	391
Capital expenditures	699	69	44	811
Long lived assets	5,706	613	642	6,960
Total assets	10,522	1,580	1,089	13,192
Net assets	5,141	784	630	6,555
Number of warehouses	309	61	27	397

Source: Company 10-K reports, 2004 and 2006.

We run a tight operation with extremely low overhead which enables us to pass on dramatic savings to our members.

Costco warehouses averaged 140,000 square feet and were constructed inexpensively with concrete floors. Because shoppers were attracted principally by Costco's low prices, its warehouses were rarely located on prime commercial real estate sites. Merchandise was generally stored on racks above the sales floor and displayed on pallets containing large quantities of each item, thereby reducing labor required for handling and stocking. In-store signage was done mostly on laser printers, and there were no shopping bags at the checkout counter—merchandise was put directly into the shopping cart or sometimes loaded into empty boxes. Warehouses generally operated on a seven-day, 69-hour week, typically being open between 10:00 a.m. and 8:30 p.m. weekdays, with earlier closing hours on the weekend; the gasoline operations outside many stores generally had extended hours. The shorter hours of operation—as compared to those of traditional retailers, discount retailers, and supermarkets—resulted in lower labor costs relative to the volume of sales.

Costco warehouse managers were delegated considerable authority over store operations. In effect, warehouse managers functioned as entrepreneurs running their own retail operation. They were responsible for coming up with new ideas about what items would sell in their stores, effectively merchandising the ever-changing lineup of treasure-hunt products and orchestrating in-store product locations and displays to maximize sales and quick turnover. In experimenting with what items to stock and what in-store merchandising techniques to employ, warehouse managers had to know the clientele who patronized their locations—for instance, big-ticket diamonds sold well at some warehouses but not at others. Costco's best managers kept their finger on the pulse of the members who shopped their warehouse location to stay in sync with what would sell well, and they had a flair for creating a certain element of excitement, hum, and buzz in their warehouses. Such managers spurred above-average sales volumes—sales at Costco's top-volume warehouses often exceeded $5 million a week, with sales exceeding $1 million on many days. Successful managers also thrived on the rat race of running a high-traffic store and solving the inevitable crises of the moment.

Costco bought the majority of its merchandise directly from manufacturers, routing it either directly to its warehouse stores or to one of nine cross-docking depots that served as distribution points for nearby stores. Depots received container-based shipments from manufacturers and reallocated these goods for combined shipment to individual warehouses, generally in less than 24 hours. This maximized freight volume and handling efficiencies. When merchandise arrived at a warehouse, it was moved straight to the sales floor; very little was stored in locations off the sales floor, thereby lowering receiving costs by eliminating many of the costs associated with multiple-step distribution channels, which include purchasing from distributors as opposed to manufacturers; using central receiving, storage, and distribution warehouses; and storing merchandise in locations off the sales floor.

Costco had direct buying relationships with many producers of national brand-name merchandise (including Canon, Casio, Coca-Cola, Colgate-Palmolive, Dell, Fuji, Hewlett-Packard, Kimberly-Clark, Kodak, Levi Strauss, Michelin, Nestlé, Panasonic, Procter & Gamble, Samsung, Sony, KitchenAid, and Jones of New York) and with manufacturers that supplied its Kirkland Signature products. No one manufacturer supplied a significant percentage of the merchandise that Costco stocked. Costco had not experienced any difficulty in obtaining sufficient quantities of merchandise, and management believed that if one or more of its current sources of supply became unavailable, the company could switch its purchases to alternative manufacturers without experiencing a substantial disruption of its business.

Costco warehouses accepted cash, checks, most debit cards, American Express, and a private-label Costco credit card. Costco accepted merchandise returns when members were dissatisfied with their purchases. Losses associated with dishonored checks were minimal because any member whose check had been dishonored was prevented from paying by check or cashing a check at the point of sale until restitution was made. The membership format facilitated strictly controlling the entrances and exits of warehouses, resulting in limited inventory losses of less than two-tenths of 1 percent of net sales—well below those of typical discount retail operations.

Costco's Membership Base and Member Demographics

Costco attracted the most affluent customers in discount retailing—the average income of individual members was about $75,000, with over 30 percent of members having annual incomes of $100,000 or more. Many members were affluent urbanites, living in nice neighborhoods not far from Costco warehouses. One loyal Executive member, a criminal defense lawyer, said, "I think I spend over $20,000–$25,000 a year buying all my products here from food to clothing—except my suits. I have to buy them at the Armani stores."[13] Another Costco loyalist said, "This is the best place in the world. It's like going to church on Sunday. You can't get anything better than this. This is a religious experience."[14]

Costco had two primary types of memberships: Business and Gold Star (individual). Gold Star memberships were for individuals who did not qualify for a Business membership. Businesses—including individuals with a business license, retail sales license, or other evidence of business existence—qualified as Business members. Business members generally paid an annual membership fee of $50 for the primary membership card, which also included a spouse membership card, and could purchase up to six additional membership cards for an annual fee of $40 each for partners or associates in the business; they could also purchase a transferable company card. A significant number of business members also shopped at Costco for their personal needs.

Gold Star members generally paid an annual membership fee of $50, which included a spouse card. In addition, members could upgrade to an Executive membership for an annual fee of $100; Executive members were entitled an additional 2 percent savings on qualified purchases at Costco (redeemable at Costco warehouses), up to a maximum rebate of $500 per year. Executive members also were eligible for savings and benefits on various business and consumer services offered by Costco, including merchant credit card processing, small-business loans, auto and home insurance, long-distance telephone service, check printing, and real estate and mortgage services; these services were mostly offered by third-party providers and varied by state. In 2006, Executive members represented 23 percent of Costco's primary membership base and generated approximately 45 percent of consolidated net sales. Effective May 1, 2006, Costco increased annual membership fees by $5 for U.S. and Canadian Gold Star, Business, and Business Add-on members; the $5 increase, the first in nearly six years, impacted approximately 15 million members.

At the end of fiscal 2006, Costco had almost 48 million cardholders:

Gold Star members (including Executive members)	17,338,000
Business members	5,214,000
Total primary cardholders	22,552,000
Add-on cardholders	25,127,000
Total cardholders	47,679,000

Recent trends in membership are shown at the bottom of Exhibit 1. Members could shop at any Costco warehouse; member renewal rates were about 86.5 percent.

Compensation and Workforce Practices

In September 2006, Costco had 71,000 full-time employees and 56,000 part-time employees, including approximately 8,000 people employed by Costco Mexico, whose operations were not consolidated in Costco's financial and operating results. Approximately 13,800 hourly employees at locations in California, Maryland, New Jersey, and New York, as well as at one warehouse in Virginia, were represented by the International Brotherhood of Teamsters. All remaining employees were non-union.

Starting wages for new Costco employees were in the $10–$12 range in 2006; on average,

Costco employees earned $17–$18 per hour, plus biannual bonuses. Employees enjoyed the full spectrum of benefits. Salaried employees were eligible for benefits on the first of the month after the date of hire. Full-time hourly employees were eligible for benefits on the first of the month after working a probationary 90 days; part-time hourly employees became benefit-eligible on the first of the month after working 180 days. The benefit package included the following:

- Health and dental care plans. Full-time employees could choose from among a freedom-of-choice health care plan, a managed-choice health care plan, and three dental plans. A managed-choice health care and a core dental plan were available for part-time employees. The company paid about 90 percent of an employee's premiums for health care (far above the more normal 50 percent contributions at many other retailers), but employees did have to pick up the premiums for coverage for family members.

- Convenient prescription pickup at Costco's pharmacies, with co-payments as low as $5 for generic drugs. Generally, employees paid no more than 15 percent of the cost for the most expensive branded drugs.

- A vision program that paid $45 for an optical exam (the amount charged at Costco's optical centers) and had generous allowances for the purchase of glasses and contact lenses.

- A 401(k) plan in which Costco matched hourly employee contributions by 50 cents on the dollar for the first $1,000 annually to a maximum company match of $500 per year. Eligible employees qualified for additional company contributions based on the employee's years of service and eligible earnings. The company's union employees on the West Coast qualified for matching contributions of 50 cents on the dollar to a maximum company match of $250 a year; eligible union employees qualified for additional company contributions based on

straight-time hours worked. Company contributions for salaried workers ran about 3 percent of salary during the second year of employment and could be as high as 9 percent of salary after 25 years. Company contributions to employee 401(k) plans were $233.6 million in fiscal 2006, $191.6 million in fiscal 2005, and $169.7 million in fiscal 2004.

- A dependent care reimbursement plan in which Costco employees whose families qualified could pay for day care for children under 13 or adult day care with pretax dollars and realize savings of anywhere from $750 to $2,000 per year.

- Confidential professional counseling services.

- Company-paid long-term disability coverage equal to 60 percent of earnings if out for more than 180 days on a non–worker's compensation leave of absence.

- All employees who passed their 90-day probation period and were working at least 10 hours per week were automatically enrolled in a short-term disability plan covering non-work-related injuries or illnesses for up to 26 weeks. Weekly short-term disability payments equaled 60 percent of average weekly wages up to a maximum of $1,000 and were tax free.

- Generous life insurance and accidental death and dismemberment coverage, with benefits based on years of service and whether the employee worked full-time or part-time. Employees could elect to purchase supplemental coverage for themselves, their spouses, or their children.

- An employee stock purchase plan allowing all employees to buy Costco stock via payroll deduction and avoid commissions and fees.

- A health care reimbursement plan in which benefit-eligible employees could arrange to have pretax money automatically deducted from their paychecks and deposited in a health care reimbursement account that could be used to pay medical and dental bills.

- A long-term care insurance plan for employees with 10 or more years of service. Eligible employees could purchase a basic or supplemental policy for nursing home care for themselves, their spouses, or their parents (including in-laws) or grandparents (including in-laws).

Although admitting that paying good wages and good benefits was contrary to conventional wisdom in discount retailing, Jim Sinegal was convinced that having a well-compensated workforce was very important to executing Costco's strategy successfully. He said, "Imagine that you have 120,000 loyal ambassadors out there who are constantly saying good things about Costco. It has to be a significant advantage for you. . . . Paying good wages and keeping your people working with you is very good business."[15] When a reporter asked him about why Costco treated its workers so well compared to other retailers (particularly Wal-Mart, which paid lower wages and had a skimpier benefits package), Sinegal replied: "Why shouldn't employees have the right to good wages and good careers. . . . It absolutely makes good business sense. Most people agree that we're the lowest-cost producer. Yet we pay the highest wages. So it must mean we get better productivity. Its axiomatic in our business—you get what you pay for."[16]

About 85 percent of Costco's employees had signed up for health insurance, versus about 50 percent at Wal-Mart and Target. The Teamsters' chief negotiator with Costco said, "They gave us the best agreement of any retailer in the country."[17] Good wages and benefits were said to be why employee turnover at Costco ran under 6 percent after the first year of employment. Some Costco employees had been with the company since its founding in 1983. Many others had started working part-time at Costco while in high school or college and opted to make a career at the company. One Costco

employee told an ABC *20/20* reporter, "It's a good place to work; they take good care of us."[18] A Costco vice president and head baker said working for Costco was a family affair: "My whole family works for Costco, my husband does, my daughter does, my new son-in-law does."[19] Another employee, a receiving clerk who made about $40,000 a year, said, "I want to retire here. I love it here."[20] An employee with over two years of service could not be fired without the approval of a senior company officer.

SELECTING PEOPLE FOR OPEN POSITIONS Costco's top management wanted employees to feel that they could have a long career at Costco. It was company policy to fill at least 86 percent of its higher-level openings by promotions from within; in actuality, the percentage ran close to 98 percent, which meant that the majority of Costco's management team members (including warehouse, merchandise, administrative, membership, front end, and receiving managers) were homegrown. Many of the company's vice presidents had started in entry-level jobs; according to Jim Sinegal, "We have guys who started pushing shopping carts out on the parking lot for us who are now vice presidents of our company."[21] Costco made a point of recruiting at local universities; Sinegal explained why: "These people are smarter than the average person, hardworking, and they haven't made a career choice."[22] On another occasion, he said, "If someone came to us and said he just got a master's in business at Harvard, we would say fine, would you like to start pushing carts?"[23] Those employees who demonstrated smarts and strong people management skills moved up through the ranks.

But without an aptitude for the details of discount retailing, even up-and-coming employees stood no chance of being promoted to a position of warehouse manager. Sinegal and other top Costco executives who oversaw warehouse operations insisted that candidates for warehouse managers be top-flight merchandisers with a gift for the details of making items fly off the shelves; Sinegal said, "People who have a feel for it just start to get it. Others, you look at them and it's like staring at a blank canvas. I'm not trying to be unduly harsh, but that's the way it works."[24] Most newly appointed warehouse managers at Costco came from the ranks of assistant warehouse managers who had a track record of being shrewd merchandisers and tuned into what new or different products might sell well given the clientele that patronized their particular warehouse—just having the requisite skills in people management, crisis management, and cost-effective warehouse operations was not enough.

EXECUTIVE COMPENSATION Executives at Costco did not earn the outlandish salaries that had become customary over the past decade at most large corporations. In fiscal 2005, both Jeff Brotman and Jim Sinegal were each paid $350,000 and earned a bonus of $100,000 (versus $350,000 salaries and $200,000 bonuses in fiscal 2004). As of early 2006, Brotman owned about 2.2 million shares of Costco stock (worth about $110 million as of December 2006) and had been awarded options to purchase an additional 1.35 million shares; Sinegal owned 2.7 million shares of Costco stock (worth about $140 million as of December 2006) and had also been awarded options for an additional 1.35 million shares. Several senior officers at Costco were paid 2005 salaries in the $475,000–$500,000 range and bonuses of $47,000–$77,000. Sinegal explained why executive compensation at Costco was only a fraction of the millions paid to top-level executives at other corporations with sales of $50 billion or more: "I figured that if I was making something like 12 times more than the typical person working on the floor, that that was a fair salary."[25] To another reporter, he said: "Listen, I'm one of the founders of this business. I've been very well rewarded. I don't require a salary that's 100 times more than the people who work on the sales floor."[26] Sinegal's employment contract was only a page long and provided that he could be terminated for cause.

Costco's Business Philosophy, Values, and Code of Ethics

Jim Sinegal, who was the son of a steelworker, had ingrained five simple and down-to-earth business principles into Costco's corporate culture and the manner in which the company operated. The following are excerpts of these principles and operating approaches:

1. **Obey the law**—The law is irrefutable! Absent a moral imperative to challenge a law, we must conduct our business in total compliance with the laws of every community where we do business. We pledge to:
   - Comply with all laws and other legal requirements.
   - Respect all public officials and their positions.
   - Comply with safety and security standards for all products sold.
   - Exceed ecological standards required in every community where we do business.
   - Comply with all applicable wage and hour laws.
   - Comply with all applicable anti-trust laws.
   - Conduct business in and with foreign countries in a manner that is legal and proper under United States and foreign laws.
   - Not offer, give, ask for, or receive any form of bribe or kickback to or from any person or pay to expedite government action or otherwise act in violation of the Foreign Corrupt Practices Act.
   - Promote fair, accurate, timely, and understandable disclosure in reports filed with the Securities and Exchange Commission and in other public communications by the Company.

2. **Take care of our members**—Costco membership is open to business owners, as well as individuals. Our members are our

reason for being—the key to our success. If we don't keep our members happy, little else that we do will make a difference. There are plenty of shopping alternatives for our members, and if they fail to show up, we cannot survive. Our members have extended a trust to Costco by virtue of paying a fee to shop with us. We will succeed only if we do not violate the trust they have extended to us, and that trust extends to every area of our business. We pledge to:

- Provide top-quality products at the best prices in the market.

- Provide high-quality, safe, and wholesome food products by requiring that both vendors and employees be in compliance with the highest food safety standards in the industry.

- Provide our members with a 100 per-cent satisfaction guaranteed warranty on every product and service we sell, including their membership fee.

- Assure our members that every product we sell is authentic in make and in representation of performance.

- Make our shopping environment a pleasant experience by making our members feel welcome as our guests.

- Provide products to our members that will be ecologically sensitive.

- Provide our members with the best customer service in the retail industry.

- Give back to our communities through employee volunteerism and employee and corporate contributions to United Way and Children's Hospitals.

3. **Take care of our employees**—Our employees are our most important asset. We believe we have the very best employees in the warehouse club industry, and we are committed to providing them with rewarding challenges and ample opportunities for personal and career growth. We pledge to provide our employees with:

- Competitive wages.

- Great benefits.

- A safe and healthy work environment.

- Challenging and fun work.

- Career opportunities.

- An atmosphere free from harassment or discrimination.

- An Open Door Policy that allows access to ascending levels of management to resolve issues.

- Opportunities to give back to their communities through volunteerism and fundraising.

4. **Respect our suppliers**—Our suppliers are our partners in business and for us to prosper as a company, they must prosper with us. To that end, we strive to:

- Treat all suppliers and their representa-tives as you would expect to be treated if visiting their places of business.

- Honor all commitments.

- Protect all suppliers' property assigned to Costco as though it were our own.

- Not accept gratuities of any kind from a supplier.

- Avoid actual or apparent conflicts of interest, including creating a business in competition with the Company or working for or on behalf of another employer in competition with the Company.

If we do these four things throughout our orga-nization, then we will achieve our ultimate goal, which is to:

5. **Reward our shareholders**—As a company with stock that is traded publicly on the NASDAQ stock exchange, our shareholders are our business partners. We can only be successful so long as we are providing them with a good return on

the money they invest in our company. . . . We pledge to operate our company in such a way that our present and future stockholders, as well as our employees, will be rewarded for our efforts.

Competition

In the discount warehouse retail segment, there were three main competitors—Costco Wholesale, Sam's Club (671 warehouses in six countries—the United States, Canada, Brazil, Mexico, China, and Puerto Rico), and BJ's Wholesale Club (165 locations in 16 states). At the end of 2006, there were just over 1,200 warehouse locations across the United States and Canada; most every major metropolitan area had one, if not several, warehouse clubs. Costco had close to a 55 percent share of warehouse club sales across the United States and Canada, with Sam's Club (a division of Wal-Mart) having roughly a 36 percent share and BJ's Wholesale Club and several small warehouse club competitors about a 9 percent share. The wholesale club and warehouse segment of retailing was estimated to be a $110 billion business, and it was growing about 20 percent faster than retailing as a whole.

Competition among the warehouse clubs was based on such factors as price, merchandise quality and selection, location, and member service. However, warehouse clubs also competed with a wide range of other types of retailers, including retail discounters like Wal-Mart and Dollar General, supermarkets, general merchandise chains, specialty chains, gasoline stations, and Internet retailers. Not only did Wal-Mart, the world's largest retailer, compete directly with Costco via its Sam's Club subsidiary but its Wal-Mart Supercenters sold many of the same types of merchandise at attractively low prices as well. Target and Kohl's had emerged as significant retail competitors in certain merchandise categories. Low-cost operators selling a single category or narrow range of merchandise—such as Lowe's,

Home Depot, Office Depot, Staples, Best Buy, Circuit City, PetSmart, and Barnes & Noble—had significant market share in their respective product categories.

Brief profiles of Costco's two primary competitors in North America are presented in the following sections; Exhibit 3 shows selected financial and operating data for these two competitors.

Sam's Club

In 2007, Sam's Club had 693 warehouse locations and more than 49 million members. Wal-Mart Stores opened the first Sam's Club in 1984, and management had pursued rapid expansion of the membership club format over the next 23 years, creating a chain of 579 U.S. locations in 48 states and 114 international locations in Brazil, Canada, China, Mexico, and Puerto Rico as of February 2007. Many Sam's Club locations were adjacent to Wal-Mart Supercenters. The concept of the Sam's Club format was to sell merchandise at very low profit margins, resulting in low prices to members.

Sam's Clubs ranged between 70,000 and 190,000 square feet, with the average being about 132,000 square feet. All Sam's Club warehouses had concrete floors; sparse decor; and goods displayed on pallets, simple wooden shelves, or racks in the case of apparel. Sam's Club stocked brand-name merchandise, including hard goods, some soft goods, institutional-size grocery items, and selected private-label items sold under the Member's Mark, Bakers & Chefs, and Sam's Club brands. Generally, each Sam's Club also carried software, electronics, jewelry, sporting goods, toys, tires and batteries, stationery and books, and most clubs had fresh-foods departments that included bakery, meat, produce, floral products, and a Sam's Café. A significant number of clubs had a one-hour photo processing department, a pharmacy that filled prescriptions, an optical department, and self-service gasoline pumps. Members could shop for a broad assortment of merchandise and services online at www.samsclub.com.

Exhibit 3

Selected Financial and Operating Data for Sam's Club and BJ's Wholesale Club, 2000–2006

	2006	2005	2004	2002	2000
Sam's Club [a]					
Sales in United States [c] ($ in millions)	$41,582	$39,798	$37,119	$31,702	$26,798
Operating income ($ in millions)	$1,512	$1,385	$1,280	$1,028	$942
Assets ($ in millions)	$6,345	$5,686	$5,685	$4,404	$3,843
Number of locations at year-end	693	670	642	596	564
United States	579	567	551	525	500
International	114	103	91	71	64
Average sales per U.S. location ($ in millions)	$71.8	$66.7	$67.4	$60.4	$3.6
Average warehouse size (square feet)	132,000	129,400	128,300	125,200	122,100
BJ's Wholesale [b]					
Net sales	$8,303	$7,784	$7,220	$5,729	$4,767
Membership fees and other	$177	$166	$155	$131	$102
Total revenues	$8,480	$7,950	$7,375	$5,860	$4,869
Selling, general, and administrative expenses	$698	$611	$556	$416	$335
Operating income	$144	$204	$179	$220	$209
Net income	$72	$129	$114	$131	$132
Total assets	$1,993	$1,990	$1,892	$1,481	$1,234
Number of clubs at year-end	172	165	157	140	118
Number of members (000s)	Not avail.	8,619	8,329	8,190	6,596
Average sales per location ($ in millions)	$48.3	$47.2	$6.0	$40.9	$40.4

[a] Fiscal years end January 31; data for 2006 are for year ending January 31, 2007; data for 2005 are for year ending January 31, 2006; and so on.

[b] Fiscal years ending on last Saturday of January; data for 2006 are for year ending January 27, 2007; data for 2005 are for year ending January 28, 2006; and so on.

[c] For financial reporting purposes, Wal-Mart consolidates the operations of all foreign-based stores into a single "international" segment figure; thus, financial information for foreign-based Sam's Club locations is not separately available.

Like Costco, Sam's Club stocked about 4,000 items, a big fraction of which were standard and a small fraction of which represented special buys and one-time offerings. The treasure-hunt items at Sam's Club tended to be less upscale and carry lower price tags than those at Costco. The percentage composition of sales was as follows:

	2006	2005	2004
Food	32%	30%	31%
Sundries	29	31	31
Hard goods	23	23	23
Soft goods	5	5	6
Service businesses	11	11	9

In 2006, Sam's Club launched a series of initiatives to grow its sales and market share:

- *Adding new lines of merchandise, with more emphasis on products for the home as opposed to small businesses.* In particular, Sam's had put more emphasis on furniture, flat-screen TVs and other electronics products, jewelry, and select other big-ticket items.

- *Instituting new payment methods.* Starting November 10, 2006, Sam's began accepting payment via MasterCard credit cards; prior to then, payment was limited to cash, check, Discover Card, and debit cards. Early results with MasterCard were favorable; company officials reported that in the week following the MasterCard acceptance, the average ticket checkout at Sam's increased by 35 percent.

- *Running ads on national TV.* Sam's spent about $50 million annually on advertising and direct mail promotions. During the 2006 holiday season, Sam's ran national TV ads on high-profile TV programs like *Deal or No Deal*, NBC's coverage of the Macy's Thanksgiving Day Parade, and the Thanksgiving Day NFL matchup between the Detroit Lions and Miami Dolphins on CBS. The TV ads and companion print ads featured Sam's Club shoppers showing off their purchases with a background sound track playing "God Only Knows" by the Beach Boys—scenes included a young man watching shark shows on a flat-screen TV from his bathtub, a well-dressed woman buying a hot dog roaster, and a Florida couple buying a supersize inflatable snow globe.

The annual fee for Sam's Club business members was $35 for the primary membership card, with a spouse card available at no additional cost. Business members could add up to eight business associates for $35 each. The annual membership fee for an individual Advantage member was $40, which included a spouse card. A Sam's Club Plus premium membership cost $100 and included health care insurance, merchant credit card processing, Web site operation, personal and financial services, and an auto, boat, and recreational vehicle program. Regular hours of operations were Monday through Friday 10:00 a.m. to 8:30 p.m., Saturday 9:30 a.m. to 8:30 p.m., and Sunday 10:00 a.m. to 6:00 p.m.

Approximately two-thirds of the merchandise at Sam's Club was shipped from the division's own distribution facilities and, in the case of perishable items, from some of Wal-Mart's grocery distribution centers; the balance was shipped by suppliers direct to Sam's Club locations. Like Costco, Sam's Club distribution centers employed cross-docking techniques whereby incoming shipments were transferred immediately to outgoing trailers destined for Sam's Club locations; shipments typically spent less than 24 hours at a cross-docking facility and in some instances were there only an hour. The Sam's Club distribution center network consisted of 7 company-owned-and-operated distribution facilities, 13 third-party-owned-and-operated facilities, and 2 third-party-owned-and-operated import distribution centers. A combination of company-owned trucks and independent trucking companies were used to transport merchandise from distribution centers to club locations.

BJ's Wholesale Club

BJ's Wholesale Club introduced the member warehouse concept to the northeastern United States in the mid-1980s. Since then it had expanded to 163 stores operating in 16 states in the Northeast and the Mid-Atlantic; it also had two ProFoods Restaurant Supply clubs and three cross-dock distribution centers. BJ's had 144 big-box warehouses (averaging 112,000 square feet) and 19 smaller-format warehouses (averaging 71,000 square feet); the two ProFoods clubs averaged 62,000 square feet. Clubs were located in both freestanding and shopping center locations. Construction and site development costs for a full-sized BJ's Club were in the $5 to $8 million range; land acquisition costs could run $5 to $10 million (significantly higher in some locations). Each warehouse generally had an investment of $3 to $4 million for fixtures and equipment. Pre-opening expenses at a new club were close to $1 million. Full-sized clubs had approximately $2 million in inventory. Merchandise was generally displayed on pallets containing large quantities of each item, thereby reducing labor required for handling, stocking, and restocking. Backup merchandise was generally stored in steel racks above the sales floor. Most merchandise was premarked by the manufacturer so that it did not require ticketing at the club.

Like Costco and Sam's, BJ's Wholesale sold high-quality, brand-name merchandise at prices that were significantly lower than the prices found at supermarkets, discount retail chains, department stores, drugstores, and specialty retail stores like Best Buy. Its merchandise lineup of about 7,500 items included consumer electronics, prerecorded media, small appliances, tires, jewelry, health and beauty aids, household products, computer software, books, greeting cards, apparel, furniture, toys, seasonal items, frozen foods, fresh meat and dairy products, beverages, dry grocery items, fresh produce, flowers, canned goods, and household products; about 70 percent of BJ's product line could be found in supermarkets. Food categories and household items accounted for approximately 59 percent of BJ's total food and general merchandise sales in 2005; about 12 percent of sales consisted of BJ's private-label products, which were primarily premium quality and typically priced well below name-brand products. In some product assortments, BJ's had three price categories for members to choose from—good, deluxe, and luxury.

There were 125 BJ's locations with home improvement service kiosks, 130 clubs with Verizon Wireless kiosks, 44 with pharmacies, and 87 with self-service gas stations. Other specialty products and services, provided mostly by outside operators that leased warehouse space from BJ's, included photo developing, full-service optical centers, brand-name fast-food service, garden and storage sheds, patios and sunrooms, vacation packages, propane tank filling services, discounted home heating oil, an automobile buying service, installation of home security services, printing of business forms and checks, and muffler and brake services.

BJ's Wholesale Club had about 8.6 million members in 2006 (see Exhibit 3). It charged $45 per year for a primary Inner Circle membership that included one free supplemental membership; members in the same household could purchase additional supplemental memberships for $20. A business membership also cost $45 per year, which included one free supplemental membership and the ability to purchase additional supplemental memberships for $20.

BJ's launched a membership rewards program in 2003 that offered members a 2 percent rebate, capped at $500 per year, on most all in-club purchases; members who paid the $80 annual fee to enroll in the rewards program accounted for 5 percent of all members and 10 percent of total merchandise and food sales in 2005. Purchases with a co-branded BJ's MasterCard earned a 1.5 percent rebate. BJ's was the only warehouse club that accepted MasterCard, Visa, Discover, and American Express cards at all locations; members could also pay for purchases by cash, check, and debit cards. BJ's accepted returns of most merchandise within 30 days after purchase.

BJ's increased customer awareness of its clubs primarily through direct mail, public relations efforts, marketing programs for newly opened clubs, and a publication called *BJ's Journal,* which was mailed to members throughout the year; during the holiday season, BJ's engaged in radio and TV advertising, a portion of which was funded by vendors.

Merchandise purchased from manufacturers was shipped either to a BJ's cross-docking facility or directly to clubs. Personnel at the cross-docking facilities broke down truckload quantity shipments from manufacturers and reallocated goods for shipment to individual clubs, generally within 24 hours.

STRATEGY FEATURES THAT DIFFERENTIATED BJ'S   Top management believed that several factors set BJ's Wholesale operations apart from those of Costco and Sam's Club:

- Offering a wide range of choice—7,500 items versus 4,000 items at Costco and Sam's Club.

- Focusing on the individual consumer via merchandising strategies that emphasized a customer-friendly shopping experience.

- Clustering club locations to achieve the benefit of name recognition and maximize the efficiencies of management support, distribution, and marketing activities.

- Trying to establish and maintain the first or second industry leading position in each major market where it operated.

- Creating an exciting shopping experience for members with a constantly changing mix of food and general merchandise items and carrying a broader product assortment than competitors.

- Supplementing the warehouse format with aisle markers, express checkout lanes, self-checkout lanes and low-cost video-based sales aids to make shopping more efficient for members.

- Being open longer hours than competitors.

- Offering smaller package sizes of many items.

- Accepting manufacturers' coupons.

- Accepting more credit card payment options.

Endnotes

[1] As quoted in Alan B. Goldberg and Bill Ritter, "Costco CEO Finds Pro-Worker Means Profitability," an ABC News original report on *20/20,* August 2, 2006, http://abcnews.go.com/2020/Business/story?id=1362779 (accessed November 15, 2006).

[2] Ibid.

[3] As described in Nina Shapiro, "Company for the People," *Seattle Weekly,* December 15, 2004, www.seattleweekly.com (accessed November 14, 2006).

[4] 2005 and 2006 annual reports.

[5] Matthew Boyle, "Why Costco Is So Damn Addictive," *Fortune,* October 30, 2006, p. 130.

[6] As quoted in ibid., pp. 128–29.

[7] Steven Greenhouse, "How Costco Became the Anti-Wal-Mart," *New York Times,* July 17, 2005, www.wakeupwalmart.com/news (accessed November 28, 2006).

[8] As quoted in Greenhouse, "How Costco Became the Anti-Wal-Mart."

[9] As quoted in Shapiro, "Company for the People."

[10] As quoted in Greenhouse, "How Costco Became the Anti-Wal-Mart."

[11] Boyle, "Why Costco Is So Damn Addictive," p. 132.

[12] Ibid., p. 130.

[13] As quoted in Goldberg and Ritter, "Costco CEO Finds Pro-Worker Means Profitability."

[14] Ibid.

[15] Ibid.

[16] Shapiro, "Company for the People."

[17] Greenhouse, "How Costco Became the Anti-Wal-Mart."

[18] As quoted in Goldberg and Ritter, "Costco CEO Finds Pro-Worker Means Profitability."

[19] Ibid.

[20] As quoted in Greenhouse, "How Costco Became the Anti-Wal-Mart."

[21] As quoted in Goldberg and Ritter, "Costco CEO Finds Pro-Worker Means Profitability."

[22] Boyle, "Why Costco Is So Damn Addictive," p. 132.

[23] As quoted in Shapiro, "Company for the People."

[24] Ibid.

[25] As quoted in Goldberg and Ritter, "Costco CEO Finds Pro-Worker Means Profitability."

[26] As quoted in Shapiro, "Company for the People."

Case 2

+CASE TUTOR The Battle in Radio Broadcasting: XM vs. Sirius vs. Local Radio vs. Internet Radio

Arthur A. Thompson Jr.
The University of Alabama

In early 2007, about 220 million people in the United States and Canada listened to radio each week. It was estimated that the average adult listened to radio about three hours daily, with the amount of listening fairly evenly distributed across gender and age groups. But the radio industry in North America was in a state of flux. New technology and changing listening habits were reshaping the competitive structure of the radio marketplace in particular and audio broadcasting in general, precipitating a battle for both listening audiences and advertising dollars. Most motor vehicle manufacturers had begun offering factory-installed or dealer-installed satellite radios in their new vehicles— of the 16 million vehicles expected to be sold in the United States in 2007, at least 5 million were expected to be equipped with satellite radio receivers. Already, almost 15 million U.S. vehicles (about 6 percent of the nation's 230 million registered vehicles) could receive satellite radio broadcasts, and increasing numbers of consumers had begun purchasing satellite radio receivers for their homes. Going into 2007, the two leading satellite radio competitors, XM Radio and Sirius Satellite Radio, had attracted over 14 million U.S. and Canadian subscribers and were expected to add another 3–5 million subscribers in 2007.

In addition, many radio stations were investing in new equipment to begin broadcasting high-definition (HD) digital radio programs. Seven of the top U.S. radio companies had formed a strategic alliance to accelerate the roll-out of HD digital radio broadcasts, and more than 15 manufacturers—including Alpine, Delphi, Panasonic, Polk, and Yamaha—were producing digital radio receivers. Clear Channel Communications, Inc., the largest owner of radio stations in the United States, had announced that it expected to install HD digital radio broadcasting capability at 1,000 of its 1,150 stations by the end of 2008. As of early 2007, more than 1,000 radio stations were broadcasting primary signals with HD radio technology, making HD-quality programming available to 80 percent of the U.S. population; another 2,000 U.S. radio stations had announced plans to initiate HD radio broadcasts within several years. HD digital radio eliminated the static, hiss, pop, and fades associated with analog radio signals so that AM-band broadcasts took on the quality of FM broadcasts; furthermore, FM-band broadcasts of HD digital signals produced CD- and DVD-quality sound. HD radio also permitted radio broadcasters to segment a single, existing radio frequency so that it could carry multiple, simultaneous, higher-quality AM and FM broadcast streams as well as wireless data. A number of local radio stations had also taken steps to have their signals relayed over the Internet; in 2007, there were thousands of free online radio stations and a half-dozen or more Internet sites that specialized in helping people locate online radio broadcasts of their liking. Many Internet radio stations are completely independent from traditional ("terrestrial") radio stations and broadcast only on the Internet. Radio listeners with broadband Internet connections had thousands of choices, including Internet-enabled radio stations anywhere in the world—it was very easy to listen to a European radio station from North America or New Zealand. Internet radio was popular with people whose interests were not being met by their local radio stations. Some people were drawn to Internet radio because of the enormously wide genre of programs that were available, because they were traveling or temporarily living in a foreign country, and/or because they were looking to expand their cross-cultural awareness.

An even newer phenomenon was podcasting—an on-the-go, on-demand technology that enabled people to listen to audio files that could be downloaded from the Internet (using some version of podcasting software) to a personal computer, an iPod, a cell phone, or other type of digital media player. Podcast-enabled devices made it simple for the user to download and listen to any of tens of thousands of podcasts whose content ranged from Spanish lessons to headline news to ESPN sports to health information to any type of music imaginable. *BusinessWeek* had emerged as the leading supplier of business-related podcasts. In 2006, podcast enthusiasts downloaded millions of files at Google, Yahoo! Podcasts, MSN, AOL, and Apple's iTunes Music Store. Web sites like Podcast.net and Podcast.com had sprung up that allowed podcast producers to post their creations and podcast listeners to sample, find, subscribe, and listen to most any of the tens of thousands of podcasts available worldwide.

Several local radio stations and some of their more entrepreneurial disc jockeys had begun assembling their own customized podcasts of music or other topics and posting the podcasts on Web sites for interested listeners to download. Brian Ibbott, an enterprising disc joskey in a Denver suburb, produced a series of 35-minute music podcasts called Coverville that focused on a new rendition of a previously recorded cover song of an album.[1] Ibbott's podcasts, which were produced in his home and delivered in an informal, relaxed style, usually featured about six selections and included information about the performing artist and source album. Coverville downloads became so popular that Ibbott turned his podcasts into a sideline business, creating his own Web site, Coverville.com, at which he sold advertising and marketed subscriptions to Coverville via Yahoo! and iTunes.

Another increasingly important competitive element in the radio broadcasting market was the exploding use of portable MP3 players; these devices, which sold for approximately $80–$350 and could store up to 20,000 songs, could also be plugged into car outlets and used as a music source while driving. Using MP3 players to listen to music instead of tuning into radio stations was commonplace in 2007 since song files could be readily obtained via numerous file-sharing software programs and on the Web sites of online music retailers, artists, and record labels. At Apple's iTunes Web site, iPod owners could download and purchase over 4 million songs, 100,000 podcasts, 20,000 audio books, 5,000 music videos, 250 feature films, and 350 television shows, as well as convert music on compact disc to digital files. Apple had sold close to 89 million iPods as of January 2007.

Still another, but lesser, competitive element was the recent entry of cable TV companies into the music broadcasting marketplace. Cable TV companies customarily included 40 or so continuous music channels as part of the digital programming package offered to consumers having digital and high-definition TVs.

In 2000, market research indicated that about 75 percent of the population 12 years and older listened to the radio daily and about 95 percent listened at least once weekly.[2] However, in 2006–2007, these percentages were believed to have fallen, particularly among younger age groups due to the enormous popularity of iPods and other brands of portable MP3 players as a primary music source for teens and young adults.

The Radio Broadcasting Industry

In 2006, there were close to 11,000 commercial radio stations in the United States licensed by the Federal Communications Commission, of which 43.2 percent were AM stations and 66.8 percent were FM stations; there were an additional 2,760 FM educational stations. The number of licensed commercial radio stations had hovered in the range of 10,200 to 11,000 since the mid-1990s. However, the number of radio station owners had been in a long-term decline as more and more stations came under the ownership of a single operator. While there were about 9,300 radio stations in 2006, according to market researcher C. Barnes & Co., the radio broadcasting industry had become increasingly dominated by such large multistation operators as Clear Channel Communications (about 1,150 stations), Cumulus Media (307 stations), Citadel Communications (223 stations), Infinity Broadcasting (178 stations), Entercom Communications (119 stations), and Cox Radio (80 stations). About 30 other operators had 20 or more stations each. In addition to the trend toward greater industry consolidation, a number of multistation operators were restructuring their radio station portfolios. Several larger operators were selling off stations in smaller audience markets in order to better concentrate their attention and resources on midsized and larger markets. Clear Channel, for example, in late 2006 announced plans to sell 448 of its stations that were outside the Top 100 Arbitron Metro areas (it also planned to divest its entire group of 42 television stations, all of which were located in small and midsized geographic areas throughout the United States).

Traditional AM and FM radio stations had a well-established market for their product offering and used an advertising-based business model that provided free broadcast reception paid for by commercial advertising. Stations chose one of several basic programming formats (music, talk, sports, religious, news, educational, ethnic), put their own differentiating spin on the selected programming format, and then tried to make money by selling a sufficient number of advertising spots at rates commensurate with their audience ratings to produce a profitable revenue stream. Radio stations competed for listeners and advertising revenues with other radio stations in their geographic listening area according to such factors as program content, on-air talent, transmitter power, and audience demographics; these factors, along with audience size and the number and characteristics of other radio stations in the area, affected the rates they were able to charge for advertising. A growing number of AM and FM radio stations had begun reducing the number of commercials per hour, expanding the range of music played on the air, improving ad copy, and experimenting with new formats in order to provide more entertaining listening and better compete with satellite radio.

Revenues for the licensed commercial stations in the United States in 2006 were about $21.2 billion, of which $20.5 billion or 96.9 percent came from ad sales. According to market research data compiled by C. Barnes & Co., radio industry revenues had grown briskly over the past three years, and the brisk growth was expected to continue through 2008:[3]

2004	$15.7 billion
2005	18.4
2006	21.2
2007	24.1
2008	27.1

Each of the 100 largest metro area markets in the United States generated annual radio advertising revenues of $40 million or more. The largest radio market, New York City and the surrounding area, generated ad revenues of just over $1 billion; between 40 and 45 U.S. metro areas generated radio advertising revenues of $100 million or more. However, there were about 650 geographic markets that generated less than $10 million in radio advertising annually.

XM Satellite Radio Inc.

XM Satellite Radio was incorporated in 1992 for the purpose of exploiting satellite radio transmission technology and creating a national radio network to compete alongside traditional AM and FM radio stations. XM became a public company in 1999 with an issue of 10.2 million shares of common stock that yielded net proceeds of $114 million. Follow-on offerings of common stock, along with preferred stock issues and secured notes, were undertaken in late 1999 and early 2000 to raise an additional $750 million in capital to help finance the launch of two high-powered Boeing satellites, arrange for the manufacture of satellite radio receivers and other equipment, install terrestrial signal repeaters and other necessary networking equipment, develop programming, conduct market research, and attract subscribers. Program broadcasts began in November 2001, and by December 2002 the company had attracted almost 350,000 subscribers at fees of $9.95 per month. Market research done in 2000–2001 indicated that as many as 49 million people might subscribe to satellite radio service by 2012, assuming a monthly fee of $9.95 and radio receiver prices of $150–$399, depending on the car or home model chosen. A 2002 market research study conducted for XM concluded that there would be about 15 million satellite radio subscribers by the end of 2006. The forecast proved fairly accurate given that both XM and Sirius had recently raised their subscription rates to $12.95 monthly; at year-end 2006, there were 13.6 million satellite radio subscribers in the United States. (XM Radio had 7.63 million subscribers and Sirius had 6.0 million subscribers.) During 2006, XM added 1.7 million new subscribers, but this was fewer than the 3 million that senior management forecast at the start of 2006.

However, XM had yet to earn a profit from its satellite service; the company had lost money every year of its existence. As shown in Exhibit 1, XM reported losses of $584.5 million in 2003, $642.4 million in 2004, $666.7 million in 2005, and $718.9 million in 2006. Exhibit 2 and 3 show XM Radio's balance sheets and cash flow performance for 2003–2006. In the fourth quarter of 2006, XM Radio reported a positive cash flow from operations despite the sizable losses.

XM Satellite Radio's Business Model and Strategy

In stark contrast to the advertising-based business model of traditional local radio, XM Radio employed a subscription-based business model. The company endeavored to offer a sufficiently broad and appealing selection of digital-quality radio programs that would attract listeners willing to pay $12.95 per month for mostly commercial-free programming. XM had a family plan that allowed subscribers to get a discounted rate of $6.99 per month for additional radios. So far, XM had been restrained in trying to cover some of its costs via ad sales, although a few XM channels did run occasional advertising spots.

PROGRAM OFFERINGS   XM's lineup of over 170 channels in early 2007 had broad listener appeal and included 69 commercial-free music channels, 5 commercial music channels, 37 news/talk/commentary channels, 38 sports channels, and 21 instant traffic and weather channels—see Exhibit 4. XM subscribers could listen to original music and talk channels created by XM's programming staff, programs and channels of leading national brand-name content providers like Fox News and ESPN, and live coverage of over 5,000 sporting events annually (including play-by-play broadcasts of Major League Baseball, college football, college men's and women's basketball, and the National Hockey League, plus coverage of PGA Tour, FIFA World Cup soccer, and NASCAR racing events. From time to time, XM added new

Exhibit 1

Consolidation Statement of Operations, XM Radio, 2003–2006 ($ in thousands, except per share amounts)

	2006	2005	2004	2003
Revenue:				
Subscriptions	$825,626	$502,612	$220,468	$78,239
Activation	16,192	10,066	4,814	1,868
Merchandise	21,720	18,182	7,261	6,692
Net ad sales	35,330	20,103	8,485	4,065
Other revenue	34,549	7,303	3,415	917
Total revenue	933,417	558,266	244,443	91,781
Operating expenses:				
Cost of revenue (excludes depreciation & amortization):				
Revenue share & royalties	149,010	93,874	50,676	26,440
Customer care & billing operations	104,871	76,222	40,887	25,945
Cost of merchandise	48,949	40,707	11,557	9,797
Ad sales	15,961	10,058	6,165	3,257
Satellite & terrestrial	49,019	42,355	35,922	39,692
Broadcast & operations:				
Broadcast	23,049	16,609	10,832	7,689
Operations	34,683	24,460	13,192	12,023
Total broadcast & operations	57,732	41,069	24,024	19,712
Programming & content	165,196	101,008	32,704	23,109
Total cost of revenue	590,738	405,293	201,935	147,952
Research & development (excludes depreciation & amortization)	37,428	31,218	23,513	12,285
General & administrative (excludes depreciation & amortization)	88,626	43,864	28,555	27,418
Marketing (excludes depreciation & amortization):				
Retention & support	31,842	22,275	13,286	7,873
Subsidies & distribution	241,601	264,719	165,704	92,521
Advertising & marketing	147,640	163,312	88,076	64,309
Amortization of GM liability	29,760	37,250	37,250	35,564
Total marketing	450,843	487,556	304,316	200,267
Depreciation & amortization	168,880	145,870	147,165	158,317
Total operating expenses	1,336,515	1,113,801	705,484	546,239
Operating loss	(403,098)	(555,535)	(461,041)	(454,458)
Other income (expense):				
Interest income	21,664	23,586	6,239	3,066
Interest expense	(121,304)	(107,791)	(85,757)	(110,349)
Loss from de-leveraging transactions	(122,189)	(27,552)	(76,621)	(24,749)
Loss from impairment of investments	(76,572)	—	—	—
Equity in net loss of affiliate	(23,229)	(482)		
Other income	5,842	3,389	2,129	1,955
Net loss before income taxes	(718,886)	(664,385)	(615,051)	(584,535)
Provision for deferred income taxes	14	(2,330)	(27,317)	—
Net loss	$(718,872)	$(666,715)	$(642,368)	$(584,535)
Preferred stock dividend requirements	(12,820)	(8,597)	(8,802)	(17,569)
Net loss on Series B and C preferred stock retirement		—		(2,776)
Net loss attributable to common stockholders	$(731,692)	$(675,312)	$(651,170)	$(604,880)
Net loss per share of common stock: basic and diluted	$(2.70)	$(3.07)	$(3.30)	$(4.83)
Weighted average shares used in computing loss per share	270,586,682	219,620,468	197,317,607	125,176,320

Sources: 2005 and 2006 10-K reports and company press release, February 26, 2007.

Exhibit 2

Consolidated Balance Sheet, XM Radio, 2004–2006 ($ in thousands)

	2006	2005	2004
ASSETS			
Current assets:			
Cash and cash equivalents	$ 218,216	$ 710,991	$ 717,867
Accounts receivable, net of allowance for doubtful accounts	62,293	47,247	20,182
Due from related parties	13,991	8,629	5,367
Related party prepaid expenses	66,946	54,752	31,160
Prepaid programming content	28,172	65,738	11,390
Prepaid and other current assets	43,040	55,811	18,197
Total current assets	$ 432,658	$ 943,168	$ 804,163
Restricted investments	2,098	5,438	4,492
System under construction	126,049	216,527	329,355
Net property and equipment	849,662	673,672	461,333
Digital Audio Radio Service (DARS) license from FCC	141,387	141,276	141,227
Intangibles, net of accumulated amortization	4,640	5,902	7,164
Deferred financing fees, net of accumulated amortization	38,601	36,735	44,466
Related party prepaid expenses, net of current portion	160,712	9,809	25,901
Equity investments	80,592	187,403	—
Prepaid and other assets, net of current portion	4,219	3,731	3,534
Total assets	$1,840,618	$2,223,661	$1,821,635
LIABILITIES AND STOCKHOLDERS' EQUITY			
Current liabilities:			
Accounts payable	$ 51,844	$ 145,691	$ 59,986
Accrued expenses	147,591	154,125	88,107
Accrued satellite liability	64,875	104,300	100,100
Accrued interest	18,482	5,603	14,146
Current portion of long-term debt	14,445	7,608	6,556
Due to related parties	46,459	60,750	27,610
Subscriber deferred revenue	340,711	275,944	114,951
Deferred income	9,915	10,137	—
Total current liabilities	$ 694,322	$ 764,158	$ 411,456
Satellite liability, net of current portion	—	23,285	15,000
Long-term debt, net of current portion	1,286,179	1,035,584	948,741
Due to related parties, net of current portion	—	53,901	38,911
Subscriber deferred revenue, net of current portion	86,482	84,694	37,396
Deferred income, net of current portion	140,695	141,073	—
Other noncurrent liabilities	40,735	40,018	33,968
Total liabilities	$2,238,498	$2,142,713	$1,485,472
Stockholders' equity			
Series A, B, C, and D preferred stock, par value $0.01	54	60	60
Class A common stock, par value $0.01; 600,000,000 shares authorized, 305,781,515 shares, 240,701,988 shares, and 208,249,188 shares issued and outstanding at December 31, 2006	3,058	2,407	2,082
Accumulated other comprehensive income	3,590	5,985	—
Unearned restricted stock compensation	—	(18,101)	—
Additional paid-in capital	3,093,894	2,870,201	2,446,910
Accumulated deficit	(3,498,476)	(2,779,604)	(2,112,889)
Total stockholders' equity (deficit)	(397,880)	80,948	336,163
Total liabilities and stockholders' equity	$1,840,618	$2,223,661	$1,821,635

Sources: 2005 and 2006 10-K reports; company press release on February 26, 2007.

Exhibit 3

Selected Cash Flow Data, XM Radio, 2003–2006 ($ in thousands)

	2006	2005	2004	2003
Cash flows from operating activities:				
Net loss	$(718,872)	$(666,715)	$(642,368)	$(584,535)
Net cash used in operating activities	(462,091)	(168,449)	(85,552)	(245,123)
Cash flows from investing activities:				
Purchase of property and equipment	$ (54,895)	$ (61,210)	$ (25,934)	$ (15,685)
Additions to system under construction	(220,124)	(118,583)	(143,978)	(4,108)
Proceeds from sale of assets	7,182	—	—	—
Purchase of equity investments	—	(25,334)	—	—
Net maturity (purchase) of restricted investments	3,390	(996)	(341)	22,750
Insurance proceeds from satellite recoveries	—	—	133,924	—
Other investing activities	—	—	—	11,664
Net cash (used in) provided by investing activities	$(264,447)	$(206,123)	$ (36,329)	$ 14,621
Cash flows from financing activities:				
Proceeds from sale of common stock, net and exercise of stock options	$ 6,420	$ 319,637	$ 236,835	$ 253,102
Proceeds from issuance of 9.75% senior notes due 2014	600,000	—	—	—
Proceeds from issuance of senior floating rate notes due 2013	200,000	—	—	—
Proceeds from issuance of 10% senior secured convertible notes	—	—	—	210,000
Proceeds from issuance of 12% senior secured notes	—	—	—	185,000
Proceeds from issuance of 1.75% convertible senior notes	—	100,000	300,000	—
Proceeds from issuance of floating rate notes	—	—	200,000	—
Proceeds from refinancing of mortgage on corporate facility	—	—	33,300	—
Payments of premiums on de-leveraging transactions	(27,398)	(3,398)	(10,347)	
Repayment of 12% senior secured notes	(100,000)	(15,000)	(70,000)	—
Repayment of 7.75% convertible subordinated notes	—	—	(6,723)	
Repayment of 14% senior secured notes	(186,545)	(22,824)	(13,028)	—
Repayment of related-party long-term debt	—	—	(81,194)	—
Repayment of senior secured floating rate notes due 2009	(200,000)	—	—	—
Payments on mortgages on corporate facilities	(578)	(381)	(28,247)	(420)
Payments on related-party credit facility	—	—	(103,034)	—
Repurchase of Series B preferred stock	(23,960)	—	—	(10,162)
Payments on other borrowings	(12,725)	(9,651)	(40,174)	(2,722)
Deferred financing costs	(21,451)	(2,419)	(13,017)	(12,084)
Net cash provided by financing activities	$ 233,763	$ 365,964	$ 411,094	$ 615,991
Net increase (decrease) in cash and cash equivalents	$(492,775)	$ (6,876)	$ 299,560	$ 385,489
Cash and cash equivalents at beginning of period	710,991	717,867	418,307	32,818
Cash and cash equivalents at end of period	$ 218,216	$ 710,991	$ 717,867	$ 418,307

Sources: 2005 and 2006 10-K reports.

Exhibit 4

Comparative Programming and Channel Offerings, XM Radio and Sirius Satellite Radio, February 2007

	XM RADIO	SIRIUS SATELLITE RADIO
Monthly subscription cost	$12.95	$12.95
Number of channels	Over 170	Over 130
Music		
Music by decades	50s, 60s, 70s, 80s, 90s	50s, 60s, 70s, 80s, 90s
Pop and Hits	11 channels	15 channels
Country	9 channels	7 channels
Rock	14 channels	13 channels
Hip-Hop/Urban/R&B	7 channels	7 channels
Christian/Gospel	3 channels	3 channels
Jazz/Blues	5 channels	5 channels
Classical	3 channels	3 channels
Latin/International	7 channels	7 channels
Dance/Electronic/Standards/ Other	9 channels	7 channels
News	Fox News, CNN, CNN Headline, ABC News & Talk, MSNBC, 5 others	Fox News, CNN, CNN Headline, ABC News & Talk, CNBC, 7 others
Talk, Variety & Entertainment	Fox News Talk, C-Span, Open Road (truckers channel), The Power (African American talk), Talk Five (a women's interest channel), Oprah & Family, E!, 6 other channels	NPR Talk, NPR Now, Fox News Talk, Political Talk, C-Span, Howard Stern, Martha Stewart Living, Court TV Radio, Playboy Radio, E!, 3 others
Sports News and Talk	ESPN Radio, ESPN News, Fox Sports Radio, NASCAR Radio, The Sporting News, PGA Tour Network, Home Ice (24/7 hockey talk and play-by-play), MLB Home Plate (24/7 MLB news & talk), 2 others	ESPN Radio, ESPN News, ESPN Deportes, NBA Radio, NFL Radio (non-stop NFL talk), Sports Byline USA, 2 others
Family/Kids	Radio Disney, XM Kids, Radio Classics, Family Talk	LIME, Radio Disney, Kids Stuff, Radio Classics, Discovery Channel Radio
Traffic & Weather	The Weather Channel, Instant Traffic & Weather in 21 urban areas, XM 24/7 Emergency Alert	Local weather & traffic in 11 areas, Canada weather, Sirius weather and emergency
Financial News	CNBC, Bloomberg Radio	CNBC, Bloomberg
Comedy	5 channels	3 channels
Religion	—	3 channels
Special Programming	Opie and Anthony programs, Major League Baseball (play-by-play of games on 14 channels, plus a Spanish language channel), College Sports (ACC, PAC-10, Big Ten, Big East), National Hockey League (play-by-play), broadcasts of 16 college football bowl games, 6 holiday channels	Dave Ramsey Show, Richard Simmons, Adam Curry (podcasts), NFL play-by-play of games, NBA play-by-play of 1,000 games, NHL play-by-play (up to 40 games per week during the season), Wimbledon tennis championships

Sources: Company Web sites, accessed December 15, 2006, and March 5, 2007.

channels and altered its programs on existing channels to enhance listener appeal and keep its offerings fresh and in step with lifestyle trends for all age groups. The company had broadcast studios in New York City; Washington, D.C.; and the Country Music Hall of Fame in Nashville, Tennessee.

XM's target market included the drivers of the 255+ million registered automobiles and trucks and the 125+ million households with home radios in both the United States and Canada. Management believed that XM Radio had broad market appeal because of its "innovative and diverse programming, nationwide coverage, many commercial-free music channels, and digital sound quality."[4]

Programming could be received via portable receivers suitable for personal and home use and receivers installed in vehicles. Subscribers had online access to more than 85 XM channels over the Internet. In November 2005, XM management partnered with DIRECTV to make 72 channels of XM's music, children's, and talk programming available to the over 16 million customers of DIRECTV. XM also offered an online service through an arrangement with AOL and had partnered with Napster to provide online music purchase and playlist management capability.

XM's Marketing Strategy and Marketing Partnerships

XM's marketing strategy was aimed at building awareness and demand among potential subscribers and in the advertising community. The company made a point of advertising that its satellite radio service had appealing features compared to traditional radio. Advertising and promotional activities were conducted via television, radio, print, and the Internet; sample programming and marketing materials were distributed at retail outlets, concert venues, and motor sports events and on the Internet to generate consumer interest. General Motors and Honda sponsored national and local print and television advertising that featured the XM logo and message. The company's 2005 holiday

season "Listen Large" marketing campaign featured TV spots with Ellen DeGeneres, Snoop Dogg, Derek Jeter, David Bowie, and Martina McBride. To leverage its extensive sports broadcasting offerings and exclusive relationships with Major League Baseball, XM promoted its "every team, all season long" play-by-play broadcasts of more than 2,500 Major League Baseball spring training, regular season, and playoff games. A free Delphi XM Roady XT satellite radio was offered to every fan at Game One of the 2005 World Series in Chicago. XM promoted its exclusive relationship with the PGA Tour by offering handheld radios for rental and purchase at PGA events. And it had a multiyear agreement with Andretti Green Racing (AGR) to be a major associate sponsor of the race car driven by IndyCar Series superstar Danica Patrick. XM Radio service was available on certain AirTran, JetBlue, and United airplanes, and the company had an exclusive multiyear strategic marketing alliance with Starbucks, which included the Starbucks Hear Music channel on XM and a multi-artist music compilation CD series.

Other subscriber acquisition promotional activities included:

- In-store promotional campaigns, including displays located in electronics, music and other retail stores, rental car agencies and automobile dealerships.
- Incentive programs for retailers.
- Jointly funded local advertising campaigns with retailers.

A central element of XM's marketing strategy to grow its business and obtain new subscribers was to have XM receivers installed in new motor vehicles—purchasers of new vehicles equipped with a factory-installed XM receiver typically got a free three-month or six-month trial subscription. Via partnerships with General Motors (an investor in XM Radio), Honda/Acura (also an investor in XM Radio), Toyota/Lexus/Scion, Hyundai, Nissan/Infiniti, Porsche, Volkswagen/Audi, and others (see Exhibit 5), XM Radio was available as a factory-installed

Exhibit 5

Motor Vehicle and Rental Car Brands That Install XM Radio and Sirius Satellite Receivers, December 2006

MOTOR VEHICLE PARTNERS	
XM RADIO	**SIRIUS SATELLITE RADIO**
Acura	Aston Martin
Alamo Car Rental	Audi
Avis Car Rental	BMW
General Motors (Buick, Cadillac, Chevrolet, Hummer, GMC, Pontiac, Saab, Saturn)	Daimler Chrysler (Chrysler, Dodge, Jeep, Mercedes)
Harley-Davidson	Fleetwood Enterprises (motorhomes)
Honda	Ford/Lincoln/Mercury
Hyundai	Hertz Car Rental
Infiniti	Infiniti
Isuzu	Jaguar
National Car Rental	Kia Motors
Nissan	Land Rover
Porsche	Lexus
Subaru	Mitsubishi
Suzuki	Rolls Royce
Toyota/Lexus/Scion	Volvo
Volkswagen/Audi	

Source: Company Web sites, as of December 2006.

or dealer-installed option in more than 140 different vehicle models for model years 2006 and 2007; in a number of these models, XM service was available to new car prospects during vehicle test drives. General Motors offered factory-installed XM receivers as an option on over 55 models; GM had installed over 4 million XM radios as of fall 2006 and expected to install as many as 1.8 million XM receivers in its 2007 models. American Honda planned to equip more than 650,000 vehicles with factory XM radios in 2007. In 2005, Hyundai Motor America became the first automaker to launch XM as standard, factory-installed equipment in every vehicle across its entire model lineup. Harley-Davidson became the first manufacturer of motorcycles to offer XM Radio as an option on all six 2006 model bikes in its touring lineup; XM was standard equipment on Harley-Davidson's Screamin' Eagle Ultra Classic Electra Glide model.

XM's marketing and promotional costs to obtain new subscribers and retain existing subscribers totaled $450.8 million in 2006, $487.6 million in 2005, $304.3 million in 2004, and $200.3 million in 2003 (Exhibit 1). The amounts spent on marketing and promotion to secure new subscribers were exceptionally burdensome, as shown in Exhibit 6.

XM RADIO EQUIPMENT   XM radios ranging in price from $200 to $400 were available at such national consumer electronics retailers as Best Buy, Circuit City, and Wal-Mart under the Delphi, Pioneer, Alpine, Audiovox, Tao, Sony, Polk, and etón/Grundig brand names. In 2006, numerous mass-market retailers sold support for XM's car stereo, home stereo, plug-and-play, and portable handheld products. The company had expanded its product line in 2006 to include several new models of XM2go portable receivers and had added both XM

Exhibit 6

Comparative Measures of XM Radio's Performance per Average Subscriber and as a Percentage of Total Revenue, 2003–2006

ANNUAL AMOUNTS PER AVERAGE SUBSCRIBER[1]					AMOUNTS AS A PERCENTAGE OF TOTAL REVENUE			
2006	2005	2004	2003		2006	2005	2004	2003
$138	$122	$107	$108	**Total revenue**	100%	100%	100%	100%
122	110	96	92	Subscription revenue	88	90	90	85
5	4	4	5	Net ad sales	4	4	3	4
(87)	(88)	(88)	(177)	**Total cost of revenue**	63	73	84	164
(22)	(20)	(22)	(31)	Revenue share & royalties	16	17	21	29
(15)	(17)	(18)	(30)	Customer care & billing operations	11	14	17	28
n.a.	(9)	(5)	(11)	Cost of merchandise	n.a.	7	5	11
(7)	(9)	(16)	(46)	Satellite & terrestrial	5	8	15	43
(9)	(9)	(10)	(26)	Broadcast & operations	6	7	10	21
(24)	(22)	(14)	(27)	Programming & content	18	18	13	25
(6)	(7)	(10)	n.a.	Research & development	4	6	10	n.a.
(13)	(10)	(12)	(33)	General & administrative	9	8	12	30
(66)	(106)	(133)	(235)	**Total marketing**	48	87	124	218
(5)	(5)	(6)	n.a.	Retention & support	3	4	5	n.a.
(36)	(58)	(72)	(108)	Subsidies & distribution	26	47	68	101
(22)	(36)	(38)	(75)	Advertising & marketing	16	29	36	70
(25)	(88)	(136)	(386)	**Adjusted EBITDA loss** [2]	18	72	128	359

[1] Average subscribers are calculated as the averages of the beginning and ending subscriber balances for each year.

[2] EBITDA — Earnings before interest, taxes, depreciation, and amortization.

Sources: Data for 2004–2006 are from the company's 2006 10-K report, p. 40; data for 2003 are from the company's 2005 10-K report, p. 36.

Connect-and-Play technology and the capability to download and play MP3 files to several of its radio models. Some models featured customizable sports and stock tickers as well as TuneSelect, which notified the listener when a favorite artist or song was playing on any XM channel. In 2005, the first generation XM2go receivers had won numerous awards for innovation and for consumer technology design and engineering. Five XM products were recognized as honorees for the Innovations 2006 Awards sponsored by the Consumer Electronics Association. XM management planned to continue to add new receiver features and expand its model lineup in 2007.

XM radios incorporated a proprietary chip set, designed by the company's technology and innovation team in conjunction with others, to decode the signal from XM's satellites and repeaters. Ongoing improvements in the chipset design had spawned a broad array of XM Radio products, including units significantly smaller and much less expensive than the first-generation models. The latest generation of XM radios included handheld units with memory features and models with customizable sports and stock tickers as well as TuneSelect, which notified the listener when a favorite artist or song was playing on XM.

XM had partnered with Sirius Satellite Radio, its principal competitor, to develop a common receiver platform for satellite radios that would enable buyers to purchase one radio receiver capable of receiving both XM and Sirius signals.

The technology was being jointly developed and funded by the two companies, with each company having an ownership interest in the technology. The joint effort to develop a common receiver platform was spurred by FCC rules that required both licensed satellite radio systems to move toward the use of technology that enabled consumers to receive XM and Sirius signals via the same receiver.

SIGNAL TRANSMISSION OPERATIONS

From 2001 to 2005, XM Radio broadcast its signals throughout the continental United States from the two satellites (known as *Rock* and *Roll*) that were launched in 2001. A third satellite (known as *Rhythm*) was launched in February 2005. In the second half of 2006, the company launched a fourth satellite (known as *Blues*) to replace signal transmission by the *Rock* and *Roll* satellites; the company expected to use *Rock* and *Roll* as in-orbit spares for the near term (the licenses for these two satellites expire in 2009). The combination of the new *Rhythm* and *Blues* satellites gave XM the capability to deliver a full complement of digital broadcasts for at least 15 more years (the length of a satellite's useful life). The license for the *Rhythm* satellite expires in 2013, and the license for the *Blues* satellite expires in 2014, but licenses could be renewed by the Federal Communications Commission absent significant misconduct on XM's part. XM also had a network of approximately 800 terrestrial repeaters, which received and retransmitted the satellite signals in 60 markets to augment the satellite signal coverage that was impaired by buildings, tunnels, or terrain.

CANADIAN OPERATIONS

In November 2005, Canadian Satellite Radio, operating under the name XM Canada, XM's exclusive Canadian licensee, launched its satellite radio service in Canada for a monthly subscription fee of CDN$12.99. XM Canada's 100+ channel lineup included XM's digital-quality commercial-free music, exclusive Canadian channels highlighting Canadian artists, National Hockey League play-by-play coverage of more than 40 games per week, and news/talk. XM Canada had 147,000 subscribers as of November 30, 2006, and had a goal of 1 million subscribers by 2010. XM Canada had an 80 percent share of all factory-installed satellite radios in current 2007 vehicles being marketed in Canada and was available as a factory-installed or dealer-installed option on 115 different models in 2007. XM Satellite Radio owned a 23 percent interest in XM Canada, had two representatives on the board of directors, and received 15 percent of XM Canada's monthly subscription revenues.

COPYRIGHT AGREEMENTS

Like all radio broadcasters, XM maintained music programming royalty arrangements with and paid license fees to such organizations as Broadcast Music Inc. (BMI) and the American Society of Composers, Authors and Publishers (ASCAP), which negotiated with copyright users, collected royalties, and distributed them to songwriters and music publishers. Under the Digital Performance Right in Sound Recordings Act of 1995 and the Digital Millennium Copyright Act of 1998, broadcasters had to negotiate royalty arrangements with the copyright owners of the sound recordings or, if negotiation is unsuccessful, have the royalty rate established by a copyright royalty board. In July 2006, XM negotiated a new five-year music licensing agreement with ASCAP; however, its other licensing and royalty agreements expired in 2006. XM Radio was participating in a Copyright Royalty Board proceeding in order to set the royalty rate for the six-year period starting in January 2007.

Sirius Satellite Radio Inc.

Sirius Satellite launched national service in July 2002. Like XM, Sirius employed a subscription-based business model and sought to attract customers with an attractive lineup of channels. By year-end 2003, it had 261,000 subscribers; three years later it had 6 million subscribers (see Exhibit 10 on page C-252). In early 2007, Sirius was broadcasting on 133 channels that included 69 channels of 100 percent commercial-free music and 64 channels of sports, news, talk, entertainment, traffic, weather, and data content for a monthly subscription fee of $12.95. Exhibit 4 shows how Sirius Satellite Radio's programming lineup compared with that of XM Radio.

But despite the company's rapidly expanding subscriber base, Sirius (just like XM) had been gushing red ink, with reported losses of $314 million in 2003, $712 million in 2004, $863 million in 2005, and $1.1 billion in 2006. However, management expected the company to generate positive free cash flow (after capital expenditures) in 2007; Sirius achieved its first ever quarter of positive free cash flow in the fourth quarter of 2006. In the 2005 annual report, Sirius CEO Mel Karmazin predicted revenues of $3 billion and positive cash flows of approximately $1 billion in 2010. Karmazin said the company was focused on achieving positive cash flow, accelerating along the path to profitability, and providing the best content in all of radio. The company's financial statements are shown in Exhibits 7, 8, and 9.

Sirius Satellite Radio's Marketing Strategy

As was the case with XM Radio, two key components of Sirius Satellite Radio's strategy to grow its subscriber base and market the concept of satellite radio, in addition to appealing programming, were to partner with motor vehicle manufacturers to install satellite radio receivers in new vehicles and to promote the sales of receivers in retail channels. Sirius had partnerships with DaimlerChrysler, Ford, Mitsubishi, BMW, Rolls-Royce, Nissan, Infiniti, Toyota, Lexus, Scion, Volkswagen, Audi, and Subaru to offer Sirius receivers as factory-installed or dealer-installed equipment (see Exhibit 5 for partnership comparisons with XM Radio). As of December 31, 2006, Sirius radios were available as a factory-installed option in 89 vehicle models and as a dealer-installed option in 19 vehicle models; Sirius service was offered to renters of Hertz vehicles at 55 airport locations nationwide. As was the case at XM Radio, Sirius had agreements with some vehicle makers to only offer Sirius brand satellite radios as a

factory-installed option. By year-end 2007, Sirius management expected that Sirius Satellite Radio receivers would be available in 150 vehicle models. Executives believed that an increasing proportion of the company's subscribers would be generated through its relationships with automakers. For instance, Sirius had projected that about 40 percent of the 2007 Chrysler, Dodge, and Jeep vehicles would come with factory-equipped Sirius radios, up from 30 percent in the 2006 model year. Mercedes was installing Sirius radios in about 70 percent of its 2007 vehicles, well ahead of its 50 percent target. Ford Motor was offering Sirius radios as an option on 21 Ford, Mercury, and Lincoln models, up from four models at the beginning of 2006 and 16 models at the end of third-quarter 2006.

As of 2006, consumers could purchase Sirius receivers at some 25,000 consumer electronics retailers and mobile audio dealers, including Best Buy, Circuit City, Crutchfield, Costco, Target, Wal-Mart, Sam's Club, RadioShack, heavy truck dealers, and many truck stops nationwide. Receivers were also available for purchase at Sirius's Web site. The receiver product line included portable and transportable Plug & Play radios with various features and functionality, radios for cars and trucks, and high-end receivers complete with motorized touch-control display screens. The company's strategy was to continue to introduce lighter, thinner, and more feature-rich models. Sirius radios were distributed by Alpine, Audiovox, Brix Group, Clarion, Delphi, Directed Electronics, Eclipse, Eton, Jensen, JVC, Kenwood, Magnadyne, Monster Cable, Pioneer, Russound, Tivoli, Thomson, and XACT Communications. To further broaden its audience and revenue base, Sirius had made its music channels available to DISH satellite television subscribers; certain music channels were offered to Sprint subscribers over multimedia handsets.

In December 2005, Sirius Canada launched service in Canada with 100 channels of commercial-free music and news, sports, talk, and entertainment programming, including 10 channels of Canadian content; as of February

Exhibit 7

Consolidated Income Statement, Sirius Satellite Radio, 2003–2006 (in 000s of $, except per share amounts)

	2006	2005	2004	2003
Revenue:				
Subscriber revenue, including effects of mail-in rebates	$ 575,404	$ 223,615	$ 62,881	$ 12,615
Advertising revenue, net of agency fees	31,044	6,131	906	116
Equipment revenue	26,798	12,271	2,898	61
Other revenue	3,989	228	169	80
Total revenue	637,235	242,245	66,854	12,872
Operating expenses:				
Satellite and transmission	39,229	27,856	31,157	32,604
Programming and content	230,215	98,607	63,353	29,820
Customer service and billing	68,137	46,653	22,341	23,657
Cost of equipment	35,233	11,827	3,467	115
Sales and marketing	222,492	170,592	154,495	121,165
Subscriber acquisition costs	419,716	349,641	173,702	74,860
General and administrative	87,538	59,831	44,028	36,211
Engineering, design and development	58,732	44,745	30,520	24,534
Depreciation	105,749	98,555	95,370	95,353
Equity granted to third parties and employees/stock-based compensation	437,918	163,078	126,725	12,083
Total operating expenses	1,704,959	1,071,385	745,158	450,402
Loss from operations	(1,067,724)	(829,140)	(678,304)	(437,530)
Other income (expense):				
Debt restructuring	—	—	—	256,538
Interest and investment income	33,320	26,878	9,713	5,287
Interest expense	(64,032)	(45,361)	(41,386)	(50,510)
Loss from redemption of debt	—	(6,214)	—	—
Income (expense) from affiliate	(4,445)	(6,938)	—	—
Other income	79	89	2,016	—
Total other income (expense)	(35,078)	(31,546)	(29,657)	211,315
Loss before income taxes	(1,102,802)	(860,686)	(707,961)	(226,215)
Income tax expense	(2,065)	(2,311)	(4,201)	—
Net loss	$(1,104,867)	$(862,997)	$(712,162)	$(226,215)
Preferred stock dividends	—	—	—	(8,574)
Preferred stock deemed dividends	—	—	—	(79,634)
Net loss applicable to common stockholders	$(1,104,867)	$(862,997)	$(712,162)	$(314,423)
Net loss per share applicable to common stockholders (basic and diluted)	$(0.79)	$(0.65)	$(0.57)	$(0.38)
Weighted average common shares outstanding (basic and diluted)	1,402,619	1,325,739	1,238,585	827,186

Source: 2005 and 2006 10-K reports and company press release, February 28, 2007.

Exhibit 8

Consolidated Balance Sheets, Sirius Satellite Radio, 2004–2006 ($ in thousands)

	FOR THE YEARS ENDING DECEMBER 31		
	2006	2005	2004
ASSETS			
Current assets:			
Cash and cash equivalents	$ 393,421	$ 762,007	$ 753,891
Marketable securities	15,500	117,250	5,277
Accounts receivable, net of allowance for doubtful accounts of $3,183, $1,550, and $532, respectively	24,189	31,688	7,559
Inventory	34,502	14,256	7,927
Prepaid expenses	52,588	18,248	12,956
Restricted investments	25,000	25,165	4,706
Other current assets	72,066	42,834	18,724
Total current assets	617,266	1,011,448	811,040
Property and equipment, net	810,389	828,357	881,280
FCC satellite radio license	83,654	83,654	83,654
Restricted investments, net of current portion	52,850	82,450	92,615
Deferred financing fees	13,166	16,303	13,140
Other long-term assets	81,203	63,150	75,884
Total assets	$1,658,528	$2,085,362	$1,957,613
LIABILITIES AND STOCKHOLDERS' EQUITY			
Current liabilities:			
Accounts payable and accrued expenses	$ 437,913	$ 331,953	$182,447
Accrued interest	24,782	23,546	5,758
Deferred revenue	412,370	251,468	81,309
Total current liabilities	875,065	606,967	269,514
Long-term debt	1,068,249	1,084,437	656,274
Deferred revenue, net of current portion	76,580	56,479	15,691
Other long-term liabilities	27,705	12,511	15,501
Total liabilities	$2,047,599	$1,760,394	$956,980
Commitments and contingencies			
Stockholders' equity:			
Common stock, $0.001 par value: 2,500,000,000 shares authorized, 1,434,635,501 shares, 1,346,226,851 shares, and 1,276,922,634 shares issued and outstanding at December 31, 2005 and 2004, respectively	1,435	1,346	1,277
Additional paid-in capital	3,443,214	3,079,169	2,916,199
Deferred compensation	—	(26,694)	(50,963)
Accumulated other comprehensive loss	—	—	(24)
Accumulated deficit	(3,833,720)	(2,728,853)	(1,865,856)
Total stockholders' equity (deficit)	(389,071)	324,968	1,000,633
Total liabilities and stockholders' equity	$1,658,528	$2,085,362	$1,957,613

Sources: 2005 and 2006 10-K reports.

Exhibit 9

Selected Cash Flow Data, Sirius Satellite Radio, 2003–2006 ($ in thousands)

	FOR THE YEARS ENDED DECEMBER 31			
	2006	**2005**	**2004**	**2003**
Cash flows from operating activities:				
Net loss	$(1,104,867)	$(862,997)	$(712,162)	$(226,215)
Net cash used in operating activities	(414,549)	(273,740)	(334,463)	(284,487)
Cash flows from investing activities:				
Additions to property and equipment	(99,827)	(49,888)	(28,589)	(20,118)
Sale of property and equipment	127	72	443	—
Purchases of restricted investments	(12,339)	(21,291)	(89,706)	—
Release of restricted investments	26,000	10,997	—	—
Purchases of available-for-sale securities	(123,500)	(148,900)	—	(24,826)
Sales of available-for-sale securities	229,715	31,850	—	—
Maturities of available-for-sale securities		5,085	25,000	150,000
Net cash (used in) provided by investing activities	20,176	(172,075)	(92,852)	105,056
Cash flows from financing activities:				
Proceeds from issuance of long-term debt, net	—	493,005	518,413	194,224
Proceeds from issuance of common stock, net	—	—	96,025	492,659
Redemption of debt	—	(57,609)		
Costs associated with debt restructuring	—	—	—	(4,737)
Proceeds from exercise of stock options	25,787	18,543	26,051	—
Proceeds from exercise of warrants	—	—	19,850	—
Other	—	(8)	(112)	(111)
Net cash provided by financing activities	25,787	453,931	660,227	682,035
Net increase (decrease) in cash and cash equivalents	(368,586)	8,116	232,912	502,604
Cash and cash equivalents at the beginning of period	762,007	753,891	520,979	18,375
Cash and cash equivalents at the end of period	$ 393,421	$ 762,007	$ 753,891	$ 520,979

Source: 2005 and 2006 10-K reports and company press release, February 28, 2007.

2007, Sirius Canada had 300,000 subscribers and was broadcasting on 110 channels. Sirius Canada enjoyed a 75 percent market share in the Canadian market for satellite radio. Sirius receivers were available in over 3,500 retail outlets in Canada.

Sirius management was concentrating future marketing efforts on (1) enhancing and refining its programming, (2) introducing Sirius radios with new features and functions, and (3) expanding the distribution of Sirius radios through arrangements with automakers and through additional retail points of sale. Sirius was reinforcing its "The Best Radio on Radio"

promotional theme with a variety of new initiatives, including the following:

- Launching Sirius Internet Radio (SIR), a CD-quality, online version of the Sirius satellite radio service. SIR delivered more than 75 channels of Sirius programming, without the use of a radio, for a $12.95 monthly subscription fee. To mark the launch of SIR, Sirius allowed free listening for two days.

- Introducing the industry's first portable satellite radio with WiFi capabilities. The model allowed users to listen for the first time to live and recorded Sirius content almost anywhere. This receiver stored up to 100 hours of live programming (two gigabytes) and could be used to access the company's Internet radio services over an accessible WiFi network and to purchase favorite songs through Yahoo! Music Engine, Yahoo! Music Jukebox, or other compatible download services.

- Devoting an entire channel to such music superstars as the Who, the Rolling Stones, and Elvis Presley (channel 13). In past years, Sirius had dedicated channels to the music of Bruce Springsteen, the E Street Band, country music star George Strait, and David Gilmour of Pink Floyd.

- Entering into a multiyear agreement with the Metropolitan Opera to establish a dedicated channel for opera lovers using Metropolitan Opera content.

- Signing an agreement with the Chelsea Football Club, the two-time defending champions of the Barclays English Premier League, to make Sirius the exclusive satellite radio provider of Chelsea soccer matches.

Sirius billed itself as the leading provider of sports radio programming, broadcasting play-by-play action for every NFL game, over 1,000 NBA games per season, 40 NHL games per week, the Wimbledon tennis championships, several top Thoroughbred horse races, and football and basketball games of 125 college teams.

RECENT PERFORMANCE AND ACCOMPLISHMENTS
In 2005–2006, Sirius achieved several important financial and operational milestones in its drive for industry leadership and long-term profitability:

- Parity with XM in distributing satellite radios through retail channels (based on a retail market share of 54 percent for 2005 and 60 percent for the fourth quarter of 2005).[5]

- Rapid acceleration of subscribers coming from motor vehicle partners.

- Extended long-term exclusive agreements with DaimlerChrysler, Ford, and BMW.

- Lower subscriber acquisition costs.

- New programming agreements with Martha Stewart, Richard Simmons, the NBA, Adam Curry's Podcast Show, and NASCAR.

- Introduction of the Sirius S50 receiver, the satellite radio industry's first wearable device with MP3/WMA capabilities.

- The launch of Sirius music on the Sprint wireless network.

- An arrangement for NASCAR to move from XM to Sirius in 2007.

On January 9, 2006, Howard Stern moved his radio show to Sirius Satellite Radio from terrestrial radio as part of two channels programmed by Howard Stern and Sirius. To attract Howard Stern, Sirius agreed to provide a budget of $100 million annually to cover total production and operating costs for the Stern show, including compensation of the show cast and staff, overhead, construction costs for a dedicated studio, and the development of additional programming and marketing concepts. Sirius management estimated that Stern's broadcast presence on Sirius would need to generate approximately 1 million new subscribers in order for Sirius to show a profit on the five-year deal. Stern's interest in moving to Sirius was said, in part, to be a response to avoid "censorship" efforts by the Federal Communications Commission (FCC)—the FCC does not regulate the content of satellite programs. Stern's terrestrial radio shows, known for their raunchy content, had an estimated audience of over 10 million in 2004 when the deal with Sirius was struck. In January 2007, Sirius paid Howard Stern a bonus in stock worth nearly $83 million for exceeding subscriber goals set back in 2004 when the five-year agreement was struck.

SUBSCRIPTION PLANS
Most customers subscribed on an annual or monthly basis. Discounts were offered for prepaid, long-term, and multiple subscriptions. In a number of

instances, automakers included a six-month or one-year subscription to Sirius service in the sale or lease price of vehicles equipped with Sirius receivers; frequently, Sirius received subscription payments from automakers in advance of the activation of its service (Sirius reimbursed automakers for a portion of the costs associated with installing Sirius receivers in their vehicles). Sirius received an average of approximately nine months of prepaid revenue per subscriber when service was activated. Other revenue sources included activation fees, the sale of advertising on nonmusic channels, and direct sale of Sirius radios and accessories.

OPERATIONS   Sirius transmitted its satellite broadcasts through a proprietary satellite radio system that consisted of three orbital satellites, 140 terrestrial repeaters that received and retransmitted Sirius signals, a satellite uplink facility, and studios in New York City, Los Angeles, Memphis, Nashville, New Orleans, Houston, and Daytona.

As shown in Exhibit 7, Sirius spent $222.5 million for sales and marketing in 2006, $170.6 million in 2005, $154.5 million in 2004, and $121.2 million in 2003. As was the case with XM Radio, Sirius had experienced very high new subscriber acquisition costs—$419.7 million in 2006, $349.6 million in 2005, and $173.7 million in 2004. While the acquisition costs *per subscriber* were trending downward, the company did not realize a positive revenue contribution above marketing costs until a customer's second year of service—see Exhibit 10 for comparisons with XM Radio.

The Profitability Forecast for XM and Sirius: Sunny or Cloudy?

While the satellite radio business was an emerging force in radio broadcasting and growing public awareness of both XM and Sirius was helping boost subscriber totals, the future of both companies was uncertain. Investors were skeptical about the abilities of the two companies to produce attractive profits and return on invested capital. The stock prices of both XM and Sirius had taken a huge beating on Wall Street during 2006, falling about 50 percent since year-end 2005. XM's stock price had traded as high as $37 in January 2005 but had been trending steadily downward since October 2005 to the $14–$15 range in January 2007. Sirius's stock price hit an all-time high of close to $8 in January 2005 and traded in the $6.00–$7.50 range for most of 2005; but nervous investors had bid the stock price down to the $3.75–$4.00 range in January 2007.

Most alarming to investors was that both XM and Sirius had recently scaled back their estimates of subscriber growth. At the beginning of 2006, XM management announced a bullish forecast of 9 million subscribers by year-end, but it was forced to issue a series of lower estimates as subscriber growth slowed. XM ended 2006 with just 7.6 million subscribers. XM's president and chief operating officer, Nate Davis, said that the slower-than-expected growth rate was not due to market indifference but rather to failure to "stimulate the market with new products."[6] Sirius management began 2006 by estimating that the number of Sirius subscribers would grow to 6 million by year-end; estimates were then raised to 6.3 million. But Sirius management had cut its estimates back to 6.1 million by November 2006, and the company ended the year with barely over 6 million subscribers. Sirius management, however, was pleased with the company's performance in 2006 and the gains it was making in challenging XM for leadership in the fledgling satellite radio industry.

XM AND SIRIUS PROPOSE A MERGER
On February 19, 2007, executives at Sirius and XM announced a plan to merge the two satellite broadcasters and bring an end to the expensive bidding war for talent and programming that had impaired the profitability of both companies. The merger deal called for Sirius to acquire XM via an exchange of shares of stock, with

Exhibit 10

Comparative Subscriber Statistics, XM Radio versus Sirius Satellite Radio, 2003–2006

	2006	2005	2004	2003
Number of subscribers at year-end				
XM Radio	7,625,000	5,932,957	3,229,124	1,360,228
Sirius	6,024,555	3,316,560	1,143,258	261,061
Gross subscriber additions				
XM Radio	3,866,481	4,130,437	2,580,515	n.a.
Sirius	3,758,163	2,519,301	986,556	255,798
Net subscriber additions				
XM Radio	1,695,595	2,703,833	1,868,896	1,013,069
Sirius	2,707,995	2,173,302	882,197	231,114
Average monthly subscription revenue per subscriber, after rebates and special promotions				
XM Radio	$10.09	$ 9.51	$ 8.68	$8.97
Sirius	10.45	10.06	10.02	9.39
Average monthly net advertising revenue per subscriber				
XM Radio	$0.43	$0.39	$0.33	$0.47
Sirius	0.56	0.28	0.14	0.09
Average revenue per subscriber from both subscriptions and advertising (includes activation, equipment, and other revenue per subscriber)				
XM Radio	$11.41	$10.57	$ 9.59	$10.52
Sirius	11.01	10.34	10.16	9.48
Subscriber acquisition costs				
XM Radio	$108	$109	$100	$137
Sirius	114	139	177	293
Customer care and billing costs per average subscriber				
XM Radio	n.r.	$1.39	$1.48	$2.53
Sirius	$1.24	2.10	3.56	6.84

n.r. = Not reported.

Sources: XM Satellite Radio 2005 and 2006 10-K reports; XM Satellite Radio press release on February 26, 2007; Sirius 2004, 2005, and 2006 10-K reports; and Sirius press release on February 28, 2007.

XM shareholders receiving 4.6 shares of Sirius for each share owned of XM stock. The merger would create a company with about $1.5 billion in revenues and 14 million subscribers. The proposed merger called for the CEO of Sirius, Mel Karmazin, to be CEO of the merged company and for Gary Parsons, the chairman and CEO of XM, to be chairman of the new company (whose name had not been announced). Hugh Panero, the CEO of XM, was scheduled to continue in his current role until the merger closed.

However, the merger proposal was expected to face tough scrutiny from antitrust regulators at the U.S. Department of Justice because it would create a satellite radio broadcasting monopoly. Also, the terms under which the Federal Communications Commission had originally granted the satellite licenses to XM and Sirius expressly prohibited one company from owning both satellite radio licenses—in January 2007, when rumors of a possible XM/Sirius merger surfaced, FCC chairman Kevin

Martin said the FCC's rules would not permit a merger between XM and Sirius. Traditional radio stations were expected to oppose the merger as well.

The ramifications of the proposed merger were expected to entail months of regulatory hearings, and many analysts were highly skeptical that merger approval would be granted by both the FCC and the Department of Justice. Nonetheless, executives at Sirius and XM expressed belief that there was greater than a 50–50 chance of winning approval for the merger. XM's chairman Gary Parsons said regulators could be convinced that the merger was in the public interest, due to the existence of competition from the iPod, Internet radio, audio services provided by cable- and satellite-television providers, and other venues. The companies also planned to argue that (1) they could provide greater programming and content choices to consumers as a single entity and (2) the merged companies would be better able to develop and introduce a wider range of lower-cost, easy-to-use, and multifunctional receivers through efficiencies in chip-set and radio design and procurement, thus helping keep satellite radio competitive in the consumer electronics–driven world of audio entertainment. Top executives at XM and Sirius were expected to counter the argument that a merger would create a satellite radio monopoly with arguments that satellite radio was in direct competition with free over-the-air AM and FM radio as well as iPods and other brands of MP3 players, mobile phone streaming, HD radio, Internet radio, the digital music channels offered by cable TV companies, and next-generation wireless technologies.[7] At February 2007 hearings before congressional committees overseeing antitrust issues, Mel Karmazin hinted that approval of the proposed XM/Sirius merger might lead to lower monthly subscription rates.

Endnotes

[1] Described in Heather Green, Tom Lowry, and Catherine Yang, "The New Radio Revolution," *BusinessWeek Online,* March 3, 2005, www.businessweek.com (accessed December 5, 2006).

[2] Radio Advertising Bureau, *Radio Marketing Guide and Factbook for Advertisers,* Fall 1999 and Spring 2000, as cited in XM Satellite Radio's 2000 10-K report, p. 2.

[3] C. Barnes & Co., *Barnes Reports: Radio Industry Broadcasting* (NAICS 51311), 2007 Edition, p. 7.

[4] Company 2006 10-K report, p.1.

[5] Based on data made available to the company by market researcher NPD Group.

[6] Eric A. Taub, "Thanks to Stern, Sirius May Be Set for a Merger," *Tuscaloosa News,* January 1, 2007, p. 5B.

[7] Sirius press release, February 19, 2007.

Case 3

Competition in the Bottled Water Industry in 2006

John E. Gamble
University of South Alabama

With global revenues exceeding $62 billion in 2005, bottled water was among the world's most attractive beverage categories. Industry revenues were forecast to grow by an additional 30 percent between 2005 and 2010, to reach approximately $82 billion. Bottled water had long been a widely consumed product in Western Europe and Mexico, where annual per capita consumption approached or exceeded 40 gallons in 2005, but until the mid-1990s bottled water had been somewhat of a novelty or prestige product in the United States. In 1990, approximately 2.2 billion gallons of bottled water were consumed in the United States and per capita consumption approximated 9 gallons. U.S. per capita consumption had grown to more than 25 gallons by 2005. The rising popularity of bottled water in the United States during the late 1990s and early 2000s had allowed the United States to become the world's largest market for bottled water, with annual volume sales of nearly 7.5 billion gallons in 2005. In 2006, emerging-country markets in Asia and South America seemed to be replicating the impressive growth of bottled water in the United States, with annual growth rates exceeding 20 percent. Exhibit 1 presents bottled water statistics for the 10 largest country markets for bottled water in 2004.

The growing popularity of bottled water in the United States was attributable to concerns over the safety of municipal drinking water, an increased focus on fitness and health, and the hectic on-the-go lifestyles of American consumers. Bottled water's convenience, purity, and portability made it the natural solution to consumers' dissatisfaction with tap water and carbonated beverages. The U.S. bottled water market, like most markets outside the United States, was characterized by fierce competitive rivalry as the world's bottled water sellers jockeyed for market share and volume gains. Both the global and U.S. bottled water markets had become dominated by a few international food and beverage producers—such as Coca-Cola, PepsiCo, and Nestlé—but they also included many small regional sellers who were required to either develop low-cost production and distribution capabilities or use differentiation strategies keyed to some unique product attributes. In 2006, competitive rivalry continued to ratchet upward as sellers launched innovative product variations, lowered prices in developed markets, used strategic agreements to strengthen positions in established markets, and acquired smaller sellers to gain footholds in rapidly growing emerging markets. Industry analysts and observers believed the recent moves undertaken by the world's largest sellers of bottled water would alter the competitive dynamics of the bottled water industry and would mandate that certain players modify their current strategic approaches to competition in the industry.

Exhibit 1

Leading Country Markets for Bottled Water, 1999, 2004 (in millions of gallons)

2004 RANK	COUNTRY	BOTTLED WATER SALES		CAGR* (1999–2004)
		1999	2004	
1	United States	4,579.9	6,806.7	8.2%
2	Mexico	3,056.9	4,668.3	8.8
3	China	1,217.0	3,140.1	20.9
4	Brazil	1,493.8	3,062.0	15.4
5	Italy	2,356.1	2,814.4	3.6
6	Germany	2,194.6	2,722.6	4.4
7	France	1,834.1	2,257.3	4.2
8	Indonesia	907.1	1,943.5	16.5
9	Spain	1,076.4	1,453.5	6.2
10	India	444.0	1,353.3	25.0
All others		6,833.5	10,535.0	9.0
Worldwide total		25,993.4	40,756.7	(Avg. CAGR) 9.4

* CAGR = Compound annual growth rate

Source: Beverage Marketing Corporation as reported by the International Bottled Water Association, 2006.

Industry Conditions In 2006

Even though it was the world's largest market for bottled water, the United States remained among the faster-growing markets for bottled water since per capita consumption rates of bottled water fell substantially below those in Western Europe, the Middle East, and Mexico. Bottled water consumption in the United States also lagged per capita consumption of soft drinks by more than a 2:1 margin, but in 2003 bottled water surpassed coffee, tea, milk, and beer to become the second largest beverage category in the United States. In 2005, more than 15.3 million gallons of carbonated soft drinks were consumed in the United States, but concerns about sugar consumption and other nutrition and fitness issues had encouraged many consumers to transition from soft drinks to bottled water. Whereas the bottled water market in the United States grew by 10.7 percent between 2004 and 2005 to reach 7.5 billion gallons, the U.S. carbonated soft drink market declined by 0.6 percent. Industry analysts expected the carbonated soft drink industry to decline by 1.5 percent annually for the foreseeable future as bottled water, energy drinks, and sports drinks gained a larger "share of the stomach." Exhibits 2, 3, and 4 illustrate the growing popularity of bottled water among U.S. consumers during the 1990s and through 2004.

Almost one-half of bottled water consumed in the United States in 1990 was delivered to homes and offices in returnable five-gallon containers and dispensed through coolers. At that time, only 186 million gallons of water were sold in one-liter or smaller single-serving polyethylene terephthalate (PET) bottles. Beginning in the late 1990s, consumers began to appreciate the convenience and portability of water bottled in single-serving PET containers that could be purchased chilled from a convenience store and drunk immediately. By 2005, bottled water sold in two-liter or smaller PET containers accounted for 60.8 percent of industry volume. The unit sales of bottled water packaged in PET containers grew by 22.5 percent between 2004 and 2005. Water sold in

Exhibit 2

Per Capita Consumption of Bottled Water by Country Market, 1999, 2004

2004 RANK	COUNTRY	PER CAPITA CONSUMPTION (IN GALLONS)		CAGR* (1999–2004)
		1999	2004	
1	Italy	40.9	48.5	3.5%
2	Mexico	30.9	44.5	7.5
3	United Arab Emirates	29	43.2	8.3
4	Belgium-Luxembourg	32.2	39.1	4.0
5	France	31	37.4	3.8
6	Spain	26.9	36.1	6.1
7	Germany	26.6	33	4.4
8	Lebanon	17.9	26.8	8.4
9	Switzerland	23.8	26.3	2.0
10	Cyprus	17.8	24.3	6.4
11	United States	16.8	23.9	7.3
12	Saudi Arabia	19.9	23.2	3.1
13	Czech Republic	16.4	23	7.0
14	Austria	19.7	21.7	2.0
15	Portugal	18.6	21.2	2.7
	Global Average	4.3	6.4	8.3

* CAGR = Compound annual growth rate

Source: Beverage Marketing Corporation as reported by the International Bottled Water Association, 2006.

Exhibit 3

Global Bottled Water Market Wholesale Value and Volume, 2001–2005, Forecasts for 2006–2010

YEAR	VOLUME SALES (IN BILLIONS OF LITERS)	ANNUAL CHANGE	INDUSTRY REVENUES ($ IN BILLIONS)	ANNUAL CHANGE
2001	92.8	—	$47.3	—
2002	99.5	7.2%	51.3	8.5%
2003	107.9	8.4	56.1	9.4
2004	113.3	5.0	59.1	5.3
2005(e)	119.7	5.6	62.9	6.4
2006(f)	125.9	5.2	66.4	5.6
2007(f)	132.9	5.6	70.4	6.0
2008(f)	139.5	5.0	74.5	5.8
2009(f)	146.4	4.9	78.5	5.4
2010(f)	153.4	4.8	81.9	4.3

(e) = estimated

(f) = forecast

Source: Global Bottled Water Industry Profile, December 2005, Datamonitor.

Exhibit 4

U.S. Per Capita Consumption of Bottled Water, 1991–2005

YEAR	PER CAPITA CONSUMPTION (IN GALLONS)	ANNUAL CHANGE
1991	9.3	—
1992	9.8	5.4%
1993	10.5	7.1
1994	11.5	9.5
1995	12.2	6.1
1996	13.1	7.4
1997	14.1	7.6
1998	15.3	8.5
1999	16.8	9.8
2000	17.8	6.0
2001	19.3	8.4
2002	21.2	9.8
2003	22.6	6.6
2004	24	6.2
2005(p)	25.7	7.1

(p) = preliminary

Source: Beverage Marketing Corporation as reported by the International Bottled Water Association, 2006.

five-gallon containers used in the home and office delivery (HOD) market accounted for only 17.8 percent of industry volume in 2005 and grew by only 0.2 percent between 2004 and 2005. Similarly, water sold in 1- or 2.5-gallon high-density polyethylene (HDPE) containers accounted for just 16.5 percent of industry volume in 2005 and grew by only 1.0 percent between 2004 and 2005.

Convenience and portability were two of a variety of reasons U.S. consumers were increasingly attracted to bottled water. A heightened emphasis on healthy lifestyles and improved consumer awareness of the need for proper hydration led many consumers to shift traditional beverage preferences toward bottled water. Bottled water consumers frequently claimed that drinking more water improved the appearance of their skin and gave them more energy. Bottled water analysts also believed that many health-conscious consumers drank bottled water because it was a symbol to others that they were interested in their health.

A certain amount of industry growth was attributable to increased concerns over the quality of tap water provided by municipal water sources. Consumers in parts of the world with inadequate water treatment facilities relied on bottled water to provide daily hydration needs, but tap water in the United States was very pure by global standards. (Municipal water systems were regulated by the U.S. Environmental Protection Agency and were required to comply with the provisions of the Safe Drinking Water Act Amendments of 2001.) Consumer concerns over the quality of drinking water in the United States emerged in 1993 when 400,000 residents of Milwaukee, Wisconsin, became ill with flu-like symptoms and almost 100 immune-impaired residents died from waterborne bacterial infections. Throughout the 1990s and into the early 2000s, the media sporadically reported cases of municipal water contamination, such as in 2000 when residents of Washington, D.C., became ill after the city's water filtration process caused elevated levels of suspended materials in the water.

Even though some consumers were concerned about the purity of municipal water, most consumers' complaints with tap water centered on the chemical taste of tap water that resulted from treatment processes that included the use of chlorine and other chemicals such as fluoride. In a tap-water tasting in Atlanta hosted by *Southpoint Magazine*, judges rated municipal water on taste and found some cities' waters very palatable. Water obtained from the municipal source in Memphis was said to have "a refreshing texture." However, other municipal systems did not fare as well with the judges—some of whom suggested Houston's water tasted "like a chemistry lab," while others said Atlanta's municipal water was akin to "a gulp of swimming pool water."[1] However, there were positive attributes to the chemicals added to tap water, as chlorine was necessary to kill any bacteria in the water and fluoride had contributed greatly to improved dental health in the United States. In addition, tap water had been shown to be no less healthy than bottled water in a number of independent studies, including a study publicized in Europe that was commissioned by the World Wide Fund for Nature and conducted by researchers at the University of Geneva.

Bottled water producers in the United States were required to meet the standards of both the Environmental Protection Agency (EPA) and the U.S. Food and Drug Administration (FDA). Like all other food and beverage products sold in the United States, bottled water was subject to such food safety and labeling requirements as nutritional labeling provisions and general good manufacturing practices (GMPs). Bottled water GMPs were mandated under the 1962 Kefauver-Harris Drug Amendments to the Federal Food, Drug and Cosmetic Act of 1938 and established specifications for plant construction and design, sanitation, equipment design and construction, production and process controls, and record keeping. The FDA required bottled water producers to test at least weekly for the presence of bacteria and to test annually for inorganic contaminants, trace metals, minerals, pesticides, herbicides, and organic compounds. Bottled water was also regulated by state agencies that conducted inspections of bottling facilities and certification of testing facilities to ensure that bottled water was bottled under federal GMPs and was safe to drink.

Bottled water producers were also required to comply with the FDA's Standard of Identity, which required bottlers to include source water information on their products' labels. Water labeled as "spring water" must have been captured from a borehole or natural orifice of a spring that naturally flows to the surface. "Artesian water" could be extracted from a confined aquifer (a water-bearing underground layer of rock or sand) where the water level stood above the top of the aquifer. "Sparkling water" was required to have natural carbonation as it emerged from the source, although carbonation could be added to return the carbon dioxide level to what was evident as the water emerged from the source. Even though sparkling water was very popular throughout most of Europe, where it accounted for approximately 54 percent of industry sales, it made up only 8 percent of the bottled water market in the United States.

The FDA's definition of "mineral water" stated that such water must have at least 250 parts per million of total dissolved solids, and its standards required water labeled as "purified" to have undergone distillation, deionization, or reverse osmosis to remove chemicals such as chlorine and fluoride. "Drinking water" required no additional processing beyond what was required for tap water but could not include flavoring or other additives that account for more than 1 percent of the product's total weight. Both "drinking water" and "purified water" had to clearly state that the water originated "from a community water system" or "from a municipal source."

Bottled water producers could also voluntarily become members of the International Bottled Water Association (IBWA) and agree to comply with its Model Code, which went beyond the standards of the EPA, FDA, or state agencies. The Model Code allowed fewer parts per million of certain organic and inorganic chemicals and microbiological contaminants than FDA, EPA, or state regulations and imposed a chlorine limitation on bottled water. Neither the FDA nor the EPA limited chlorine content. IBWA members were monitored for compliance through annual, unannounced inspections administered by an independent third-party organization.

Distribution and Sale of Bottled Water

Consumers could purchase bottled water in nearly any location in the United States where food was also sold. The distribution of bottled water varied depending on the producer and the distribution channel. Typically, bottled water was distributed to large grocers and wholesale clubs directly by the bottled water producer, whereas most producers used third parties like beer and wine distributors or food distributors to make sales and deliveries to convenience stores, restaurants, and delis.

Because of the difficulty for food service distributors to restock vending machines and provide bottled water to special events, Coca-Cola and PepsiCo were able to dominate such channels since they could make deliveries of bottled water along with their deliveries of other beverages. Coca-Cola's and PepsiCo's vast beverage distribution systems made it easy for the two companies to make Dasani and Aquafina available anywhere Coke or Pepsi could be purchased. In addition, the two cola giants almost always negotiated contracts with sports stadiums, universities, and school systems that made one of them the exclusive supplier of all types of nonalcoholic beverages sold in the venue for a specified period. Under such circumstances, it was nearly impossible for other brands of bottled water to gain access to the account.

PepsiCo and Coca-Cola's soft drink businesses had allowed vending machine sales to account for 8 percent of industry sales volume in 2005 and had also aided the two companies in making Aquafina and Dasani available in supermarkets, supercenters, wholesale clubs, and convenience stores. Soft drink sales were important to all types of food stores since soft drinks made up a sizable percentage of the store's sales and since food retailers frequently relied on soft drink promotions to generate store traffic. Coca-Cola and PepsiCo were able to encourage their customers to purchase items across their product lines to ensure prompt and complete shipment of key soft drink products. As a diversified food products company, PepsiCo had exploited the popularity of its soft drinks, Gatorade sports drinks, Frito-Lay snack foods, and Tropicana orange juice in persuading grocery accounts to purchase not only Aquafina but also other non–soft drink brands such as FruitWorks, SoBe, Lipton's Iced Tea, and Starbucks Frappuccino.

Since most supermarkets, supercenters, and food stores usually carried fewer than seven branded bottled waters plus a private-label brand, bottled water producers other than Coke and Pepsi were required to compete aggressively on price to gain access to shelf space. Supermarkets and discount stores accounted for 43.5 percent of U.S. industry sales in 2005 and were able to require bottled water suppliers to pay slotting fees in addition to offering low prices to gain shelf space. Natural foods stores could also require annual contracts and slotting fees but were much more willing than traditional supermarkets to pay higher wholesale prices for products that could contribute to the store's overall level of differentiation. In fact, most natural foods stores would not carry brands found in traditional supermarkets.

Convenience stores were also aggressive in pressing bottled water producers and food distributors for low prices and slotting fees. Most convenience stores carried only two to four brands of bottled water beyond what was distributed by Coca-Cola and Pepsi and required bottlers to pay annual slotting fees of $300 to $400 per store in return for providing 5 to 10 bottle facings on a cooler shelf. Some bottlers offered to provide retailers with rebates of approximately 25 cents per case to help secure distributors for their brand of bottled water. Food and beverage distributors usually allowed bottled water producers to negotiate slotting fees and rebates directly with convenience store buyers.

There was not as much competition among bottled water producers to gain shelf space in delis and restaurants since that channel accounted for only 6.5 percent of U.S. industry sales in 2005. PepsiCo and Coca-Cola were among the better-suited bottled water producers to economically distribute water to restaurants since they likely provided fountain drinks to such establishments.

Suppliers to the Industry

The suppliers to the bottled water industry included municipal water systems; spring operators; bottling equipment manufacturers; deionization, reverse osmosis, and filtration equipment manufacturers; manufacturers of PET and HDPE bottles and plastic caps; label printers; and secondary packaging suppliers. Most packaging supplies needed for the production of bottled water were readily available from a large number of suppliers. Large bottlers able to commit to annual purchases of more than 5 million PET bottles could purchase bottles for as little as 5 cents per bottle, whereas regional bottlers purchasing smaller quantities of bottles or making only one-time purchases of bottles could expect to pay as much as 15 cents per bottle. Suppliers of secondary packaging like cardboard boxes, shrink-wrap, and six-pack rings and suppliers of printed film or paper labels were numerous and aggressively competed for the business of large bottled water producers.

Bottling equipment used for water purification and filling bottles was manufactured and marketed by about 50 different companies in the United States. A basic bottle-filling line could be purchased for about $125,000, whereas a large state-of-the-art bottling facility could require a capital investment of more than $100 million. Bottlers choosing to sell spring water could expect to invest about $300,000 for source certification, road grading, and installation of pumping equipment, fencing, holding tanks, and disinfecting equipment. Bottlers that did not own springs were also required to enter into lease agreements with spring owners that typically ranged from $20,000 to $30,000 per year. Companies selling purified water merely purchased tap water from municipal water systems at industrial rates prior to purifying and bottling the water for sale to consumers. Sellers of purified water were able not only to pay less for water they bottled, but also to avoid spring water's inbound shipping costs of 5 to 15 cents per gallon since water arrived at the bottling facility by pipe rather than by truck.

Key Competitive Capabilities in the Bottled Water Industry

Bottled water did not enjoy the brand loyalty of soft drinks, beer, or many other food and beverage products but was experiencing some increased brand loyalty, with 10 to 25 percent of consumers looking for a specific brand and an additional two-thirds considering only a few brands acceptable. Because of the growing importance of brand recognition, successful sellers of bottled water were required to possess well-developed brand-building skills. Most of the industry's major sellers were global food companies that had built respected brands in soft drinks, dairy products, chocolates, and breakfast cereals prior to entering the bottled water industry.

Bottled water sellers also needed to have efficient distribution systems to supermarket, wholesale club, and convenience store channels to be successful in the industry. It was imperative for bottled water distributors (whether direct store delivery by bottlers or delivery by third parties) to maximize the number of deliveries per driver since distribution included high fixed costs for warehouses, trucks, hand-held inventory tracking devices, and labor. It was also critical for distributors and bottlers to provide on-time deliveries and offer responsive customer service to large customers in the highly price-competitive market. Price competition also mandated high utilization of large-scale plants to achieve low production costs. Volume and market share were also key factors in keeping marketing expenses at an acceptable per-unit level.

Recent Trends in the Bottled Water Industry

As the annual growth rate of bottled water sales in the United States slowed from double-digit rates, signs had begun to appear that price competition in the bottled water industry might mirror that of the carbonated soft drink industry. Fierce price competition could be expected to bring volume gains but result in flat or declining revenues for the bottled water industry. Coca-Cola, Nestlé, and PepsiCo had avoided strong price competition through 2004, but during the first six months of 2005 all three of the industry's largest sellers began to offer considerable discounts on 12- and 24-bottle multipacks to boost unit volume. Exhibit 5 presents average U.S. retail prices for 24-bottle

Exhibit 5

Average Retail Prices of Multipack Bottled Water Marketed by Nestlé Waters, Coca-Cola, and PepsiCo, 2003–2005

BRANDS	2003 AVERAGE 24-PACK PRICE	2004 AVERAGE 24-PACK PRICE	2005 AVERAGE 24-PACK PRICE*
Poland Spring (Nestlé Waters)	$5.89	$5.17	$5.10
Dasani (Coca-Cola)	$5.36	$5.88	$5.80
Dannon (Coca-Cola)	$4.70	$4.70	$4.35
Aquafina (PepsiCo)	$5.24	$5.40	$5.01

* January 2005–June 2005.

Source: Morgan Stanley, as reported by the *Atlanta Journal-Constitution,* June 21, 2005.

multipacks marketed by Nestlé Waters, Coca-Cola, and PepsiCo between 2003 and the first six months of 2005.

The world's largest sellers of bottled water appeared to be positioning for industry maturity by purchasing smaller regional brands. Nestlé had acquired bottled water producers and entered into joint ventures in Poland, Hungary, Russia, Greece, France, Turkey, Algeria, South Korea, Indonesia, and Saudi Arabia between 2000 and 2006. Danone Waters also made a number of acquisitions and entered into strategic alliances and joint ventures during the early 2000s to increase penetration of selected emerging and developed markets.

Danone and Nestlé had long competed against each other in most country markets, but PepsiCo and Coca-Cola were also becoming global sellers of bottled water. Coca-Cola had used a joint venture with Danone Waters to increase its bottled water product line in the United States beyond Dasani and acquired established brands in Europe and Australia to build strength in markets outside the United States. PepsiCo expanded into international markets for bottled water by allowing foreign bottling franchisees to license the Aquafina brand. The strategic maneuvering had created a more globally competitive environment in which the top sellers met each other in almost all of the world's markets and made it difficult

for regional sellers to survive. California-based Palomar Mountain Spring Water was one of many casualties of intensifying competitive rivalry. Like many other independent bottled water companies launched in the 1990s, Palomar was forced into bankruptcy in 2003 after losing key supermarket and discount store contracts. After Palomar lost much of its distribution in California supermarkets and discount stores to Nestlé, its 2003 revenues fell to $7 million from $30 million just two years earlier. Exhibit 6 illustrates the extent to which the U.S. bottled water market had consolidated by 2003 and 2004.

The introduction of enhanced waters or functional waters was the most important product innovation since bottled water gained widespread acceptance in the United States, with most sellers in 2006 having introduced variations of their products that included flavoring, vitamins, carbohydrates, electrolytes, and other supplements. The innovation seemed to be a hit with U.S. consumers, as the market for enhanced bottled waters expanded from $20 million in 2000 to approximately $1 billion in 2006. Most sellers of bottled water had yet to make functional waters widely available outside the United States. Energy Brands helped create the enhanced water segment in the United States with its 2000 launch of Glacéau Vitamin Water, which contained a variety of

Exhibit 6

Top Four U.S. Bottled Water Marketers, 2003–2004

RANK	COMPANY	LEADING BRANDS	2004 MARKET SHARE	2003 MARKET SHARE
1	Nestlé Waters	Poland Spring, Deer Park, Arrowhead, Zephyrhills, Ozarka, Ice Mountain	42.1%	39.1%
2	Coca-Cola	Dasani, Evian, and Dannon	21.9	24.1
3	PepsiCo	Aquafina	13.6	14.5
4	CG Roxanne	Crystal Geyser	7.4	7.0
	Others/Private-Label		15.0	15.3
	TOTAL		100.0%	100.0%

Source: Morgan Stanley, as reported by the *Atlanta Journal-Constitution,* June 21, 2005.

vitamins promoting mental stimulation, physical rejuvenation, and overall improved health. Glacéau was the best-selling brand of enhanced water in 2000 and 2001, but it fell to the number two position in the segment upon PepsiCo's launch of Propel Fitness Water. Propel Fitness Water remained the market leader in the U.S. enhanced water segment in 2006. Energy Brands had achieved a compounded annual growth rate of more than 200 percent between 2000 and 2005, to record estimated sales of $350 million and maintain its number two position in the U.S. functional water category.

Coca-Cola, Nestlé, and Danone Waters had begun testing vitamin-enhanced waters in as early as 2002, but all three had changed their approaches to functional waters by 2006. Coke had given up on vitamin-enhanced waters in favor of flavored water, while Nestlé Waters and Danone Waters retained only a fluoride-enhanced water. Like those at Coca-Cola, managers at Nestlé and Danone believed that flavored waters offered substantial growth opportunities in most country markets. The Tata Group, an Indian beverage producer, showed greater confidence in the vitamin-enhanced bottled water market with its purchase of a 30 percent stake in Energy Brands in 2006 for $677 million. The Tata Group's chairman believed that Energy Brands had the potential to become a $3 billion company within 10 years.

Profiles of the Leading Bottled Water Producers

Nestlé Waters

Nestlé was the world's leading seller of bottled water, with a worldwide market share of 18.3 percent in 2006. It was also the world's largest food company, with 2005 sales of 91 billion Swiss francs (approximately $71 billion). The company was broadly diversified into 10 food and beverage categories that were sold in almost every country in the world under such recognizable brand names as Nescafé, Taster's Choice, Perrier, Vittel, Carnation, PowerBar, Friskies, Alpo, Nestea, Libby's, Stouffer's, and, of course, Nestlé. The company produced bottled water as early as 1843, but its 1992 acquisition of Perrier created the foundation of what has made Nestlé Waters the world's largest seller of bottled water, with 75 brands in 130 countries. In 2005, Nestlé recorded bottled water sales of 8.8 billion Swiss francs (approximately $6.9 billion) and was the global leader in the bottled water industry, with an 18.3 percent worldwide market share in 2005. Nestlé Waters was the number one seller of bottled water in the United States with a 42.1 percent market share in 2004 and the number one seller in Europe with a 20 percent market share. Nestlé was also the number one seller in Africa and the

Middle East and was aggressive in its attempts to build market-leading positions in emerging markets in Asia and Latin America through the introduction of global Nestlé products and the acquisition of established local brands. The company acquired nearly 20 bottled water producers between 2001 and 2003. In 2006, Nestlé Waters was the number one brand of bottled water in Pakistan, Vietnam, and Cuba; the number two brand in Indonesia and Argentina; and the number three brand in Thailand.

The company's bottled water portfolio in 2006 included two global brands (Nestlé Pure Life and Nestlé Aquarel), five international premium brands (Perrier, Vittel, Contrex, Acqua Panna, and S. Pellegrino), and 68 local brands. Nestlé Pure Life was a purified water product developed in 1998 for emerging markets and other markets in which spring water was not an important differentiating feature of bottled water. Nestlé Aquarel was developed in 2000 for the European market and markets that preferred still spring water over purified water or sparkling spring water. Nestlé's other waters marketed in Europe were either spring water with a higher mineral content or sparkling waters such as Perrier and S. Pellegrino. Almost all brands marketed outside of Europe were either spring water or mineral water with no carbonation. Its brands in the United States included Pure Life, Arrowhead, Ice Mountain, Calistoga, Deer Park, Zephyrhills, Ozarka, and Poland Spring.

During the early 2000s, Nestlé Waters management believed that its broad portfolio of local water brands was among the company's key resource strengths. However, the notable success of Nestlé's two global brands had caused management to reorganize the division in 2006. Pure Life and Aquarel had grown from just 2.5 percent of the division's sales in 2002 to 12.0 percent of the division's 2005 sales. Consumers in the United States seemed to accept the Pure Life brand as well as long-established local brands, with sales of Nestlé Pure Life in the United States increasing by 50 percent between 2004 and 2005. Flavored varieties of Pure Life had also achieved notable success in Canada

by capturing a 70 percent share of the flavored water market within the first six months on the market. Nestlé's 68 local brands had accounted for as much as 75.7 percent of division sales in 2002, but local brands had declined to 64.8 percent of sales in 2005. The company's five premium international brands accounted for an additional 23.2 percent of 2005 sales.

Nestlé had test-marketed functional waters fortified with vitamins and plant extracts between 2003 and 2004, but offered only fruit-flavored enhanced waters in 2006. Contrex Lemon Meringue and Strawberry Melba were two innovative calorie-free flavors introduced in 2006. The company had also used packaging innovations to differentiate its bottled water brands, including a spill-proof cap for child-sized bottles of Poland Spring, Deer Park, and Arrowhead. Nestlé Waters also developed a bubble-shaped bottle that was designed to appeal to children. Perrier's new PET container was part of a strategy to revitalize the prestigious brand, which had experienced annual sales declines since the mid-1990s. The new plastic bottle was intended to better match the on-the-go lifestyles of young consumers than Perrier's heavy one-liter glass containers. Nestlé would still package Perrier in glass bottles for consumers who preferred the brand's traditional packaging for dinner parties and other formal settings.

Home and office delivery (HOD) was also an important component of Nestlé's strategy—especially in North America, Europe, and the Middle East. HOD made up nearly 30 percent of Nestlé Waters' sales volume in the United States and was recording double-digit growth in most other country markets in 2005. In 2005, Nestlé competed in the HOD market for bottled water in 30 countries. Between 2000 and 2004, the company had made 8 acquisitions in the European HOD segment to grow from no presence to the leading position, with 32 percent market share. Nestlé had also made acquisitions and entered into joint ventures to develop market-leading positions in countries located in the Middle East, Northern Africa, and the Far East. Nestlé's market-leading positions in

Europe and the United States in HOD and PET channels allowed it to earn the status of low-cost leader in the United States. Exhibit 7 illustrates Nestlé Waters' cost and wholesale pricing advantages relative to Coca-Cola and PepsiCo in U.S. markets. Nestlé Waters' management stated in mid-2002 that it expected to double the division's revenues by 2010.

Groupe Danone

Groupe Danone was established through the 1966 merger of two of France's leading glass makers, who foresaw the oncoming acceptability of plastic as a substitute to glass containers. The management of the newly merged company believed that, rather than shifting its focus to the manufacture of plastic containers, the company should enter markets for products typically sold in glass containers. Groupe Danone's diversification outside of glass containers began in 1969 when the company acquired Evian—France's leading brand of bottled water. Throughout the 1970s and 1980s, Groupe Danone acquired additional food and beverage companies that produced beer, pasta, baby food, cereals, sauces, confectionery, dairy products, and baked goods. In 1997, the company slimmed its portfolio of businesses to dairy products, bottled water, and a baked goods division producing cereal, cookies, and snacks. In 2005, Groupe Danone was a leading global food company, with annual sales of €13 billion, and was the world's largest producer of dairy products; the number two producer of cereal, cookies, and baked snacks; and the second

Exhibit 7

Value Chain Comparison for the Bottled Water Operations of Nestlé, PepsiCo, and Coca-Cola

	NESTLÉ WATERS	PEPSICO	COCA-COLA
Retailer price per case	$8.44	$8.52	$8.65
Retailer margin	35.0%	17.5%	17.6%
Wholesale price per case	$5.49	$7.03	$7.13
Wholesale sales	$5.49	$7.03	$7.13
Support revenue	0.00	0.41	0.52
Total bottler revenue	$5.49	$7.44	$7.65
Expenses			
Water*	$0.01	$1.67	$1.70
PET bottles	1.03	1.16	1.16
Secondary packaging	0.61	0.68	0.68
Closures	0.21	0.23	0.23
Labor/manufacturing	0.70	0.70	0.77
Depreciation	0.07	0.08	0.08
Total cost of goods sold	2.63	4.52	4.62
Gross profit	$2.86	$2.92	$3.03
Selling, general, & administrative	2.29	2.25	2.53
EBITA	$0.57	$0.67	$0.50
EBITA margin	10.4%	9.0%	6.5%

* Includes licensing fees and royalties paid by Coca-Cola and PepsiCo bottlers to Coca-Cola and PepsiCo.

Source: Goldman Sachs Global Equity Research as reported by *Beverage World,* April 2002.

largest seller of bottled water. The company had been the largest seller of bottled water by volume in 2005 but was displaced by Nestlé in terms of both volume and dollar sales during 2006.

Danone recorded worldwide bottled water sales of €3.4 billion in 2005. Among Groupe Danone's most important beverage brands were Evian, the world's leading brand of spring water, and Wahaha, the leading brand of bottled water in China. Each brand accounted for more than €1 billion in sales during 2005. During that year, 40 percent of Danone's bottled water sales originated in Europe, 47 percent were in China, and 13 percent were in emerging markets outside of Asia. Danone's local and regional brands held number one shares in many country markets such as Denmark, Germany, Spain, the United Kingdom, Poland, Indonesia, Mexico, and Morocco.

Like Nestlé, Danone had made a number of acquisitions of regional bottled water producers during the late 1990s and early 2000s. During 2002, Danone acquired a controlling interest in Poland's leading brand of bottled water for an undisclosed amount and purchased Canada's Sparkling Spring brand of waters for an estimated $300–$400 million. The company also entered into a joint venture with Kirin Beverage Company to strengthen its distribution network in Japan and embarked on a partnership with the Rachid Group, an Egyptian firm, to accelerate its development of market opportunities in North Africa and the Near and Middle East. During 2003 and 2004, Groupe Danone acquired three HOD bottled water sellers in Mexico. Danone acquired the leading brand of bottled water in Serbia and an HOD seller in Spain in 2004. In 2006, the company acquired a 49 percent stake in Denmark's leading seller of bottled water.

Danone Waters' revenues had declined by nearly 20 percent between 2000 and 2005 as its U.S. distribution agreement with Coca-Cola began to suffer. Prior to Coca-Cola's launch of Dasani, its bottlers distributed Evian and other non-Coke bottled water brands. Before the introduction of Dasani, about 60 percent of

Evian's U.S. distribution was handled by Coca-Cola bottlers. With Coca-Cola bottlers' attention directed toward the sale of Dasani, Evian lost shelf space in many convenience stores, supermarkets, delis, restaurants, and wholesale clubs.

Danone Waters and Coca-Cola entered into a joint venture in 2002 that allowed Evian and Dannon water brands to be distributed along with Dasani to convenience stores, supermarkets, and other retail locations serviced by Coca-Cola's bottling operations. In addition, the agreement made Coke responsible for the production, marketing and distribution of Dannon in the United States. Coca-Cola provided Danone an up-front cash payment in return for 51 percent ownership of the joint venture. Danone contributed its five plants and other bottled water assets located in the United States to the joint venture. However, Evian and Dannon continued to suffer under the new distribution arrangement as Coca-Cola continued to put most of its marketing muscle behind Dasani. Danone sold its 49 percent interest in the North American bottled water joint venture to Coca-Cola in 2005.

Danone's home and office delivery businesses were not included in the agreement with Coca-Cola and were combined with Suntory Water Group's assets to form DS Waters in 2003. The combination of Danone Waters' and Suntory Waters' assets made the joint venture the largest HOD distributor in the United States, with sales of approximately $800 million. Brands marketed by DS Waters included Alhambra, Crystal Springs, Sierra Springs, Hinckley Springs, Kentwood Springs, Belmont Springs, and Sparkletts. Groupe Danone and Suntory sold 100 percent of DS Waters to a private investment fund in 2005 for an undisclosed sum. The sale resulted in a €315 million loss for Groupe Danone and completed Groupe Danone's exit from the North American bottled water market. Danone's HOD business remained the worldwide leader in the category with number one rankings in Asia, Argentina, and Canada. Groupe Danone was the second largest HOD provider in Europe in

2005 through a joint venture with Swiss-based Eden Springs.

Groupe Danone had made functional and flavored waters a strategic priority for its beverage business. The company introduced flavored and vitamin-rich versions of Volvic in Europe during 2003 and 2004, and by 2005 it was selling flavored and functional waters in most of its markets. The company held a number one ranking in functional beverage categories in New Zealand and Argentina. Functional and flavored waters accounted for 25 percent of the group's beverage sales in 2005.

The Coca-Cola Company

With 300 brands worldwide, the Coca-Cola Company was the world's leading manufacturer, marketer, and distributor of nonalcoholic beverage concentrates. The company produced soft drinks, juice and juice drinks, sports drinks, water, and coffee and was best known for Coca-Cola, which has been called the world's most valuable brand. In 2005, the company sold more than 20.6 billion cases of beverages worldwide to record revenues of $23.1 billion. Coca-Cola's net income for 2005 was nearly $4.9 billion. Seventy-three percent of Coke's gallon sales were generated outside of North America, with four international markets (Mexico, Brazil, China, and Japan) accounting for 27 percent of Coca-Cola's sales by volume. Sales in the United States also accounted for 27 percent of the company's total volume.

Along with the universal appeal of the Coca-Cola brand, Coca-Cola's vast global distribution system that included independent bottlers, bottlers partially owned by Coca-Cola, and company-owned bottlers made Coke an almost unstoppable international powerhouse. Coca-Cola held market-leading positions in most countries in the cola segment of the soft drink industry, and the strength of the Coca-Cola brand aided the company in gaining market share in most other soft drink segments such as the lemon-lime and diet segments. The company had also been able to leverage Coke's appeal with consumers to gain access to retail distribution channels for new beverages included in its portfolio such as Minute Maid orange juice products, Powerade isotonic beverages, and Dasani purified water.

The Coca-Cola Company did not market and distribute its own brand of bottled water until 1999, when it introduced Dasani. The company created a purified water that included a combination of magnesium sulfate, potassium chloride, and salt to recreate what Coke researchers believed were the best attributes of leading spring waters from around the world. The Dasani formula was a closely guarded secret and was sold to bottlers, just as the company sold its Coke concentrate to bottlers. The Dasani name was developed by linguists who suggested the dual "a"s gave a soothing sound to the name, the "s" conveyed crispness and freshness, and the "i" ending added a foreign ring. Dasani was supported with an estimated $15 million advertising budget during its first year on the market and was distributed through all retail channels where Coke was available. Coca-Cola's U.S. advertising budget for Dasani was $20 million in 2005. Coca-Cola's marketing expertise and vast U.S. distribution system allowed Dasani to become the second largest brand of water sold in the United States by 2001—a position it continued to hold in 2006.

Coca-Cola's 2002 joint venture with Danone Waters allowed Coca-Cola to jump to the rank of second largest bottled water producer in the United States and third largest bottled water producer in the world. The joint venture provided Coke with bottled water products at all price points, with Dasani positioned as an upper-midpriced product, Evian as a premium-priced bottled water, and Dannon as a discount-priced water. Coke management believed the addition of Dannon would allow the company to protect Dasani's near-premium pricing, while gaining spring water brands that could be marketed nationally to challenge Nestlé's regional brands in the spring water segment.

Even though the joint venture allowed Coca-Cola's sales of bottled water to increase from $765 million in 2002 to $1.3 billion in 2003, the three-tier strategy seemed to be failing in some regards since Coke's three water brands had collectively lost 2.2 market share points between 2003 and 2004. Coca-Cola's loss of market share seemed to be attributable, to some degree, to Nestlé's growth during 2004 and the increasing popularity of private-label brands, which had grown by more than 60 percent during 2004. However, some lost market share for the three brands combined might have been a result of weak support for Evian and Dannon brands. Coca-Cola had committed to increasing advertising and promotion for Evian by 20 percent between 2005 and 2010, but beverage industry analysts believed it was unlikely that Evian would ever return to its previous top-five ranking in the United States.

Coca-Cola tested a vitamin- and flavor-enhanced Dasani NutriWater sub-brand during 2002 and 2003, but it abandoned the concept after poor test-market performance. In 2005, the company did go forward with Splenda-sweetened lemon- and raspberry-flavored varieties of Dasani. The company later added strawberry and grape flavors to the Dasani line. Fruit-flavored Dasani had proved to be successful in the market by 2006, with most retailers stocking at least two flavors of Dasani in addition to unflavored Dasani water. Coca-Cola extended the Dasani line in 2006 with the introduction of Dasani Sensations—a flavored water with light carbonation. Like other varieties of Dasani, Dasani Sensations contained no calories. Powerade Option was another functional water developed by Coca-Cola that was introduced in 2005. Powerade Option was a competing product to Gatorade Propel Fitness Water and was available in grape and strawberry flavors in 2006. As of 2006, Powerade Option had been largely unsuccessful in capturing share from Propel Fitness Water and was unavailable in many retail locations.

Coca-Cola had long produced and marketed bottled water in foreign countries under local brand names, such as its Bon Aqua brand in the German market and NaturAqua in Hungary, but began efforts to make Dasani an international brand in 2004 with expansion into Africa, Brazil, and the United Kingdom. Coca-Cola management chose the United Kingdom as its entry point to Western Europe with launches planned for 20 additional European countries by mid-2004. Coca-Cola supported the March 2004 launch of Dasani in the United Kingdom with a $3.2 million advertising budget and a 4-million-bottle sampling campaign but voluntarily recalled all Dasani bottles from retailers' shelves just two weeks after the launch.

The recall was predicated on test results performed by the company that indicated the bottles were tainted with bromate—a cancer-causing agent. Bromate became introduced to the product when calcium, a mandatory ingredient for bottled waters sold in the United Kingdom, was added to Coca-Cola's proprietary formula of minerals used to distinguish Dasani from other bottled waters. The bromate levels present in Dasani exceeded regulatory limits in the United Kingdom but met standards for purity on the European continent. Nevertheless, Coke management believed it best to recall the product and discontinue immediate plans to distribute Dasani not only in the United Kingdom but also in all other European markets. The Dasani launch was viewed by many in the business press as one of the all-time great marketing disasters and resulted in Coke's abandoning the Dasani brand in Europe. Coca-Cola management announced during a June 2006 Deutsche Bank conference for consumer goods that it would expand its line of noncarbonated beverages in Europe through acquisitions. Within two weeks of the announcement, Coca-Cola had acquired the Italian mineral water company Fonti del Vulture and the Apollinaris mineral water brand sold in Germany by Orangina. Coca-Cola also acquired two HOD bottled water producers in Australia during 2006.

PepsiCo Inc.

In 2006, PepsiCo was the world's fourth largest food and beverage company, with sales of approximately $32 billion. The company's brands were sold in more than 200 countries and included such well-known names as Lay's, Tostitos, Mountain Dew, Pepsi, Doritos, Lipton

Iced Tea, Gatorade, Quaker, and Cracker Jack. Six of PepsiCo's products were among the top-15 largest selling products sold in U.S. supermarkets. PepsiCo also produced and marketed Aquafina—the best-selling brand of bottled water in the United States between 2002 and 2006.

PepsiCo had made attempts to enter the bottled water market in as early as 1987, when it purchased a spring water company, but its attempts were unsuccessful until its 1997 introduction of Aquafina. After experimenting with spring water and sparkling water for several years, Pepsi management believed it would be easier to produce a national brand of bottled water that could utilize the same water purification facilities in Pepsi bottling plants that were used to produce the company's brands of soft drinks. Pepsi management also believed that the company could distinguish its brand of purified bottled water from competing brands by stripping all chlorine and other particles out of tap water that might impart an unpleasant taste or smell. PepsiCo began testing a filtration process for Aquafina in 1994 when it installed $3 million worth of reverse osmosis filtration equipment in its Wichita, Kansas, bottling plant to further purify municipal water used to make soft drinks. The system pushed water through a fiberglass membrane at very high pressure to remove chemicals and minerals before further purifying the water using carbon filters. The water produced by Pepsi's process was so free of chemicals that the company was required to add ozone gas to the water to prevent bacteria growth.

Since the company's introduction of Aquafina, PepsiCo had expanded its water brands in the United States to include Gatorade Propel Fitness Water, SoBe Life Water, and functional versions of Aquafina. The product lines for its water business were developed around customer type and lifestyle. Propel was a flavor- and vitamin-enriched water marketed to physically active consumers, while Life Water was a vitamin-enhanced water similar to Glacéau Vitamin Water in formulation and packaging that was marketed to image-driven consumers. The company targeted mainstream water consumers with unflavored Aquafina, Aquafina FlavorSplash (offered in four flavors), and Aquafina Sparkling (a zero-calorie, lightly carbonated citrus or berry-flavored water). Aquafina Alive, planned for a 2007 launch, included vitamins and natural fruit juices. The company's strategy involved offering a continuum of healthy beverages from unflavored Aquafina to nutrient-rich Gatorade. In 2006, Gatorade, Propel, and Aquafina were all number one in their categories, with market shares of 80 percent, 34 percent, and approximately 14 percent, respectively.

PepsiCo was slowly moving into international bottled water markets, with its most notable effort occurring in Mexico. In 2002, PepsiCo's bottling operations acquired Mexico's largest Pepsi bottler, Pepsi-Gemex SA de CV, for $1.26 billion. Gemex not only bottled and distributed Pepsi soft drinks in Mexico but also was Mexico's number one producer of purified water. After its acquisition of Gemex, PepsiCo shifted its international expansion efforts to bringing Aquafina to selected emerging markets in Eastern Europe, the Middle East, and Asia. In 2006, Aquafina was the number one brand of bottled water in Russia and Vietnam and the number two brand in Kuwait.

Other Sellers

In addition to the industry's leading sellers of bottled water, there were hundreds of regional and specialty brands of bottled water in the United States. Most of these companies were privately held bottlers with distribution limited to small geographic regions that competed aggressively on price to make it onto convenience store and supermarket shelves as third-tier brands. Many of these bottlers also sought out private-label contracts with discounters and large supermarket chains to better ensure full capacity utilization and to achieve sufficient volume to purchase bottles and other packaging at lower prices. CG Roxanne was the most successful privately owned bottled water company in the United States. The company's

Crystal Geyser brand made it the fourth largest seller of bottled water in the United States in 2004, with a 7.4 percent market share. Crystal Geyser competed at the lower price points in U.S. supermarkets and convenience stores and was bottled from springs in California, Tennessee, South Carolina, and New Hampshire. The company did not disclose its financial performance.

Another group of small bottlers such as Fiji, Voss, Penta, and Trinity Springs used differentiating features to avoid the fierce price competition at the low end of the market and sold in the superpremium segment, where bottled water retailed from $1.50 to $2.25 per 16-ounce PET container. Superpremium brands were most often sold in natural foods stores, with Trinity Springs being among the leaders in the channel in 2005. Trinity's differentiation was based on its water source, which was a 2.2-mile-deep artesian well located in the Trinity Mountains of Idaho. Trinity Springs' distribution halted in March 2006 when a court invalidated the 2004 sale of the company to Amcon Distributing. Amcon, which had lost $2 million in fiscal 2005 and another $1.8 million during the first six months of fiscal 2006, shut down its Trinity Springs water division after the ruling and was negotiating a settlement with Trinity Springs shareholders in late 2006.

Penta's differentiation was based on a proprietary purification system that the company claimed removed 100 percent of impurities from tap water. The company had also built brand recognition through product placements in motion pictures, music videos, and more than 25 television series. Penta also sponsored a large number of triathlons across the United States and was endorsed by a wide variety of entertainers and professional athletes. In 2006, Penta was distributed in more than 5,000 health food stores in the United States. Penta was also available in Australia, Japan, the United Kingdom, and Canada. Fiji was also among the best-selling brands of superpremium water sold in natural foods stores in 2006 but was also sold in many supermarkets, convenience stores, and drugstores across the United States. Like Penta, Fiji received considerable exposure from its placement in network television series and motion pictures.

Voss achieved differentiation not only from the purity of its source in Norway but also through its distinctive glass bottle and limited channels of distribution. The brand was available only in the most exclusive hotels, spas, and resorts. Another superpremium brand, Eon, achieved its differentiation through its anti-aging claims. The company's anti-aging properties were said to result from the basic atomic structure of Eon water, which was altered through a proprietary reverse osmosis technology. The structure of Eon was similar to that naturally occurring in snowflakes and glacier ice and was suggested to improve cellular hydration and cell detoxification properties better than unstructured water. Many other superpremium brands of bottled water were sold in the United States during 2006, with each attempting to support its premium pricing with some unique characteristic.

Endnote

[1] As quoted in "The Taste of Water," Bottled Water Web, www.bottledwaterweb.com/watertaste.htm.

Case 4

Blue Nile Inc.: World's Largest Online Diamond Retailer

Arthur A. Thompson Jr.
The University of Alabama

A 2006 issue of *Kiplinger's Personal Finance* cited the experience of a couple in Hawaii who were shopping for an engagement ring.[1] The bride-to-be knew what she wanted, so she took a lead role in conducting the search. Several retail jewelry stores in Honolulu quoted her a price of about $7,900 for a nearly flawless diamond ring just under a carat. But the bride-to-be, a policewoman who took pride in thorough investigations, decided to continue her search online. She found a similar ring at BlueNile.com for $4,263 and her fiancé agreed to buy it. As soon as the order was placed, Blue Nile acquired the diamond, which had been selected from the New York diamond cutter whose diamond inventory was displayed on BlueNile.com, and the cutter shipped the diamond overnight to Blue Nile's 13,000-square-foot warehouse in Seattle. A Blue Nile bench jeweler, using a magnifying visor and assorted tools of the trade, mounted the diamond in the setting that the bride-to-be had selected. The ring was cleaned in a tiny hot tub, blasted with steam, placed in a blue-and-silver box that was packed inside a cardboard shipping box, and shipped via FedEx for overnight delivery to the bride in Honolulu. The whole process took just three days. According to the bride-to-be, "It looks absolutely brilliant. It blinds you."[2]

Founded in 1999, Blue Nile had grown to become the world's largest online retailer of certified diamonds and fine jewelry, with sales of

$251.6 million in 2006 (up from $169.2 million in 2004). According to *Internet Retailer* magazine, in 2006 Blue Nile was larger than the next three largest online jewelers combined; the magazine had ranked Blue Nile number 48 in its "Top 400 Guide to Retail Web Sites"; in its December 2006 issue, the magazine went a step further and named Blue Nile an Internet Retailer Best of the Web 2007 company (one of five companies cited).[3] *Forbes* magazine had selected Blue Nile as a Forbes Favorite every year during 2000–2005. The company had been awarded the BizRate.com Circle of Excellence Platinum Award, which recognized the best in online customer service as ranked by actual consumers; Blue Nile was the only jeweler to have ever received this award, and had been the recipient of this award every year since 2002. *Kiplinger's Personal Finance* named Blue Nile as the best online jeweler in November 2006.[4] Blue Nile had also received notice in *Time* and *Money* magazines.

In 2006, jewelry in the United States was an estimated $55–$60 billion industry.[5] Annual sales of diamond jewelry were in the $30–$35 billion range, with diamond engagement rings accounting for sales of $4–$5 billion. About 72 percent of Blue Nile's 2005 revenues involved sales of engagement rings; Blue Nile's average engagement ring sale in 2005 was $5,600. Blue Nile management believed that the company's market share of online sales of engagement rings exceeded 50 percent and that its 2005 share of the overall engagement ring market in the United States was approximately 3.2 percent.[6] Sales of diamond jewelry other than engagement rings accounted for 18 percent of Blue Nile's 2005 sales; management considered this segment to present significant growth opportunities because satisfied buyers of Blue Nile engagement rings would likely consider Blue Nile in their future purchases of diamond jewelry. Blue Nile provided engagement rings for over 80,000 couples from 2000 to mid-2006. Sales of jewelry not containing diamonds accounted for 10 percent of Blue Nile's 2005 revenues; sales of these typically lesser-priced items were considered important because they helped develop both trial and repeat purchase opportunities.

Blue Nile's Business Model and Strategy

In an industry famous for big markups, frequent closeout sales, and myriad judgments of value that often mystified consumers, the marketing challenge for online jewelers was to convince understandably skittish shoppers to purchase fine jewelry online. It was one thing to shop for a diamond in a reputable jewelry store where one could put on a ring or other jewelry item to see how it looked, perhaps inspect a stone with a magnifying glass or microscope, and have a qualified jeweler describe the features of various stone(s) and cuts, compare the character and merit of various settings, and explain why some items carried higher price tags than others. It was quite another thing to commit to buying expensive jewelry based on pictures and information provided on an Internet Web site.

Blue Nile's strategy to attract customers had two core elements. The first was offering high-quality diamonds and fine jewelry at competitively attractive prices. The second entailed providing jewelry shoppers with a host of useful information and trusted guidance throughout their purchasing process. Top management believed its strategy of providing educational information, in-depth product information,

and grading reports—coupled with its wide product selection and attractive prices—was the key driver of the company's success and, ideally, would lead to customers looking upon Blue Nile as their jeweler for life:

> We have established and are continuing to develop a brand based on trust, guidance and value, and we believe our customers view Blue Nile as a trusted authority on diamonds and fine jewelry. Our goal is for consumers to seek out the Blue Nile brand whenever they purchase high quality diamonds and fine jewelry.[7]

Competitive Pricing, Lean Costs, and Supply Chain Efficiency

Blue Nile's domestic and international Web sites showcased as many as 60,000 independently certified diamonds and hundreds of styles of fine jewelry. The product offerings ranged from simple classic designs suitable for wearing every day to an impressive signature collection of some of the finest diamonds in the world. Diamonds were the most significant component of Blue Nile's merchandise offerings, but the selection was limited chiefly to high-quality stones in terms of shape, cut, color, clarity, and carat weight. Complementing the large selection of individual diamonds and gems was a broad range of diamond, platinum, gold, pearl, and sterling silver jewelry that included settings, rings, wedding bands, earrings, necklaces, pendants, bracelets, and watches.

Blue Nile offered a Build Your Own feature that allowed customers to customize diamond rings, pendants, and earrings. Customers could select a diamond and then choose from a variety of ring, earring, and pendant settings that were designed to match the characteristics of each individual diamond.

Blue Nile's economical supply chain and comparatively low operating costs allowed it to sell comparable-quality diamonds, gemstones, and fine jewelry pieces at substantially lower prices than those of reputable local jewelers. The supply chain bypassed the markups of traditional layers of diamond wholesalers and brokers, thus generally allowing Blue Nile to obtain most of its product offerings more cost-efficiently than traditional brick-and-mortar jewelers. The distinctive feature of Blue Nile's supply chain was its set of arrangements that allowed it to display leading diamond and gem suppliers' products on its Web site; some of these arrangements entailed multiyear agreements whereby designated diamonds were offered only at Blue Nile. Blue Nile's suppliers represented more than half of the total supply of high-quality diamonds in the United States.[8] Blue Nile did not actually purchase a diamond or gem from these suppliers until a customer placed an order for it; this enabled Blue Nile to minimize the costs associated with carrying large inventories and limited its risk of potential markdowns. However, Blue Nile did selectively purchase finished pieces (usually bracelets, necklaces, earrings, pendants, wedding bands, and watches), stocking them in its own inventory until customers purchased them. Even so, Blue Nile had inventories of only $11.7 million at year-end 2005 (versus sales of $203.2 million). In contrast, traditional jewelers had far bigger inventories relative to annual sales. For example, Zale Corporation—which not only sold online but also was the parent of Zales Jewelers (780 stores in the United States and Puerto Rico), Zales Outlet, Gordon's Jewelers, Bailey Banks & Biddle (a luxury retail jeweler with 70 locations in 31 states and Puerto Rico), Peoples Jewelers (the largest Canadian jeweler), Mappins Jewelers (another Canadian jewelry chain), and Piercing Pagoda—reported year-end inventories of $853.6 million on 2005 sales of $2.4 billion. Luxury jewelry retailer Tiffany & Co. reported year-end inventories of $1.06 billion on 2005 sales of $2.4 billion.

Blue Nile's supply chain savings gave it a significant pricing advantage. For every dollar that Blue Nile paid suppliers for stones, settings, and other purchased items, it sold its finished jewelry for a markup of about 33 percent over cost (equal to a gross profit margin of 22 percent). In contrast, Zale sold at an average markup of 100 percent over cost of goods sold and Tiffany sold an average markup over cost

of goods sold of 127 percent in 2005 (equal to a gross profit margin of 56 percent).

Another cost-saving element of Blue Nile's strategy was lean operating costs. The company had only 146 employees as of early 2006, of whom 133 were full-time; independent contractors and temporary personnel were hired on a seasonal basis. Blue Nile conducted its operations via a combination of proprietary and licensed technologies. It licensed third-party information technology systems for financial reporting, inventory management, order fulfillment, and merchandising. Also, it used redundant Internet carriers to minimize service interruptions and downtime. Management continuously monitored various operating systems using third-party software, and an on-call team responded to any emergencies or technology issues. Management also continuously explored avenues to improve operating efficiency, refine the company's supply chain, and leverage its investment in fixed-cost technology. Blue Nile's selling, general, and administrative (SG&A) expenses were only 13.3 percent of 2005 annual sales, down from 14.1 percent in 2003 and 19.6 percent in 2002; in contrast, SG&A expenses were 41.2 percent of 2005 sales at Zale Corporation and 40.1 percent of 2005 sales at Tiffany & Co.

Blue Nile's agreements with suppliers and low operating costs enabled it to earn respectable profits while selling at prices that ranged from 20 to 40 percent below those of local retail jewelry stores. Blue Nile had a net profit margin of 6.5 percent in 2005, compared to 2005 net profit margins of 4.5 percent at Zale and 10.6 percent at Tiffany.

Blue Nile cut the retail prices of its diamonds in the second quarter of 2006 in an effort to drive sales gains; the price cuts helped produce a 30 percent sales gain in the quarter, the largest increase of the past six quarters. Sales in the second quarter of 2006 included seven customer sales above $100,000 and one sale above $200,000. In the third quarter, the company's biggest sale was a premium-quality seven-carat engagement ring purchased for $324,000. CEO Mark Vadon, in an interview with The Motley

Fool, talked about Blue Nile's sales of diamonds at six-figure prices:

> Back in Q2, I believe we announced we had seven transactions in the quarter above $100,000, and over time, as the business has established more of a brand name out there, that part of the market for us is very, very active. We have always had products in that type of price range, and it used to be unusual for us to see a six-figure purchase. Now those are becoming pretty common around here.
>
> What we typically do as our price points rise, we drop our percentage gross margin. So if you look at a purchase at, say, $100,000 price point, we are only making 8% or 9% gross margin on something like that. We are being as aggressive as possible to make the sale, so we will make more selling $100,000 of small rings as opposed to a single $100,000 ring, but we are really excited to have those types of sales.
>
> We are obviously looking at the dollars of profit we are making on the transaction, and we just love that people walk around with a Blue Nile ring that is that extraordinary and [tell] people where they bought it.[9]

Educational Information and Certification

Blue Nile went to considerable lengths to put to rest any concerns shoppers might have about buying fine jewelry online. It employed an informative sales process, striving to demystify and simplify the process of choosing a diamond or some other gemstone. Blue Nile's Web site provided a wealth of easy-to-understand information about the five C's of purchasing diamonds and gems (carat, cut, color, clarity, and cut grade—see Exhibit 1), allowing shoppers to educate themselves about what characteristics determined the quality and value of various stones. In addition to providing substantial educational information, Blue Nile's Web site and its extensively trained customer service representatives provided detailed product information that enabled customers to objectively compare diamonds and fine jewelry products and to make informed decisions in choosing a stone of suitable size/weight, cut, clarity, look, and price.

Blue Nile's management believed that having reputable industry professionals certify and grade each gemstone offered for sale had many advantages. The grading reports provided valuable guidance to consumers in choosing a stone that was right for them and their pocketbook—the carat weight, color, cut, and clarity of a diamond were critical in providing the buyer with the desired sparkle, brilliance, and dazzling or sophisticated look. In addition, a jewelry shopper's ability to immediately review professionally prepared grading reports for a gemstone of particular interest instilled confidence in shopping for fine jewelry at Blue Nile, typically quelling any fears that the stone might not live up to expectations. Furthermore, the grading reports that Blue Nile provided facilitated comparison shopping, allowing jewelry shoppers not only to compare alternative Blue Nile gems but also to see how Blue Nile's products stacked up against the products they might be considering at competing jewelers.

Customers interested in a particular diamond displayed at Blue Nile's Web site could view or print out an accompanying diamond grading or certification report, prepared by an independent team of professional gemologists, that documented the specific characteristics of the diamond—see Exhibit 2. A diamond grading report (also called a diamond certificate or diamond quality document) was a report created by a team of gemologists who evaluated, measured, and scrutinized the diamond using trained eyes, a jeweler's loupe, a microscope, and other industry tools. A completed certificate included an analysis of the diamond's dimensions, clarity, color, polish, symmetry, and other characteristics. Many round diamonds had a cut grade on the report. Every loose diamond sold by Blue Nile was analyzed and graded by either the Gemological Institute of America (GIA) or the American Gem Society Laboratories (AGSL):

- The GIA was regarded as the world's foremost authority in gemology; its mission was to promote public trust in gems and jewelry. In the 1950s, the GIA had created an International Diamond Grading System and established standards that revolutionized the diamond industry. Most recently, the GIA had introduced a new Diamond Cut Grading System, which used computer modeling to assess and predict the cut quality in round brilliant cut diamonds. The GIA's research revealed that there was no single set of proportions that defined a

Exhibit 1

Determining a Diamond's Value: The Five C's

Carat

Refers to a diamond's weight, not its size. One carat equals one-fifth of a gram. While lighter diamonds often carry a lower price per carat, a 1.0 carat diamond might sparkle more than a 1.25 carat diamond if it is cut differently or has better color and clarity.

Clarity

The degree to which a diamond is free of flaws or inclusions—blemishes, internal imperfections, scratches, trace minerals, or other tiny characteristics that can detract from a diamond's beauty. Diamonds that are absolutely clear are the most sought after and therefore the most expensive. The lower the clarity (and the greater the flaws and inclusions), the lower the value of the diamond. The naked eye can see flaws in diamonds with very poor clarity, but even using a magnifying glass an untrained person would have trouble seeing flaws in a high-clarity diamond. The 11 grades of clarity—ranging from flawless to included—are based on the number, location, size, and type of inclusions present in a diamond. Inclusions and flaws are more visible to the naked eye in lower-grade emerald cuts than in lower-grade round diamonds.

Color

Concerns a diamond's transparency. Acting as a prism, a diamond can divide light into a spectrum of colors and reflect this light as colorful flashes called fire. Like colored glass, color in a diamond will act as a filter and will diminish the spectrum of color emitted. The less color in a diamond, the more colorful the fire and the better the color grade. A little color in a white diamond could diminish its brilliance. White diamonds with very little color were the most highly valued and are priced accordingly. Color grades range from D (absolutely colorless and extremely rare) to Z. White diamonds with grade of D, E, or F are considered "colorless" grade and very high quality; diamonds with grades of G or H are near colorless and offer excellent value; diamonds with grades of I or J have slightly detectable color but still represent good value; the color in diamonds graded K–Z detracts from the beauty of the stone and is especially noticeable in platinum or white gold settings. (Blue Nile only sold diamonds with color grades of J or higher.) Yellow diamonds (some of which are fancy and highly valued) are graded on a different scale than white diamonds.

Cut

A diamond's shape (round, square, oval, pear, heart, marquise, and so on) and style (width, depth, symmetry, polish, and number/position of flat surfaces). Most diamonds are cut with 58 facets, or separate flat surfaces; it is the diamond cutter's job, using precise mathematical formulas, to align the facets at precise angles in relation to each other to maximize the reflection and refraction of light. Cut style affects how light travels within a diamond, thus determining its brightness, fire, and face-up appearance. The cutter's goal is to transform a diamond in the rough into a sparkling, polished stone of the largest possible size and greatest optical beauty; a poor or less desirable cut can dull the look and brilliance of diamonds with excellent color and clarity. There is no single measurement of a diamond that defines its cut, but rather a collection of measurements and observations that determine the relationship between a diamond's light performance, dimensions, and finish.

Cut Grade

This newest of the 5 C's is perhaps the overall best measure or indicator of a diamond's brilliance, sparkle, and "wow effect." Fewer than 5% of diamonds on the market qualified for the highest cut grade rating. Cut grade was a summary rating that took into account such measures as the diamond's table size (the flat surface at the top of the diamond) as a percentage of the diamond's girth (the widest part of the diamond), the crown of the diamond (the portion above the girth) and the crown angle, the pavilion (the portion of the diamond below the girth)—the height of the pavilion contributed to its brilliance; the pavilion angle, the depth of the diamond (from the top facet to the culet); culet size, the diamond's polish and symmetry; and several other factors affecting sparkle, radiance, and brilliance.

(continued)

Exhibit 1 (concluded)

The following table shows price variations in diamonds with varying clarity but the same carat weight and color grade.

Price Comparison: 1 carat, H-color, ideal cut diamond

CLARITY GRADE	DESCRIPTION	PRICE
FL	**Flawless** No internal or external finish flaws.	**$7,500**
IF	**Internally flawless** No internal flaws.	**$7,200**
VVS1	**Very very slightly included**	**$6,900**
VVS2	Very difficult to see inclusions under 10× magnification.	**$6,600**
VS1	**Very slightly included**	**$6,100**
VS2	Difficult to see inclusions under 10× magnification, typically unable to see inclusions with unaided eye.	**$5,600**
SI1	**Slightly included**	**$5,000**
SI2	Easy to see inclusions under 10× magnification, may not be able to see inclusions with unaided eye.	**$4,300**

The following table compares the prices of diamonds with varying color grades but the same clarity grade (VS1) and carat weight:

Price comparison: 1–1.09 carat VS1 round diamond

	COLORLESS			NEAR-COLORLESS			
	D	**E**	**F**	**G**	**H**	**I**	**J**
Ideal	$8,000	$7,600	$7,200	$6,800	$6,000	$5,200	$4,300
Very Good	$7,500	$7,200	$6,900	$6,200	$5,600	$4,700	$4,200
Good	$7,200	$6,800	$6,700	$6,000	$5,200	$4,600	$4,000
Fair	$7,000	$6,700	$6,600	$5,200	$4,700	$4,200	$3,700

Source: Compiled from a variety of sources, including the educational information posted at www.bluenile.com and www. diamonds.com (accessed August 23, 2006). The two price tables are from www.bluenile.com (accessed August 23, 2006).

well-cut round brilliant diamond; according to the GIA, many different proportions could produce attractive diamonds. The GIA had also developed software that provided a method of estimating a cut grade—and a database that was embedded into a number of leading diamond measuring devices so that cut grade estimation could be automated. As a result, manufacturers could plan and, in effect, predict cut grades; buyers could compare cut qualities; and retailers could communicate the effects of cut on round brilliant diamonds. On January 1, 2006, the GIA laboratory introduced new versions of the GIA Diamond Grading Report and Diamond Dossier that provided a single, comprehensive cut grade for all standard round brilliant diamonds falling in the GIA D-to-Z color scale and Flawless-to-I3 clarity scale. Diamonds received one of five cut grades, from Excellent to Poor.

- Founded in 1996, the AGSL was the only diamond grading laboratory to offer a unique 0 to 10 grading system that provided easy-to-read, clear, and accurate information about each diamond it graded. A cut grade of 10 was the lowest quality, and a grade of 000 was the absolute finest or ideal quality, but so far AGSL had only awarded cut grades to select round and square-cut diamonds. (It was, however, considering expanding the grading system to other cuts.) AGSL grading reports were

Exhibit 2

Diamond Characteristics Documented in a GIA Diamond Grading Report

Shape and Cutting Style: The diamond shape and cutting style.

Measurement: The diamond's dimensions in millimeters.

Carat Weight: The weight of the diamond listed to the nearest hundredth of a carat.

Color Grade: A grading that assesses the absence of color in a diamond.

Clarity Grade: Clarity grade determined under 10× magnification.

Cut Grade: A grade of cut as determined by a diamond's face-up appearance, design, and craftsmanship. A GIA cut grade was available on round diamonds graded after January 1, 2006. The addition of cut grade to grading reports was particularly important because cut grade was the best indicator of a diamond's sparkle, brilliance, and "wow effect." (A diamond's cut concerned its shape and number of facets but was not a reliable indicator of the sparkle and brilliance across the stone when looking at it face up.) The GIA's cut grades used a five-point scale from Poor to Excellent; in 2006, GIA cut grades were available only for select round diamonds, the most popular cut for engagement rings. GIA was said to be considering expanding its cut grade ratings to stones in other shapes (square, pear, and marquise). (According to one source, fewer than 5 percent of diamonds qualified for the highest cut grade.)

Finish: Grades that represent a diamond's surface and facet placement.

Polish: Rating the overall smoothness of the diamond's surface.

Symmetry: Measuring the shape, alignment, and placement of the diamond's facets in relation to one another as well as the evenness of the outline.

Fluorescence: Color and strength of color when diamond is viewed under ultraviolet light.

Comments: A description of additional diamond characteristics not already mentioned in the report.

Clarity Plot: A map of the approximate size, type, and position of inclusions as viewed under a microscope.

Proportion Diagram: A map of the diamond's actual proportions that typically includes information about the following:

- **Culet:** Appearance, or lack thereof, of the culet facet. The culet (pronounced "que-let" or the French-sounding "que-lay") was a tiny flat surface formed by polishing off the tip at the bottom of a diamond. The presence of a culet protected the fragile tip of the diamond from chipping during the cutting, handling, and setting of the diamond. However, Asians often preferred diamonds without a culet, so the practice of downgrading diamonds without culets had been discontinued.
- **Table:** Located at the top of the diamond, the table was the largest facet (or flat surface) of a diamond.
- **Depth:** The height of a gemstone measured from the culet to the table.
- **Girdle:** Range of girdle thickness.

based on the gemological industry's highest standards of evaluating the four C's of cut, color, clarity, and carat weight. AGSL grades allowed a shopper to compare the quality of the diamond against the price.

These two laboratories, among the most respected laboratories in the diamond industry, were known for their consistency and unbiased diamond grading systems. Diamonds that were accompanied by GIA and AGSL grading reports were the most highly valued in the industry.

In addition to being graded by the GIA or AGSL, all diamonds in Blue Nile's signature collection were also certified by the Gem Certification and Appraisal Lab (GCAL). This provided a second authoritative analysis of the diamond. GCAL verified that a diamond met all the specific quality requirements of the Blue Nile Signature Collection—see Exhibit 3.

Marketing

Blue Nile's marketing strategy was designed to increase Blue Nile brand recognition, generate consumer traffic, acquire customers, build a loyal customer base, and promote repeat purchases. Top executives at Blue Nile believed

Exhibit 3

Contents of a Certificate of Authenticity Issued by the Gem Certification and Appraisal Lab (GCAL)

Actual Size Photo—A photo of the diamond at its true size.

Laser Inscription Photo—A close-up shot of the laser inscription on the diamond taken at $50\times$ magnification.

Proportion Diagram—A diagram noting the diamond's actual scale, and noting its specific measurements. These measurements were used to determine the cut grade.

Enlarged Photomicrograph—A photo of the diamond from top and bottom.

An Optical Brilliance Analysis—Images of the diamond were captured using a controlled lighting environment and carefully calibrated amounts of light at specific viewing angles. These tests showed the amount of light return or brilliance as it exited the diamond's crown.

Optical Symmetry Analysis—A test analyzing the light exiting the diamond and showing the discrepancies in the balance of the diamond. An even and symmetrical pattern showed that the light was well balanced and indicated exceptional diamond quality.

Certification Statement—A statement signed by the GCAL laboratory director verifying the quality of the graded diamond.

Diamond Grading Analysis—This analysis noted the diamond's shape, measurements, carat weight, and cut grade based on its proportions, polish, symmetry, color, and clarity grades. It also contained any comments regarding the diamond.

Source: www.bluenile.com (accessed August 8, 2006).

that jewelry shoppers preferred to seek out high-quality diamonds and fine jewelry from a trusted source in a nonintimidating environment, where information, guidance, reputation, convenience, and value were important characteristics. Hence, a major portion of Blue Nile's marketing effort was focused on making sure that site visitors had a positive, informative experience shopping at Blue Nile, one that inspired their confidence to buy diamonds and fine jewelry from the company. One key initiative to provide a good customer experience was the development of a user-friendly interactive search tool that allowed shoppers to customize their search and quickly identify diamonds with the characteristics they were looking for. An advanced version of Blue Nile's diamond search tool launched in March 2006 allowed site visitors to search Blue Nile's diamond collection according to any of 12 criteria, including price, carat weight, cut, color, clarity, polish, symmetry, fluorescence, culet, diamond grading report, depth percentage, and table percentage. The Blue Nile customer experience was designed to empower customers with

knowledge and confidence as they evaluated, selected, and purchased diamonds and fine jewelry.

The company's efforts to draw more shoppers to its site and boost awareness of Blue Nile included both online and offline marketing and advertising efforts. Most of Blue Nile's advertising dollars went for ads at Web portals (Yahoo!, America Online, and MSN), search engine sites (Google), and select other sites. The company also did some direct online marketing. Advertising expenses were $4.5 million in 2003, $6.5 million in 2004, $7.6 million in 2005, and $9.7 million in 2006.

Blue Nile pulled back on advertising during December 2005 because the cost to buy keywords on Internet search engines rose dramatically. Search keyword bidding pushed up Blue Nile's cost per click on Google to more than 50 percent above December 2004 levels; moreover, the price of Google's top five keywords rose by over 80 percent. According to Blue Nile's CEO, Mark Vadon, the aggressive competition in the crowded search market converted fewer searchers into Blue Nile buyers.

Customer Service and Support

Blue Nile strove to provide a high level of customer service and was continuously engaged in refining the customer service aspects in every step of the purchase process. Complementing the extensive information resources on its Web site was a call center staffed with knowledgeable, highly trained support personnel. Blue Nile diamond and jewelry consultants were trained to provide guidance on all steps in the process of buying diamonds and fine jewelry, including the process for selecting an appropriate item, the purchase of that item, financing and payment alternatives, and shipping services. Customers with questions could call a prominently displayed toll-free number or send an e-mail to service@bluenile.com; most calls to the Blue Nile call center were answered within 10 seconds.[10] There were personnel assigned to creating and enhancing the features and functionality of the company's Web site and order processing and fulfillment systems. Policies relating to privacy, security, product availability, pricing, shipping, refunds, exchanges, and special orders were readily accessed at the company's Web site.

Order Fulfillment Operations

Order fulfillment at Blue Nile was designed to enhance customer value and confidence by filling customer orders accurately and delivering them quickly and securely. When an order for a customized diamond jewelry piece was received, the supplier holding the diamond in inventory generally shipped it to Blue Nile (or an independent third-party jeweler with whom Blue Nile maintained an ongoing relationship for assembly) within one business day. Upon receipt at Blue Nile, the diamond was sent to assembly for setting and sizing, tasks performed by either Blue Nile bench jewelers or independent third-party bench jewelers. Each diamond was inspected upon arrival from suppliers; additionally, each finished setting or sizing was inspected prior to shipment to a customer. Prompt and secure delivery was a high priority, and Blue Nile shipped nearly all diamond and fine jewelry products via FedEx. The company had an on-time order delivery rate of 99.96 percent, which it was striving to push to 100 percent.[11]

Order fulfillment costs, which were included as part of SG&A expenses, totaled $1.5 million in 2003, $1.6 million in 2004, $1.8 million in 2005, and $2.4 million in 2006. These costs included all expenses associated with operating and staffing the Seattle warehouse and order fulfillment center, including costs attributable to receiving, inspecting, and warehousing inventories and picking, preparing, and packaging customers' orders for shipment.

Product Line Expansion

Blue Nile was selectively expanding its product offerings in terms of both price points and product mix. New product offerings included both customized and noncustomized jewelry items. Management believed that the online nature of Blue Nile's business, coupled with its supply arrangements where diamonds and other gemstones were purchased from suppliers only when an order was placed, allowed it to readily test shopper response to new diamond and gemstone offerings and to efficiently add promising new merchandise to its overall assortment of fine jewelry.

Expansion into International Markets

Blue Nile was selectively pursuing opportunities in those international markets where management believed the company could leverage its existing infrastructure and deliver compelling customer value. The decision to enter a new country market was based on the volume of consumer spending on jewelry, the extent to which consumers in a country were adopting online purchasing, the competitive landscape, and other factors. In August 2004, Blue Nile launched a Web site in the United Kingdom (www.bluenile.co.uk) offering a limited number of products; in September 2005, Blue Nile began providing customers at its U.K. Web site with the ability to customize their diamond jewelry purchases and to buy wedding bands. A Web site in Canada (www.bluenile.ca) was launched in January 2005. In 2006, both the U.K. and Canadian Web sites had more limited merchandise selections than the U.S. Web site and less developed search and educational features; the two international sites had combined sales of only $3.3 million in 2005.

Other Strategy Elements

Blue Nile's strategy had three other key elements:

- Blue Nile had a 30-day return policy that gave customers plenty of time to consider their purchase and make sure they had made a good decision. If customers were not satisfied for any reason, they could return any item without custom engraving in its original condition within 30 days of the date of shipment for a refund or an exchange. Requests for a refund or a different item were processed within a few days.

- Blue Nile offered free shipping with every order delivered to a U.S. address; orders were shipped via FedEx Express, FedEx Ground, or U.S. Postal Service, depending on order value and destination. All orders under $250 were shipped via FedEx Ground if within the 48 contiguous states or by U.S. Postal Service for destinations in Hawaii and Alaska. Orders between $250 and $1,000 were shipped via FedEx two-day delivery. All orders over $1,000 and all loose diamond orders were shipped via FedEx Priority Overnight. Customers had the option to upgrade the delivery of items under $1,000 to FedEx Priority Overnight for a $15 charge.

- Blue Nile automatically provided an appraisal stating the approximate retail replacement value of the item to customers who bought (1) a preset engagement ring priced under $2,500; (2) a diamond jewelry item priced $1,000 and over (except preset solitaire engagement rings, preset earrings, or preset solitaire pendants priced $2,500

or over that come with International Gemological Institute appraisals); or (3) any custom diamond ring, earring, or pendant. The appraisal value was based on current market data, typical retail prices, the weight of precious metal included in the item, craftsmanship, and the cut, color, clarity, and carat weight of the gemstone(s). Included with the appraisal was a brief description of the item being appraised, a photograph of the item, and the cut, color, clarity, and either carat weight for any diamonds, or millimeter dimensions for any gemstones. An appraisal represented value-added to customers because a customer had to have one to obtain insurance coverage and determine what constituted equal replacement in case of loss, theft, or damage.

Blue Nile's Financial and Strategic Performance

During the 2001–2006 period, Blue Nile's sales jumped from $48.7 million to $251.6 million, a compound average growth rate of almost 39 percent. Gross profits (sales minus cost of goods sold) rose from $11.1 million in 2001 to $50.9 million in 2006, equal to a compound average growth rate of 35.6 percent. And the company's bottom-line performance was vastly improved, going from a net loss of $7.4 million in 2001 to a net profit of $13.1 million in 2006 (although net profit was flat from 2005 to 2006). The company generated $40.5 million in cash from operations in 2006 and had a largely debt-free balance sheet going into both 2006 and 2007. Exhibit 4 presents highlights of Blue Nile's financial results from fiscal years 2001 through 2006. In fiscal year 2007, Blue Nile's management expected that net sales would be between $290 million and $300 million, with net income in the range of $0.80 to $0.85 per diluted share.

One of the big appeals of Blue Nile's business model was the ability to generate cash 40 to 55 days ahead of the need to pay suppliers; in a

Exhibit 4

Selected Financial Data, Blue Nile Inc., 2001–2006 ($ in thousands, except per share data)

	YEAR ENDED JAN. 3, 2007	YEAR ENDED JAN. 2, 2006	YEAR ENDED JAN. 1, 2005	YEARS ENDED DECEMBER 31		
				2003	2002	2001
Income Statement Data						
Net sales	$251,587	$203,169	$169,242	$128,894	$72,120	$48,674
Cost of sales*	200,734	158,025	131,590	99,476	53,967	37,551
Gross profit	50,853	45,144	37,652	29,418	18,153	11,123
Selling, general and administrative expenses	34,296	27,095	22,295	18,207	14,126	15,421
Restructuring charges	—	—	—	(87)	400	1,017
Operating income (loss)	16,557	18,049	14,857	11,298	3,627	(5,315)
Other income (expense)	3,423	2,504	772	(12)	(2,000)	(2,045)
Income (loss) before income taxes	19,980	20,553	15,629	11,286	1,627	(7,360)
Income tax expense (benefit)	6,916	7,400	5,642	(15,700)	—	—
Net income (loss)	$ 13,064	$ 13,153	$ 9,987	$ 26,986	$ 1,627	$ (7,360)
Basic net income (loss) per share	$0.79	$0.75	$0.80	$6.98	$0.49	$(2.44)
Diluted net income (loss) per share	$0.76	$0.71	$0.51	$1.65	$0.11	$(2.44)
Weighted average shares outstanding:						
Basic	16,563	17,550	12,450	3,868	3,336	3,015
Diluted	17,278	18,597	17,885	16,363	14,160	3,015
Balance Sheet Data						
Cash and cash equivalents	$ 78,540	$ 71,921	$ 59,499	$ 30,383	$22,597	$16,298
Marketable securities	19,767	42,748	41,868	—	—	—
Accounts receivable	1,640	1,877	1,028	916	481	92
Inventories	14,616	11,764	9,914	10,204	5,181	6,619
Total current assets	116,018	132,496	121,529	47,595	n.a.	n.a.
Accounts payable	66,625	50,157	37,775	26,288	15,791	5,253
Total current liabilities	74,137	55,627	43,691	30,932	n.a.	n.a.
Working capital	41,881	76,869	77,838	16,663	1,795	9,021
Total assets	122,106	138,005	128,382	62,305	30,914	26,545
Total long-term obligations	666	863	1,071	1,126	1,091	10,789
Total stockholders' equity (deficit)	47,303	81,515	83,620	(27,238)	(54,560)	(56,199)
Cash Flow Data						
Net cash provided by operating activities	$ 40,518	$ 31,272	$ 29,751	$ 19,816	$16,730	$ 4,460
Net cash used in investing activities	21,065	(2,053)	(43,296)	(3,503)	(1,041)	n.a.
Net cash provided by (used in) financing activities	(54,964)	(16,797)	42,661	(8,527)	(9,390)	n.a.

*Cost of sales included purchases from suppliers, inbound and outbound shipping costs, insurance on shipments, and jewelry assembly costs.

n.a. = not available.

Source: Company 10-K reports, 2004, 2005, and 2006, and company press release, February 12, 2007.

very real sense, Blue Nile's business model was self-funding because suppliers financed Blue Nile's sales growth—see Exhibit 5. Moreover, the company's business model was readily scalable to substantially higher sales volumes with minimal additional capital investment. Blue Nile's capital expenditures for facilities and equipment were a meager $3.5 million in 2003, $1.4 million in 2004, $1.1 million in 2005, and $1.9 million in 2006. Capital expenditures for fiscal 2007 were budgeted at $4.0 million.

Blue Nile executives believed the company's market position was highly defensible. The company had negotiated exclusive and highly favorable arrangements with a number of diamond and gemstone suppliers that allowed it to offer a broad range and selection of fine jewelry products with minimal inventory, it had a very lean cost structure, and it had created a premium brand name and brand awareness that competitors would have difficulty replicating. While Blue Nile's competitiveness was dependent on maintaining favorable arrangements with its suppliers, the company was somewhat protected by having negotiated agreements with a variety of suppliers, thus limiting its dependence on particular suppliers—in 2004 and 2005, the top three suppliers accounted for only 25 percent of the company's purchases. Moreover, the supply arrangements were favorable to suppliers, providing them with real-time market intelligence about what items were selling, the potential of high sales volume through a single account, and a way to achieve more inventory turns and otherwise manage their own inventories more efficiently.

Stock Issues and Repurchases

Blue Nile became a public company in 2004, selling some 2.3 million shares of common stock at $20.50 per share and realizing proceeds of $42.5 million after expenses. Trading of the company's stock began on May 20, 2004, on the NASDAQ exchange under the symbol NILE. Since trading began, the stock had traded as low as $22.50 (August 2004) and as high as $43 (December 2005); the stock price hovered in the $30 to $35 range during the January–August 2006 period.

Exhibit 5

The Cash-Generating Capability of Blue Nile's Business Model

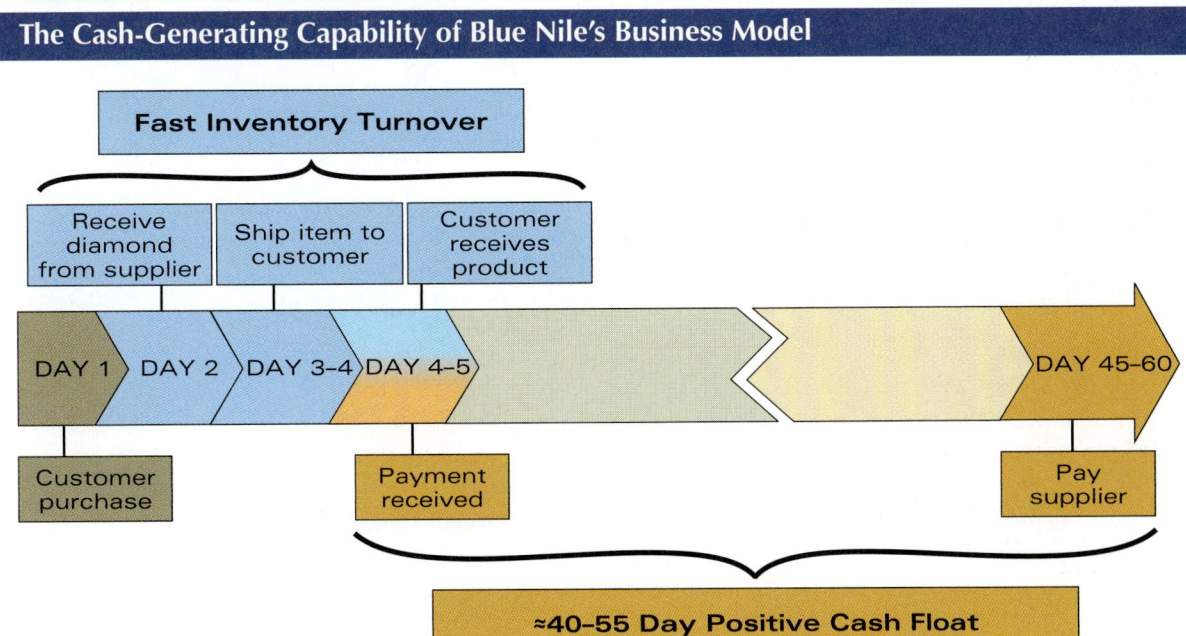

Source: Blue Nile Management Presentation, Goldman Sachs Seventh Annual Internet Conference, May 24, 2006.

Blue Nile had several stock-based compensation plans, under which stock options could be issued to officers, employees, nonemployee directors, and consultants. Going into 2006, stock options for just over 2 million shares were outstanding, about 1.1 million of which were exercisable in 2006. Blue Nile also had an employee stock purchase plan, but no shares had been issued as of January 1, 2006.

Blue Nile repurchased about 3.3 percent of its outstanding shares of common stock in 2005 at a cost of $17.4 million; the company spent $57.4 million to repurchase about 1.8 million shares in 2006.

Industry Growth and Competition

According to U.S. Department of Commerce data, total U.S. jewelry sales, including watches and fashion jewelry, were $59 billion in 2005, up from $57 billion in 2004. The U.S. jewelry market had grown at a compound annual growth rate of 5.7 percent over the last 25 years. Jewelry sales in the United States grew by 4.6 percent in 2004, 2.9 percent in 2003, 8.0 percent in 2004, and 2.7 percent in 2005; they were forecast to grow 6.0 percent in 2006.[12] Sales were somewhat seasonal, with relatively higher sales in February

Exhibit 6

Major U.S. Retailers of Jewelry, 2005

	GENERAL RETAILERS OF JEWELRY		SPECIALTY RETAILERS OF JEWELRY	
RANK	**RETAILER**	**2005 SALES (IN BILLIONS)**	**RETAILER**	**2005 SALES (IN BILLIONS)**
1	Wal-Mart	$2.7	Zale Corp. (2,300+ locations in the United States, Canada, and Puerto Rico)*	$2.4
2	QVC	1.4	Sterling (Kay Jewelers, Jared, and assorted regional retailers)*	2.3
3	JCPenney	1.2	Tiffany (150 stores in U.S. and international locations)	1.2
4	Sears	1.1	Helzberg Diamonds (270 locations)	0.5
5	Finlay	1.0	Fred Meyer (430 stores in 34 states under the brands Fred Meyer Jewelers, Littman Jewelers, and Barclay Jewelers)	0.5
6	Costco	0.4	Whitehall (386 stores in 38 states under the brands Whitehall, Lundstrom, and Marks Bros.)	0.3
7	Home Shopping Network	0.4	Friedman's (420+ locations in 20 states)	0.3
8	Target	0.4	Ross-Simon (14 stores in 9 states, plus catalog sales)	0.3
9	Jewelry Television	0.4	Tourneau (30 locations in 13 states)***	0.3
10	Neiman-Marcus	0.4	Ben Bridge Jeweler (70+ stores in 12 mostly western states)**	0.2
	Share of Overall Market	**15.9%**	**Share of Overall Market**	**13.7%**

*Sterling was a wholly owned subsidiary of Britain-based Signet Group, PLC; Sterling operated 781 Kay's Jewelry stores in 50 states, 110 Jared Galleria of Jewelry showrooms in 26 states, and 330 other regional stores under a variety of brand names in 31 states.

**Became a subsidiary of Warren Buffet's Berkshire Hathaway in 2000.

***Tourneau's sales were heavily concentrated in fine watches.

Source: Company Web sites, plus information posted at www.signetgroupplc.com (accessed August 25, 2006).

(Valentine's Day), May (Mother's Day), and the October–December holiday shopping season. Sales of diamond jewelry in the United States were an estimated $32.5 billion in 2005 and were believed to represent about 50 percent of the global diamond jewelry market.[13]

The diamond and fine jewelry retail market was intensely competitive, with sales highly fragmented among locally owned jewelry stores (34 percent); retail jewelry store chains with 100+ stores (13 percent); numerous chain department stores (12 percent); online retailers that sold fine jewelry and online auction sites (4 percent); television shopping retailers (4 percent); mass merchants, such as discount superstores and wholesale clubs whose merchandise offerings included fine jewelry (10 percent); and all other retailers, such as general merchandise and clothing stores and catalog retailers (23 percent). The Jewelry Board of Trade estimated that there were some 24,500 specialty jewelry firms in the United States in 2005, down from 26,750 specialty jewelry retailers in 1999. However, the number of stores operated by specialty jewelry retailers increased by about 700 stores over the same period, reflecting a continuing industry trend toward consolidation; the five largest specialty jewelry retailers in the United States had increased their collective share from about 18 percent to about 24 percent of specialty jewelry sales since 1999. Nonetheless, independent jewelers, including those with fewer than 100 stores, accounted for about 70 percent of the sales made by specialty jewelry retailers.

Blue Nile's primary competition came from both online and offline retailers that offered products within the higher-value segment of the jewelry market. Many brick-and-mortar jewelry retailers (including market leaders Zale, Sterling, Tiffany, and Helzberg, among many others) had recently begun selling jewelry online at their Web sites. The principal competitive factors in the fine jewelry market were product selection and quality, price, customer service and support, brand recognition, reputation, reliability and trust, and, in the case of online retailers, Web site features and functionality, convenience, and speed of delivery.

The Online Jewelry Industry

Jewelry e-tailers sold approximately $340 million worth of engagement rings in 2005; online sales of other types of rings and jewelry items were another $2 billion in 2005.[14] A majority of those sales were said to be to men, chiefly because they were more amenable than women to shopping for jewelry online. The primary appeal of buying diamonds and jewelry online was lower prices. Most online jewelry retailers employed a business model similar to Blue Nile's, keeping their inventories lean, purchasing stones from suppliers only when an order for a specific stone was received, and delivering the merchandise a few days after the order was placed.

Blue Nile's Online Competitors

There were dozens of online retailers of diamonds in 2006. Some were more reputable than others, and the sites varied considerably in terms of diamond selection, prices, customization options, educational information, product information, and access to professional grading reports, responsive customer service, and return policies. Popular sites, in addition to market leader Blue Nile, included Diamonds.com, Whiteflash.com. Ice.com, JamesAllen.com, Overstock.com, and Amazon.com.

DIAMONDS.COM Diamonds.com was founded in 2000 and headquartered in Las Vegas; the principal owners had over 25 years' experience in all areas of the diamond industry. The company's product offering included over 40,000 loose diamonds sourced from New York City's famed 47th Street diamond district, along with a selection of settings, rings, bracelets, necklaces, and earrings. There was extensive educational information on the Diamonds.com Web site; the discussion of the four C's of purchasing a diamond was lucid and informative. There was a search function that allowed site visitors to search the loose diamond inventory based on shape, carat size, cut, color, clarity, and price. Shoppers had the ability to customize their purchase by choosing a stone and a setting. Diamond grading reports issued by either the Gemological Institute of America or the American Gemological Society Laboratory could be viewed online for all loose diamonds, shipping was free, and orders came with an identifying grading report and warranty document. Customers could return noncustomized orders for a full refund (excluding shipping, handling, and insurance) for up to 30 days after delivery; returns were not accepted on custom work or special orders unless an error had been made. The staff at Diamonds.com included expert gemologists trained at the world's leading gemological laboratories; shoppers could call a toll-free number for assistance or to place a phone order.

WHITEFLASH.COM   About half of Whiteflash's sales involved orders for customized jewelry. Whiteflash had a small inventory (about 1,000 stones) and was said to charge higher prices than Blue Nile and many other e-tailers.[15] One distinctive strategy element was its trade-up program, whereby a customer could trade in a jewelry item purchased from Whitehall for a higher-priced item and only pay the difference between the new item and the previously purchased item. Whiteflash had a policy of not accepting returns on customized jewelry products unless an error had been made in doing the custom work; for loose stones and standard settings, Whiteflash offered a full refund 10 days from receipt for any reason. The education materials at the Whiteflash Web site included video tutorials.

ICE.COM   Over 300,000 customers had made purchases at Ice.com since it began online operations in 2001. Ice's product line included rings, necklaces, earrings, bracelets, pendants, and watches. Its product offerings were all finished products; no customization options were available. The average purchase was about $210 (versus over $1,600 at Blue Nile). The company had a monthly payment option, provided free shipping on orders over $150, and had an unconditional 30-day money-back guarantee.

Bridal and engagement rings came with an appraisal certificate. There was no educational information on the company's Web site, and the information provided about the quality of its diamond jewelry was limited. Customers could make inquiries via a toll-free number or e-mail.

JAMESALLEN.COM   Founded in 1998 by James Allen Schultz and his wife Michele Sigler, JamesAllen.com had grown to be one of the largest online diamond retailers. The firm's strategy centered around offering "the world's most beautiful engagement rings coupled with the finest laboratory graded diamonds, all at an extraordinary value." It had been featured in such trade magazines as *National Jeweler* and profiled by the *Washington Post, U.S. News & World Report,* NBC News, and National Public Radio. While an estimated 3 percent of the round diamonds sold in the United States qualified as "Ideal" under AGSL grading standards, over 90 percent of the customers shopping at JamesAllen.com chose diamonds from the retailer's Signature Ideal, Ideal, or Premium categories. All stones came with grading reports from either the Gemological Institute of America or the American Gemological Society Laboratory.

Management claimed that no other company offered a finer collection of top-quality cut diamonds. The product offerings at JamesAllen.com included 55,000 loose diamonds, preset engagement rings, preset wedding and anniversary rings, diamond studs, diamond jewelry, and designer jewelry by Amy Levine, Danhov, and Leo Popov. Shoppers could customize their own diamond rings, studs, and pendants. The JamesAllen.com Web site had a comprehensive Education section that featured an interactive demonstration of the importance of diamond cut, 3D viewing, and tips and search tools. An expert staff answered questions via phone or e-mail. Payment options included credit card, wire transfer, personal check, certified check, or money order. JamesAllen.com provided free overnight shipping via FedEx or UPS on all orders within the United States. Orders outside the United States had to be prepaid via wire transfer and carried a shipping fee of $100. The company had a full 30-day return policy, but loose diamond returns that did not include the original laboratory grading report were subject to a charge of $150.

Endnotes

[1] Sean O'Neill, "Clicks and Stones," *Kiplinger's Personal Finance,* February 2006, www.kiplinger.com/personalfinance/magazine/archives/2006/02/diamonds.html (accessed August 7, 2006).

[2] Ibid.

[3] According to information posted at www.bluenile.com (accessed August 8, 2006).

[4] Sean O'Neill, "Get a Diamond Deal Online," *Kiplinger's Personal Finance,* November 14, 2006, www.kiplinger.com/features/archives/2006/11/diamonds.html (accessed February 1, 2007).

[5] Blue Nile management presentation, Goldman Sachs Seventh Annual Internet Conference, May 24, 2006, available at www.bluenile.com (accessed August 8, 2006).

[6] Ibid.

[7] Blue Nile's 2005 10-K report, p. 4.

[8] Citigroup securities analyst Mark Mahaney, "The Long Case for Online Jewelry Retailer Blue Nile," March 31, 2006, available at http://internet.seekingalpha.com/article/8418 (accessed August 25, 2006).

[9] Shruti Basavaraj, "The $324,000 Question," The Motley Fool, November 28, 2006, www.fool.com (accessed February 1, 2007).

[10] Sean O'Neill, "Clicks and Stones" *Kiplinger's Personal Finance,* February 2006, www.kiplinger.com/personalfinance/magazine/archives/2006/02/diamonds.html (accessed August 7, 2006).

[11] As cited in "Internet Retailer Best of the Web 2007," *Internet Retailer,* December 2006, www.internetretailer.com (accessed February 1, 2007).

[12] IDEX Online Research, "U.S. Jewelry Sales Strong in June," August 15, 2006, www.idexonline.com (accessed August 25, 2006).

[13] Information posted at www.signetgroupplc.com (accessed August 25, 2006).

[14] O'Neill, "Clicks and Stones."

[15] Ibid.

Case 5

Panera Bread Company

Arthur A. Thompson Jr.
The University of Alabama

As Panera Bread Company headed into 2007, it was continuing to expand its market presence swiftly. The company's strategic intent was to make great bread broadly available to consumers across the United States. It had opened 155 new company-owned and franchised bakery-cafés in 2006, bringing its total to 1,027 units in 36 states. Plans were in place to open another 170 to 180 café locations in 2007 and to have nearly 2,000 Panera Bread bakery-cafés open by the end of 2010. Management was confident that Panera Bread's attractive menu and the dining ambience of its bakery-cafés provided significant growth opportunity, despite the fiercely competitive nature of the restaurant industry.

Already Panera Bread was widely recognized as the nationwide leader in the specialty bread segment. In 2003, Panera Bread scored the highest level of customer loyalty among quick-casual restaurants, according to a study conducted by TNS Intersearch.[1] J. D. Power and Associates' 2004 restaurant satisfaction study of 55,000 customers ranked Panera Bread highest among quick-service restaurants in the Midwest and Northeast regions of the United States in all categories, which included environment, meal, service, and cost. In 2005, for the fourth consecutive year, Panera Bread was rated among the best of 121 competitors in the Sandleman & Associates national customer satisfaction survey of more than 62,000 consumers. Panera Bread had also won "best of" awards in nearly every market across 36 states.

Company Background

In 1981, Louis Kane and Ron Shaich founded a bakery-café enterprise named Au Bon Pain Company Inc. Units were opened in malls, shopping centers, and airports along the East Coast of the United States and internationally throughout the 1980s and 1990s; the company prospered and became the dominant operator within the bakery-café category. In 1993, Au Bon Pain Company purchased Saint Louis Bread Company, a chain of 20 bakery-cafés located in the St. Louis, Missouri, area. Ron Shaich and a team of Au Bon Pain managers then spent considerable time in 1994 and 1995 traveling the country and studying the market for fast-food and quick-service meals. They concluded that many patrons of fast-food chains like McDonald's, Wendy's, Burger King, Subway, Taco Bell, Pizza Hut, and KFC could be attracted to a higher-quality, quick-dining experience. Top management at Au Bon Pain then instituted a comprehensive overhaul of the newly acquired Saint Louis Bread locations, altering the menu and the dining atmosphere. The vision was to create a specialty café anchored by an authentic, fresh-dough artisan bakery and upscale quick-service menu selections. Between 1993 and 1997, average unit volumes at the revamped Saint Louis Bread units increased by 75 percent, and over 100 additional Saint Louis Bread units were opened. In 1997, the Saint Louis Bread bakery-cafés were renamed Panera Bread in all markets outside St. Louis.

By 1998, it was clear that the reconceived Panera Bread units had connected with consumers. Au Bon Pain management concluded the

Panera Bread format had broad market appeal and could be rolled out nationwide. Ron Shaich believed that Panera Bread had the potential to become one of the leading fast-casual restaurant chains in the nation. Shaich also believed that growing Panera Bread into a national chain required significantly more management attention and financial resources than the company could marshal if it continued to pursue expansion of both the Au Bon Pain and Panera Bread chains. He convinced Au Bon Pain's board of directors that the best course of action was for the company to go exclusively with the Panera Bread concept and divest the Au Bon Pain cafés. In August 1998, the company announced the sale of its Au Bon Pain bakery-café division

for $73 million in cash to ABP Corporation; the transaction was completed in May 1999. With the sale of the Au Bon Pain division, the company changed its name to Panera Bread Company. The restructured company had 180 Saint Louis Bread and Panera Bread bakery-cafés and a debt-free balance sheet.

Between January 1999 and December 2006, close to 850 additional Panera Bread bakery-cafés were opened, some company-owned and some franchised. Panera Bread reported sales of $829.0 million and net income of $58.8 million in 2006. Sales at franchise-operated Panera Bread bakery-cafés totaled $1.2 billion in 2006. A summary of Panera Bread's recent financial performance is shown in Exhibit 1.

Exhibit 1

Selected Consolidated Financial Data for Panera Bread, 2002–2006 ($ in millions, except for per share amounts)

	2006	2005	2004	2003	2002
Income Statement Data					
Revenues:					
Bakery-café sales	$666,141	$499,422	$362,121	$265,933	$212,645
Franchise royalties and fees	61,531	54,309	44,449	36,245	27,892
Fresh dough sales to franchisees	101,299	86,544	72,569	61,524	41,688
Total revenues	828,971	640,275	479,139	363,702	282,225
Bakery-café expenses:					
Food and paper products	197,182	142,675	101,832	73,885	63,370
Labor	204,956	151,524	110,790	81,152	63,172
Occupancy	48,602	37,389	26,730	18,981	15,408
Other operating expenses	92,176	70,003	51,044	36,804	27,971
Total bakery-café expenses	542,916	401,591	290,396	210,822	169,921
Fresh dough costs of sales to franchisees	85,618	75,036	65,627	54,967	38,432
Depreciation and amortization	44,166	33,011	25,298	18,304	13,794
General and administrative expenses	59,306	46,301	33,338	28,140	24,986
Pre-opening expenses	6,173	3,241	2,642	1,531	1,051
Total costs and expenses	738,179	559,180	417,301	313,764	248,184
Operating profit	90,792	81,095	61,838	49,938	34,041
Interest expense	92	50	18	48	32
Other (income) expense, net	(1,976)	(1,133)	1,065	1,592	467
Provision for income taxes	33,827	29,995	22,175	17,629	12,242
Net income	$ 58,849	$ 52,183	$ 38,430*	$ 30,669	$ 21,300
Earnings per share					
Basic	$1.88	$1.69	$1.28	$1.02	$0.74
Diluted	1.84	1.65	1.25	1.00	0.71

(*continued*)

Exhibit 1   (concluded)

	2006	2005	2004	2003	2002
Weighted average shares outstanding					
Basic	31,313	30,871	30,154	29,733	28,923
Diluted	32,044	31,651	30,768	30,423	29,891
Balance Sheet Data					
Cash and cash equivalents	$ 52,097	$ 24,451	$ 29,639	$ 42,402	$ 29,924
Investments in government securities	20,025	46,308	28,415	9,019	9,149
Current assets	127,618	102,774	58,220	70,871	59,262
Total assets	542,609	437,667	324,672	256,835	195,431
Current liabilities	109,610	86,865	55,705	44,792	32,325
Total liabilities	144,943	120,689	83,309	46,235	32,587
Stockholders' equity	397,666	316,978	241,363	193,805	151,503
Cash Flow Data					
Net cash provided by operating activities	$104,895	$110,628	$ 84,284	$ 73,102	$ 46,323
Net cash used in investing activities	(90,917)	(129,640)	(102,291)	(66,856)	(40,115)
Net cash provided by financing activities	13,668	13,824	5,244	6,232	5,664
Net (decrease) increase in cash and cash equivalents	27,646	(5,188)	(12,763)	12,478	11,872

* After adjustment of $239,000 for cumulative effect of accounting change.

Sources: 2006 10-K report, pp. 36–38; 2005 10-K report, pp. 16–17; 2003 10-K report, pp. 29–31; and company press release, February 8, 2007.

The Panera Bread Concept and Strategy

The driving concept behind Panera Bread was to provide a premium specialty bakery and café experience to urban workers and suburban dwellers. Its artisan sourdough breads made with a craftsman's attention to quality and detail and its award-winning bakery expertise formed the core of the menu offerings. Panera Bread specialized in fresh baked goods, made-to-order sandwiches on freshly baked breads, soups, salads, custom roasted coffees, and other café beverages. Panera's target market was urban workers and suburban dwellers looking for a quick-service meal and a more aesthetically pleasing dining experience than that offered by traditional fast food restaurants.

In his letter to shareholders in the company's 2005 annual report, Panera chairman and CEO Ron Shaich said:

We think our continued commitment to providing crave-able food that people trust, served in a warm, community gathering place by associates who make our guests feel comfortable, really matters. When this is rooted in our commitment to the traditions of handcrafted, artisan bread, something special is created. As we say here at Panera, it's our Product, Environment, and Great Service (PEGS) that we count on to deliver our success—year in and year out.

Panera Bread's distinctive menu, signature café design, inviting ambience, operating systems, and unit location strategy allowed it to compete successfully in five submarkets of the food-away-from-home industry: breakfast, lunch, daytime "chill out" (the time between breakfast and lunch and between lunch and dinner when customers visited its bakery-cafés to take a break from their daily activities), light evening fare for eat-in or take-out, and take-home bread. In 2006, Panera began enhancing its menu in ways that would attract more diners during the evening meal hours. Management's long-term objective and strategic intent was

Exhibit 2

Selected Operating Statistics, Panera Bread Company, 2000–2006

	2006	2005	2004	2003	2002	2001	2000
Revenues at company-operated stores (in millions)	$ 666.1	$ 499.4	$ 362.1	$ 265.9	$ 212.6	$ 157.7	$ 125.5
Revenues at franchised stores (in millions)	$1,245.5	$1,097.2	$ 879.1	$ 711.0	$ 542.6	$ 371.7	$ 199.4
Systemwide store revenues (in millions)	$1,911.6	$1,596.6	$1,241.2	$ 976.9	$ 755.2	$ 529.4	$ 324.9
Average annualized revenues per company-operated bakery-café (in millions)	$ 1.967	$ 1.942	$ 1.852	$ 1.830	$ 1.764	$ 1.636	$ 1.473
Average annualized revenues per franchised bakery-café (in millions)	$ 2.074	$ 2.016	$ 1.881	$ 1.860	$ 1.872	$ 1.800	$ 1.707
Average weekly sales, company-owned cafés	$ 37,833	$ 37,348	$ 35,620	$35,198	$33,924	$31,460	$28,325
Average weekly sales, franchised cafés	$ 39,894	$ 38,777	$ 36,171	$35,777	$35,997	$34,607	$32,832
Comparable bakery-café sales percentage increases*							
Company-owned	3.9%	7.4%	2.9%	1.7%	4.1%	5.8%	8.1%
Franchised	4.1%	8.0%	2.6%	(0.4)%	6.1%	5.8%	10.3%
Systemwide	4.1%	7.8%	2.7%	0.2%	5.5%	5.8%	9.1%
Company-owned bakery-cafés open at year-end	391	311	226	173	132	110	90
Franchised bakery-cafés open at year-end	636	566	515	429	346	259	172
Total bakery-cafés open	1,027	877	741	602	478	369	262

* The percentages for comparable store sales are based on annual changes at stores open at least 18 months.

Sources: Company 10-K reports, 2000, 2001, 2003, 2005, and 2006; company press releases, January 4, 2007, and February 8, 2007.

to make Panera Bread a nationally recognized brand name and to be the dominant restaurant operator in the specialty bakery-café segment. According to Scott Davis, Panera's senior vice president and chief concept officer, the company was trying to succeed by "being better than the guys across the street" and making the experience of dining at Panera so attractive that customers would be willing to pass by the outlets of other fast-casual restaurant competitors to dine at a nearby Panera Bread bakery-café.[2] Davis maintained that the question about Panera Bread's future was not *if* it would be successful but *by how much.*

Management believed that its concept afforded growth potential in suburban markets sufficient to expand the number of Panera bread locations by 17 percent annually through 2010 (see Exhibit 3 and 4) and to achieve earnings per share growth of 25 percent annually. Panera Bread's growth strategy was to capitalize on Panera's market potential by opening both company-owned and franchised Panera Bread locations as fast as was prudent. So far, franchising had been a key component of the company's efforts to broaden its market penetration. Panera Bread had organized its business around company-owned bakery-café operations, the franchise operations, and fresh dough operations; the fresh bread unit supplied dough to all Panera Bread stores, both company-owned and franchised.

Exhibit 3

Areas of High and Low Market Penetration of Panera Bread Bakery-Cafés, 2006

	HIGH PENETRATION MARKETS			LOW PENETRATION MARKETS	
AREA	NUMBER OF PANERA BREAD UNITS	POPULATION PER BAKERY-CAFÉ	AREA	NUMBER OF PANERA BREAD UNITS	POPULATION PER BAKERY-CAFÉ
St. Louis	40	67,000	Los Angeles	17	1,183,000
Columbus, OH	19	83,000	Miami	2	1,126,000
Jacksonville	12	98,000	Northern California	10	1,110,000
Omaha	12	101,000	Seattle	5	860,000
Cincinnati	26	108,000	Dallas/Fort Worth	10	590,000
Pittsburgh	25	142,000	Houston	12	335,000
Washington, D.C./ Northern Virginia	26	152,000	Philadelphia	25	278,000

Untapped Markets

New York City	Phoenix	Austin
Salt Lake City	Tucson	San Antonio
Memphis	District of Columbia	Green Bay/Appleton
New Orleans	Spokane	Shreveport
Atlantic City	Baton Rouge	Toronto
Albuquerque	Little Rock	Vancouver

Source: Panera Bread management presentation to securities analysts, May 5, 2006.

Exhibit 4

Comparative U.S. Market Penetration of Selected Restaurant Chains, 2006

RESTAURANT CHAIN	NUMBER OF LOCATIONS	POPULATION PER LOCATION
Subway	19,965	15,000
McDonald's	13,727	22,000
Starbucks Coffee	7,700	39,000
Applebee's	1,800	166,000
Panera Bread	910	330,000

Note: Management believed that a 17 percent annual rate of expansion of Panera Bread locations through 2010 would result in 1 café per 160,000 people.

Source: Panera Bread management presentation to securities analysts, May 5, 2006.

Panera Bread's Product Offerings and Menu

Panera Bread's signature product was artisan bread made from four ingredients—water, natural yeast, flour, and salt; no preservatives or chemicals were used. Carefully trained bakers shaped every step of the process, from mixing the ingredients, to kneading the dough, to placing the loaves on hot stone slabs to bake in a traditional European-style stone deck bakery oven. Exhibit 5 shows Panera's lineup of breads.

The Panera Bread menu was designed to provide target customers with products built on the company's bakery expertise, particularly its 20-plus varieties of bread baked fresh throughout the day at each café location. The key menu groups were fresh baked goods, made-to-order sandwiches and salads, soups, light entrées, and café beverages. Exhibit 6 shows a sampling of the items on a typical Panera Bread menu.

The menu offerings were regularly reviewed and revised to sustain the interest of regular customers, satisfy changing consumer preferences, and be responsive to various seasons of the year. The soup lineup, for example, changed seasonally. Product development was focused on providing food that customers would crave

Exhibit 5

Panera's Lineup of Bread Varieties, 2006

Sourdough

Panera's signature sourdough bread that featured a golden, crackled crust and firm, moderately structured crumb with a satisfying, tangy flavor. *Available in Baguette, Loaf, XL Loaf, Roll, and Bread Bowl.*

Asiago Cheese

Chunks of Asiago cheese were added to the standard sourdough recipe and baked right in, with more Asiago cheese sprinkled on top. *Available in Demi and Loaf.*

Focaccia

A traditional Italian flatbread made with Panera's artisan starter dough, olive oil, and chunks of Asiago cheese. *Available in three varieties—Asiago Cheese, Rosemary & Onion, and Basil Pesto.*

Nine Grain

Made with cracked whole wheat, rye, corn meal, oats, rice flour, soy grits, barley flakes, millet, and flaxseed plus molasses for a semisweet taste. *Available in Loaf.*

Tomato Basil

A sourdough-based bread made with tomatoes and basil, topped with sweet walnut streusel. *Available in XL Loaf.*

Cinnamon Raisin

A light raisin bread with a swirl of cinnamon, sugar, and molasses. *Available in Loaf.*

Artisan Sesame Semolina

Made with enriched durum and semolina flours to create a golden yellow crumb, topped with sesame seeds. *Available in Loaf and Miche.*

Artisan Multigrain

Nine grains and sesame, poppy, and fennel seeds blended with molasses, topped with rolled oats. *Available in Loaf.*

Artisan French

Made with Panera's artisan starter to create a nutty flavor with a wine-like aroma. *Available in Baguette and Miche.*

Whole Grain

A moist, hearty mixture of whole spelt flour, millet, flaxseed, and other wheat flours and grains, sweetened with honey, and topped with rolled oats. *Available in Loaf, Miche, and Baguette.*

French

A classic French bread characterized by a thin, crackly crust, slightly sweet taste and a lighter crumb than our sourdough. *Available in Baguette, Loaf, XL Loaf, and Roll.*

Ciabatta

A flat, oval-shaped loaf with a delicate flavor and soft texture; made with Panera's artisan starter and a touch of olive oil. *Available in Loaf.*

Honey Wheat

A mild wheat bread with tastes of honey and molasses; the soft crust and crumb made it great for sandwiches. *Available in Loaf.*

Rye

Special natural leavening, unbleached flour, and chopped rye kernels were used to create a delicate rye flavor. *Available in Loaf.*

Sunflower

Made with honey, lemon peel, and raw sunflower seeds and topped with sesame and honey-roasted sunflower seeds. *Available in Loaf.*

Artisan Three Seed

The addition of sesame, poppy, and fennel seeds created a sweet, nutty, anise-flavored bread. *Available in Demi.*

Artisan Three Cheese

Made with Parmesan, Romano, and Asiago cheeses and durum and semolina flours. *Available in Demi, Loaf, and Miche.*

Artisan Stone-Milled Rye

Made with Panera's artisan starter, chopped rye kernels, and caraway seeds, topped with more caraway seeds. *Available in Loaf and Miche.*

Artisan Country

Made from artisan starter with a crisp crust and nutty flavor. *Available in Loaf, Miche, and Demi.*

Lower-Carb Pumpkin Seed

Made from Panera's artisan starter dough, pumpkin seeds, and flax meal to create a subtle, nutty flavor. *Available in Loaf.*

(continued)

Exhibit 5 (concluded)

White Whole Grain

A new bread created especially for Panera Kids sand-wiches; a sweeter alternative to the Whole Grain bread with a thin, caramelized crust sweetened with honey and molasses. *Available in Loaf.*

Lower-Carb Italian Herb

Made from Panera's artisan starter dough, roasted garlic, dried herbs, and sesame seed topping. *Available in Loaf.*

Source: www.panerabread.com (accessed July 28, 2006).

Exhibit 6

Sample Menu Selections, Panera Bread Company, 2006

Bakery

Loaves of Bread (22 varieties)
Bagels (11 varieties)
Cookies (5 varieties)
Scones (5 varieties)
Cinnamon Rolls/Pecan Rolls
Croissants
Coffee Cakes
Muffins (5 varieties)
Artisan and Specialty Pastries (8 varieties)
Brownies (3 varieties)
Mini-Bundt Cakes (3 varieties)

Signature Sandwiches

Pepperblue Steak
Garden Veggie
Tuscan Chicken
Asiago Roast Beef
Italian Combo
Bacon Turkey Bravo
Sierra Turkey
Turkey Romesco
Mediterranean Veggie

Café Sandwiches

Smoked Turkey Breast
Chicken Salad
Tuna Salad
Smoked Ham and Cheese

Hot Panini Sandwiches

Turkey Artichoke
Frontega Chicken
Smokehouse Turkey
Portobello and Mozzarella

Soups

Broccoli Cheddar
French Onion
Baked Potato
Low-Fat Chicken Noodle
Cream of Chicken and Wild Rice
Boston Clam Chowder
Low-Fat Vegetarian Garden Vegetable
Low-Fat Vegetarian Black Bean
Vegetarian Roasted Red Pepper and Lentil
Tuscan Chicken and Ditalini
Tuscan Vegetable Ditalini

Hand Tossed Salads

Asian Sesame Chicken
Fandango
Greek
Caesar
Grilled Chicken Caesar
Bistro Steak
Classic Café
California Mission Chicken
Fuji Apple Chicken
Strawberry Poppyseed and Chicken
Grilled Salmon

Side Choices

Portion of French Baguette
Portion of Whole Grain Baguette
Kettle-cooked or Baked Chips
Apple

Panera Kids

Grilled Cheese
Peanut Butter and Jelly
Kids Deli

Exhibit 6   (concluded)

Baked Egg Souffles	**Beverages**
Four Cheese	Coffee
Spinach and Artichoke	Hot and Iced Teas
Spinach and Bacon	Sodas
	Bottled Water
	Juice
	Organic Milk
	Organic Chocolate Milk
	Hot Chocolate
	Orange Juice
	Organic Apple Juice
	Espresso
	Cappuccino
	Lattes
	Mango Raspberry Smoothie

Source: Sample menu posted at www.panerabread.com (accessed July 29, 2006).

and trust to be tasty. New menu items were developed in test kitchens and then introduced in a limited number of the bakery-cafés to determine customer response and verify that preparation and operating procedures resulted in product consistency and high-quality standards. If successful, they were then rolled out systemwide. New product rollouts were integrated into periodic or seasonal menu rotations, which Panera referred to as "Celebrations."

Panera recognized in late 2004 that significantly more customers were conscious about eating "good" carbohydrates, prompting the introduction of whole grain breads. In 2005, several important menu changes were made. Panera introduced a new line of artisan sweet goods made with gourmet European butter, fresh fruit toppings, and appealing fillings; these new artisan pastries represented a significantly higher level of taste and upgraded quality. To expand its breakfast offerings and help boost morning-hour sales, Panera introduced egg soufflés baked in a flaked pastry shell. And, in another health-related move, Panera switched to the use of natural, antibiotic-free chicken in all of its chicken-related sandwiches and salads. During 2006, the chief menu changes involved the addition of light entrées to jump-start dinner appeal; one such menu addition was crispani (a pizzalike topping on a thin crust). In 2006, evening-hour sales represented 20 percent of Panera's business.

Panera Fresh Catering

In 2004–2005, Panera Bread introduced a catering program to extend its market reach into the workplace, schools, parties, and gatherings held in homes. Panera saw catering as an opportunity to grow lunch and dinner sales with making capital investments in additional physical facilities. By the end of 2005, catering was generating an additional $80 million in sales for Panera Bread. Management foresaw considerable opportunity for future growth of Panera's catering operation.

Marketing

Panera's marketing strategy was to compete on the basis of providing an entire dining experience rather than by attracting customers on the basis of price only. The objective was for customers to view dining at Panera as being a good value—meaning high-quality food at reasonable prices—so as to encourage frequent visits. Panera Bread performed extensive market research, including the use of focus groups, to determine customer food and drink preferences and price points. The company tried to grow sales at existing Panera locations through menu development, product merchandising, promotions at everyday prices, and sponsorship of local community charitable events.

Historically, marketing had played only a small role in Panera's success. Brand awareness had been built on customers' satisfaction with their dining experience at Panera and their tendency to share their positive experiences with friends and neighbors. About 85 percent of consumers who were aware that there was a Panera Bread bakery-café in their community or neighborhood had dined at Panera on at least one occasion.[3] The company's marketing research indicated that 57 percent of consumers who had "ever tried" dining at Panera Bread had been customers in the past 30 days. This high proportion of trial customers to repeat customers had convinced management that getting more first-time diners into Panera Bread cafés was a potent way to boost store traffic and average weekly sales per store.

Panera's research also showed that people who dined at Panera Bread very frequently or moderately frequently typically did so for only one part of the day. Yet 81 percent indicated "considerable willingness" to try dining at Panera Bread at other parts of the day.[4]

Franchise-operated bakery-cafés were required to contribute 0.7 percent of their sales to a national advertising fund and 0.4 percent of their sales as a marketing administration fee and were also required to spend 2.0 percent of their sales in their local markets on advertising. Panera contributed similar amounts from company-owned bakery-cafés toward the national advertising fund and marketing administration. The national advertising fund contribution of 0.7 percent had been increased from 0.4 percent starting in 2006. Beginning in fiscal 2006, national advertising fund contributions were raised to 0.7 percent of sales, and Panera could opt to raise the national advertising fund contributions as high as 2.6 percent of sales.

In 2006, Panera Bread's marketing strategy had several elements. One element aimed at raising the quality of awareness about Panera by continuing to feature the caliber and appeal of its breads and baked goods, by hammering the theme "food you crave, food you can trust," and by enhancing the appeal of its bakery-cafés as a neighborhood gathering place. A second marketing initiative was to raise awareness and boost trial of dining at Panera Bread at multiple meal times (breakfast, lunch, "chill out" times, and dinner). Panera avoided hard-sell or in-your-face marketing approaches, preferring instead to employ a range of ways to softly drop the Panera Bread name into the midst of consumers as they moved through their lives and let them "gently collide" with the brand; the idea was to let consumers "discover" Panera Bread and then convert them into loyal customers by providing a very satisfying dining experience. The third marketing initiative was to increase perception of Panera Bread as a viable evening meal option and to drive early trials of Panera for dinner (particularly among existing Panera lunch customers).

Franchise Operations

Opening additional franchised bakery-cafés was a core element of Panera Bread's strategy and management's initiatives to achieve the company's growth targets. Panera Bread did not grant single-unit franchises, so a prospective franchisee could not open just one bakery-café. Rather, Panera Bread's franchising strategy was to enter into franchise agreements that required the franchise developer to open a number of units, typically 15 bakery-cafés in six years. Franchisee candidates had to be well capitalized, have a proven track record as excellent multi-unit restaurant operators, and agree to meet an aggressive development schedule. Applicants had to meet eight stringent criteria to gain consideration for a Panera Bread franchise:

- Experience as a multi-unit restaurant operator.
- Recognition as a top restaurant operator.
- Net worth of $7.5 million.

- Liquid assets of $3 million.
- Infrastructure and resources to meet Panera's development schedule for the market area the franchisee was applying to develop.
- Real estate experience in the market to be developed.
- Total commitment to the development of the Panera Bread brand.
- Cultural fit and a passion for fresh bread.

The franchise agreement typically required the payment of a franchise fee of $35,000 per bakery-café (broken down into $5,000 at the signing of the area development agreement and $30,000 at or before a bakery-café opened) and continuing royalties of 4–5 percent on sales from each bakery-café. Franchise-operated bakery-cafés followed the same standards for in-store operating standards, product quality, menu, site selection, and bakery-café construction as did company-owned bakery-cafés. Franchisees were required to purchase all of their dough products from sources approved by Panera Bread. Panera's fresh dough facility system supplied fresh dough products to substantially all franchise-operated bakery-cafés. Panera did not finance franchisee construction or area development agreement payments or hold an equity interest in any of the franchise-operated bakery-cafés. All area development agreements executed after March 2003 included a clause allowing Panera Bread the right to purchase all bakery-cafés opened by the franchisee at a defined purchase price, at any time five years after the execution of the franchise agreement.

Exhibit 7 shows estimated costs of opening a new franchised Panera Bread bakery-café. As of 2006, the typical franchise-operated bakery-café averaged somewhat higher average weekly and annual sales volumes than company-operated cafés (see Exhibit 2), was equal to or slightly more profitable, and produced a slightly higher return on equity investment than company-operated cafés (partly because many franchisees made greater use of debt in financing their operations than did Panera, which had no long-term debt at all).[5] During the 2003–2006 period, in four unrelated transactions, Panera purchased 38 bakery-cafés from franchisees.

Exhibit 7

Estimated Initial Investment for a Panera Bread Bakery-Café, 2007

INVESTMENT CATEGORY	ACTUAL OR ESTIMATED AMOUNT	TO WHOM PAID
Franchise fee	$35,000	Panera
Real property	Varies according to site and local real estate market conditions	
Leasehold improvements	$350,000 to $1,250,000	Contractors
Equipment	$250,000 to $300,000	Equipment vendors, Panera
Fixtures	$60,000 to $90,000	Vendors
Furniture	$50,000 to $70,000	Vendors
Consultant fees and municipal impact fees (if any)	$20,000 to $120,000	Architect, engineer, expeditor, others
Supplies and inventory	$19,000 to $24,175	Panera, other suppliers
Smallwares	$24,000 to $29,000	Suppliers
Signage	$20,000 to $72,000	Suppliers
Additional funds (for working capital and general operating expenses for 3 months)	$175,000 to $245,000	Vendors, suppliers, employees, utilities, landlord, others
Total	$1,003,000 to $2,235,175, plus real estate and related costs	

Source: www.panerabread.com (accessed February 9, 2007).

Panera provided its franchisees with market analysis and site selection assistance, lease review, design services and new store opening assistance, a comprehensive 10-week initial training program, a training program for hourly employees, manager and baker certification, bakery-café certification, continuing education classes, benchmarking data regarding costs and profit margins, access to company developed marketing and advertising programs, neighborhood marketing assistance, and calendar planning assistance. Panera's surveys of its franchisees indicated high satisfaction with the Panera Bread concept, the overall support received from Panera Bread, and the company's leadership. The biggest franchisee issue was the desire for more territory. In turn, Panera management expressed satisfaction with the quality of franchisee operations, the pace and quality of new bakery-café openings, and franchisees' adoption of Panera Bread initiatives.[6]

As of April 2006, Panera had entered into area development agreements with 42 franchisee groups covering 54 markets in 34 states; these franchisees had commitments to open 423 additional franchise-operated bakery-cafés. If a franchisee failed to develop bakery-cafés on schedule, Panera had the right to terminate the franchise agreement and develop its own company-operated locations or develop locations through new area developers in that market. As of mid-2006, Panera Bread did not have any international franchise development agreements but was considering entering into franchise agreements for several Canadian locations (Toronto and Vancouver).

Site Selection and Café Environment

Bakery-cafés were typically located in suburban, strip mall, and regional mall locations. In evaluating a potential location, Panera studied the surrounding trade area, demographic information within that area, and information on competitors. Based on analysis of this information, including the use of predictive modeling using proprietary software, Panera developed projections of sales and return on investment for candidate sites. Cafés had proved successful as freestanding units, as both in-line and end-cap locations in strip malls, and in large regional malls.

The average Panera bakery-café was approximately 4,600 square feet. The great majority of the locations were leased. Lease terms were typically for 10 years with one, two, or three 5-year renewal option periods thereafter. Leases typically entailed charges for minimum base occupancy, a proportionate share of building and common-area operating expenses and real estate taxes, and a contingent percentage rent based on sales above a stipulated sales level. The average construction, equipment, furniture and fixture, and signage cost for the 66 company-owned bakery-cafés opened in 2005 was $920,000 per bakery-café after landlord allowances.

Each bakery-café sought to provide a distinctive and engaging environment (what management referred to as "Panera Warmth"), in many cases using fixtures and materials complementary to the neighborhood location of the bakery-café. In 2005–2006, the company had introduced a new G2 café design aimed at further refining and enhancing the appeal of Panera bakery-cafés as a warm and appealing neighborhood gathering place (a strategy that Starbucks had used with great success). The G2 design incorporated higher-quality furniture, cozier seating areas and groupings, and a brighter, more open display case. Many locations had fireplaces to further create an alluring and hospitable atmosphere that patrons would flock to on a regular basis, sometimes for a meal, sometimes to meet friends and acquaintances for a meal, sometimes to take a break for a light snack or beverage, and sometimes to just hang out with friends and acquaintances. Many of Panera's bakery-cafés had outdoor seating, and virtually all cafés featured free wireless high-speed (Wi-Fi) Internet access—Panera considered free Wi-Fi part of its commitment to making its bakery-cafés open community gathering places where people could catch up on some work, hang out with friends, read the paper, or just relax. All Panera cafés used real china and stainless silverware instead of paper plates and plastic utensils.

Bakery-Café Supply Chain

Panera had invested about $52 million in a network of 17 regional fresh dough facilities (16 company-owned and one franchise-operated) to supply fresh dough daily to both company-owned and franchised bakery-cafés. These facilities, totaling some 313,000 square feet, employed about 830 people who were largely engaged in preparing the fresh doughs, a process that took about 48 hours. The dough-making process began with the preparation and mixing of Panera's all-natural starter dough, which then was given time to rise; other all-natural ingredients were then added to create the different bread and bagel varieties (no chemicals or preservatives were used). Another period of rising then took place. Next the dough was cut into pieces, shaped into loaves or bagels, and readied for shipment in fresh dough form. There was no freezing of the dough, and no partial baking was done at the fresh dough facilities. Each bakery-café did all of the baking itself, using the fresh doughs delivered daily. The fresh dough facilities manufactured about 50 different products, with 11 more rotated throughout the year.

Distribution of the fresh bread and bagel doughs was accomplished through a leased fleet of about 140 temperature-controlled trucks operated by Panera personnel. Trucks on average delivered dough to six bakery-cafés, with trips averaging about 300 miles (but in some cases extending to as much as 500 miles—management believed the optimal trip length was about 300 miles). The fresh dough was sold to both company-owned and franchised bakery-cafés at a delivered cost not to exceed 27 percent of the retail value of the product. Exhibit 8 provides financial data relating to each of Panera's three business segments: company-operated bakery-cafés, franchise operations, and fresh dough facilities. The sales and operating profits associated with the fresh doughs supplied to company-operated bakery cafés are included in the revenues and operating profits of the company-owned bakery-café segment. The sales and operating profits of the fresh dough facilities segment shown in Exhibit 8 all represent transactions with franchised bakery-cafés.

Management claimed that the company's fresh-dough-making capability provided a competitive advantage by ensuring consistent quality and dough-making efficiency. It was more economical to concentrate the dough-making operations in a few facilities dedicated to that function than it was to have each bakery-café equipped and staffed to do all of its baking from scratch.

Panera obtained ingredients for its doughs and other products manufactured at the fresh dough facilities from a variety of suppliers. While some ingredients used at the fresh dough facilities were sourced from a single supplier, there were numerous suppliers of each ingredient and Panera could obtain ingredients from another supplier when necessary. Panera contracted externally for the supply of sweet goods to its bakery-cafés. In November 2002, it entered into a cost-plus agreement with Dawn Food Products Inc. to provide sweet goods for the period 2003–2007. Sweet goods were completed at each bakery-café by professionally trained bakers—completion entailed finishing with fresh toppings and other ingredients and baking to established artisan standards.

Panera had arrangements with independent distributors to handle the delivery of sweet goods and other materials to bakery-cafés. Virtually all other food products and supplies for retail operations, including paper goods, coffee, and smallwares, were contracted for by Panera and delivered by the vendors to the designated distributors for delivery to the bakery-cafés. Individual bakery-cafés placed orders for the needed supplies directly from a distributor two to three times per week. Franchise-operated bakery-cafés operate under individual contracts with one of Panera's three primary independent distributors or other regional distributors.

Exhibit 8

Business Segment Information, Panera Bread Company, 2003–2006 ($ in thousands)

	2006	2005	2004	2003
Segment revenues:				
Company bakery-café operations	$666,141	$499,422	$362,121	$265,933
Franchise operations	61,531	54,309	44,449	36,245
Fresh dough operations	159,050	128,422	103,786	93,874
Intercompany sales eliminations	(57,751)	(41,878)	(31,217)	(32,350)
Total revenues	$828,971	$640,275	$479,139	$363,702
Segment operating profit:				
Company bakery-café operations	$123,225	$ 97,831	$ 71,725	$ 55,111
Franchise operations	54,160	47,652	39,149	32,132
Fresh dough operations	15,681	11,508	6,942	6,557
Total segment operating profit	$193,066	$156,991	$117,816	$ 93,800
Depreciation and amortization:				
Company bakery-café operations	$ 32,741	$ 23,345	$ 17,786	$ 12,256
Fresh dough operations	7,097	6,016	4,356	3,298
Corporate administration	4,328	3,650	3,156	2,750
Total	$ 44,166	$ 33,011	$ 25,298	$ 18,304
Capital expenditures:				
Company bakery-café operations	$ 86,743	$ 67,554	$ 67,374	$ 33,670
Fresh dough operations	15,120	9,082	9,445	8,370
Corporate administration	7,433	5,420	3,610	3,721
Total capital expenditures	$109,296	$ 82,056	$ 80,429	$ 45,761
Segment assets:				
Company bakery-café operations	$374,795	$301,517	$204,295	$147,920
Franchise operations	3,740	2,969	1,778	1,117
Fresh dough operations	59,919	37,567	39,968	33,442
Other assets	104,155	95,614	78,631	74,356
Total assets	$542,609	$437,667	$324,672	$256,835

Sources: Company 10-K reports, 2004, 2005, and 2006.

Competition

According to the National Restaurant Association, sales at the 925,000 food service locations in the United States were forecast to be about $511 billion in 2006 (up from $308 billion in 1996) and account for 47.5 percent of consumers' food dollars (up from 25 percent in 1955). Commercial eating places accounted for about $345 billion of the projected $511 billion in total food service sales, with the remainder divided among drinking places, lodging establishments with restaurants, managed food service locations, and other types of retail, vending, recreational, and mobile operations with food service capability. The U.S. restaurant industry had about 12.5 million employees in 2006, served about 70 billion meals and snack occasions, and was growing about 5 percent annually.[7] Just over 7 out of 10 eating and drinking places in the United States were independent single-unit establishments with fewer than 20 employees.

Even though the average U.S. consumer ate 76 percent of meals at home, on a typical day, about 130 million U.S. consumers were food service patrons at an eating establishment—sales at commercial eating places averaged close to $1 billion daily. Average household expenditures for food away from home in 2004 were $2,434, or $974 per person. In 2003, unit sales averaged $755,000 at full-service restaurants and $606,000 at limited-service restaurants; however, very popular restaurant locations achieved annual sales volumes in the $2.5 million to $5 million range. The profitability of a restaurant location ranged from exceptional to good to average to marginal to money-losing.

The restaurant business was labor-intensive, extremely competitive, and risky. Industry members pursued differentiation strategies of one variety or another, seeking to set themselves apart from rivals via pricing, food quality, menu theme, signature menu selections, dining ambience and atmosphere, service, convenience, and location. To further enhance their appeal, some restaurants tried to promote greater customer traffic via happy hours, lunch and dinner specials, children's menus, innovative or trendy dishes, diet-conscious menu selections, and beverage/appetizer specials during televised sporting events (important at restaurants/bars with big-screen TVs). Most restaurants were quick to adapt their menu offerings to changing consumer tastes and eating preferences, frequently featuring heart-healthy, vegetarian, organic, low-calorie, and/or low-carb items on their menus. It was the norm at many restaurants to rotate some menu selections seasonally and to periodically introduce creative dishes in an effort to keep regular patrons coming back, attract more patrons, and remain competitive.

Consumers (especially those who ate out often) were prone to give newly opened eating establishments a trial, and if they were pleased with their experience to return, sometimes frequently—loyalty to existing restaurants was low when consumers perceived there were better dining alternatives. It was also common for a once-hot restaurant to lose favor and confront the stark realities of a dwindling clientele, forcing it to either reconceive its menu and dining environment or go out of business. Many restaurants had fairly short lives; there were multiple causes for a restaurant's failure—a lack of enthusiasm for the menu or dining experience, inconsistent food quality, poor service, a bad location, meal prices that patrons deemed too high, and superior competition by rivals with comparable menu offerings.

While Panera Bread competed with specialty food, casual dining, and quick-service restaurant retailers—including national, regional, and locally owned restaurants—its closest competitors were restaurants in the so-called fast-casual restaurant category. Fast-casual restaurants filled the gap between fast-food and casual, full-table-service dining. Fast-casual restaurants provided quick-service dining (much like fast-food enterprises) but were distinguished by enticing menus, higher food quality, and more inviting dining environments; typical meal costs per guest were in the $7–$12 range. Some fast-casual restaurants had limited table service and some were self-service (like fast-food establishments). Exhibit 9 provides information on prominent national and regional chains that were competitors of Panera Bread.

Exhibit 9

Representative Fast-Casual Restaurant Chains and Selected Full-Service Restaurant Chains in the United States, 2006

COMPANY	NUMBER OF LOCATIONS, 2005–2006	SELECT 2005 FINANCIAL DATA	KEY MENU CATEGORIES
Atlanta Bread Company	160 bakery-cafés in 27 states	Not available (privately held company)	Fresh-baked breads, waffles, salads, sandwiches, soups, wood-fired pizza and pasta (select locations only), baked goods, and desserts

(continued)

Exhibit 9   (continued)

COMPANY	NUMBER OF LOCATIONS, 2005–2006	SELECT 2005 FINANCIAL DATA	KEY MENU CATEGORIES
Applebee's Neighborhood Grill and Bar*	1,730+ locations in 49 states, plus some 70 locations in 16 other countries	2005 revenues of $1.2 billion; average annual sales of $2.5 million per location; alcoholic beverages accounted for about 12 percent of sales	Beef, chicken, pork, seafood, and pasta entrées plus appetizers, salads, sandwiches, a selection of Weight Watchers branded menu alternatives, desserts, and alcoholic beverages
Au Bon Pain	190 company-owned and franchised bakery-cafés in 23 states; 222 locations internationally	Systemwide sales of about $245 million in 2005	Baked goods (with a focus on croissants and bagels), soups, salads, sandwiches and wraps, and coffee drinks
Baja Fresh	300+ locations across the United States	A subsidiary of Wendy's International	Tacos, burritos, quesadillas, fajitas, salads, soups, sides, and catering services
Bruegger's	260 bakery-cafés in 17 states	2005 revenues of $155.2 million; 3,500 full-time employees	Several varieties of bagels and muffins, sandwiches, salads, and soups
California Pizza Kitchen*	190+ locations in 27 states and 5 other countries	2005 revenues of $480 million; average annual sales of $3.2 million per location	Signature California-style hearth-baked pizzas; creative salads, pastas, soups, and sandwiches; appetizers; desserts, beer, wine, coffees, teas, and assorted beverages
Chili's Grill and Bar* (a subsidiary of Brinker International**)	1,074 locations in 49 states and 23 countries	Average revenue per meal of ≈$12.00; average capital investment of $2.4 million per location	Chicken, beef, and seafood entrées, steaks, appetizers, salads, sandwiches, desserts, and alcoholic beverages (13.6 percent of sales)
Chipotle Mexican Grill	500+ locations (all company-owned)	2005 sales of $628 million; 13,000 employees	A selection of gourmet burritos and tacos
Corner Bakery Café (a subsidiary of Brinker International**)	90 locations in 8 states and District of Columbia	Average revenue per meal of ≈$7.44; average capital investment of $1.7 million per location	Breakfast selections (egg scramblers, pastries, mixed berry parfaits); lunch/dinner selections (hot and cold sandwiches, salads, soups, and desserts); catering (≈21 percent of sales)
Cracker Barrel	527 combination retail stores and restaurants in 42 states	Restaurant sales of $2.1 billion in 2005; average restaurant sales of $3.3 million	Two menus (breakfast and lunch/dinner); named "Best Family Dining Chain" for 15 consecutive years
Culver's	330 locations in 16 states	Not available (a privately held company)	Signature hamburgers served on buttered buns, fried battered cheese curds, value dinners (chicken, shrimp, cod with potato and slaw), salads, frozen custard, milkshakes, sundaes, and fountain drinks

Exhibit 9   (continued)

COMPANY	NUMBER OF LOCATIONS, 2005–2006	SELECT 2005 FINANCIAL DATA	KEY MENU CATEGORIES
Fazoli's	380 locations in 32 states	Not available (a privately held company)	Spaghetti and meatballs, fettuccine Alfredo, lasagna, ravioli, submarinos and panini sandwiches, salads, and breadsticks
Fuddruckers	200+ locations in the United States and 6 Middle Eastern countries	Not available (a privately held company)	Exotic hamburgers (the feature menu item), chicken and fish sandwiches, French fries and other sides, soups, salads, and desserts
Jason's Deli	150 locations in 20 states	Not available (a privately held company)	Sandwiches, extensive salad bar, soups, loaded potatoes, desserts; catering services, party trays, and box lunches
McAlister's Deli	200+ locations in 18 states	Not available (a privately held company)	Deli sandwiches, loaded baked potatoes, soups, salads, and desserts, plus sandwich trays and lunch boxes
Moe's Southwest Grill	200+ locations in 35 states	Not available (a privately held company)	Tex-Mex foods prepared fresh—tacos, burritos, fajitas, quesadillas, nachos, salads, chips and salsa
Noodles & Company	120+ urban and suburban locations in 16 states	Not available (a privately held company)	Asian, Mediterranean, and American noodle/pasta entrées, soups, and salads
Nothing But Noodles	39 locations in 20 states	Not available (a privately held company)	Starters, a wide selection of American and Italian pastas, Asian dishes with noodles, pasta-less entrées, soups, salads, and desserts
Qdoba Mexican Grill	280+ locations in 40 states	A subsidiary of Jack in the Box, Inc.; Jack in the Box had 2005 revenues of $2.5 billion, 2,300+ Jack in the Box and Qdoba locations, and 44,600 employees	Signature burritos, a "Naked Burrito" (a burrito served in a bowl without the tortilla), nontraditional taco salads, three-cheese nachos, five signature salsas, and a Q-to-Go Hot Taco Bar catering alternative
Rubio's Fresh Mexican Grill	150 locations in 5 western states	2005 revenues of $141 million; average sales of $960,000 per location	Signature fish tacos; chicken, beef, and pork tacos; burritos and quesadillas; salads; proprietary salsas; sides; and domestic and imported beers

continued

Exhibit 9 (concluded)

COMPANY	NUMBER OF LOCATIONS, 2005–2006	SELECT 2005 FINANCIAL DATA	KEY MENU CATEGORIES
Starbucks	7,500+ company-operated and licensed locations in the United States, plus ≈3,000 international locations	2005 revenues of $6.4 billion; estimated retail sales of $1.1 million per company-operated location	Italian-style espresso beverages, teas, sodas, juices, assorted pastries and confections; some locations offer sandwiches and salads

* Denotes a full-service restaurant.

** Brinker International was a multi-concept restaurant operator with over 1,500 restaurants including Chili's Grill & Bar, Chili's Too, Corner Bakery Café, Romano's Macaroni Grill, On the Border Mexican Grill & Cantina, and Maggiano's Little Italy. Brinker had 2005 sales of $3.9 billion.

Sources: Company Web sites and en.wikipedia.org/wiki/Fast_casual_restaurant (accessed August 2, 2006).

Endnotes

[1] According to information in Panera Bread's press kit; the results of the study were reported in a 2003 *Wall Street Journal* article.

[2] As stated in a presentation to securities analysts, May 5, 2006.

[3] As cited in Panera Bread's presentation to securities analysts on May 5, 2006.

[4] Ibid.

[5] Ibid.

[6] Ibid.

[7] Information posted at www.restaurant.org (accessed August 1, 2006).

Case 6

Coach Inc.: Is Its Advantage in Luxury Handbags Sustainable?

John E. Gamble
University of South Alabama

In the six years following its October 2000 initial public offering (IPO), Coach Inc.'s net sales had grown at a compounded annual rate of 26 percent and its stock price had increased by 1,400 percent as a result of a strategy keyed to a concept called accessible luxury. Coach created the accessible luxury category in women's handbags and leather accessories by matching key luxury rivals on quality and styling, while beating them on price by 50 percent or more. Not only did Coach's $200–$500 handbags appeal to middle-income consumers wanting a taste of luxury, but affluent consumers with the means to spend $2,000 or more on a handbag regularly snapped up its products as well. By 2006, Coach had become the best-selling brand of women's luxury handbags and leather accessories in the United States, with a 25 percent market share, and was the second best-selling brand of such products in Japan, with an 8 percent market share. Beyond its winning combination of styling, quality, and pricing, the attractiveness of Coach retail stores and high levels of customer service contributed to its competitive advantage.

Much of the company's growth in net sales was attributable to its rapid growth in company-owned stores in the United States and Japan. Coach stores ranged from prominent flagship stores on Rodeo Drive and Madison Avenue to factory outlet stores. In fact, Coach's

factory stores had achieved higher comparable store growth during 2005 and 2006 than its full-price stores. At year-end 2006, comparable store sales in Coach factory stores had increased by 31.9 percent since year-end 2005, while comparable store sales for Coach full-price stores experienced a 12.3 percent year-over-year increase. In 2006, Coach products were sold in 218 full-price company-owned stores, 86 factory stores, 900 U.S. department stores, 118 locations in Japan, and 108 international locations outside Japan.

Going into 2007, the company's executives expected to sustain its impressive growth through monthly introductions of fresh new handbag designs and the addition of retail locations in the United States, Japan, and rapidly growing luxury goods markets in Asia. The company planned to add three to five factory stores per year to eventually reach 105 stores in the United States, add 30 full-price stores per year in the United States to reach 300, and add at least 10 stores per year in Japan to reach as many as 180 stores. The company also expected its licensed international distributors to open new locations in Hong Kong and mainland China. Other growth initiatives included strategic alliances to bring the Coach brand to such additional luxury categories as women's knitwear and fragrances. Only time would tell if Coach's growth could be sustained and its advantage would hold in the face of new accessible luxury lines recently launched by such industry elites as Giorgio Armani, Dolce & Gabbana, and Gianni Versace.

Company History

Coach was founded in 1941 when Miles Cahn, a New York City leather artisan, began producing women's handbags. The handbags crafted by Cahn and his family in their SoHo loft were simple in style and extremely resilient to wear and tear. Coach's classic styling and sturdy construction proved popular with discriminating consumers, and the company's initial line of 12 unlined leather bags soon developed a loyal following. Over the next 40 years, Coach was able to grow at a steady rate by setting prices about 50 percent lower than those of more luxurious brands, adding new models, and establishing accounts with retailers such as Bloomingdale's and Saks Fifth Avenue. The Cahn family also opened company-owned stores that sold Coach handbags and leather accessories. After 44 years of family management, Coach was sold to diversified food and consumer goods producer Sara Lee.

Sara Lee's 1985 acquisition of Coach left the handbag manufacturer's strategy and approach to operations more or less intact. The company continued to build a strong reputation for long-lasting classic handbags. However, by the mid-1990s, the company's performance began to decline as consumers developed a stronger preference for stylish French and Italian designer brands such as Gucci, Prada, Louis Vuitton, Dolce & Gabbana, and Ferragamo. By 1995, annual sales growth in Coach's best-performing stores fell from 40 percent to 5 percent as the company's traditional leather bags fell out of favor with consumers.

In 1996, Sara Lee made 18-year Coach veteran Lew Frankfort head of its listless handbag division. Frankfort's first move was to hire Reed Krakoff, a top Tommy Hilfiger designer, as Coach's new creative director. Krakoff believed that new products should be based on market research rather than on designers' instincts about what would sell. Under Krakoff, Coach conducted extensive consumer surveys and held focus groups to ask customers about styling, comfort, and functionality preferences. The company's research found that consumers were looking for edgier styling, softer leathers, and leather-trimmed fabric handbags. Once prototypes had been developed by a team of designers, merchandisers, and sourcing specialists, hundreds of previous customers were asked to rate prototype designs against existing handbags. The prototypes that made it to production were then tested in selected Coach stores for six months before a launch was announced. The design process developed by Krakoff also allowed Coach to launch new collections every month. Prior to his arrival, Coach had introduced only two collections per year.

Frankfort's turnaround plan also included a redesign of the company's flagship stores to complement Coach's contemporary new designs. Frankfort abandoned the stores' previous dark wood-paneled interiors in favor of minimalist architectural features that provided a bright and airy ambience. The company also improved the appearance of its factory stores, which carried test models, discontinued models, and special lines that sold at discounts ranging from 15 to 50 percent. Such discounts were made possible by the company's policy of outsourcing production to 40 suppliers in 15 countries. The outsourcing agreements allowed Coach to maintain a sizable pricing advantage relative to other luxury handbag brands in its full-price stores as well. Handbags sold in Coach full-price stores ranged from $200 to $500, which was well below the $700–$800 entry-level price charged by other luxury brands.

Coach's attractive pricing enabled it to appeal to consumers who would not normally consider luxury brands, while the quality and styling of its products were sufficient to satisfy traditional luxury consumers. In fact, a *Women's Wear Daily* survey found that Coach's quality, styling, and value mix was so powerful that affluent women in the United States ranked Coach ahead of much more expensive luxury brands such as Hermès, Ralph Lauren, Prada, and Fendi.[1] By 2000, the changes to Coach's strategy and operations allowed the brand to build a sizable lead in the accessible luxury segment of the leather handbags and accessories industry and made it a solid performer in Sara Lee's business lineup. With the turnaround successfully executed, Sara Lee management elected to spin off Coach through an IPO in October 2000 as part of a restructuring initiative designed to focus the corporation on food and beverages.

Coach Inc.'s performance proved to be stellar as an independent public company. The company's annual sales had increased from $500 million in 1999 to more than $2.1 billion in 2006. Its earnings over the same time frame improved from approximately $16.7 million to $494 million. By late 2006, Coach Inc.'s share price had increased by nearly 15 times from the 2000 IPO price. Exhibit 1 presents income statements for Coach Inc. for fiscal 1999 through fiscal 2006. Its balance sheets for fiscal 2005 and fiscal 2006 are presented in Exhibit 2. Coach's market performance between its October 2000 IPO date and December 2006 is presented in Exhibit 3.

Overview of the Global Luxury Goods Industry in 2006

The world's most well-to-do consumers spent more than $105 billion on luxury goods such as designer apparel, fine watches, writing instruments, jewelry, and select quality leather goods in 2005. The global luxury goods industry was expected to grow by 7 percent during 2006, to reach $112 billion. Italian luxury goods companies accounted for a 27 percent share of industry sales in 2005, while French luxury goods companies held a 22 percent share, Swiss companies owned a 19 percent share, and U.S. companies accounted for a 14 percent share.

Growth in the luxury goods industry had been attributed to increasing incomes and wealth in developing countries in Eastern Europe and Asia and changing buying habits in the United States. Although traditional luxury consumers in the United States ranked in the top 1 percent of wage earners, with household incomes of $300,000 or better, a growing percentage of luxury goods consumers earned substantially less but still aspired to own products with higher levels of quality and styling. The growing desire for luxury goods by middle-income consumers was thought to be a result of a wide range of factors, including effective advertising and television programming that glorified conspicuous consumption. The demanding day-to-day rigor of a two-income household was another factor suggested to urge middle-income consumers to reward themselves with luxuries.

An additional factor contributing to rising sales of luxury goods was the growth of big-box discounters such as Wal-Mart and Target. Discounters' low prices on everyday items had facilitated a "trade up, trade down"[2] shopping strategy, whereby consumers could buy necessities at very low prices and then splurge on indulgences ranging from premium vodka to $4,000 Viking stoves. The combined effect of such factors had allowed spending on luxury goods to grow at four times the rate of overall spending in the United States.

Both retailers and luxury goods manufacturers had altered their strategies in response to the changing buying preferences of middle-income consumers in the United States. Much of Target's success was linked to its merchandising strategy, which focused on relationships with designers such as Philippe Starck, Todd Oldham, Michael Graves, and Isaac Mizrahi. Target's growth had not gone unnoticed by Wal-Mart, which in 2004 began to closely watch haute couture fashion trends for inspiration for new apparel lines. Wal-Mart hosted fashion shows in Manhattan and Miami's South Beach to launch its Metro 7 collection of women's apparel in fall 2005. Exsto was a designer-inspired menswear line that Wal-Mart introduced in summer 2006.

Wal-Mart also had begun to evaluate new store concepts that might appeal to upscale consumers. In 2006, the company was testing a stylish new Supercenter store in Plano, Texas, that stocked gourmet cheeses, organic produce, and 1,200 different wines. The new store also included a Wi-Fi coffee shop and a sushi bar. A Wal-Mart spokesperson explained

Exhibit 1

Coach Inc.'s Consolidated Statements of Income, 1999–2006 ($ in thousands, except share amounts)

	2006	2005	2004	2003	2002	2001	2000	1999
Net sales	$2,111,501	$1,710,423	$1,321,106	$953,226	$719,403	$600,491	$537,694	$500,944
Cost of sales	472,622	399,652	331,024	275,797	236,041	218,507	220,085	226,190
Gross profit	1,638,879	1,310,771	990,082	677,429	483,362	381,984	317,609	274,754
Selling, general, and administrative expenses	874,275	738,208	584,778	458,980	362,211	275,727	261,592	248,171
Reorganization costs	—	—	—	—	3,373	4,569	—	7,108
Operating income	764,604	572,563	405,304	218,449	117,778	101,688	56,017	19,475
Interest income (expense), net	32,623	15,760	3,192	1,059	(299)	(2,258)	(387)	(414)
Income before provision for income taxes and minority interest	797,227	588,323	408,496	219,508	117,479	99,430	55,630	19,061
Provision for income taxes	302,950	216,070	152,504	81,219	41,695	35,400	17,027	2,346
Minority interest, net of tax		13,641	18,043	7,608	184	—	—	—
Net income	$ 494,277	$ 358,612	$ 237,949	$130,681	$ 75,600	$ 64,030	$ 38,603	$ 16,715
Net income per share*								
Basic	$1.30	$0.95	$0.64	$0.36	$0.21	$0.20	$0.14	$0.06
Diluted	$1.27	$0.92	$0.62	$0.35	$0.21	$0.19	$0.14	$0.06
Shares used in computing net income per share:								
Basic	379,635	378,670	372,120	359,116	352,192	327,440	280,208	280,208
Diluted	388,495	390,191	385,558	371,684	363,808	337,000	280,208	280,208

* The two-for-one stock splits in April 2005, October 2003, and July 2002 have been retroactively applied to all prior periods.

Source: Coach Inc. 10-K reports.

Exhibit 2

Coach Inc.'s Balance Sheets, Fiscal 2005–Fiscal 2006 (in thousands)

	JULY 1, 2006	JULY 2, 2005
ASSETS		
Cash and cash equivalents	$ 143,388	$ 154,566
Short-term investments	394,177	228,485
Trade accounts receivable, less allowances		
of $6,000 and $4,124, respectively	84,361	65,399
Inventories	233,494	184,419
Deferred income taxes	78,019	50,820
Prepaid expenses and other current assets	41,043	25,671
Total current assets	974,482	709,360
Long-term investments		122,065
Property and equipment, net	298,531	203,862
Goodwill	227,811	238,711
Indefinite life intangibles	12,007	12,088
Deferred income taxes	84,077	54,545
Other noncurrent assets	29,612	29,526
Total assets	$1,626,520	$1,370,157
LIABILITIES AND STOCKHOLDERS' EQUITY		
Accounts payable	$ 79,819	$ 64,985
Accrued liabilities	261,835	188,234
Revolving credit facility		12,292
Current portion of long-term debt	170	150
Total current liabilities	341,824	265,661
Deferred income taxes	31,655	4,512
Long-term debt	3,100	3,270
Other liabilities	61,207	40,794
Total liabilities	$ 437,786	$ 314,237
Stockholders' equity		
Preferred stock: (authorized 25,000,000 shares; $0.01 par value) none issued		
Common stock: (authorized 1,000,000,000 shares; $0.01 par value) issued and outstanding 369,830,906 and 378,429,710 shares, respectively	$ 3,698	$ 3,784
Additional paid-in-capital	775,209	566,262
Retained earnings	417,087	484,971
Accumulated other comprehensive (loss) income	(7,260)	903
Total stockholders' equity	1,188,734	1,055,920
Total liabilities and stockholders' equity	$1,626,520	$1,370,157

Source: Coach Inc. 2006 10-K report.

the company's experimentation by commenting, "We've always been a top choice for the budget-minded customers. What we're trying to do now is expand our product line, and sell products more relevant to folks who are more discerning in their shopping."[3] Like Wal-Mart, other middle-market retailers had altered their merchandising strategies to accommodate consumers' desires for luxury. During the 2006 Christmas shopping season, J. Crew offered

Exhibit 3

Performance of Coach Inc.'s Stock Price, 2000–2006

(a) Trend in Coach's Common Stock Price

12/06/06

Stock Price (in dollars)

Year

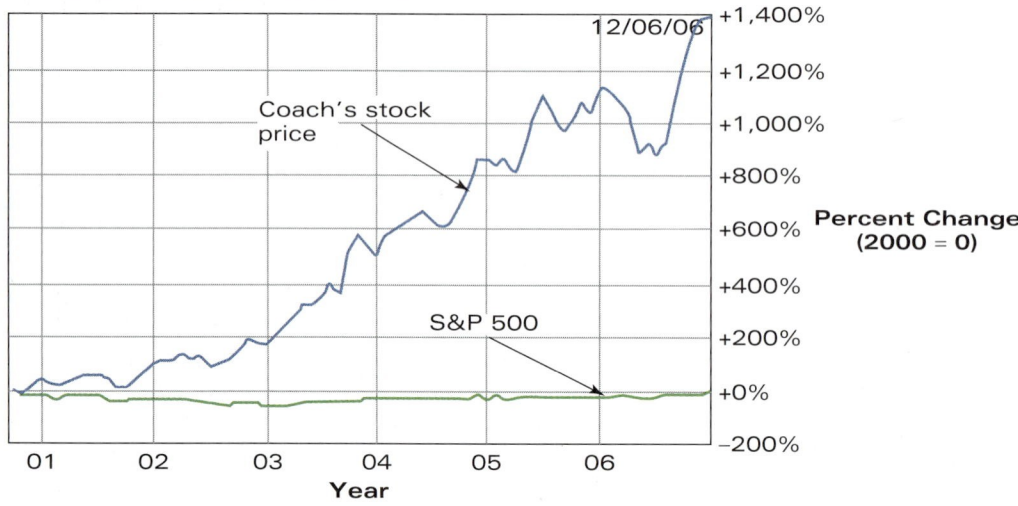

(b) Performance of Coach's Stock Price versus the S&P 500 Index

12/06/06

Coach's stock price

S&P 500

Percent Change (2000 = 0)

Year

$1,400 cashmere overcoats and Home Depot stocked $2,800 HDTVs for consumers looking for extraordinary gifts.

Manufacturers of the finest luxury goods sought to exploit middle-income consumers' desire for such products by launching "diffusion lines" that offered affordable or accessible luxury.[4] In 2006, most leading designer brands had developed sub-brands that retained the styling and quality of the marquee brand, but sold at considerably more modest price points. For example, while Dolce & Gabbana dresses might sell at price points between $1,000 and $1,500, very similar-appearing dresses under Dolce & Gabbana's affordable luxury brand— D&G—were priced at $400 to $600. Giorgio Armani's Emporio Armani line and Gianni Versace's Versus lines typically sold at price points about 50 percent less than similar-looking items carrying the marquee labels. Profit margins on marquee brands approximated 40–50 percent, while most diffusion brands carried profit margins of about 20 percent. Luxury goods manufacturers believed that diffusion brands' lower profit margins were offset by the growing size of the accessible luxury market and protected margins on such products by sourcing production to low-wage countries.

Growing Demand for Luxury Goods in Emerging Markets

In 2004, the worldwide total number of households with assets of at least $1 million increased by 7 percent, to reach 8.3 million. The number of millionaires was expected to increase by another 23 percent by 2009, to reach 10.2 million. With much of the increase in new wealth occurring in Asia and Eastern Europe, demand for luxury goods in emerging markets was projected to grow at annual rates approaching 10 percent. Rising incomes and new wealth had allowed Chinese consumers to account for 11 percent of all luxury goods purchases in 2004. The Chinese market for luxury goods was predicted to increase to 24 percent of global revenues by 2014, which would make it the world's largest market for luxury goods. In 2006, a number of prestigious Western retailers such as Saks Fifth Avenue had opened retail stores in China to build a first-mover advantage in the growing market. Similarly, most luxury goods companies had opened stores in China's largest cities, with Louis Vuitton operating 12 stores in 10 cities in 2006.

Luxury goods producers were also opening retail stores in India, which was another rapidly growing market for luxury goods. In 2005, approximately 50,000 households earned more than 10 million rupees (approximately $250,000) and were the backbone of India's $500 million luxury goods market. The number of households in India with annual incomes of over 10 million rupees was expected to double by 2010. As of 2006, Versace, Louis Vuitton, Dior, Chanel, Hugo Boss, and Tommy Hilfiger

had opened retail locations in India. Gucci and Giorgio Armani had announced plans to open flagship stores in India by 2008. LVMH, which was the parent company of Louis Vuitton, Givenchy, Fendi, and others, planned to expand its network of 50 stores in 18 Indian cities to 100 luxury stores in 23 cities by 2008.

Counterfeiting

In 2006, more than $500 billion worth of counterfeit goods were sold in countries throughout the world. European and American companies that produced highly sought-after branded products were most vulnerable to counterfeiting, with fakes plaguing almost every industry. Fake Rolex watches and Ralph Lauren Polo shirts had long been a problem, but by the mid-2000s, counterfeiters were even making knockoffs of branded auto parts and prescription drugs. Counterfeiting had become so prevalent that the Global Congress on Combating Counterfeiting estimated that 9 percent of all goods sold worldwide were not genuine. The European Union's trade commission categorized the problem as "nothing short of an economic crisis."[5] Interpol believed in 2005 that terrorist organizations such as al Qaeda commonly used counterfeiting to fund their activities since fake brands were as profitable as drugs and because there was very little risk of being prosecuted if caught. About two-thirds of all counterfeit goods were produced by manufacturers in China.

One problem in combating counterfeiting was the demand for knockoffs. In the United States, China, and Europe, vendors and consumers who traded in outdoor street markets knowingly bought and sold fakes and had few reservations about doing so. Using Great Britain as an illustration of the problem, experts there believed that 100 million fake luxury goods were sold in Britain in 2005 and that one in eight adult Britons had purchased a fake in the past year. The European Union and the Chinese government took a step toward combating piracy in 2005 with the signing of an agreement that would fine owners of outdoor bazaars in China if vendors were caught selling counterfeit goods.

In addition, the agreement called for landlords to terminate the lease of any vendor caught selling counterfeit goods a second time. The Chinese government convicted more than 5,500 individuals of intellectual property rights crimes in 2005. However, many piracy and counterfeiting experts believed the problem would not subside until the Chinese government adopted a zero tolerance policy against fakes.

Coach's Strategy and Industry Positioning

In 2006, Coach Inc. designed and marketed women's handbags; leather accessories such as key fobs, belts, electronics accessories, and cosmetics cases; and outerwear such as gloves, hats, and scarves. Coach also designed and marketed leather business cases and luggage. The company entered into a licensing agreement with the Movado Group in 1998 to make Coach-branded watches available in Coach retail stores. Coach entered into a similar agreement with the Jimlar Corporation in 1999 that gave Jimlar the right to manufacture and market Coach-branded women's footwear. In 2006, Coach footwear was available in 500 locations in the United States, including department stores and Coach retail stores. Marchon Eyewear became a licensee for Coach-branded eyewear and sunglasses in 2003. Coach sunglasses were sold in Coach retail stores, department stores, and specialty eyewear stores. Coach frames for prescription glasses were sold through Marchon's network of optical retailers.

Handbags accounted for 67 percent of Coach's 2006 sales, while women's accessories accounted for 23 percent of the company's sales, men's accessories accounted for 2 percent of sales, and outerwear made up 2 percent of 2006 net sales. Business cases and luggage each accounted for 1 percent of company 2006 revenues. Royalties from Coach's licensing agreements with Movado, Jimlar, and Marchon accounted for 1 percent, 2 percent, and 1 percent of the company's 2006 net sales, respectively.

Coach held a 25 percent share of the U.S. luxury handbag market and was the second best-selling brand of luxury handbags in Japan, with an 8 percent market share. Through 2006, Coach had focused on Japan and the United States since those two countries ranked numbers one and two, respectively, in global luxury goods spending. Coach's sales in Japan had increased from $144 million in 2002 to more than $420 million in 2006, while the company's market share in the United States had more than doubled from the 12 percent it held in 2002.

Approach to Differentiation

The market research design process developed by Coach's executive creative director, Reed Krakoff, provided the basis of the company's differentiated product line, but the company's procurement process (which selected only the highest-quality leathers) and its sourcing agreements with quality offshore manufacturers were additional contributors to the company's reputation for high quality. Monthly product launches enhanced the company's voguish image and gave consumers reason to make purchases on a regular basis. The company's market research found that its best customers visited a Coach store once every two months and made a purchase once every seven months. In 2006, the average Coach customer purchased four handbags per year, a figure that had doubled since 2002. Lew Frankfort said the increase was attributable to monthly product launches that "increase the frequency of consumer visits" and women's changing style preference of "using bags to complement their wardrobes in the same way they used to use shoes."[6] A retail analyst agreed with Frankfort's assessment of the importance of frequent product introductions, calling it "a huge driver of traffic and sales and has enabled them to capture the . . . customer who wants the newest items and fashions."[7] Seventy percent of Coach's 2006 sales came from products introduced within the fiscal year.

The aesthetic attractiveness of Coach's full-price stores, which were designed by an in-house architectural group under the direction of Krakoff, further enhanced the company's luxury image. A 2006 survey of 2,000 wealthy shoppers by the Luxury Group ranked Coach store environments 10th among luxury brands. The surveyed shoppers found few differences among the 10 highest-rated store atmospheres, with number one Louis Vuitton scoring 88.1 out of 100; number two Hermès scoring 87.9; Armani and Gucci scoring 86; Versace, Ferragamo, and Prada all scoring 85; and Burberry and Coach tying at 84.

Coach sought to make customer service experiences an additional differentiating aspect of the brand. Coach had agreed since its founding to refurbish or replace damaged handbags, regardless of the age of the bag. In 2006, the company provided store employees with regular customer service training programs and scheduled additional personnel during peak shopping periods to ensure that all customers were attended to satisfactorily. Through the company's Special Request service, customers were allowed to order merchandise for home delivery if the particular handbag or color wasn't available during a visit to a Coach store.

Retail Distribution

Coach's channels of distribution included direct-to-consumer channels and indirect channels. Direct-to-consumer channels included full-price and factory stores in the United States, Internet sales, catalog sales, and stores in Japan. Wholesale accounts with department stores in the United States and in international markets outside Japan represented the company's indirect sales. Exhibit 4 provides selected financial data for Coach Inc. by channel of distribution.

In the United States, Coach products could be found in approximately 900 department stores, 218 Coach full-price stores, and 86 Coach factory outlet stores. U.S. consumers could also order Coach products through either the company's Web site or its printed catalog. The company mailed about 4.1 million catalogs to strategically selected households in the United States during 2006 and placed another 3.5 million catalogs in Coach retail stores for customers to pick up during a store visit. Sales from catalogs were incidental since the catalogs were primarily used to build brand awareness, promote store traffic, and help shoppers evaluate styles before visiting a Coach retail store. Coach's Web site accomplished the same goals as its catalogs but had become a significant contributor to overall sales. In 2006, the Web site had 40 million unique visitors and generated $54 million in net sales. The company also sent promotional e-mails to 55 million selected customers in 2006.

FULL-PRICE STORES Coach's full-price U.S. retail stores accounted for 54 percent of Coach's 2006 net sales. Beginning in 2003, full-price stores were divided into three categories—core locations, fashion locations, and flagship stores. Under Coach's tiered merchandising strategy, the company's flagship stores carried the most sophisticated and highest-priced items, while core stores carried widely demanded lines. The company's fashion locations tended to stock a blend of Coach's best-selling lines and chic specialty bags. By 2006, the company had successfully graduated many core locations to fashion locations. Management believed that Coach had remaining opportunities in the United States to move core stores to fashion stores and fashion stores to flagship stores.

Coach's site-selection process placed its core and fashion stores in upscale shopping centers and downtown shopping areas, while flagship stores were restricted to high-profile fashion districts in cities such as New York, Chicago, Beverly Hills, and San Francisco. Even though flagship stores were "a beacon for the brand,"[8] as Frankfort described them, the company had been very prudent in the number of flagship stores it operated since such stores, by

Exhibit 4

Selected Financial Data for Coach Inc. by Channel of Distribution, Fiscal 2004–Fiscal 2006 ($ in thousands)

	DIRECT-TO-CONSUMER	INDIRECT	CORPORATE UNALLOCATED*	TOTAL
Fiscal 2006				
Net sales	$1,610,691	$500,810		$2,111,501
Operating income (loss)	717,326	313,689	(266,411)	764,604
Income (loss) before provision for income taxes and minority interest	717,326	313,689	(233,788)	797,227
Depreciation and amortization expense	43,177	5,506	16,432	65,115
Total assets	$ 743,034	$ 91,247	792,239	$1,626,520
Additions to long-lived assets	$ 70,440	$ 6,036	57,400	$ 133,876
Fiscal 2005				
Net sales	$1,307,425	$402,998		$1,710,423
Operating income (loss)	548,520	243,276	(219,233)	572,563
Income (loss) before provision for income taxes and minority interest	548,520	243,276	(203,473)	588,323
Depreciation and amortization expense	37,275	4,362	8,763	50,400
Total assets	$ 646,788	$ 69,569	$653,800	$1,370,157
Additions to long-lived assets	$ 70,801	$ 4,778	$ 19,013	$ 94,592
Fiscal 2004				
Net sales	$1,002,737	$318,369		$1,321,106
Operating income (loss)	403,884	178,390	(176,970)	405,304
Income (loss) before provision for income taxes and minority interest	403,884	178,390	(173,778)	408,496
Depreciation and amortization expense	30,054	3,509	6,537	40,100
Total assets	$ 328,530	$ 64,770	$666,979	$1,060,279
Additions to long-lived assets	$ 57,589	$ 3,884	$ 12,186	$ 73,659

* Breakdown of Coach Inc.'s unallocated corporate expenses, 2004–2006 ($ in thousands):

	FISCAL YEAR ENDED		
	JULY 1, 2006	JULY 2, 2005	JULY 3, 2004
Production variances	$ 14,659	$ 11,028	$ 12,581
Advertising, marketing, and design	(91,443)	(70,234)	(56,714)
Administration and information systems	(148,846)	(125,217)	(102,682)
Distribution and customer service	(40,781)	(34,810)	(30,155)
Total corporate unallocated	($266,411)	($219,233)	($176,970)

Source: Coach Inc. 2006 10-K report.

definition, were required to be located on the world's most expensive parcels of real estate.

FACTORY STORES   Coach's factory stores in the United States were generally located 50 or more miles from its full-price stores and made up about 19 percent of the company's 2006 net sales. About 75 percent of factory store inventory was produced specifically for Coach's factory stores, while the remaining 25 percent was made up of overstocked items and discontinued models. Coach's 10–50 percent discounts offered in factory stores allowed the company to maintain a year-round full-price policy in full-price stores. Coach's CEO, Lew Frankfort, believed that discounted prices were critical to success in retailing since 80 percent of women's apparel sold in the United States was bought on sale or in a discount store. "Women in the U.S. have been trained to expect to be able to find a bargain if they either go through the hunt . . . or are willing to buy something after the season," said Frankfort.[9]

Coach had found that there was very little overlap between shoppers in full-price stores and factory stores. The company's market research found the typical full-price store shopper was a 35-year-old, college-educated, single or newly married working woman. The typical factory store shopper was a 45-year-old, college-educated, married, professional woman with children. The average annual spending in a Coach store by full-price shoppers was $1,100. Factory store shoppers spent about $770 annually on Coach products, with 80 percent spent in factory stores and 20 percent spent in a full-price store. The 80:20 ratio of spending also applied to full-price store customers. A retail analyst characterized the difference between the two types of Coach customers as "one wants fashion first and the other is a discount shopper. . . . There is no question it is a very different mindset."[10] Coach had found its full-price customers and factory store customers were equally brand loyal.

Coach's factory stores had outperformed full-price stores in terms of comparable store sales growth during 2005 and 2006, with comparable factory store sales increasing by 31.9 percent during 2006 and comparable full-price store sales increasing by 12.3 percent during the year. The company's impressive overall growth in comparable store sales was attributable, to some degree, to its policy of charting sales for every store and every type of merchandise on a daily basis. During holiday shopping periods, management received sales updates two or three times per day. The frequent updates allowed management to shift production to the hottest-selling items to avoid stockouts.

The company's top-performing factory store during 2005 was its Woodbury Common outlet store, located about 50 miles outside New York City. The store's 2005 sales of $20 million and estimated 2006 sales of $25 million made it as productive as the company's Madison Avenue flagship store. Some degree of Coach's success with its outlet stores resulted from its strategy that valued factory stores as much as full-price stores. The company was committed to providing factory store customers with service and quality equal to that provided to full-price customers. A May 2006 *Consumer Reports* review of outlet stores rated Coach number one in terms of merchandise quality and customer service.

At year-end 2006, Lew Frankfort stated the company would add 3 to 5 factory stores per year until it reached 105, and 30 full-price stores per year to reach 300. Frankfort believed that North America could support 400 full-price Coach stores long term. He did not want factory outlet stores to grow too rapidly, noting, "Our destiny lies in our ability to grow full-price stores."[11] Some analysts were worried that Coach's highly successful factory stores might someday dilute its image. A Luxury Institute analyst described the dilemma faced by Coach and luxury diffusion brands by commenting, "To be unique and exclusive you cannot be ubiquitous."[12] Exhibit 5 shows Coach's growth in retail stores by type and geographic region between 2001 and 2006.

U.S. WHOLESALE Wholesale sales of Coach products to U.S. department stores increased by 23 percent during 2006, to reach $232 million. Department stores were becoming less relevant in U.S. retailing, with the average consumer spending less time in malls and shopping in fewer stores during visits to malls. The share of the U.S. retail market held by department stores declined from about 30 percent in 1990 to approximately 20 percent in 2000. However, handbags and accessories remained a better-performing product category for such retailers. Coach had eliminated 500 department store accounts between 2002 and 2006. Macy's, Bloomingdale's, Lord & Taylor, Dillard's, Nordstrom, Saks Fifth Avenue, and Parisian

Exhibit 5

Coach Inc.'s Retail Stores by Geographic Region, Fiscal 2001–Fiscal 2006

	2006	2005	2004	2003	2002	2001
North America						
Full price company-owned stores	218	193	174	156	138	121
Net increase vs. prior year	25	19	18	18	17	15
Percentage increase vs. prior year	11.5%	9.8%	10.3%	11.5%	12.3%	12.4%
Retail square footage	562,553	490,925	431,617	363,310	301,501	251,136
Net increase vs. prior year	71,628	59,308	68,307	61,809	50,365	42,077
Percentage increase vs. prior year	12.7%	12.1%	15.8%	17.0%	16.7%	16.8%
Average square footage	2,581	2,544	2,481	2,329	2,185	2,076
Factory stores	86	82	76	76	74	68
Net increase vs. prior year	4	6	0	2	6	5
Percentage increase vs. prior year	4.7%	7.3%	0.0%	2.6%	8.1%	7.4%
Factory square footage	281,787	252,279	231,355	232,898	219,507	198,924
Net increase vs. prior year	29,508	20,924	(1,543)	13,391	20,583	16,414
Percentage increase vs. prior year	10.5%	8.3%	(0)	5.7%	9.4%	8.3%
Average square footage	3,277	3,077	3,044	3,064	2,966	2,925
Coach Japan						
Total locations	118	103	100	93	83	76
Net increase vs. prior year	15	3	7	10	7	6
Percentage increase vs. prior year	12.7%	2.9%	7.0%	10.8%	8.4%	7.9%
Total square footage	194,375	161,632	119,291	102,242	76,975	63,371
Net increase vs. prior year	32,743	42,341	17,049	25,267	13,604	7,229
Percentage increase vs. prior year	16.8%	26.2%	14.3%	24.7%	17.7%	11.4%
Average square footage	1,647	1,569	1,193	1,099	927	834
Other International						
International freestanding stores	21	14	18	n.a.	n.a.	n.a.
International department store locations	63	58	70	n.a.	n.a.	n.a.
Other international locations	24	22	27	n.a.	n.a.	n.a.
Total international wholesale locations	108	94	115	n.a.	n.a.	n.a.

n.a. = Not available

Source: Coach Inc. 10-K reports.

were the highest volume department store sellers of Coach merchandise in 2006.

International Markets

INTERNATIONAL WHOLESALE   Coach's wholesale distribution in international markets involved department stores, freestanding retail locations, shop-in-shop locations, and specialty retailers in 18 countries. The company's largest international wholesale accounts were the DFS Group, Lotte Group, Shila Group, Tasa Meng Corporation, and Imaginex. The largest portion of sales by these companies was to traveling Japanese consumers. Coach's largest wholesale country markets were Korea, Hong Kong, Taiwan, Singapore, Japan, Saudi Arabia, Australia, Mexico, Thailand, Malaysia, the Caribbean, China, New Zealand, and France. In 2006, international wholesale accounts amounted to $147 million.

COACH JAPAN   Coach products in Japan were sold in shop-in-shop department store locations, full-price Coach stores, and Coach factory stores. The company had 118 retail locations in Japan in 2006, although company managers believed Japan could support as many as

180 retail outlets. Coach's expansion plan for Japan called for at least 10 new stores annually, which would more than double its number of flagship stores to 15. Coach management believed the increase in stores would allow the company to increase its market share in Japan to 15 percent. The number of Coach retail locations in Japan and other international markets for 2001 through 2006 is presented in Exhibit 5. Coach Inc.'s sales and assets by geographic region are provided in Exhibit 6.

Coach's Strategic Options in 2007

Going into 2007, Lew Frankfort's key growth initiatives involved store expansion in the United States, Japan, Hong Kong, and mainland China; increasing sales to existing customers to drive comparable store growth; and creating alliances to exploit the Coach brand in additional luxury categories. The company's managers believed that there was an opportunity to double the number of full-price retail stores in North America and increase the number of North American factory stores by a third. They also believed that Japan could support approximately 70 additional Coach stores. Licensed distributors in Hong Kong operated

13 locations there and planned to open at least 10 locations on mainland China by 2007.

The company's second growth initiative was to increase same-store sales through continued development of new styles, the development of new usage collections, and the exploitation of gift-giving opportunities. The company had recently begun to prewrap items during holiday shopping periods and had created a new section of its Web site for gift-givers. Coach. com's gift guide recommended items that might appeal to women based on their needs. For example, the Web site recommended handbags preferred by professional women, handbags for formal events, items for fashion-oriented teens, and essential handbags.

During late 2006, Coach launched a women's knitwear collection through a strategic alliance with Lutz & Patmos. The leather- and fur-trimmed cashmere and wool knits ranged from $300 to $1,500. The company also entered into an agreement with a division of the Estée Lauder Company for the development of a fragrance that would be sold in Coach stores beginning in spring 2007.

For the first quarter of fiscal 2007, Coach's comparable store sales for full-price stores increased by 16 percent relative to the same period in 2006. Coach factory stores achieved

---

Exhibit 6

Coach Inc.'s Net Sales and Assets by Geographic Region, Fiscal 2004–Fiscal 2006 ($ in thousands)

	UNITED STATES	JAPAN	OTHER INTERNATIONAL	TOTAL
Fiscal 2006				
Net sales	$1,574,285	$420,509	$116,707	$2,111,501
Long-lived assets	266,190	298,087	3,684	567,961
Fiscal 2005				
Net sales	$1,253,170	$372,326	$ 84,927	$1,710,423
Long-lived assets	314,919	288,338	2,995	606,252
Fiscal 2004				
Net sales	$ 982,668	$278,011	$ 60,427	$1,321,106
Long-lived assets	280,938	55,487	2,384	338,809

Source: Coach Inc. 2006 10-K report.

year-over-year comparable store sales growth of 27.1 percent. The company's indirect sales improved by 11 percent between the first quarter of 2006 and the first quarter of fiscal 2007. Operating income during the first quarter of 2007 increased by 36 percent, while operating margins improved by 340 basis points to reach 35.7 percent. Lew Frankfort attributed the company's continuing sales and profit growth to 19 new store openings in the United States; new handbag collections such as Coach Signature Stripe, Chelsea, Hamptons silhouettes, and Legacy lifestyle; and the increased assortment of gifts under $100 geared to price-sensitive holiday shoppers. The company's stock provided nearly a 35 percent return to shareholders during the 2006 calendar year. The challenge for Lew Frankfort and other key Coach executives was to defend against competitive attacks from French and Italian luxury goods makers and sustain the impressive growth rate the company had achieved since its 2000 IPO.

Endnotes

[1] "How Coach Got Hot," *Fortune* 146, no. 8 (October 28, 2002).

[2] As quoted in "Stores Dancing Chic to Chic," *Houston Chronicle,* May 6, 2006.

[3] Ibid.

[4] "Some Fashion Houses Bolster Lower Priced Lines," *The Wall Street Journal,* September 25, 2006.

[5] As quoted in "Gumshoe's Intuition: Spotting Counterfeits at Port of Antwerp," *The Wall Street Journal,* December 14, 2006, p. A1.

[6] As quoted in "Fashions Keep Retailer Busy," *Investor's Business Daily,* February 10, 2005, p. A4.

[7] Ibid.

[8] As quoted in "Coach's Split Personality," *BusinessWeek,* November 7, 2005.

[9] As quoted in "Coach Sales Strategy Is in the Bag," *Financial Times,* April 18, 2006, p. 22.

[10] Ibid.

[11] As quoted in "Coach's Split Personality."

[12] As quoted in "Expansion into U.S.: Extending the Reach of the Exclusive Lifestyle Brands," *Financial Times,* July 8, 2006, p. 17.

Nucor Corporation: Competing against Low-Cost Steel Imports

Arthur A. Thompson Jr.
The University of Alabama

In the 1950s and early 1960s, Nuclear Corporation of America was involved in the nuclear instrument and electronics business. After suffering through several money-losing years and facing bankruptcy in 1964, the company's board of directors opted for new leadership and appointed F. Kenneth Iverson as president and CEO. Shortly thereafter, Iverson concluded that the best way to put the company on sound footing was to exit the nuclear instrument and electronics business and rebuild the company around its profitable South Carolina–based Vulcraft subsidiary, which was in the steel joist business—Iverson had been the head of Vulcraft prior to being named president. Iverson moved the company's headquarters from Phoenix, Arizona, to Charlotte, North Carolina, in 1966 and proceeded to expand the joist business with new operations in Texas and Alabama. Then, in 1968, management decided to integrate backward into steelmaking, partly because of the benefits of supplying its own steel requirements and partly because Iverson saw opportunities to capitalize on newly emerging technologies to produce steel more cheaply. The company adopted the name Nucor Corporation in 1972, and Iverson initiated a long-term strategy to grow Nucor into a major player in the U.S. steel industry.

By 1985, Nucor had become the seventh largest steel company in America, with revenues of $758 million, six joist plants, and four state-of-the-art steel mills that used electric arc furnaces to produce new steel products from recycled scrap steel. Nucor was regarded as an excellently managed company, an accomplished low-cost producer, and one of the most competitively successful manufacturing companies in the country.[1] A series of articles in the *New Yorker* related how Nucor, a relatively small American steel company, had built an enterprise that led the whole world into a new era of making steel with recycled scrap steel. NBC did a business documentary that used Nucor to make the point that American manufacturers could be successful in competing against low-cost foreign manufacturers.

At the turn of the century, Nucor was the second largest steel producer in the United States and charging to overtake longtime leader U.S. Steel. Nucor's sales in 2000 exceeded 11 million tons, and revenues were nearly $4.8 billion. Several years thereafter, Nucor surpassed U.S. Steel as the largest steelmaker in North America, but Nucor fell back into second place in 2006 when a global steel company in Europe made a series of acquisitions in the United States to create a U.S.-based subsidiary (Mittal Steel USA) with greater production capacity than Nucor. (However, Nucor shipped more tons of steel

Nucor's Growth in the Steel Business, 1970–2006

YEAR	TONS SOLD TO OUTSIDE CUSTOMERS	AVERAGE PRICE PER TON	NET SALES (IN MILLIONS)	EARNINGS BEFORE TAXES (IN MILLIONS)	PRETAX EARNINGS PER TON	NET EARNINGS (IN MILLIONS)
1970	207,000	$245	$ 50.8	$ 2.2	$ 10	$ 1.1
1975	387,000	314	121.5	11.7	30	7.6
1980	1,159,000	416	482.4	76.1	66	45.1
1985	1,902,000	399	758.5	106.2	56	58.5
1990	3,648,000	406	1,481.6	111.2	35	75.1
1995	7,943,000	436	3,462.0	432.3	62	274.5
2000	11,189,000	425	4,756.5	478.3	48	310.9
2001	12,237,000	354	4,333.7	179.4	16	113.0
2002	13,442,000	357	4,801.7	230.1	19	162.1
2003	17,473,000	359	6,265.8	66.9	4	62.8
2004	19,109,000	595	11,376.8	1,731.3	96	1,121.5
2005	20,465,000	621	12,701.0	2,016.4	104	1,310.3
2006	22,118,000	667	14,751.3	2,693.8	129	1,757.7

Source: Company records posted at www.nucor.com (accessed October 3, 2006, and January 31, 2007).

to customers in 2005 than did Mittal Steel.) At the end of 2006, Nucor was solidly entrenched as the second largest steel producer in North America based on total production capacity, with 18 plants having the capacity to produce 25 million tons of steel annually, 2006 revenues of $14.8 billion, and net profits of $1.8 billion. It was the most profitable steel producer in North America in both 2005 and 2006. The company was regarded as the low-cost steel producer in the United States and one of the most efficient and technologically innovative steel producers in the world. Nucor had earned a profit in every quarter and every year since 1966—a truly remarkable accomplishment in a mature and cyclical industry where it was common for companies to post losses when demand for steel sagged. Going into 2007, Nucor had paid a dividend for 135 consecutive quarters. Exhibit 1 provides highlights of Nucor's growth since 1970.

Nucor In 2007

Ken Iverson, the architect of Nucor's climb from obscurity to prominence in the steel industry, was regarded by many as a "model company president." Under Iverson, who served

as CEO until late 1998, Nucor was known for its aggressive pursuit of innovation and technical excellence, rigorous quality systems, strong emphasis on employee relations and workforce productivity, cost-conscious corporate culture, and ability to achieve low costs per ton produced. The company had a streamlined organizational structure, incentive-based compensation systems, and steel mills that were among the most modern and efficient in the United States. Iverson proved himself as a master in crafting and executing a low-cost leadership strategy, and he made a point of making sure that he practiced what he preached when it came to holding down costs. The offices of executives and division general managers were simply furnished. There were no company planes and no company cars, and executives were not provided with company-paid country club memberships, reserved parking spaces, executive dining facilities, or other perks. To save money on his own business expenses and set an example for other Nucor managers, Iverson flew coach class and took the subway when he was in New York City.

When Iverson left the company in 1998 following disagreements with the board of directors, he was succeeded briefly by John Correnti and then Dave Aycock, both of whom had worked in various roles under Iverson for a number of years. In 2000, Daniel R. DiMicco, who had joined Nucor in 1982 and risen up through the ranks to executive vice president, was named president and CEO. Under DiMicco, Nucor continued to pursue a rapid-growth strategy, expanding capacity via both acquisition and new plant construction and boosting tons sold from 11.2 million in 2000 to 22.1 million in 2006. Exhibit 2 provides a summary of Nucor's financial and operating performance for 2000–2006.

Product Line

Over the years, Nucor had expanded progressively into the manufacture of a wider and wider range of steel products, enabling it in 2006 to offer steel users one of the broadest product lineups in the industry. Steel products were considered commodities. While some steelmakers had plants where production quality was sometimes inconsistent or on occasions failed to meet customer-specified metallurgical characteristics, most steel plants turned out products of comparable metallurgical quality— one producer's reinforcing bar was essentially the same as another producer's reinforcing bar, a particular grade of sheet steel made at one plant was essentially identical to the same grade of sheet steel made at another plant. The commodity nature of steel products forced steel producers to be price-competitive, with the market price of each particular steel product being driven by demand–supply conditions for that product.

STEEL PRODUCTS Nucor's first venture into steel in the late 1960s, via its Vulcraft division, was principally one of fabricating steel joists and joist girders from steel that was purchased from various steelmakers; the joists and girders were sold mainly to construction contractors. Vulcraft expanded into the fabrication of steel decking in 1977, most of which was also sold to construction-related customers. Vulcraft's joist, girder, and decking products were used mainly for roof and floor support

systems in retail stores, shopping centers, warehouses, manufacturing facilities, schools, churches, hospitals, and, to a lesser extent, multistory buildings and apartments.

In 1979, Nucor began fabricating cold finished steel products. These consisted mainly of cold drawn and turned, ground, and polished steel bars or rods of various shapes—rounds, hexagons, flats, channels, and squares—and were made of carbon, alloy, and leaded steels as per customer specifications or end-use requirements. Cold finished steel of one type or another was used in tens of thousands of products, including anchor bolts, farm machinery, ceiling fan motors, garage door openers, air conditioner compressors, and lawn mowers. Nucor sold cold finished steel directly to large customers in the automotive, farm machinery, hydraulic, appliance, and electric motor industries and to independent steel distributors (usually referred to as steel service centers) that supplied manufacturers buying steel products in relatively small quantities. The total market for cold finished products in the United States was an estimated 2 million tons annually. In 2006, Nucor Cold Finish was the largest producer of cold finished bars in the United States, with a market share of about 17 percent; its 4 cold finish facilities (in Nebraska, South Carolina, Utah, and Wisconsin) had annual capacity of 490,000 tons. Nucor Cold Finish obtained virtually all of the steel needed to produce cold finished bars from Nucor's bar mills.

Nucor's line of steel products also included metal building systems, light-gauge steel framing, and steel fasteners (bolts, nuts, washers, screws, and bolt assemblies). These were produced by the company's building system and fasteners divisions. Nucor Building Systems began operations in 1987 and had four manufacturing facilities (Indiana, South Carolina, Texas, and Utah) in 2007; its wall and roof systems were mainly used for industrial and commercial buildings, including distribution centers, automobile dealerships, retail centers, aircraft hangars, churches, office buildings, warehouses, and manufacturing facilities. Complete metal building packages could be customized and combined with other materials

Exhibit 2

Seven-Year Financial and Operating Summary, Nucor Corporation, 2000–2006 ($ in millions, except per share data and sales per employee)

	2006	2005	2004	2003	2002	2001	2000
FOR THE YEAR							
Net sales	$14,751.3	$12,701.0	$11,376.9	$6,265.8	$4,801.8	$4,333.7	$4,756.5
Costs, expenses, and other:							
Cost of products sold	11,283.1	10,085.4	9,128.9	5,996.5	4,332.3	3,914.3	3,929.2
Marketing, administrative, and other expenses	592.5	493.6	415.0	165.4	175.6	150.7	183.2
Interest expense (income), net	(37.4)	4.2	22.4	24.6	14.3	6.5	(.8)
Minority interests	219.2	110.7	80.9	24.0	79.5	103.1	151.5
Other income	—	(9,200)	(1,596)	(11.6)	(29.9)	(20.2)	—
Total	12,057.5	10,684.6	9,645.6	6,199.0	4,571.7	4,154.3	4,263.0
Earnings before income taxes	2,693.8	2,016.4	1,731.3	66.9	230.1	179.4	493.5
Provision for income taxes	936.1	706.1	609.8	4.1	68.0	66.4	182.6
Net earnings	$ 1,757.7	$ 1,310.3	$ 1,121.5	$ 62.8	$ 162.1	$ 113.0	$ 310.9
Net earnings per share:							
Basic	$5.73	$4.17	$3.54	$0.20	$0.52	$0.37	$0.95
Diluted	5.68	4.13	3.51	0.20	0.52	0.37	0.95
Dividends declared per share	$0.90	$0.925	$0.235	$0.20	$0.19	$0.17	$0.15
Percentage of net earnings to net sales	11.9%	10.3%	9.9%	1.0%	3.4%	2.6%	6.5%
Return on average equity	38.6%	33.9%	38.7%	2.7%	7.2%	5.2%	14.2%
Capital expenditures	$ 338.4	$ 331.5	$ 285.9	$ 215.4	$ 243.6	$ 261.1	$ 415.4
Depreciation	363.9	375.1	383.3	364.1	307.1	289.1	259.4
Sales per employee (000s)	1,273	1,159	1,107	637	528	531	619
AT YEAR END							
Current assets	$ 4,675.0	$ 4,071.6	$ 3,174.9	$1,620.7	$1,415.4	$1,373.7	$1,379.5
Current liabilities	1,450.0	1,255.7	1,065.8	629.6	591.5	484.2	558.1
Working capital	3,225.0	2,815.9	2,109.2	991.0	823.8	889.5	821.5
Cash provided by operating activities	2,251.2	2,136.6	1,024.8	493.8	497.2	495.1	820.8
Current ratio	3.2	3.2	3.0	2.6	2.4	2.8	2.5
Property, plant, and equipment	$ 2,856.4	$ 2,855.7	$ 2,818.3	$2,817.1	$2,932.1	$2,365.7	$2,329.4
Total assets	7,885.0	7,138.8	6,133.2	4,492.4	4,381.1	3,759.3	3,710.9
Long-term debt	922.3	923.6	923.6	903.6	894.6	460.5	460.5
Stockholders' equity	4,826.0	4,279.8	3,456.0	2,342.1	2,323.0	2,201.5	2,131.0
Shares outstanding (000s)	301.2	310.2	319.0	314.4	312.8	311.2	310.4
Employees	11,900	11,300	10,600	9,900	9,800	8,400	7,900

Source: 2005 and 2006 10-K reports and company press release, January 25, 2007.

such as glass, wood, and masonry to produce a cost-effective, aesthetically sound building of up to 1 million square feet. The buildings were sold through a builder distribution network. Nucor Building Systems obtained a significant portion of its steel requirements from Nucor's bar and sheet mills.

The fastener division, located in Indiana, began operations in 1986 with the construction of a $25 million plant. At the time, imported steel fasteners accounted for 90 percent of the U.S. market because U.S. manufacturers were not competitive on cost and price. Iverson said, "We're going to bring that business back; we can make bolts as cheaply as foreign producers." Nucor built a second fastener plant in 1995, giving it the capacity to supply about 20 percent of the U.S. market for steel fasteners.

STEELMAKING In 1968 Nucor got into basic steelmaking, building a mill in Darlington, South Carolina, to manufacture steel bars. The Darlington mill was one of the first plants of major size in the United States to use electric arc furnace technology to melt scrap steel and cast molten metal into various shapes. Electric arc furnace technology was particularly appealing because the labor and capital requirements to melt steel scrap and produce crude steel were far lower than those at conventional integrated steel mills, where raw steel was produced using coke ovens, basic oxygen blast furnaces, ingot casters, and multiple types of finishing facilities to make crude steel from iron ore, coke, limestone, oxygen, scrap steel, and other ingredients. By 1981, Nucor had four bar mills making carbon and alloy steels in bars, angles, and light structural shapes; in 2006, Nucor had 10 such plants with a total annual capacity of approximately 7.7 million tons. The products of bar mills were widely used in metal buildings, farm equipment, automotive products, furniture, and recreational equipment; many types of construction required the use of steel reinforcing rods, or rebar.

In the late 1980s, Nucor entered into the production of sheet steel at a newly constructed plant in Crawfordsville, Indiana. Flat-rolled sheet steel was used in the production of motor vehicles, appliances, steel pipes and tubes, and other durable goods. The Crawfordsville plant was the first in the world to employ a revolutionary thin-slab casting process that substantially reduced the capital investment and costs to produce flat-rolled sheet steel. Thin-slab casting machines had a funnel-shaped mold to squeeze molten steel down to a thickness of 1.5–2.0 inches, compared to the typical 8- to 10-inch-thick slabs produced by conventional casters. It was much cheaper to then build and operate facilities to roll thin-gauge sheet steel from 1.5- to 2-inch-thick slabs than from 8- to 10-inch-thick slabs. The Crawfordsville plant's costs were said to be $50 to $75 per ton below the costs of traditional sheet steel plants, a highly significant cost advantage in a commodity market where the going price at the time was $400 per ton. *Forbes* magazine described Nucor's pioneering use of thin-slab casting as the most substantial technological/industrial innovation in the past 50 years.[2] By 1996, two additional sheet steel mills that employed thin-slab casting technology were constructed and a fourth mill was acquired in 2002, giving Nucor the capacity to produce 10.8 million tons of sheet steel products annually as of 2006.

Also in the late 1980s, Nucor added wide-flange steel beams, pilings, and heavy structural steel products to its lineup of product offerings. Structural steel products were used in buildings, bridges, overpasses, and similar such projects where strong weight-bearing support was needed. Customers included construction companies, steel fabricators, manufacturers, and steel service centers. To gain entry to the structural steel segment, in 1988 Nucor entered into a joint venture with Yamato-Kogyo, one of Japan's major producers of wide-flange beams, to build a new structural steel mill in Arkansas; a second mill was built on the same site in the 1990s that made the Nucor-Yamato venture in Arkansas the largest structural beam facility in the Western Hemisphere. In 1999, Nucor began production at a third structural steel mill in South Carolina. All three mills used a special continuous casting method that was quite cost-effective. As of 2006,

Nucor had the capacity to make 3.7 million tons of structural steel products annually.

Starting in 2000, Nucor began producing steel plate of various thicknesses and lengths that was sold to manufacturers of heavy equipment, ships, barges, rail cars, refinery tanks, pressure vessels, pipes and tubes, and similar products. Steel plate was made at mills in Alabama and North Carolina that had combined capacity of about 2.8 million tons.

Exhibit 3 shows Nucor's sales by product category for 1990–2006. The breadth of its product line made Nucor the most diversified steel producer in North America. The company had market leadership in several product categories—it was the largest U.S. producer of steel bars, structural steel, steel joist, steel deck, and cold-rolled bars. Nucor had an overall market share of shipments to U.S.-based steel customers (including imports) of about 17 percent in both 2005 and 2006.

Strategy

Starting in 2000, Nucor embarked on a four-part growth strategy that involved new acquisitions, new plant construction, continued plant upgrades and cost reduction efforts, and joint ventures.

STRATEGIC ACQUISITIONS The first element of the four-part strategy was to make acquisitions that would strengthen Nucor's customer base, geographic coverage, and lineup of product offerings. Beginning in the late 1990s, Nucor management concluded that growth-minded companies like Nucor might well be better off purchasing existing plant capacity rather than building new capacity, provided the acquired plants could be bought at bargain prices, economically retrofitted with new equipment if need be, and then operated at costs comparable to (or even below) those of newly constructed state-of-the-art plants. At the time, the steel industry worldwide had far more production capacity than was needed to meet market demand, forcing many companies to operate in the red. Nucor had not made any

acquisitions since about 1990, and a team of five people was assembled in 1998 to explore acquisition possibilities.

For almost three years, no acquisitions were made. But then the economic recession that hit Asia and Europe in the late 1990s reached the United States in full force in 2000–2001. The September 11, 2001, terrorist attacks further weakened steel purchases by such major steel-consuming industries as construction, automobiles, and farm equipment. Many steel companies in the United States and other parts of the world were operating in the red. Market conditions in the United States were particularly grim. Between October 2000 and October 2001, 29 steel companies in the United States, including Bethlehem Steel Corporation and LTV Corporation, the nation's third and fourth largest steel producers, respectively, filed for bankruptcy protection. Bankrupt steel companies accounted for about 25 percent of U.S. capacity. The *Economist* noted that of the 14 steel companies tracked by Standard & Poor's, only Nucor was indisputably healthy. Some experts believed that close to half of the U.S. steel industry's production capacity might be forced to close before conditions improved; about 47,000 jobs in the U.S. steel industry had vanished since 1997.

One of the principal reasons for the distressed market conditions in the United States was a surge in imports of low-priced steel from foreign countries. Outside the United States, weak demand and a glut of capacity had driven commodity steel prices to 20-year lows in 1998. Globally, the industry had about 1 billion tons of annual capacity, but puny demand had kept production levels in the 750 to 800 million tons per year range during 1998–2000. A number of foreign steel producers, anxious to keep their mills running and finding few good market opportunities elsewhere, had begun selling steel in the U.S. market at cut-rate prices in 1997–1999. Nucor and other U.S. companies reduced prices to better compete and several filed unfair trade complaints against foreign steelmakers. The U.S. Department of Commerce concluded in March 1999 that steel companies

Exhibit 3

Nucor's Sales of Steel Products, by Product Category, 1990–2006

TONS SOLD TO OUTSIDE CUSTOMERS (IN THOUSANDS)

	STEEL					STEEL JOISTS (2006 CAPACITY OF ≈ 715,000 TONS)	STEEL DECK (2006 CAPACITY OF ≈ 435,000 TONS)	COLD FINISHED STEEL (2006 CAPACITY OF ≈ 490,000 TONS)	OTHER STEEL PRODUCTS*	TOTAL TONS
YEAR	SHEET (2006 CAPACITY OF ≈ 10.8 MILLION TONS)	BARS (2006 CAPACITY OF ≈ 7.7 MILLION TONS)	STRUCTURAL (2006 CAPACITY OF ≈ 3.7 MILLION TONS)	PLATE (2006 CAPACITY OF ≈ 2.8 MILLION TONS)	TOTAL (2006 CAPACITY OF ≈ 25 MILLION TONS)					
2006	8,495	6,513	3,209	2,432	20,649	570	398	327	174	22,118
2005	8,026	5,983	2,866	2,145	19,020	554	380	342	169	20,465
2004	8,078	5,244	2,760	1,705	17,787	522	364	271	165	19,109
2003	6,954	5,530	2,780	999	16,263	503	353	237	117	17,473
2002	5,806	2,947	2,689	872	12,314	462	330	226	110	13,442
2001	5,074	2,687	2,749	522	11,032	532	344	203	126	12,237
2000	4,456	2,209	3,094	20	9,779	613	353	250	194	11,189
1995	2,994	1,799	1,952	—	6,745	552	234	234	178	7,943
1990	420	1,382	1,002	—	2,804	443	134	163	104	3,648

* Includes steel fasteners (steel screws, nuts, bolts, washers, and bolt assemblies), metal building systems, and light-gauge steel framing.

Source: Company records posted at www.nucor.com (accessed October 3, 2006, and January 31, 2007).

in six countries (Canada, South Korea, Taiwan, Italy, Belgium, and South Africa) had illegally dumped stainless steel in the United States, and the governments of Belgium, Italy, and South Africa further facilitated the dumping by giving their steel producers unfair subsidies that at least partially made up for the revenues lost by selling at below-market prices. Congress and the Clinton administration opted to not impose tariffs or quotas on imported steel, which helped precipitate the number of bankruptcy filings. However, the Bush administration was more receptive to protecting the U.S. steel industry from the dumping practices of foreign steel companies. In October 2001, the U.S. International Trade Commission (ITC) ruled that increased steel imports of semifinished steel, plate, hot-rolled sheet, strip and coils, cold-rolled sheet and strip, and corrosion-resistant and coated sheet and strip were a substantial cause of serious injury, or threat of serious injury, to the U.S. industry. In March 2002, the Bush administration imposed tariffs of up to 30 percent on imports of selected steel products to help provide relief from Asian and European companies dumping steel in the United States at ultra-low prices.

Even though market conditions were tough for Nucor in 2001–2003, management concluded that oversupplied steel industry conditions and the number of beleaguered U.S. companies made it attractive to expand Nucor's production capacity via acquisition. The company proceeded to make a series of acquisitions:

- In 2001, Nucor paid $115 million to acquire substantially all of the assets of Auburn Steel Company's 400,000-ton steel bar facility in Auburn, New York. This acquisition gave Nucor expanded market presence in the Northeast and was seen as a good source of supply for a new Vulcraft joist plant being constructed in Chemung, New York.

- In November 2001, Nucor announced the acquisition of ITEC Steel Inc. for a purchase price of $9 million. ITEC Steel had annual revenues of $10 million and produced load-bearing light-gauge steel framing for

the residential and commercial market at facilities in Texas and Georgia. Nucor was impressed with ITEC's dedication to continuous improvement and intended to grow ITEC's business via geographic and product line expansion. ITEC Steel's name was changed to Nucon Steel Commercial Corporation in 2002.

- In July 2002, Nucor paid $120 million to purchase Trico Steel Company, which had a 2.2-million-ton sheet steel mill in Decatur, Alabama. Trico Steel was a joint venture of LTV (which owned a 50 percent interest), and two leading international steel companies—Sumitomo Metal Industries and British Steel. The joint venture partners had built the mill in 1997 at a cost of $465 million, but Trico was in Chapter 11 bankruptcy proceedings at the time of the acquisition and the mill was shut down. The Trico mill's capability to make thin sheet steel with a superior surface quality added competitive strength to Nucor's strategy to gain sales and market share in the flat-rolled sheet segment. By October 2002, two months ahead of schedule, Nucor had restarted operations at the Decatur mill and was shipping products to customers.

- In December 2002, Nucor paid $615 million to purchase substantially all of the assets of Birmingham Steel Corporation, which included four bar mills in Alabama, Illinois, Washington, and Mississippi. The four plants had capacity of approximately 2 million tons annually. The purchase price also included approximately $120 million in inventory and receivables, the assets of Port Everglade Steel Corporation, the assets of Klean Steel, Birmingham Steel's ownership interest in Richmond Steel Recycling, and a mill in Memphis, Tennessee, that was not currently in operation. Top executives believed that the Birmingham Steel acquisition would broaden Nucor's customer base and build profitable market share in bar steel products.

- In August 2004, Nucor acquired a cold-rolling mill in Decatur, Alabama, from

Worthington Industries for $80 million. This 1-million-ton mill, which opened in 1998, was located adjacent to the previously acquired Trico mill and gave Nucor added ability to service the needs of sheet steel buyers located in the southeastern United States.

- In June 2004, Nucor paid a cash price of $80 million to acquire a plate mill owned by Britain-based Corus Steel that was located in Tuscaloosa, Alabama. The Tuscaloosa mill, which currently had capacity of 700,000 tons that Nucor management believed was expandable to 1 million tons, was the first U.S. mill to employ a special technology that enabled high-quality wide steel plate to be produced from coiled steel plate. The mill produced coiled steel plate and plate products that were cut to customer-specified lengths. Nucor intended to offer these niche products to its commodity plate and coiled sheet customers.

- In February 2005, Nucor completed the purchase of Fort Howard Steel's operations in Oak Creek, Wisconsin; the Oak Creek facility produced cold finished bars in size ranges up to six-inch rounds and had approximately 140,000 tons of annual capacity.

- In June 2005, Nucor purchased Marion Steel Company located in Marion, Ohio, for a cash price of $110 million. Marion operated a bar mill with annual capacity of about 400,000 tons; the Marion location was in proximity to 60 percent of the steel consumption in the United States.

- In May 2006, Nucor acquired Connecticut Steel Corporation for $43 million in cash. Connecticut Steel's bar products mill in Wallingford had annual capacity to make 300,000 tons of wire rod and rebar and approximately 85,000 tons of wire mesh fabrication and structural mesh fabrication, products that complemented Nucor's present lineup of steel bar products provided to construction customers.

- In late 2006, Nucor purchased Verco Manufacturing Company for approximately $180 million; Verco produced steel floor and roof decking at one location in Arizona and two locations in California. The Verco acquisition further solidified Vulcraft's market-leading position in steel decking, giving it total annual capacity of 530,000 tons.

- In January 2007, Nucor announced plans to acquire all of the shares of Canada-based Harris Steel for a total cash purchase price of about $1.07 billion. Harris Steel had 2005 sales of Cdn$1.0 billion and earnings of Cdn$64 million. The company's operations consisted of (1) Harris Rebar, which was involved in the fabrication and placing of concrete reinforcing steel and the design and installation of concrete post-tensioning systems; (2) Laurel Steel, which manufactured and distributed wire and wire products, welded wire mesh, and cold finished bar; and (3) Fisher & Ludlow, which manufactured and distributed heavy industrial steel grating, aluminum grating, and expanded metal. In Canada, Harris Steel had 24 reinforcing steel fabricating plants, two steel grating distribution centers, and one cold finished bar and wire processing plant; in the United States, it had 10 reinforcing steel fabricating plants, two steel grating manufacturing plants, and three steel grating manufacturing plants. Harris had customers throughout Canada and the United States and employed about 3,000 people. For the past three years, Harris had purchased a big percentage of its steel requirements from Nucor. Nucor planned to operate Harris Steel as an independent subsidiary.

By 2005–2006, steel industry conditions worldwide had improved markedly. Prices in the United States were about 50 percent higher than in 2000 and Nucor's sales and earnings were at all-time highs (see Exhibits 1 and 3). But dumping of foreign-made steel into the U.S. market at below-market prices was still a problem. In April 2005, the U.S. International Trade Commission extended the antidumping and countervailing duty orders and suspension agreement covering imports of hot-rolled steel from Brazil, Japan, and the Russian Federation for an additional five years.

THE COMMERCIALIZATION OF NEW TECHNOLOGIES AND NEW PLANT CONSTRUCTION

The second element of Nucor's growth strategy was to continue to be a technology leader and to be aggressive in constructing new plant capacity, particularly when such construction offered the opportunity to be first-to-market with new steelmaking technologies. Nucor management made a conscious effort to focus on the introduction of disruptive technologies (those that would give Nucor a commanding market advantage and thus be disruptive to the efforts of competitors in matching Nucor's cost competitiveness and/or product quality) and leapfrog technologies (those that would allow Nucor to overtake competitors in terms of product quality, cost per ton, or market share).

One of Nucor's biggest and most recent successes in pioneering new technology had been at its Crawfordsville facilities, where Nucor had the world's first installation of direct strip casting of carbon sheet steel—a process called Castrip. After several years of testing and process refinement at Crawfordsville, Nucor announced in 2005 that the Castrip process was ready for commercialization; Nucor had exclusive rights to Castrip technology in the United States and Brazil. The process, which had proved to be quite difficult to bring to commercial reality, was a major technological breakthrough for producing flat-rolled, carbon, and stainless steels in very thin gauges; it involved far fewer process steps to cast metal at or very near customer-desired thicknesses and shapes. The Castrip process drastically reduced capital outlays for equipment and produced savings on operating expenses as well—major expense savings included ability to use lower-quality scrap steel and requiring 90 percent less energy to process liquid metal into hot-rolled steel sheets. A big environmental benefit of the Castrip process was cutting greenhouse gas emissions by up to 80 percent. Nucor's Castrip facility at Crawfordsville had the capacity to produce 500,000 tons annually and employed 55 people. In 2006, Nucor was building its second Castrip facility on the site of the Nucor-Yamato beam mill in Arkansas.

Nucor's growth strategy also included investing in the construction of new plant capacity whenever management spotted opportunities to strengthen its market presence:

- In 2006, Nucor announced that it would construct a new facility to produce metal building systems in Brigham City, Utah. The new plant, Nucor's fourth building systems plant, was to have capacity of 45,000 tons, employ over 200 people, and cost about $27 million; operations were expected to begin in the first quarter of 2008. The new plant gave Nucor national market reach in building systems products and total annual capacity of more than 190,000 tons.

- In 2006, Nucor announced plans to construct a state-of-the-art steel mill in Memphis, Tennessee, to produce special-quality steel bars; the mill was expected to cost $230 million, employ more than 200 people, and have annual capacity of 850,000 tons. Management believed the mill would not only give Nucor one of the industry's most diverse lineups of special-quality steel bar products but also provide a significantly better cost structure compared to both foreign and domestic competitors in the special-quality steel bar segment. Nucor already had special-quality bar mills in Nebraska and South Carolina.

THE DRIVE FOR PLANT EFFICIENCY AND LOW-COST PRODUCTION

A key part of Nucor's strategy was to continue making capital investments to improve plant efficiency and keep production costs low. From its earliest days in the steel business, Nucor had built state-of-the-art facilities in the most economical fashion possible and then made it standard company practice to invest aggressively in plant modernization and efficiency improvements as technology advanced and new cost-saving opportunities emerged. Nucor management made a point of staying on top of the latest advances in steelmaking around the world, diligently searching for emerging cost-effective technologies it could adopt or adapt in its facilities. Executives at Nucor had a long-standing commitment to provide the company's workforce with the best technology available to get the job done right in a safe working environment.

Nucor management also stressed continual improvement in product quality and cost at each one of its production facilities. Many Nucor locations were ISO 9000 and ISO 14001 certified. The company had a program called BESTmarking aimed at being the industry-wide best performer on a variety of production and efficiency measures. Managers at all Nucor plants were accountable for demonstrating that their operations were competitive on both product quality and cost vis-à-vis the plants of rival companies. One trait of Nucor's corporate culture was the expectation that plant-level managers would be aggressive in implementing methods to improve product quality and keep costs per ton low relative to rival plants.

The company's latest initiative involved investments to upgrade and fully modernize the operations of its production facilities. Examples included a three-year bar mill modernization program and the addition of vacuum degassers to its four sheet steel mills. Adding the vacuum degassers not only improved Nucor's ability to produce some of the highest-quality sheet steel available but also resulted in expanded capacity at low incremental cost. Nucor's capital expenditures for new technology, plant improvements, and equipment upgrades totaled $415 million in 2000, $261 million in 2001, $244 million in 2002, $215 million in 2003, $286 million in 2004, $331 million in 2005, and $338 million in 2006. Capital expenditures for 2007 were projected to be $930 million; the big increase over 2006 capital spending was intended to ensure that Nucor plants were kept in state-of-the-art condition and globally competitive on cost. Top executives expected that all of Nucor's plants would have

ISO 14001 certified Environmental Management Systems in place by the end of 2007.

GLOBAL GROWTH VIA JOINT VENTURES

The fourth component of Nucor's strategy was to grow globally with joint ventures and the licensing of new technologies. Nucor had recently entered into a joint venture with Companhia Vale do Rio Doce (CVRD) to construct and operate an environmentally friendly pig iron project in northern Brazil. Production began in the fourth quarter of 2005. The joint venture at the Brazilian plant involved using fast-growing eucalyptus trees as fuel.[3] Eucalyptus trees reached a mature height of 70 feet in seven years and immediately began to grow back when harvested the first two times, after which they had to be replanted. The project appealed to Nucor because it counteracted global warming. As eucalyptus trees grow, they take in carbon dioxide from the atmosphere and sequester it in their biomass; some goes back into the soil as leaves and twigs fall to the ground, with the remainder being stored in the wood of the tree. While burning the eucalyptus wood to create the charcoal fuel on which this project depended resulted in the release of some of the stored carbon dioxide to the atmosphere and still more was released when the charcoal was combined with iron ore in a mini blast furnace to create pig iron, some of the carbon dioxide was locked up in the pig iron. But the net effect on any global warming due to the release of carbon dioxide was overwhelmingly positive, given that about 500,000 tons of pig iron were being produced and that over 200,000 acres, or about 312 square miles, of eucalyptus forest were being restored or protected. In the overall scheme, the production of pig iron at the Brazilian plant removed about 2,400 pounds of carbon dioxide from the atmosphere for every ton of pig iron produced; this compared quite favorably with the conventional method of producing pig iron, which increased the carbon dioxide in the atmosphere by 4,180 pounds for every ton of pig iron produced.

Nucor had recently partnered with the Rio Tinto Group, Mitsubishi Corporation, and Chinese steelmaker Shougang Corporation to pioneer Rio Tinto's HIsmelt technology at a new plant located in Kwinana, Western Australia. The HIsmelt plant converted iron ore to liquid metal or pig iron and was both a replacement for traditional blast furnace technology and a hot metal source for electric arc furnaces. Rio Tinto had been developing the HIsmelt technology for 10 years and believed that it had the potential to revolutionize iron making and provide low-cost, high-quality iron for making steel. Nucor had a 25 percent ownership in the venture and had a joint global marketing agreement with Rio Tinto to license the technology to other interested steel companies. The Australian plant represented the world's first commercial application of the HIsmelt technology. Production started in January 2006; the plant had a capacity of over 800,000 metric tons and was expandable to 1.5 million metric tons at an attractive capital cost per incremental ton. Nucor viewed the Australian plant as a future royalty stream and raw material source. The technology had also been licensed to a Chinese steelmaker that planned to construct an 800,000-ton steel plant in China using the HIsmelt process for its iron source.

Nucor's third principal international project involved a raw materials strategy initiative to develop a low-cost substitute for scrap steel. Nucor was already the largest purchaser of scrap steel in North America, and the company's rapid growth strategy made it vulnerable to rising prices for scrap steel. In an effort to curtail its dependence on scrap steel as a raw material input, Nucor acquired an idled direct reduced iron plant in Louisiana in September 2004, relocated its operation to Trinidad (an island off the coast of South America near Venezuela), and expanded the project to a capacity of 1.8 million metric tons. Nucor was currently purchasing 6 to 7 million tons of iron annually to use in making higher-quality grades of sheet steel; integrating backward into supplying 25 to 30 percent of its own iron requirements held promise of raw material savings and less reliance on outside iron suppliers. The Trinidad site was chosen because it had a long-term and very cost-attractive supply of natural gas, along with favorable logistics for receiving iron ore and shipping direct reduced iron to Nucor's sheet steel mills in the United States. Production began in January 2007.

Nucor was looking for other opportunities globally. But so far, Nucor's strategy to participate in foreign steel markets was via joint ventures involving pioneering use of new steel-making technologies. The company did not currently have any plans to build and operate its own steel mills outside the United States—its only company-operated foreign facility was the one in Trinidad.

Operations

Nucor had 49 facilities in 17 states and was the largest recycler of scrap steel in North America. The company recycled over 23 million tons of scrap in 2005 and over 21 million tons in 2006. At Nucor's steel mills, scrap steel and other metals were melted in electric arc furnaces and poured into continuous casting systems. Sophisticated rolling mills converted the billets, blooms, and slabs produced by various casting equipment into rebar, angles, rounds, channels, flats, sheet, beams, plate, and other finished steel products. Nucor's steel mill operations were highly automated, typically requiring fewer operating employees per ton produced than the mills of rival companies. High worker productivity at all Nucor steel mills resulted in labor costs equal to about 8 percent of revenues in 2005–2006—a considerably lower percentage than the labor costs at the integrated mills of companies using union labor and conventional blast furnace technology. Nucor's value chain (anchored in using electric arc furnace technology to recycle scrap steel) involved far fewer production steps, far less capital investment, and considerably less labor than the value chains of companies with integrated steel mills that made crude steel from iron ore.

Nucor's two big cost components at its steel plants were scrap steel and energy. Scrap steel prices were driven by market demand–supply conditions and could fluctuate significantly—see Exhibit 4. Nucor implemented a raw material surcharge in 2004 to cope with sharply increasing scrap steel prices in 2004 and help protect operating profit margins. Total energy costs increased by approximately $7 per ton from 2004 to 2005 as natural gas prices increased by approximately 31 percent and electricity prices increased by approximately 19 percent; energy costs rose another $1 per ton in 2006. Due to the efficiency of Nucor's steel mills, however, energy costs remained less than 10 percent of revenues in 2004, 2005, and 2006. In 2006, Nucor hedged a portion of its exposure to natural gas prices out into 2007 and also entered into contracts with natural gas suppliers to purchase natural gas in amounts needed to operate its direct reduced iron facility in Trinidad from 2006 through 2028.

Nucor plants were linked electronically to each other's production schedules, and each plant strived to operate in a just-in-time inventory mode. Virtually all tons produced were shipped out very quickly to customers; consequently, finished goods inventories at Nucor plants were relatively small.

Exhibit 4

Nucor's Costs for Scrap Steel and Scrap Substitute, 2005–2006

PERIOD	AVERAGE SCRAP AND SCRAP SUBSTITUTE COST PER TON USED
2000	$120
2001	101
2002	110
2003	137
2004	238
2005	
Quarter 1	272
Quarter 2	246
Quarter 3	217
Quarter 4	240
2006	
Quarter 1	237
Quarter 2	247
Quarter 3	257
Quarter 4	243

Source: Nucor's 10-K reports and information posted at www. nucor.com (accessed October 25, 2006, and January 31, 2007).

Organization and Management Philosophy

Nucor had a simple, streamlined organization structure to allow employees to innovate and make quick decisions. The company was highly decentralized, with most day-to-day operating decisions made by division or plant-level general managers and their staff. The three building systems plants and the four cold-rolled products plants were headed by a group manager, but otherwise each plant operated independently as a profit center and was headed by a general manager, who in most cases also had the title of vice president. The group manager or plant general manager had control of the day-to-day decisions that affected the group or plant's profitability.

The organizational structure at a typical plant had three management layers:

- General Manager
- Department Manager
- Supervisor/Professional
- Hourly Employee

Group managers and plant managers reported to one of four executive vice presidents at corporate headquarters. Nucor's corporate staff was exceptionally small, consisting of only 66 people in 2006, the philosophy being that corporate headquarters should consist of a small cadre of executives who would guide a decentralized operation where liberal authority was delegated to managers in the field. Each plant had a sales manager who was responsible for selling the products made at that particular plant; such staff functions as engineering, accounting, and personnel management were performed at the group/plant level. There was a minimum of paperwork and bureaucratic systems. Each group/plant was expected to earn about a 25 percent return on total assets before corporate expenses, taxes, interest, or profit sharing. As long as plant managers met their profit targets, they were allowed to operate with minimal restrictions and interference from corporate headquarters. There was a very friendly spirit of competition from one plant to the next to see which facility could be the best performer, but since all of the vice presidents and general managers shared the same bonus systems, they functioned pretty much as a team despite operating their facilities individually. Top executives did not hesitate to replace group or plant managers who consistently struggled to achieve profitability and operating targets.

Workforce Compensation Practices

Nucor was a nonunion "pay for performance" company with an incentive compensation system that rewarded goal-oriented individuals and did not put a maximum on what they could earn. All employees were covered under one of four basic compensation plans, each featuring incentives related to meeting specific goals and targets:

1. *Production Incentive Plan*—Production line jobs were rated on degree of responsibility required and assigned a base wage comparable to the wages paid by other manufacturing plants in the area where a Nucor plant was located. But in addition to their base wage, operating and maintenance employees were paid weekly bonuses based on the number of tons by which the output of their production team or work group exceeded the standard number of tons. All operating and maintenance employees were members of a production team that included the team's production supervisor, and the tonnage produced by each work team was measured for each work shift and then totaled for all shifts during a given week. If a production team's weekly output beat the weekly standard, team members (including the team's production supervisor) earned a specified percentage bonus for each ton produced above the standard—production bonuses were paid weekly (rather than quarterly or annually) so that workers and supervisors would be rewarded immediately for their efforts. The standard rate was calculated based on the capabilities of the equipment

employed (typically at the time plant operations began), and no bonus was paid if the equipment was not operating (which gave maintenance workers a big incentive to keep a plant's equipment in good working condition)—Nucor's philosophy was that everybody suffered when equipment was not operating and the bonus for downtime ought to be zero. Production standards at Nucor plants were seldom raised unless a plant underwent significant modernization or important new pieces of equipment were installed that greatly boosted labor productivity. It was common for production incentive bonuses to run from 50 to 150 percent of an employee's base pay, thereby pushing their compensation levels up well above those at other nearby manufacturing plants. Worker efforts to exceed the standard and get a bonus involved not so much working harder as practicing good teamwork and close collaboration in resolving problems and figuring out how best to exceed the production standards.

2. *Department Manager Incentive Plan*—Department managers earned annual incentive bonuses based primarily on the percentage of net income to dollars of assets employed for their division. These bonuses could be as much as 80 percent of a department manager's base pay.

3. *Professional and Clerical Bonus Plan*—A bonus based on a division's net income return on assets was paid to employees that were not on the production worker or department manager plan.

4. *Senior Officers Incentive Plan*—Nucor's senior officers did not have employment contracts and did not participate in any pension or retirement plans. Their base salaries were set at approximately 90 percent of the median base salary for comparable positions in other manufacturing companies with comparable assets, sales, and capital. The remainder of their compensation was based on Nucor's annual overall percentage of net income to stockholders'

equity (i.e., return on equity, or ROE) and was paid out in cash and stock. Once Nucor's ROE reached a threshold of not less than 3 percent or more than 7 percent (as determined annually by the compensation committee of the board of directors), senior officers earned a bonus equal to 20 percent of their base salary. If Nucor's annual ROE exceeded 20 percent, senior officers earned a bonus equal to 225 percent of their base salary. Officers could earn an additional bonus of up to 75 percent of their base salary based on a comparison of Nucor's net sales growth with the net sales growth of members of a steel industry peer group. There was also a long-term incentive plan that provided for stock awards and stock options; this incentive covered a three-year performance period and was linked to Nucor's return on average invested capital relative to that of other steel industry competitors. The structure of these officer incentives was such that Nucor officers could find their bonus compensation swinging widely—from close to zero (in years like 2003 when industry conditions were bad and Nucor's performance was subpar) to 400 percent (or more) of their base salaries (when Nucor's performance was excellent, as had been the case in 2004–2006).

Nucor management had designed the company's incentive plans for employees so that bonus calculations involved no discretion on the part of a plant/division manager or top executives. This was done to eliminate any concerns on the part of workers that managers or executives might show favoritism or otherwise be unfair in calculating or awarding bonuses. Based on labor costs equal to about 8 percent of revenues, a typical Nucor employee earned close to $91,300 in 2005 in base pay and bonuses. (The average in 2000–2002, when the steel market was in the doldrums, was about $60,000 per employee.)[4] Total worker compensation at Nucor could run double the average earned by workers at other manufacturing companies in the states where Nucor's plants were located. At Nucor's new $450 million plant in Hertford County, North Carolina, where jobs were scarce and poverty was common, Nucor employees earned three times the local average manufacturing wage. Nucor management philosophy was that workers ought to be excellently compensated because the production jobs were strenuous and the work environment in a steel mill was relatively dangerous.

Employee turnover in Nucor mills was extremely low; absenteeism and tardiness were minimal. Each employee was allowed four days of absences and could also miss work for jury duty, military leave, or the death of close relatives. After this, a day's absence cost a worker the entire performance bonus pay for that week, and being more than a half-hour late to work on a given day resulted in no bonus payment for the day. When job vacancies did occur, Nucor was flooded with applications; plant personnel screened job candidates very carefully, seeking people with initiative and a strong work ethic.

Employee Relations and Human Resources

Employee relations at Nucor were based on four clear-cut principles:

1. Management is obligated to manage Nucor in such a way that employees will have the opportunity to earn according to their productivity.

2. Employees should be able to feel confident that if they do their jobs properly, they will have a job tomorrow.

3. Employees have the right to be treated fairly and must believe that they will be.

4. Employees must have an avenue of appeal when they believe they are being treated unfairly.

The hallmarks of Nucor's human resources strategy were its incentive pay plan for production exceeding the standard and the job security provided to production workers—despite being in an industry with strong down cycles, Nucor had made it a practice not to lay off workers.

Nucor took an egalitarian approach to providing fringe benefits to its employees; employees had the same insurance programs, vacation schedules, and holidays as upper-level management. However, certain benefits were not available to Nucor's officers. The fringe benefit package at Nucor included:

- *Profit sharing*—Each year, Nucor allocated 10 percent of its operating profits to profit-sharing bonuses for all employees (except senior officers). Depending on company performance, the bonuses could run anywhere from 1 percent to over 20 percent of pay. Twenty percent of the bonus amount was paid to employees in the following March as a cash bonus, and the remaining 80 percent was put into a trust for each employee, with each employee's share being proportional to his or her earnings as a percent of total earnings by all workers covered by the plan. An employee's share of the profits became vested after one full year of employment. Employees received a quarterly statement of their balance in profit sharing.

- *401(k) plan*—Both officers and employees participated in a 401(k) plan, in which the company matched from 5 percent to 25 percent of each employee's first 7 percent of contributions; the amount of the match was based on how well the company was doing.

- *Medical and dental plan*—The company had a flexible and comprehensive health benefit program for officers and employees that included wellness and health care spending accounts.

- *Tuition reimbursement*—Nucor reimbursed up to $2,750 of an employee's approved educational expenses each year and up to $1,250 of a spouse's educational expenses.

- *Employee stock purchase plan*—Nucor had a monthly stock investment plan for employees whereby Nucor added 10 percent to the amount an employee contributed toward the purchase of Nucor shares; Nucor paid the commission on all share purchases.

- *Service awards*—After each five years of service with the company, Nucor employees received a service award consisting of five shares of Nucor stock.

- *Scholarships*—Nucor provided the children of employees (except senior officers) up to $2,750 worth of scholarship funding each year to be used at accredited academic institutions.

- *Other benefits*—Long-term disability, life insurance, vacation. In 2004, 2005, and 2006 Nucor paid each employee (excluding officers) a special year-end bonus of $2,000; this was in addition to record profit-sharing bonuses and 401(k) matching contributions of $272.6 million in 2006, $206.0 million in 2005, and $172.3 million in 2004 (versus only $8.9 million in 2003). The extra $2,000 bonuses resulted in additional profit-sharing costs of approximately $23.8 million in 2006, $22.6 million in 2005, and $21.0 million in 2004.

Most of the changes Nucor made in work procedures and in equipment came from employees. The prevailing view at Nucor was that the employees knew the problems of their jobs better than anyone else and were thus in the best position to identify ways to improve how things were done. Most plant-level managers spent considerable time in the plant, talking and meeting with frontline employees and listening carefully to suggestions. Promising ideas and suggestions were typically acted on quickly and implemented—management was willing to take risks to try worker suggestions for doing things better and to accept the occasional failure when the results were disappointing. Teamwork, a vibrant team spirit, and a close worker–management partnership were much in evidence at Nucor plants.

Nucor plants did not use job descriptions. Management believed job descriptions caused more problems than they solved, given the teamwork atmosphere and the close collaboration among work group members. The company saw formal performance appraisal systems as added paperwork and a waste of time. If a Nucor employee was not performing well, the problem was dealt with directly by supervisory personnel and the peer pressure of work group members (whose bonuses were adversely affected).

Employees were kept informed about company and division performance. Charts showing the division's results in return on assets and bonus payoff were posted in prominent places in the plant. Most all employees were quite aware of the level of profits in their plant or division. Nucor had a formal grievance procedure, but grievances were few and far between. The corporate office sent all news releases to each division, where they were posted on bulletin boards. Each employee received a copy of Nucor's annual report; it was company practice for the cover of the annual report to consist of the names of all Nucor employees.

All of these practices had created an egalitarian culture and a highly motivated workforce that grew out of former CEO Ken Iverson's radical insight: that employees, even hourly clock punchers, would put forth extraordinary effort and be exceptionally productive if they were richly rewarded, treated with respect, and given real power to do their jobs as best they saw fit.[5] There were countless stories of occasions when managers and workers had gone beyond the call of duty to expedite equipment repairs (in many instances even blowing their weekends to go help personnel at other Nucor plants solve a crisis); the company's workforce was known for displaying unusual passion and company loyalty even when no personal financial stake was involved. As one Nucor worker put it, "At Nucor, we're not 'you guys' and 'us guys.' It's all of us guys. Wherever the bottleneck is, we go there, and everyone works on it."[6]

It was standard procedure for a team of Nucor veterans, including people who worked on the plant floor, to visit with their counterparts as part of the process of screening candidates for acquisition.[7] One of the purposes of such visits was to explain the Nucor compensation system and culture face-to-face, gauge reactions, and judge whether the plant would fit into "the Nucor way of doing things" if it was acquired. Shortly after making an acquisition, Nucor management moved swiftly to institute its pay-for-performance incentive system and to begin instilling the egalitarian Nucor culture and idea sharing. Top priority was given to looking for ways to boost plant production using fewer people and without making substantial capital investments; the take-home pay of workers at newly acquired plants typically went up dramatically. At the Auburn Steel plant, acquired in 2001, it took Nucor about six months to convince workers that they would be better off under Nucor's pay system; during that time, Nucor paid people under the old Auburn Steel system but posted what they would have earned under Nucor's system. Pretty soon, workers were convinced to make the changeover—one worker saw his pay climb from $53,000 in the year prior to the acquisition to $67,000 in 2001 and to $92,000 in 2005.[8]

NEW EMPLOYEES Each plant/division had a "consul" responsible for providing new employees with general advice about becoming a Nucor teammate and serving as a resource for inquiries about how things were done at Nucor, how to navigate the division and company, and how to resolve issues that might come up. Nucor provided new employees with a personalized plan that set forth who would give them feedback about how well they were doing and when and how this feedback would be given; from time to time, new employees met with the plant manager for feedback and coaching. In addition, there was a new employee orientation session that provided a hands-on look at the plant/division operations; new employees also participated in product group meetings to provide exposure to broader business and technical issues. Each year, Nucor brought all recent college hires to the Charlotte headquarters for a forum intended to give the new hires a chance to network and provide senior management with guidance on how best to leverage their talent.

Pricing and Marketing

The commodity nature of steel products meant that the prices a company could command were driven by market demand–supply conditions that changed more or less continually. As a consequence, Nucor's average sales prices per ton varied considerably from quarter to quarter—see Exhibit 5. Nucor's pricing strategy was to quote the same price and sales terms to all customers, with the customer paying all shipping charges. Its prices were customarily the lowest or close to the lowest in the U.S. market for steel. Nucor's status as a low-cost producer with reliably low prices had resulted in numerous customers entering into noncancelable 6- to 12-month contracts to purchase steel mill products from Nucor. These contracts contained a pricing formula tied to raw material costs (with the cost of scrap steel being the primary driver of price adjustments during the contact period). In 2005–2006, about 45 percent

of Nucor's steel mill production was committed to contract customers. All of Nucor's steel mills planned to pursue profitable contract business in the future.

Nucor had recently begun developing its plant sites with the expectation of having several customer companies co-locate nearby to save shipping costs on their steel purchases. In order to gain the advantage of low shipping costs, two tube manufacturers, two steel service centers, and a cold-rolling facility had located adjacent to Nucor's Arkansas plant. Four companies had announced plans to locate close to a new Nucor plant in North Carolina.

Approximately 92 percent of the production of Nucor's steel mills was sold to outside customers in 2005–2006; the balance was used internally by Nucor's Vulcraft, Cold Finish, Building Systems, and Fasteners divisions. Steel joists and joist girder sales were obtained by competitive bidding. Vulcraft supplied price quotes to contractors on a significant percentage of the domestic buildings that had steel joists and joist girders as part of their support systems. Nucor's pricing for steel joists, girders, and decking included delivery to the job site. Vulcraft maintained a fleet of trucks to ensure and control on-time delivery; freight costs for

Exhibit 5

Nucor's Average Sales Prices (per ton) for Steel Products, by Product Category, 2005–2006

PERIOD	SHEET	BARS	STRUCTURAL	PLATE	STEEL JOISTS	STEEL DECK	COLD FINISHED STEEL	OVERALL PRICE PER TON
2005								
Qtr 1	$675	$514	$605	$763	$1,102	$1,020	$1,012	$663
Qtr 2	609	499	574	708	1,084	972	1,067	621
Qtr 3	523	496	561	625	1,056	935	1,003	571
Qtr 4	583	542	634	684	1,077	931	1,069	630
2006								
Qtr 1	594	543	649	698	1,104	938	1,010	631
Qtr 2	625	567	667	712	1,092	930	1,033	654
Qtr 3	673	601	703	746	1,122	946	1,067	702
Qtr 4	624	576	727	732	1,175	1,031	998	683

Source: Company records posted at www.nucor.com (accessed October 23, 2006, and January 31, 2007).

deliveries were less than 10 percent of revenues in 2005–2006. In 2005, Vulcraft had a 40 percent share of the U.S. market for steel joists. Steel deck was specified in the majority of buildings using steel joists and joist girders. In 2005 and 2006, Vulcraft supplied more than 30 percent of total domestic sales of steel deck; the 2006 Verco acquisition gave Nucor the capability to substantially increase its sales and market share of steel deck in 2007.

Competition in the Steel Industry

The global marketplace for steel was considered to be relatively mature and highly cyclical as a result of ongoing ups and downs in the world economy or the economies of particular countries. In general, competition within the steel industry, both in the United States and globally, was intense and expected to remain so. Numerous steel companies had declared bankruptcy during the past 10 years, either ceasing production altogether or more usually continuing to operate after being acquired and undergoing restructuring to become more cost-competitive.

Worldwide demand had grown by about 6 percent annually since 2000 (well above the 1.1 percent growth rate from 1975 to 2000), but there had been periods of both strong and weak demand during 2000–2006 (see Exhibit 6). Prices for steel products were near record levels throughout most of 2004–2006, driven by strong global demand for steel products (see Exhibit 7). Worldwide sales of steel products were in the $770 to $790 billion range in 2004–2005; prior to 2004, global sales had never exceeded $500 billion in any one year, according to data compiled by the International Iron and Steel Institute.

Nonetheless, steelmaking capacity worldwide still exceeded global demand in 2005–2006. Many foreign steelmakers, looking to operate their plants as close to capacity as possible or seeking to take advantage of favorable foreign currency fluctuations, had begun exporting steel products to the U.S. market, where strong demand and tight domestic supplies had

Exhibit 6

Estimated Worldwide Production of Crude Steel, with Compound Average Growth Rates, 1975–2005

YEAR	ESTIMATED VALUE OF WORLD STEEL PRODUCTION (IN BILLIONS OF $)	WORLD CRUDE STEEL PRODUCTION (MILLIONS OF TONS)	COMPOUND AVERAGE GROWTH RATES IN STEEL PRODUCTION	
			PERIOD	PERCENTAGE RATE
1975	n.a.	710	1975–1980	2.2%
1980	n.a.	790	1980–1985	0.1
1985	$250	792	1985–1990	1.4
1990	415	849	1990–1995	−0.5
1995	470	828	1995–2000	2.4
2000	385	934	2000–2005	6.0
2001	270	937		
2002	330	996		
2003	465	1,068		
2004	790	1,176		
2005	770	1,247		

n.a. = not available

Source: International Iron and Steel Institute, *World Steel in Figures, 2006,* www.worldsteel.org (accessed November 6, 2006).

Exhibit 7

Estimated Consumption of Steel Products, by Geographic Region, 2000–2005 (in millions of tons)

REGION	2000	2001	2002	2003	2004	2005
European Union (25 countries)	177.6	174.6	173.2	176.0	185.2	176.8
Other European countries, Russia, and Ukraine	60.8	64.1	63.0	71.8	75.6	80.1
North America	161.6	145.6	145.9	143.5	164.2	149.7
Central and South America	31.0	31.8	30.4	30.4	36.0	35.8
Africa	17.0	18.4	20.3	21.0	22.6	24.7
Middle East	21.7	25.5	27.9	33.3	33.7	38.2
Asia	353.0	382.7	432.8	496.2	546.7	602.8
Australia, New Zealand	7.4	6.9	7.9	8.3	8.8	8.7
World total	830.2	849.6	901.5	980.6	1,072.9	1,116.8

Source: International Iron and Steel Institute, *World Steel in Figures, 2006,* www.worldsteel.org (accessed November 6, 2006).

pushed steel prices to highly profitable levels. According to U.S. Department of Commerce data, steel imports into the United States rose by over 70 percent between November 2005 and September 2006 and were expected to reach a record level of over 45 million tons in 2006 (see Exhibit 8); companies in China, Russia, Korea, Turkey, Taiwan, Japan, India, Australia, and Brazil were particularly aggressive in exporting their production to the U.S. market.[9] Steel imports from China, for example, jumped from 139,300 tons in November 2005 to a monthly average of over 575,000 tons in July, August, and September 2006. Steel imports from Taiwan rose from 48,400 tons in November 2005 to nearly 265,000 tons in September 2006. Steel imports from Russia were 121,300 tons in November 2005 and 517,000 tons in August 2006. Steel imports from Korea were about 115,700 tons in November 2005 and over 260,000 tons in September 2006; imports from Australia were 60,000 tons in November 2005 and 162,000 tons in September 2006. In 2005, foreign steelmakers captured a 22.8 percent share of the U.S. market for steel products (based on tons); foreign steelmakers were expected to achieve close to a 30 percent share of the U.S. market in 2006. Many non-U.S. steel producers were owned and/or subsidized by their governments, a condition that often meant their production and sales decisions were driven by political and economic

policy considerations rather than by prevailing market conditions. Steel supplies in the United States (and other countries) were also subject to shifting foreign exchange rates, with more imports pouring in when the local currency was strong and more exports flowing out when the local currency was weak.

In February 2007, Nucor CEO Dan DiMicco applauded the announcement that the U.S. government had requested World Trade Organization (WTO) dispute settlement consultations with China regarding claims that China was violating WTO rules by providing subsidies to Chinese steel exporters.[10] Under the WTO dispute settlement procedures, a request for consultations was the first step in resolving the U.S. claim that the Chinese government was violating WTO rules. If a WTO panel found that China was indeed breaking WTO rules, it could order China to provide compensation to the United States by allowing the United States to impose higher tariffs on Chinese goods or take similar measures. Under U.S. countervailing duty law, if a U.S. Department of Commerce investigation confirmed that foreign plants exporting steel to the United States were being subsidized by their government and if the U.S. International Trade Commission determined that the subsidized imports had injured the domestic steel industry, then the United States could apply countervailing duties to offset the

Exhibit 8

The U.S. Market for Steel Products, 1995–2005 (in millions of tons)

YEAR	U.S. SHIPMENTS OF STEEL PRODUCTS	U.S. EXPORTS OF STEEL MILL PRODUCTS	U.S. IMPORTS OF STEEL MILL PRODUCTS	APPARENT U.S. CONSUMPTION OF STEEL MILL PRODUCTS*
1995	97.5	7.1	24.4	114.8
1996	100.9	5.0	29.2	125.0
1997	105.9	6.0	31.2	131.0
1998	102.4	5.5	41.5	138.4
1999	106.2	5.4	35.7	136.5
2000	109.1	6.5	38.0	140.5
2001	98.9	6.1	30.1	122.9
2002	100.0	6.0	32.7	126.7
2003	106.0	8.2	23.1	120.9
2004	111.4	7.9	35.8	139.3
2005	105.0	9.4	32.1	127.7

* Apparent U.S. consumption equals total shipments minus exports plus imports.

Source: American Iron and Steel Institute, as reported in Standard & Poor's Industry Surveys.

subsidies. While the U.S. government had not previously applied countervailing duties when authorized to do so, the Commerce Department was currently considering whether to change this practice. DiMicco saw the U.S. government's request for WTO settlement consultations as only a first step toward leveling the playing field for U.S. steel producers; he said:

> This request does not cover the vast majority of the massive domestic subsidies China

provides to its steel industry and other manufacturers. Nor does it address China's gross manipulation of its currency, which provides Chinese exports with a huge advantage in international trade. Free trade is possible only if everyone follows the rules—and China hasn't.[11]

Exhibit 8 shows steel production, steel exports, and steel imports for the U.S. market for 1995–2005. Exhibit 9 shows the value of steel mill shipments by U.S.-based steelmakers

Exhibit 9

Dollar Value of Shipments of Steel Mill Products by U.S.-Based Steelmakers, by Product Category, 2004–2005 ($ in billions)

PRODUCT CATEGORY	2004	2005
Steel ingot and semifinished shapes	$ 4.9	$ 5.7
Hot-rolled sheet and strip, including tin mill products	25.2	24.8
Hot-rolled bars and shapes, plates, structural shapes, and pilings	14.9	17.1
Steel pipe and tube	9.5	10.9
Cold-rolled sheet steel and strip	12.2	13.5
Cold finished steel bars and steel shapes	2.0	2.1
Steel wire	2.3	2.3
All other steel mill products	1.3	1.3
Total	$72.7	$78.3

Source: U.S. Department of Commerce, "Current Industrial Reports, Steel Mill Products, 2005," www.census.gov/mcd (accessed November 2, 2006).

Exhibit 10

Top 20 Countries: Total Steel Production, Steel Exports, and Steel Imports, 2004–2005 (in millions of tons)

RANK	TOTAL STEEL PRODUCTION, 2005		STEEL EXPORTS, 2004		STEEL IMPORTS, 2004	
1	China	385.0	Japan	38.3	China	36.6
2	Japan	124.0	Russia	33.5	United States	36.4
3	United States	104.6	Ukraine	31.1	Germany	21.9
4	Russia	72.8	Germany	30.1	Italy	21.4
5	South Korea	52.7	Belgium	25.9	South Korea	19.5
6	Germany	49.0	China	22.2	France	18.2
7	Ukraine	42.5	France	20.6	Belgium	16.4
8	India	42.0	South Korea	16.5	Taiwan, China	15.1
9	Brazil	34.8	Italy	14.7	Spain	13.0
10	Italy	32.3	Turkey	14.5	Thailand	12.2
11	Turkey	23.1	Brazil	13.2	Canada	10.2
12	France	21.5	Taiwan, China	10.4	United Kingdom	9.6
13	Taiwan, China	20.5	Netherlands	9.9	Turkey	9.0
14	Spain	19.6	United Kingdom	8.6	Iran	8.7
15	Mexico	17.9	United States	8.0	Malaysia	8.3
16	Canada	16.9	Spain	7.1	Netherlands	7.2
17	United Kingdom	14.5	Austria	6.4	Hong Kong	6.9
18	Belgium	11.0	Mexico	6.1	Mexico	6.4
19	South Africa	10.5	India	6.1	Vietnam	6.0
20	Iran	10.4	Canada	6.0	United Arab Emirates	5.1

Source: International Iron and Steel Institute, *World Steel in Figures, 2006,* www.worldsteel.org (accessed November 6, 2006).

for 2004–2005, broken down by product category. Exhibit 10 shows data for the top 20 countries worldwide as concerns total steel production, steel exports, and steel imports; Exhibit 11 shows the 20 largest steel companies worldwide as of 2005.

Steel Production

Steel was produced by either integrated steel facilities or minimills that employed electric arc furnaces. Integrated mills used blast furnaces to produce hot metal typically from iron ore pellets, limestone, scrap steel, oxygen, assorted other metals, and coke. (Coke was produced by firing coal in large coke ovens and was the major fuel used in blast furnaces to produce hot metal.) Hot metal from the blast furnace process was then run through the basic oxygen process to produce liquid steel. To make flat-rolled steel products, liquid steel was either fed into a continuous caster machine and cast into slabs or else cooled in slab form for later processing. Slabs were further shaped or rolled at a plate mill or hot strip mill. In making certain sheet steel products, the hot strip mill process was followed by various finishing processes, including pickling, cold-rolling, annealing, tempering, or galvanizing. These various processes for converting raw steel into finished steel products were often distinct steps undertaken at different times and in different on-site or off-site facilities rather than being done in a continuous process in a single plant facility—an integrated mill was thus one that had multiple facilities at a single plant site and could therefore not only produce crude (or raw) steel but also run the crude steel through various facilities and finishing processes to make hot-rolled and cold-rolled sheet steel products, steel bars and beams, stainless steel, steel wire and nails, steel pipes and tubes, and other finished steel products. The steel produced

Exhibit 11

Top 20 Steel Companies Worldwide, Based on Crude Steel Production, 2005

		CRUDE STEEL PRODUCTION (IN MILLIONS OF TONS)	
2005 RANK	**COMPANY (HEADQUARTERS)**	**2005**	**2004**
1	Mittal Steel* (Netherlands)	69.4	47.2
2	Arcelor* (Luxembourg)	51.5	51.7
3	Nippon Steel (Japan)	35.3	35.7
4	POSCO (South Korea)	33.6	33.3
5	JFE (Japan)	32.9	34.8
6	Baosteel (China)	25.0	23.6
7	U.S. Steel (USA)	21.3	22.9
8	Nucor (USA)	20.3	19.7
9	Corus Group** (Great Britain)	20.1	20.9
10	Riva (Italy)	19.3	18.4
11	ThyssenKrupp (Germany)	18.2	19.4
12	Tangshan (China)	17.7	7.8
13	Evraz (Russia)	15.3	15.1
14	Gerdau (Brazil)	15.1	16.1
15	Severstal (Russia)	15.0	14.1
16	Sumitomo (Japan)	14.9	14.3
17	SAIL (India)	14.8	13.3
18	Wuhan (China)	14.3	10.2
19	Anshan (China)	13.1	12.5
20	Magnitogorsk (Russia)	12.6	12.5

* Mittal Steel and Arcelor merged in 2006.

** Corus Group was acquired by Tata Steel (India) in 2006; Tata Steel was the world's 56th largest producer of steel in 2005.

Source: International Iron and Steel Institute, *World Steel in Figures, 2006,* www.worldsteel.org (accessed November 6, 2006).

by integrated mills tended to be purer than steel produced by electric arc furnaces since less scrap was used in the production process. (Scrap steel often contained nonferrous elements that could adversely affect metallurgical properties.) Some steel customers required purer steel products for their applications.

Minimills used an electric arc furnace to melt steel scrap or scrap substitutes into molten metal, which was then cast into crude steel slabs, billets, or blooms in a continuous casting process; as was the case at integrated mills, the crude steel was then run through various facilities and finishing processes to make hot-rolled and cold-rolled sheet steel products, steel bars and beams, stainless steel, steel wire and nails, steel pipes and tubes, and other finished steel products. Minimills could accommodate short production runs and had relatively fast product

change-over time. Minimills typically were able to produce a narrower range of steel products than integrated producers, and their products tended to be more commodity-like. The electric arc technology employed by minimills offered two primary competitive advantages: capital investment requirements that were 75 percent lower than those of integrated mills and a smaller workforce (which translated into lower labor costs per ton shipped).

Global Steel Industry Trends

Over the past five decades, changes in steelmaking technology had revolutionized the world's steel industry. Up until the 1960s, steel was produced in large-scale plants using capital-intensive basic oxygen blast furnace technology and open hearth furnace technology where steel was made from scratch using iron ore, coke, scrap steel, limestone, and other raw materials—such companies were referred to as integrated producers because the value chains at such plants involved a number of production steps and processes to convert the raw materials into finished steel products. But starting in the 1960s, the advent of electric arc furnace technology spurred new start-up companies to enter the steelmaking business. These new companies, called minimills because their plants produced steel on a much smaller scale than did the integrated mills, used low-cost electric arc furnaces to melt scrap steel and cast the molten metal directly into a variety of steel products at costs substantially below those of integrated steel producers.

Initially, minimills were able to only make low-end steel products (such as reinforcing rods and steel bars) using electric arc furnace technology. But when thin-slab casting technology came on the scene in the 1980s, minimills were able to compete in the market for flat-rolled carbon sheet and strip products; these products sold at substantially higher prices per ton and thus were attractive market segments for minimill companies. Carbon sheet and strip steel products accounted for about 50–60 percent of total steel production and represented the last big market category controlled by the producers employing basic oxygen furnace and blast furnace technologies. Thin-slab casting technology, which had been developed by SMS Schloemann-Siemag AG of Germany, was pioneered in the United States by Nucor at its plants in Indiana and elsewhere. Other minimill companies in the United States and other countries were quick to adopt thin-slab casting technology because the low capital costs of thin-slab casting facilities, often coupled with the lower labor costs per ton, gave minimill companies a cost and pricing advantage over integrated steel producers, enabling them to grab a growing share of the global market for flat-rolled sheet steel and other carbon steel products. Many integrated producers also switched to thin-slab casting as a defensive measure to protect their profit margins and market shares.

By 2005, electric arc furnace technology was being used to produce about 33 percent of the world's steel; basic oxygen furnace technology was used to produce about 65 percent of all steel products. Limited supplies of scrap steel and upward-trending prices for scrap steel were said to be the main factors constraining greater use of electric arc technology across the world. Open hearth technology had largely been abandoned as of 2005 and was used only at plants in Russia, the Ukraine, India, and a few other Eastern European countries. In 2003–2006, about 90 percent of the world's production of steel involved the use of continuous-casting technology.

INDUSTRY CONSOLIDATION In both the United States and across the world, the last two industry downturns had resulted in numerous mergers and acquisitions. Some of the mergers/acquisitions were the result of a financially and managerially strong company seeking to acquire a high-cost or struggling steel company at a bargain price and then pursue cost reduction initiatives to make newly acquired steel mill operations more cost competitive. Other mergers/acquisitions reflected the strategies of growth-minded steel companies looking to expand both their production capacity and their geographic market presence.

In 2006, the world's two largest steel producers, Mittal Steel and Arcelor, both headquartered in Europe but with operations in various parts of the world, merged to form a giant company with total steel production of over 116 million tons (equal to about a 10 percent market share worldwide). Prior to its merger with Arcelor, Mittal Steel in 2005 had acquired International Steel Group, the second largest steel producer in the United States, with 13 major plants in eight states, and Inland Steel, another struggling U.S. steel producer. In 2006, Arcelor Mittal had total production capacity of nearly 125 million tons, annual revenues of $77 billion, earnings of $13.3 billion, plants in 27 countries on five continents (North America, South America, Europe, Asia, and Africa), and 330,000 employees.

Also in 2006, Tata Steel in India acquired Corus Steel (Great Britain), the world's eighth largest steel company; the new company produced over 27 million tons in 2005. Tata Steel was one of the lowest-cost steel producers in the world, with access to low-cost iron ore deposits, and was adding new production capacity at three sites in India, a plant in Iran, and a plant in Bangladesh; Corus was regarded as a relatively high-cost producer but had been profitable in 2004–2005 after posting huge losses in 2000–2003. Corus had a 50 percent share of the steel market in Great Britain and substantial sales in parts of Europe; it was formed in 1999 as the result of a merger between troubled British Steel and Koninklijke Hoogovens, a well-regarded steel company based in the Netherlands.

Jinan Iron and Steel and Laiwu Steel, the 6th and 7th largest steel producers in China and the 23rd and 24th largest producers in the world, merged in October 2006 to form a company with total sales of almost 23 million tons in 2005; the merged company was named Shandong Iron and Steel. Industry observers believed the Jinan-Laiwu merger was an attempt by Chinese steelmakers to better compete with Arcelor Mittal and other foreign rivals.

In the United States, U.S. Steel, headquartered in Pittsburgh, had acquired National Steel in 2003, giving it steelmaking capability of 26.8 million tons annually as of 2006. In 2006, U.S. Steel had 12 steelmaking facilities in the United States, one in Slovakia, and two in Serbia. U.S. Steel had a labor-cost disadvantage versus Nucor and Mittal Steel USA (the U.S.-based operations of Arcelor Mittal), partly due to the lower productivity of its unionized workforce and partly due to its pension costs. While Mittal Steel USA also had a union workforce, it had recently downsized the labor force at some of its plants by close to 75 percent and now operated many of its U.S. plants with a very lean workforce in a manner akin to Nucor. Arcelor Mittal's recent acquisitions of Inland Steel and International Steel Group in the United States had transformed Mittal Steel USA into North America's largest steel producer, with operations in 12 states and annual raw steel production

capability of about 31 million tons. Mittal Steel USA's principal products included a broad range of hot-rolled, cold-rolled, and coated sheets; tin mill products; carbon and alloy plates; wire rod; rail products; and bars and semi-finished shapes to serve the automotive, construction, pipe and tube, appliance, container, and machinery markets. All of these products are available in standard carbon grades as well as high-strength, low-alloy grades for more demanding applications.

Nucor's Chief Domestic Competitors

Consolidation of the industry into a smaller number of larger and more efficient steel producers had heightened competitive pressures for Nucor and most other steelmakers. Nucor had three major rivals headquartered in the United States—Mittal Steel USA, U.S. Steel, and AK Steel. Mittal Steel USA competed only in carbon steel product categories; it had seven integrated mills, three plants that used electric arc furnaces, and four rolling and finishing facilities. About 17,200 of its approximately 20,500 employees were represented by unions. U.S. Steel had mostly integrated steel mills, a unionized workforce, worldwide annual raw steel production capacity of 26.8 million tons, and worldwide raw steel production of 21.2 million tons in 2005. AK Steel had seven steel mills and finishing plants in four states; about 6,300 of its approximately 8,000 employees were represented by unions. It sold much of its output to automotive companies—its two biggest customers were General Motors and Ford. Exhibit 12 presents selected financial and operating data for these three competitors.

In addition to the three major domestic rivals, there were a number of lesser-sized U.S.-based steelmakers with plants that competed directly against Nucor plants. However, Nucor's most formidable competitive threat in the U.S. market consisted of Mittal Steel USA and foreign steelmakers that were intent on exporting some of their production to the United

Exhibit 12

Selected Financial and Operating Data for Nucor's Three Largest U.S.-Based Competitors

COMPANY	2005	2004	2003
Mittal Steel USA			
Net sales	$12,237	$12,174	
Cost of goods sold	10,617	10,315	
Selling, general, and administrative expenses	371	301	
Net income	$ 491	$ 1,286	
Net income as a percent of net sales	4.0%	10.6%	
Shipments of finished steel products (millions of tons)	18.8	21.1	
Raw steel production (millions of tons)	20.0	23.9	
U.S. Steel			
Net sales	$14,039	$13,975	$9,328
Cost of sales	11,601	11,368	8,458
Selling, general, and administrative expenses	698	739	673
Income (loss) from operations	1,439	1,625	(719)
Net income	$ 892	$ 1,117	$ (436)
Net income as a % of net sales	10.3%	8.0%	(4.7)%
Shipments of steel products (millions of tons)	19.7	21.8	19.2
Raw steel production (millions of tons)	21.2	23.0	19.8
Domestic	15.3	17.3	14.9
Foreign	5.9	5.7	4.9
Production as a % of total capability			
Domestic	79.1%	89.0%	90.1%
Foreign	79.5	76.8	87.9
AK Steel Group			
Net sales	$ 5,647.4	$ 5,217.3	$4,041.7
Cost of products sold	4,996.8	4,553.6	3,886.9
Selling and administrative expenses	208.4	206.4	243.6
Operating profit (loss)	113.1	(79.7)	(651.8)
Net income (loss)	$ (2.3)	$ 38.4	$ (560.4)
Operating profit as a % of net sales	2.0%	(1.5)%	6.0%
Net income as a % of net sales	(0.04)%	4.6%	(13.9)%
Shipments of finished steel products (millions of tons)	6.4	6.3	5.8

Source: Company 10-K reports.

States; there were many foreign steel producers that had costs on a par with or even below those of Nucor, although their competitiveness in the U.S. market varied significantly according to the prevailing strength of their local currencies versus the U.S. dollar.

Endnotes

[1] Tom Peters and Nancy Austin, *A Passion for Excellence: The Leadership Difference* (New York: Random House, 1985), and "Other Low-Cost Champions," *Fortune,* June 24, 1985.

[2] According to information posted at www.nucor.com (accessed October 11, 2006).

[3] This discussion is based on information posted at www.nucor.com (accessed October 17, 2006).

[4] Nanette Byrnes, "The Art of Motivation," *BusinessWeek,* May 1, 2006, p. 59.

[5] Ibid., p. 57.

[6] Ibid., p. 60.

[7] Ibid.

[8] Ibid.

[9] Based on information in the STAT-USA database, U.S. Department of Commerce, http://ia.ita.doc.gov/steel/license/SMP/Census/GDESC52/MMT_ALL_ALL_12M.htm (accessed October 27, 2006).

[10] Company press release, February 2, 2007.

[11] Ibid.

Case 8

Competition in Video Game Consoles: Sony, Microsoft, and Nintendo Battle for Supremacy

John E. Gamble
University of South Alabama

About 250 to 300 million people worldwide played video games in 2007. Historically, games were typically played by preteens, teens, and young adults, but by 2005 the average game player age had increased to 33, and 25 percent of gamers were over age 50. In 2000, only 13 percent of gamers were over age 50. In addition to video games appealing to a broader demographic base, gamers were spending more time playing video games. In 2003, the average American was said to spend 75 hours annually playing video games, which was more than double the amount of time spent playing video games in 1997.

More than $35 billion was spent on video game consoles, game software, handheld game devices, mobile games, and online games in 2005. Next-generation consoles launched by Microsoft in November 2005 and by Nintendo and Sony in November 2006 were expected to drive video game–related sales to more than $51 billion by 2010—see Exhibit 1. Sony's PlayStation 3, Microsoft's Xbox 360, and Nintendo's Wii were all equipped with powerful microprocessors, hard drives, Internet connectivity, and high-definition (HD) resolution graphics, giving them new capabilities and visual effects that were expected to spur sufficient interest in video games by traditional gamers and current

nongamers to drive sales of video game consoles from $3.9 billion in 2005 to $5.8 billion in 2010.

In 2007, Nintendo, Sony, and Microsoft were locked into a fierce battle for control of the projected $5.8 billion pie. Each company used differing business models to generate revenues and profits and varying strategies to try to build competitive advantage in the marketplace. With the next-generation battle of video game hardware in full swing in 2007, the early results made it unclear who the eventual winner might be. Microsoft's one-year head start with next-generation technology gave it an installed base of more than 10 million Xbox 360 units by January 2007, while Sony's installed base of PlayStation 3 units stood at just over 2 million units. Nintendo had been able to sell more than 3 million Wii video game consoles between November 2006 and January 2007. Some analysts believed that Microsoft could sustain its first-mover advantage and achieve a market-leading position by 2011. Others were convinced that Sony's 100-million-plus dedicated PlayStation 2 owners would eventually migrate to the PlayStation 3—giving it another 100-million-unit-selling console by 2012. It was unclear how appealing Nintendo's Wii would prove among video game players, but the Wii was the winner of the 2006 holiday season sales battle. In fact, the combined sales of the Wii

Exhibit 1

Size of the Global Video Games Market, by Sector, 2000, 2003, and 2005, with Projections for 2010 ($ in millions)

	2000	2003	2005	2010
Console hardware	$ 4,791	$ 6,047	$ 3,894	$ 5,771
Console software (both sales and rentals)	9,451	16,449	13,055	17,164
Handheld hardware	1,945	1,501	3,855	1,715
Handheld software (both sales and rentals)	2,872	2,238	4,829	3,113
PC software (both sales and rentals)	5,077	3,806	4,313	2,955
Broadband	70	497	1,944	6,352
Interactive TV	81	249	786	3,037
Mobile	65	587	2,572	11,186
Total	$24,352	$31,370	$35,248	$51,292

Source: Informa Telecoms & Media, "Games Market to Score Big in 2007," press release, October 24, 2005, and "Game Industry Boom Continues," press release, July 24, 2003, both at www.informamedia.com (accessed September 8, 2006).

and Nintendo's handheld DS and Game Boy Advance systems allowed Nintendo to account for 55 percent of all video game sales during the 2006 holiday gift-buying season. There was some thought that the Wii's innovative wireless wand controller would prove to be a fad and the battle would ultimately be between Microsoft and Sony. With the next-generation battle already fierce, but only into its first months, there was ample opportunity for additional maneuvering by all three rivals.

History of Video Game Systems

The development of video games began as early as 1947 when engineers working on television projects began to tinker with programs to play simple games using cathode ray tubes. Two noteworthy developments were the creation of Tennis for Two by Brookhaven National Laboratory researcher William A. Higinbotham in 1958 and the invention of Spacewar in 1962 by a trio of Massachusetts Institute of Technology graduate students. Ralph Baer, an engineer at Loral, filed the first patent for a video game in 1968, which led to the development of the Magnavox Odyssey. The Odyssey video game

system, introduced to U.S. consumers in 1972, allowed users to play such games as table tennis, hockey, shooting gallery, and football on their black-and-white televisions. The graphics were limited to white lines, dots, and dashes projected on the picture tube, so Magnavox provided users with color transparencies to place on their TV screens to provide the appropriate background for each game. The Odyssey system sold approximately 350,000 units by 1975.

The introduction of Pong, an arcade game produced by Atari, was another key video game launch that occurred in 1972. Atari developed a Pong system for televisions in 1975, but its 1977 launch of the Atari 2600 was the first home game system to achieve success in the marketplace. The Atari 2600 offered full-color output, sound, and cartridge-based games such as Space Invaders. Atari eventually sold more than 30 million 2600 game systems.

By 1983, consumers had tired of simple arcade-type games and, for all practical purposes, the industry was dying. Nintendo rescued the video game industry in 1985 with its introduction of its Nintendo Entertainment System (NES), which was bundled with the soon-to-be ubiquitous Super Mario Brothers video game. Nintendo sold 61.9 million NES systems before its 1991 introduction of the Super NES.

Nintendo built on the success of the NES with the launch of the Game Boy handheld model, which allowed users to take their games outside the home. Nearly 120 million Game Boy units had been sold by 2001. Nintendo's ability to resurrect the industry with innovative game systems created a competitive, technology-driven industry environment that remained prevalent into 2007. Exhibit 2 presents a brief description of key video game systems along with their launch prices and number of units sold.

Overview of the Global Market for Video Game Consoles

The dramatic increase in the amount of time consumers spent playing video games during the late 1990s and early 2000s was primarily attributable to the improved capabilities of game consoles launched at the turn of the 21st century. The processing capabilities of the Sony PlayStation 2, in particular, allowed game developers to create complex games that were presented at a high screen resolution. Sports games such as NCAA Football, racing games such as Need for Speed, and shooter games like Call of Duty provided game players with high levels of interaction and backgrounds that were surprisingly realistic looking compared to early video game systems.

The sale of game systems and software tended to decline as the installed base grew and consumers had purchased most "must-have" titles. Industry sales slowed considerably between 2003 and 2005 as gamers postponed purchases until the eagerly awaited Xbox 360, PlayStation 3, and Wii became available. With sales of game software, hardware accessories, and online games expected to exceed $50 billion in 2010, spending on video game hardware and software was projected to account for a larger share of U.S. consumers' entertainment dollars than the motion picture industry. In 2005, U.S. sales of video game hardware exceeded $10 billion, while Americans spent approximately $9 billion at movie theater box offices.

Competition Among the Makers of Video Game Consoles

Technological leadership in computing power and graphics rendering were critical competitive capabilities needed in the console segment of the video game industry. However, such capabilities did not guarantee success in the industry. Sega consistently beat Nintendo and Sony to the market with next-generation computing capabilities but was unable to achieve success and eventually withdrew from the console market in 2001. Sonic the Hedgehog had been Sega's only legitimate "hit" game title, which was not enough incentive for gamers to abandon their Nintendo or Sony systems. With Sega's installed base failing to grow, game software developers focused their efforts on Nintendo and Sony. The small number of new game titles becoming available for Sega's systems further compounded its problems in the marketplace. A survey of 16,670 players of video games conducted by the NPD Group found that, for 87 percent of survey respondents, "appealing game titles" was the single most important feature in choosing a game system.[1]

With the availability of intriguing games so important to gaining sales and increasing the installed base of consoles, Nintendo and, to a lesser extent, Microsoft had established internal game development capabilities. In fact, Nintendo's most popular game titles, including Mario Brothers, Pokémon, and Donkey Kong, had been developed by the company's own software development teams. Software operating profit margins that ranged from 35 to 40 percent had been a consistent contributor to Nintendo's profitability. Independent game publishers such as Electronic Arts, Activision, Take Two Interactive, THQ, Square Enix, Capcom, Atari, and Sega paid console makers royalties on each software copy sold. Independent game publishers tended to spend the lion's share, if not all, of game development budgets on new games for video game consoles with a large installed base

Exhibit 2

Selected Information for the Best-Selling Video Game Hardware Systems, 1972–2006

LAUNCH DATE	MANUFACTURER	SYSTEM NAME	LAUNCH PRICE	KEY FEATURES	UNITS SOLD
1972	Magnavox	Odyssey	$100	Black-and-white display, color overlays	350,000
November 1977	Atari	Atari 2600	$200	Color output, sound, cartridge-based games	30 million
October 1985	Nintendo	NES	$199	8-bit processor	61.9 million
August 1989	Sega Enterprises	Sega Genesis	$200	16-bit processor	13 million
August 1989	Nintendo	Game Boy	$109	Handheld system	118.7 million
August 1991	Nintendo	Super NES	$199	16-bit processor	49.1 million
April 1995	Sega Enterprises	Sega Saturn	$399	32-bit processor	1.4 million
September 1995	Sony Computer Entertainment	PlayStation	$299	32-bit processor	102.5 million
September 1996	Nintendo	Nintendo 64	$199	64-bit processor	32.9 million
September 1999	Sega Enterprises	Sega Dreamcast	$199	200 MHz processor, 3D graphics	8.2 million
October 2000	Sony Computer Entertainment	PlayStation 2	$299	294 MHz processor, DVD, backward compatibility with PS One	106.2 million as of December 2006
June 2001	Nintendo	Game Boy Advance	$100	Handheld system, 32-bit processor, 32,000 color video resolution	75.8 million as of December 2006
November 2001	Microsoft	Xbox	$299	733 MHz processor, hard drive, Ethernet port	24 million
November 2001	Nintendo	GameCube	$199	485 MHz processor	20.9 million as of December 2006
November 2004	Nintendo	Nintendo DS/DS Lite	$199	Handheld system, Wi-Fi connection, touchpad	21.3 million as of December 2006
March 2005	Sony	PlayStation Portable	$249	Handheld system, 333 MHz processor, 3D graphics, music and movie playback	20 million as of December 2006
November 2005	Microsoft	Xbox 360	$299–$399	3.2 GHz processor, 500 MHz graphics card, Wi-Fi, 1080p HD resolution, 12x DVD, wireless controllers ($399 version only), 20 GB hard drive ($399 version only)	10.4 million as of December 2006
November 2006	Sony	PlayStation 3	$499–$599	3.2 GHz processor, 550 MHz graphics card, Wi-Fi ($599 version only), 1080p HD resolution, Blu-ray optical drive, wireless controllers, 20 or 60 GB hard drive	1.8 million as of December 2006
November 2006	Nintendo	Wii	$249	729 MHz processor, 243 MHz graphics card, Wi-Fi, 512 MB embedded flash memory, motion sensitive wireless controllers	3.2 million as of December 2006

Source: www.businessweek.com (accessed March 1, 2007).

and continuing sales growth; consequently, there were far fewer games developed for slow-selling video game systems than was the case for the best-selling consoles.

In addition to cooperative relationships with independent game publishers, makers of video game consoles were also required to collaborate with micro processor and graphics accelerator producers to develop next-generation game systems. None of the established console manufacturers had the capability to produce all components needed for the assembly of game consoles—especially technologically advanced core components. In developing the PlayStation 3, Xbox 360, and Wii consoles that were launched in 2005 and 2006, Microsoft, Nintendo, and Sony each allied with IBM in the development of the console microprocessor. In all three cases, IBM and the console maker began with standard PowerPC microprocessor technology but customized the microprocessor to perform the complex calculations needed to run game software. The processing tasks needed to run video game software were much different from the processing tasks executed when running productivity software. All three companies maintained similar relationships with makers of graphics processing units (GPUs) to develop the technological capabilities to display HD-quality graphics and 3D effects. Companies such as Nvidia frequently co-developed graphics chips for more than one of the three console makers.

PC manufacturers also collaborated with micro processor and GPU manufacturers to build computers capable of running 3D and HD video games. AMD's four core, or "brain," microprocessors were developed to perform tasks similar to what the nine-brain PowerPC chip used in the PlayStation 3 could do. Intel released its Core 2 Extreme microprocessor in 2006, which allowed gamers to play processing-intense games on personal computers (PCs). In 2007, AMD was developing an eight-core microprocessor that would allow extreme gamers to simultaneously play the most graphically intense video game, burn a DVD, download an HD movie, and make a Voice over Internet

Protocol (VoIP) telephone call. The Mach V PC marketed by boutique computer maker Falcon Northeast used two gigabytes of memory, an Intel Core 2 Extreme CPU, and a $600 Nvidia 3D GPU to perform such multiple tasks. The Mach V sold for $16,000 and included a 30-inch LCD display and a wireless keyboard and mouse. Dell Inc., the world's leading manufacturer of desktop and laptop computers in 2006, was broadening its product line to include PC models with advanced graphics, wide-screen displays, and multiple processors that greatly enhanced the online gaming experience. Michael Dell believed that Microsoft's new Vista operating system was a great platform for gamers, and Dell Inc. had an advanced technology group working with game developers to explore how to make the PC the best platform for gaming.

Competition in the industry also mandated that game console manufacturers establish relationships with such value chain allies as discounters, electronics retailers, and toy stores. Big-box retailers such as Wal-Mart, Target, Best Buy, Circuit City, Toys "R" Us, and specialty retailers like Gamestop dedicated ample square footage to video game systems, accessories, and software. There was little price competition among retailers in the sale of video game consoles and software. More price competition at the retailer level was found with video game accessories—especially accessories manufactured and marketed by third parties. Sony, Nintendo, or Microsoft accessories tended to sell at comparable price points across retailers.

Changes in the Competitive Landscape

CONSOLE TECHNOLOGY Future generations of game systems would undoubtedly include even more impressive technological capabilities than the next-generation consoles launched in 2005 and 2006. Jen-Hsun Huang, CEO of graphic accelerator maker Nvidia, believed there was ample opportunity for higher levels of photorealism in video games since no console was yet able to deliver the industry's aspirational "Toy Story standard."[2] Huang believed the industry was still "a good solid 10 years away from photorealism" and summarized the industry's innovation focus by commenting:

> In the next several years, we will still just be learning to do the basics of film, like motion, blur, depth of field—all of that stuff alone chews up a lot of graphics processing. We're pretty excited about moving to high-dynamic range where the color system has the fidelity of what we see in real life. The images don't seem realistic yet. Articulating a human form and human animation, the subtleties of humans and nature, are still quite a ways away for us.[3]

ONLINE GAMING   The manner in which video game software would be delivered to gamers was also set for change. The addition of Ethernet ports and Wi-Fi cards to video game consoles, coupled with the increased percentage of homes with broadband access, had given rise to online games. As shown in Exhibit 1, online game-playing via broadband connections was expected to constitute a $6.4 billion market worldwide by 2010, up from $1.9 billion in 2005. However, most online game revenue was expected to come from PC gamers, with only about 25 percent of online game subscription revenues in 2010 coming from games played on consoles. Even though online games were expected to grow dramatically, DFC Intelligence expected that by 2011 less than 25 percent of those owning consoles capable of playing online games would actually subscribe to an online game service.[4]

MOBILE GAMING   Historically, Nintendo's handheld devices had been the dominant leaders in the mobile video game player market segment. The company sold nearly 120 million Game Boy systems between 1989 and 2001. Nintendo introduced the Game Boy Advance in 2001, which was succeeded by the Nintendo DS. Going into 2007, Nintendo had sold more than 75 million Game Boy Advance players, 330 million Game Boy Advance game

cartridges, 21 million Nintendo DS devices, and over 60 million games for Nintendo DS models. Sony entered the handheld/mobile gaming segment in 2005 with its PlayStation Portable (PSP), quickly becoming an important market contender, with worldwide sales approaching 20 million units by year-end 2006. Despite the historical popularity of traditional handheld devices (Game Boy, Nintendo DS, and PSP) for game playing, the market for games software for such devices was expected to be stagnant, with projected sales of only $3.1 billion for gaming software on handheld sets in 2010 versus $4.8 billion in 2005.

However, mobile gaming on cellular phones and other wireless devices was expected to explode from a $2.6 billion market in 2005 to a $11.2 billion market in 2010 (see Exhibit 1). In the fall of 2006, Apple announced that it was launching video games for its fifth-generation iPod models, with the games being downloadable directly from Apple's iTunes store. (Buyers of these iPod models could also download over 75 movies and 220 TV shows from iTunes.)

Mobile gaming was a fast-developing market segment because advancing technology made it possible to incorporate high-resolution color displays, greater processing power, and improved audio capabilities on cellular handsets, iPods and other brands of MP3 players, and other sophisticated handheld devices (including those designed just for playing video games). There were over 1.5 billion cell phones in active operation across the world (about 35 percent of which were game enabled), and new models with enhanced game-playing capability were selling briskly—most cell phone users, intrigued by the new features of next-generation models, upgraded their phones every few years. While playing video games on handheld devices had historically been a favorite pastime of preteens and teenagers, the popularity of game-capable cell phones, iPods, and other sophisticated handheld devices was expected to spur increases in mobile gaming among the young adult population worldwide in the years ahead.

The Three Main Contenders in Video Game Consoles: Microsoft, Sony, and Nintendo

In 2007, there were only six leading video game consoles that had enough global market visibility and appeal to generate large-volume sales of new units: Microsoft's Xbox 360; Sony's Play-Station 3 and handheld PSP; and Nintendo's Wii, Game Boy Advance, and DS/DS Lite. The makers of all the other game consoles were niche players for the most part. And, significantly, Microsoft, Sony, and Nintendo each had a differing history in the video game industry and differing competitive approaches.

Microsoft

In the 30 years since its founding in 1976, Microsoft had become the most important software company in the world through the development and sale of such omnipresent software packages as Windows, Word, Excel, Power-Point, and Internet Explorer. In 2006, Microsoft's software business, software consulting services business, online MSN service, and entertainment and devices division contributed to total revenues of $44.3 billion and net earnings of $12.6 billion. Microsoft spent almost 15 percent of its revenues on research and development activities in 2006 to ensure its future products offered levels of innovation and functionality necessary to sustain its advantage in the technology sector.

MICROSOFT'S HOME AND ENTERTAINMENT DIVISION Microsoft entered the video console industry in November 2001 with the introduction of the Xbox system, which was the industry's most technologically advanced game console until the November 2005 launch of the Xbox 360. The original Xbox sold 24 million units by 2006. The company's home and entertainment division included the Xbox 360 business and other such products and services as Xbox Live, video game software, Encarta learning products, PC keyboards and

mice, and Internet Protocol Television (IPTV). Microsoft's IPTV venture sought to change the delivery of television programming such that viewers could use broadband access and their home computers (or an Xbox 360) to watch TV broadcasts, on-demand programming, or archived episodes of classic TV series.

Revenues and operating losses for the division between 2004 and 2006 are shown in the following table:

	2006	2005	2004
Revenue (in millions)	$ 4,256	$3,140	$ 2,737
Operating Loss (in millions)	$(1,262)	$ (485)	$(1,337)

Source: Microsoft 2006 annual report.

Revenue increases in 2006 were a result of the sale of 5 million Xbox 360 consoles during fiscal 2006, the popularity of Microsoft PC game titles such as Age of Empires III, and an increase in revenues from IPTV. The division's operating loss in 2006 was largely the result of a $1.64 billion increase in costs related to Xbox 360 production and the development of Halo 2. The division's relatively small operating loss in 2005 resulted from declining Xbox production costs and an increase in the sale of high-margin video games for the Xbox. Microsoft discontinued the sale of Xbox units once the Xbox 360 was in production and Xbox inventory was cleared. The company expected the division's operating loss in future years to decline as Xbox 360 production costs became lower and as the volume of video game software for the Xbox 360 increased.

THE XBOX 360 Microsoft contracted its manufacturing activities for its game consoles and video game disks to third parties in Asia. The company had multiple sources for the commodity-like components used in the production of the Xbox 360, but it used single sources for core components. The company purchased all microprocessors from IBM, all GPUs from Taiwan Semiconductor Manufacturing Company, and all memory chips from

NEC Corporation. Microsoft expected the life cycle for the Xbox 360 to reach five to seven years.

Upon its release, video game industry analysts were quite satisfied with the Xbox 360's capabilities. The Xbox 360's HD graphics impressed many, as did its ease of use. Reviewers were also very pleased with game titles that accompanied the Xbox 360 launch and Microsoft's Xbox Live Arcade games, which could be played over the Internet. Analysts were particularly struck by Xbox 360 games that had been co-developed by Microsoft Game Studios and proven Hollywood screenwriters, directors, and producers. A full list of Xbox 360 features is presented in Exhibit 3.

The November 2005 Xbox 360 launch came one year earlier than the release of next-generation consoles by Sony and Nintendo. The one-year lead in technology gave Microsoft a temporary advantage in building Xbox's installed base and variety of video games. By year-end 2006, more than 160 game titles were available for the Xbox 360. With more than 5 million Xbox 360s installed prior to the launch of the PlayStation 3 or Wii, third-party game developers had little choice but to develop games for the Xbox 360. Gamers were unlikely to buy new software for current-generation consoles once they began to anticipate the launch of a new-generation system. With the exception of annually updated games like Tiger Woods 2007, there was little point in developing new games for the PlayStation 2 or GameCube in 2005 and 2006.

XBOX LIVE Microsoft's one-year head start in making its next-generation console available also helped it build traffic to its Xbox Live Web site. Xbox Live provided Xbox users having broadband access the capability to play online games, chat, watch game trailers, demo new game titles, maintain a profile, participate in forums, download television programming and movies, and access massively multiplayer online games (MMOGs). Xbox Live generated revenue from advertising, subscription fees to its premium-level Xbox Live Gold, movie

and television program download fees, and download fees charged to Xbox Silver members. Counting the complimentary Xbox Silver memberships, Xbox Live had approximately 6 million registered users by March 2007. The company found that approximately 25 percent of Xbox Silver members purchased the full version of free demo versions of new games.

In late 2006, Microsoft was testing a cross-platform version of Xbox Live called Xbox Live Anywhere that would allow users to play Xbox games from Xbox consoles, cell phones, handheld systems, or PCs. Some industry analysts believed that revenue gains from a cross-platform online gaming site would be limited since surveys had shown that only 18 percent of all gamers play games on consoles, cell phones, handheld systems, and PCs. Of that 18 percent, only 31 percent were interested in cross-platform play. However, 40 percent of gamers who regularly played games on both PCs and console systems were highly interested in cross-platform play.[5] As of March 2007, Microsoft had not made a formal announcement about its plans for Xbox Live Anywhere. Even if Microsoft did not go forward with a launch of Xbox Live Anywhere, PC users using Microsoft's Vista operating system would be able to connect to Xbox Live to play video games.

The addition of downloadable television programs and motion pictures to Xbox Live had the potential to change how Xbox 360 consoles were used. Xbox 360 owners could download TV shows and movies onto their hard drives from Xbox Live's 1,000-hour library of programming for on-demand viewing at a later time. Xbox Live offered movie downloads from Paramount, Lionsgate, and Warner Bros., as well as selected television programming from all major networks and cable channels. Programming pricing was based on usage of points purchased online at Xbox Live or through Xbox 360 retailers. In March 2007, a 1,000-point card sold for $12.50, while a 1,600-point card sold for $19.50. The price of a standard-definition television program download was 160 points. HD programs sold for 240 points. Microsoft charged Xbox Live users 320 points

Exhibit 3

Comparative Features of Microsoft Xbox 360, Sony PlayStation 3, and Nintendo Wii

	XBOX 360	PLAYSTATION 3	WII
U.S. launch date	May 12, 2005	November 17, 2006	November 19, 2006
Price	$299—core system	$499—20 GB version	$249
	$399—premium system	$599—60 GB version	
Microprocessor	3.2 GHz IBM PowerPC	3.2 GHz IBM PowerPC	729 MHz IBM PowerPC
Graphics processor	ATI 500 MHz	RSX 550 MHz	ATI 243 MHz
Video resolution	720p, 1080i, 1080p	480i, 480p, 720p, 1080i, 1080p	480p
System memory	512 MB (shared with video)	256 MB dedicated	64 MB (shared with video)
Video memory	512 MB (shared with system)	256 MB dedicated	64 MB (shared with system)
Optical drive	12x DVD; optional HD-DVD priced at $199	Blu-ray HD	DVD available on models produced after late 2007
Storage/hard drive	64 MB memory card with core system; 20 GB hard drive with premium system	20 GB or 60 GB hard drive	512 MB embedded flash memory
Ethernet port	Yes	Yes	Optional Ethernet adapter priced at $29
Wireless networking	Wi-Fi	Wi-Fi available on 60 GB version only	Wi-Fi
Controllers	Wired controller with core system; wireless with premium system	Bluetooth wireless controller w/limited motion-sensing capabilities	Bluetooth wireless, full motion-sensing controller
Online services	Free Xbox Live Silver service including online gaming and voice chat and text messaging; Premium Xbox Live service at $49/year; downloadable full-length movies and television programming starting at $2 per download	Web browser; free PlayStation online gaming Network service providing game demos and game add-ons; online Sony store	Wii Network includes online shopping, weather, news, Web browsing, and e-mail, instant messaging
Game prices	$40–$60	$50–$60	$30–$50
Compatibility with previous generations	Compatible with approximately 300 Xbox titles	Compatible with most PlayStation 2 and PlayStation titles	Compatible with all GameCube titles; online access to titles originally released for Nintendo 64, SNES, NES, Sega Genesis, and TurboGrafx consoles

Sources: Product information published at www.gamestop.com, www.circuitcity.com, www.amazon.com, www.maxconsole.com, www.zdnet.com, and www.biz.gamedaily.com.

for standard-definition movie downloads and 360 points for downloads of HD movies.

The Xbox 360's 20-gigabyte hard drive could store 16 hours of standard definition programs or about 4½ hours of HD programming. Users who deleted programs to free hard drive space were allowed to download previously purchased programs at no charge. Standard-definition programming could be downloaded in minutes, while an HD movie might take hours to download. Even though HD downloads were lengthy, Xbox Live was the only HD programming download service available for televisions in March 2007. Movies downloaded to PCs could be watched only on a PC monitor. Peter Moore, a Microsoft vice president, explained to *The Wall Street Journal* that gaming was the primary selling point for the Xbox 360, but "we look at the console as an entertainment amplifier for the living room."[6]

MARKETING   Microsoft used a variety of approaches to market the Xbox 360 and Xbox Live to consumers. The company supported the Xbox 360 with a $150 million ad campaign in fiscal 2007 and regularly entered into promotions to increase awareness of the Xbox 360. In 2006, Microsoft and Burger King agreed to a promotion that made Xbox 360 games available for purchase in Burger King restaurants. Microsoft also established a promotion with the Kellogg Company that placed Xbox-branded green fruit roll-ups on store shelves. In addition, Microsoft provided co-op advertising with its retail partners. During late 2006, Sears ran TV ads that showed a young boy dreaming about playing Xbox 360 games.

Microsoft had also developed highly innovative viral marketing campaigns for the Xbox 360 and its game titles. Viral marketing had proved to be important with gamers since many young consumers did not respond to, and even resented, traditional advertising. One such campaign involved Perfect Dark Zero, an Xbox Live game that relied on users sending links to friends asking them to join in to expand its subscriber base. The viral marketing campaign for Viva Piñata was highly sophisticated. Viva

Piñata was Microsoft's attempt at developing a game that might have the same level of appeal with young children that was achieved by Nintendo's Super Mario Brothers and Donkey Kong. The campaign included a new Saturday-morning cartoon based on Viva Piñata characters that aired on Fox Television and a line of electronic action figures produced by Playmates Toys. The Viva Piñata toy could interact with Xbox Live by allowing users to download and upload "special powers" that added to the experience of playing with the toy or playing the video game.

XBOX 360'S EARLY LEAD   Some analysts believed that Microsoft had developed a first-mover advantage by beating Nintendo and Sony to market with next-generation technology by a year. In an interview with *BusinessWeek* prior to the launch of the PlayStation 3 and Wii, Kevin Bachus, the former Microsoft executive who originally proposed the Xbox idea to Bill Gates, stated:

> [The] 360 still has a chance of winning the next-gen battle, but it's far from a certainty. If our industry's brief history has taught us anything it's that there are no set "laws" regarding console adoption—despite what the manufacturers might claim. This generation will be decided not on production capabilities or technology, but on brand, price, and content. If Sony can leverage its brand, aggressively cut prices on both hardware and software, and deliver just a few platform-driving franchises as they've done in the past with Final Fantasy, Grand Theft Auto, and others, they can quickly reverse Microsoft's early lead.[7]

By year-end 2006, Microsoft had sold more than 10.4 million Xbox 360 units, with more than 1.1 million units selling in December alone. By comparison, Sony sold 491,000 PlayStation 3 units in December 2006, while Nintendo sold 604,000 Wii systems. Microsoft expected to sell an additional 2 million units during the first six months of 2007. Microsoft was using its early sales lead to reduce production costs and increase accessories sales to speed profitability.

In fact, by November 2006, it was estimated that Microsoft's production costs for the Xbox 360 had fallen to $306 per unit. Microsoft executives expected for the company's entertainment and devices division to become profitable by fiscal 2008. An NPD Group analyst believed that "Xbox is now poised to really take advantage of its lead in this generation's race, provided they (and third-party supporters) keep bringing the games to market that keep consumers wanting to play on that system."[8]

Sony

The Sony Corporation was the world's leading manufacturer and marketer of audio, video, communications, and information technology products, with fiscal 2006 revenues of $64 billion. Sony's video game business contributed $7.8 billion to the company's 2006 total revenues and had generated as much as two-thirds of Sony's total operating profits in past years. However, Sony was confronted with a number of challenges in 2006 and 2007. The company had been unable to capitalize on the exploding growth in digital audio players, was losing market share in the liquid crystal display (LCD) flat-panel TV market, and expected its profits to fall by about 40 percent during fiscal 2007 because of an extensive laptop battery recall and excessive PlayStation 3 development costs and production problems.

SONY'S PLAYSTATION AND PLAYSTATION 2 Introduced in 1995, the Sony PlayStation was an instant success, selling more than 100,000 units in North America during its first weekend on store shelves. By the PlayStation's six-month anniversary, more than 1 million units had been sold in North America and the company hit the 4 million mark in North America in just over two years. The PlayStation's cutting-edge graphics, CD optical drive, 32-bit processor, and variety of game titles made it much more appealing to adolescents and young adults than Nintendo's Super NES system. Over 100 million PlayStation consoles were eventually sold, which was more than twice the number of Nintendo SNES units sold. By 2001, one in three U.S. households had purchased a PlayStation game console.

Nintendo launched its 64-bit Nintendo 64 console a year after the PlayStation was introduced, but it failed to take a considerable number of sales away from the PlayStation because of Nintendo's limited game categories. While Sony's third-party game developers were creating games that would be appealing to preteens, teenagers, and young adults, Nintendo's game development focus was on smaller children. Because Sony targeted older gamers, it was able to add features to the PlayStation 2 (PS2) that might be difficult for young children to operate. The PS2 was able to play DVDs and could be connected to the Internet with an Ethernet adaptor. The $299 PS2 was powered by a 294-megahertz microprocessor, which was the most powerful game processor until the introduction of the Xbox.

As with the PlayStation, Sony's third-party game developers took advantage of the massive installed base and directed their resources toward developing blockbuster game titles for Sony consoles. Third-party-developed games like Gran Turismo, Final Fantasy, Grand Theft Auto, Madden NFL, Medal of Honor, and Need for Speed were games likely to be found in most game collections. The Sony PS2 was also backward compatible with the game titles that had made the PlayStation a marketplace success. The combination of technological superiority and large number of hit game titles allowed Sony to sell more than 100 million PS2 consoles and achieve a 70 percent worldwide market share in game consoles. Even though Sony introduced the PlayStation 3 in November 2006, it planned to continue producing the PS2. Sony lowered the retail price of the PS2 to $129 in the United States once it began shipping PlayStation 3 consoles.

THE SONY PSP In 2005, Sony challenged Nintendo's dominance in handheld systems with the introduction of the $249 PlayStation Portable (PSP). The PSP used a 333-megahertz microprocessor and a 4.3-inch LCD screen to allow gamers to play 3D games, watch television programs recorded with TiVo, connect to wireless Internet networks, review pictures from digital cameras, listen to MP3s, and watch full-length movies that were available on Universal Media Disc (UMD) minidisks. In addition, up to 16 PSP players in close proximity could connect wirelessly to play multiplayer games. The PSP achieved the status of top-selling hand-held game in the United States shortly after its release, but users complained that PSP games were "just rehashes of what you would play on the console."[9] Sony had sold more than 20 million PSP handheld systems by December 2006.

SONY PLAYSTATION 3   Sony hoped to replicate the success of the PlayStation 2 by following a similar strategy with the PlayStation 3. The PlayStation 3 (PS3) was packed with technological features that would allow game developers to create 3D and HD game titles that could exploit the processing power of its 3.2-gigahertz nine-brain processor and Nvidia GPU. (A full list of PlayStation 3 features is presented in Exhibit 3.) The PS3 also had the opportunity to become the central component of a home entertainment system since it included a state-of-the-art Blu-ray HD optical drive and Internet connectivity. Blu-ray was a next-generation DVD drive developed by Sony that could show movies in HD resolution. At the time of the PS3 launch, Sony was in a battle with Toshiba, which had developed a competing HD-DVD player, to become the video disk platform of the future. Clearly, the industry could support only one type of HD disk player. Sony's expectation was that its massive installed base would migrate to the PS3—making it the dominant design in video game consoles and making its Blu-ray drive the industry standard for HD disks.

One of the few flaws evident in Sony's strategy in the first months after the November 2006 launch of the PS3 was the pricing of the console. The PS3 sold at either $499 or $599, depending on hard drive size. Sony's production cost for the PS3 was estimated at $805 for the 20-gigabyte version and $840 for the 60-gigabyte version. The company justified its PS3 pricing by noting the retail price of a Blu-ray player was $1,000. Sony hoped consumers would make the determination that purchasing a PS3 was at least $400 less expensive than purchasing a Blu-ray player and that they would get all of the video game capabilities of the PS3 as an added bonus. Analysts believed that Sony might lose as much as $2 billion on the PS3 in fiscal 2007, but could begin to achieve break-even on its production costs once about 20 million PS3 units had been sold.

In some ways, the November 2006 launch of the PS3 was a deviation from Sony's intended strategy. Sony had not planned to launch the PS3 when it did, but it was forced into an early launch date because of the November 2005 launch of the Xbox 360 by Microsoft. The PS3 was designed to be backward compatible with more than 16,000 PlayStation and PS2 game titles, but the launch of the system was accompanied by only 24 PS3 game titles. The PS3 had tremendous graphics and processing capabilities, but all of this was not needed to play PS2 games. A PlayStation or PS2 video game was not going to look any better played on a PS3. In addition, the 24 HD games that accompanied the launch did not fully utilize the capabilities of the PS3 since third-party software developers had been forced to shorten their planned development times. Whether or not a consumer owned an HDTV was another consideration that would have to be made before upgrading to a PS3.

Sony was barely able to get the PS3 to market in time for 2006 holiday shopping because of a variety of production problems. Some of its production problems centered on the use of the Blu-ray optical drive. An initial holdup involved the development of copy-protection technology for the Blu-ray drive, which was followed by a problem producing the laser component needed in the assembly of Blu-ray drives. Production problems also affected the PS3's backward compatibility capacity, with many PS2 game titles not working on the PS3 when it was first launched. The cumulative effect of Sony's supply chain and production problems allowed it to ship only an estimated 125,000 to 175,000 units for its North American launch. The company had planned to support the launch with 400,000 units. Sony was eventually able to ship nearly 500,000 units before the 2006 holiday season ended. However, the production problems continued into 2007, with Sony delaying its European launch of the PS3 until March 2007. Sony expected that 30 PS3 game titles would be available by its European launch.

Another factor that might hinder the sales of PS3 units for some time was the tremendous video game development costs necessary to produce games that could fully utilize the console's capabilities. Even with the PS2, game development costs typically ran $2 to $7 million. Game developers were willing to make such an investment to develop games for the PS2 since a hit could easily sell 5 to 10 million units at $50 per unit. Analysts had projected that game development costs for the PS3 would average $20 million, with some titles requiring much higher investments. Game developers willing to make such an investment based on the PS3's modest installed base of just over 2 million units in early 2007 were taking a huge risk. The president and CEO of game developer THQ commented in November 2006: "Using a crack development team to only sell a few hundred thousand units is not a good use of resources."[10]

With new game titles arriving to the market slowly, Sony could not rely on its PlayStation Network to satisfy the gaming expectations of consumers. Most video game industry analysts found the site's online games to be very limited and no match for Xbox Live. However, the PlayStation Network did offer users free access to a limited number of multiplayer online games and text, voice, and video chat. The combination of the PS3's high price, limited game titles, limited production, and uninspiring online experience made the PS2 its strongest competing game console during late 2006 and early 2007. During the 2006 holiday season, 1.4 million PS2s were sold in the United States, compared to 1.1 million Xbox 360s, 604,000 Nintendo Wii consoles, and 491,000 PS3 systems. Analysts expected that

Sony would sell 11 million PS2s in 2007 and the PS2 would continue to outsell the PS3 through 2008. Even given its problems, the Sony PS3 hit the 2 million sales mark in fewer months than the PlayStation or the PlayStation 2.

Nintendo

The playing card manufacturer founded in 1889 in Kyoto, Japan, eventually became known as the Nintendo Company Ltd. in 1963 when it expanded outside playing cards to other types of games. The company had produced electronic toys as early as 1970, but its 1981 introduction of a coin-operated video game called Donkey Kong transformed the company into a household name in North America, Asia, and Europe. By 2007, Nintendo had sold more than 387 million game consoles and 2.2 billion video games worldwide. In the United States, one in four households had a Nintendo game system of one generation or another.

In fiscal 2006, Nintendo recorded revenues of $4.3 billion and earned profits of $840 million through the sale of Nintendo game systems and video game software. The company projected fiscal 2007 revenues and earnings of $7.6 billion and $1.0 billion, respectively.

NINTENDO'S STRATEGY   With the company's business limited to the sale of game consoles, handheld game systems, and game software, the company pursued a different strategic approach than that used by Sony and Microsoft. The company focused on earning profits from the sale of game consoles as well as from game software sales. A company senior vice president commented, "We don't have other sister divisions that can underwrite big losses in our area. So we have to be able to get to breakeven, or profitability pretty quickly on the hardware and then the software-tie ratio becomes the icing on that."[11]

Based on that business model, Nintendo had never held a technological advantage in the industry and didn't attempt to battle Sony and Microsoft for the allegiance of hardcore gamers. It had succeeded by developing game systems that were intuitive and easy to operate. Its video games were fun to play but didn't offer a cinematic experience. Nintendo's strategy was well matched to the interests of children and casual gamers. Nintendo's president, Satoru Iwata, explained in the company's annual report, "Nintendo has implemented a strategy which encourages people around the world to play video games regardless of their age, gender or cultural background. Our goal is to expand the gaming population."[12]

THE NINTENDO GAMECUBE At the time of the November 2001 launch of the GameCube system, its processing capabilities were nearly twice as great as that of the PS2 but far less than what the Xbox was capable of performing. The middle-path strategy did not give consumers much of a reason to get excited about the GameCube, since those wanting cutting-edge graphics might find the Xbox appealing and those enamored with PlayStation's action games were still quite pleased with their PS2s. With no clear point of differentiation, the GameCube was Nintendo's least successful game console in its history—selling just over 20 million units by year-end 2006. Even though the GameCube's successor, the Wii, was introduced in November 2006, the company retained the GameCube in its product line for especially price-sensitive buyers. The GameCube's retail price in early 2007 was $99.99.

GAME BOY ADVANCE AND DS/DS LITE Few in the video game industry anticipated the runaway success of Nintendo's Game Boy handheld system when it was introduced in 1989. Nintendo paired the Game Boy with its new Pokémon video game in 1996, which was accompanied by an animated series and a line of trading cards. With the help of Pokémon, the low-screen-resolution Game Boy player sold nearly 120 million units. Even though the Game Boy had a life cycle of more than a decade, Nintendo kept its appearance fresh by making the handheld game in different colors and eventually adding a color display. Such cosmetic changes to handheld games were critical to

sustaining sales since many children thought of the Game Boy as a fashion accessory.

Nintendo's next-generation successor to the Game Boy was the Game Boy Advance. The Game Boy Advance allowed users to play Pokémon and other games on a larger, higher-resolution screen. Nintendo had sold more than 75 million Game Boy Advance units between its June 2001 launch and December 2006. Even though Nintendo launched the DS (a newer-generation handheld system) in November 2004, it continued to offer the Game Boy Advance through 2007 as a low-priced ($79.99) alternative to the Nintendo DS.

The Nintendo DS was developed to appeal to Nintendo's core youth market as well as to such historically nongamers as women and those over age 35. The system included dual screens, a stylus-operated touchpad, voice recognition, and Wi-Fi capabilities to make operation of the system intuitive rather than an exercise in dexterity. The company developed innovative new games for the DS that would appeal to those who were uninterested in first-person shooters or other genres preferred by the PlayStation aficionados. Nintendo DS games such as Nintendogs, which allowed gamers to play with a virtual pet, and Brain Training for Adults, which asked gamers to solve arithmetic puzzles, weren't very popular with 18- to 30-year-old males, but they were a huge hit with people who had never before shown an interest in video games. Nintendo planned to introduce 20 new game titles during the first quarter of 2007 to appeal to the interests of new gamers and children.

The retail price of the DS was also an aspect of Nintendo's handheld systems attractive to casual gamers. In March 2007, the retail price of the Nintendo DS Lite was $129.99, compared to a retail price of $199.99 for the Sony PSP. The DS Lite was a slightly smaller and more brightly lit successor to the DS. The Nintendo DS Lite had been the top-selling video game system during the 2006 holiday shopping period, with more than 1 million units sold in November alone. In addition, more than 641,000 Game Boy Advance systems were sold in November 2006, which made it the number three best-selling system during the month. The PS2 was the best-selling console and second best-selling system overall, with 664,000 units sold during November 2006.

THE WII Nintendo followed its game plan used with the Nintendo DS in developing the Wii. As with the DS, Nintendo attempted to develop a game system that would appeal to nongamers—especially moms. Shigeru Miyamoto, a key Wii developer, explained this key consideration to *BusinessWeek* writers in 2006:

> Our goal was to come up with a machine that moms would want—easy to use, quick to start up, not a huge energy drain, and quiet while it was running. Rather than just picking new technology, we thought seriously about what a game console should be. [CEO Satoru] Iwata wanted a console that would play every Nintendo game ever made. Moms would hate it if they had to have several consoles lying around.[13]

His colleague on the development team, Ken'ichiro Ashida, added, "We didn't want wires all over the place, which might anger moms because of the mess."[14]

The development team considered a variety of controller types that could be wireless and intuitive. Nintendo rejected such design inspirations as cell phones, car navigation remotes, and touch panels for a wireless wand. The wand took over one year to develop and was able to respond to hand motions that were used in throwing a ball, casting a fishing line, swinging a baseball bat, or pointing a gun. A separate "nunchuk" device allowed the user to create motion necessary to play games needing two hands. A Wedbush Morgan Securities analyst commented on the brilliance of the design by pointing out, "With the Wii remote, the learning curve for most games is 15 minutes or less. I think that will eliminate the intimidation factor and will attract a broader audience."[15]

Although Nintendo executives knew early during the development of the Wii that it would be unable to compete with the next-generation consoles soon to be launched by Microsoft and Sony, they believed the wireless wand controller would have appeal with the masses. Reggie Fils-Aime, the president of Nintendo of America explained:

> What makes the Wii so special is obviously the Wii Remote: the ability to play tennis with a flick of the wrist, to play baseball like you do it on the ball field. That allows the consumer to get more in the game by having a totally different type of interface, plus it allows game developers to create all new different types of games. We have everything from a game like "Trauma Center" from Atlas, where you're the doctor, and you're using the precision of the Wii remote to stitch up a patient and take shards of glass out of their arm—things of that nature. The new way to play "Madden Football," a brand new Madden where you act like the quarterback, where you hike the ball, pass. All of that allows for totally unique game play.[16]

Another consideration was creating a game console that would easily fit within the family budget. Miyamoto explained, "Originally, I wanted a machine that would cost $100. My idea was to spend nothing on the console technology so all the money could be spent on improving the interface and software."[17] As a result, Nintendo wound up using a microprocessor that, although twice as fast as that used in the GameCube, was less powerful than what Microsoft had used in the original Xbox. Also, the Wii contained only a 512 MB flash memory card to store data instead of a hard drive and could not play DVDs. The Wii could connect to the Internet through a wireless home network, but not with an Ethernet cable. A full list of Wii features is presented in Exhibit 3. Analysts believed that, at launch, Nintendo would earn a profit on every Wii console sold because of its modest components' costs.

One additional benefit of Nintendo's low-tech approach to a next-generation console was the low relative development costs needed for Wii video games. Analysts expected that on average the development cost for a Wii video game would be less than half of that necessary to develop games for the Xbox 360 or PS3. As a result, game developers were very interested in creating new games for the Wii. Electronic Arts announced six Nintendo Wii titles during a July 2006 industry trade show, while it said little of its plans for new PS3 games. A video game analyst believed developers saw more opportunity for immediate profits from Wii games than those for PS3 and were "holding off on creating games for Sony" until its installed base grew.[18] In addition to new games, Wii users could also access all older games on Nintendo's Wii Connect24 online gaming site. Wii Connect24 also offered a weather channel, news channel, shopping channel, and Web browser. The Wii console also allowed users to view digital pictures stored on an SD memory card and create personalized Wii interfaces for each member of the family.

The Winner of the Battle for Supremacy: Sony or Microsoft or Nintendo?

In early 2007, there were varying opinions about which company would end up as the market leader in video game consoles in 2010—Sony or Microsoft or Nintendo. During the 2006 holiday season, Nintendo had done surprisingly well, capturing a 55 percent market share based on the combined unit sales of the Wii, DS, DS Lite, and Game Boy Advance. In addition, Nintendo sold more than 1.5 million extra controllers for the Wii during the holidays. Buyers of Wii consoles during November–December 2006 purchased, on average, three video game titles for the Wii. Even so, some observers contended that Microsoft had been the winner of

the 2006 holiday season since sales of the Xbox 360 exceeded sales of either the PlayStation 3 or the Wii (although only limited supplies of the PS3 and Wii were available during that period since their production was still in the startup phase). By year-end 2006, Microsoft had sold over 10 million units of the Xbox 360, giving it a sizable lead over the PS3 and the Wii in terms of total users.

But whether Microsoft's first-to-market strategy would translate into a sustainable first-mover advantage was debatable. Microsoft had more than 160 game titles available for the Xbox 360, compared to fewer than 30 for the PS3— but a wave of new games for both the PS3 and the Wii were coming to market in 2007. The Wii was no match for the Xbox 360's HD video resolution, but there were indications that its innovative controller had big appeal to a number of ardent game players. There were also analysts who believed that once Sony opted to lower the price of the PS3 (if indeed Sony management did decide to be more price-competitive), it would replicate the success it had achieved with the PlayStation and PS2. Market research firm Strategy Analytics had forecast that Sony would sell more than 100 million PS3 units by 2012, while Microsoft would sell approximately 60 million Xbox 360s and Nintendo would sell a meager 20–25 million Wii consoles. Merrill Lynch analysts foresaw a much closer contest, forecasting that Microsoft would achieve a 39 percent market share of the video console market by 2011, with Sony at a 34 percent share and Nintendo at 27 percent. According to one analyst, "There will always be a short-term winner, but there's definitely room in the long run for all three."[19]

Endnotes

1 "Report from The NPD Group Provides Insight into Consumer Purchase Intent of Next Generation Video Game Consoles," *Business Wire*, November 13, 2006.

2 As quoted in "Nvidia CEO Talks Console War," *BusinessWeek* (online), July 26, 2006.

3 Ibid.

4 "Console Makers Online and on Top," *BusinessWeek* (online), April 5, 2006.

5 As described in "Microsoft Plays It Cool on Games," *BusinessWeek* (online), September 28, 2006.

6 As quoted in "Coming to Xbox 360: Films and TV," *The Wall Street Journal* (online), November 7, 2006, p. B3.

7 As quoted in "Kevin Bachus on Next-Gen Console Wars," *BusinessWeek* (online), April 17, 2006.

8 As quoted in "Report: Sony Sold 490,700 PS3s in U.S.," *AFX International Focus*, January 13, 2007.

[9] As quoted in "In the Game Wars, Nintendo's All Charged Up," *BusinessWeek* (online), July 28, 2006.

[10] As quoted in "Mysteries of the PS3 and Wii Launch Solved!" *CNNMoney* (online), November 9, 2007.

[11] As quoted in "Nintendo Wii Enters Video Game Fray," *Investor's Business Daily,* November 20, 2006, p. A4.

[12] As quoted in Nintendo's 2006 annual report.

[13] As quoted in "The Big Ideas behind Nintendo's Wii," *BusinessWeek* (online), November 16, 2006.

[14] Ibid.

[15] As quoted in "Nintendo Brings the Games to the People," *BusinessWeek* (online), October 31, 2006.

[16] As quoted in "Nintendo's U.S. Head: We're Doing Things Right with the New Console," Associated Press State & Local Wire, November 17, 2006.

[17] As quoted in "The Big Ideas behind Nintendo's Wii."

[18] As quoted in "Will Sony's Pricey PS3 Pay Off?" *BusinessWeek* (online), July 20, 2006.

[19] As quoted in "PS3, Wii Get All the Buzz, but Xbox Could Have the Happiest Holidays," *Advertising Age,* October 30, 2006, p. 3.

Case 9

+CASE TUTOR

Electronic Arts in 2007: Can It Retain Its Global Lead in Video Game Software?

Arthur A. Thompson Jr.
The University of Alabama

With fiscal 2007 sales of $3.1 billion, Electronic Arts (EA) was the world's leading independent developer, publisher, and marketer of video games. It developed games for play on all the leading home video game consoles (Sony's PlayStation 2 and PlayStation 3, Microsoft's Xbox 360, and Nintendo's Wii); wireless phones and handheld devices such as Nintendo's Game Boy Advance and Sony's PlayStation Portable (PSP); personal computers; and Web sites. EA had more ability than any other game publisher to distribute, market, and sell its game titles to consumers all over the world. It had 31 game titles that sold over 1 million units each in fiscal year 2005 and 27 titles that exceeded sales of 1 million units each in fiscal 2006. EA released sequels of its popular sports titles annually—Madden NFL (professional football), NBA Live (professional basketball), FIFA (professional soccer), NCAA Football, and Tiger Woods PGA Tour. When Madden NFL 07 was introduced in August 2006, it sold a record 2 million copies at retail prices of $59.99 a copy in its first week; the new release of NCAA Football 06 sold over 1 million copies in the first week.

In 2003, Lawrence Probst, EA's chairman and CEO, had confidently predicted the company was on course to become the "biggest and best entertainment company in the world" with revenues eventually rivaling those of Disney (2002 revenues of $25.3 billion) and Time Warner (2002 revenues of $42 billion). But EA's revenues had apparently topped out, having hovered in the $2.8–$3.1 billion range since 2004. Moreover, EA's net profits had suffered for three years running, partly because of changes in the way that consumers purchased and played video games, partly because of a slower-than-expected transition to next-generation video game platforms, and partly because of significantly higher costs to develop new video games. The company's best year on the bottom line had been in its fiscal year ending March 31, 2004, when it reported earnings of $577 million; since then, net profits had fallen to $504 million in fiscal 2005, $236 million in fiscal 2006, and $76 million in the 2007 fiscal year ending March 31, 2007. Nonetheless, Lawrence Probst believed the company's outlook was quite promising despite the rather profound changes under way in the industry; Probst said:

> Transition is never easy and the combination of new technology, new platforms and new markets makes this one particularly complex. Today, EA is investing ahead of revenue in what we believe will be another period of strong and sustained growth for the interactive entertainment industry. No

other company is investing in as many strategic areas; no other company has as much opportunity. Our commitment of financial and creative resources is significant, but so is the potential for long-term growth.[1]

Probst and other EA executives believed that high-speed broadband Internet connections and the newly introduced generation of powerful game-playing consoles gave EA the opening it needed to take video games to heights far beyond what consumers could experience with movies and TV entertainment.

The Video Game Industry

In 2005, the video game industry represented a $35 billion global market. The market was expected to mushroom to a record-setting $58 billion in 2007 as (1) video game enthusiasts rushed to purchase Sony's PlayStation 3 (PS3) or Microsoft's Xbox 360 or Nintendo's Wii (pronounced "we") and video games that exploited the powerful capabilities of these new consoles and (2) mobile gaming on cell phones and online gaming via broadband took off—see Exhibit 1. The industry consisted of makers of devices that played video games (consoles, handheld players, and arcade machines), game developers who developed games for play on all the various types of game-playing devices, retailers of video game players and video games, and companies that had Web sites for online game play.

Sony, Microsoft, and Nintendo had incorporated faster processing speeds, digital and high-definition graphics capability, online connectivity, and assorted other innovative features that took the playing of video games on their latest generation of consoles to dramatic new heights. Sony's PS3, for instance, included Blu-ray technology that exploited the full power of high-definition graphics. Nintendo's Wii had a unique controller. Game developers had responded by creating increasingly sophisticated and exotic games that allowed players to compete in a host of sports and racing events, pilot supersonic fighter jets and spacecraft to defend against all manner of enemies, and enter mystical worlds to untangle ancient webs of treachery and deceit. In 2007, there were games covering all genres, games for players of

Exhibit 1

Size of the Global Video Games Market, by Sector, 2000, 2003, and 2005, with Projections for 2010 ($ in millions)

	2000	2003	2005	2010
Console hardware	$ 4,791	$ 6,047	$ 3,894	$ 5,771
Console software (both sales and rentals)	9,451	16,449	13,055	17,164
Handheld hardware	1,945	1,501	3,855	1,715
Handheld software (both sales and rentals)	2,872	2,238	4,829	3,113
PC software (both sales and rentals)	5,077	3,806	4,313	2,955
Broadband	70	497	1,944	6,352
Interactive TV	81	249	786	3,037
Mobile	65	587	2,572	11,186
Total	$24,352	$31,370	$35,248	$51,292*

* Note: Industry analysts expected that industrywide sales would reach a peak of $58 million in 2007 (as game players rushed to buy the new PS3, Wii, and Xbox 360) and then taper off to $51.3 million in 2010 as sales of the newly introduced game-playing consoles tapered off.

Source: Informa Telecoms & Media, "Games Market to Score Big in 2007," press release, October 24, 2005, and "Game Industry Boom Continues," press release, July 24, 2003, both at www.informamedia.com (accessed September 8, 2006).

all ages, and games targeted to both hard-core and casual game players.

Retail sales of video game software soared to record levels in the 1990s, with sales that climbed steadily toward $15 billion annually by 2000. From 1985 to 1994, Nintendo and Sega dominated the market for video game consoles, with combined market shares of around 90 percent. The two rivals sparred back and forth in an escalating battle for market leadership in making the platforms or consoles on which most video games were played. Then, in 1995, competitive rivalry in video games took on a new dimension when Sony entered the market with its new PlayStation. Nintendo and Sega, the longtime industry leaders, found themselves in a fierce battle with Sony, and other small-share console makers scrambled to generate enough sales to survive. There was a huge industry shakeout. By 1998, Sony emerged as the undisputed leader worldwide. In the United States, Sony's PlayStation captured a 70 percent market share, with Nintendo at 26 percent and Sega at only 4 percent. All other video console makers faded into oblivion, and Sega, unable to make any headway in regaining lost market share, exited the market for video consoles in 2001 and turned its full attention to developing video games. The entry of Microsoft's Xbox in 2002 made the video console business a fierce three-way contest.

In 2006, Sony was the undisputed global leader in video game hardware, having shipped more than 100 million PlayStation 2 (PS2) units since its launch in 2000; Sony and independent game developers had introduced more than 7,000 titles for the PS2, and more than 1 billion units had been sold as of 2006. During 2001–2005, the PS2 had about a 70 percent share of the console market. Such market acceptance made PS3 the odds-on favorite for Sony to remain the market leader in video game hardware. But despite PS2's market dominance and huge base of installed users, Microsoft's Xbox 360 and Nintendo's Wii were expected to gain market share against the new PS3. For the first time, the three major console platforms were strongly differentiated from one another, as well as from prior-generation platforms. The Xbox 360 was said to have the best online capabilities, the PS3 the best high-definition graphics, and Nintendo's Wii, while lacking the raw graphics power of the PS3 and Xbox 360, had a novel motion-sensitive controller that allowed users to play games by wielding the controller like a tennis racket, sword, gun, or fishing pole.

In 2007, Sony, Microsoft, and Nintendo were waging an intense global battle for market share in video game consoles. Microsoft's Xbox 360 had a solid first-mover advantage, having been introduced in late 2005 (barely in time for the 2005 holiday sales season). Sony's PS3 had been delayed due to various design and production problems and did not hit the market in Japan and the United States until November 2006—and then only in limited numbers (about 1.5 million units); moreover, it retailed at a hefty $599 per console ($410 in Japan), a far higher price than the $250–$300 introduction prices of prior-generation consoles. The PS3 did not launch in Europe until March 2007, so it would be well into 2008 before a big fraction of the 100 million PS2 users would be able to upgrade to PS3 in the event they chose to do so.

Nintendo's strategy with the Wii was to gain market share by pricing the Wii below both the Xbox 360 and the PS3—at around $250 retail in the United States and $213 in Japan; the Wii, introduced in November 2006, was also late to market because of delays in working out bugs and glitches. Microsoft's Xbox 360 retailed for $399.99 in North America, €299 in Europe, and £209.99 in Great Britain; Microsoft was selling a low-end version of the Xbox 360 at about $255 in Japan (along with two free games) to boost flagging sales. Microsoft expected that its shipments of the Xbox 360 would reach 10 million units worldwide by the end of 2006 and 13–15 million units by June 2007; there were some 160 game titles available for the Xbox 360 in August 2006. Nintendo expected to sell 4 million Wiis by year-end 2006, which would give both Nintendo's Wii and Microsoft's Xbox 360 a nice sales lead over Sony's PS3 heading into 2007. Sony's announced pricing for the PS3 had met strong resistance in some quarters, raising questions about whether the high price would hurt the PS3's chances of attracting a wide audience or whether Sony would be forced into making price cuts early on.

Because the three console makers also developed and marketed games for their respective platforms, independent game publishers were said not to want any single console to dominate the market for this latest generation of game players. A more balanced market share distribution among Sony, Microsoft, and Nintendo would weaken the long-standing leverage that platform manufacturers had in demanding sizable royalty payments from game publishers who wanted to create games played on their platforms. Square Enix, an influential Japan-based games developer that heretofore had made games only for PlayStation (including the showcase Final Fantasy series, with worldwide sales of over 68 million units, and the Dragon Quest series, with worldwide sales of over 40 million units), had announced that it would make games for all three of the new consoles. According to a Square Enix executive, "We don't want the PlayStation 3 to be the overwhelming loser, so we want to support them. But we don't want them to be the overwhelming winner either, so we can't support them too much."[2]

The Demographics of Video Game Players

About 250 to 300 million people worldwide were very active or frequent players of video games; game enthusiasts usually owned consoles, handheld players, PCs, or game-capable cell phones and spent six or more hours weekly playing video games. The average American was said to spend 75 hours annually playing video games, more than double the amount spent gaming in 1997 and more than was spent watching rented movies on DVDs or videocassettes.[3] The average gamer in the United States spent over 350 hours annually playing video games; hard-core gamers often spent 700 or more hours annually. Perhaps another

Exhibit 2

Size of the U.S. Market for Video Games, 1996–2005

YEAR	UNIT SALES*	DOLLAR SALES
1996	74.1 million	$2.6 billion
1997	108.4	3.7
1998	153.0	4.8
1999	185.2	5.5
2000	197.1	5.6
2001	211.0	6.1
2002	226.4	7.0
2003	241.4	7.1
2004	250.0	7.4
2005	228.5	7.0

* Includes video games played on PCs as well as games played on video game consoles and handheld devices.

Source: U.S. data are from the NPD Group, point-of-sale information, as reported in "Essential Facts about the Computer and Video Game Industry," Entertainment Software Association, www.theesa.com (accessed September 7, 2006).

100 million people were infrequent or casual players, using arcade machines in malls and other retail locations, their own personal computers (PCs) during idle moments or as a diversion, the consoles and handheld players of friends and acquaintances, or cell phones.

The majority of video game players were preteens, teenagers, and young adults (those between the ages of 20 and 40). The average age of game players was rising, as people who became game players as preteens or teenagers continued to play in their adult years—in 2005, the average game player age in the United States was 33 and 25 percent were over 50.[4] To broaden the appeal of video games for adults, game developers were creating a growing number of games with mature content. Hardcore gamers purchased 10–15 new games annually and were also among those most attracted to playing games online. Exhibit 3 provides game-player demographics and other video game–related statistics. A substantial number of consumers were not attracted to playing video games, partly because of a lack of interest, partly because they lacked the patience to

Exhibit 3

Video Game–Playing Statistics, U.S. Households, 2005

- The average player spent about 6.8 hours per week playing games.
- 31% of all game players in the United States were under age 18, 44% were in the 18–49 age group, and 25% were over age 50 (up from 13% in 2000).
- The average game player in the United States in 2003 was 33 years old.
- 62% of gamers were male.
- The average age of the most frequent game purchaser was 40; 89% of the time parents were present when games were purchased or rented.
- The top four reasons parents played video games with their children:
    Because they were asked to—79%
    It's fun for the entire family—75%
    It's a good opportunity to socialize with the child—71%
    It's a good time to monitor game content—62%
- 44% of most frequent game players played games online, up from 19% in 2000.
- Best-selling video games by type of genre, 2002 and 2005:

| | 2002 | | 2005 | |
GAME CATEGORIES	PC GAMES	CONSOLE GAMES	PC GAMES	CONSOLE GAMES
Sports	6.3%	19.5%	3.7%	17.3%
Action	—	25.1	4.7	30.1
Strategy/role-playing	35.4	7.4	43.2	—
Racing	4.4	16.6	—	11.1
Fighting	0.1	6.4	—	4.7
Shooting	11.5	5.5	14.4	8.7
Family/child	25.6	—	19.8	9.3
Adventure	—	5.1	5.8	—
Edutainment	—	7.6	—	—

Note: The categories were "redefined" between 2002 and 2005.

- Computer and video game sales by rating, 2001 and 2005:

	2001	2005
Everyone	62.3%	49.0%
Teen	24.6	32.0
Mature	9.9	15.0
Everyone 10+	2.1	4.0

- 16 of the top 20 best-selling console games and 16 of the top 20 best-selling PC games were rated Everyone or Teen.

Source: Interactive Digital Software Association, "Essential Facts about the Computer and Video Game Industry," 2002, www.idsa.com (accessed November 12, 2003), and Entertainment Software Association, "Essential Facts about the Computer and Video Game Industry," 2006, www.theesa.com (accessed September 7, 2006).

learn complex controls, and partly because they were unwilling to spend the 20 to 30 hours it took to navigate a game successfully.

The development of video games was considered by some observers to be a niche business, with each game targeted to appeal to a particular subculture. In 2006, increasing numbers of games were being targeted to narrowed-in genres and consumers with specific game-playing preferences. Thinking of the gamers as consisting of just two primary segments—power or hard-core gamers and casual gamers—was overly simplistic. The size of the target niche for a game and the following a game could attract were thus crucial. Unless a game could attract a sizable audience and produce unit sales sufficient to cover development costs, production and packaging costs, and marketing costs, then it ended up a moneyloser. According to one renowned game designer, "Only the top 20 percent is going to make money at any given moment. Most of what we make is destined for the garbage heap of history."[5] Moreover, unless the content of a game could be adapted to other media, the revenue-generating capability of a video game quickly eroded after a few months on the market (and certainly after next-generation consoles were introduced). For instance, even a top-selling title like Madden NFL, usually introduced in August just before the start of football season, generated few sales after December.

Industry Growth

A number of factors had contributed to growth of the video game industry during the 1990–2006 period:[6]

- *Broader game content.* The number and variety of video games had expanded over the years to the point where there were games for all tastes and all ages.

- *Quantum leaps in the quality of both graphics and play.* The latest generation of consoles introduced in 2005–2007 offered a huge leap in the game-playing experience and had entertainment functions well beyond that of just playing video games. The PS3, Xbox 360, and Wii consoles had high-definition graphics that rendered real-life images, wireless connectivity for surfing the Internet or playing games online, parental controls, hard drives for saving downloaded games, and multichannel surround sound; they could accommodate wired or wireless controllers and were formatted with a 16:9 widescreen format for high-definition

televisions. (However, games would play on standard TVs as well.)

- *The evolution of video game consoles into multifaceted entertainment devices.* The latest generation of consoles had the ability to record TV shows, play music, rip CDs onto the hard drive, and stream video and digital pictures stored on a PC, thus expanding the entertainment value for families.

- *Growing interest in video games by adults.* Demographic research indicated that growing numbers of young adults were continuing to play video games past their teenage and college years. Sports games involving professional and college sports and NASCAR racing were appealing to adults, as were games with mature content.

- *Collaboration between Hollywood movie studios and video game developers to translate popular action movies into video games.* Game developers and Hollywood movie studios had seen the merits of working hand in hand on projects that had both the action component and widespread interest (especially among teenagers) to make a good game. Releasing a game in conjunction with a hit movie—such as a Harry Potter or James Bond movie or *Spider-Man* or *Lord of the Rings*—could increase sales three or four times. Sometimes, film stars recorded dialogue for video games and special scenes were filmed specifically for use in the video game. Game designers would take a movie script and add to the storyline, making it more mission-rich and multifaceted than what appeared onscreen.

- *The growing capability to play games online, often in head-to-head competition with other online players.* Online gaming had allowed game designers to extend their storylines by providing new chapters, adding new missions, and introducing new characters, thus hooking enthusiasts into playing through a never-ending story. Sequels of sports games with the latest player rosters and team schedules spurred continuing interest on the part of online players.

Competitive Structure of the Video Game Software Business

The video game software business was part of the broader entertainment business. Video games competed for the leisure time and discretionary spending of consumers against such other forms of entertainment as motion pictures, television, and music. Industry participants varied in size—from small companies with limited resources to large, diversified companies with considerable financial and marketing clout. Sony, Nintendo, and to a lesser extent Microsoft had in-house personnel assigned to developing game titles exclusively for their respective platforms and were actively marketing their own games against the games of independent game publishers like Electronic Arts, Activision, Take Two Interactive, THQ, Square Enix, Capcom, Atari, Sega, Lucas Arts Entertainment, NCsoft, and numerous others. Well-known media giants such as Disney, Fox, Viacom, and Time Warner, attracted by the growth opportunities in video games and the emergence of related entertainment technologies, were expanding their software game publishing efforts.

Competition among the publishers of video game software was vigorous, revolving around engaging content and game play, number and variety of product offerings, the incorporation of cutting-edge technologies and innovative game features that captured the attention and interest of game players, continuous introduction of new titles, building a brand name that inspired buyer trust and confidence in game quality, gaining access to retail shelf space and visibility in other distribution channels, effective marketing and sales promotion, pricing, and ability to complete game development and time new product releases to match peak sales periods. Success in the marketplace depended heavily on a company's prowess in developing a stream of new titles with mass appeal, marketing them effectively, and having at least several hit titles, outcomes that required ever-increasing budgets for creative game development, advertising, and sales promotion. As a consequence, only companies that could marshal the financial resources needed to support a sizable and talented game development staff and fund a potent sales and marketing effort were likely to prosper or even survive.

Emerging Video Game Distribution Channels and Market Segments

Aside from the transition to next-generation consoles that began in 2005–2006, several other factors were driving market change in video games.

DIGITAL DISTRIBUTION Retail sales where consumers bought packaged video games were the industry's most important distribution channel in 2006. Thousands of retail outlets across the world stocked video games—not surprisingly, Wal-Mart was the world's biggest video game retailer, with a market share of about 18 percent. Other key retailers in North America were Target, Best Buy, Circuit City, Blockbuster, Toys "R" Us, and GameStop. In many instances, retailers demanded hefty slotting fees to stock lesser-known or slower-selling games. While some industry observers believed that retailers would remain the primary point of purchase for the foreseeable future, others were less sure. One of the biggest market trends in 2006 was the growing propensity of mainstream consumers to use the Internet to purchase and play video games. Digital distribution via Internet downloads was gaining rapid acceptance because more and more households had broadband or high-speed Internet connections. A broadband connection enabled a consumer to purchase a video game online and download it to a hard drive (on either a PC or a console equipped with a hard drive). In 2006, most PC-based video games were being offered for sale digitally in addition to being available at retail. Moreover, it was becoming quite common for online retailers to promote game sales by offering free downloadable demos. Digital distribution was expected to grow significantly as the installed of new consoles grew—all three of the leading consoles had hard drives and wireless Internet connections that facilitated downloading of online game purchases. The weaknesses of digital distribution were that downloaded files were not portable (could not be taken to a friend's house or sold at garage sales) and their large file sizes took up considerable hard drive space.

A second driver of digital distribution was the "unlimited shelf space" of Web-based game retailers that enabled them to offer a far wider selection of games than most retailers. With more than 500 titles for PlayStation, 200 titles for Xbox, and 150 titles for GameCube during much of 2003–2006, the big majority of brick-and-mortar retailers tended to award shelf space to only the most popular titles (perhaps 25 to 75, depending on store size and the amount of space devoted to video games) and select new releases. Wal-Mart, for example, generally stocked only about 80–90 games. The shelf life of the average newly released video game was about five weeks, even with expensive in-store merchandising campaigns. Popular video games seldom remained on retail shelves longer than 120 days. Internet retailers, however, could offer a very wide selection of game titles at low incremental cost—indeed, it made sense for Amazon.com or other Internet retailers specializing in video games to stock a big selection of both new releases and older games for all types of platforms and target audiences. Digital distribution had considerable economical appeal to game developers, allowing them to bypass the costs of such game-publishing activities as physical production, packaging, shipping, inventory management, and return processing. In addition, the lower-cost economics of digital distribution created room for game e-tailers to employ price-cutting tactics to spur sales toward the end of a game's life cycle or to induce bargain hunters to purchase a disappointingly slow-selling game.

RISING POPULARITY OF MASSIVELY MULTIPLAYER ONLINE GAMES

High-speed Internet connections greatly enhanced the online game-playing experience, enabling players to compete directly with other online players in what were called massively multiplayer online games (MMOGs). In 2006, with millions of households across the world already having broadband connections and millions

more households getting them annually, participation in MMOGs was booming; many enthusiastic online gamers had joined online communities dedicated to the playing of a particular game. Online game-playing via broadband connections was expected to constitute a $6.4 billion market worldwide by 2010, up from $1.9 billion in 2005 (see Exhibit 1). Forecasters expected the growth would be driven not only by PC-based subscriptions but also by the rapidly growing number of video game console systems with online capability—about 75 percent of the online game subscription revenue in 2010 was expected to come from games played on PCs and 25 percent was expected to come from games played on consoles. By 2008, the installed base of MMOG-capable consoles and PCs was projected to exceed 100 million worldwide. In 2005, over 50 percent of the subscription revenue from online game play came from Asian countries outside Japan, most notably South Korea, China, and Taiwan. In the future online game playing was expected to be more evenly distributed across Asia, North America, and Europe.

The boom in MMOGs had spawned the formation of online communities. A key to success for MMOGs was easy interaction among the players—making it simple to chat with other players, heckle opponents, talk trash, or cooperate with other players to complete certain tasks and missions. MMOG players enjoyed being part of an online gaming community in which they could hang out, chat, engage in head-to-head duels, and check statistics showing their skills versus those of other players. Game play in MMOGs was thus not a solitary interaction between an individual and a technology. Rather, MMOG communities functioned as "third places" (gathering places outside the home and workplace that people used for informal social interaction) where players could hold multiple real-time conversations with fellow players through text or voice, build relationships with other players in different cities and countries, and become exposed to a diversity of worldviews.[7]

The most popular MMOG worldwide in 2006 was said to be World of Warcraft, which had attracted a global following and was available in six languages (English, Korean, German, French, and both simplified and traditional Chinese)—a Spanish version was in development. Online play of World of Warcraft (created by Blizzard Entertainment, a subsidiary of Vivendi International) generated more than $100 million in subscription revenues in each of several countries in its first year alone. MMOG play in major markets like South Korea, China, Japan, and the United States was big enough in 2007 that a highly popular MMOG could generate $100 million in annual revenues per country.

However, MMOGs were more tedious and expensive to build than traditional games (World of Warcraft took nine years to develop), and there were ongoing costs for game masters, servers, technology support, and new content development. Revenues to cover the costs of online game sites came from annual or monthly subscription fees, pay-to-play fees, onsite advertising, and selling digital downloads of games. The business model for profiting from MMOGs was heavily dependent on subscription revenues, whereas the business model of casual game sites (which typically had higher traffic) entailed a more diverse revenue stream that included site advertising, selling digital downloads, and, to a lesser but increasing extent, subscriptions. In 2006, the business of operating an online game-playing site was considered very risky. A host of online game sites seeking to capitalize on the anticipated market growth in online gaming had sprung up in the 2002–2006 period; many had since gone out of business, and a big majority of the remaining ones were struggling to generate sufficient revenues to be profitable.

Some of the more prominent online gaming sites in North America in 2006 were Microsoft's Xbox Live (which had 2 million subscribers), Sony Online Entertainment's PlayStation site (where games installed on a PlayStation Portable, PlayStation 2, or PlayStation 3 could be played online for monthly fees of $21.99), Electronic Arts' www.ea.com, and CNET

Networks Entertainment's www.gamespot.com. Vivendi's Blizzard Entertainment had set up a special Web site, www.worldofwarcraft.com, to handle online play of World of Warcraft. In Asia, there were about 10 companies with significant subscription revenues from online game play, led by South Korean company Ncsoft, which had $300 million in online game revenue in 2005.[8] So far, relatively few companies had generated sizable subscription revenues from online play of MMOGs and casual games—video game developers were finding that earning a profit from online game play with a subscription-based business model was more elusive than relying on the proven business model of selling packaged games through retail channels.

THE EMERGENCE OF MOBILE GAMING

Historically, Nintendo's Game Boy, Game Boy Color, and Game Boy Advance handheld devices had been the dominant leaders in the mobile video game play market segment. To solidify its market-leading position in 2004–2006, Nintendo introduced the Nintendo DS and Nintendo DS Lite portable game players to complement its Game Boy Advance model. Going into 2006, Nintendo had sold over 75 million Game Boy Advance players, 330 million Game Boy Advance game cartridges, 17 million Nintendo DS devices, and over 60 million games for Nintendo DS models. Sony entered the handheld/mobile gaming segment in 2005 with its PlayStation Portable (PSP), quickly becoming an important market contender with worldwide sales approaching 20 million units by year-end 2006. Despite the historical popularity of traditional handheld devices for game playing (Game Boy, Nintendo DS, and PSP), the market for gaming software for such devices was expected to be stagnant, with projected sales of only $3.1 billion for gaming software on handheld sets in 2010 versus $4.8 billion in 2005.

However, mobile gaming on cellular phones and other wireless devices was expected to explode from a $2.6 billion market in 2005 to an $11.2 billion market in 2010 (Exhibit 1). In the fall of 2006, Apple announced that it was launching video games for its fifth-generation iPod models, with the games being downloadable directly from Apple's iTunes store. (Buyers of these iPod models could also download over 75 movies and 220 TV shows from iTunes.)

Mobile gaming was a fast-developing market segment because advancing technology made it possible to incorporate high-resolution color displays, greater processing power, and improved audio capabilities on cellular handsets, iPods and other brands of digital music players, and other sophisticated handheld devices (including those designed just for playing video games). There were over 1.5 billion cell phones in active operation across the world (about 35 percent of which were game enabled), and new models with enhanced game-playing capability were selling briskly—most cell phone users, intrigued by the new features of next-generation models, upgraded their phones every few years. While playing video games on handheld devices had historically been a favorite pastime of preteens and teenagers, the popularity of game-capable cell phones, iPods, and other sophisticated handheld devices was expected to spur increases in mobile gaming among the young adult population worldwide in the years ahead.

To capitalize on the growth opportunities in mobile gaming via cellular handsets and MP3 players, independent game developers had come up with games that customers could download on their cell phones or MP3 players. Cell phone users usually purchased video games through a wireless carrier's branded e-commerce service that was directly accessible from the handset. Purchasers were charged a one-time or monthly subscription fee on their cellular handset invoice for the game; the wireless carrier generally retained a portion of the fee and paid the rest to the game developer. Such wireless distribution also eliminated such traditional game publishing activities as physical production, packaging, shipping, inventory management, and return processing.

PC GAMES: A SEGMENT IN DECLINE OR POISED FOR GROWTH?

A number of observers believed the market for PC-based games was in irreversible decline; one forecasting group had predicted that sales and rentals of PC gaming software would represent a worldwide market of only $3.0 billion in 2010, down from $4.3 billion in 2005 (Exhibit 1). Those who saw the market for PC games as fading contended that PCs were not as well suited to playing the most popular video games as were consoles and that the new generation of consoles widened this gap even further. Michael Dell, cofounder and chairman of Dell Inc. and an occasional player of World of Warcraft, believed that multimedia-equipped PCs had a bright future as a gaming platform.[9] Dell Inc. was broadening its product lineup to include models with advanced graphics, widescreen displays, and multiple processors that greatly enhanced the online gaming experience, particularly MMOGs; further advances in the video performance of PCs were coming to market soon. Michael Dell believed that Microsoft's new Vista operating system was a great platform for gamers and Dell Inc. had an advanced technology group working with game developers to explore how to make the PC the best platform for gaming. At the Austin Game Conference in September 2006, Michael Dell had a private meeting at his house for 12 game developers.[10] Dell Inc. was the world's leading manufacturer of desktop and laptop computers.

Also in 2006, Microsoft launched a strategic initiative to reenergize the PC gaming market segment by introducing a Games for Windows branding for games that were optimized for play on Windows XP and Vista. Game publishers whose PC-based games met a set of technical guidelines that provided users with easy game installation, high reliability, wide-screen viewing, ability to launch from the Windows Media Center, support for the Xbox 360 Controller for Windows, and support for key Windows Vista features (such as the Game Explorer function and parental controls) were authorized to display a Games for Windows logo on the CD or DVD cases of their PC titles. Microsoft's strategic intent in promoting global Games for Windows branding was to help convince PC users that the Windows Vista operating system was a first-class vehicle for gaming.

SHARPLY RISING DEVELOPMENT COSTS

In the early 1980s, a game for an eight-bit Nintendo game player could be developed for less than $100,000. In the early 1990s, game publishers customarily spent around $300,000 to develop a game for Nintendo's Super NES, Sega's Genesis, or PCs. In 1996, a typical PlayStation game cost just under $1 million to develop and retailed for $49. In 2003, development costs for a PlayStation 2 or Xbox game usually ran from $2 to $7 million per title, with retail prices running at $49.99 for hit titles. By 2005, development costs for frontline titles ranged from $5 to $20 million. The costs to develop high-profile hit games for the PS3, Xbox 360, and Wii were predicted to *average* as high as $20 million. Development costs for video console games were climbing for several reasons:

- It took ever bigger and more talented development teams to brainstorm the content of a new game, capitalize on the computing speed and graphics capabilities of each new generation of consoles, and wow game enthusiasts. The gifted and artistic skills it took to conceptualize and flesh out an innovative game were in short supply. As a consequence, talented game developers were becoming a more and more valuable resource, commanding ever higher salaries and bonuses. As game-playing transitioned to PS3, Xbox 360, and Wii, most industry observers believed a large and capable staff of game developers would prove an even more important key success factor.
- Games to fully exploit the capabilities of the latest console generation and capture the rapt attention of game enthusiasts for long periods required far more complicated and detailed animation, graphics, and

coding than older 64-bit consoles, making them increasingly time-intensive to prepare and debug. Game development cycles for the PS2, Xbox, GameCube, PCs, and the PSP were typically 12 to 24 months, but developing games for the PS3, Xbox 360, and Wii could take from 12 to 36 months, depending on game complexity and scope. Game development times were typically 6 to 9 months for the Game Boy, 9 to 12 months for the Nintendo DS (Dual Screen), and 6 to 9 months for wireless phones.[11] After initial development of an all-new game for a particular platform, it could take 9 to 12 months to develop a title for other platforms.[12]

- Costs went up when a game had to be reworked or when developers decided to push the technology envelope a bit further and add new or more elaborate features. Game developers often did not know how long it would take or what it would cost to program some games because aspects of many new games had never been done before and it took several rounds of programming to create the desired effects.

- Payments for licensed content or the use of intellectual property owned by others (for rights to use certain characters or celebrities in games or to tie in with hit movies), coupled with the need for special film crews and backdrops to stage certain scenes, could cost game publishers an additional $1 to $10 per game unit.

According to one knowledgeable source, since 1993–1994 the inflation-adjusted budget for creating a game had gone up by 22 times and the amount of data included in a game had grown by 40 to 150 times, yet the industry had only gotten 6 times better at making the content.[13]

Video Game Prices

Retail prices for video games in packaged form varied, depending on popularity, length of time on the market, and the age and popularity of the console for which they were developed. For example, Madden NFL 07 retailed for $59.99 on the Xbox 360; $49.99 on PlayStation 2 and Xbox; $39.99 on GameCube, PSP, and PCs; and $29.99 on Game Boy Advance and Nintendo DS. Hit titles for the newest console generation commanded a premium price as high as $59.99 in 2006, with less popular sellers retailing for $49.99 and $39.99. The prices of titles with lagging sales were frequently discounted after being on the market for several weeks; price discounting was a sales tactic used by many Internet retailers and by big-box retailers like Wal-Mart.

On average, game prices tended to decline once a generation of consoles had been on the market for a significant period (see Exhibit 4), chiefly because there were so many game titles competing for the attention of game players and because the shelf space of game retailers was limited. There were about 50 high-profile games scheduled for release during the September–November 2006 period.[14] About 750 new games (or sequels of existing games) were expected to hit the market during 2007–2008; most all game developers were developing new games in expectation that booming sales of PS3, Xbox 360, and Wii would spur big gains in video game purchases. If past sales statistics held true, the top 100 games would account for 50 percent of total sales and half of those might be able to command a premium price.

Royalties Paid to Console Manufacturers

Sony, Nintendo, and Microsoft, aside from creating their own games with in-house staff, licensed independent game developers to create software for use with their respective game-playing systems. The license agreements gave the platform manufacturer the right to set the fee structure that developers had to pay in order to publish games for their platforms. The customary royalty was in the $8 to $10 range on newly released games, but the royalty payment typically decreased as game prices fell. Because royalties did not have to be paid to console manufacturers on PC-based games, the retail prices of PC-based games published by independent game developers were often about $10 cheaper.

The license agreement also gave manufacturers an assortment of controls in other areas. Typically, the game developer was required to

Exhibit 4

Average Retail Prices of Video Games, 1995–2002

TYPE OF CONSOLE	1995	1996	1997	1998	1999	2000	2001	2002
16-bit (1989 debut)								
Sega Genesis	$41	$29	$21	$14	$13	$10	$10	$ 7
Super Nintendo	$43	$41	$29	$22	$17	$11	$10	$ 9
32-bit (1995 debut)								
PlayStation	$53	$49	$39	$35	$31	$28	$23	$18
Sega Saturn	$55	$47	$35	$20	$11	$ 5	$14	$ 6
64-bit (1996 debut)								
Nintendo 64		$65	$61	$51	$46	$42	$38	$28
128-bit (2000 debut)								
GameCube							$50	$46
Xbox							$50	$45
PlayStation 2						$49	$48	$41

Source: The NPD Group/NPD FunWorld and www.msnbc.com/news (accessed September 8, 2006).

submit a prototype for evaluation and approval that included all artwork to be used in connection with packaging and marketing of the product. The console manufacturer had final approval over all games for its consoles (sometimes limiting the number of games approved in a given time frame) and could specify the dates on which new games could be released. Sony and Nintendo were the exclusive producers of the DVDs or game cartridges for their platforms, requiring royalties to be paid based on the number of units manufactured. Microsoft did not engage in production activities but required that titles for Xbox be manufactured by preapproved manufacturers. The manufacture of game titles required that the game publisher place a purchase order with Sony, Nintendo, or a Microsoft-preapproved manufacturer for the desired number of units drawn on its line of credit with the manufacturer for 100 percent of the order cost; the publisher then submitted software code, related artwork, user instructions, warranty information, and brochure and packaging designs for approval. Orders were generally shipped within two weeks of receipt of the purchase order.

All these royalty requirements and the need to maintain good collaborative relationships with console manufacturers tended to increase developer lead times and costs for getting a new game to market. This was especially true when platform manufacturers opted to bring out next-generation platforms with capabilities that entailed more demanding specifications. Moreover, when next-generation platforms were introduced, platform manufacturers required a new license of developers, giving them an opportunity to alter the fee structure and impose new terms and conditions on licensees. Next-generation platforms posed two other risks to game developers. If manufacturers were delayed in introducing next-generation platforms, then the introduction of their new games was delayed as well. And if a manufacturer's new platform met with a poor reception in the marketplace, then the accompanying games of developers had shorter-than-expected life cycles and often ended up as money-losers.

In addition, as online capabilities emerged for video game platforms, platform manufacturers had control over the financial terms on which online game play would be offered to players using their consoles. In each case, compatibility code and the consent of the platform manufacturer were required before a game developer could include online capabilities in their games for a manufacturer's consoles and handheld devices. (This, of course, was not the case for PC-based games.) The forward integration of Microsoft, Sony, and Nintendo into online game sites thus put their strategies and business models in head-on competition with the strategies and business models of independent game developers, like Electronic Arts, that had their own online game-playing businesses.

Marketing and Distribution Costs

Competition for shelf space and efforts to make games into top sellers had prompted game publishers to boost their advertising and promotion efforts. By and large, the video game software business was hit-title driven and required significant expenditures for marketing and advertising. Game publishers usually promoted their games in several ways:

- Television, print, radio, outdoor, and Internet ads.
- Company Web sites.
- In-store promotions, displays, and retailer-assisted cooperative advertising.
- Trade shows.
- Product sampling through demonstration software.
- Consumer contests and promotions.

Television advertising was often required to create mass-market demand for an altogether new game; a minimal TV advertising campaign for a game cost about $2 million.

About 50 percent of annual video game sales occurred in the fourth quarter of the calendar year; many holiday shoppers considered video game hardware and software as ideal gifts.

Exhibit 5

Representative Value Chain for Video Games, 2006

	PC GAME DOWNLOADED FROM INTERNET	PACKAGED DVD FOR CONSOLE
Retail price	$39.99	$59.99
Retailer margin	$ 8.00	$12.00
Wholesale price received by publisher	$31.99	$47.99
Publisher costs		
Manufacturing/packaging	$ 0.00	$ 3.00
Hardware royalty fee (paid to console maker)	$ 0.00	$ 8.00
Licensed content royalties	$0.00–$10.00	$0.00–$10.00
Margin for game development and programming, marketing, other costs, and profit	$21.99–$31.99	$26.99–$36.99

Source: Developed by the case author from information available from Wedbush Morgan Securities and www.msnbc.com/news/924871.asp (accessed September 8, 2006).

Exhibit 5 shows a representative value chain for video games.

Electronic Arts

Electronic Arts began operations in 1982 in California and was headquartered in Redwood City, just outside San Francisco. The company developed, published, distributed, and marketed video games for in-home video game consoles (such as Sony's PlayStation 2 and 3, Microsoft's Xbox and Xbox 360, and Nintendo's Game Cube and Wii), personal computers, handheld video game players (such as the PlayStation Portable or PSP, Nintendo DS, and Game Boy Advance), cellular phones, and online play. Like other entertainment companies, EA focused on the creation, acquisition, exploitation, and protection of intellectual property; its intellectual property was primarily lodged in software code, patented technology, and the trade secrets used to develop games and make them run properly on a variety of gaming platforms. In 2006, it had about 7,200 employees, of whom 4,000 were outside the United States.

EA's revenues had more than doubled since 2000 (see Exhibit 6). The company's profits had suffered because of huge operating losses in its online business; as shown in Exhibit 7, the EA.com business segment reported operating losses of $154 million in fiscal 2001, $151 million in fiscal 2002, and $157 million in fiscal 2003. Starting in fiscal 2004, EA eliminated separate reporting for its online operations at EA.com, a move that concealed the financial performance of EA's online operations from public view.

EA's Creative Process

EA's game design staff of 4,100 people consisted of digital animators, programmers, and creative individuals who in many instances had backgrounds in television, the music industry, and the movie industry and were attracted by the creative opportunities in video games and EA's attractive compensation packages of high pay and stock options. Game design personnel were located in five principal design studios in Los Angeles, Redwood Shores (outside San Francisco), Orlando, Vancouver (Canada), and Guildford (England) and smaller design studios in Chicago, Montreal, Shanghai, Chertsey (England), and Tokyo. The dispersion of design studios helped EA to design games that were specific to different cultures—for example, the London studio took the lead in designing the popular FIFA Soccer game to suit European tastes and to replicate the stadiums, signage, and team rosters. No other game software company had EA's ability to localize games or to

Exhibit 6

Summary of Electronic Arts' Financial Performance, Fiscal Years 2000–2007 ($ in millions, except for per share data)

	FISCAL YEAR ENDING MARCH 31						
	2007	**2006**	**2005**	**2004**	**2003**	**2002**	**2000**
Statement of Operations Data							
Net revenues	$3,091	$2,951	$3,129	$2,957	$2,482	$1,725	$1,420
Cost of goods sold	1,212	1,181	1,197	1,103	1,073	815	711
Gross profit	1,879	1,770	1,932	1,854	1,409	910	709
Operating expenses:							
Marketing and sales	466	431	391	370	332	241	189
General and administrative	288	215	221	185	131	107	92
Research and development	1,041	758	633	511	401	381	256
Amortization of intangibles	27	7	3	3	7	25	12
Charge for acquired in-process technology	3	8	13	—	—	—	7
Restructuring charges	15	26	2	9	15	7	—
Asset impairment charges	—	—	—	—	66	13	—
Total operating expenses	1,840	1,445	1,263	1,078	953	774	555
Operating income (loss)	39	325	669	776	456	135	154
Interest and other income, net	99	64	56	21	5	13	16
Income (loss) before provision for income taxes and minority interest	138	389	725	797	461	148	170
Provision for income taxes	66	147	221	220	143	46	53
Income (loss) before minority interest	72	242	504	577	318	102	117
Minority interest in consolidated joint ventures	4	(6)	—	—	(1)	—	—
Net income (loss)	$ 76	$ 236	$ 504	$ 577	$ 317	$ 102	$ 117
Net income per share—diluted	$ 0.25	$ 0.75	$ 1.59	$ 1.87	$ 1.08	$0.35	$0.44
Balance Sheet Data at Fiscal Year End							
Cash, cash equivalents, and short-term investments	$2,635	$2,272	$2,958	$2,414	$1,588	$ 797	$ 340
Marketable securities	341	160	140	1	1	7	—
Working capital	2,571	2,143	2,899	2,185	1,334	700	440
Total assets	5,146	4,386	4,370	3,464	2,429	1,699	1,192
Long-term liabilities	88	97	54	42	54	—	—
Total liabilities	1,114	966	861	786	640	453	265
Minority interest	—	12	11	—	4	3	4
Total stockholders' equity	4,032	3,408	3,498	2,678	1,785	1,243	923
Cash Flow Data							
Net cash provided by operating activities	$ 397	$ 596	$ 634	$ 669	$ 714	$ 288	$ 78
Net cash provided by (used in) investing activities	(487)	(108)	(1,726)	288	(464)	(240)	(180)
Net cash provided by (used in) financing activities	190	(503)	200	225	133	84	106

Source: Company 10-K reports, 2001, 2003, and 2006; company press release, May 8, 2007.

Exhibit 7

EA's Financial Performance by Business Segment, Fiscal Years 2001–2003 ($ in thousands)

	FISCAL YEARS		
	2003	**2002**	**2001**
Operations of EA Core (or non-online) Business Segment			
Net revenues	$2,400,669	$1,647,502	$1,280,172
Cost of goods sold	1,056,385	797,894	650,330
Gross profit	1,344,284	849,608	629,842
Total operating expenses	730,747	563,146	506,427
Operating income (loss)	613,537	286,462	123,415
Identifiable assets	$2,287,743	$1,529,422	$1,167,846
Capital expenditures	58,328	38,406	51,460
Operations of EA.com Business Segment			
Net revenues	$ 81,575	$ 77,173	$ 42,101
Cost of goods sold	16,417	16,889	14,661
Gross profit	65,158	60,284	27,440
Total operating expenses	222,468	211,307	181,171
Operating income (loss)	(157,310)	(151,023)	(153,731)
Identifiable assets	$ 71,790	$ 169,952	$ 211,072
Capital expenditures	780	13,112	68,887

Note: During 2001–2003, EA defined its two business segments as EA Core (which included all non-online operations worldwide) and EA.com (which consisted of all online activities worldwide). Beginning in April 2003 (the start of EA's 2004 fiscal year), EA consolidated the operations of EA.com into its core business operations and eliminated the distinction between the two segments.

Source: 2003 10-K report, pp. 110–12.

launch games on multiple platforms in multiple countries in multiple languages. EA's Harry Potter and the Chamber of Secrets was released simultaneously in 75 countries, in 31 languages, and on seven platforms.[15]

Developing a game from scratch took about 18 months. To create a new game, small teams of EA game developers put together quick prototypes to demonstrate one small scene that represented the "creative center" of a potential game, usually focusing on the activity that would make the game fun to play.[16] If the game was green-lighted, the team fleshed out the idea and created storyboards of every scene, much like moviemakers would illustrate a script. State-of-the-art tools were used to allow for more cost-effective product development and to efficiently convert games designed on one game platform to other platforms. Every 90 days, a large group of EA managers and executives listened to game developers update

their works in progress. If the presentation of a game did not come across as promising, EA pulled the plug on further work. Only a few new original games made it through to production and distribution each year.

In the course of creating a number of its games, EA acquired intellectual property and other licensed content from sports leagues, player associations, performing artists, movie studios, music studios, and book authors. Many of its games included the likenesses or voices of various artists, sports personalities, and cartoon characters, along with the musical compositions and performances of film stars and musicians. J. K. Rowling, the author of the Harry Potter books, had written portions of the script for EA's Harry Potter games.

EA's policy was to design only those games that it could be proud of. While some of EA's rivals developed and marketed games with profanity, sex, crime, and violence (e.g., Take-Two

Interactive's best-selling Grand Theft Auto game involved doing drug deals, blowing up cars, consorting with a prostitute, and then hacking her to death), EA did not create games that would likely be given a "Mature" rating even though such games could generate millions of dollars in revenues. The chief guardian of this policy was EA's CEO, Lawrence Probst, who had declared, "EA will not publish games with gratuitous sex and violence."[17] In years past, when EA had acquired smaller game developers whose game portfolio included games with Mature ratings, EA had ceased further production and sale of those games. But while forbidding gore and raunchy graphics, EA did include trash talk in its sports games. During the past 25 years, EA had won over 700 awards for outstanding software in the United States and Europe.

Brands and Product Lines

Electronic Arts marketed its video games under four brand names:

- EA SPORTS—Games for this brand included EA's series of realistic sports simulation games for professional and college football, professional and college basketball, World Cup soccer, professional golf, NASCAR racing, rugby, boxing, and fantasy football.

- EA—This brand covered a variety of games (mostly nonsports) and included such titles as Need for Speed, Most Wanted, The Sims 2, Harry Potter and the Goblet of Fire, and Burnout Revenge.

- EA SPORTS BIG—This brand, used for arcade-style extreme sports games and modified traditional sports games, included such titles as SSX On Tour (skiing and snowboarding) and FIFA Street 2 (soccer).

- Pogo—The Pogo brand was used for EA's online and downloadable casual games (card games, puzzle games, and word games) made available at www.pogo.com; there were three sub-brands of casual games: (1) Pogo (a free online games service),

(2) Club Pogo (a premium subscription-based online games service), and
(3) Pogo-To-Go (downloadable games).

EA had been highly successful in boosting unit sales volumes and revenues through the development of product families or "franchise" games. For example, most of the new versions of most of EA SPORTS titles were released annually, so as to include the latest team rosters, event schedules, venue locations, and so on. Likewise, EA had been successful in creating and marketing sequels for many of its best-selling EA and EA SPORTS BIG products. The company also released "expansion packs" for certain PC titles that provided additional content (characters, storylines, settings, missions) for previously published games—for example, The Sims 2 Open for Business expanded the characters, settings, and game play of the original The Sims 2 game. Annual release games, sequels, and games that spawned expansion packs were considered "franchise" titles.

CO-PUBLISHING AND DISTRIBUTION PRODUCTS Electronic Arts partnered with other game development companies to assist them in developing their own interactive games, which EA then published, marketed, and distributed on the partner's behalf—an arrangement the company referred to as co-publishing. Another product category, termed distribution products, involved distributing and marketing video games that were developed and published by other companies.

Distribution Channels

Electronic Arts distributed its games through four channels: retailers, online sellers, cellular handsets, and other manufacturers that bundled EA games with their own products. The console, PC, and handheld games that EA published were usually made available to consumers on a disk that was packaged and typically sold in retail stores and through various online stores (including EA's own online store at www.ea.com). EA referred to these as packaged goods products. EA's games were available in approximately 80,000 retail locations worldwide. In North America, EA's largest market, packaged goods products were sold primarily to mass-market retailers (such as Wal-Mart, Target, and Kmart), electronics specialty stores (such as Best Buy and Circuit City), and specialty retailers (such as Toys "R" Us, Blockbuster, and game software retailer GameStop); about 94 percent of EA's North American revenues were derived from packaged goods sales to retailers. In Europe, sales to about 10 retailers accounted for about 40 percent of sales. In Japan, the biggest fraction of EA's sales were made through a distribution relationship with Sony. Sales to Wal-Mart constituted 13–15 percent of EA's total revenues worldwide.

Online distribution consisted of (1) online-only casual games that EA made available to consumers at www.pogo.com and on certain online services provided by America Online; (2) MMOGs sold to consumers in the form of a CD, DVD, or download file containing the necessary software to play the game online (EA's two MMOGs were Ultima Online and The Sims Online); and (3) including capability features in certain packaged PC, PlayStation, PSP, and Xbox games that enabled consumers to participate in online communities and play against one another via the Internet at either EA's site (in the case of PC games) or the sites of the console/handheld makers. Online downloads for certain games were available at the EA.com site, third-party sites such as Gametap and GameStop, and Microsoft's Xbox Live service.

Consumers with cellular phones could purchase and download EA games from wireless carrier services operated by Verizon, Cingular, Sprint, and Vodafone, among others. In an effort to better capitalize on the growth opportunities in this distribution channel, Electronic Arts in 2006 had acquired JAMDAT Mobile, a global publisher of wireless games and other wireless entertainment applications, and merged it with EA's existing cellular handset software game development operations to form EA Mobile. EA executives believed the added resources and expertise provided by the JAMDAT acquisition would enable EA Mobile to rapidly grow

the $19 million in cellular game revenues the company received in fiscal 2006.

The fourth and smallest distribution channel involved supplying games to manufacturers in related industries (primarily the makers of PCs and computer software). It was common for PC and other software manufacturers to pay fees to EA for the licensing and distribution rights to include EA games as part of the manufacturer's package sold to consumers. EA called such sales OEM bundles.

Pricing and Marketing

The retail selling prices in North America of EA's games, excluding older titles marketed as classics, typically ranged from $39.99 to $59.99. Classics titles had retail prices from $10 to $30. Outside North America, prices varied widely according to local market conditions.

EA's business was highly seasonal. Retail sales were highest in the calendar year-end holiday season (about 40–50 percent of the annual total) and lowest in the April–May–June period.

EA's expenditures for sales and marketing were climbing (see Exhibit 6). A big part of EA's marketing effort was devoted to promoting the EA SPORTS brand. Management saw sports as a particularly attractive genre. Sports games were appealing to males between the ages of 16 and 40 because they had nearly photo-realistic graphics and gave game-playing sports fans the chance to carry on rivalries that were the trademark of professional and collegiate teams. Sports games were regularly endorsed by the biggest stars in professional sports, which helped spur sales (as well as providing big-name sports stars with lucrative endorsement contracts).

EA had sales offices in 36 countries and was actively pursuing sales in most all parts of the world. The company used a field sales organization and a group of telephone sales representatives to market its games directly to retailers. In markets where direct sales were uneconomical, EA used specialized and regional distributors and rack jobbers to get its products on retailer shelves. Orders from retailers were typically shipped upon receipt, resulting in little or no order backlog. However, sales of digital downloads at EA.com and other online sites were becoming a bigger factor.

Foreign sales were expected to account for a significant and growing portion of EA's revenues. Exhibit 8 shows the geographic distribution of EA's sales for fiscal years 2001–2007.

EA's Suppliers

Electronic Arts used two types of suppliers:

- Sony, Nintendo, and Microsoft's preapproved manufacturers that produced the packaged games for EA titles played on their platforms.
- Third-party vendors that handled the production of EA's PC-based game titles—pressing of CDs or DVDs, printing of user manuals and other packaging-related materials, the packaging of the disk in jewel cases, and shipping.

EA was able to negotiate volume discounts in many cases, and it was the company's practice to have multiple sources of supply for all the functions that were outsourced to third-party suppliers. It was usually able to receive shipment of orders from these suppliers within two weeks. The costs to press a disk, print game instruction booklets, and package a DVD were typically less than $2 per unit.

EA kept only a small inventory of its games on hand because (1) it could obtain additional supplies and fill retailer orders from replenished inventories within two or three weeks and (2) historically, most sales of a particular game occurred 60–90 days after initial release.

EA's Strategy

EA's near-term strategic objective was to maintain and grow its leadership position in games for the Xbox 360, PS3, and Wii. Toward this end, EA had spent heavily on R&D to develop altogether new games and sequels of existing games (with expanded missions, more elaborate graphics, and other fresh options and features); R&D spending, the lion's share of which was for games development, totaled $1.04 billion in fiscal 2007, $758 million in fiscal 2006, and $633 million in fiscal 2005, amounts about triple the R&D spending in 2000 (see Exhibit 6). The early results on EA's new games for the Xbox 360 were encouraging; in fiscal 2006, 3 of the top 10 games for the Xbox 360 in North America and Europe were EA games. EA had introduced a total of 360 games for the Xbox 360 platform (many of which were upgraded and/or more elaborate versions of games for the original Xbox).

To further capitalize on the opportunities that management saw in the global market for video games, EA management had established a number of strategic objectives and was pursuing initiatives to achieve them:

- *Exploit the opportunity for digital downloading*—To respond to the growing affinity of consumers for buying and downloading games from the Internet, in 2006 EA began offering digital downloads of most of its PC games. Further, starting

Exhibit 8

EA's Net Revenues by Geographic Area, Fiscal Years 2001–2007 ($ in millions)

	2007	2006	2005	2004	2003	2002	2001
North America	$1,666	$1,584	$1,665	$1,610	$1,436	$1,093	$ 832
Europe	1,261	1,174	1,284	1,180	879	519	387
Asia-Pacific	164	193	180	167	167	112	104
Total	$3,091	$2,951	$3,129	$2,957	$2,482	$1,724	$1,323

Sources: 2003 10-K report, p.113; 2005 10-K report, p. 96; 2006 10-K report, p. 40; and company press release, May 8, 2007.

with the launch of its new Xbox 360 titles, EA had begun promoting several of its newly introduced games by offering free demos at EA.com. As of early 2006, EA's demo for Fight Night Round 3 had been downloaded more than 400,000 times and was the most popular demo on Xbox Live. Although PC game sales via digital downloads had initially been small, EA management believed that growing consumer use of digital downloads would help EA generate incremental revenue and improve operating margins.

- *Grow revenues via "microtransactions"*—This strategy element involved offering buyers of EA games the ability to purchase additional content and game-enhancing features (characters, storylines, settings, missions, and strategy guides) for games they already owned. Players of EA sports games could pay a modest fee to download new uniforms for their athletes, customized parts for their racing cars, and strategy guides to improve their skills. In fiscal year 2006, EA began offering premium content at price points between $9.99 and $29.99 for its Ultima Online, Club Pogo, Battlefield 2, and The Sims 2 games played on PCs and quickly sold more than 200,000 downloads. Premium content for EA games played on new generation consoles started being sold online via microtransactions in late 2006 and in 2007. EA saw these microtransactions as creating an entirely new revenue stream for many of its most popular games.

- *Make greater use of in-game dynamic advertising technology*—In recent years, EA had begun programming into certain of its games a small number of static ads (quick product messages embedded in the game) that would not intrude on the player's entertainment experience. However, new technology had become available that would allow it to stream ever-changing advertising messages into games played online. For instance, a roadside billboard in Need for Speed could display a soft drink message on one day, a fast-food ad the next day, and an ad to shop at Wal-Mart the third day. While this technology was at an early stage, EA game designers were building additional dynamic ads into online games to enable EA to grow advertising revenues. According to Nielsen Entertainment, in-game advertising was expected to be a $75 million market in 2006 and grow to $1 billion by 2010.[18]

- *Grow revenue from subscriptions for online game play*—In early 2007, more than 1.5 million players were paying fees of $5 monthly or $30 annually to play games and participate in EA's Club Pogo community. More than half of the subscribers at www.pogo.com were women over the age of 35. EA was planning to launch Pogo in China and Europe. As of mid-2006, subscription revenues for playing MMOGs at EA.com had been disappointingly small. Total subscription service revenues were $61 million in fiscal 2006 and $79 million in fiscal 2007, amounts that were less than the revenues from just one of EA's best-selling game titles.

- *Grow revenues from games played on cellular handsets*—To position itself to capitalize on the expected growth in mobile gaming, EA had entered into agreements with 90 wireless carriers in 40 countries to distribute EA's games and applications for wireless phones. These agreements set forth how the amount of the one-time and/or monthly subscription fee would be divided between EA and the carrier. In the years to come, EA expected to enter into agreement with additional wireless carriers. The JAMDAT Mobile acquisition was made specifically to bolster EA's competitiveness in mobile gaming. EA had what management believed was an aggressive plan to migrate many of EA's popular game franchises to the mobile platform, grow its mobile games business in North America where it was already the market leader, and expand its presence in Europe and Asia.

- *Pursue sales in countries and market segments where EA's presence is low and increase the company's global market share*—EA was unrivaled in its ability to market, sell, and distribute its game titles to consumers all over the world. Creating new online games and cultivating new customers was an important part of the company's growth strategy. By early 2007, EA expected to have more than 300 people dedicated to production, marketing, and sales in emerging markets like China, India, and Eastern Europe.

- *Capitalize on the expected mushrooming game player interest in MMOGs*—This strategy element had two related components: develop more PC games (since consumers who played games on their PCs were strong candidates for online game play) and strengthen EA's capabilities in designing games well suited for multiplayers. By some order of magnitude, EA was the world's number one publisher of games for the PC. In fiscal 2006, EA had 4 of the top 10 best-selling PC game titles in North America and 5 of the top 10 in Europe. Flagship franchises like The Sims, Battlefield, and Command & Conquer had millions of loyal players, and new versions were being prepared to extend that success. Several new PC games were in development. In 2006, EA acquired Mythic Entertainment, a critically acclaimed developer of MMOGs with a product line consisting of 15 MMOGs, the best known of which was Dark Age of Camelot. Mythic was based in Virginia and had a staff of more than 170 people. EA management believed that Mythic's proprietary technology, innovative game design, and record of exemplary customer service would enhance EA's resource capabilities and competitiveness in the MMOG segment.

- *Decrease reliance on game content licensed from others and increase the number of games based on ideas from EA's own game development staff*—Because escalating licensing costs involving the use of content owned by the

NFL, the NBA, FIFA, and movie studios (for movie titles like *Harry Potter and the Sorcerer's Stone* and *The Godfather*) was putting heavy pressure on operating margins, EA management had set a goal of increasing the percentage of its revenues from games with wholly owned content from 40 percent to 50 percent in the next cycle of game releases. Management believed that by tapping more heavily into the ideas and creativity of its own game design staff, it would be able to improve both game quality and profit margins. During 2006, EA's game designers were responding to the challenge to create more in-house games—two supposedly innovative games, SPORE and Army of Two, were scheduled for release in 2007, and creative sequels to six other popular EA franchise titles were in the works.

While top executives at Electronic Arts saw online gaming as a critical component of their overall strategy to grow sales of the company's existing and future products, they recognized that there were many questions surrounding the global market for online gaming. At what pace would households continue to switch from dial-up to broadband Internet connections? What fraction of video game enthusiasts would become enamored with playing games online? How fast would online gaming grow, and how big would the global market for online gaming get? Would interest in online gaming prove to be permanent or a passing fad? Would other innovative online entertainment experiences emerge to erode the interest in online gaming? To what extent would gamers be willing to pay for online game content (game-enhancing microtransactions and/or monthly subscriptions)? Should EA concentrate on developing online games with global market appeal or games targeted at the preferences of consumers in just a few countries?

Exhibit 9 shows the number of new title releases by console for fiscal years 2005–2007. Roughly 70 percent of EA revenues came from new releases of existing games. Exhibit 10

Exhibit 9

New EA Game Titles for Selected Platforms, Fiscal Years 2005–2007

PLATFORM	NUMBER OF NEW GAME TITLE RELEASES		
	FISCAL 2007	FISCAL 2006	FISCAL 2005
PlayStation 2		28	27
PlayStation 3	8–12	—	—
PlayStation Portable	n.a.	16	3
Xbox		28	26
Xbox 360	15–20	7	—
Nintendo Wii	4+	—	—
GameCube		14	20

n.a. = Not available.

Source: Company annual reports and press releases.

presents a breakdown of EA's revenues by game platform and product category for fiscal years 2001–2007. Management expected that revenues from prior-generation platforms would continue to erode while those from current and future generation platforms would rise.

EA's Competitors

Electronic Arts faced several different groups of competitors. In the console and handheld segment, EA's main rivals included Sony, Microsoft, and Nintendo (all of which made games for their own platform brands), along with perhaps 20 other independent game developers, including Activision, Atari, Sega, Square Enix (a big game developer in Japan), Take Two Interactive, and THQ. Diversified media companies like Disney, Viacom, and Fox were expanding their efforts in publishing and marketing video games. In the casual games portion of the online market segment, EA's chief rivals included Yahoo!, Popcap, MSN, and Real

Exhibit 10

EA's Revenues by Product Line, Fiscal Years 2001–2007 ($ in millions)

REVENUE SOURCE	2007	2006	2005	2004	2003	2002	2001
Games for Consoles							
Sony PlayStation 3	$ 93	—	—	—	—	—	—
Sony PlayStation 2	885	$1,127	$1,330	$1,315	$ 911	$ 483	$ 259
Sony PlayStation	—	1	10	30	100	190	310
Microsoft Xbox 360	481	140	—	—	—	—	—
Microsoft Xbox	157	400	516	384	219	78	—
Nintendo Wii	65						
Nintendo GameCube	61	135	212	200	177	52	—
All consoles	1,742	1,803	2,068	1,929	1,407	803	569
Games for PCs	498	418	531	470	500	456	405
Games for Mobile Devices							
Nintendo Game Boy Advance and Game Boy Color	39	55	77	78	105	82	—
PlayStation Portable (PSP)	248	252	18	—	—	—	—
Nintendo DS	104	67	23	—	—	—	—
Cellular handsets	139	19	—	—	—	—	—
All mobile devices	530	393	118	78	105	82	
Co-publishing and distribution	175	213	283	398	376	269	222
Internet subscription services	79	61	55	49	38	31	29
Licensing, advertising, and other	57	63	74	33	57	84	97
Total	$3,091	$2,951	$3,129	$2,957	$2,482	$1,725	$1,322

Source: EA's 2003, 2006, and 2007 10-K reports; company press release, May 8, 2007.

Networks. In MMOGs, EA competed against NCsoft, Sony, Atari, Blizzard Entertainment, and an assortment of lesser-known Asian companies. In the cell phone segment, EA's principal competitors included Disney, Gameloft, Sony, Yahoo!, THQ Wireless, Infospace, Mforma, Sorrent, and Verisign.

Small game developers were struggling to absorb the rising costs of developing games in preparation for wide-scale market adoption of the new generation of consoles. They were more capital constrained, had less predictable revenues and cash flow, lacked product diversity, and were forced to spread fixed costs over a smaller revenue base—factors that were prompting the industry to consolidate to a smaller number of larger developers. Since 2000, a number of game developers across the world had merged or been acquired. Several had gone bankrupt (including 3DO and Acclaim Entertainment) and several more (including Atari and Midway Games) were in financial distress as of 2006. Many struggling developers were having trouble convincing potential buyers that the value of their game titles and development teams outweighed the risks of taking on their entire enterprise, given that they were either losing money or barely breaking even.

Brief profiles of selected rivals are presented in the following paragraphs. Exhibit 11 provides summary information on these and other rivals.

ACTIVISION   Activision was founded in 1979 and headquartered in Santa Monica, California; its mission was to be one of the largest, most profitable, and most highly respected interactive entertainment companies in the world. In 2006, Activision was the second largest independent U.S. publisher of video game software (behind Electronic Arts). It released 17 major titles in fiscal 2006, versus 14 in fiscal 2005. The company posted net revenues of $1.47 billion for the fiscal year ended March 31, 2003, almost double the $786 million reported for fiscal 2002. It reported 2006 net income of $41.9 million, versus a net of $138.3 million in 2005 and $77.7 million in 2004, and ended its 2006 fiscal year with $1 billion in cash. Geographically,

Activision's 2006 revenues were divided almost equally between the United States and Europe; only $40 million in revenues came from other parts of the world market.

Activision management believed that the revenue opportunities created by the new-generation platforms would produce the greatest growth period in the industry's history. It expected that online gaming, wireless gaming, and in-game advertising would play significant roles in both the company's and the industry's long-term performance.

Activision's strategy was grounded around four elements:

- Developing and marketing games for a wide range of product categories and target audiences.

- Focusing on games that were, or had the potential to become, "franchise properties" with sustainable consumer appeal and brand recognition.

- Strengthening the company's international presence—the company had recently begun selling its games in Norway, Austria, and Denmark.

- Exerting stronger control over game development costs and variable marketing expenses so as to improve profit margins—the company was working to improve the efficiency of the game development process and have its various development studios share tools and technologies.

Activision's biggest competitive strength was in games based on superheroes such as Spider-Man and James Bond, animated characters such as Shrek, and skateboard legend Tony Hawk—the company's series of Tony Hawk games had generated combined revenues exceeding $1 billion. It was also strong in action sports games other than skateboarding, having signed long-term agreements with athletes in biking, surfing, snowboarding, and wakeboarding. Activision released four new game titles concurrent with the launch of the Xbox 360 and, as of early 2006, had the top-selling game on the Xbox 360, Call of Duty 2. It released three new titles to correspond with

Exhibit 11

Financial Performance of Selected Game Developers, 2004–2006 ($ in millions)

	FISCAL YEARS		
	2006	**2005**	**2004**
Activision *			
Net revenues	$1,468.0	$1,405.9	$ 947.7
Cost of sales—product costs	734.9	658.9	475.5
Cost of sales—intellectual property licenses and royalties	205.5	186.0	91.6
Net income	41.9	138.3	77.7
Net cash provided by operating activities	86.0	215.3	67.4
Cash and cash equivalents	923.9	915.4	675.8
THQ *			
Net sales	$ 806.6	$ 756.7	$ 640.8
Cost of sales	287.9	255.2	234.6
License amortization and royalties	80.5	85.9	71.1
Software development amortization	116.4	93.6	105.6
Product development	84.2	73.0	36.9
Selling and marketing	123.6	110.5	87.1
Net income	34.3	63.0	35.8
Net cash provided by operating activities	42.8	60.5	71.2
Cash and cash equivalents	371.6	331.2	253.0
Take Two Interactive **			
Net revenues	$1,037.8	$1,202.6	$1,127.7
Product costs	538.8	593.4	619.7
Royalties	206.8	164.3	114.1
Software development costs	79.9	28.4	15.9
Selling and marketing	139.3	157.7	117.6
Research and development	64.3	73.2	43.3
Net income	(184.9)	37.5	65.4
Net cash provided by operations	43.4	40.0	20.5
Cash and cash equivalents	132.5	107.2	155.1
Midway Games **			
Net revenues	$ 165.6	$ 150.1	$ 161.6
Product costs and distribution	67.3	56.2	62.7
Royalties and product development	68.9	75.8	41.3
Research and development expense	37.0	39.7	25.6
Selling and marketing expense	43.2	57.2	41.2
Net loss	(77.8)	(112.5)	(24.7)
Net cash used in operations	(92.9)	(100.4)	(46.1)
Cash and cash equivalents	73.4	98.4	118.3

* Fiscal years ending March 31.

** Fiscal years ending December 31.

Source: Company 10-K reports and press releases.

the introduction of the PS3, and three new titles concurrent with the introduction of Wii.

In June 2006, in the latest of a series of acquisitions over the past nine years, Activision purchased video game publisher RedOctane, the developer of the popular Guitar Hero franchise; this acquisition gave Activision early leadership in music-based gaming, which management believed would be one of the fastest-growing genres in the coming years.

TAKE TWO INTERACTIVE SOFTWARE INC.

Take Two's games were concentrated in the action, racing, strategy, sports, and simulation genres and were marketed under four brands: Rockstar Games, 2K Games, 2K Sports, and Global Star Software. In 2005, Take Two released 14 new internally developed titles and 28 new titles developed by third parties; in 2005, the company released 15 new internally developed titles and 18 titles developed by third parties. Of the total of 29 internally developed titles developed in 2005 and 2006, six sold more than 1 million units across all platforms and four sold more than 500,000 units; five of the 46 externally developed titles sold more than 500,000 units. Many of Take Two Interactive's titles were rated M (age 17 and over) or AO (age 18 and over)—Take Two was the leading publisher of games for mature audiences. The company's top franchise was its M-rated Grand Theft Auto series, which had sales of over 7 million copies in 2005 and accounted for 38.1 percent of Take Two's 2005 revenues. Management saw the Grand Theft Auto series as a "uniquely original popular culture phenomenon." Take Two expected to release at least 25 new titles during 2007.

The company had 12 game development studios in the United States, Canada, and England and a game development staff of 1,140 employees as of October 2005. Its game development personnel had the technical capabilities to develop and localize software titles for all major hardware platforms and the PC. Its localization capabilities included both translating game content into foreign languages and making changes in game content to enhance local appeal. Management closed 3 of the company's 12 game development studios in 2006 in response to declining sales and mounting losses.

Take Two had sales offices in 13 countries and a marketing and sales staff of about 256 people. During 2003–2005, the company spent progressively larger amounts for advertising—$56 million in 2003, $72 million in 2004, and $101 million in 2005—but trimmed its advertising and promotional activities in 2006 as an economizing measure due to a downturn in sales revenues. In 2006, the company derived 69 percent of its revenues from sales in North America, 28 percent from sales in Europe, and 3 percent from sales in other parts of the world. Sales to Take Two's largest five customers accounted for almost 41 percent of 2005 revenues and over 49 percent of 2006 revenues; Wal-Mart was Take Two's largest customer, accounting for 15.4 percent of 2006 revenues. Financial data on Take Two Interactive are shown in Exhibit 11.

THQ INC.

THQ was one of the world's fastest-growing video game publishers with a diverse portfolio of game titles catering to every segment of the gaming audience. With fiscal 2006 revenues of $807 million, it was the fourth largest independent U.S. developer and publisher of video games. Headquartered in Los Angeles, THQ employed 1,700 people; its game development resources included some 1,300 people in 15 studio locations in North America, the United Kingdom, and Australia. THQ developed games for all console and handheld game systems, PCs, and cell phones; it was the leading independent publisher of games for handheld systems (the Game Boy, Nintendo DS, and PSP). THQ games were on retail shelves in more than 75 countries and it distributed wireless content in every major worldwide market. In fiscal 2005, 39 percent of THQ's sales were outside North America, up from 29 percent in 2004. The company's revenues had grown for 11 consecutive years.

At the end of fiscal 2006, THQ had shipped more than 25 million units of games based on its series of World Wrestling Entertainment games, 17 million units of its SpongeBob SquarePants games, more than 8.5 million units of games based on *Finding Nemo,* and more than 7.5 million units of games based on *The Incredibles.* It had a number of other "franchise" titles and several all-new games scheduled for release in 2006–2007. THQ's financial and strategic priorities were to grow revenues at above-market rates, increase operating margins, and boost sales outside North America. The company's strategy to grow revenues in 2007–2008 was to expand its share of games sold to core gamers, emphasize more casual game content suitable for cellular phones, continue to acquire small developers and thereby expand its internal game development capabilities, acquire additional licensed intellectual content, expand its digital downloading and microtransaction offerings, and incorporate additional in-game advertising.

Selected financial performance data for THQ are shown in Exhibit 11. Management had forecast that sales for fiscal 2007 would rise by 12–18 percent, resulting in sales of $900 to $950 million.

MIDWAY GAMES INC.   In 2006, Midway was struggling, having lost over $330 million in 2003–2006. (Recent financial data are shown in Exhibit 11.) To help stem the tide of losses, the company reduced the size of its workforce by about 10 percent during 2006. About 88 percent of the company's stock was owned by Sumner Redstone, CEO and chairman of Viacom.

Historically, Midway had been strong in games for mature audiences—versions of its best-known title, Mortal Kombat, had sold over 20 million copies. The company also developed over-the-top sports games characterized by extreme game play and the exaggerated abilities of characters; its best-seller in this genre was NBA Ballers. Over 86 percent of the company's 2005 revenues came from games played on the PlayStation 2 and Xbox; about 19 percent of the company's revenues came from sales of Mortal Kombat.

Midway had six game design studios and an internal product development staff of 650 employees, up from 330 in 2003. Four new studios had been added since 2004, and one in Australia was closed. The company released 12 new titles in 2004, 18 new titles in 2005, and 28 titles in 2006. Midway spent $27.7 million for advertising in 2006, $41.2 million in 2005, and $28.3 million in 2004. To conserve on game development costs in 2006, Midway was standardizing its preproduction and planning process, sharing technology across all studios, and instituting peer review and intrastudio resource sharing. Midway's costs to develop games for the PlayStation 2 and Xbox had ranged from $4 million to $16 million; management expected that development costs for PS3 and Xbox 360 games would run between $10 and $25 million per game and take 24 to 36 months.

To try to capitalize on the expected surge in spending for games for newly introduced platforms, Midway had bolstered its distribution capabilities in Europe, opened a new sales office in the United Kingdom to orchestrate sales of Midway titles in Europe and Australia, increased its product development efforts in games for children and for PCs (neither of which had been a significant part of the company's business in recent years), and increased its development efforts in multiaction games that allowed players to have multiple experiences (such as shooting, driving, and fighting) within a single game. In September 2006, Midway released The Grim Adventures of Billy and Mandy, a humorous animated fighting/adventure game for children based on licensed content from a popular TV show on Cartoon Network. Management expected these initiatives along with its portfolio of new titles for 2007 (which included *The Lord of the Rings Online*) to produce full-year 2007 revenues of $225 million and reduced losses of $40 million.

Endnotes

[1] Letter to the stockholders, 2006 proxy statement, and annual report, p. 3.

[2] As quoted in Yukari Kane and Nick Wingfield, "Problems for PlayStation 3 Could Bring Other Sony Setbacks," *The Wall Street Journal*, September 25, 2006, p. B6.

[3] Peter Lewis, "The Biggest Game in Town," *Fortune*, September 15, 2003, p. 135.

[4] Entertainment Software Association, "Essential Facts about the Computer and Video Game Industry," 2006, www.theesa.com (accessed September 7, 2006).

[5] Raph Koster, "The Age of Dinosaurs," speech to Austin Game Conference on September 7, 2006; as reported by Mark Wallace in "AGC: Koster Says Game Industry Dinosaur 'Doomed,'" www.gamsutra.com (accessed September 13, 2006).

[6] Paul A. Paterson, "Synergy and Expanding Technology Drive Booming Video Industry," *TD Monthly* 2, no. 8 (August 2003), www.toydirectory.com/monthly/Aug2003 (accessed November 15, 2003).

[7] Constance Steinkuehler and Dmitri Williams, "Where Everybody Knows Your (Screen) Name: Online Games as 'Third Places,'" *Journal of Computer-Mediated Communication* 11, no. 4 (July 2006), Article 1, http://jcmc.indiana.edu (accessed September 12, 2006).

[8] DFC Intelligence, "Who Will Benefit from the Growth of Online Game Subscription Revenue?" press release, March 7, 2006.

[9] Mark Wallace, "Michael Dell on the Future of PC Gaming," a transcript of a public Q&A session with Michael Dell at the Austin Game Conference in September 2006, September 11, 2006, www.gamsutra.com (accessed September 13, 2006).

[10] Lilly Rockwell, "Dell Forges Closer Ties to Gamers," *Austin American-Statesman,* September 9, 2006, www.statesman.com (accessed September 14, 2006).

[11] As cited in THQ Inc.'s 2006 10-K report, pp. 6–7.

[12] According to information in Take Two Interactive Software's 2005 10-K report, p. 6.

[13] Statistics attributed to MMOG designer Raph Koster and reported in Carolyn Koh, "AGC Talk: Raph Koster's 'The Age of Dinosaurs,'" *Game News,* September 13, 2006, http://home.nestor.minsk.by/game/news/2006/09/1303.html (accessed September 13, 2006).

[14] Lou Kesten, "Video-Game News in Brief: Fall Releases; a 'Madden' Record; Ads in Games," September 7, 2006, www.deseretnews.com (accessed September 11, 2006).

[15] Associated Press, "Electronic Arts: A Powerhouse Well-Attuned to Public Tastes," news release, August 18, 2003.

[16] Dean Takahashi, "Electronic Arts Grows to $2.5 Billion in Annual Sales," *San Jose Mercury News,* May 5, 2003.

[17] As quoted in Ashby Jones, "The Rules of the Game," *Corporate Counsel* 3, no. 7 (July 1, 2003), pp. 72ff., www.law.com/jsp/cc/pubarticleCC.jsp?id=1055463668855 (accessed December 4, 2003).

[18] As cited in Activision's 2006 annual report, p. 12.

Manpower Australia: Using Strategy Maps and the Balanced Scorecard Effectively

Suresh Cuganesan
Macquarie Graduate School of Management

Guy Ford
Macquarie Graduate School of Management

Haider Khan
Macquarie Graduate School of Management

The 2004 financial performance was very encouraging for Varina Nissen, who was then in the second year of her role as managing director for Manpower Australia. Revenue had increased by 10 percent, while costs were well below target. The overall measure of performance, return on sales, had been improved. Scott McLachlan, the CFO and director of corporate services, announced confidently, "We have achieved the budget targets. It's never happened before in the history of Manpower Australia." The corporate strategy developed by Nissen and her team, and executed through the balanced scorecard (BSC), had achieved the short-term financial objectives for the company and a turnaround in a relatively short time. However, future challenges awaited Nissen and McLachlan, not least of which was how to use the BSC to secure further performance improvements.

The recruitment industry in Australia heading into 2005 continued to become more challenging. Since the industry had reached relative maturity, profit margins were being eroded. Manpower's major competitors had also focused on improving productivity and were often able to offer clients better prices. This had affected the company's core business of temporary placements, which had been flat for the last couple of years. There were also candidate shortages in certain segments of the market, while customers were demanding total solutions for their human resource management needs, ranging from the existing recruiting services to learning/development and performance management/succession planning activities. An opportunity existed for growth through innovation—developing and marketing new products and services to target customers.

Under Nissen's leadership, a new strategic vision had been developed and communicated: Manpower was to become a "leader in innovative people solutions." The emphasis was on innovation and growth of higher-margin business, such as human resource services, while maintaining high service-delivery speed at lower costs in Manpower's core business of recruitment. To help communicate and implement her strategy, Nissen had developed and implemented a Strategy Map and BSC for the organization in 2004. According to Manpower's senior management, the BSC at Manpower had been important in communicating the key behaviors required for improved productivity and demonstrating the financial impacts of doing so, with the improved financial performance in 2004 being seen as proof that it worked.

However, given the changing business environment, Nissen wanted to know whether the value propositions were being delivered to targeted customers and, if so, whether they were leading to improved customer and financial outcomes. Was the company progressing fast enough in performing activities and services that were valued by targeted customers? In addition, the CFO of Manpower's global operations was still concerned over the slow pace of productivity gains in Manpower Australia as compared to Manpower's global standards. Beating the productivity targets agreed on with the parent company represented another challenge for Manpower Australia, where return on revenue had to be increased by 2 percent and the expense to gross profit ratio decreased by 10 percent.

Nissen and McLachlan both felt that the BSC could help the business implement its strategy more effectively and attain a higher level of performance than that already achieved. However, they were also aware that the BSC was not being used as extensively as they had envisaged in some parts of the business and, in some cases, was being totally ignored in managerial decision making. Also, there was a lack of consistent communication to teams on effective progress on performance. Overall, they thought that the BSC needed to be improved if it was to focus the entire organization on the critical leading indicators of success for the business.

The Australian Recruitment Employment Services Industry

Market Size

The Australian market for employment services was estimated at A$12.5 billion (US$8.1 billion) in 2003, and had grown by 13.0 percent from 2002. During the last five years, the market had grown by over 60 percent. One of the major drivers for this growth was that companies were focusing more on investing and strengthening their core competencies, and turning to strategic alliances with employment service providers to manage and operate noncore activities such as staff recruitment and related human resource management activities.

General temporary jobs, growing by 107.9 percent during 1999–2003 (see Exhibit 1), constituted the largest sector in the employment services industry, with 37.7 percent (A$4.7 billion) of the total revenue mix. Temporary employment provided flexibility for organizations in

Exhibit 1

Sizes of Market Sectors in Employment Services Industry in Australia, 1999–2003 (A$ in millions)

	1999	2003
Executive search	A$ 579.5	A$1,191.2
General permanent jobs	2,429.1	2,883.9
General temporary jobs	2,273.2	4,727.1
Outplacement consultancy	497.5	877.7
Specialist agencies	2,038.7	2,858.9

Source: Euromonitor International.

times of economic uncertainty as well as flexibility on the side of employees. Although the executive employment market remained flat during 2003, there was consistent growth in this sector due to increased pressure to improve corporate performance and the growth of global firms. In Australia, the demand for talent and experience had increased at most levels in organizations, particularly in information technology (IT) and financial services–related jobs.

Competitor Dynamics

Industry statistics revealed that there were approximately 2,750 organizations in the employment services (recruiting) industry in 2002/2003. The employment services industry in Australia was highly fragmented, with low barriers to entry and the nondominance of global players. Adecco Group SA had been the market leader for the last six years, with a market share of 11.6 percent. Manpower Services (Australia) Pty. Ltd. had the second largest market share (6.0 percent), while Skilled Engineering, a strong performer in temporary placement, was third with a market share of 5.8 percent (see Exhibit 2). There were also a number of niche service providers that focused on higher-margin areas such as executive search specifically.

Market Growth Forecasts

The recruiting (employment services) market was forecast to grow 61.7 percent from 2003 to 2008, to reach a value of A\$20.3 billion (US\$13.2 billion). The major drivers for growth were the positive economic outlook, existing low unemployment levels (which, at 5.6 percent, were the lowest in 14 years), and high confidence levels positively affecting investments in human resources. While general temporary jobs were projected to continue to be the largest sector in the Australian employment services market, with a value of A\$7.6 billion and 37.5 percent of total industry revenues, the other forecasted growth sector was executive search, with a forecast of 61 percent growth.

In addition, companies were looking to outsource more of the human resource management function. Alongside the provision of core recruiting and staff services, opportunities existed for participants in the employment services industry to provide core human resource management functions such as employee records maintenance, payroll services, and health/wealth benefits services, together with learning/development and performance/succession planning advice. Overall, opportunities existed for recruitment firms to become more proactive

---

Exhibit 2

Market Shares of Leading Employment Services Providers in Australia, 2003

Adecco Group SA	11.6%
Manpower Services (Australia) Pty. Ltd.	6.0
Skilled Engineering Ltd.	5.8
Hudson Global Resources	4.6
Chandler Macleod Group Pty. Ltd.	3.1
Hays Personnel Services (Australia) Pty. Ltd.	3.0
Kelly Services Australia	2.5
Spherion Group	1.7
Julia Ross	1.6
Candle Australia Ltd.	1.6
Drake	1.5
Integrated Group	1.5
Michael Page	0.7

Source: Euromonitor International.

in offering solutions to their clients across the entirety of the human resource management spectrum.

Manpower Global

Manpower Inc., established in 1948 in Milwaukee, Wisconsin, was a world leader in the employment services industry, offering customers a continuum of services to meet their needs throughout the employment and business cycle. A Fortune 500 company, it specialized in permanent, temporary, and contract recruitment; employee assessment; training; career transition; and organizational consulting services. Manpower's global network of 4,300 offices in 74 countries and territories enabled the company to meet the needs of its 440,000 customers per year. These ranged from small and medium-sized enterprises across all industry sectors to some of the world's largest multinational corporations. During 2003, the company's 21,400 staff employees and 1.6 million temporary workers worldwide supplied 780 millions of hours of work. Manpower Inc. claimed to be able to help any company—no matter where it was in its business evolution—to raise productivity through improved strategy, quality, efficiency, and cost reduction, thereby enabling clients to concentrate more on their core business activities.

Manpower had shown impressive financial performance worldwide during financial year 2004. Revenues from services increased by 22.5 percent, to US$14.9 billion; gross profit increased by 30.5 percent, to US$2.8 billion; and net earnings per share, diluted, increased by 53.3 percent, to US$2.59. The company's global vision, strategies, and values (see Exhibit 3) represented a framework for direction and priorities in making decisions, developing opportunities, and building relationships for Manpower's people and customers around the world.

Manpower Australia

Manpower had been operating in Australia and New Zealand as a human resources solution provider for over three decades. It was first established as a franchised operation in 1965 but was later purchased by Manpower Inc. in 1996. There were 72 offices in Australia/New Zealand, with 34,000 temporary workers. During 2003, over 85,000 permanent and temporary jobs were filled in Australia/New Zealand by Manpower. In Australia, Manpower operated under the brand names of Manpower, Right Management Consultants, Manpower Executive, Elan, and Manpower City. The company's current organization structure is shown in Exhibit 4.

The company had four divisions: Recruitment & Staffing Solutions (R&SS), Major Client Services (MCS), Corporate Services, and Strategic Services. R&SS, the retail arm of the company, operated through a network of 58 branches and was generally organized by regions, whereas MCS was generally structured into teams that serviced the needs of high-volume clients such as major information technology companies. The core business of R&SS and MCS was the fulfilment of both temporary jobs (temps) and permanent jobs (perms). Across both business units, the Manpower consultant was responsible for servicing client needs through the sourcing of the right candidate.

In general, the MCS business was considered to be at the lower-margin end of the spectrum of Manpower's offerings, while executive permanent recruitment and human resources (HR) services tended to be of higher margin. In recognition of this, a significant effort had been made to augment the existing portfolio of clients with volume business with HR services as well as compete in retail and, in particular, expand its executive placement business.

The Strategy

Varina Nissen joined Manpower Australia and New Zealand as managing director in 2003. According to Nissen and McLachlan, when Nissen joined Manpower, the company was facing a number of significant challenges:

- Manpower Australia had experienced flat growth for the past two years against the Manpower global standard of year-on-year growth.

Exhibit 3

Manpower Global: Vision, Strategies, and Values

Vision

To be the best worldwide provider of higher-value staffing services and center for quality employment opportunities.

Strategies

- **Revenue**—Rigorously focus on industries, geographies and customers that have the strongest long-term growth opportunities for staffing services and solutions.
- **Efficiency**—Continuously improve profit margins and returns through disciplined internal processes and increased productivity.
- **Acquisitions**—Identify and pursue opportunities for strategic acquisitions that have the best potential to catalyze and enrich the core temporary staffing business.
- **Technology**—Aggressively explore and implement the transformational opportunities of information technology and e-commerce to continuously develop defensible competitive advantage in all aspects of the company's activities.
- **Organization and culture**—Capitalize on our entrepreneurial corporate culture to make the most of our internal talent and develop meaningful career paths for employees, striving toward "best practices" in everything we do throughout the global organization.

Values

Manpower global core values are based on three principles pertaining to people, knowledge, and innovation.

People—*We care about people and the role of work in their lives.*

- We respect all our people as individuals, enabling and trusting them to meet the needs of colleagues, customers and the community.
- We are committed to developing professional service according to our high quality and ethical standards.
- We recognize everyone's contribution to our success.
- We help people develop their careers through planning, work experience, coaching, and training.

Knowledge—*We learn and grow by sharing knowledge and resources.*

- We actively listen to our people and customers and act upon this information to improve our relationships and services.
- We pursue the adoption of the best practices worldwide.
- We share one global identity and act as one company while recognizing the diversity of national cultures and working environments.
- We reward team behavior.

Innovation—*We dare to innovate and be pioneers.*

- We thrive on our entrepreneurial spirit and speed of response.
- We take risks, knowing that we will not always succeed.
- We are willing to challenge each other and not accept the status quo.
- We lead by example.

- There had been little successful new product development.
- The company had been underperforming against the Manpower global standard for the measure of gross profit/total salary cost.

- The company was challenged by competitor discounting.
- Culture and processes did not support innovation or have the capability of the company's rapid commercialization.

Exhibit 4

Manpower Organizational Chart

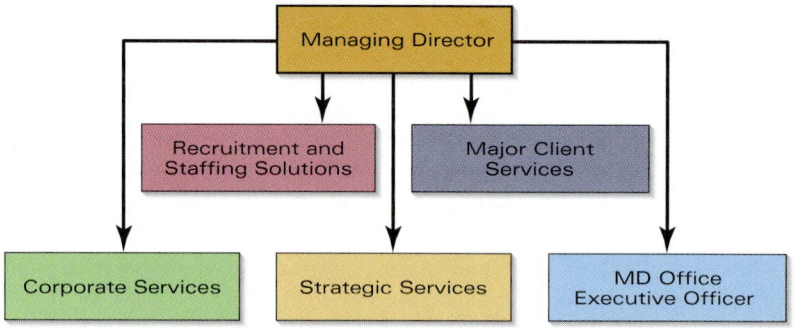

All key areas of the business were thus challenged to create value and improve the company's financial performance; however, there was no explicit strategy in place to give managers direction and focus. In the absence of a specific Australian strategy, the newly appointed managing director decided to develop a corporate strategy based on the corporate vision: "To be recognised as the Australian Leader in delivering innovative people solutions." Three strategic themes were identified:

1. A focus on clients and candidates.

2. The expansion of service offerings to provide people solutions throughout the HR value chain.

3. Supply capability to grow communities and sectors/industries.

To make these strategic themes operational, Manpower required significant marketplace repositioning, cultural change, operational redirection, and an overall improvement in all major aspects of the business. Five strategic initiatives were proposed to address these challenges:

- Grow market share in growth industries and sectors.

- Contribute to the employment growth in communities.

- Meet industry benchmarks.

- Reposition the Manpower brand as "the authority on work."

- Proactively manage risk.

In Australia, the market conditions for the recruiting industry were volatile. According to Scott McLachlan, the CFO of Manpower:

> The recruiting industry in Australia is highly competitive and extremely fragmented. The market leader has only 10–11 percent of total market share and there are around 3,000 agencies in the country. There are all types of competitors across the board and also competitors in key categories and niche providers. The market has shifted from being volume and price driven to being profitable growth driven. It is a low return, low cost of entry market and therefore the purchasing power is starting to shift. The successful company is one that is both a low-cost provider and delivers products that are better than the competitors'. Also, 70 percent of cost is related to people; therefore, the best gross profit return per consultant is important to achieve.

Initially, the focus was mainly on developing and clarifying Manpower Australia's vision and strategy. However, Nissen was also concerned about the organization's agility in aligning itself with the rapidly changing business environment and the strategy that had been developed. She knew that the mind-set and behaviors of the Manpower consultant, being the customer- and candidate-facing resource, were the keys to achieving this agility. In one meeting, she raised her concerns with other members of her team:

> Recruiting is a commoditized industry with competitive margins at retail and margin squeeze in volume accounts. Therefore, in order to perform, our front-line staff,

whether consultant or support staff, must be able to understand and implement the company's strategy. This could also be where we have our single-most potential point of failure—in the field. Our people need to understand, from the company's strategy, what they can deliver to our customers and candidates, and how to price it, with effective operations and sales tools.

To help communicate and drive strategic priorities, Nissen developed a strategy map and a balanced scorecard (BSC) at Manpower.

The Strategy Map and Balanced Scorecard

After developing and finalizing strategic initiatives, the next challenge was to implement the strategy and measure the impact on business performance. Nissen and her team chose the BSC as the strategy implementation tool. According to both Nissen and McLachlan, the BSC was selected by Manpower because:

- Manpower's vision and strategy needed to be translated into actions, with a common language, particularly a common, fact-based approach to measurement.

- Key changes were required in the measurement systems that would impact customer relationships, core competencies, and organizational capabilities.

- There was a need for a measurement and management framework that could link long-term financial success to current customers, internal processes, employees, and systems performance.

- BSC used measurements to inform employees about the drivers of current and future success.

- With BSC it was easier to channel collective energy, enthusiasm, knowledge, and abilities in the pursuit and achievement of long-term common goals.

According to Nissen, "The balanced scorecard is an easy to adopt methodology and is value focused. It clarifies the cause and effect linkages between employee, customers and financials. It's a modern tool that helps

analyse business effectively." McLachlan was likewise happy with the selection of the BSC as the company's strategic measurement system; he said, "The scorecard will monitor how we are going in our journey." The CFO added, "Previously, the management was more focused on short term gains. With balanced scorecard, the management team started looking across at least a year's horizon and the operational team started focusing on quarterly horizons."

The management team decided to implement the BSC first in the R&SS division. It was envisaged that once successes were created, the program could then be rolled out efficiently and effectively to the entire organization. R&SS was selected because the company wanted to leverage its branch network to focus on growth sectors and occupations through the implementation of various strategic initiatives, and it was felt that the BSC framework could help this process.

To achieve clarity around Manpower's strategy, a strategy map (see Exhibit 5) was first developed during various strategy sessions with the executive management. The strategy map was used to describe the corporate strategy and elaborate how the value would be created through the execution of strategy.

One of Manpower's directors highlighted how Varina Nissen supported the strategy mapping process: "The major reason for adopting the strategy map was its cause and effect linkage and it was Varina who focused the team towards the cause and effect relationship. She repeatedly conveyed during various strategy meetings how the employee engagement and customer measures drove financial results." The first version of the strategy map was developed by Nissen prior to discussion with senior management, most of whom agreed to its cause-and-effect linkages. A key feature of the strategy map was the integration and alignment of all levels of her management team and the overall organization. Nissen said, "The strategy map was developed to unite the leadership team by linking the divisions and business units through higher corporate goals like ROS, Expenses as a percent of gross profit, etc."

Exhibit 5

Manpower Australia's Strategy Map, 2003–2004

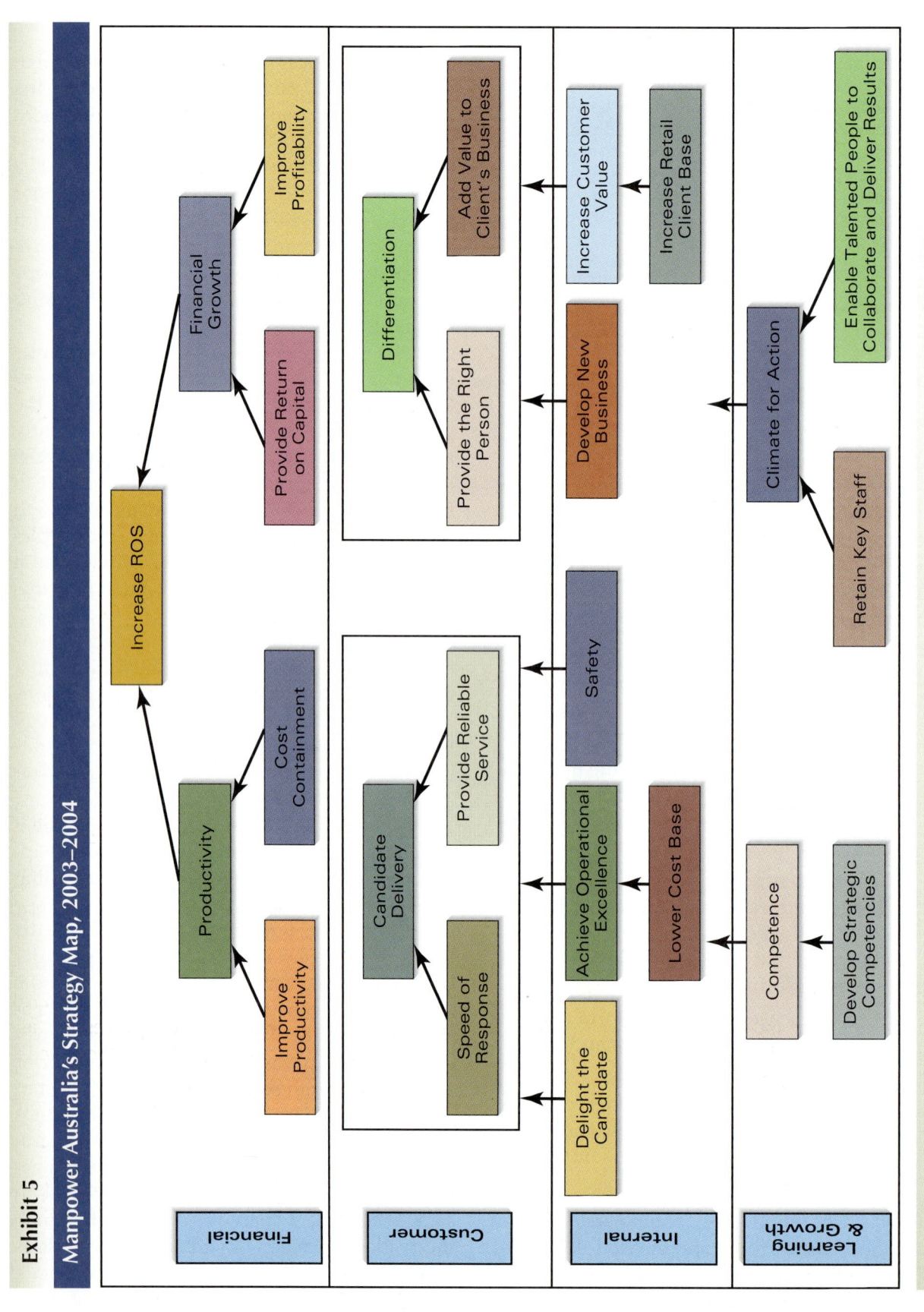

Exhibit 6

Manpower Australia's Recruiting & Staffing Solution (R&SS) Scorecard, 2004

THEMES	OBJECTIVES	MEASURES
Financial Perspective		
Growth	• Provide return on capital • Improve profitability	• YTD return on sales • Sales revenue • Gross profit • Operating unit profit • YTD gross profit margin • Gross profit growth YoY
Productivity	• Improve productivity • Cost containment	• Debtors over 29 days • DSO days • SG&A growth YoY • SG&A as % of gross profit • YTD gross profit/total personnel cost
Customer Perspective		
Candidate delivery	• Speed of response	• Job fill rate contract • Job fill rate perm • Job fill rate temp • Job vacancy days contract • Job vacancy days permanent • Job vacancy days temporary
Internal Business Process Perspective		
Increase customer value	• Increase the retail client base as a % of gross profit	• Client retention—lapsed
Achieve operational excellence	• Lower the cost base of the business	• Pay bill error rate
Safety	• Safety	• Lost time injury frequency rate (LTIFR) rolling average
Learning and Growth Perspective		
Climate for action	• Retain key staff	• Staff retention

Having developed the strategy map, the R&SS scorecard (see Exhibit 6) was developed and implemented in 2004. The scorecard was built from the top down using four steps:

1. Financial outcomes were set.

2. Key customer outcomes that created related financial outcomes were identified.

3. Internal processes relating to customers and productivity outcomes were identified.

4. The infrastructure needed to achieve all of the above was identified.

Initially, effort was not directed toward developing new measures for processes, as shown in the strategy map, but rather focus was on leveraging the existing information. Nissen emphasized, "Initially the focus was on capturing what was already available."

The R&SS scorecard consisted of four perspectives, seven strategic themes, nine objectives, and 21 measures. The four perspectives of the BSC were:

1. Financial

2. Customer

3. Internal Business Processes
4. Learning & Growth

FINANCIAL PERSPECTIVE   Financial measures indicated whether a company's strategy, implementation, and execution were contributing to bottom-line improvement. Manpower was in the "sustain" stage of its life cycle, as the recruiting industry had reached maturity. Most companies in the sustain stage used measures related to accounting income, such as operating profit and gross margins. Manpower had chosen both growth and productivity themes for maximizing income (see Exhibit 7).

The financial perspective of the R&SS scorecard had two strategic themes, four objectives, and 11 measures. Return on sales (ROS) as the overall financial objective was driving the business toward operational efficiency. Thus, debtor measures were incorporated to improve asset utilization through improvement in the cash cycle, and the measures on the selling, general, and administration expenses focused on cost reduction. The productivity focus highlighted the company's strategy to deal with the highly competitive market conditions with squeezing margins, while the various growth metrics were aimed at capturing the performance of Manpower in expanding its scale of business, share of revenue, and profit.

CUSTOMER PERSPECTIVE   The customer perspective articulated the customer- and market-based strategy that would deliver superior future financial returns. This perspective usually included identification of the customer and market segments, with common metrics comprising outcome measures and attributes of the specific value proposition offered that would drive the outcomes sought by the business. Common outcome measures usually included customer satisfaction, customer retention, customer acquisition, customer profitability, and market and account share in targeted segments. Measures of the value proposition typically focused on product/service attributes, the customer relationship, and/or brand image and reputation.

The customer perspective of the R&SS scorecard had one strategic theme, one objective, and six measures (see Exhibit 8). The focus on speed in candidate delivery clearly indicated the company's emphasis on productivity, which was considered one of the major requirements for efficient branch operations.

INTERNAL BUSINESS PROCESS PERSPECTIVE   In the internal business process perspective, critical processes were identified at which the organization must excel to achieve its financial and customer objectives. Internal

Exhibit 7

Financial Perspective

THEMES	OBJECTIVES	MEASURES
Growth	• Provide return on capital • Improve profitability	• YTD return on sales • Sales revenue growth • Gross profit • Operating unit profit • YTD gross profit margin • Gross profit growth YoY
Productivity	• Improve productivity • Cost containment	• Debtors over 29 days • DSO days • SG&A growth • SG&A as % of gross profit • YTD gross profit/total personnel cost

Exhibit 8

Customer Perspective

THEME	OBJECTIVE	MEASURES
Candidate delivery	• Speed of response	• Job fill rate contract • Job fill rate permanent • Job fill rate temporary • Job vacancy days contract • Job vacancy days permanent • Job vacancy days temporary

processes accomplished two vital components of an organization's strategy: (1) they produced and delivered the value proposition for customers and (2) they directly impacted the productivity theme in the financial perspective. The organization's internal processes could be grouped into four clusters: operations management processes, innovation processes, customer management processes, and regulatory and social processes.

Manpower had focused mainly on three clusters of internal processes. Manpower's corporate scorecard had three strategic themes, three objectives, and three measures under the internal business process perspective (see Exhibit 9). The customer and candidate management processes were focused on client retention and ensuring the longevity of the customer base. The operational excellence theme was geared to reducing the cost structure by reducing invoicing and other errors/disputes that impacted prompt client payments. Safety was given priority under the regulatory and social processes of the company, with the Lost Time Injury Frequency Rate (LTIFR) metric focused on candidates' occupational health and safety issues, risk management, and cost related to injury compensation.

LEARNING AND GROWTH PERSPECTIVE The objectives in the learning and growth perspective provided the infrastructure to enable objectives in the other three perspectives to be achieved. This perspective focused on the longer-term enablers of the business and its readiness to implement the chosen strategy. Enablers were grouped into human capital readiness focused on employee skills and competencies (with common outcome measures comprising employee retention, productivity, and satisfaction), information system capabilities, and overall cultural alignment and values.

The learning and growth perspective in the R&SS scorecard had one theme, one objective, and one measure (see Exhibit 10). The main focus was on retaining key staff. Staff retention was arguably an outcome measure for employees' satisfaction.

Exhibit 9

Internal Business Process Perspective

THEMES	OBJECTIVES	MEASURES
Increase customer value	• Increase the retail client base as a % of gross profit	• Client retention—lapsed
Achieve operational excellence	• Lower the cost base of the business	• Pay bill error rate
Safety	• Safety	• Lost time injury frequency rate (LTIFR) rolling average

Exhibit 10

Learning and Growth Perspective

THEME	OBJECTIVE	MEASURE
Climate for action	• Retain key staff	• Staff retention

The Implementation Process

Having developed the BSC for R&SS, Nissen developed BSCs for the other business units and cascaded down to regions and branches within R&SS. The monthly business review meeting, led by Nissen and comprising her senior management team, undertook to assess the development of BSCs, the selection of right measures, and the linking of initiatives with strategy, and to review the progress at each meeting. In addition, the initial implementation and rollout of the BSC at Manpower was made the responsibility of the general manager of human resources, and the BSC and strategic initiatives progress were reported in the monthly intranet communication to all staff.

A BSC evaluation interview-survey conducted at Manpower revealed that the BSC formulation process had been relatively top-down, with most of the respondents indicating that they had not been directly involved in the formulation of BSC objectives (see Exhibit 11). For most of the survey respondents, their journey started after receiving instructions from Nissen or her senior management team to develop the scorecard,

with the majority of these adopting the strategic objectives and metrics that were prescribed.

A series of road shows and education workshops were held throughout Manpower and its branches to communicate the rationale for the BSC and how it was to be used, with a number of these led by Nissen. To ensure adoption and take-up of the BSC, periodic BSC reviews were made a part of the management reviews early in the implementation phase. These reviews monitored the progress of the BSC and its impact on the business. In addition, the BSC reporting and analysis was to be facilitated through technology and Manpower's intranet. According to Nissen, "It was important to signal our revitalization of our Manpower company, that everyone should have a modern looking tool—not an Excel spreadsheet but a tool through which they could analyze the data and reach a fact-based conclusion." As many measures were already in the company's management information system, personnel responsible for maintaining this were also given responsibility to feed the data manually into the BSC reporting tool. Within R&SS in particular, a scoreboard form (Exhibit 12) was developed to ensure that

Exhibit 11

Survey Results on Role in BSC Development

ROLE IDENTIFIED	% RESPONSE*
Not a part of strategic objective formulation	39%
Only responsible for metrics in my business area	22
I adopted the objectives suggested	11
Involved in initial conversations and workshops	11
Reviewed objectives with my team	6
Senior management developed it along with IT	6
Change scorecard to suit business needs	6
	100%

* Responses rounded to the next whole number.

Exhibit 12

Scoreboard Form

FINANCIALS		CUSTOMER		INTERNAL BUSINESS		LEARNING & GROWTH	
Operating profit margin (ROS as % revenues)		Temporary job fill rate/ cycle time		Pay bill error rate		Retention	
Gross profit/total salary cost		Temporary job fill rate/ cycle time		Last time injury frequency rate		Fill rate of internal jobs	
Gross profit/branch personnel cost		Temporary job fill rate/ cycle time					

	From this period	To next period	Target period

Sales	From what	To what	Target
	Action points:		

Staffing	From what	To what	Target
	Action points:		

Skills	From what	To what	Target
	Action points:		

System	From what	To what	Target
	Action points:		

Safety	From what	To what	Target
	Action points:		

Team name	
Date agreed	
Next review date	

the BSC was reviewed at the branch level on a timely basis and actions were taken by the branch managers in five areas: sales, staffing, skills, systems, and safety.

The BSC measures were also linked to compensation. Quarterly bonuses were introduced that were linked to the achievement of the financial numbers, with the BSC aimed at enabling learning about which lead indicators drove financial results. Nissen encouraged the team, "It's okay to be away from your numbers. This is an opportunity for understanding and learning. Learn from the deviations and understand what to do in the future to meet the numbers." In addition, the company also developed 27 incentive plans that were linked with the other nonfinancial measures on the BSC. While there was a common perception that these plans needed to be simplified and rationalized, linking incentives with the BSC measures suggested that Manpower's leadership strongly believed in the BSC. One of the directors claimed, "HR incentive plans at Manpower are in place for sustainable performance and they are aligned with the balanced scorecard objectives and measures."

In mid-2004, responsibility for the BSC was handed over to the directors of the individual business units to drive to lower levels of their respective areas. The BSC Evaluation Survey indicated that significant benefits had been achieved through the BSC implementation at Manpower (see Exhibit 13) in addition to the improvement in the company's financial performance. Specifically, 85 percent of responses to an interview survey pointed out that the BSC had provided a better understanding of business, more focus on key issues, and learning and development of management team. However, the perception of the BSC as a strategic management system was still low among the participants, with 11 percent of responses indicating that Manpower would not be different without the BSC and 3 percent indicating that it did not drive business decision making.

Problems and Challenges

The Balanced Scorecard

Although the initial implementation of the BSC had resulted in productivity gains for Manpower, Nissen and McLachlan didn't want to

Exhibit 13

Survey Results: Benefits of BSC

BENEFITS IDENTIFIED	% RESPONSE*
Helped in understanding of business	22%
Gives focus and insight on key issues	19
Helped in developing management team	14
Nothing will happen if BSC taken out	11
Consistency of communication by providing a common language	8
Gives a good snapshot of business	5
Improved decision making	3
Helped improve business results	3
Drives behavior	3
Helps in changing culture	3
Doesn't drive business decision making	3
Greater visibility	3
Mechanism for rewarding people	3
Drives business	3
	100%

* Responses rounded to the next whole number.

stop there. They were focused on leveraging this success by refining the BSC so that innovative and growth objectives could be better achieved. However, one problem was that there appeared to be a blockage in the business using the information embedded in the BSC to identify and better manage the critical lead indicators that would lead to success. Information from the BSC evaluation survey found low usage of the BSC (see Exhibit 14), especially by teams working under the senior to middle management. When the leadership team was questioned regarding the extent of their direct reports usage of the BSC, 65 percent of them reported low or no usage by their direct reports. They attributed this low take-up to the quality of the information presented on the scorecard. The measures were limited to past performance, lagging, not relevant, and at times inaccurate. Only 17 percent of responses claimed that the direct reports used it for business analysis purposes.

Business Challenges

The external business environment was also becoming increasingly challenging for the company. Discussions among Manpower's senior and middle managers revealed issues relating to the external environment of clients, candidates, and competitors, while internal factors related to systems/processes, employees, and culture.

The major issues and challenges related to clients were identified as comprising:

- Pressure for low price.
- Required speedy service.
- Lack of understanding of customer needs.
- High level of service expectations.
- Increasing customer bargaining power.

The customers' focus was on price, speed, and quality. However, there was a need for better understanding at Manpower for the customer needs and requirements. One of the general managers explained, "There are different industrial sectors and each sector is at a different stage of life cycle—therefore their demands and needs are different. There is no one-fits-all solution. We need to be more focused and analyze each of the sectors in detail to successfully execute our strategy."

The major candidate issues were:

- Candidate shortage.
- Decreasing candidate loyalty and stability.
- Poor candidate care.

Exhibit 14	
Survey Results: BSC Usage	
USAGE IDENTIFIED	**% RESPONSE***
Use it extensively for business analysis	17%
BSCs don't have any new info to review	17
Only interested in summary level data on monthly basis	14
Weekly financial reports are more relevant and useful	14
BSC information lagging—not useful	7
Drive behavior as it impacts incentives	7
It's part of their job	7
Measures not relevant to business	7
Not interested	3
Don't have access to BSC	3
Accuracy of BSC questionable	3
	100%

* Responses rounded to the next whole number.

There was a severe shortage of candidates, especially in certain skill categories. A regional operations manager of Manpower within R&SS raised the candidate-related issues: "Sourcing candidates with the right skill set is a big issue. In addition to this shortage, candidate loyalty is another issue. Whether we are the preferred supplier or not, it is a candidate-driven market and the candidate will move even for an extra 50 cents per hour."

In relation to competition, the market had already matured with rivalry intensifying and a number of niche competitors emerging targeting higher margin business. In this scenario, the main issues and challenges that Manpower currently faced from this highly competitive market were:

- Offering low prices.
- Growth of niche agencies.
- Developing brands.

Another R&SS regional operations manager explained the market conditions as follows: "It's a very competitive market. Pricing has become an issue as we choose to be profitable and the competition chooses to get the business at any cost." Similarly, the general manager of one of the business units was worried about the increasing number of niche agencies, commenting: "As the market entry barriers are low there is a huge growth of consultants, usually a one-person or two-person company. This increasing competition has meant that clients preferred to maintain more suppliers on their preferred list."

Internally, Manpower's systems and processes were identified as an area that needed improvement. Key issues were identified as being:

- Lack of standardization/consistency in branches and between teams.
- Old and slow processes.
- Inefficient candidate handling processes.
- Too many applications and no end-to-end solution.

One of the R&SS regional operations managers identified processes as one of the greatest challenges: "Our processes are very long. They are not fully integrated and therefore we double handle a lot of work." Furthermore, the lack of integration was seen as having competitive impacts, with one of the members of the senior management team explaining: "Our technology needs continuous upgrading. We don't have an end-to-end recruiting system. We've got various brilliant applications but at times we lose speed as they are not totally integrated. We need to focus on our databases and make them more aligned towards customers' and consultants' needs and requirements. They should be made more user friendly and precise. For example, one should be quickly able to search for job specs or other requirements. We have got legacy systems and there is a cost of changing them."

The nature of the industry also posed significant challenges in relation to the management of human capital. While the consultant was important—being the candidate- and client-facing resource—hiring and retaining skilled and effective consultants was difficult. McLachlan, who was also director of corporate services, claimed, "For the company there is a continuous battle in finding the right consultant, the client- and candidate-facing resources. The industry has a large attrition rate that we need to manage. We are continuously bridging the gaps, if any, in the leadership and management skills at the business unit level." The current issues with the people side of the business were many, but the most important were:

- Finding the right consultant.
- Low staff retention.
- Slow career growth.

Finally, in implementing the new strategic direction, the whole organization was going through a change management process. Many within the organization considered it important to inculcate the right culture to support these initiatives. Challenges identified related to developing a high performance culture were:

- Changing the bureaucratic corporate culture.

- Shift required from customer service to sales culture.

The issues relating to the cultural readiness of Manpower to pursue the new strategic initiatives were summarized by one member of the senior management team as follows: "We need to focus on staff advocacy and engagement for achieving our targets. There is a service culture. Our people do selling but not as a selling culture. A selling culture is that if you have ten candidates you will place all of them, but in a service culture you will only focus on what is demanded by the customer and not what you can sell. We want to move to that culture of selling."

What Next?

Varina Nissen and her team believed their biggest challenge was to use the available information to evaluate the implementation and achievement of current strategic objectives and the initiatives, to help focus the business on the lead indicators of success, and refine the current strategic thinking if required to adapt to the emerging conditions and issues.

Abercrombie & Fitch: An Upscale Sporting Goods Retailer Becomes a Leader in Trendy Apparel

Janet L. Rovenpor
Manhattan College

On November 10, 2005, Abercrombie & Fitch (A&F) celebrated the opening of a new 36,000-square-foot, four-level flagship store on Fifth Avenue and 56th Street in Manhattan. The timing was perfect—right ahead of the busy Christmas shopping season during which the retailer hoped to sell large quantities of cashmere sweaters, Henley long-sleeved fleeces, hand-knit wool sweaters, polo shirts, and jeans. The Fifth Avenue store, considered a prototype for other flagship stores, featured dark interiors, oak columns, bronze fixtures, and a central staircase with frosted glass-block flooring. A mural by the artist Mark Beard of muscular, skin-showing rope climbers in a setting from the 1930s was prominently displayed. "We're really excited to be back on Fifth Avenue. We're really trying to build the character of the brand. We had a little store in Trump Tower that closed in 1986, and we have been looking on Fifth Avenue for a few years. This is a prestige location and great for the positioning of the brand," commented CEO Michael Jeffries.[1]

In an attempt to gauge customer reaction to the opening of the new store, *New York Magazine* surveyed 75 teenagers, asking them what the A&F brand meant to them. Answers were varied: "It's gross." "It's overpriced." "It's stylish and sleek." "It's very logotistical." "It projects the typical image of the perfect American male—good at school and masculine." "It was cool up until we were 16. Then it got this dumb-jock-meathead image."[2] Perhaps such contradictory statements were just what A&F's senior executives wanted. Consumers either loved or hated the company, its products, and its image. Part of the trendy retailer's competitive strategy, in fact, was to stir up controversy, go against convention, and appeal emotionally to its youthful customers.

A&F's Fifth Avenue store symbolized the values the retailer held: sensuality, a youthful lifestyle, a love for the outdoors, and fun with friends. It was the culmination of the retailer's creative endeavors to design and implement an exciting store format that drew shoppers in and captivated them. The loud music, appealing visuals, and perfumed interiors encouraged teenagers to hang out and browse.

A&F had come a long way from its early beginnings in 1892. Back then, A&F was considered a luxury sporting goods retailer with conservative tastes that appealed to affluent clients, including adventurers, hunters, presidents, and heads of royal families. President Theodore Roosevelt, for example, purchased snake-proof sleeping bags for a 1908 African safari at an Abercrombie store. Admiral Richard Byrd bought equipment for his 1950s expedition to Antarctica.

A&F's competitive strategies seemed to be working. In 2006, the specialty retailer operated 850 stores in 49 states, the District of Columbia, and Canada. It had 6,900 full-time and 69,200 part-time employees. Its 2005 revenues were $2.78 billion, and its net income was $334 million. It planned to open its first European store in London in 2007. *Apparel* magazine ranked A&F number four in terms of profitability (net income as a percentage of sales) among apparel retailers in 2006 (up from number five in 2005).

At the same time, questions existed regarding the retailer's long-term success. Would teenagers, A&F's primary target market, remain loyal to the company and its products? Could A&F bring back some of the shoppers it had alienated because of its treatment of minority employees and its racy slogans on its T-shirts? Would A&F be able to maintain its competitive advantage in a fragmented industry in which new entrants from both the United States as well as from overseas markets were intent on imitating A&F's strategies? Should CEO Jeffries be concerned with the exodus of talented senior executives from his top management team? Who would eventually succeed Jeffries? Would the retailer's new corporate governance and diversity initiatives pay off?

The U.S. Specialty Apparel Industry

A&F was considered a specialty retailer. Retailers in this category sold products in specific merchandise categories (e.g., apparel, footwear, office supplies, home furnishings, books, jewelry, toys). Numerous small to midsized firms existed. They survived by catering to local tastes and preferences. Sometimes, their financial performance was adversely affected when a competitor entered their niche or when the preferences, lifestyles, and demographics of

their target markets changed. As young people became interested in electronics and began spending more and more time playing video games, for example, the fortunes of retailers like Best Buy rose at the expense of retailers like Toys "R" Us.[3]

Specialty apparel retailers opened stores in shopping malls and constructed freestanding units along major roadways. The firms enhanced their capabilities to sell products via directing mailings of catalogs and through Web sites equipped with shopping-cart technologies. To compete with mass merchandisers and department stores, they tried to: (1) maintain high prices and high-quality merchandise; (2) cultivate customer loyalty through various membership programs; and (3) promote their own private-label brands. J. Crew, for example, offered high-end, limited-edition items (e.g., crocodile sling backs and silk wedding dresses) that created excitement and enticed consumers to buy early at full prices. Chico's FAS Inc. offered a customer loyalty program, Passport Club, that gave customers discounts and other benefits when their purchases exceeded $500.

In 2005 and 2006, the price of oil surged above $70 a barrel. This contributed to a corresponding rise in gasoline prices (e.g., the average retail price for a gallon of gasoline reached $3.07 in 2005, up 65.9 percent from 2004).[4] As consumers used more of their income on fuel and drove their vehicles less frequently, they spent less on goods and services. Retailers who catered primarily to low- to moderate-income Americans (e.g., Gap Inc.'s Old Navy division) experienced a decline in same-store sales. Retailers who served more affluent Americans (e.g., Chico's FAS and Nordstrom's) or who served teenagers and children (e.g., A&F, American Eagle Outfitters, and Wet Seal) benefited from an increase in same-store sales. The latter group of retailers was not significantly affected by rising energy costs.[5]

Believing that "trend transcends age," A&F catered to cool, attractive, fashion-conscious consumers offering products to meet their needs through different life stages—from elementary school to postcollege.[6] The retailer managed four brands:

- A&F: Repositioned in 1992, A&F offered apparel that reflected the youthful lifestyle of the East Coast and Ivy League traditions for college students. In 2006, there were 361 A&F brand stores in the United States (close to its capacity of 400 stores).

- Abercrombie: Launched in 1998, Abercrombie targeted customers ages 7–14 with fashions similar to the A&F line. There were 163 stores in 2006.

- Hollister Company: Launched in 2000, Hollister Company targeted high school students with lower-priced casual apparel, personal care products, and accessories. It promoted the laid-back, California surf lifestyle. There were 318 stores in 2006, a number that had the potential to double.

- Ruehl: Launched in 2004, Ruehl sold casual sportswear, trendy apparel, and leather goods to postcollege consumers ages 22 to 35. Its line of clothing was inspired by the lifestyle of New York City's Greenwich Village. The merchandise was more upscale and more expensive than the A&F line. There were eight stores in 2006.

A&F had three main competitors. Two—American Eagle Outfitters Inc. (AEOS) and Gap Inc.—were publicly held firms, and one—J. Crew Group, Inc. (JC)—was a privately held firm. For basic comparative financial data, see Exhibit 1. Data for JC were unavailable because the retailer was privately held.

Based in Warrendale, Pennsylvania, AEOS sold lower-priced casual apparel and accessories to men and women ages 15–25. The Schottenstein family (who held interests in Value City Department and Furniture Stores) owned 14 percent of the retailer. AEOS operated over 850 stores in the United States and Canada, with approximately 40 percent of its stores located west of the Mississippi River. Revenues in 2005 were $2.3 billion (an increase of 22.7 percent from 2004); net income reached $294 million (an increase of 38 percent from

2004). AEOS planned to launch two new store concepts in 2006. Martin + Osa would be a clothing store selling denim and active sportswear targeting men and women ages 24–40. Aerie was an intimate apparel sub-brand that would be operated adjacent to existing AEOS stores and as stand-alone stores.

JC operated 200 retail and outlet stores in the United States. With a joint venture partner, it also had 45 stores in Japan. Millard "Mickey" Drexler, former CEO of Gap Inc., headed the retailer; Texas Pacific Group (a private equity firm) owned 56 percent of JC. While revenues in 2005 were $804 million (up 14 percent from 2004), the company suffered a net loss of $100 million (double the losses in 2004). JC planned to launch Madewell, a casual clothing store for women selling merchandise at prices 20 to 30 percent lower than JC prices. It also was preparing an initial public offering of common stock of $355 million.

Whereas JC was the smallest of A&F's direct competitors, Gap was the largest, with 3,000 stores worldwide. Gap stores sold basic casual clothing and accessories for children, men, and women. Revenues in 2005 were $16 billion (a decrease of 1.5 percent from 2004); net income was $1.1 billion (a decrease of 3 percent from 2004). Gap Inc. also operated Banana Republic (high-quality, fashionable apparel) and Old Navy (low-priced trendy clothing). Its most recent entry was Forth & Towne (stylish apparel for women over 35). Gap's CEO, Paul Pressler, struggled to turn around the retailer's poor performance, which began in 2000 (before he arrived) when the company overexpanded, assumed too much debt, and made a few fashion-related miscalculations.

A&F's Early Beginnings

A&F was founded in 1892 by David T. Abercrombie (see Exhibit 2 for key milestones in A&F's history). Abercrombie was a civil engineer, topographer, and colonel in the Officers Reserve Corps. He was also an avid hunter and fisherman. The first store was located on

Exhibit 1

Comparative Financial Information for Abercrombie & Fitch (A&F), American Eagle Outfitters, and Gap, 2002–2005

	A&F				AMERICAN EAGLE OUTFITTERS				GAP			
	2005	2004	2003	2002	2005	2004	2003	2002	2005	2004	2003	2002
Operating revenues (in millions)	$2,785	$2,021	$1,708	$1,596	$2,309	$1,881	$1,520	$1,463	$16,023	$16,267	$15,854	$14,455
Net income (in millions)	$334	$216.4	$204.8	$194.9	$294	$213.3	$60	$88.7	$1,113	$1,150	$1,030	$477.5
Net income as a % of operating revenues	12.0%	10.7%	12.0%	12.2%	12.7%	11.3%	3.9%	6.1%	6.9%	7.1%	6.5%	3.3%
Earnings per share ($)	$3.83	$2.33	$2.12	$1.98	$1.94	$1.55	$0.59	$0.62	$1.26	$1.29	$1.15	$0.55
Return on assets	18.7%	15.8%	17.2%	22.1%	18.3%	16.0%	7.5%	12.6%	12.6%	11.3%	10.2%	5.4%
Return on equity	33.6%	28.3%	25.5%	29.0%	27.8%	26.7%	9.8%	16.4%	20.5%	23.7%	24.4%	14.3%
Current ratio	1.9	1.6	2.4	2.8	2.99	3.3	2.8	3.0	2.7	2.8	2.7	2.1
Debt/capital ratio (%)	0	0	0	0	0	0	2.1%	2.8%	16.5%	27.6%	34.2%	44.2%
Debt as a % of net working capital	0	0	0	0	0	0	4.1%	5.7%	NA	46.4%	59.3%	96.1%
Annual high-low stock price	$74.10–44.17	$ 47.45–23.07	$33.65–20.65	$33.85–14.97	$34.04–19.45	$23.88–7.91	$11.69–6.60	$15.22–4.88	$22.70–15.90	$25.72–18.12	$23.47–12.01	$17.14–8.35

NM = Not meaningful.

NA = Not available.

Sources: Standard & Poor's Industry Surveys: Retailing Specialty; data for 2005 from company 10-K reports and Hoover's.

Exhibit 2

Key Milestones in A&F's History

1892	A&F was founded by David T. Abercrombie, an engineer, topographer, outdoorsman and colonel.
1900	Ezra Fitch, a lawyer from Kingston, New York, became Abercrombie's business partner.
1907	Abercrombie resigned from the company.
1917	A&F's 12-story building on Madison Avenue and 45th Street opened.
1928	Ezra Fitch resigned as president. He was succeeded by James S. Cobb.
1929	A&F acquired an interest in Von Lengerke & Detmold, a gun, camp, and fishing chain based in Chicago.
1935	A&F earned a net profit of $148,123, up from $123,424 in the previous year.
1940	Otis Guernsey was elected president and CEO.
1943	A&F earned a net profit of $286,694.
1958	A store in San Francisco opened.
1961	John H. Ewing became president and CEO, succeeding Guernsey. Earle Angstadt became the president and CEO in the mid-1960s.
1962	A&F opened a store in Colorado Springs.
1963	A&F opened a store in Short Hills, New Jersey.
1967	A&F acquired the Crow's Nest, a nautical supply store with a national mail order business.
1968	Sales peaked at $28 million and net income rose to $866,000.
1970	Angstadt resigned. He was replaced by William Humphreys. Henry Haskell, a major shareholder, soon replaced Humphreys as CEO. A&F lost money every year until 1977.
1972	A store in a Chicago suburb opened.
1977	A&F declared bankruptcy.
1978	A&F was acquired by Oshman's Sporting Goods Inc.
1988	The Limited acquired A&F from Oshman's.
1989	Sally Frame-Kasaks was named president and chief executive of A&F. She left the company in 1992.
1992	Michael Jeffries became president and chief executive of A&F.
1996	A&F was spun off from The Limited as an independent company.
1999	There were 186 A&F stores and 13 Abercrombie stores.
2001	A&F opened a new 260,000-square-foot corporate office and a 700,000-square-foot distribution center in New Albany, Ohio.

Water Street in lower Manhattan. Ezra Fitch, a lawyer and one of Abercrombie's best customers, became a partner in 1900. The two men frequently argued. Fitch continued to run the company after Abercrombie resigned in 1907.

A&F's 12-story building on Madison Avenue and 45th Street opened in 1917. It featured a log cabin and casting pool on the roof and a rifle range in the basement. The store's location was excellent. By 1923, Madison Avenue and 45th Street had become the "heart" of the "specialized shop trade."[7] Near A&F's flagship store were Brooks Brothers, Tiffany Studios, Eastman Kodak, and Maillard's. The Roosevelt Hotel was just undergoing construction. Abercrombie died in 1931 at the age of 64; Fitch died of a stroke aboard his yacht in Santa Barbara, California, in 1930 at the age of 65.

A&F's managers promoted it as "The Finest Sporting Goods Store in the World." An early advertisement announcing the opening of a new store on 36th Street appears in Exhibit 3. A&F was known for its expensive and exotic goods as well as for its affluent clientele. It was possible to buy an antique miniature cannon for $300, a custom-made rifle for $6,000, or a Yukon dog sled for $1,188. Presidents William Taft and Warren Harding purchased golf clubs at A&F.

Exhibit 3

An Early A&F Advertisement in the New York Times 1912

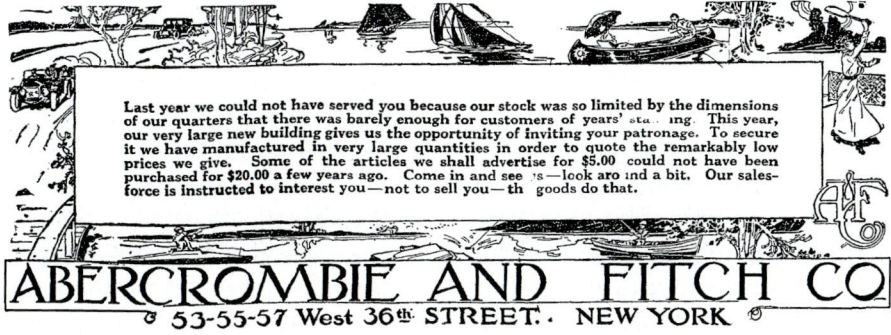

Opening

We Cordially Invite You to Inspect Our New Store

We maintain at this address, the finest Sporting Goods Store in the world. We want you to visit the establishment—we are proud of it, and we are proud of the stock we have to show you. It comprises everything for the Great Out of Doors, each article the BEST for its purpose and most of them exclusive. You can't get them elsewhere.

For a good many years, this concern, The Abercrombie & Fitch Co., occupied a small, exclusive store at 57 Reade Street, in the dingy downtown district where buyers came only because they HAD to—because they could not buy elsewhere the things they bought from us. We have been known the world over not only as the one place where the big Nimrods, Explorers, Hunters, Trappers, Fishermen,—the whole Out-of-Door Brotherhood were outfitted, but as a sort of informal clearing house of information for them. We outfitted Col. Roosevelt for his trip into Africa—Stewart Edward White speaks of our outfits in his textbooks—our peculiar specialty of having the RIGHT thing, the CORRECT thing and finally the EXCLUSIVE thing was recognized by the adept many years ago. Our business grew by word of mouth—by talks over camp fires and at club tables, because when once a man or woman found us, they had found the ONLY one there was and took a pride in passing on the good news. We outgrew our store—we outgrew the building—and now we have our own building on 36th Street. So long as we

had to move, we moved to a place where you could get at us—right in the centre of your shopping district.

We have the finest store of its kind in the world. We have not merely the finest stock of our sort in the world, but we carry the ONLY correct things for the purpose. We have broadened our business and to bring this about, we have manufactured in quantities impossible before because of the restrictions of space in our old quarters. All the economies due to manufacturing and buying on a wholesale plan are reflected in the very low prices of the goods we offer you.

We want you to see our Out-of-Door Clothing for Men and Women and for Boys. We want you to see our complete outfits for camping, for canoeing, for fishermen, for golfers, for every 'one of the sports. We want you to see to what lengths we have gone to provide not only the best, but the exactly RIGHT and the EXCLUSIVE thing for your favorite sport, the thing you have always wanted but couldn't get elsewhere because it didn't EXIST elsewhere.

EZRA H. FITCH, President

Last year we could not have served you because our stock was so limited by the dimensions of our quarters that there was barely enough for customers of years' standing. This year, our very large new building gives us the opportunity of inviting your patronage. To secure it we have manufactured in very large quantities in order to quote the remarkably low prices we give. Some of the articles we shall advertise for $5.00 could not have been purchased for $20.00 a few years ago. Come in and see 's—look around a bit. Our salesforce is instructed to interest you—not to sell you—the goods do that.

ABERCROMBIE AND FITCH CO
53-55-57 West 36th STREET. NEW YORK

President Dwight Eisenhower bought hunting boots for $55 for his walks in the woods at Camp David. Other famous customers were: Amelia Earhart, Greta Garbo, Charles Lindberg, Clark Gable, the Duke of Windsor, Howard Hughes, and Ernest Hemingway.

A&F was not just a place to purchase sporting goods and rugged apparel. It was also a place where individuals could learn new skills and get involved in the community. In 1923, the Adirondack Club held its annual meeting in A&F's log cabin. Its members discussed whether or not an open season should be declared on beavers whose dam-building activities were causing floods that damaged timber and ruined trout streams. In 1966, A&F held a lecture on how to capture a musk ox barehanded without harming it. In 1967, A&F ran a fishing clinic in which experts discussed tackle, knot tying, and trout angling techniques. In 1973, A&F served flambé quail, prepared in the log cabin's fireplace, in celebration of a talking cookbook it had produced. The cookbook contained two 40-minute cassettes and a booklet of recipes printed on waterproof and greaseproof plastic.

Throughout its early history, A&F did a good job keeping up with its customers and with changing fashions. During World War II, when activities such as parlor skeet and military board games were popular, A&F sold a wooden box that could be filled with water and used to blow sailboats from side to side. In the 1940s, barbeque picnics in fields outside country homes became the latest fad arriving from the West. A&F sold high-quality BBQ equipment and insulated canvas bags to keep drinks cold. In 1964, A&F made a splash when it developed the capacity to sell a cashmere sweater with a lifelike reproduction of one's pet embroidered on it. It sold resort wear with a fruit motif in the 1940s and Bermuda length culottes in the 1960s. A&F had a clearly defined target market. CEO Earle K. Anstadt, Jr. said, "We aren't out for the teenage business. Our customers are on the go and have the time and the money to enjoy travel and sport."[8]

A&F had its share of problems. Some were typical of all retailers throughout the decades, and some were atypical. During the early 1940s, A&F stores were low on inventory. Commerce had been disrupted by the wartime effort. It was difficult to import goods from abroad. Manufacturers were busy making binoculars, field glasses, saddles, and marine clocks for use by the Army and Navy. A&F wrote to its customers, asking them if they would like to sell optical or sporting goods in satisfactory condition back to the retailer so that the items could be refurbished and resold to new customers.

One year, the Office of Price Administration placed limits on civilian consumption of rubber products. This caused a rush on golf balls sold by A&F. A&F joined other retailers in asking customers to do their Christmas shopping early—in November. A lack of manpower had overwhelmed the postal services and caused delays.

At least twice in A&F's history, a customer used one of the guns on display in an A&F shop to commit suicide. The first shooting occurred in 1932, when the son of a famous horse breeder killed himself. The second shooting occurred in 1968 when an immigrant from Czechoslovakia killed himself. Subsequently, extra care was taken to ensure that every gun was fitted with a trigger lock and kept in locked showcases. Customers were no longer handed guns or ammunition over the counter; upon purchase, the firearms were delivered to their homes.

Employee theft and shoplifting occurred. In 1915, for example, Gustave Touchard Jr., a champion tennis player, was charged with stealing 48 dozen golf balls worth $288 from an A&F store on 36th Street. He had worked at the store as a manager of its sporting department. In 1923, a well-dressed woman was caught with 21 yards of Scotch tweed cloth hidden in the ulster (i.e., a bulky overcoat) she was wearing. The theft occurred a few weeks after two sisters who shopped at Macy's while carrying small dogs in their arms were caught with stolen items in their wide sleeves. In 1969, inventory shrinkage (from bookkeeping errors, internal theft, and shoplifting) totaled $1 million (up from between $600,000 and $700,000 the previous year). This contributed to the retailer's pretax loss for the year.[9]

Between 1970 and 1976, A&F continued to incur financial losses. In the fiscal year ending January 31, 1976, A&F incurred a net loss of $1 million on sales of $23.8 million.[10] The loss followed annual deficits ranging from $287,000 to $540,000 every year since 1970.[11] A&F's best year had been in 1968, when it reported pretax earnings of $866,000 on sales of $28 million.[12] Managers began to search for a possible buyer of the firm. No one was seriously interested.

In August 1976, A&F filed for bankruptcy. It held a sale to liquidate its inventory of $8.5 million. A sign in the retailer's Madison Avenue store read: "They say we're stuffy so we're moving the stuff out at tremendous reductions on all floors."[13] After the sale, the stores were closed. A&F's difficulties were attributed to several factors: competition from mass marketers (e.g., Hermann's World of Sporting Goods) that sold discounted merchandise; the lack of professional managers and leadership turnover (the retailer had had three different CEOs in its last six years); high overhead costs; and a dearth of customers who could afford its exotic, high-priced items.

In 1978, Oshman's Sporting Goods Inc. of Houston acquired A&F's name, trademark, and mailing list for $1.5 million. A&F's slogan was changed from "The Finest Sporting Goods Store in the World" to "The Adventure Goes On." The new owners had studied A&F's business model for two years. According to A&F president Jerry Nanna, "We examined the original business, took it apart and retained the good qualities. We also retained some of the legendary old products that Abercrombie had and expanded their variety. But we dropped most of the tailored clothing that proved to be a drain."[14] The owners believed that they could bring A&F styles up-to-date for the 1980s. The chain expanded to 12 stores; sales of $20 million were expected in 1982.

In 1988, The Limited Inc. acquired 25 A&F stores and the A&F catalog business for $47 million from Oshman's. Two additional stores were closed. At the time, The Limited operated a chain of 3,100 stores that sold women's apparel. In 1992, Michael Jeffries became president and chief executive of A&F, a retailing unit of The Limited. A new format was introduced. The chain began to carry casual, classic American clothes for 20-something men and women. A&F became one of The Limited's fastest-growing divisions. The number of stores grew from 40 in 1992 to 113 in 1996. Its sales increased at a compounded annual rate of 40.3 percent during those same years.[15] In 1996, The Limited spun off A&F. Jeffries stayed on as CEO.

Senior Executives and Corporate Governance

Michael Jeffries got his start in retailing at an early age when he helped his father select the toys that were sold in the family's chain of party supply stores. He also enjoyed organizing and designing the window and counter displays. Born in 1944, Jeffries received a BA in economics from Claremont McKenna College and an MBA from Columbia University. He entered the management training program of Abraham & Straus (a New York department store that belonged to Federated) in 1968. From there, he went on to start a women's clothing store, Alcott & Andrews, which later failed. He worked in merchandising at Paul Harris, which also went bankrupt.[16]

In his flip-flops, polo shirt, and torn jeans, Jeffries embodied the casual look of A&F more than anyone else. He made sure that A&F's apparel reflected the lifestyles of college students. Teams of designers, merchandisers, and marketers visited college campuses once a month to talk to students and find out what they liked and how they spent their time. On one of those visits in 1998, Jeffries saw someone wearing nylon wind pants. A&F was quick to make its own version of the pants. Tom Lennox, A&F's director of corporate communications and investor relations once said, "We just believe that it is our job to position Abercrombie and Fitch as the coolest brand, the brand with the greatest quality, the aspirational brand of college students."[17]

A&F's success did not make Jeffries complacent. He was quoted as saying, "Every morning I'm scared. I'm superstitious. I come in every morning being afraid to look at yesterday's figures, and I want everyone else to have that same kind of fear."[18] He worked hard and constantly traveled from store to store. He was always thinking of ways to extend the A&F brand, with a fifth concept in the planning stage. Jeffries had a few eccentric habits. He went through revolving doors twice, parked his black Porsche at an odd angle in the company's parking lot, and wore the same lucky shoes when he reviewed financial reports.[19] It was almost as if he felt that his firm's good fortune could change at any time. Perhaps he realized that his primary target audience—teenagers—was fickle and that trendy apparel quickly became outdated.

Between 2003 and 2006, A&F had three different chief financial officers and two different chief operating officers. The latter position remained unfilled. In July 2003, Wesley McDonald, who had been A&F's chief financial officer (CFO) for four years, left to become CFO of Kohl's Corporation. He was replaced in February 2004 by Susan Riley, who had held CFO positions at Mount Sinai Medical Center, Dial Corporation, and Tambrands Inc. In August 2005, Riley resigned for family reasons and returned to her home in New York City. Michael Kramer became A&F's new CFO. He had been the CFO of the retail unit of Apple Inc. He also had retail experience working for Gateway Inc., The Limited, and Pizza Hut. He had a BA in business administration and accounting from Kansas State University and was a certified public accountant.

Seth Johnson was A&F's chief operating officer (COO) between 2000 and 2004. Before that, he had been its CFO. Johnson was credited with keeping costs down by reducing payroll and travel expenses. He was responsible for installing computer systems to help A&F's distribution system run more efficiently. He had aspired to a CEO position and was offered such an opportunity at Pacific Sunwear of California Inc. Robert Singer, the former CFO of Gucci, became the next president and COO in 2004. After 15 months on the job, Singer resigned to become the CEO of Barilla Holdings SpA. Disagreements about international expansion were cited as the reason for his departure. Singer's duties were divided between John Lough (executive vice president of logistics and store operations) and Michael Kramer (CFO). Search for a replacement began.

Unlike other retailers, A&F did not have division presidents for its brands. Merchants from different businesses reported directly to the CEO. They did not work within a particular brand. Instead, they led categories (e.g., denim or outerwear). They were responsible for these brands across each of the company's divisions. That way, their expertise and knowledge could best be leveraged and exploited.

A&F encountered criticism from shareholders regarding executive compensation and the composition of its board of directors. In February 2005, shareholders charged A&F directors with wasting corporate assets by paying CEO Jeffries $22.9 million in salary, bonus, and stock options. The company settled the lawsuit and Jeffries agreed to reduce his $12 million bonus to $6 million and to forgo new stock options for two years. The bonus was contingent on meeting specific earnings targets. Jeffries would receive the full $6 million bonus if A&F's earnings per share increased by 13.5 percent between February 1, 2005, and January 31, 2009.[20]

Shareholders also expressed concern over the independence of A&F's board of directors. John W. Kessler, chair of the compensation committee, had financial ties to the retailer. As chair of a real estate development firm owned by The Limited's CEO, Les Wexner (Jeffries's former boss), Kessler sold the land on which A&F built its headquarters in 1999. He received a fee for finding the site. Kessler's son-in-law, Thomas D. Lennox, was A&F's director of investor relations and communications. Samuel Shahid, president and creative director of the advertising agency that received $2 million a year from A&F for its services, was a board member until May 2005. He was replaced by Allan A. Tuttle, an attorney for the luxury goods maker Gucci Group. While Tuttle did not have financial ties to A&F, he was a friend of Robert Singer, who at the time was A&F's president and COO.

A&F denied wrongdoing and settled the lawsuits to "avoid the uncertainty, harm and expense of litigation."[21] As part of its agreement with shareholders, A&F promised to provide more public information about executive compensation and to add independent members to its board and its compensation committee.

A&F underwent a formal investigation by the U.S. Securities and Exchange Commission regarding insider selling of stock. In June and July 2005, when A&F's stock price was high, Jeffries sold 1.6 million shares worth $120 million. In August, share prices declined after the company announced it would miss Wall Street expectations regarding its second-quarter earnings. A&F was also sued for making false and misleading statements of monthly and quarterly sales figures and for failing to disclose that profit margins were declining and inventory rising. The company announced that it was cooperating with the SEC and that the shareholder lawsuit had no merit.

Store Concept and Marketing Strategies

When customers walked into an A&F clothing store in a local mall, they were often greeted by a young, handsome salesperson wearing the latest fashion in casual attire. The store's lights were dimmed and posters of attractive models wearing its trademark cargo pants and polo shirts adorned the walls. In some stores, chandeliers made of fake deer antlers or whitewashed moose antlers hung from the ceilings. Apparel was neatly folded and placed on long wooden tables. The retailer's hip, trendy, all-American look was reinforced by the playing of loud dance music and the spraying of men's cologne. The intent was to provide a sensual experience that appealed to a shopper's senses of sight, smell, and sound. According to marketing expert Pam Danziger, "Shoppers are rejecting the old concept of 'hunting and gathering' shopping in favor of a more involved, interesting, dynamic retail experience."[22] A&F was able to successfully implement an exciting store format.

Every A&F store was designed according to one of several specific models created at company headquarters. The retailer wanted complete control over its brand and to communicate a consistent message in all stores across the nation. Jeffries himself made sure the model stores were "perfect."[23] The prototypes were photographed and sent to the store managers of the individual outlets for replication. Jeffries was known for paying attention to every detail. He visited stores and made sure that the clothes were folded correctly. He approved of the background music to be played in the stores and selected the appropriate volume level for all locations. He even gave suggestions on how mannequins could be made to look more rugged and masculine.

A&F's Web site (www.abercrombie.com/anf/lifestyles/) was created to match the feel and aura of its stores as much as possible. It featured striking black-and-white images of young people in outdoor settings. Through the "A&F Lifestyle" link, Web surfers could download screen savers or send e-postcards to one another. According to *Forbes* magazine, the A&F Web site's best feature was the photo gallery showing images of the models that made A&F famous. Its worst feature was that the models pictured did not have the effect of showcasing the company's line of clothing.[24]

A&F had an enviable target market. It catered to teenagers, whose population in the United States was expanding. In 2003, there were 32 million teens living in the United States This number was expected to rise to 35 million by 2010. Moreover, teens spent approximately $170 billion on goods and services in 2002, with one-third of that amount going toward apparel.[25] Spending in 2005 was lower—$159 billion[26]—but teen retailing was considered to be somewhat recession-proof. Although teens worked for low wages, they had multiple revenue streams—babysitting, paper routes, part-time jobs, and assistance from parents.[27] They usually did not have financial obligations (no mortgages or bills to pay). Also, parents were more likely to spend money on their children than on themselves.

A&F's busy seasons were spring and fall. The company hired extra employees during the back-to-school and holiday seasons. A&F was typically able to sell its merchandise at its customary premium prices without resorting to frequent off-price sales and deep discounting. Management feared that greatly reduced sale prices would cheapen the A&F brand. The company economized on advertising and promotional expenditures by relying extensively on word-of-mouth advertising. The retailer claimed that it spent less than 2 percent of net sales on marketing in 2004.[28] It also kept careful watch on administrative expenses and bargained hard for lower prices from its suppliers. Premium prices and economical operating costs were a merchandising formula that worked well for A&F.

A&F tried to introduce two or three new items in its stores every week. It launched a new men's line, Ezra Fitch, which featured high-quality apparel made from cashmere, velvet, and leather. A&F cultivated brand loyalty. Shoppers could join Hollister's Club Cali and receive gift cards based on how much they spent. Instead of marking down items the day after Thanksgiving (the start of the busy Christmas shopping season), the company issued invitations to after-hours parties with new bands. In 2004, preferred customers who spent $1,000 a year or more were invited to a live concert given by Ryan Cabrera. The concert was also shown on big-screen televisions in 50 other Hollister stores around the nation.

A&F generated controversy. Adults often reacted negatively to the company's catalog photographs, revealing clothes, and racy slogans. But teenagers and young adults were thought to respond positively to A&F's provocative advertising, perhaps in a show of rebellion against the traditional values and/or because they closely identified with the lifestyle images and hip trends portrayed in A&F ads. Teens were reluctant to shop in the same stores as their parents. Some observers believed that A&F purposely created controversy and engaged in risky practices to attract attention, draw in shoppers, and sell more products. As an analyst with Midwest Research in Cleveland remarked, "Abercrombie is not a company that really cares about backing away from controversy. They use controversy as a free

advertising gig and are successful in driving traffic into the stores."[29]

The following is a list of some of A&F's controversial moves:

- In July 1998, a story entitled "Drinking 101" appeared in an A&F back-to-school catalog. It featured recipes for alcoholic beverages and a game for helping students decide which drink to mix. After being criticized by Mothers Against Drunk Driving (MADD), A&F deleted the story and sent postcards to students who received the publication by mail reminding them to "be responsible, be 21, and don't ever drink and drive."[30]

- In April 2002, A&F sold a line of T-shirts with Asian cartoon characters and matching ethnic slogans: "Wong Brothers Laundry Service Two Wongs Can Make It White"; "Wok-N-Bowl"; "Buddha Bash: Get Your Buddha on the Floor." The retailer took the T-shirts off store shelves after protests from college students from campuses around the country. A&F's spokesperson Hampton Carney apologized, saying, "It is not, and never has been, our intention to offend anyone. These were designed to add humor and levity to our fashion line. Since some of our customers were offended by these T-shirts, we removed them from all our stores."[31]

- In May 2002, A&F sold thong underwear for girls ages 10 and up with sexual phrases such as "Eye Candy" and "Wink, Wink" printed on the front. Family-advocacy groups and Christian organizations protested. The line was recalled in Washington, D.C., area stores.[32]

- In December 2003, under heavy criticism from parents and consumer groups, A&F decided to stop publishing its provocative catalog, A&F Quarterly. Its holiday issue featured nude models and articles about group sex and masturbation.[33]

- In March 2004, Bob Wise, governor of West Virginia, asked A&F to pull from its shelves

T-shirts with the slogan "It's All Relative in West Virginia." Wise explained that the slogan was offensive because it referred to a stereotype that West Virginia was a state that condoned incest.[34]

- In October 2004, officials of USA Gymnastics sought the immediate removal of a T-shirt depicting a male gymnast performing on the still rings alongside the phrase "L is for Loser." They wrote a letter to Jeffries saying its members would be encouraged to withdraw their support of the chain.[35]

- In May 2005, A&F quietly pulled a line of T-shirts from its stores with slogans that read "I Brews Easily," "Candy is Dandy but Liquor is Quicker," and "Don't Bother I'm Not Drunk Yet." The company was criticized for glorifying underage drinking and promoting a lifestyle that was illegal for its target audience. Pressure came from the International Institute for Alcohol Awareness, a public advocacy group that worked to reduce underage drinking. This time, A&F responded to criticism before the issue was reported in national newspapers.[36]

- In November 2005, 24 participants in the Allegheny County Girls as Grantmakers program organized a "girlcott" of A&F stores to protest its "attitude T-shirts," which featured such slogans as "Who needs brains when you have these?"; "Blondes Are Adored, Brunettes Are Ignored"; "All Men Like Tig Old Bitties." Other groups—such as Peace Project, an antidiscrimination student club in Norwalk, Connecticut, and the Women & Girls Foundation of Southwestern Pennsylvania—joined in. A&F pulled two of the more offensive T-shirts, and its executives agreed to meet with several of the protestors. The girls suggested that the retailer print more appropriate slogans, such as "All This and Brains to Match" and "Your Future Boss." They hoped the firm would launch such a line and donate a portion of revenue to groups like theirs.[37]

Logistics and Supply Chain Management

A&F operated solely as a retailer. It assumed responsibility for creating and managing its brands. Unlike other businesses, A&F did not distribute its apparel and accessories through wholesaling, licensing, or franchising. Abercrombie clothing could not be purchased in department stores or in discount stores. It could, however, be purchased online via the A&F Web site. E-commerce transactions generated over $100 million in business a year.[38]

During 2005, A&F purchased merchandise from approximately 246 factories and suppliers located around the globe, primarily in Southeast Asia and Central and South America. It did not source more than 50 percent of its apparel from any single factory or supplier. The design and development process for a garment took anywhere from 6 to 12 weeks.[39] Retailers struggled to reduce this time so as not to get stuck with merchandise that had lost its fashion appeal. A&F made the process more efficient by centralizing its design services at its New Albany, Ohio, headquarters, which reduced overseas travel of executives.

A&F also operated a distribution center in New Albany, Ohio. Merchandise was received, inspected, and then distributed to stores via contract carriers. It was here that concepts for new divisions were created and prototypes for new stores were constructed. The new formats were kept secret until their launch dates.

A&F launched an anticounterfeiting program in an effort to protect its brand and prevent low-cost manufacturers in Asian factories from making imitations of its products. Local authorities seized 300,000 pairs of fake Abercrombie jeans (worth $20 million) in a raid of a Chinese warehouse in 2006. The retailer hired a former FBI agent to head a 10-person department to conduct investigations overseas and to work with foreign authorities.[40]

A&F began experimenting with radio frequency identification (RFID) technology in its Ruehl stores, which sold higher-priced and higher-quality merchandise than its other stores. Tags that could be monitored electronically were sewn into the seams of garments. Employees could thus track garments, enabling them to quickly return items that had been left in dressing rooms or placed in the wrong spots on the sales floor. The technology could also be used to prevent theft and to differentiate between authentic products and counterfeit goods.

A&F's Financial Performance

In 2005, A&F achieved revenues of $2.785 billion, an increase of 37.8 percent from 2004. Its net income rose to $334 million, an increase of 54.3 percent from 2004 (see Exhibit 4). Earnings per share rose to $3.66 from $2.28. A&F opened 63 new stores and added 20,600 employees to its payroll. It had no long-term debt. It repurchased

1.8 million shares of common stock for $103.3 million and paid dividends of 60 cents a share, for a total of $52.2 million.

A&F's Socially Responsible Practices

A&F held fund-raising activities that benefited local charities and communities. Every Christmas holiday season, shoppers were invited into its stores to have their picture taken with its models. The fee was $1, which the retailer matched. The proceeds were donated to foundations such as Toys for Tots or the Juvenile Diabetes Research Foundation. It held the "A&F Challenge," an action-packed outdoor event, at its headquarters in New Albany, Ohio. Participants, who paid an entry fee of $25, went on a 20-mile cycling tour, a 5K inline skating tour, and a 5K run. They heard live music from

Exhibit 4

Summary of A&F's Financial Performance, 2001–2005

	2005	2004	2003	2002	2001
Operating revenues (in thousands)	$2,784,711	$2,021,253	$1,707,810	$1,595,757	$1,364,853
Gross profit (in thousands)	1,851,416	1,341,224	1,083,170	980,555	817,325
Operating income (in thousands)	542,738	347,635	331,180	312,315	268,004
Net income (in thousands)	$333,986	$216,376	$204,830	$194,754	$166,600
Earnings per share	$3.66	$2.28	$2.06	$1.94	$1.62
Dividends declared per share	$0.60	$0.50	0	0	0
Total assets (in thousands)	$1,789,718	$1,386,791	$1,401,369	$1,190,615	$ 929,978
Capital expenditures (in thousands)	$256,422	$185,765	$159,777	$145,662	$171,673
Long-term debt (in thousands)	0	0	0	0	0
Shareholders' equity (in thousands)	$995,227	$669,326	$857,765	$736,307	$582,395
Number of stores	851	788	700	597	491
Gross square feet of store space	6,025,000	5,590,000	5,016,000	4,358,000	3,673,000
Number of employees	69,100	48,500	30,200	22,000	16,700

Source: A&F 10-K report.

a band, enjoyed food and drinks, and received a T-shirt. All proceeds went to the Center for Child and Family Advocacy in Columbus, Ohio. The company's largest donation—$10 million—went to a children's hospital in Columbus in June 2006. The hospital's new trauma center would bear the A&F name.

A&F also sometimes got involved in issues at the supplier end of its business. In 2004, it joined a boycott of Australian merino wool in an effort to force ranchers to end a cruel procedure known as mulesing; although intended to protect lambs from flies, the procedure was said to cause pain and suffering. Even though A&F did not purchase much Australian wool, wool producers feared that the retailer would set a precedent and that other retailers would soon join the boycott. They agreed to end the practice of mulesing by 2010 or sooner.[41]

Organizational Culture and Human Resource Management

A&F's core corporate values were "nature, friendships and having fun."[42] These values were reflected in everything from the decor of the retailer's stores and the casual attire of its employees to the layout of A&F's headquarters in New Albany, Ohio, and to the firm's advertising messages. If there were no customers to serve, employees might throw a football to one another in the store. The retailer's home page on its Web site featured a tree house that could be downloaded as wallpaper.

A&F's headquarters, built in 2001, was situated in the woods along Blacklick Creek in New Albany, Ohio. Its campuslike setting served as a continual reminder to employees that the firm's target audience was college students. It was also designed to encourage teamwork and creativity. Instead of sitting at desks in individual cubicles, employees engaged in collaborative work at long tables in doorless conference rooms. Employees could walk along paths in the woods to relax, think, or seek inspiration for a new idea. There was no executive suite.

Jeffries had no desk or office. He also worked in a conference room with a view of the grounds from large windows.

Employees enjoyed healthy meals that included roast chicken, international dishes, salads, fruit juices, and gourmet coffees in the full-service cafeteria. They traveled from building to building on scooters and were allowed to bring their skateboards. A bonfire pit provided the atmosphere of an outdoor summer camp. Employees worked out in the gym. One of the architects said, "A&F wants to give back to the people who work there. That's why they can go to that rusty barn the first thing in the morning, or get sweaty in the gym and then go to work, have a great meal and then go back to work again. It reinforces the idea that this is community."[43]

Store managers visited nearby fraternities and sororities to recruit salespeople, or "brand representatives." They were encouraged to ask attractive shoppers in their stores if they wanted to apply for a sales position. Tom Lennox, A&F's investor relations and communications director, acknowledged that the firm liked to hire job candidates who looked great. "Brand representatives are ambassadors to the brand. We want to hire brand representatives that will represent the Abercrombie & Fitch brand with natural classic American style, look great while exhibiting individuality, project the brand and themselves with energy and enthusiasm, and make the store a warm, inviting place that provides a social experience for the customer," Lennox said.[44] The company ran a manager-in-training program for seniors and graduates. Promotion to store manager could occur one year after completing the training.

Brand representatives were expected to adhere to a dress code outlined in an Abercrombie Associate's Handbook. Hair was to be neatly combed and attractive; makeup was to be worn to enhance natural features and create a fresh, natural appearance; fingernails were not to extend more than a quarter of an inch beyond the tip of the finger, and nail polish was to be a natural color; mustaches, goatees, and beards were unacceptable; jewelry was to be simple and classic—only women were allowed to wear earrings, they could have no more than two earrings in each ear, and each earring could be no larger than a dime and could not dangle.[45]

In 2000, the California Department of Industrial Relations received complaints from several A&F employees who said that they were forced to buy and wear the company's clothes on the job. One woman, in another part of the country, later claimed that she spent more on clothes for work than she earned at the store. Such company policy might have violated a state work uniform law that required employers to supply the clothing when they wanted workers to wear specific apparel. In 2003, A&F settled the lawsuit in California for $2.2 million without admitting wrongdoing. Employees received reimbursements ranging from $180 to $490 depending on their job status and the amount of money spent on clothing.[46] The case spurred similar lawsuits across the state and the rest of the nation against The Limited, Gap, Chico's, and Polo Ralph Lauren. In some states, lawyers used the federal Fair Labor Standards Act, which required employers to pay minimum wage, to argue that sales associates ended up with less than minimum wage after spending their earnings on store clothing.

A&F's legal problems were only just beginning. In July 2003, two former A&F employees filed a lawsuit accusing the company of failing to pay overtime wages when they were required to work 50–60 hours a week. The plaintiffs claimed that they were sales associates, with no management responsibilities, but were classified as managers so that the retailer could avoid paying overtime. According to the Federal Fair Labor Standards Act and the Ohio Minimum Fair Wage Standards Act, nonexempt employees had to be paid time and a half for work in excess of 40 hours a week.

In June 2003, lawyers for nine plaintiffs filed a lawsuit against the retailer for discriminating against minorities in its hiring practices and job placement. It allegedly cultivated an "overwhelmingly white workforce" and steered minority applicants into less visible jobs.[47] Former

A&F employees appeared on CBS's television program *60 Minutes* and said that A&F was interested in hiring employees who fit a certain look. Anthony Ocampo worked at an Abercrombie store during his Christmas break from Stanford University. When he returned to get a summer job, he was told that he could not be rehired because the store already had too many Filipinos working there. Eduardo Gonzalez, another Stanford University student who was Latino, was told that he could only work in the store's stockroom or as part of the overnight crew; at Banana Republic, he was asked if he was applying for a management position. Carla Grubb, an African American student at California State University at Bakersfield, felt she was not treated fairly because she was scheduled to work only during closing times and was asked to wash the front windows, vacuum, and clean the mannequins.

In November 2003, another lawsuit was filed against A&F on behalf of a New Jersey woman who claimed that her application for a sales-associate position was denied because she was African American. A&F denied that it discriminated against minorities. It claimed that minorities represented 13 percent of all its store associates (which exceeded national averages). The U.S. Equal Employment Opportunity Commission also initiated a lawsuit, claiming that A&F violated parts of the Civil Rights Act of 1964. Store managers reported that they were instructed to discard job applications if the candidates did not possess the right look.

In November 2004, A&F paid $50 million (including legal fees) to settle the discrimination lawsuits. It agreed to hire a vice president of diversity, provide training in diversity and inclusion to its employees and managers, increase the number of minority employees in sales and store management positions, enhance its compliance and oversight processes, and use more minority models in its advertising. The retailer promised that within two years its sales force would consist of 9 percent African Americans, 9 percent Latinos, its current percentage of Asians, and 53 percent women.[48] A&F was told to stop recruiting from predominantly white fraternities and sororities. It agreed to hire 25 full-time diversity recruiters who would seek new hires from historically black colleges, minority job fairs, and minority recruiting events. Michael Jeffries issued a statement: "We have, and always have had, no tolerance for discrimination. We decided to settle this suit because we felt that a long, drawn-out dispute would have been harmful to the company and distracting to management."[49]

Todd Corley became A&F's new vice president of diversity. Due to his efforts, A&F established a $300,000 grant for scholarships for the United Negro College Fund, became a sponsor of the Organization of Chinese Americans' College Leadership Summit, became a sponsor of the National Black MBA Association, and offered internships for minority college juniors seeking retail-management careers through Inroads Inc.

A&F's Future

A&F was likely to face increased competition. One of its direct rivals, American Eagle Outfitters, was able to outperform A&F in terms of profitability and assume the number three rank (compared to A&F's fourth-place rank) among U.S. publicly traded apparel companies in 2006, as listed by *Apparel* magazine. Newcomers to the specialty apparel industry, as well as large department stores, sought to imitate A&F's product offerings. Metropark, for example, a West Coast chain for 20- to 35-year-old shoppers, opened its 15th store in Atlanta, Georgia. It planned to open an additional 50 stores by 2007. The retailer sold brand-name casual apparel made by such designers as True Religion and Joe's Jeans. It also tried to create a nightclub-like atmosphere in its stores with flat-screen televisions playing music videos and a lounge offering energy drinks and magazines.

Department stores, too, began to diversify their lines by stocking merchandise from new suppliers and by promoting their own in-house labels. Oved Apparel launched Company 81 in 2005 as "an Abercrombie for department stores."[50] It began to sell distressed denim,

chinos, shorts, golf jackets, blazers, and graphic T-shirts at the wholesale level. It provided department stores with in-store signage and imagery from its advertising campaign to complement its merchandise. Federated Department Stores, which operated Macy's and Bloomingdale's, created an in-house label called American Rag. Its merchandise was similar in style to A&F's but priced more moderately.

As if sensing the encroachment of competitors, A&F began an unusual effort to improve its customer service. In the past, brand representatives acted more like models than salespeople. They were known for their snobbish disregard of shoppers. They did not talk to customers until they were within five feet of each other.[51] Some customers felt intimidated. Under COO Singer, store greeters were positioned in the entrance to each store and salespeople were posted in every section. A vice president of training was hired to work with store staff. The number of employees was increased and hours of store operations were extended. The added attention helped reduce merchandise shrinkrage.[52] Nonetheless, progress in customer service may have been derailed by the departure of Singer from the company.

A&F also needed to be vigilant regarding the needs and preferences of its target markets. Teenagers were perceived as being fickle. According to experts on the reactions of millennials to pop culture, they were difficult to influence because they thought more independently and changed their minds more frequently than previous generations. They would find the "emphasis on the physicality of models" in A&F advertisements unappealing.[53] The emerging trend toward ethical consumption was also something to be watched. Young people began to purchase food products and clothing with Fair Trade labels. They were committed, for example, to purchasing coffee that was organically grown from suppliers who paid bean pickers higher wages than the going rate. They bought T-shirts that were not made in overseas sweatshops.

The challenges for A&F executives in 2006 and beyond were to anticipate competitor moves, to improve customer service, and to maintain consumer loyalty. They needed to hire talented top managers who could work well alongside CEO Jeffries. These domestic imperatives came at a critical time for the retailer. It was just about to enter the European market, with its first store on Savile Row in London. Pamela Quintiliano, a WR Hambrecht retail analyst, gave the expansion plan a nod of approval: "Abercrombie is an incredibly strong brand name, and there's a hunger for American brands around the world."[54]

Endnotes

[1] J. E. Palmierie and D. Moin, "A&F Hits Fifth Avenue Fray," *DNR* 35 (November 14, 2005), p. 4. Retrieved April 19, 2006, from ABI/Inform (ProQuest) database.

[2] D. Penny, "The Abercrombie Report," *New York* 38 (November 21, 2005), p. 6. Retrieved April 19, 2006, from ABI/Inform (ProQuest) database.

[3] M. Souers and M. Normand, "Specialty Retailers Demonstrate Resilience in Face of Adversity," *Standard & Poor's Industry Surveys: Retailing: Specialty,* January 12, 2006.

[4] Ibid.

[5] Ibid.

[6] A&F, 10-K report; J. Sheban, "Oh, Canada!" *Knight Ridder Tribune Business News,* February 26, 2006, p. 1. Retrieved April 18, 2006, from ABI/Inform (ProQuest) database.

[7] "Rapid Growth in Specialized Shop Trade Madison Avenue in the Forties The Centre," *New York Times,* February 18, 1923. Retrieved April 21, 2006, from ProQuest Historical Newspapers database.

[8] "New Face for Fashion at Abercrombie & Fitch," *New York Times,* September 11, 1965, p. 14. Retrieved April 21, 2006, from ProQuest Historical Newspapers database.

[9] "Changes Weighed for Abercrombie," *New York Times,* September, 1970, p. 73. Retrieved April 21, 2006, from ProQuest Historical Newspapers database.

[10] "Abercrombie Reports Loss of $1 Million in Fiscal Year," *New York Times,* August 26, 1976, p. 68. Retrieved April 21, 2006, from ProQuest Historical Newspapers database.

[11] R. Hanley, "Abercrombie & Fitch Put Up for Sale," *New York Times,* July 20, 1976. Retrieved April 21, 2006, from ProQuest Historical Newspapers database.

[12] I. Barmash, "Abercrombie & Fitch in Bankruptcy Step," *New York Times,* August 7, 1976, p. 47. Retrieved April 21, 2006, from ProQuest Historical Newspapers database.

[13] C. G. Fraser, "'Stuffy' Abercrombie's Gets Sale Relief," *New York Times,* August 29, 1976, p. 47. Retrieved April 21, 2006, from ProQuest Historical Newspapers database.

[14] I. Barmash, "New Guise for Abercrombie's," *New York Times,* November 9, 1982, p. D1. Retrieved April 21, 2006, from ProQuest Historical Newspapers database.

[15] D. Canedy, "After Unbuttoning Its Image, a Retail Legend Comes to Market," *New York Times,* September 1996, p. F3. Retrieved April 21, 2006, from ProQuest Historical Newspapers database.

[16] R. Berner, "Flip-Flops, Torn Jeans—And Control," *BusinessWeek,* May 30, 2005, p. 68. Retrieved December 12, 2005, from ABI/Inform (ProQuest) database.

[17] M. Cole, "Facing a Brave New World," *Apparel* 45 (July 2004), p. 22. Retrieved April 20, 2006, from ProQuest Historical Newspapers database.

[18] M. Pledger, "Abercrombie & Fitch Focuses on American College Audience," *The Plain Dealer,* June 22, 1999, p. 2S. Retrieved April 19, 2006, from Lexis/Nexis Academic database.

[19] Berner, "Flip-Flops."

[20] "Abercrombie CEO Benefits Settlement OKd," *Los Angeles Times,* June 15, 2005. Retrieved May 18, 2006, from ABI/Inform (Proquest) database.

[21] Ibid.

[22] M. Wilson, "The 'Pop' Factor," *Chain Store Age* 82 (April 2006), p. 78. Retrieved May 18, 2006, from ABI/Inform (Proquest) database.

[23] B. Denizet-Lewis, "The Man Behind Abercrombie & Fitch," www.salon.com (January 24, 2006).

[24] "Web Site Reviews: Abercrombie & Fitch," Forbes.com, www.forbes.com/bow/b2c/review.jhtml?id=6833 (accessed May 1, 2006).

[25] J. Ablan, "Trend Setter," *Barron's* 83 (March 31, 2003), p. 21. Retrieved April 20, 2006, from ABI/Inform (ProQuest) database.

[26] P. B. Erikson, "Companies Focus on Youthful Influence for Prosperity," *Knight Ridder Tribune Business News,* April 16, 2006, p. 1. Retrieved April 21, 2006, from ABI/Inform (ProQuest) database.

[27] Ibid.; Ablan, "Trend Setter."

[28] Presentation at the Merrill Lynch Retailing Leaders & Household Products & Cosmetics Conference, March 25, 2005, www.abercrombie.com (accessed April 22, 2006).

[29] T. Turner, "Retailer Abercrombie & Fitch Angers West Virginia Residents with New T-Shirt," *Knight Ridder Tribune Business News,* March 24, 2004, p. 1. Retrieved November 8, 2004, from ABI/Inform (ProQuest) database.

[30] "Abercrombie & Fitch Plans to Delete Drinking Section," *The Wall Street Journal,* July 30, 1998, p. 1. Retrieved November 8, 2004, from ABI/Inform (ProQuest) database.

[31] G. Kim, "Racism Doesn't Belong on T-shirts," *Knight Ridder Tribune Business News,* April 28, 2002, p. 1. Retrieved April 21, 2006, from ABI/Inform (ProQuest) database.

[32] D. DeMarco, "Abercrombie & Fitch Pulls Children's Thong," *Knight Ridder Tribune Business News,* May 23, 2002, p. 1. Retrieved November 8, 2004, from ABI/Inform (ProQuest) database.

[33] J. Caggiano, "Abercrombie & Fitch Drops Racy Publication," *Knight Ridder Tribune Business News,* December 11, 2003, p. 1. Retrieved November 8, 2004, from ABI/Inform (ProQuest) database.

[34] Turner, "Retailer Abercrombie & Fitch."

[35] "USA Gymnastics Upset with Abercrombie & Fitch," *Washington Post,* October 8, 2004, p. D2. Retrieved November 8, 2004, from ABI/Inform (ProQuest) database.

[36] K. S. Shalett, "Shamed off Shelves," *Times-Picayune,* May 20, 2005, p. 1. Retrieved December 12, 2005, from ABI/Inform (ProQuest) database.

[37] M. Haynes, "'Girlcott' Organizers Meet with Abercrombie & Fitch Execs over T-shirts," *Knight Ridder Tribune Business News,* December 6, 2005, p. 1. Retrieved December 12, 2005, from ABI/Inform (ProQuest) database.

[38] "Abercrombie & Fitch Co. at Banc of America Securities Consumer Conference," *Fair Disclosure Wire,* March 17, 2005. Retrieved May 24, 2006, from ABI/Inform (ProQuest) database.

[39] K. Showalter, "A&F Readies $10 Million Expansion," *Business First of Columbus,* March 11, 2005, http://columbus.bizjournals.com/columbus/stories/2005/03/14/story5.html (accessed April 29, 2006).

[40] J. Sheban, "Fighting Fakes: Abercrombie Enlists Expert to Help It Combat Counterfeiting," *Knight Ridder Tribune Business News,* February 3, 2006, p. 1. Retrieved April 23, 2006, from ABI/Inform (ProQuest) database.

[41] J. Sheban, "Abercrombie & Fitch's Wool Boycott Helps End 'Mulesing' Practice," *Knight Ridder Tribune Business News,* November 12, 2004, p. 1. Retrieved April 19, 2006, from ABI/Inform (ProQuest) database.

[42] D. Gebolys, "Inside Abercrombie & Fitch," *Columbus Dispatch,* May 24, 2001, p. 1F. Retrieved April 19, 2006, from LexisNexis Academic database.

[43] K. Showalter, "Abercrombie & Fitch: Campus Reflects the True Nature of New Albany Firm's Culture," *Business First of Columbus,* August 24, 2001, http://columbus.bizjournals.com/columbus/stories/2001/08/27/focus1.html?page=3 (accessed April 29, 2006).

[44] S. Greenhouse, "Going for the Look, but Risking Discrimination," *New York Times,* July 13, 2003, p. 12. Retrieved November 9, 2004, from ABI/Inform (ProQuest) database.

[45] B. Paynter, "Don't Hate Me Because I'm Beautiful," *Kansas City Pitch Weekly,* September 4, 2003. Retrieved February 12, 2005, from LexisNexis Academic database.

[46] "Abercrombie & Fitch Settles Dress Code Case," *Houston Chronicle,* June 25, 2003, p. 2. Retrieved November 4, 2004, from ABI/Inform (ProQuest) database.

[47] T. Turner, "Cincinnati Suit Charges Abercrombie & Fitch with Failing to Pay Overtime," *Knight Ridder Tribune Business News,* July 9, 2003, p. 1.

[48] J. Sheban, "Abercrombie & Fitch: The Face of Change," *Columbus Dispatch,* July 31, 2005, p. F1. Retrieved April 19, 2006, from ABI/Inform (ProQuest) database.

[49] S. Greenhouse, "Abercrombie & Fitch Bias Case Is Settled," *New York Times,* November 17, 2004, p. A16. Retrieved May 24, 2006, from ABI/Inform (ProQuest) database.

[50] L. Bailey, "The New South: Young Men's & Streetwear," *DNR* 35 (August 22, 2005), p. 94. Retrieved June 1, 2006, from ABI/Inform (ProQuest) database.

[51] Paynter, "Don't Hate."

[52] S. King, "Style and Substance: Abercrombie & Fitch Tries to Be Less Haughty," *The Wall Street Journal,* June 17, 2005, p. B1. Retrieved June 23, 2005, from ABI/Inform (ProQuest) database.

[53] V. Seckler, "Brands' Challenge: Bridging Gap with Young People," *Women's Wear Daily* 77 (April 12, 2006). Retrieved June 1, 2006, from ABI/Inform (ProQuest) database.

[54] J. Sheban, "Oh Canada!"

Monitoring Foreign Suppliers: The Challenge of Detecting Unethical Practices

Arthur A. Thompson Jr.
The University of Alabama

Importers of goods from China, Indonesia, Cambodia, Vietnam, Malaysia, Korea, Pakistan, Bangladesh, Sri Lanka, India, the Philippines, Peru, Honduras, the Dominican Republic, Tunisia, and other less developed countries had long had to contend with accusations by human rights activists that they sourced goods from sweatshop manufacturers that paid substandard wages, required unusually long work hours, used child labor, operated unsafe workplaces, and habitually engaged in assorted other unsavory practices. Since the 1990s, companies had responded to criticisms about sourcing goods from manufacturers in developing nations where working conditions were often substandard by instituting elaborate codes of conduct for foreign suppliers and by periodically inspecting the manufacturing facilities of these suppliers to try to eliminate abuses and promote improved working conditions. In several industries where companies sourced goods from common foreign suppliers, companies had joined forces to conduct plant monitoring; for example, Hewlett-Packard, Dell, and other electronics companies that relied heavily on Asia-based manufacturers to supply components or assemble digital cameras, handheld devices, and PCs had entered into an alliance to combat worker abuse and poor working conditions in supplier factories.

But a number of unscrupulous foreign manufacturers had recently gotten much better at concealing human rights abuses and substandard working conditions. In November 2006, *BusinessWeek* ran a cover story detailing how shady foreign manufacturers were deceiving inspection teams and escaping detection.[1] According to the *BusinessWeek* special report, Ningbo Beifa Group—a top Chinese supplier of pens, mechanical pens, and highlighters to Wal-Mart, Staples, Woolworth, and some 400 other retailers in 100 countries—was alerted in late 2005 that a Wal-Mart inspection team would soon be visiting the company's factory in the coastal city of Ningbo. Wal-Mart was Beifa's largest customer and on three previous occasions had caught Beifa paying its 3,000 workers less than the Chinese minimum wage and violating overtime rules; a fourth offense would end Wal-Mart's purchases from Beifa. But weeks prior to the audit, an administrator at Beifa's factory in Ningbo got a call from representatives of Shanghai Corporate Responsibility Management & Consulting Company offering to help the Beifa factory pass the Wal-Mart inspection.[2] The Beifa administrator agreed to pay the requested fee of $5,000. The consultant advised management at the Beifa factory in Ningbo to create fake but authentic-looking records regarding pay scales and overtime work and make sure to get any workers with grievances out of the plant on the day of the audit.

Beifa managers at the factory were also coached on how to answer questions that the auditors would likely ask. Beifa's Ningbo factory reportedly passed the Wal-Mart inspection in early 2006 without altering any of its practices.[3] A lawyer for Beifa confirmed that the company had indeed employed the Shanghai consulting firm but said that factory personnel engaged in no dishonest actions to pass the audit; the lawyer indicated that the factory passed the audit because it had taken steps to correct the problems found in Wal-Mart's prior audits.

Growing Use of Strategies to Deliberately Deceive Plant Inspectors

In 2007, substandard wages and abusive working conditions were thought to be prevalent in factories in a host of countries—China, Indonesia, Cambodia, Vietnam, Malaysia, Korea, Pakistan, Bangladesh, Sri Lanka, India, the Philippines, Peru, Honduras, the Dominican Republic, Tunisia, and several other countries in Latin America, Eastern Europe, the Middle East, and Africa. (See Exhibit 1 for a sample of the problems in eight countries.) Factories in China were particularly in the spotlight because of China's prominence as the world's biggest source of low-priced goods. China was the largest single source of goods imported into both the United States and the 25 countries comprising the European Union. U.S. imports from Chinese manufacturers amounted to about $280 billion in 2006.

Political support in many countries for growing trade ties with offshore manufacturers, especially those in China, often hinged on the ability of companies with global sourcing strategies to convince domestic governmental officials, human rights groups, and concerned citizens that they were doing all they could do to police working conditions in the plants of suppliers in low-wage, poverty-stricken countries where sweatshop practices were concentrated. A strong program of auditing the offshore plants of suspect employers was a way for a company to cover itself and negate accusations that it was unfairly exploiting workers in less developed countries.

Workplace Rules in China

Minimum wages in China were specified by local or provincial governments and in 2006 ranged from $45 to $101 per month, which equated to hourly rates of $0.25 to $0.65 based on a 40-hour workweek.[4] According to Chinese government income data compiled by the U.S. Bureau of Labor Statistics and a Beijing consulting firm, the average manufacturing wage in China was $0.64 per hour (again assuming a 40-hour workweek). While the standard workweek in Chinese provinces officially ranged from 40 to 44 hours, there were said to be numerous instances where plant personnel worked 60 to 100 hours per week, sometimes with only one or two days off per month. Such long work hours meant that the actual average manufacturing wage in China was likely well below $0.64 per hour in 2005–2006. According to estimates made by a veteran inspector of Chinese factories, employees at garment, electronics, and other plants making goods for export typically worked more than 80 hours per week and earned an average of $0.42 per hour.[5]

Overtime pay rules in Chinese provinces officially called for time-and-a-half pay for all work over eight hours per day and between double and triple pay for work on Saturdays, Sundays, and holidays. However, it was commonplace for Chinese employers to disregard overtime pay rules, and governmental enforcement of minimum wage and overtime requirements by both Beijing officials and officials in local Chinese provinces was often minimal to nonexistent. At a Hong Kong garment plant where 2,000 employees put in many overtime hours operating sewing and stitching machines, worker pay averaged about $125 per month—an amount that the owner acknowledged did not meet Chinese overtime pay requirements. The owner said that overtime rules were "a fantasy. Maybe in two or three decades we can meet them."[6] Many young Chinese factory

Exhibit 1

Comparative Labor and Workplace Conditions in Eight Countries, 2006

COUNTRY	LABOR AND WORKPLACE OVERVIEW
Brazil	Primary problems in the manufacturing workplace are forced labor, inadequate occupational safety (work accidents are common in several industries), and wage discrimination (wages paid to females are 54% to 64% of those paid to males).
China	Factories are most prone to ignore minimum wage requirements, underpay for overtime work, subject workers to unsafe and unhealthy working conditions, and suppress worker attempts to join independent unions.
India	Most common issues concern underpayment of minimum wages, overtime pay violations, use of child labor (according to one estimate some 100 million children ages 5 to 14 work and at least 12.6 million work full-time), the use of forced labor (perhaps as many as 65 million people), and inattention to occupational safety.
Indonesia	The stand-out issues concern weak enforcement of minimum-wage rules and work hours in factories, overtime pay violations in factories, subpar occupational safety (especially in mining and fishing), and use of underage labor (particularly in domestic service, mining, construction, and fishing industries).
Mexico	Problem areas include sweatshop conditions in many assembly plants near the U.S. border and elsewhere, fierce opposition to unions, insistence on pregnancy tests for female job applicants of child-bearing age, and use of child labor in nonexport economic sectors.
Peru	Worst workplace conditions relate to lack of enforcement of wage and overtime provisions in factories, mandatory overtime requirements for many workers, and inattention to occupational safety.
South Africa	Most frequent offenses entail failure to observe minimum-wage and overtime pay rules (particularly in garment industry), use of child labor, occupational safety violations (especially in nonexport sectors where outside monitoring is nonexistent), and low pay for women.
Sri Lanka	Most frequent violations relate to underpayment of wages, forced overtime requirements, compulsory work on Sundays and holidays, and inattention to worker health and safety (such as excessive noise, blocked exits, and disregard for worker safety—one study found 60% of grain and spice mill workers lost fingers in work-related accidents and/or contracted skin diseases).

Source: Compiled by the author from information in "How China's Labor Conditions Stack Up Against Those of Other Low-Cost Nations," *BusinessWeek Online,* November 27, 2006, www.businessweek.com (accessed January 26, 2007). The information was provided to *BusinessWeek* by Verité, a Massachusetts-based nonprofit social auditing and research organization with expertise in human rights and labor abuses in supplier factories around the world.

workers were tolerant of long hours and less than full overtime pay because they wanted to earn as much as possible, the idea being to save enough of their income to return to their homes in the countryside after a few years of factory employment.

Chinese export manufacturing was said to be rife with tales of deception to frustrate plant monitoring and escape compliance with local minimum wage and overtime rules and supplier codes of conduct. Indeed, a new breed of consultants had sprung up in China to aid local manufacturers in passing audits conducted both by customer companies and by industry alliance groups.[7]

Emerging Strategies to Frustrate Plant Monitoring Efforts

The efforts of unscrupulous manufacturers in China and other parts of the world to game the plant monitoring system and use whatever deceptive practices it took to successfully pass plant audits had four chief elements:

1. *Maintaining two sets of books*—Factories generated a set of bogus payroll records and time sheets to show audit teams that their workers were properly paid and received the appropriate overtime pay; the genuine records were kept secret. For example, at an onsite audit of a Chinese maker of lamps

for Home Depot, Sears, and other retailers, plant managers provided inspectors with payroll records and time sheets showing that employees worked a five-day week from 8 a.m. to 5:30 p.m. with a 30-minute lunch break and no overtime hours; during interviews, managers at the plant said the records were accurate. But other records auditors found at the site, along with interviews with workers, indicated that employees worked an extra three to five hours daily with one or two days off per month during peak production periods; inspectors were unable to verify whether workers at the plant received overtime pay.[8] According to a compliance manager at a major multinational company who had overseen many factory audits, the percentage of Chinese employers submitting false payroll records had risen from 46 percent to 75 percent during the past four years; the manager also estimated that only 20 percent of Chinese suppliers complied with local minimum-wage rules and that just 5 percent obeyed hour limitations.[9]

2. *Hiding the use of underage workers and unsafe work practices*—In some instances, factories in China, parts of Africa, and select other countries in Asia, Eastern Europe, and the Middle East employed underage workers. This was disguised either by falsifying the personnel records of underage employees, by adeptly getting underage employees off the premises when audit teams arrived, or by putting underage employees in back rooms concealed from auditors. A memo distributed in one Chinese factory instructed managers to "notify underage trainees, underage full-time workers, and workers without identification to leave the manufacturing workshop through the back door. Order them not to loiter near the dormitory area. Secondly, immediately order the receptionist to gather all relevant documents and papers."[10] At a toy plant in China, a compliance inspector, upon smelling strong fumes in a poorly ventilated building, found young female employees on a production line using spray guns to paint figurines; in a locked back room that a factory official initially refused to open, an apparently underage worker was found hiding behind co-workers.[11]

3. *Meeting requirements by secretly shifting production to subcontractors*—On occasions, suppliers met the standards set by customers by secretly shifting some production to subcontractors who failed to observe pay standards, skirted worker safety procedures, or otherwise engaged in abuses of various kinds.

4. *Coaching managers and employees on answering questions posed by audit team members*—Both managers and workers were tutored on what to tell inspectors should they be interviewed. Scripting responses about wages and overtime pay, hours worked, safety procedures, training, and other aspects related to working conditions was a common tactic for thwarting what inspectors could learn from interviews. However, in instances where plant inspectors were able to speak confidentially with employees away from the worksite, they often got information at variance with what they were told during onsite interviews—plant personnel were more inclined to be truthful and forthcoming about actual working conditions and pay practices when top-level plant management could not trace the information given to inspectors back to them.

There was a growing awareness among companies attempting to enforce supplier codes of conduct that all factories across the world with substandard working conditions and reasons to hide their practices from outside view played cat-and-mouse games with plant inspectors. In many less-developed countries struggling to build a manufacturing base and provide jobs for their citizens, factory managers considered deceptive practices a necessary evil to survive, principally because improving wages and working conditions to comply with labor codes and customers' codes of conduct for suppliers raised costs and imperiled already thin profit margins. Violations were said to be most prevalent at factories making apparel, but more violations were surfacing in factories making furniture, appliances, toys, and electronics.

However, large global corporations such as General Electric, Motorola, Dell, Nestlé, and Toyota that owned and operated their own offshore manufacturing plants in China and other low-wage countries had not been accused of mistreating their employees or having poor working conditions. The offshore factories of well-known global and multinational companies were seldom subject to monitoring by outsiders because the workplace environments in their foreign plants were relatively good in comparison to those of local manufacturing enterprises who made a business of supplying low-cost components and finished goods to companies and retailers in affluent, industrialized nations.

Foreign Supplier Compliance Programs at Nike and Wal-Mart

Corporate sensitivity to charges of being socially irresponsible in their sourcing of goods from foreign manufacturers had prompted hundreds of companies to establish supplier codes of conduct and to engage in compliance monitoring efforts of one kind or another manner. Most companies with global sourcing strategies and factory compliance programs worked proactively to improve working conditions globally, preferring to help suppliers achieve the expected standards rather than abruptly and permanently cutting off purchases. The most commonly observed problems worldwide related to benefits such as pensions and insurance (medical, accident, unemployment) not being paid. Other frequent issues included workers not being paid for all hours worked, the use of false books, and incomplete or insufficient documentation.

Nike and Wal-Mart were two companies with supplier codes of conduct and rather extensive programs to monitor whether suppliers in low-wage, low-cost manufacturing locations across the world were complying with their codes of conduct. Both companies initiated such efforts in the 1990s because they came under fire from human rights activist groups for allegedly sourcing goods from sweatshop factories in China and elsewhere.

Nike's Supplier Code of Conduct and Compliance Monitoring Program

Nike was the world's leading designer, distributor, and marketer of athletic footwear, sports apparel, and sports equipment and accessories, but it did no manufacturing. All Nike products were sourced from contract manufacturers. In April 2005, Nike reported that there were over 730 factories actively engaged in manufacturing its products; of these, about 135 were in China (including Hong Kong and Macau); 73 in Thailand, 39 in Indonesia, 35 in Korea, 34 in Vietnam, 33 in Malaysia, 25 in Sri Lanka, and 18 in India.[12] Nike's contract factories employed roughly 625,000 workers, the majority of whom were women between the ages of 19 and 25 performing entry-level, low-skill jobs.

Nike drafted a code of conduct for its contract factories in 1991, distributed the code to all of its contract factories in 1992, and directed them to post the code in a visible place and in the appropriate local language. The code had been modified and updated over the years, and in 2007 also included a set of leadership standards that was adopted in 2002. Nike's code of conduct is presented in Exhibit 2. In 1998, in a move to strengthen its opposition to the use of child labor in factories, Nike directed its contract factories to set age standards for employment at 16 for apparel and 18 for footwear; these age standards were more demanding than those set in 1991 and exceeded the International Labor Organization's age minimum of 15 years.

NIKE'S SYSTEM FOR MONITORING CONTRACT MANUFACTURERS During 2003–2006, Nike used three approaches to plant monitoring:[13]

- *Basic monitoring or SHAPE inspections:* SHAPE inspections, used since 1997, sought to gauge a factory's overall compliance performance, including environment, safety,

Exhibit 2

Nike's Code of Conduct for Its Suppliers and Contract Manufacturers, 2006

Nike, Inc., was founded on a handshake

Implicit in that act was the determination that we would build our business with all of our partners based on trust, teamwork, honesty and mutual respect. We expect all of our business partners to operate on the same principles. At the core of the NIKE corporate ethic is the belief that we are a company comprised of many different kinds of people, appreciating individual diversity, and dedicated to equal opportunity for each individual.

NIKE designs, manufactures, and markets products for sports and fitness consumers. At every step in that process, we are driven to do not only what is required by law, but what is expected of a leader. We expect our business partners to do the same. NIKE partners with contractors who share our commitment to best practices and continuous improvement in:

1. Management practices that respect the rights of all employees, including the right to free association and collective bargaining
2. Minimizing our impact on the environment
3. Providing a safe and healthy workplace
4. Promoting the health and well-being of all employees

Contractors must recognize the dignity of each employee, and the right to a workplace free of harassment, abuse or corporal punishment. Decisions on hiring, salary, benefits, advancement, termination or retirement must be based solely on the employee's ability to do the job. There shall be no discrimination based on race, creed, gender, marital or maternity status, religious or political beliefs, age or sexual orientation.

Wherever NIKE operates around the globe we are guided by this Code of Conduct and we bind our contractors to these principles. Contractors must post this Code in all major workspaces, translated into the language of the employee, and must train employees on their rights and obligations as defined by this Code and applicable local laws.

While these principles establish the spirit of our partnerships, we also bind our partners to specific standards of conduct. The core standards are set forth below.

Forced Labor

The contractor does not use forced labor in any form—prison, indentured, bonded or otherwise.

Child Labor

The contractor does not employ any person below the age of 18 to produce footwear. The contractor does not employ any person below the age of 16 to produce apparel, accessories or equipment. If at the time Nike production begins, the contractor employs people of the legal working age who are at least 15, that employment may continue, but the contractor will not hire any person going forward who is younger than the Nike or legal age limit, whichever is higher. To further ensure these age standards are complied with, the contractor does not use any form of homework for Nike production.

Compensation

The contractor provides each employee at least the minimum wage, or the prevailing industry wage, whichever is higher; provides each employee a clear, written accounting for every pay period; and does not deduct from employee pay for disciplinary infractions.

Benefits

The contractor provides each employee all legally mandated benefits.

Hours of Work/Overtime

The contractor complies with legally mandated work hours; uses overtime only when each employee is fully compensated according to local law; informs each employee at the time of hiring if mandatory overtime is a condition of employment; and on a regularly scheduled basis provides one day off in seven, and requires no more than 60 hours of work per week on a regularly scheduled basis, or complies with local limits if they are lower.

Environment, Safety and Health (ES&H)

The contractor has written environmental, safety and health policies and standards, and implements a system to minimize negative impacts on the environment, reduce work-related injury and illness, and promote the general health of employees.

(continued)

Exhibit 2 (concluded)

Documentation and Inspection

The contractor maintains on file all documentation needed to demonstrate compliance with this Code of Conduct and required laws; agrees to make these documents available for Nike or its designated monitor; and agrees to submit to inspections with or without prior notice.

Source: www.nike.com (accessed January 25, 2007).

---

and health. They were typically performed by Nike's field-based production staff and could be completed in one day or less. Nike's stated goal was to conduct two SHAPE audits on each active factory each year, but the actual number of such audits had fallen short of that target.

- *In-depth M-Audits:* The M-Audit was designed to provide a deeper measure of the working conditions within contract factories. As a general rule, Nike focused its plant inspection efforts on factories where noncompliance was most likely to occur. Factories located in highly regulated countries where workers were more informed about their rights and workplace laws and regulations were enforced were deemed less likely to be out of compliance. In 2003, Nike focused its M-audits on factories presumed to have the highest risk of noncompliance and the greatest size (as measured by worker population). In 2004 M-audits were focused on factories believed to be of medium risk for noncompliance. Nike's stated goal was to conduct M-audits for approximately 25–33 percent of its active factory base each year. The M-Audit included four major categories of inquiry (hiring practices, worker treatment, worker–management communications, and compensation) and covered more than 80 labor–management issues.

In 2004 Nike had 46 employees who regularly conducted M-Audits. The typical M-Auditor was under the age of 30, and 74 percent were women. Nike tried to hire auditors who were local nationals and understood the local language and culture. In 2003–2004, over 9,200 factory workers were individually interviewed

as part of the M-Audit process. Each interview took approximately 30 minutes. The typical M-Audit took an average of 48 hours to complete, including travel to and from the factory—travel hours accounted for between 25 and 30 percent of total M-Audit time.

- *Independent external monitoring:* Beginning in 2003, Nike became a member of the Fair Labor Association, an organization that conducted independent audits of factories that provided goods to members. The FLA applied a common set of compliance standards in all of its factory audits. About 40 factories supplying goods to Nike were audited by the FLA in 2003.

In 2004, Nike's compliance team consisted of 90 people based in 24 offices in 21 countries. The typical Nike compliance team in each country spent about one-third of their time on monitoring and auditing activities, about half their time assisting and tracking factory remediation activities, and the remainder of their time on troubleshooting and collaboration/outreach work.[14] In its 2004 Corporate Responsibility Report, Nike said:

> With an average of one compliance staff for more than 10 factories—some of which are remote and some of which are large and complex businesses with 10,000 or more employees—tracking and assisting factory remediation is at times an overwhelming and incomplete body of work.[15]

Nike's factory audits were announced rather than unannounced because "much of the information we require in our evaluation of a factory is dependent upon access to relevant records and individuals within factory management."[16] When a factory was found to be out of compliance with the code of conduct, Nike's compliance team worked with factory management and the Nike business unit for which products were being manufactured to develop a Master Action Plan (MAP) that specified the factory's needed remediation efforts. The Nike production manager responsible for the business relationship with the contract factory monitored MAP progress and exchanged information about progress or obstacles with Nike's country compliance team. The Nike general manager for production monitored the progress of all factories within his or her purview, and weighed in when factory remediation progress was too slow.

To further facilitate factory compliance with Nike's Code of Conduct for suppliers, the company conducted or sponsored training and education programs for factory personnel. In 2004, over 16,500 factory managers and workers attended programs relating to labor issues, worker health and safety, and environmental protection.[17]

NIKE'S COMPLIANCE RATING SYSTEM

Nike's factory ratings for SHAPE and M-Audits resulted in numeric scores ranging from 0 to 100 (a score of 100 indicated full compliance); these numeric scores were then converted to one of four overall grades:[18]

Exhibit 3 presents a summary of Nike's latest available factory ratings.

CUTTING OFF ORDERS TO NONCOMPLYING OR NONPERFORMING SUPPLIERS

A factory was cut from Nike's supplier base when, over a specified period, Nike management determined that factory management lacked the capacity or the will to correct serious issues of noncompliance. One supplier in China, for example, was cited for repeated violations of overtime standards and falsification of records. The compliance team established action plans, which three different Nike business units worked with the factory to implement. After six months of continuous efforts, and no improvement, the factory was dropped. In November 2006, Nike severed its business relationship with a Pakistani supplier of soccer balls that failed to correct serious code of conduct violations.

More typically, Nike's decision to end a business relationship with problem suppliers was based on a balanced scorecard of factory performance that took into account labor code compliance along with such measures as price, quality, and delivery time. For example, a manufacturing group in South Asia had performed poorly on a range of issues, from overtime and

GRADE	CRITERIA
A	No more than 5 minor violations on a factory's Master Action Plan for improving working conditions and achieving higher levels of compliance with Nike's Code of Conduct, and no more than 20 percent of MAP items past due.
B	No more than 5 minor violations, but no serious or critical issues outstanding on the MAP and no more than 30 percent of MAP items past due.
C	One or more C-level compliance issues outstanding on the MAP and no more than 30 percent of MAP items past due—examples of C-level issues included excessive work hours per week (more than 60 but less than 72), not providing 1 day off in 7, verbal or psychological harassment of workers, exceeding legal annual overtime work limit for 10% or more of workforce, conditions likely to lead to moderate injury or illness to workers, and conditions likely to lead to moderate harm to environment or community.
D	One or more D-level issues outstanding on the factory's MAP or past due correction of prior D-level issues; or more than 40 percent of open MAP items past due. Examples of D-level issues included unwillingness to comply with code standards, falsified records, coaching of workers to falsify information, use of underage workers or forced labor, paying below the legal wage, no verifiable timekeeping system, exceeding daily work hour limit or work in excess of more than 72 hours per week for more than 10% of workforce, not providing one day off in 14, and conditions that could lead to serious worker injury or harm to the environment.

Note: A grade of E was assigned to factories for which there was insufficient information.

Exhibit 3

Summary Results of Nike's Compliance Ratings for Contract Suppliers, Fiscal Years 2003–2004

	GEOGRAPHIC REGION				
	AMERICAS	EUROPE, MIDDLE EAST, AFRICA	NORTHERN ASIA	SOUTHERN ASIA	WORLDWIDE TOTAL
Number of SHAPE audits in 2004	178	157	378	303	1,016
Number of M-Audits in 2003 and 2004	148	56	198	167	569
M-Audit Numeric Scores in 2003–2004					
Lowest score	46	49	25	20	20
Average score	78	70	58	58	65
Highest score	94	96	95	95	99
Compliance Ratings for Contact Factories as of June 2004					
Grade of A	32	15	34	25	106 (15%)
Grade of B	64	40	147	76	327 (44%)
Grade of C	18	7	33	65	123 (17%)
Grade of D	5	35	14	8	62 (8%)
Grade of E	18	7	22	70	117 (16%)

Note: Worker population in M-Audited factories was 375,000 in fiscal year 2003 and 213,000 in fiscal year 2004.

Source: Nike's 2004 Corporate Responsibility Report, pp. 20, 34, and 35.

worker–management communication to the quality of product and shipping dates. After a series of performance reviews, Nike management informed the factory group that it would not be placing orders for the next season. Nike did not report on factories dropped solely from noncompliance reasons related to its code of conduct because, management said, "it is often difficult to isolate poor performance on compliance as the sole reason for terminating a business relationship."[19]

To give its contract manufacturers greater incentive to comply with Nike's workplace standards and expectations, during crunch production periods Nike management and plant auditors had given some factories latitude to institute long workweeks (above 72 hours) and not hold them to a strict standard of 1 day off out of every 14 days if the employer gave workers more days off during slack production periods. Nike was also working to streamline its methods of designing shoes and placing orders with key suppliers and helping foreign factories develop more efficient production techniques, so as to help contract factories eliminate the need to institute long workweeks and excessive overtime. According to Nike's vice president for global footwear operations, "If you improve efficiency and innovation, it changes the cost equation" for factories.[20]

Wal-Mart's Supplier Code of Conduct and Compliance Monitoring Program

In 1992, Wal-Mart established a set of standards for its suppliers and put in place an ethical standards program to monitor supplier compliance with these standards.[21] Since then, Wal-Mart's standards for suppliers had been periodically evaluated and modified based on experience and feedback from the ethical sourcing community. The company's standards for suppliers covered compensation, working hours, forced labor, underage labor, discrimination, compliance with applicable national laws and regulation, health and safety practices, environmental abuse, freedom of association and collective bargaining, rights concerning foreign contract workers, and the right of audit by Wal-Mart.

Prior to contracting with any supplier, Wal-Mart required suppliers to review and sign a supplier agreement, which incorporated an expectation that the supplier would comply with Wal-Mart's standards for suppliers. In addition, it was mandatory that all suppliers display Wal-Mart's "Standards for Suppliers" poster in all of the suppliers' factories. Factory management was required to sign that it had read and fully understood the "Standards for Suppliers" poster, and a copy of the poster in the relevant language had to be posted in a public place within the factory. Wal-Mart's "Standards for Suppliers" poster was available in 25 languages.

In February 2002, Wal-Mart created the Global Procurement Services Group (GPSG), which was charged with identifying new suppliers, sourcing new products, building partnerships with existing suppliers, managing Wal-Mart's global supply chain of direct imports, providing workplace standards training to suppliers, and enforcing compliance with Wal-Mart's supplier standards. All Wal-Mart personnel engaged in monitoring supplier compliance became part of the GPSG organization. In 2007, GPSG consisted of about 1,600 people working from offices in 23 countries, including China, Indonesia, India, Pakistan, Sri Lanka, Bangladesh, Honduras, Nicaragua, Guatemala, Mexico, Brazil, and Turkey (countries where supplier compliance presented big challenges).

In 2005–2006, Wal-Mart purchased goods from about 7,200 factories in over 60 countries; about 2,000 of the 7,200 factories had recently come into Wal-Mart's compliance and factory audit system due to mergers, acquisitions, and new factory construction. About 200 Wal-Mart personnel scattered across GPSG's offices in all 23 countries were engaged in monitoring

suppliers for compliance with Wal-Mart's standards for suppliers. Suppliers covered by Wal-Mart's ethical standards program had to disclose the factory (or factories) used to fulfill each order placed by Wal-Mart.

Wal-Mart's Supplier Auditing Program and Compliance Rating System

During 2005, Wal-Mart audited more factories than any other company in the world, performing 14,750 initial and follow-up audits of 7,200 supplier factories; in 2004, Wal-Mart conducted 12,561 factory audits. The company's audit methodology and its factory rating system are described in Exhibit 4. A summary of Wal-Mart's audit findings for 2004 and 2005 is contained in Exhibit 5. Wal-Mart management said that the greater incidence of violations in 2005 compared to 2004 was primarily due to a 100 percent increase in unannounced audits, increased rigor of supplier standards, a reclassification of violations to strengthen and reinforce their severity, the implementation of team audits, and greater auditor familiarity with the factories and their workers.

Rather than banning the placement of orders at supplier factories receiving Yellow (medium-risk violations) and Orange (high-risk violations) ratings, Wal-Mart's policy was to work with supplier factories to reduce violations and achieve steady improvement of workplace conditions, a position widely endorsed by most human rights activists, concerned citizens groups, and nongovernmental agencies striving for better factory conditions for low-wage workers. To help promote higher levels of supplier compliance, Wal-Mart trained more than 8,000 supplier personnel in 2004 and another 11,000 suppliers and members of factory management in 2005. The training focused on increasing supplier familiarity with Wal-Mart's standards for suppliers and encouraging an exchange of information about factory operating practices. Wal-Mart also actively worked with its foreign suppliers on ways to do better production planning, enhance plant efficiency,

Exhibit 4

Wal-Mart's Factory Audit Methodology and Factory Ratings System, 2005

- **Opening Meeting**—The Opening Meeting consisted of (1) confirmation of the factory and its information, (2) an introduction by the Wal-Mart auditors to factory management and supplier representatives, (3) a presentation and signing of the Wal-Mart Gifts & Gratuity Policy (which forbids any offer or receipt of gifts or bribes by the factory or the auditor), and (4) a request by the auditors of factory documentation related to personnel, production, and time and pay records.

- **Factory Tour**—The auditors conducted a factory walk-through to examine factory conditions. The walk-through had minimal factory managers present because auditors asked production employees questions about machinery operation and other working conditions. Auditors also followed up with workers interviewed in previous audits about conditions since the last audit. The tour lasted up to three hours, depending on the size of the factory.

- **Worker Interviews**—During factory tours, auditors typically chose workers off the shop floor to interview, although additional workers could be requested to verify factory records during the documentation review process. Factory management had to provide a private location for interviews, and under no circumstances were interviews conducted with factory management or supplier representatives present. Workers were interviewed in same-sex groups. The objectives of the interviews were to discover what interviewees had to say relevant to the audit, verify findings and observations made by the auditors, and ensure that workers understood their rights. A minimum of 15 workers were interviewed. The number of workers interviewed depended on the size of the factory.

- **Factory Documentation Review**—Auditors conducted an on-site inspection of appropriate production documents. For Initial and Annual audits, document review required records dating back at least three months and up to one year. Follow-up audits not only included reviewing findings from the previous audit, but also always included review of hours and compensation. Any factory that failed or refused to comply with this requirement was subject to immediate cancellation of any and all outstanding orders.

- **Closing Meeting**—Auditors summarized the audit findings, described any violations found, made recommendations to remedy the violations, and gave factory management a chance to ask any questions about the audit. Factory management and the auditor both signed the on-site audit report. Auditors left a copy of the signed audit findings and recommendations. Factory management was expected to act on all the recommendations in the on-site report and to present a completed action plan to the auditor during the follow-up audit opening meeting so auditors could validate that the actions were taken. Suppliers and factory management were encouraged to contact the regional Wal-Mart Ethical Standards office to discuss any concerns or questions about the on-site report and recommendations.

- **Factory Ratings**—Factories were rated Green, Yellow, Orange, or Red. A Green assessment was assigned for no or minor violations; a Yellow rating signified medium-risk violations; an Orange rating entailed high-risk violations (and was an automatic rating for factories where the use of one or two underage workers was discovered); and a Red rating indicated failure to pass the audit (factories found to use prison or forced labor, have extremely unsafe working conditions, have more than two underage workers, engage in serious worker abuse, or have other serious violations were immediately assigned a Red rating). Red-rated factories were permanently banned from producing merchandise for Wal-Mart. Starting in 2006, Green-rated factories had re-audits every 2 years instead of annually. Yellow- and Orange-rated factories had follow-up audits after 120 days to allow time for corrections and verification that corrective actions had been implemented. Factories rated Orange with underage labor violations for only one or two workers were an exception to the timeline for re-audits; such factories were re-audited within 30 days. If the follow-up audit for these factories indicated that the use of underage labor had been corrected, the factory could continue production for Wal-Mart; a failure on the follow-up 30-day audit resulted in a Red rating and a permanent order ban. A factory receiving an Orange assessment four times in a two-year period was banned from producing for Wal-Mart for up to one year (the ban on orders for such factories was extended from 90 days to one year starting January 1, 2005, in order to strengthen the seriousness of program noncompliance).

- **Use of Outside Auditors**—When Wal-Mart sourced goods for its foreign stores from suppliers in the same country in which the foreign stores were located, it used outside auditors to check supplier compliance. In 2005, the outside auditing firms used were Accordia, Bureau Veritas, Cal Safety Compliance Corporation (CSCC), Global Social Compliance, Intertek Testing Services, and Société Générale de Surveillance.

Source: Wal-Mart's 2005 Report on Ethical Sourcing, posted at www.walmart.com (accessed January 25, 2007).

Exhibit 5

Comparison of Wal-Mart's 2004 and 2005 Factory Audit Results

	2004	2005
Number of factory audits	12,561	14,750
Audits resulting in Green ratings	20.7%	9.6%
Audits resulting in Yellow ratings	42.6%	37.0%
Audits resulting in Orange ratings	35.6%	52.3%
Number of factories permanently banned from receiving orders	1,211	164 (141 of these related to the use of underage labor)

Source: Wal-Mart's 2005 Report on Ethical Sourcing, posted at www.walmart.com (accessed January 25, 2007).

better educate and train workers, make supply chain improvements, and adopt better factory operating practices. Wal-Mart also consulted with knowledgeable outside experts and organizations on ways to accelerate ethical compliance and the achievement of better working conditions in supplier factories.

Upon learning of the incident in the *Business-Week* report cited in the opening of this case, Wal-Mart began an investigation of the Beifa factory in Ningbo. Wal-Mart acknowledged that some of its suppliers were trying to deceive plant monitors and avoid complying with Wal-Mart's standards for suppliers.

Compliance Efforts of Industry Groups and Nongovernmental Organizations—The Fair Labor Association

Some companies, rather than conducting their own supplier monitoring and compliance effort, had banded together in industry groups or multi-industry coalitions to establish a common code of supplier conduct and to organize a joint program of factory inspections and compliance efforts. For example, Hewlett-Packard, Dell, and other electronics companies that relied heavily on Asia-based manufacturers to supply components or else assemble digital cameras, handheld devices, and personal computers had entered into an alliance to combat worker abuse and poor working conditions in the factories of their suppliers.

The Fair Labor Association

One of the most prominent and best organized coalitions was the Fair Labor Association (FLA), whose members and affiliates included 194 colleges and universities, a number of concerned nongovernmental organizations, and a group of 35 companies that included Nike, the Adidas Group (the owner of both Reebok and Adidas brands), Puma, Eddie Bauer, Liz Claiborne, Patagonia, Cutter & Buck, Russell Corporation, and Nordstrom. As part of its broad-based campaign to eliminate human rights abuses and improve global workplace conditions, the FLA had established its Workplace Code of Conduct, a document to which all members and affiliates had subscribed. To aid in winning supplier compliance with the Workplace Code of Conduct, the FLA conducted unannounced audits of factories across the world that supplied its members and affiliates.

In 2004, FLA's teams of independent plant monitors conducted inspections at 88 factories in 18 countries, the results of which were published in FLA's 2005 annual public report. The audits, all of which involved factories that were supplying goods to one or more FLA members, revealed 1,603 instances of noncompliance with FLA's Workplace Code of Conduct, an average of 18.2 violations per factory (versus an average of 15.1 per factory in 2003).[22] The violations included excessive work hours, underpayment of wages and overtime, failure to observe legal holidays and grant vacations (27.5 percent); health and safety problems (44 percent); and worker harassment (5.1 percent). The FLA concluded that the actual violations relating to underpayment of wages, hours of work, and overtime compensation were probably higher than those discovered because "factory personnel have become sophisticated in concealing noncompliance relating to wages. They often hide original documents and show monitors falsified books."[23]

In its 2006 public report, the FLA said that accredited independent monitors conducted unannounced audits of 99 factories in 18 countries in 2005; the audited factories employed some 77,800 workers.[24] The audited factories were but a small sample of the 3,753 factories employing some 2.9 million people from which the FLA's 35 affiliated companies sourced goods in 2005; however, 34 of the 99 audited factories involved facilities providing goods to 2 or more of FLA's 35 affiliated companies. The 99 audits during 2005 revealed 1,587 violations, an average of 15.9 per audit. The greatest incidence of violations was found in Southeast Asia (chiefly factories located in China, Indonesia, Thailand, and India), where the average was about 22 violations per factory audit. As was the case with the audits conducted in 2004, most of the violations related to health and safety (45 percent); wages, benefits, hours of work, and overtime compensation (28 percent); and worker harassment and abuse (7 percent). Once again, the FLA indicated that the violations relating to compensation and benefits were likely higher than those detected in its 2005 audits because "factory personnel have become accustomed to concealing real wage documentation and providing falsified records at the time of compliance audits, making any noncompliances difficult to detect."[25]

The Fair Factories Clearinghouse

The Fair Factories Clearinghouse (FFC)—formed in 2006 by World Monitors Inc. in partnership with L. L. Bean, Timberland, Federated Department Stores, Adidas/Reebok, the Retail Council of Canada, and several others—was a collaborative effort to create a system for managing and sharing factory audit information that would facilitate detecting and eliminating sweatshops and abusive workplace conditions in foreign factories; membership fees were based on a company's annual revenues, with annual fees ranging from as little as $5,000 to as much as $75,000 (not including one-time initiation fees of $2,500 to $11,500). The idea underlying the FFC was that members would pool their audit information on offshore factories, creating a database on thousands of manufacturing plants. Once a plant was certified by a member company or organization, other members could accept the results without having to do an audit of their own.

Audit sharing had the appeal of making factory audit programs less expensive for member companies; perhaps more important, it helped reduce the audit burden at plants having a large number of customers that conducted their own audits. Some large plants with big customer bases were said to undergo audits as often as weekly and occasionally even daily; plus, they were pressured into having to comply with varying provisions and requirements of each auditing company's code of supplier conduct—being subject to varying and conflicting codes of conduct was a factor that induced cheating. Another benefit of audit sharing at FFC was that members sourcing goods from the same factories could band together and apply added pressure on a supplier to improve its working conditions and comply with buyers' codes of supplier conduct.[26]

The Obstacles to Achieving Supplier Compliance with Codes of Conduct in Low-Wage, Low-Cost Countries

Factory managers subject to inspections and audits of their plants and work practices complained that strong pressures from their customers to keep prices low gave them a big incentive to cheat on their compliance with labor standards. As the general manager of a factory in China that supplied goods to Nike said, "Any improvement you make costs more money. The price [Nike pays] never increases one penny but compliance with labor codes definitely raises costs."[27]

The pricing pressures from companies sourcing components or finished goods from offshore factories in China, India, and other low-wage, low-cost locations were acute. Since 1996, the prices paid for men's shirts and sweaters sourced in China were said to have dropped by 14 percent, while the prices of clocks and lamps had dropped 40 percent and the prices of toys and games had fallen by 30 percent.[28] Such downward pressure on prices made it financially difficult for foreign manufacturers to improve worker compensation and benefits, make their workplaces safer and more pleasant, introduce more efficient production methods, and overhaul inefficient plant layouts. Many factory managers believed that if they paid workers a higher wage, incurred other compliance costs, and then raised their prices to cover the higher costs that their customers would quickly cut and run to other suppliers charging lower prices. Hence, the penalties and disincentives for compliance significantly outweighed any rewards.

In a 2006 interview with *BusinessWeek,* the CEO of the Fair Labor Association, Auret van Heerden, offered a number of reasons why underpayment of wages and excessive overtime in supplier factories in China were such difficult problems to resolve:

> The brands book and confirm orders really late. And they often change their orders after booking. The brands want to order later and they don't want to hold product. Then you add price pressures into that and it is really tough for the supplier [to not overwork its workers].
>
> But the factory often doesn't order the materials until too late and they are often delivered late [to the factory], too. The factory production layout is often a mess, so the supplier gets behind schedule and over budget even before they know it. Then they have to catch up. And to save money, they extend hours, but don't pay overtime premiums. And the suppliers also lack proper training. The styles [of clothing and footwear] are becoming more complicated and are changing more frequently.
>
> Multiple codes are a big problem. The classic example is the height that a fire extinguisher should be kept off the ground—how high varies according to different codes. Companies like McDonald's, Disney, and Wal-Mart are doing thousands of audits a year that are not harmonized. That's where audit fatigue comes in.
>
> And auditing in itself tells you a little about the problem, but not enough, and not why there is a problem. So you have an overtime problem, but you don't know why. Is it because of electricity shortages, labor shortages, or a shorter order turnaround time? You don't know.[29]

Endnotes

[1] Dexter Roberts and Pete Engardio, "Secrets, Lies, and Sweatshops," *BusinessWeek,* November 27, 2006, pp. 50–58.

[2] Ibid., p. 50.

[3] Ibid.

[4] Ibid., p. 52.

[5] Ibid., p. 54.

[6] Ibid.

[7] Ibid., p. 50.

[8] Ibid., p. 55.

[9] Ibid., p. 53.

[10] Ibid., pp. 55–56.

[11] Ibid., p. 53.

[12] Information posted at www.nike.com/nikebiz/nikebiz.jhtml?page=25&cat=activefactories (accessed January 26, 2007).

[13] Information posted at www.nikebiz.com (accessed January 26, 2007); Nike's 2004 Fiscal Year Corporate Responsibility Report, pp. 21–24.

[14] Nike's 2004 Fiscal Year Corporate Responsibility Report, p. 28.

[15] Ibid., p. 29.

[16] Ibid., p. 20.

[17] Ibid., p. 30.

[18] Ibid., p. 25.

[19] Ibid., p. 26.

[20] Pete Engardio and Dexter Roberts, "How to Make Factories Play Fair," *BusinessWeek,* November 27, 2007, p. 58.

[21] The content of this section was developed by the case author from information posted in the supplier section at www.walmartstores.com (accessed January 25, 2007).

[22] These results of the audits were published in the Fair Labor Association's 2005 annual public report, posted at www.fairlabor.org (accessed January 23, 2007).

[23] Fair Labor Association, 2005 annual public report, p. 38; also quoted in Roberts and Engardio, "Secrets, Lies, and Sweatshops," p. 54.

[24] Fair Labor Association, 2006 annual public report, posted at www.fairlabor.org (accessed January 23, 2007).

[25] Ibid., p. 40.

[26] Roberts and Engardio, "Secrets, Lies, and Sweatshops," p. 58.

[27] As quoted in ibid., p. 53.

[28] Ibid., p. 58.

[29] As quoted in Dexter Roberts, "A Lion for Worker Rights," *Business-Week Online,* November 27, 2006, www.businessweek.com (accessed January 23, 2007).

Case 13

+CASE TUTOR Spectrum Brands' Diversification Strategy: A Success or a Failure?

Arthur A. Thompson Jr.
The University of Alabama

John E. Gamble
University of South Alabama

In 2003, top executives at Rayovac Corporation, concerned about fierce competition and limited growth opportunities in its global consumer battery business, decided to embark on a long-term program to diversify the company's revenue stream away from such heavy dependence on selling alkaline and rechargeable AA and AAA batteries, coin batteries for watches and calculators, hearing aid batteries (where it was the worldwide leader), and flashlight products. Three years later, via a series of acquisitions, Rayovac had transformed itself into a global branded consumer products company with positions in seven major product categories: consumer batteries, portable lighting, pet supplies, lawn and garden, electric shaving and grooming, electric personal care products, and household insect control. The resulting change in the company's revenue mix was dramatic:

PRODUCT CATEGORY	PERCENTAGE OF COMPANY NET SALES, FISCAL YEAR ENDING SEPTEMBER 30			
	2003	2004	2005	2006
Consumer batteries	90%	67%	42%	34%
Portable lighting	10	6	4	3
Pet supplies	—	—	12	21
Lawn and garden	—	—	18	20
Electric shaving and grooming	—	19	12	10
Electric personal care products	—	8	6	6
Household insect control	—	—	6	6
	100%	100%	100%	100%

In recognition of the strategic shift in its business composition, Rayovac changed its name to Spectrum Brands in May 2005.

But while the company's revenues had jumped from $573 million in fiscal 2002 to $2.55 billion at the end of fiscal 2006, its financial performance and financial condition were less than inspiring. Net income had dropped from $55.8 million in fiscal 2004 to $46.8 million in fiscal 2005 to a loss of $434 million in fiscal 2006. Despite the company's much bigger size and revenue stream, net cash flows from operations in 2006 were below the level in 2002. The company had long-term debt of more than

Exhibit 1

Consolidated Statement of Operations for Spectrum Brands, Fiscal Years 2002–2006 ($ in millions, except per share data)

	FISCAL YEARS ENDING SEPTEMBER 30				
	2006	2005	2004	2003	2002
Net sales	$2,551.8	$2,307.2	$1,417.2	$922.1	$572.7
Cost of goods sold	1,576.1	1,427.1	1,417.2	922.1	334.1
Restructuring and related charges, cost of goods sold	22.5	10.5	(0.8)	21.1	1.2
Gross profit	953.2	869.5	606.1	351.5	237.4
Operating expenses					
Selling	557.3	475.6	293.1	185.2	104.4
General and administrative	182.0	142.6	121.3	80.9	56.9
Research and development	30.6	29.3	23.2	14.4	13.1
Restructuring and related charges	33.6	15.8	12.2	11.5	—
Goodwill and intangibles impairment	433.0	—	—	—	—
Total operating expenses	1,236.5	673.5	449.9	291.9	174.4
Operating income (loss)	(283.2)	196.1	156.2	59.6	63.0
Interest expense	177.0	134.1	65.7	37.2	16.0
Other income, net	(4.1)	0.9	0.0	0.6	(1.3)
Income (loss) from continuing operations before income taxes	(456.1)	62.9	90.5	23.0	45.7
Income tax expense (benefit)	(27.6)	21.5	34.4	7.6	16.4
Income (loss) from continuing operations	(428.5)	41.3	56.2	15.5	29.2
Income (loss) from discontinued operations, net of tax benefits	(5.5)	5.5	(0.4)	—	—
Net income (loss)	$ (434.0)	$ 46.8	$ 55.8	$ 15.5	$ 29.2
Net income (loss) per common share					
Basic	$ (8.77)	$ 1.07	$ 1.67	$ 0.49	$ 0.92
Diluted	(8.77)	1.03	1.61	0.48	0.90
Weighted average shares of common stock outstanding					
Basic	49.5	43.7	33.4	31.8	31.8
Diluted	49.5	45.6	34.6	32.6	32.4

Source: Company 10-K reports, 2006 and 2003.

$2.2 billion and interest expenses of $177 million in 2006 versus long-term debt of $188 million and interest expenses of $16 million in 2002. Moreover, investors were a bit uneasy about Spectrum Brands' future prospects. Spectrum's stock price, which had traded as high as $46 in February 2005, traded in the $6 to $12 range between July 2006 and February 2007. Exhibits 1 and 2 present recent financial performance data for Spectrum Brands.

Company Background

In 1906, a company founded as the French Battery Company began operations in a plant in Madison, Wisconsin; French Battery was

Exhibit 2

Selected Consolidated Balance Sheet and Cash Flow Data for Spectrum Brands, Fiscal Years 2002–2006 ($ in millions)

	FISCAL YEARS ENDING SEPTEMBER 30				
	2006*	2005*	2004*	2003**	2002**
Balance Sheet Data					
Cash and cash equivalents	$ 28.4	$ 29.9	$ 14.0	$ 107.8	$ 9.9
Inventories	460.7	451.6	264.7	219.3	84.3
Current assets	959.8	1,048.0	648.7	675.3	259.3
Property, plant, and equipment, net	311.8	304.3	182.4	150.4	102.6
Goodwill	1,130.2	1,429.0	320.6	398.4	30.6
Intangible assets, net	1,016.1	1,154.4	422.1	253.1	88.9
Total assets	3,549.3	4,022.1	1,634.2	1,576.5	533.2
Current liabilities	562.6	557.4	396.8	405.5	118.8
Long-term debt, net of current maturities	2,234.5	2,268.0	806.0	870.5	188.5
Total shareholders' equity	452.2	842.7	316.0	202.0	174.8
Cash Flow and Related Data					
Net cash provided by operating activities	$ 44.5	$ 216.6	$ 96.1	$ 76.2	$ 66.8
Capital expenditures	60.4	62.8	26.9	26.1	15.6
Depreciation and amortization	87.5	68.6	40.6	35.0	20.3
Working capital	397.2	490.6	251.9	269.8	140.5

* Figures for 2004–2006 are as reported in the company's 10-K reports for 2005 and 2006.

** Figures for 2002 and 2003 are as reported in the company's 10-K report for 2003.

Sources: Company 10-K Reports, 2006, 2005, and 2003.

renamed Ray-O-Vac in 1930. Over the next several decades, Ray-O-Vac gained a reputation for innovation in batteries and flashlights: In 1946, company sales surpassed 100 million batteries for the first time; Ray-O-Vac produced its one billionth leakproof cell battery

1933	Patented the first wearable hearing aid tube
1939	Introduced the first leak-proof "sealed in steel" dry cell battery
1949	Introduced the crown cell alkaline for hearing aids and launched its soon-to-be-famous steel Sportsman flashlight
1970	Patented a silver oxide button cell battery
1972	Introduced the first heavy-duty, all-zinc chloride battery with double the life of general-purpose batteries
1984	Introduced the Workhorse premium flashlight with lifetime warranty
1988	Introduced a battery to power the real-time clocks of personal computers
1993	Introduced a line of long-life rechargeable batteries
2001	Introduced breakthrough chargers for high-capacity Nickel Metal Hydride (NiMH) batteries; developed a new zinc air battery that combined long life and unprecedented power for hearing aids used by the severely hearing impaired
2002	Introduced 15-minute battery recharging technology

in 1950.[1] In 1981, Ray-O-Vac debuted a new logo and a new corporate name minus the hyphens, Rayovac. During the 1970s and 1980s, Rayovac firmly established itself as the leading marketer of value-priced batteries in North America—the company's core competitive strategy was to sell a battery comparable in quality to those of competing brands but at prices averaging about 10–15 percent less.

During the early 1990s, Rayovac suffered an erosion of market share to its two primary competitors, Duracell and Energizer, becoming a distant third in market share. In 1996, a private-equity company, Thomas H. Lee Partners, purchased Rayovac and instituted a number of restructuring initiatives and organizational changes. David A. Jones was made chairman and CEO in September 1996. In 1997, Thomas H. Lee Partners took the company public with an initial offering of common stock; trading of shares began on the New York Stock Exchange in November 1997. However, Thomas H. Lee Partners retained a sizable ownership share in the company; it was the company's largest shareholder as of early 2007, controlling about 23 percent of the company's outstanding shares. Rayovac had sales of $427 million and profits of $6 million in 1997, the year it went public.

Shortly after Rayovac became a public company, CEO David Jones put it on a long-term course to rejuvenate its battery business and spur sales growth. The strategy to reshape Rayovac and grow market share was comprehensive, involving efforts to (1) build the Rayovac brand via increased advertising and promotion, (2) broaden the battery lineup via technological innovation, (3) improve merchandising and attractiveness of packaging, (4) expand distribution to include more retailers of Rayovac in more countries, (5) revamp battery manufacturing operations to slash production costs and increase plant capacity, (6) refine the supply chain and consolidate purchasing, (7) offer very attentive customer service, and (8) create a results-oriented, entrepreneurial culture.

Starting in 1999, Jones embarked on a strategy to globalize Rayovac's battery and flashlight business via a series of acquisitions in key foreign markets:[2]

1999:	Acquired ROV Limited for $155 million; ROV had been spun off from Rayovac as an independent company in 1982 and was Rayovac's largest distributor of batteries in Latin America. ROV had sales of approximately $100 million compared to Rayovac's sales in Latin America of about $20 million.
2002:	Acquired the consumer battery business of Germany-based Varta AG for $258 million. Varta was the leading European maker of general batteries, with 2001 revenues of $390 million. About 86 percent of Varta's sales came from Europe, but both Rayovac and Varta had operations in Latin America. Following the acquisition, redundant manufacturing plants were closed and the Latin American production and distribution operations of the two companies were combined to generate expected cost savings of $30–$40 million. The acquisition solidified Rayovac's market lead in Latin America (with the exception of Brazil) and made Rayovac the second leading battery producer in Europe and the market leader in consumer batteries in Austria and Germany.
2004:	Acquired 85 percent of Ningbo Baowang Battery Company in Ninghai, China, for a cash price of $17 million plus $14 million in assumed debt. Ningbo Baowang was a producer of high-performance alkaline and heavy-duty batteries and had a modern manufacturing facility that Rayovac believed was among the lowest-cost battery manufacturing operations in the world; the plant had manufacturing capacity of up to a billion batteries per year and gave Rayovac strong access to export markets around the globe. Baowang was also a leading battery brand in China with 2004 sales approaching $35 million, and the acquired company had an established sales and marketing organization that would help Rayovac penetrate the rapidly growing battery market in China.

(concluded)

2004:   Acquired Microlite, a low-cost battery manufacturer headquartered in São Paulo, Brazil, for a price of $21 million plus $8 million in assumed debt and contingent cash payments of up to $7 million depending on Microlite's performance through June 30, 2005. Microlite was Brazil's leading battery company with $53 million in net sales in 2003 and a 49 percent market share. Microlite manufactured and sold both alkaline and zinc carbon batteries as well as battery-operated lighting products; it operated two battery manufacturing facilities in Recife, Brazil, and had several sales and distribution centers throughout Brazil. The Microlite acquisition gave Rayovac an even stronger number-one market position in Latin America (Brazil was the largest market for batteries in Latin America). Moreover, since Microlite owned the Rayovac brand name in Brazil, the acquisition secured rights to the Rayovac name worldwide.

Following these moves, Rayovac established itself as the leading value brand of alkaline batteries in North America and Latin America, the top supplier of rechargeable batteries in the United States and Europe, and the world's largest manufacturer and marketer of hearing aid batteries (with a market share approximating 60 percent). Since 1997, the company's sales of battery and lighting products had grown from $427 million to just over $1 billion at the end of fiscal 2004. Going into fiscal 2005, Rayovac's battery and lighting products were sold by 19 of the world's 20 largest retailers and were available in 1 million store locations in 120 countries.[3] It had a full lineup of battery products and was continuing to introduce new products. Rayovac had more hearing aid battery patents than all of its competitors combined.

Spectrum Brands' Diversification Strategy

Starting in 2003, David Jones and other top executives at Rayovac determined that the company needed to expand beyond its battery and lighting products business, partly due to stiff competition in batteries and partly due to a maturing global market demand for batteries that diminished the company's prospects for achieving 8–10 percent annual growth in revenues and profits. Just as the strategy for becoming a global battery company had been predicated largely on acquisition, so also was the strategy to diversify into new businesses and product categories. During the 2003–2005 period, the company made four important diversification-related acquisitions:[4]

2003:   Acquired Remington Products Company, a leading designer and distributor of battery-powered electric shavers, beard and mustache trimmers, grooming products, and personal care appliances. The purchase price was $222 million, including the assumption of Remington's debt; in the 12 months prior to the acquisition, Remington had sales of $360 million and net income of $20 million.

Headquartered in Bridgeport, Connecticut, Remington was the number one selling brand in the United States in the combined dry shaving and personal grooming products categories based on units sold. Remington had acquired Clairol's worldwide personal care appliance business (consisting of hair dryers, stylers, hot rollers, and lighted mirrors) in 1993.

Remington products were sold in more than 20,000 retail outlets in the United States; more than 70 percent of Remington's sales were in North America. Remington's core North American shaving and grooming products business had grown an average of 18 percent per year from 1998 through 2002. Internationally, Remington products were sold through a network of subsidiaries and distributors in more than 85 countries.

(continued)

(concluded)

Following the acquisition, Rayovac closed Remington's headquarters, transferred all of Remington's headquarters operations to Rayovac's headquarters, moved all of Remington's manufacturing operations to a Rayovac plant in Wisconsin, merged Remington and Rayovac R&D functions into a single department, and closed Remington's distribution operations and 65 U.S. service centers and relocated their functions to Rayovac's North American and European facilities. In North America, Rayovac and Remington sales management, field sales operations, and marketing were merged into a single North American sales and marketing organization.

2005:   Acquired privately owned United Industries Corporation, for a total value of approximately $1.2 billion including the assumption of approximately $880 million of United Industries debt and a cash tax benefit of $140 million. United Industries, based in St. Louis, was a leading manufacturer and marketer of consumer products for lawn and garden care and household insect control; United also manufactured and marketed premium-branded specialty pet supplies. In lawn and garden products and household insect control, United operated as Spectrum Brands in the United States and NuGro in Canada. In pet supplies, it operated as United Pet Group. United's brands included Spectracide, Vigoro, Sta-Green, Schultz, and C.I.L. in the lawn and garden market; Hot Shot, Cutter and Repel in the household insect control market; and Marineland, Perfecto, and Eight in One in pet supply products. United had sales of approximately $950 million in 2004; major customers included Home Depot, Lowe's, Wal-Mart, PETCO, and PETsMart.

2005:   Acquired Tetra Holding, a privately held supplier of fish and aquatics supplies headquartered in Melle, Germany. The purchase price was approximately €415 million. Tetra was the leading global brand in foods, equipment, and care products for fish and reptiles, along with accessories for home aquariums and ponds. Tetra currently operated in over 90 countries worldwide and held leading market positions in Germany, the United States, Japan, and the United Kingdom. It had approximately 700 employees and annual sales of about € 200 million. The Tetra acquisition strengthened Rayovac's newly created strategic position in pet supplies. According to CEO David Jones, "Tetra's superior brand equity and demonstrated record of product innovation make it a premiere property in this industry. The combination of Tetra with our United Pet Group business means Rayovac becomes the world's largest manufacturer of pet supplies, a position with which we can leverage our company's worldwide operations, supply chain and information systems infrastructure to better meet the needs of our global retailer customers." United Pet Group President John Heil stated, "The Tetra brand is arguably the most recognized global brand name in the pet supplies industry. The acquisition of Tetra is a linchpin to our goal of becoming the most important pet supplies provider in the world."

2005:   Acquired Jungle Labs for $29 million, with the potential for additional payments contingent on Jungle Labs' meeting defined future growth objectives. Based in San Antonio, Texas, Jungle Labs had sales of approximately $14 million and was a leading manufacturer and marketer of premium water and fish care products, including water conditioners, plant and fish foods, fish medications, and other products designed to maintain an optimal environment in aquariums or ponds. Jungle was known for such innovative high-end products as Tank Buddies fizz tablets for easy fish and water care and Quick Dip test strips for fast, accurate water testing. Spectrum Brands' CEO David Jones believed that Jungle Labs' product line and its strong track record of innovative product development and marketing in water and fish care complemented the previously acquired Tetra, Marineland, ASI, and Perfecto aquatics brands and strengthened Spectrum's position in aquatic supplies.

These acquisitions drove Rayovac's decision to change its name to Spectrum Brands and prompted management to begin touting Spectrum Brands as "a brand new 100-year-old company."[5] Exhibit 3 shows the performance of Spectrum Brands' stock price as it became a more broadly diversified company.

Exhibit 3

Performance of Spectrum Brands' Stock Price, November 1997–December 2006

(a) Performance of Spectrum Brands' Stock Price and Key Acquisition Dates

(b) Performance of Spectrum Brands' Stock Price versus the S&P 500

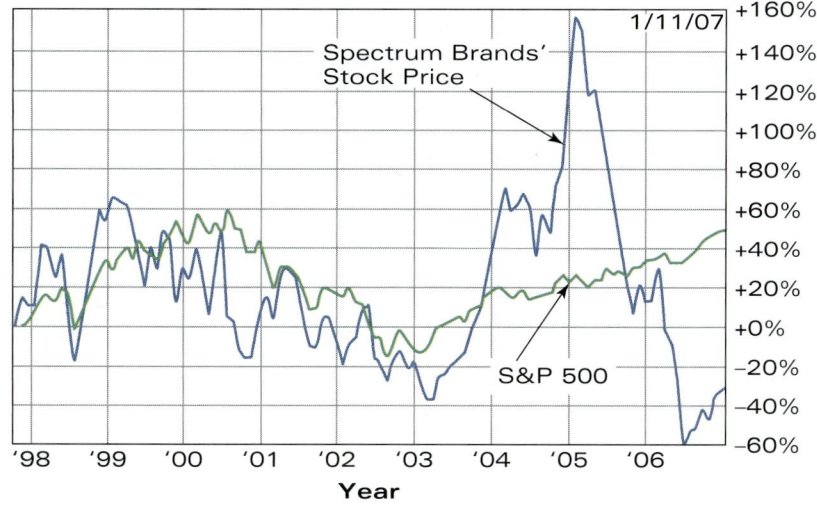

An Overview of Spectrum Brands' Businesses and Product Categories

Beginning with fiscal year 2006, Spectrum Brands began managing its business in four reportable segments:

1.   North America, which consisted of the sales and operations of its consumer battery, shaving and grooming, personal care, lawn and garden, household insect control, and portable lighting product categories in the United States and Canada.

2.   Latin America, which consisted of the sales and operations of its consumer battery, shaving and grooming, personal care, lawn and garden, household insect control, and portable lighting product categories in

Mexico, Central America, South America, and the Caribbean ("Latin America").

3. Europe/Rest of the World, which consisted of the sales and operations of its consumer battery, shaving and grooming, personal care, lawn and garden, household insect control, and portable lighting product categories in the United Kingdom, continental Europe, China, Australia, and all other countries not included in the first two segments.

4. Global Pet, which consists of the acquired operations of United Pet Group, Tetra Holdings, and Jungle Labs.

Exhibit 4 shows the company's operating performance and selected financial data for these four segments for the period 2003–2006.

The Global Battery Business

Going into 2007, most consumer batteries around the world were manufactured and marketed by one of four companies: Procter & Gamble (manufacturer/distributor of the Duracell brand), Energizer Holdings (the maker/distributor of the Energizer brand of batteries), Spectrum Brands (the maker/distributor of VARTA batteries in Europe and Rayovac batteries in the rest of the world), and Matsushita (manufacturer/distributor of the Panasonic brand).[6] Some major retailers, especially in Europe, marketed private-label brands of batteries. Duracell was the market leader worldwide, followed in order by Energizer, Rayovac/VARTA, and Panasonic.

Batteries were used chiefly to power toys and games; remote-control devices for a variety of electronics products (TVs, DVD players); handheld video game players; MP3 players like the Apple iPod; digital cameras; clocks and watches; hearing aids; and flashlights. Growth in consumer battery sales was in the low single digits in the United States and much of Europe, owing to already widespread battery use and a mature marketplace. In Latin America and Southeast Asia (particularly China), consumer use of batteries was much lower and there was

good long-term potential for sales growth in the high single digits as consumers purchased more devices powered by batteries. In North America and Europe, most consumers purchased alkaline batteries; less expensive zinc carbon batteries were most popular in Latin America, but the Latin American market was slowly converting to alkaline batteries as disposable incomes increased.

In 2001, the global market for batteries was about a $21 billion industry and had grown at a historical rate of about 6–7 percent. About one-third of total sales occurred in the United States. Since 2001, global growth had slowed to an average of 4–5 percent, resulting in global sales close to $25 billion in 2006. However, battery sales were affected by ups and downs in the economy and by the strength of sales of battery-using products.

Spectrum Brands manufactured and distributed alkaline and zinc carbon batteries, hearing aid batteries, rechargeable batteries and battery chargers, photo batteries, lithium batteries, silver oxide batteries, keyless entry batteries, and coin cells for use in watches, cameras, calculators, communications equipment, and medical instrumentation. A full line of alkaline batteries (AA, AAA, C, D, and nine-volt sizes) was sold to both retail and industrial customers, primarily under the VARTA brand in Europe and under the Rayovac brand in the rest of the world. Alkaline batteries were also manufactured for sellers of private-label batteries. Zinc carbon batteries (used primarily for low- and medium-drain battery-powered devices), Nickel Metal Hydride (NiMH) rechargeable batteries, and a variety of battery chargers were marketed primarily under the Rayovac and VARTA brands.

In the U.S. alkaline battery marketplace, the Rayovac brand was positioned as a value brand offering comparable performance to the Duracell and Energizer brands at a lower price. In Europe, the VARTA brand was competitively priced with other premium brands. In Latin America, where zinc carbon batteries outsold alkaline batteries, the Rayovac brand was also competitively priced against other leading brands. In 2005–2006, Rayovac was the

Exhibit 4

Selected Data for Spectrum Brands, by Business Segment and/or Geographic Area, Fiscal Years 2002–2006 ($ in millions)

	FISCAL YEARS ENDING SEPTEMBER 30				
	2006	**2005**	**2004**	**2003**	**2002**
Net Sales to External Customers					
North America	$1,212.4	$1,155.8	$ 654.0	$ 375.6	$435.6
Europe/ROW	559.9	657.7	618.0	421.5	52.5
Latin America	236.2	208.1	145.3	125.0	84.7
Global Pet	543.2	285.6	—	—	—
Segment total	$2,551.7	$2,307.2	$1,417.2	$ 922.1	$572.7
Segment Profit					
North America	$ 146.4	$ 164.8	$ 130.7	$ 64.8	$ 85.5
Europe/ROW	55.2	94.5	96.2	53.8	5.1
Latin America	23.4	19.0	11.7	17.7	5.3
Global Pet	83.6	28.7	—	—	—
Segment total	$ 308.6	$ 307.0	$ 238.7	$ 136.3	$ 95.9
Product Line Net Sales					
Batteries	$ 861.0	$ 968.3	$ 939.1	$ 832.3	$506.9
Lighting products	88.0	93.8	90.1	89.8	65.8
Electric shaving and grooming	252.0	273.0	271.7	—	—
Personal care	150.0	141.0	116.3	—	—
Lawn and garden	507.0	402.0	—	—	—
Household insect control	151.0	143.0	—	—	—
Pet products	543.0	285.6	—	—	—
Segment total	$2,552.0	$2,307.0	$1,417.2	$ 922.1	$572.7
Segment Total Assets					
North America	$1,503.6	$2,246.4	$ 684.8	$ 625.5	$256.4
Europe/ROW	551.3	556.5	619.5	537.4	31.4
Latin America	239.6	368.5	322.2	203.9	191.0
Global Pet	1,170.8	790.9	—	—	—
Segment total	3,465.4	3,962.3	1,626.5	1,366.8	478.8
Corporate	83.9	59.8	7.7	209.7	54.4
Company total	$3,549.3	$4,022.1	$1,634.2	$1,576.5	$533.2
Depreciation and Amortization					
North America	$ 50.8	$ 36.3	$ 20.5	$ 15.5	$ 15.4
Europe/ROW	10.6	15.7	16.2	13.5	0.7
Latin America	4.5	5.0	3.9	2.6	2.9
Global Pet	21.7	11.6	—	—	—
Segment total	$ 87.5	$ 68.6	$ 40.6	$ 31.6	$ 19.0
Capital Expenditures					
North America	$ 23.5	$ 22.8	$ 14.6	$ 14.6	$ 13.2
Europe/ROW	18.6	23.2	9.1	9.5	1.0
Latin America	5.1	8.5	3.1	2.0	1.5
Global Pet	13.2	8.2	—	—	—
Segment total	$ 60.4	$ 62.8	$ 26.9	$ 26.1	$ 15.7

Note: Totals may not add due to rounding; segment accounting treatments and allocation methodology may not be entirely consistent for 2002 and 2003 data versus 2004–2006 data.

Sources: Company 10-K reports, 2006, 2005, and 2003.

third-ranked brand in North America, with an estimated 19 percent market share (based on dollar sales).[7] VARTA was the second-ranked brand in Europe, with an estimated market share of 25 percent; in Latin America, Rayovac was the leading brand.

The retailers of private-label batteries typically sold their batteries at prices below the leading name brands; however, private-label brands were normally not supported by advertising or promotional activities. On the whole, competition in the global battery marketplace was relatively strong, but competitive pressures varied by geographic location. Competitive factors included distribution capability (as measured by the ability to win the battle for limited space on retailer's shelves), brand-name recognition (affected by advertising and promotion strategies), perceived product quality, price, product performance, and product packaging and design innovation. The main barriers to entry for new competitors were investment in technology research, the cost of building manufacturing capacity, and the expense of building retail distribution channels and brand awareness.

Industry leader Duracell had a 45 percent U.S. market share in 2005 and extended its lead in 2006. Some of Duracell's growth in the United States came at Rayovac's expense as Spectrum Brands' U.S. battery sales declined by $18 million between 2005 and 2006. Spectrum Brands' battery sales declined by $89 million outside the United States as consumers showed a growing preference for private-label alkaline batteries and since the company had elected not to bid on certain private-label contracts. Declining sales of VARTA batteries in Europe took the company partly by surprise because sales of private-label batteries grew unexpectedly fast in Germany, France, Italy, and several other countries.

Spectrum Brands' battery business also suffered from declining gross margins in 2006 as increases in raw materials prices reduced gross profit by $18 million. However, market leaders Duracell and Energizer were able to avoid margin declines by increasing prices in the United

States. Spectrum Brands management addressed the cost disadvantage in batteries in 2005 and 2006 by relocating production from Europe to its recently acquired manufacturing facilities in China. The company also restructured operations in its German packaging center to reduce its total workforce in Europe by 350.

Pet Supplies

The United Industries, Tetra, and Jungle Labs acquisitions resulted in a global pet supplies group with broad representation in products for fish, dogs, cats, birds, and other small domestic animals.[8] The aquatics lineup included such consumer and commercial aquatics products as integrated aquarium kits, stand-alone tanks and stands, filtration systems, heaters, pumps, sea salt, aquarium hoods and lights, and other aquarium supplies and accessories. The largest aquatics brands were Tetra (aquarium and pond supplies, world's leading brand of fish flakes); Marineland (aquarium heaters, filters, and décor); Perfecto (aquariums and fish tanks; aquarium stands, hoods, lights, and filters); Jungle (aquariums, pond kits, fountain maintenance, fizz and water conditioner products for ponds); and Instant Ocean (aquarium salt). The lineup of products for birds and animals included animal treats, stain and odor removal products, grooming aids, bedding products, premium food, medications, and vitamin supplements. The largest specialty pet brands were 8in1 (dog shampoos and conditioners, bird food and health care products, cat litter and health care products, stain and odor products); Nature's Miracle (stain and odor products); Dingo (dog chews and bones); Wild Harvest (bird food); and Firstrax (pet bedding, crates, and toys).

John Heil, the president of the United Pet Group at Spectrum Brands, was bullish on the group's growth prospects in 2007 and beyond due to several key trends:[9]

- Projected continued growth in the number of households owning pets (pet ownership was growing fastest in the 55–64 age group).

- Increases in the number of pets per household (47 percent of households had more than one pet).

- Pets were increasingly viewed as family members.

- Spending by pet owners on pet supplies was relatively insensitive to ups and downs in the economy.

- The number of major retailers of pet supplies was consolidating—in the United States, for example, Wal-Mart, Target, PETsMart, PETCO, and large supermarket chains were accounting for a bigger percent of total pet supply sales.

Spectrum Brands had also begun accelerating plans to source its pet supply production from Chinese contract manufacturers.

The global pet supply industry was highly fragmented, consisting primarily of small companies with limited product lines; in the United States alone, there were over 500 manufacturers. Global sales of pet supplies of all types were an estimated $60 billion in 2006. Global growth in specialty pet supplies was in the 4–6 percent range. Spectrum Brands' management estimated that the retail value of the U.S. pet supplies industry in just those product categories where it competed was about $8 billion in 2004, with another $4 billion in Europe. The industry had grown at a 6–8 percent rate annually in the United States since the mid-1990s and was expected to grow in the 4–7 percent range in the near future.

Spectrum Brands' global pet supplies group had an estimated 8 percent market share worldwide in the product categories where it competed, with broad distribution in North America, Europe, and Japan.[10] Its largest competitors in North America were Hartz Mountain and Central Garden & Pet Company. Hartz Mountain, acquired by Sumitomo Corporation in 2004, marketed over 1,500 products for dogs, cats, birds, hamsters, reptiles, and other animals; Hartz's acquisition by Sumitomo had provided the resources to pursue the development of new markets and distribution

channels in Asia and Europe. Central Garden and Pet's product line consisted of six brands of aquatics products, seven brands of dog and cat products, three brands of bird and small animal products, and five brands of animal health and insect control products. Sales of pet products at Central Garden and Pet were $569 million in fiscal 2004, $639 million in fiscal 2005, and $819 million in fiscal 2006; operating income from sales of pet products before deduction of corporate-level expenses totaled $61 million in 2004, $84 million in 2005, and $105 million in 2006.[11] Central marketed its pet products only in the United States, where its sales of $819 million in 2006 made it far and away the sales leader—Spectrum Brands and Hartz were tied at second, with U.S. sales of approximately $350 million in 2006. (However, Spectrum's international sales were greater than Hartz Mountain's, making it number two in terms of worldwide sales.) Central management estimated that total U.S. sales of pet products in 2006 amounted to about $39 billion, that the product categories in which it competed had total U.S. sales of $13 billion, and that its brands typically ranked first or second in market share in their respective segments.

Doskocil, the fourth largest seller of pet supplies in the United States, with 2006 sales of $160 million, was the only other U.S. manufacturer of pet supplies that competed in a broad number of product categories. Most other manufacturers had limited product lines that included only such specialized products as sea salt, aquariums, pet treats, or bird seed.

Lawn and Garden

Spectrum Brands' lawn and garden business consisted of several leading lawn and garden care products, including lawn fertilizers, professional fertilizers, lawn control products, herbicides, garden and indoor plant foods, plant care products, potting soils and other growing-media products and grass seed. During fiscal 2006, three new lawn and garden products were introduced—Mulch with Weed Stop (the first premium landscape mulch with weed preventer), the Smart Seeder (the first ready-to-use combination grass seed container and spreader), and the only termite killing stakes product for the do-it-yourself market. Brands with the largest sales were Spectracide, Schultz, Real-Kill, Garden Safe, and Vigoro. The company distributed its branded products primarily through Wal-Mart, Lowe's, and Home Depot and also produced private-label fertilizers for all three retailers. Sta-Green fertilizer was produced exclusively for Lowe's, Vigoro was produced exclusively for Home Depot, and Expert Gardener fertilizers were made exclusively for Wal-Mart. In Canada, lawn and garden products were sold under the Wilson, Nu-Gro, and So-Green brands.

In lawn and garden products, as in batteries, Spectrum Brands targeted value-conscious consumers who preferred products that sold at lower prices than premium-priced brands but that were still very comparable in quality and packaging. Management believed that its lawn and garden business had a strong second-place market share of 23 percent in the North American lawn and garden segments where it had product offerings, with its brands primarily positioned as value-priced alternatives.[12]

Primary competitors in the lawn and garden market were:[13]

- The Scotts Miracle-Gro Company, which marketed lawn and garden products under the Scotts, Ortho, Roundup, Osmocote, and Miracle-Gro brand names. Scotts Miracle-Gro products were number one in every major category in which the company competed—management believed the company had an overall market share of 52 percent in the segments where it had product offerings. Scotts also owned Smith & Hawken, a leading retailer of garden-inspired products that included pottery, watering equipment, gardening tools, outdoor furniture, and live plants. Scotts had sales of $2.1 billion in 2004, $2.4 billion in 2005, and $2.7 billion in 2006; over 80 percent of sales were in the United States, with the remainder in Europe. Net income was $101 million in 2004, $101 million in 2005, and $133 million in 2006. Scotts recorded market share and revenue gains in all categories during 2006, with sales of Scotts fertilizer increasing by 14 percent, sales of Miracle-Gro garden soils increasing by 17 percent, and sales of Ortho insect control products increasing by 7 percent.

- Central Garden & Pet Company, which had a product line consisting of wild bird feed, grass seed, lawn and garden chemicals and fertilizers, and indoor and outdoor pottery products. Products were marketed under 20 brands, including AMDRO (fire ant bait), Sevin (insecticides), and Pennington (the leader in both grass seed and wild bird feed). Sales of lawn and garden products at Central Garden and Pet were $698 million in fiscal 2004, $741 million in fiscal 2005, and $802 million in fiscal 2006; operating income from sales of lawn and garden products before deduction of corporate level expenses totaled $43 million in 2004, $47 million in 2005, and $57 million in 2006. Management estimated that the lawn and garden categories in which it participated had total U.S. sales of approximately $27 billion in 2006.

- Bayer AG, which marketed lawn and garden products under the Bayer Advanced brand name in North America, Europe, and Latin America and was the fourth leading seller behind Scotts, Central Garden, and Spectrum. Bayer's product line consisted of weed and insect control products, fire ant killer granules, lawn disease control products, potting mixes, and fertilizers for flowers, shrubs, and trees. Bayer, headquartered in Germany and best known for its aspirin and other health care products, had 2006 sales of about €28 billion worldwide, of which about €6 billion involved crop protection and seed treatment products, fungicides, insecticides, herbicides, fertilizers, and other crop, lawn, and garden products. Bayer's 2006 sales in the United States were said to be about $125 million.

Favorable demographic trends were expected to continue to spur sales of lawn and garden products, leading to mid-single-digit growth. Gardening was the number one leisure activity in the United States, with approximately 80 percent of homeowners working in their lawns on a regular basis. The industry, with $5 billion in 2006 retail sales, was expected to grow at 3–5 percent as the number of retirees grew and spent more time at home. Due to the rapid expansion of mass merchants with lawn and garden departments (Home Depot, Lowe's, and others) and full-line lawn and garden centers in the past 15 years, the buying power of retailers selling lawn and garden supplies had increased considerably.

Electric Shaving and Grooming

This product/business group consisted of Remington-branded men's rotary and foil shavers, women's shavers, beard and mustache trimmers, nose and ear trimmers, haircut kits, and related accessories. During fiscal 2006, several new products designed to improve the comfort and closeness of the shaving experience were introduced. These products were distributed broadly in North America and the United Kingdom and had been recently introduced in continental Europe and Latin America.

The worldwide retail sales of men's and women's electric shavers totaled $3.3 billion in 2006. The industry grew by 3 percent in 2006 and was expected to grow at a comparable rate during the next five years. Remington's two primary competitors in the electric shaving and grooming market were Norelco, a division of Koninklijke Philips Electronics NV (Philips), which sold and marketed rotary shavers, and Braun, a division of the Procter & Gamble Company, which sold and marketed foil shavers (Remington sold both foil and rotary shavers). Philips Norelco had long held the number one position in every geographic region of the world and increased its market share in North America from 46 percent in 2005 to 53 percent in 2006. Similarly, Norelco's share of the Western European market for men's and women's electric shavers increased from 56 percent in 2005 to 59 percent in 2006. The keys to Philips Norelco's growth were design and performance innovations. Test-marketing results indicated that the company's new Williams F1 electric shaver, which resembled a handheld industrial power tool and could be washed and cleaned in seconds, would prove to be very popular in 2007. Procter & Gamble's Braun was the world's best-selling brand of foil shavers and the second largest seller of men's and women's electric shavers overall, with 28 percent of the worldwide market in 2006.

Remington-branded shaving products had an overall market share of approximately 30 percent in North America. In North America, Spectrum management estimated that the Remington brand was number two in men's rotary shavers; number one in men's foil shavers; number one in women's shavers; and number one in men's beard and mustache trimmers, nose and ear trimmers, haircut kits, and related accessories.[14] Worldwide, Remington shavers were estimated to be the third best-selling brand. Both Braun and Remington experienced sales declines in North America and Europe due to Norelco's gains in market share in 2006. Braun's sales in other parts of the world increased during 2006.

Household Insect Control

The company's household insect control business was comprised of several leading products that enabled consumers to maintain a pest-free household and repel insects. These included spider, roach, and ant killer; flying insect killer; insect foggers; wasp and hornet killer; flea and tick control products; and roach and ant baits. It also manufactured and marketed a line of insect repellents. The largest brands were Hot Shot, Cutter, and Repel. The company enjoyed broad distribution of its insect control products across North America and a second-ranking market share of about 23 percent.[15] The North American market for insect control products was growing at around 4–6 percent.

Chief competitors in the household insect control market were (1) S. C. Johnson & Son, Inc., which marketed the Raid and OFF! brands of insecticide and repellent products; (2) the Scotts Miracle-Gro Company, the marketer of Ortho household insect control products; and (3) Henkel KGaA, which marketed Combat brand products.

Spectrum Brands estimated the size of the U.S. household insect control industry at approximately $1 billion in 2003. The company's management expected the industry to slightly exceed its historical 4 percent annual growth rate over the next several years because of an increasing awareness of the West Nile virus and eastern equine encephalitis. Spectrum Brands' Hot Shot, Cutter, and Repel were distant seconds to the Raid and OFF! brands marketed by S. C. Johnson. S. C. Johnson was a privately held business that also produced such well-known household products as Windex glass cleaner, Ziploc bags, Glade air freshener, and Pledge furniture polish.

Electric Personal Care Products

Electric personal care products were marketed under the Remington brand name and included hair dryers, straightening irons, curling irons, and hair setters. Remington personal care products had an estimated 21 percent share in the United Kingdom, and Remington was the number two brand in Western Europe.[16]

The global market for such electric personal care products as hair dryers, curling irons, hair straighteners, and lighted mirrors grew by 1.2 percent in 2006, to approximately $2.6 billion. Conair had been the worldwide best-selling brand of such products for decades. In addition to electrical hair care products, Conair also manufactured and marketed Cuisinart and Waring kitchen appliances, Weight Watchers bathroom scales, and Pollenex shower heads. Conair management believed that its success in the industry was related to its low-cost production capabilities and its ability to quickly bring products popularized in salons to consumers.

Vidal Sassoon, Remington, and Revlon were other brands of personal care products frequently carried by U.S. retailers. In 2005, about 59 percent of electric personal care products were sold by discounters like Wal-Mart or Target, 7 percent were sold by department stores, 23 percent were sold by drugstores and supermarkets, 7 percent were sold by specialty stores, and 4 percent were sold by other types of retailers.

Portable Lighting

Spectrum Brands sold a broad line of flashlights, lanterns, and other portable battery-powered devices for both retail and industrial markets. These were marketed under both the Rayovac and VARTA brand names, under several other brand names, and under licensing arrangements with third parties. The three major competitors were Energizer Holdings, Mag Instrument, and Eveready. Sales of Rayovac and VARTA lighting products had been flat for the past four years (see Exhibit 3).

Global retail sales of flashlights and lanterns had remained flat at about $1.5 billion during 2003–2006; no significant market growth was expected in the future. However, flashlights equipped with light emitting diodes (LEDs) were growing in popularity because of their small size, bright light, and low power usage. The industry was fragmented geographically and included few global brands. Maglite, Rayovac, and Eveready were the best-selling brands of portable lights in the United States. Mag Instruments' flashlights were considered the highest quality in the industry since the 1979 introduction of the Maglite. The all-aluminum flashlights were first marketed to police departments because of their exceptionally bright light, durability, and reliability, but consumers quickly became the biggest purchasers of the superior Mag flashlights. Maglite flashlights had been recognized for design excellence by the Japan Institute of Design and by the Museum for Applied Art in Cologne, Germany, and were named by *Fortune* as one of the 100 products "America makes best."[17] Eveready and Rayovac produced much less expensive plastic flashlights and lanterns.

Spectrum Brands' Organization and Operating Practices

Sales and Distribution

Spectrum Brands used a variety of distribution channels, including retailers, wholesalers and distributors, hearing aid professionals, industrial products distributors, and original equipment manufacturers (OEMs). Sales to Wal-Mart stores accounted for about 18 percent of consolidated net sales in fiscal 2005 and for about 19 percent in fiscal 2006; no other customer accounted for more than 10 percent of total sales in fiscal 2005 or 2006. Sales and distribution practices in each of the four reporting segments were as follows:[18]

- *North America:* Spectrum Brands' sales force in North America was organized by distribution channel, with separate sales groups for (1) retail sales and distribution channels, (2) hearing aid professionals, and (3) industrial distributors and original equipment manufacturers (OEMs). In some cases, independent brokers were used to service customers in selected North American distribution channels.

- *Latin America:* The sales force in Latin America was organized by both distribution channel and geographic territory. The Latin American sales force sold directly to large retailers, wholesalers, distributors, food and drug chains, and retail outlets in both urban and rural areas. In Latin American countries having no company sales representatives, the company used independent distributors who marketed Spectrum products through all channels in that country.

- *Europe/ROW:* A sales force group, supplemented by an international network of distributors, promoted the sale of Spectrum products in Europe and the rest of the world (ROW). Sales operations throughout Europe/ROW were organized by geographic territory and three different sales channels: (1) food/retail, which includes mass merchandisers, discounters, drugstores, and food stores; (2) specialty trade, which includes wholesale clubs, consumer electronics stores, department stores, photography stores, and wholesalers/ distributors; and (3) industrial, government, hearing aid professionals, and OEMs.

- *Global Pet:* The sales force for pet supplies was aligned by type of customer—mass merchandisers, grocery and drug chains, pet superstores, independent pet stores, and other retailers.

Manufacturing, Raw Materials, and Suppliers

Spectrum operated two major alkaline battery plants (one in Wisconsin and one in Germany), a combination zinc carbon/alkaline battery plant in China, three zinc carbon manufacturing plants and a zinc carbon battery component plant in Latin America, and two plants that made zinc air button cell batteries, one of which also produced lithium cell batteries and foil shaver components for its Remington shavers.[19] Substantially all of the company's rechargeable batteries and chargers, portable lighting products, hair care and other personal care products, and electric shaving and grooming products were manufactured by third-party suppliers primarily located in the Asia/Pacific region. The lawn and garden group had four combination production-distribution facilities; eight blend, pack, and warehouse facilities; and three distribution facilities that were shared with other Spectrum product groups. The pet supplies group had five production facilities (four in the United States and one in Germany), a specialty pet facility, and three distribution centers, one of which was shared with lawn and garden products. A number of manufacturing facilities had been closed during the past five years. Management believed that existing facilities were adequate for the company's present and foreseeable needs.

The principal raw materials used in manufacturing battery products—zinc powder, granular urea, electrolytic manganese dioxide powder, and steel—were sourced on either a global or a regional basis. The prices of these raw materials were susceptible to price fluctuations due to supply/demand trends, energy costs, transportation costs, government regulations and tariffs, changes in currency exchange rates, price controls, economic conditions, and other unforeseen circumstances. As a consequence, Spectrum regularly engaged in forward purchase and hedging derivative transactions to manage raw material costs in the upcoming 12 to 24 months.

Research and development activities were centralized at a single facility in Madison, Wisconsin. The company's R&D strategy was focused on new product development and performance enhancements of existing products.[20] Management saw efforts to introduce innovative products and improve the designs and functionality of existing products as keys to organic sales growth and enhanced value to consumers. However, while R&D expenditures had increased from $13.1 million in fiscal 2002 to $30.6 million in fiscal 2006, R&D expenditures as a percentage of net sales had declined from 2.3 percent in fiscal 2002 to 1.2 percent in fiscal 2006 (see Exhibit 1).

Recent Events at Spectrum Brands

In January 2006, Spectrum Brands sold its fertilizer technology and Canadian professional fertilizer products businesses of Nu-Gro (Nu-Gro Pro and Tech) to Agrium Inc. for net proceeds of approximately $83 million. Monies from the sale were used to reduce outstanding debt. Spectrum management was using earnings and cash flows from operations to reinvest in its businesses and to pay down debt—since going public in 1997, the company had never paid a dividend to shareholders and did not expect to pay a dividend in the near future. Exhibit 5 shows the composition of the company's long-term debt and the repayment schedule as of year-end fiscal 2006.

Late in fiscal 2006, Spectrum management began to contemplate the divestiture of portions of its business portfolio in order to better sharpen the company's focus on strategic growth businesses, reduce outstanding indebtedness, and increase the company's lackluster stock price. Wall Street advisers were engaged to assist with any divestitures; the plan was to complete any asset sales by mid-2007. Proceeds from any asset sales were expected to be used for debt repayment.

Spectrum Brands failed to capture all of the expected $100 million in cross-business strategic fits by year-end 2006, but management believed the company would be more successful in 2007. Kent Hussey pinpointed the difficulties in April 2006:

> When you make acquisitions in categories that are outside your core competency, there's a certain amount of learning that takes place, developing your own business model and dealing with new competitors in new marketplaces. So far, we think we've been very successful, but we're still in the early stages of the acquisitions in lawn and garden and pet supplies.[21]

Top executives at Spectrum Brands announced a new organizational structure in January 2007 that was expected to aid efforts to capture the expected cost-savings from cross-business strategic fits. Starting in 2007, management decided to abandon the four-operating-segment structure in favor of a three-business-segment structure—Global Batteries & Personal Care, Home & Garden, and Global Pet Supplies. According to CEO David Jones, the new structure would enable "Spectrum to operate more efficiently and profitably by eliminating duplicative staff functions and overhead in each of our business units, and downsizing our corporate infrastructure."[22] In addition, Jones said:

> By streamlining the business into three product-oriented operating units, we will significantly enhance our competitive focus and improve our cost structure. These changes will allow us to go to market faster with new, innovative products, as well as improve our ability to efficiently allocate resources on a worldwide basis. This business

Exhibit 5

Spectrum Brands' Debt Obligations, Fiscal Years 2005 and 2006

| | SEPTEMBER 30, | | | |
| | 2006 | | 2005 | |
	AMOUNT	RATE	AMOUNT	RATE
Senior Subordinated Notes, due February 1, 2015	$ 700,000	7.4%	$ 700,000	7.4%
Senior Subordinated Notes, due October 1, 2013	350,000	8.5%	350,000	8.5%
Term Loan, US Dollar, expiring February 6, 2012	604,827	8.6%	651,725	5.8%
Term Loan, Canadian Dollar, expiring February 6, 2012	72,488	7.4%	74,081	4.9%
Term Loan, Euro, expiring February 6, 2012	134,721	6.3%	137,142	4.7%
Term Loan, Euro Tranche B, expiring February 6, 2012	332,315	6.2%	338,288	4.4%
Term C Loan, expiring September 30, 2009	—	—	—	—
Euro Term C Loan, expiring September 30, 2009	—	—	—	—
Revolving Credit Facility, expiring February 6, 2011	26,200	10.3%	—	—
Revolving Credit Facility, expiring September 30, 2008	—	—	—	—
Euro Revolving Credit Facility, expiring February 6, 2011	—	—	—	—
Other notes and obligations	42,698	5.7%	38,701	—
Capitalized lease obligations	13,922	5.0%	17,396	—
Total long-term debt	2,277,171		$2,307,333	
Less current maturities payable in upcoming fiscal year	42,713		39,308	
Long-term debt outstanding	$2,234,458		$2,268,025	

Aggregate scheduled maturities of debt as of September 30, 2006:

2007	$ 42,713
2008	9,575
2009	8,939
2010	8,711
2011	242,172
Thereafter	$1,965,061
	$2,277,171

Source: Company 10-K report, 2006, pp.105–106.

unit realignment will also facilitate the orderly execution of the asset sale process we announced in July.[23]

In February 2007, Spectrum announced net sales of $564.6 million and a net loss of $0.38 per share for the first quarter of fiscal 2007 that ended December 31, 2006. Global battery sales declined 6 percent as compared to the first quarter of fiscal 2006, as strong results from Latin America were offset by sales declines in North America and Europe/ROW. Sales of Remington-branded products increased by 7 percent on a worldwide basis. Global Pet reported sales growth of 4 percent. Favorable foreign exchange rates had a $16.2 million positive impact on net sales during the quarter, mostly driven by the strong euro. The company generated operating income of $37.5 million versus $67.6 million in fiscal 2006's first quarter. The primary reasons for the decline in operating income were increased advertising and marketing expense of approximately $14 million and higher commodity costs, including an increase of $7 million in zinc costs.

Endnotes

[1] Information posted at www.spectrumbrands.com (accessed January 28, 2007).

[2] Various company press releases; 2004 10-K report, p. 15.

[3] 2004 annual report, p. 2.

[4] Various company press releases; company 10-K reports for 2003 and 2005.

[5] 2005 annual report.

[6] 2006 10-K report, p. 6.

[7] Company annual report, 2005, p. 8.

[8] 2006 10-K report.

[9] Investor presentation by John Heil, March 24, 2006; posted at www.spectrumbrands.com (accessed January 29, 2007).

[10] 2005 annual report, p. 9.

[11] Central Garden and Pet Company, 2006 10-K report, p. 66.

[12] Company annual report, 2005, p. 9.

[13] Company Web sites, SEC filings, and annual reports.

[14] 2005 annual report, p. 8.

[15] Ibid., p. 9.

[16] Ibid., p. 8.

[17] Mag Instruments Company History (www.maglite.com/history.asp).

[18] 2006 10-K report, pp. 3–4.

[19] Ibid., p. 5.

[20] Ibid.

[21] As quoted in an interview with *The Wall Street Transcript,* April 2006.

[22] Company press release, January 10, 2007.

[23] Ibid.

Sara Lee Corporation: Retrenching to a Narrower Range of Businesses

Arthur A. Thompson Jr.
The University of Alabama

John E. Gamble
University of South Alabama

In February 2005, Brenda Barnes, Sara Lee's newly appointed president and CEO, announced a bold and ambitious multiyear strategic plan to transform Sara Lee into a more tightly focused food, beverage, and household products company. The centerpiece of Barnes's transformation plan was the divestiture of weak-performing business units and product categories accounting for $8.2 billion in sales (40 percent of Sara Lee's annual revenues). While the divestitures would cut Sara Lee's revenues from $19.6 billion to about $11.4 billion, Barnes believed that Sara Lee would be better off concentrating its financial and managerial resources on a smaller number of business segments where market prospects were promising and Sara Lee's brands were well positioned.[1] Once the retrenchment initiatives were completed, the plan was to drive the company's growth via initiatives to boost the sales, market shares, and profitability of the key remaining brands: Sara Lee breads and bakery products, Ball Park meats, Douwe Egberts coffees, Hillshire Farm meats, Jimmy Dean sausage, Kiwi shoe care products, Sanex personal care products, Ambi Pur air fresheners, and Senseo single-serve coffee products.

By focusing on strong brands with good growth potential, company executives estimated that Sara Lee's sales revenues would grow to $14 billion in fiscal 2010 and that the company's operating profit margin would increase to at least 12 percent (versus an 8.1 percent operating profit margin in fiscal 2004).[2] The improved operating margin was expected to result from a combination of an increase in the mix of more profitable and innovative value-added products plus expected annual cost savings of between $575 and $800 million. However, some of the annual cost savings would be partially offset by spending an incremental $250 million annually on media advertising and promotion and on research and development. In addition, Sara Lee executives believed that the retrenchment strategy would generate sufficient cash flows to pay the company's total debt down to between $1.5 and $2 billion by fiscal 2010 (versus total debt of $4.8 billion in fiscal 2004), pay substantial dividends to shareholders, and repurchase shares of common stock.

Company Background

Sara Lee Corporation originated in 1939 when Nathan Cummins acquired C. D. Kenny Company, a small wholesale distributor of sugar, coffee, and tea that had net sales of $24 million. The purchase of Sprague, Warner & Company in 1942 prompted a name change to Sprague Warner–Kenny Corporation and a shift in the headquarters location from Baltimore to Chicago; the company's shares began trading on the New York Stock Exchange in 1946. In 1954, the company's name was changed to Consolidated

Foods Corporation to emphasize its diversified role in food processing, packaging, and distribution. In 1956, Consolidated Foods acquired Kitchens of Sara Lee and also entered the retail food business by acquiring 34 Piggly Wiggly supermarkets (later divested in 1966). The next 40 years were marked by a series of related and unrelated acquisitions:

John H. Bryan, former head of Bryan Foods (which the company acquired in 1968), became president and CEO in 1975 and served as CEO until 2000; Bryan was appointed chairman in 1976, a position he held until 2001. Bryan was the chief architect of the company's acquisition strategy during 1975–2000, guiding both its diversification efforts and its emergence as a

1962:	Jonker Fris, a Dutch producer of canned goods
1966:	Oxford Chemical Corporation
	E. Kahn's Sons Company, a producer of meats
1968:	Bryan Foods, a meat products producer
	Electrolux, a direct seller of vacuum cleaners
	Gant, an apparel producer
	Country Set, an apparel producer
	Canadelle, a producer of women's intimate apparel
1969:	Aris Gloves (later renamed Aris Isotoner)
1971:	Hillshire Farm, a meat producer
	Rudy's Farm, a meat producer
1972:	Erdal, a Dutch company that produced and marketed personal care products (later renamed Intradal)
1978:	Chef Pierre, a manufacturer/distributor of frozen prepared desserts
	Douwe Egberts, a Dutch coffee and grocery company
1980:	Productos Cruz Verde, a Spanish household products company
1982:	Standard Meat Company, a processor of meat products
1984:	Jimmy Dean Meats, a manufacturer of various meat, food, and leather products
	Nicholas Kiwi Limited, an Australian-based manufacturer and marketer of personal, household, shoe, and car care products and home medicines
1987:	Bil Mar Foods, a producer of turkey-based products
	Dim SA, the leading hosiery brand in France
1988:	Adams-Millis Corporation, a manufacturer of hosiery products (provided an entry into the men's basic sock business)
1989:	Champion Products, manufacturer of professional-quality knit athletic wear
	Van Nelle, a Dutch company active in coffee and tea
	Hygrade Food Products, a manufacturer of hot dogs, luncheon meats, bacon, and ham (which included the Ball Park and Hygrade hot dog brands)
1990:	Henson-Kickernick Inc., a manufacturer of high-quality foundations and daywear
1991:	Playtex Apparel Inc., an international manufacturer and marketer of intimate apparel products
	Rinbros, a manufacturer/marketer of men's and boys' underwear in Mexico
1992:	BP Nutrition's Consumer Foods Group
	Giltex Hosiery
	Bessin Corporation
	The furniture care businesses of SC Johnson Wax
	A majority interest in Maglificio Bellia, SpA
	Select assets of Mark Cross Inc.
1993:	SmithKline Beecham's European bath and body care brands
1997:	Aoste, a French meats company
	Lovable Italiana SpA, an Italian intimate apparel manufacturer
	Brossard France SA, a French manufacturer of bakery products
1998:	NutriMetics
	Café do Ponto

(continued)

(concluded)

1999:	Wechsler Coffee
	Chock full o'Nuts
	Continental Coffee
2000:	Hills Bros., MJB, and Chase & Sanborn coffee brands (acquired from Nestlé USA)
	Courtaulds Textiles, UK-based producer of intimate apparel brands Gossard and Berlei
	Café Pilão, the number one coffee company in Brazil
	Sol y Oro, the leading company in women's underwear in Argentina
2001:	The Earthgrains Company, the number two player in the U.S. bakery market
	A major European bakery company

global corporation. By 1980, sales had reached $5 billion. In 1985, Consolidated Foods changed its name to Sara Lee Corporation. Sales reached $10 billion in 1988, $15 billion in 1994, and $20 billion in 1998. But revenues peaked at the $20 billion level in 1998–1999, as management struggled to manage the company's broadly diversified and geographically scattered operations.

In 2000, C. Steven McMillan succeeded John Bryan as CEO and president of Sara Lee; Bryan remained chairman until he retired a year later, at which time McMillan assumed the additional title. McMillan launched strategic initiatives to narrow Sara Lee's focus on a smaller number of global branded consumer packaged goods segments—Food and Beverage, Intimates and Underwear, and Household Products. McMillan orchestrated several divestitures to begin the process of sharpening Sara Lee's business focus:

1966:	Piggly Wiggly supermarket chains
2000:	PYA/Monarch (sold to Royal Ahold's U.S. Foodservice for nearly $1.6 billion)
	Champion Europe
	Coach
	The International Fabrics division of Courtaulds
	The international bakery businesses in France, India, China, and the United Kingdom
2004:	Filodoro, an Italian intimate apparel business

Brenda C. Barnes, a former president of PepsiCo North America from 1996 to 1998, joined Sara Lee as president and chief operating officer in July 2004. At the time of her appointment, Barnes, age 50, was a board of directors member at Avon Products, the New York Times Company, Sears Roebuck, and Staples. During her 22-year career at PepsiCo, Barnes held a number of senior executive positions in operations, general management, manufacturing, sales, and marketing. From November 1999 to March 2000, she served as interim president and chief operating officer of Starwood Hotels & Resorts. Brenda Barnes's appointment as president and CEO of Sara Lee was announced on February 10, 2005, the same day as the announcement of the plan to transform Sara Lee into an even more tightly focused company. McMillan, in announcing Barnes's elevation to CEO, said:

> Our decision to fundamentally transform Sara Lee presents an ideal time for Brenda Barnes to transition to her new role as chief executive officer. We recruited Brenda last year to be my successor, and her contributions and leadership have exceeded all expectations. Brenda has played a key leadership role in designing our transformation plan and, for continuity and focus, it is appropriate that she lead its execution from the outset. Also, to ensure a smooth transition, I will remain chairman through the annual shareholders meeting in October. During these nine months, I will focus on the divestitures included in our plan.[3]

Sara Lee's Retrenchment Initiatives

The first phase of Brenda Barnes's transformation plan for Sara Lee was to exit seven businesses that had been targeted as nonstrategic:

- **Direct Selling**—A $450 million business that sold cosmetics, skin care products, fragrances, toiletries, household products, apparel, and other products to consumers through a network of independent salespeople in 18 countries around the world, most notably in Mexico, Australia, the Philippines, and Japan. In August 2005, Sara Lee announced a definitive agreement to sell its direct selling business to Tupperware Corporation for $557 million in cash.[4] The sale included products being sold under such brands as Avroy Shlain, House of Fuller, House of Sara Lee, Natur-Care, Nutrimetics, Nuvó Cosméticos, and Swissgarde.

- **U.S. Retail Coffee**—A $213 million business that marketed well-known Chock full o'Nuts, Hills Bros., MJB, and Chase & Sanborn coffees plus several private-label coffees. Not included in the divestiture plan was the sale of Sara Lee's fast-growing global coffee brand, Senseo, which had sales of approximately $85 million. The U.S. retail coffee business was sold to Italy-based Segafredo Zanetti Group for $82.5 million in late 2005.[5]

- **European Apparel**—A Sara Lee business unit that marketed such well-known brands as Dim, Playtex, Wonderbra, Abanderado, Nur Die, and Unno in France, Germany, Italy, Spain, the United Kingdom, and much of Eastern Europe; it also included Sara Lee Courtaulds, a UK-based maker of private-label clothing for retailers. The branded European apparel business had nearly $1.2 billion in sales in fiscal year 2005, ending July 2, 2005; the Sara Lee Courtaulds business had fiscal 2005 sales of about $560 million. In November 2005, Sara Lee sold the branded apparel portion of the European apparel business unit to an affiliate of Sun Capital Partners, a U.S. private equity company, based in Boca Raton, Florida, for about $115 million plus possible contingent payments based on future performance.[6] In May 2006, a big fraction of Sara Lee Courtaulds was sold to PD Enterprise Ltd., a global garment producer with

nine facilities that produced more than 120 million garments annually, including bras, underwear, nightwear, swim- and beachwear, formal wear, casual wear, jackets and coats, baby clothes, and socks; the deal with PD Enterprise did not include three Sara Lee Courtaulds facilities in Sri Lanka. (Sara Lee was continuing its efforts to find a buyer for the Sri Lanka operations.) Sara Lee received no material consideration as a result of the sale and remained liable for certain obligations of Sara Lee Courtaulds after the disposition, the most significant of which was the defined benefit pension plans that were underfunded by $483 million at the end of 2005.

- **European Nuts and Snacks**—A business with approximately €88 million in annual sales in fiscal 2005 that marketed products under the Duyvis brand in the Netherlands and Belgium as well as the Bénénuts brand in France. Sara Lee sold its European nuts and snacks business in the Netherlands, Belgium, and France to PepsiCo for approximately $150 million in November 2005.[7]

- **U.S. Meat Snacks**—A small unit with annual sales of $33 million in fiscal 2005 and $25 million in fiscal 2006. This business was sold in June 2006 for $9 million.[8]

- **European Meats**—A $1.1 billion packaged-meats business in Europe that had respectable market positions in France, the Benelux region, and Portugal and included such brands as Aoste, Justin Bridou, Cochonou, Nobre, and Imperial. Headquartered in Hoofddorp, the Netherlands, Sara Lee's European meats operation generated $1.1 billion in sales in fiscal 2005 and employed approximately 4,500 people. In June 2006, Sara Lee completed the sale of this unit to Smithfield Foods for $575 million in cash; based in Smithfield, Virginia, Smithfield Foods was the world's largest grower of hogs and producer of pork products and had subsidiaries in France, Poland,

Romania, and the United Kingdom that marketed meats under various brands, including Krakus and Stefano's.[9]

- **Sara Lee Branded Apparel**—Sara Lee's strategy for exiting branded apparel (2004 sales of $4.5 billion) was to spin the entire business off as an independent company named Hanesbrands Inc. The operations of Sara Lee Branded Apparel consisted of producing and marketing 10 brands of apparel: Hanes, L'eggs, Champion, Bali, Barely There, Playtex, Wonderbra, Just My Size, Duofold (outdoor apparel), and Outer Banks (golf, corporate, and stylish sportswear); sales of these brands were chiefly in North America, Latin America, and Asia. Two top executives of Sara Lee Branded Apparel were named to head the new company. The spin-off was completed in September 2006 when Sara Lee distributed 100 percent of the common stock of Hanesbrands to Sara Lee shareholders; shares were traded on the New York Stock Exchange under the symbol HBI.

Sara Lee management expected the retrenchment initiatives would generate combined net after-tax proceeds in excess of $3 billion. Exhibit 1 provides financial data relating to the divested businesses. The next section provides additional details about the Hanesbrands spin-off.

The Spin-Off of Hanesbrands

Sara Lee management's decision to exit the branded apparel business was driven principally by eroding sales and weak returns on its equity investment in branded apparel (Exhibit 2). But rather than sell the business, management determined that shareholders would be better served by spinning off the branded apparel business as a stand-alone company. Sara Lee shareholders received one share of Hanesbrands stock for every eight shares owned. Hanesbrands began independent operations in September 2006 and organized its business around four product/geographic segments, as shown in Exhibit 3.

However, the spin-off of Hanesbrands had some unique financial features. The terms of the spin-off called for Hanesbrands to make a one-time "dividend" payment of $2.4 billion to Sara Lee immediately following the commencement of independent operations. But in order to make the $2.4 billion payment to Sara Lee and to fund its own operations, Hanesbrands borrowed $2.6 billion, thus saddling itself with a huge debt that prompted Standard & Poor's to assign the company a B+ credit rating (which put Hanesbrands in the bottom half of apparel companies from a credit rating standpoint). The company's debt-to-equity ratio was extraordinarily high, raising some questions about whether the interest expenses associated with the high debt would still leave Hanesbrands with sufficient funds and financial flexibility to invest in revitalizing its brands and growing its business. Exhibit 4 shows the impact of the $2.4 billion payment to Sara Lee on Hanesbrands' balance sheet.

A *BusinessWeek* reporter speculated that the reason for the unusually outsized dividend payment to Sara Lee was that the proceeds Sara Lee realized from the sales of the divested units (Exhibit 1) fell far short of the hoped-for $3 billion that was an integral part of the retrenchment strategy and restructuring announced by CEO Brenda Barnes in February 2005.[10] To make up for the shortfall, Sara Lee supposedly opted to get more cash out of the Hanesbrands spin-off.

In February 2007, Hanesbrands reported that sales for the first six months of fiscal 2007 were $2.25 billion, down 3 percent from the comparable period in fiscal 2006. Net income for the six-month period was $74.1 million, down 60.7 percent from $188.6 million in the first two quarters of fiscal 2006. The decrease in net income reflected increased interest expense, reduced operating profit, and a higher income tax rate. However, strong cash flows from operations allowed the company to pay down long-term debt by more than $106 million and make a voluntary $48 million contribution to reduce the underfunded liability for qualified pension

Exhibit 1

Financial Data for Sara Lee's Divested Businesses, Fiscal Years 2004–2006

(a) Sales and Income of Divested Businesses, Fiscal Years 2004–2006 ($ in millions)

	FISCAL YEARS		
	2006	2005	2004
Net Sales of Divested Businesses			
Direct selling	$ 202	$ 473	$ 447
U.S. retail coffee	122	213	206
European branded apparel	641	1,184	1,276
European nuts and snacks	54	64	66
Sara Lee Courtaulds	437	558	536
U.S. meat snacks	25	30	33
European meats	1,114	1,176	1,111
Total net sales	$2,595	$3,698	$3,675
Pretax Income (Loss) of Divested Businesses			
Direct selling	$ 14	$ 55	$ 55
U.S. retail coffee	(46)	(39)	(2)
European branded apparel	(186)	(302)	67
European nuts and snacks	8	7	12
Sara Lee Courtaulds	(69)	—	14
U.S. meat snacks	(14)	(1)	(1)
European meats	(57)	90	101
Total pretax income (loss)	$ (350)	$ (190)	$ 246
After-Tax Income (Loss) of Divested Businesses			
Direct selling	$ 54	$ (12)	$ 34
U.S. retail coffee	(39)	(33)	—
European branded apparel	(153)	(296)	68
European nuts and snacks	3	3	7
Sara Lee Courtaulds	(71)	(1)	26
U.S. meat snacks	(9)	(1)	—
European meats	(41)	(22)	86
Total after-tax income (loss)	$ (256)	$ (362)	$ 221

(b) Proceeds Realized from the Sales of the Divested Businesses ($ in millions)

	SALE PRICE	PRETAX GAIN ON SALE	TAX BENEFIT (CHARGE)	AFTER-TAX GAIN
Direct selling	$ 557.0	$327	$(107)	$220
U.S. retail coffee	82.5	5	(2)	3
European branded apparel	≈115.0	45	41	86
European nuts and snacks	≈150.0	66	4	70
Sara Lee Courtaulds	No material consideration **	22	—	22
U.S. meat snacks	9.0	1	(1)	—
European meats *	575.0	42	(2)	40
Totals	$1,488.5 ***	$508	$ (67)	$441

* This unit was divested in early fiscal 2007; data regarding the gains from the sale are from company press release on November 7, 2006, reporting results for first quarter of fiscal 2007.

** Sara Lee retained liability for unfunded pension benefits of $483 million at Sara Lee Courtaulds and made payments of approximately $93 million to remedy its liability during 2006.

*** The actual amount realized from the sales of these businesses was closer to $1.3 billion after taking into account the payments made to remedy unfunded pension liabilities at Sara Lee Courtaulds and other costs incurred in discontinuing the operations of all these businesses.

Sources: Company 2006 10-K report, p. 56, and various company press releases announcing the sale and disposition of the businesses.

Exhibit 2

Performance of Hanesbrands Prior to Spin-Off by Sara Lee, Fiscal Years 2002–2006 ($ in thousands)

	FISCAL YEARS ENDING				
	JUNE 29, 2002	JUNE 28, 2003	JULY 3, 2004	JULY 2, 2005	JULY 1, 2006
Statements of Income Data					
Net sales	$4,920,840	$ 4,669,665	$4,632,741	$ 4,683,683	$4,472,832
Cost of sales	3,278,506	3,010,383	3,092,026	3,223,571	2,987,500
Gross profit	1,642,334	1,659,282	1,540,715	1,460,112	1,485,332
Selling, general, and administrative expenses	1,146,549	1,126,065	1,087,964	1,053,654	1,051,833
Charges for (income from) exit activities	27,580	(14,397)	27,466	46,978	(101)
Income from operations	468,205	547,614	425,285	359,480	433,600
Interest expense	2,509	44,245	37,411	35,244	26,075
Interest income	(13,753)	(46,631)	(12,998)	(21,280)	(8,795)
Income before income taxes	479,449	550,000	400,872	345,516	416,320
Income tax expense (benefit)	139,488	121,560	(48,680)	127,007	93,827
Net income	$ 339,961	$ 428,440	$ 449,552	$ 218,509	$ 322,493
Balance Sheet Data					
Cash and cash equivalents	$ 106,250	$ 289,816	$ 674,154	$ 1,080,799	$ 298,252
Total assets	$4,064,730	$ 3,915,573	$4,402,758	$ 4,237,154	$4,891,075
Noncurrent liabilities:					
Noncurrent capital lease obligations	12,171	10,054	7,200	6,188	2,786
Noncurrent deferred tax liabilities	10,140	6,599	—	7,171	5,014
Other noncurrent liabilities	37,660	32,598	28,734	40,200	42,187
Total noncurrent liabilities	59,971	49,251	35,934	53,559	49,987
Total Sara Lee equity investment	$1,762,824	$ 2,237,448	$2,797,370	$ 2,602,362	$3,229,134

Source: Hanesbrands fiscal 2006 10-K report.

Exhibit 3

Hanesbrands' Lineup of Products and Brands, 2006

PRODUCT/GEOGRAPHIC SEGMENTS	PRIMARY PRODUCTS	PRIMARY BRANDS
Innerwear	Intimate apparel, such as bras, panties, and bodywear	Hanes, Playtex, Bali, Barely There, Just My Size, Wonderbra
	Men's underwear and kids' underwear	Hanes, Champion, Polo Ralph Lauren**
	Socks	Hanes, Champion
Outerwear	Activewear, such as performance T-shirts and shorts	Hanes, Champion, Just My Size
	Casual wear, such as T-shirts	Hanes, Just My Size, Outerbanks
Hosiery	Hosiery	L'eggs, Hanes, Just My Size
International	Activewear, men's underwear, kids' underwear, intimate apparel, socks, hosiery, and casual wear	Hanes, Wonderbra,* Playtex,* Champion, Rinbros, Bali

* Terms of the February 2006 sale of Sara Lee's European branded apparel business prevented Hanesbrands from selling Wonderbra and Playtex branded products in the European Union, several other European countries, and South Africa.

** Hanesbrands had a license agreement to sell men's underwear and kids' underwear under the Polo Ralph Lauren label.

Source: Company 10-K report for fiscal 2006.

Exhibit 4

Balance Sheet for Hanesbrands, Just Prior to and Immediately Following the 2006 Spin-Off ($ in thousands)

	SEPTEMBER 30, 2006 (JUST AFTER THE SPIN-OFF)	JULY 1, 2006 (PRIOR TO THE SPIN-OFF)*
Assets		
Cash and cash equivalents	$ 209,080	$ 298,252
Accounts receivable, less allowances of $44,380 at September 30, 2006, and $41,628 at July 1, 2006	516,778	523,430
Inventories	1,262,961	1,236,586
Deferred tax assets and other current assets	168,810	151,263
Due from related entities	—	273,428
Notes receivable from parent companies	—	1,111,167
Funding receivable with parent companies	—	161,686
Total current assets	$2,157,629	$3,755,812
Property, net	609,048	617,021
Trademarks and other identifiable intangibles, net	138,395	136,364
Goodwill	278,725	278,655
Deferred tax assets and other noncurrent assets	417,406	103,223
Total assets	$3,601,203	$4,891,075
Liabilities and Owners' Equity		
Accounts payable and bank overdrafts	$ 203,972	$ 483,033
Accrued liabilities and other	403,905	368,561
Notes payable to banks	4,751	3,471
Current portion of long-term debt	26,500	—
Due to Sara Lee Corporation	26,306	—
Due to related entities	—	43,115
Notes payable to parent companies	—	246,830
Notes payable to related entities	—	466,944
Total current liabilities	665,434	1,611,954
Long-term debt	2,573,500	—
Other noncurrent liabilities	346,034	49,987
Total liabilities	$3,584,968	$1,661,941
Stockholders' or parent companies' equity:		
Common stock (500,000,000 authorized shares; $.01 par value)		
Issued and outstanding—96,306,232 as of September 30, 2006	963	—
Additional paid-in capital	73,074	—
Retained earnings (for the period subsequent to September 5, 2006)	9,230	—
Accumulated other comprehensive loss	(67,032)	(8,384)
Sara Lee's equity investment	—	3,237,518
Total owners' equity	16,235	3,229,134**
Total liabilities and owners' equity	$3,601,203	$4,891,075

* Equity investment of Hanesbrands shareholders.
** Equity investment of Sara Lee Corporation in its branded apparel business unit.
Source: Hanesbrands 10-Q Report for the quarter ending September 30, 2006.

plans to $173 million. In its first six months, Hanesbrands announced the closure of four plants and three distribution centers as part of a plan to create a lower-cost global supply chain; it also notified retirees and employees that the company would phase out premium subsidies for early retiree medical coverage, move to an access-only plan for early retirees by the end of 2007, and eliminate the medical plan for retirees aged 65 and older as a result of recently expanded Medicare coverage.

Hanesbrands' stock price, which began trading at around $22 per share in early September 2006, had trended upward to the $25–$27 range as of February 2007. Exhibit 5 compares Sara

Lee's financial situation at the end of fiscal 2004 (just prior to the transformation plan) with that at the end of fiscal 2006 (when the divestitures and the Hanesbrands spin-off were completed).

Sara Lee's Postretrenchment Strategy: Initiatives to Revitalize Sales and Boost Profitability

Upon the completion of Sara Lee Corporation's disposition of "nonstrategic" businesses in September 2006, Sara Lee management turned its full attention to growing the sales, market

Exhibit 5

Sara Lee's Financial Performance in the Fiscal Years Before and After the Divestitures and the Spin-off of Hanesbrands ($ in millions)

	FISCAL YEARS ENDING	
	JULY 1, 2006	JULY 3, 2004
Results of Continuing Operations		
Net sales	$11,471	$19,566
Cost of sales	7,035	12,017
Gross profit	4,436	7,549
Gross profit margin	38.7%	38.6%
Selling, general, and administrative expenses	3,791	5,897
SG&A expenses as a % of net sales	33.0%	30.1%
Operating income	477	1,485
Operating profit margin	4.2%	8.1%
Interest expense	288	271
Interest income	(71)	(90)
Income from continuing operations before taxes	267	1,542
Income taxes	179	270
Net income	$ 233	$ 1,272
Net profit margin	2.0%	8.0%
Other Financial and Operating Information		
Cash and cash equivalents	$ 1,933	$ 638
Inventories	916	2,779
Total assets	9,631	14,883
Net cash flow from operating activities	721	2,042
Number of employees	60,000	150,400

Note: Data for fiscal 2004 are from Sara Lee's 2004 10-K report. Data for fiscal 2006 reflect case author adjustments to the figures in Sara Lee's 2006 10-K report, made in order to account for the spin-off of Hanesbrands business and consequent exit from the branded apparel business; Sara Lee's financial results for fiscal 2006 included branded apparel because the spin-off was not effective until a few weeks after fiscal 2006 ended.
Sources: Sara Lee's 10-K reports for fiscal 2004 and fiscal 2006; Hanesbrands 10-K report for fiscal 2006.

shares, and profitability of its remaining businesses. The two chief goals were to boost top line sales by 2–4 percent annually to reach $14 billion by 2010 and to achieve a 12 percent operating profit margin by 2010. Sara Lee planned to achieve its objectives by developing three competitive capabilities in all of its remaining businesses. The company believed all of its business units must develop a strong focus on consumer and customer needs and on operating excellence. The company's management believed that competitive pricing, innovative new products, and brand-building capabilities were essential to its efforts to please consumers. Category management and leverage through size were thought to be necessary for the company to win new accounts with supermarket and discount store customers. Operating excellence was the third key element of its corporate strategy, which was critical to competitive pricing. Major operations initiatives under way at Sara Lee included lean manufacturing, centralized purchasing to achieve economies of scope, and the implementation of a common corporatewide information systems platform.

The organizational structure developed by Brenda Barnes and other key Sara Lee managers that would best enable its businesses to contribute to corporate goals was a three-division structure built around customer types. The Sara Lee Food & Beverage division included the company's North American meats brands, North American bakery products, and Senseo single-serving coffee products sold in North American supermarkets and discount stores. Sara Lee Foodservice included the sales of meat products, bakery products, and coffee and tea products sold to food-service accounts in North America. The Sara Lee International division included sales of coffee and tea products, bakery goods, and household and body care brands sold outside North America.

Sara Lee Food & Beverage

Sara Lee's Food & Beverage division (SLFB) included Ball Park franks, Jimmy Dean sausage, Hillshire Farm deli meats, Sara Lee deli meats, Sara Lee bakery products, Sara Lee frozen desserts, and Senseo single-serving coffeemakers and coffee pods. Sara Lee's sales of Hillshire Farm, Jimmy Dean, Ball Park, State Fair, and Sara Lee meat products made it the second-largest seller of such products in the $9.6 billion North American packaged-meat industry. The combined sales of Sara Lee's meat products gave it a 19.6 percent share of the North American retail meat industry in 2006. Kraft was the largest seller of packaged meats in North America, with a 21 percent market share during 2006. Smithfield Foods, ConAgra, and Hormel were the next largest meat producers in North America in 2006, with respective market shares of 9 percent, 8 percent, and 5 percent.

NORTH AMERICAN RETAIL MEAT   Sales of meats in North America improved by 5 percent and operating income increased by 36 percent relative to 2005 through new product innovations like Jimmy Dean Breakfast Bowls, Hillshire Farms Chicken Caesar Entrée Salads, and Sara Lee Thin Sliced Virginia Brand Baked Ham. In 2007, SLFB had four times as many products under development than were under development in 2005. Promotions tied to key holidays and sports events helped Sara Lee increase the sales of its meat products during 2006. The company's Power Events used a combination of in-store displays, newspaper ads, and discounts to boost sales volume of deli meats by 22 percent, on average, during event dates. The company also used Power Events for other division products, including Jimmy Dean frozen breakfast items, Sara Lee fresh bread, and Sara Lee frozen desserts. The combination of product innovations and effective promotions was expected to allow the Jimmy Dean brand to increase sales from approximately $400 million in 2005 to more than $500 million in 2007, even though sales of Jimmy Dean sausage and bacon were expected to remain level.

NORTH AMERICAN RETAIL BAKERY   The company's chief managers also expected significant growth from its fresh bakery business. Sara Lee's fresh bakery sales had improved from $91 million in 2003 to $697 million in 2006. SLFB's ability to negotiate with supermarket buyers to increase shelf space allocated for its bakery products accounted for much of the growth in bakery sales during 2006. In several cases, SLFB was able to increase space on the bread aisle from 18 inches to four feet. Average weekly sales tripled in stores where Sara Lee gained shelf space. Sara Lee's sales growth in the fresh bakery sales had made it the number one national brand of bread, with a 7.2 percent market share. Number two Pepperidge Farm recorded sales of $509 million in 2006 and held 5.3 percent of the market. Innovations that contributed to Sara Lee's boost in sales of fresh bread included wide-pan loaf breads and Hearty & Delicious thick-sliced sandwich loaves.

In addition to producing the number one brand of fresh loaf bread, Sara Lee was also the number one brand of hot dog buns, hamburger buns, and bagels and other breakfast breads in North America in 2006. Sara Lee's 2006 breakfast bread sales total of $21.2 million was more than seven times greater than the second best-selling brand's 2006 sales of $3 million. Similarly, the sales of Sara Lee's thick-sliced Hearty & Delicious fresh bread of $22.2 million was five times greater than the second best-selling brand of thick-sliced bread in 2006. The company's whole-grain white bread 2006 sales total of $90 million was more than twice that of its closest rival. Sara Lee's combined sales of fresh bread, breakfast breads, buns and rolls, bagels, and specialty breads gave it a 14 percent share of the $101 billion North American retail bread industry in 2006. Wesson was the largest baked-goods maker in North America, with a 22 percent market share in 2006, while IBC was the third largest national bakery, with a 13 percent market share. Flowers Bread was the fourth largest bakery in North America, with a 10 percent market share in 2006. Exhibit 6 presents sales and operating profits for Sara Lee's three divisions and major business segments for 2005 and 2006.

Exhibit 6

Sales and Operating Profits for Sara Lee Corporation's Three Business Units after the Restructuring and Retrenchment, 2005–2006

	2006		2005	
	SALES	OPERATING PROFIT	SALES	OPERATING PROFIT
Sara Lee Food & Beverage				
North America Retail Meats	$ 2.5 billion	$ 197 million	$ 2.4 billion	$144 million
North America Retail Bakery	$ 1.8 billion	$ 9 million	$ 1.8 billion	($10) million
Subtotal	$ 4.3 billion	$ 206 million	$ 4.2 billion	$134 million
Significant items	$ 38 million	($254) million	$ 36 million	$ 41 million
Total	$ 4.4 billion	($48) million	$ 4.3 billion	$175 million
Sara Lee Foodservice	$ 2.2 billion	$ 141 million	$ 2.1 billion	$179 million
Significant items	—	($20) million	—	$ 3 million
Total	$ 2.2 billion	$ 121 million	$ 2.1 billion	$182 million
Sara Lee International				
International Beverage	$ 2.4 billion	$ 400 million	$ 2.2 billion	$417 million
H&BC	$ 1.8 billion	$ 244 million	$ 1.8 billion	$300 million
International Bakery	$742 million	$ 64 million	$739 million	$ 72 million
Subtotal	$ 4.9 billion	$ 708 million	$ 4.8 billion	$789 million
Significant items	—	($88) million	$174 million	($4) million
Total	$ 4.9 billion	$ 620 million	$ 5.0 billion	$785 million

Source: Presentations by Sara Lee Management Team Members at the 2006 "Meet the Management" Analyst Day, www.saralee.com (accessed March 23, 2007).

Sara Lee did not anticipate significant growth for its frozen desserts like cheesecake, pound cake, pies, coffeecakes, or croissants, with projected 2007 sales approximating $75 million. Consumer eating patterns did not favor growth in home desserts, and sales of Sara Lee frozen desserts had experienced no meaningful growth in five years. The division's Senseo single-serving coffeemakers and coffee pods had also experienced little growth in 2006. Only 5 percent of coffeemakers sold during 2006 were single-serving coffeemakers, according to an NPD Group survey. The survey also found that one-half of those who purchased single-serving coffeemakers rated them as "fair" or "poor." Only about one-third of survey respondents said coffee pods were convenient to find.[11]

Sara Lee Foodservice

Sara Lee's food-service division marketed and sold products available to consumers in North American supermarkets to food service distributors such as U.S. Foodservice and Sodexho. Sara Lee Foodservice (SLF) also sold meat, bakery, and coffee products to national restaurant chains like Sonic, Dunkin' Donuts, Waffle House, Quiznos Sub, and Burger King. Most of the division's sales were standard Sara Lee, Jimmy Dean, Hillshire Farm, Ball Park, and State Farm branded products, although the division did customize meat and bakery products for its largest customers. Coffee brands sold to North American food-service accounts included Douwe Egberts and Superior Coffee. SLF also provided commercial-grade coffee machines and espresso makers to food-service customers.

The food-service industry offered Sara Lee a considerable growth opportunity since industry sales were projected to grow from $476 billion in 2006 to $522 billion in 2010 as Americans continued to eat a higher percentage of meals away from home. In 2006, industrywide sales of meats to the food-service industry exceeded $7 billion, while sales of frozen bakery products amounted to $2 billion and fresh bakery item sales approximated $5 billion. The sales

of coffee and tea to the food-service industry also approximated $5 billion in 2006. In 2006, the coffee and tea and meat segments grew by nearly 5 percent, while the bakery segment of the food-service industry grew by about 2 percent. SLF was positioned to capture a significant portion of industry growth, since in 2006 it held a 9 percent market share in deli meats sold to food-service customers, an 11 percent market share in relevant baked goods, and an 18 percent share of coffee and tea products sold to food-service customers. Beverages made up $836 million of the division's 2006 sales of $2.2 billion. Baked goods sales and meat product sales amounted to $748 million and $616 million, respectively, in 2006.

Sara Lee Foodservice had benefited from the innovations developed by Sara Lee Food & Beverage since the food-service trends mirrored those in the grocery industry. For example, presliced deli meats that were intended to satisfy consumers' desires for convenience also made sense for food-service accounts. Food-service customers had found that it was more cost effective and more sanitary to purchase presliced meat than to purchase bulk meat for restaurant employees to slice. SLF had also provided complete sandwich solutions to customers such as Quiznos that dramatically lowered restaurants' labor costs and customer wait times. Sara Lee Signature Sandwiches were made with premium Sara Lee presliced meats and Sara Lee sandwich loaves. Sara Lee's dessert and bakery brands like Sara Lee, Bistro Collection, and ChefPierre also benefited from innovations developed for consumers. Lower calorie pies developed by SLFB helped SLF capture 50 percent of the market for pies in the food-service industry. The company held 5–15 percent market shares in upscale desserts and cheesecakes, pastries, cake, bread, and muffins sold to the food-service industry.

Sara Lee International

Sara Lee's international brands included Douwe Egberts and Maison du Café coffee, Pickwick teas, Bimbo bread, Kiwi shoe care products,

Sanex body care products, Ridsect, Vapona, and GoodKnight insecticides, and Ambi Pur air fresheners. Seventy-three percent of the division's 2006 sales of $4.9 billion were made in Western Europe. Twelve percent of the division's sales were made in Asia/Australia, while 7 percent of division sales originated in Eastern Europe, 6 percent originated in South America, and 2 percent of sales were made in Africa.

During 2006, management in the division had focused on improving marketing and sales, sharing administrative services, establishing a culture of continuous improvement, and accelerating the product development process. In addition, Sara Lee International (SLI) had undergone restructuring during 2006 that eliminated 1,300 jobs. SLI management had implemented continuous improvement programs in five European factories in 2005 and 2006 and expected to bring continuous improvement programs to all 30 factories outside the United States by May 2008.

INTERNATIONAL BEVERAGE Sara Lee was the world's second largest seller of coffee in retail channels, with a global market share of about 9 percent. The total value of coffee sales in retail channels was approximately $24.5 billion in 2006. SLI recorded sales of $1.7 in retail channels in Europe during 2006, with Douwe Egberts generating 2006 sales of $379 million. Senseo's single-serving coffee pods were its second best-selling coffee product in Europe with 2006 sales of $336 million. SLI had sold more than 11 million Senseo coffeemakers and 11 billion coffee pods in Europe since 2001. The company expected sales of Senseo coffeemakers and coffee pods to continue to grow in Europe, as it launched new Senseo coffee products in 2007 that included cappuccino, espresso, and mug-size pods. The company also planned to launch ready-to-drink hot and cold coffee drinks in European retail channels in 2007. About $700 million of SLI's beverage sales of $2.4 billion were to restaurants and other out-of-home channels. SLI's European sales of tea in retail channels totaled $136 million in 2006.

INTERNATIONAL BAKERY Bimbo was the number one brand of packaged bread in Spain with a 54 percent market share. Bimbo's strongest rival in packaged bread in 2006 was private-label brands, which accounted for 25 percent of the market. Private-label brands were expected to grow faster than branded bread sales between 2007 and 2010. SLI's limited ability to increase sales in other European countries was a result of consumer preference for fresh-baked bread. In 2005, packaged bread made up only 12 percent of the €4 billion total bread market in Europe. Packaged bread was expected to grow by 7–8 percent annually to account for 25 percent of industry sales by 2015.

HOUSEHOLD & BODY CARE SLI's Household & Body Care unit's Kiwi brand was the number one shoe care brand worldwide, with distribution in 200 countries and a global market share of 63 percent in 2006. Kiwi accounted for $280 million of the business unit's 2006 sales of $1.8 billion. Sanex was the number one brand of bath and shower products in Europe with a 14.7 percent share of the $1.7 billion market. Bath and shower care products grew by 0.9 percent during 2006. Sanex was also the fourth largest deodorant brand in Europe in 2006. Sanex's 2006 sales reached $800 million, with significant sales in Spain, France, the Netherlands, the United Kingdom, Germany, Italy, South Africa, the Philippines, and Indonesia.

The company's insecticide brands held a collective market share of 28.1 percent in Europe during 2006 and contributed $205 million to the unit's revenues during 2006. SLI's largest country markets for its insecticides were India, Malaysia, Spain, and France. SLI had focused growth initiatives for its insecticides and other household and body care products on emerging markets in Asia. Its fastest-growing markets in Asia were Malaysia, India, Indonesia, and the Philippines. SLI's European strategy was keyed to maintenance of market share and product innovations such as exfoliator bath products and dermoactive deodorants.

Ambi Pur was the third largest brand of air freshener in the $2.3 billion European air care market, with 2006 sales of $335 million. The European air care market declined by 1.4 percent between 2005 and 2006. Ambi Pur was strongest in Spain, the United Kingdom, the Netherlands, Italy, and France, where its market share was as high as 25 percent. There was reason to believe that Ambi Pur could dramatically increase its market share in Europe based on the dramatic results achieved by the Ambi Pur 3volution air freshener launched in the United Kingdom in March 2006. The 3volution air freshener cycled through three different fragrances every 45 minutes since research had indicated that individuals quit detecting a scent once they have been continuously exposed to it for 30 minutes to an hour. Ambi Pur's market share in the United Kingdom increased from 16 percent at the time of the 3volution launch to nearly 26 percent at year-end 2006.

The Future

Top executives at Sara Lee believed that fiscal 2007 would be an inflection point for the company's performance, resulting in positive top- and bottom-line growth trends across all businesses. New product introductions, new marketing programs, increased in-store promotions, and improved product placement were expected to drive sales increases. Brenda Barnes said that the company expected to grow sales by 2 to 4 percent annually and achieve steady expansion in profit margins in the coming years.[12]

As a result of raising more than $3.7 billion from the disposition of businesses, management said the company had ample cash to invest in the business and return to shareholders. The company's chief financial officer expected cash from operations to be between $400 and $500 million, although the cash costs to repatriate money from outside the United States cut into the company's ability to deploy all of these funds for corporate purposes.[13] Management expected to return significant value to shareholders in fiscal 2007 by delivering a healthy $370 million dividend payout, repurchasing $500 million of shares, and reducing net debt by $1 to $2 billion. Executives indicated that the previously stated long-term targets, while aggressive, were attainable.

Endnotes

[1] Company press release, February 10, 2005.

[2] Company press releases on February 10, 2005, and February 25, 2005.

[3] Company press release, February 10, 2005.

[4] Company press release, August 10, 2005.

[5] Company press release, October 26, 2005.

[6] Company press release, November 14, 2005.

[7] Company press release, November 22, 2005.

[8] Company 10-K report for fiscal 2006.

[9] Company press release, June 27, 2006.

[10] Jane Sasseen, "How Sara Lee Left Hanes in Its Skivvies," *Business-Week,* September 18, 2006, p. 40.

[11] As discussed in "Kraft Foods' Beverage Machine Is Slow to Sell," *The Morning Call,* February 11, 2007.

[12] Letter to Shareholders, 2006 annual report, p.13.

[13] Company press release, September 16, 2006.

Indexes

Organization Index

Subject Index

478   Indexes

t

Tariffs, 70–71, 167, 181
Teams, 13–14
Technology
  advances, 77
  information systems, 135–136
  transfer, 78
Think global, act global strategy, 171–172
Think global, act local strategy, 172
Think local, act local strategy, 170–171
Threats; *see* SWOT analysis
Total quality management (TQM), 131, 132
Trade; *see also* International markets
  dumping, 181
  export strategies, 168–169
  tariffs, 70–71, 167, 181

u

Universalism, ethical, 150
Unrelated diversification, 189
  benefits, 193–194
  combined with related businesses, 195–196
  managerial requirements, 194–195
  pitfalls, 194–195
  screening candidates, 192

v

Value, signaling, 41
Value chains; *see also* Strategic fits
  analysis, 96, 98
  costs, 98, 106–107
  critical activities, 118–119
  definition, 96
  industry systems, 101–102, 103
  primary activities, 98, 99
  of related businesses, 189, 190–192
  support activities, 98, 99
  of unrelated businesses, 189
  vertical integration, 102–105
Vertical integration
  advantages, 103–104
  backward, 102, 103–104, 105
  disadvantages, 104–105
  forward, 102, 104, 105
Video game console industry, 343–358
Video game software industry, 360–385
Visions; *see* Strategic visions

w

Weaknesses; *see* SWOT analysis
Wholesale clubs, 215–233
Work climates; *see also* Corporate cultures
  caring, 135
  quality of life, 153
  results-oriented, 27
  retaining employees, 138

Name Index

a